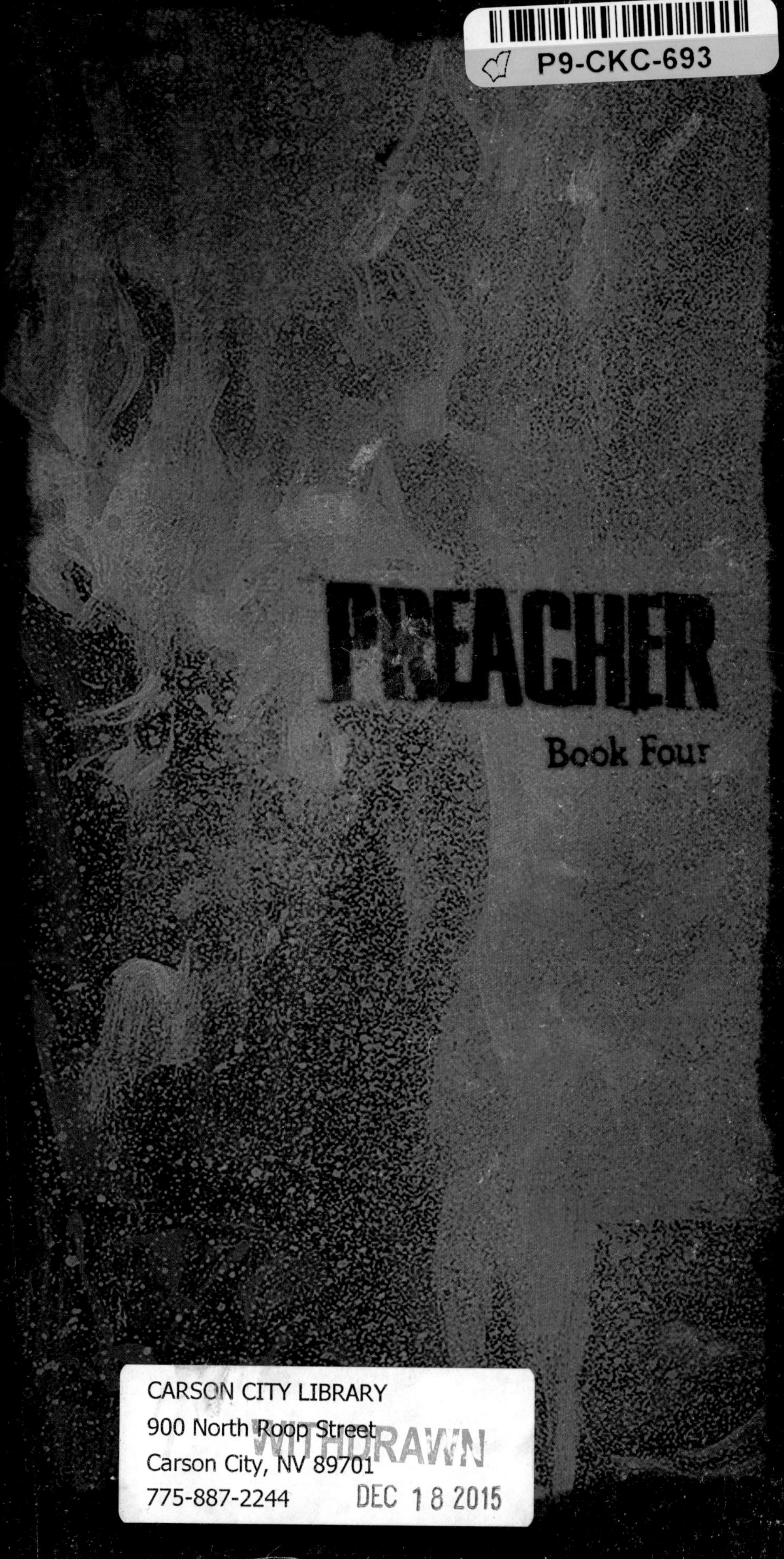
PREACHER
Book Four

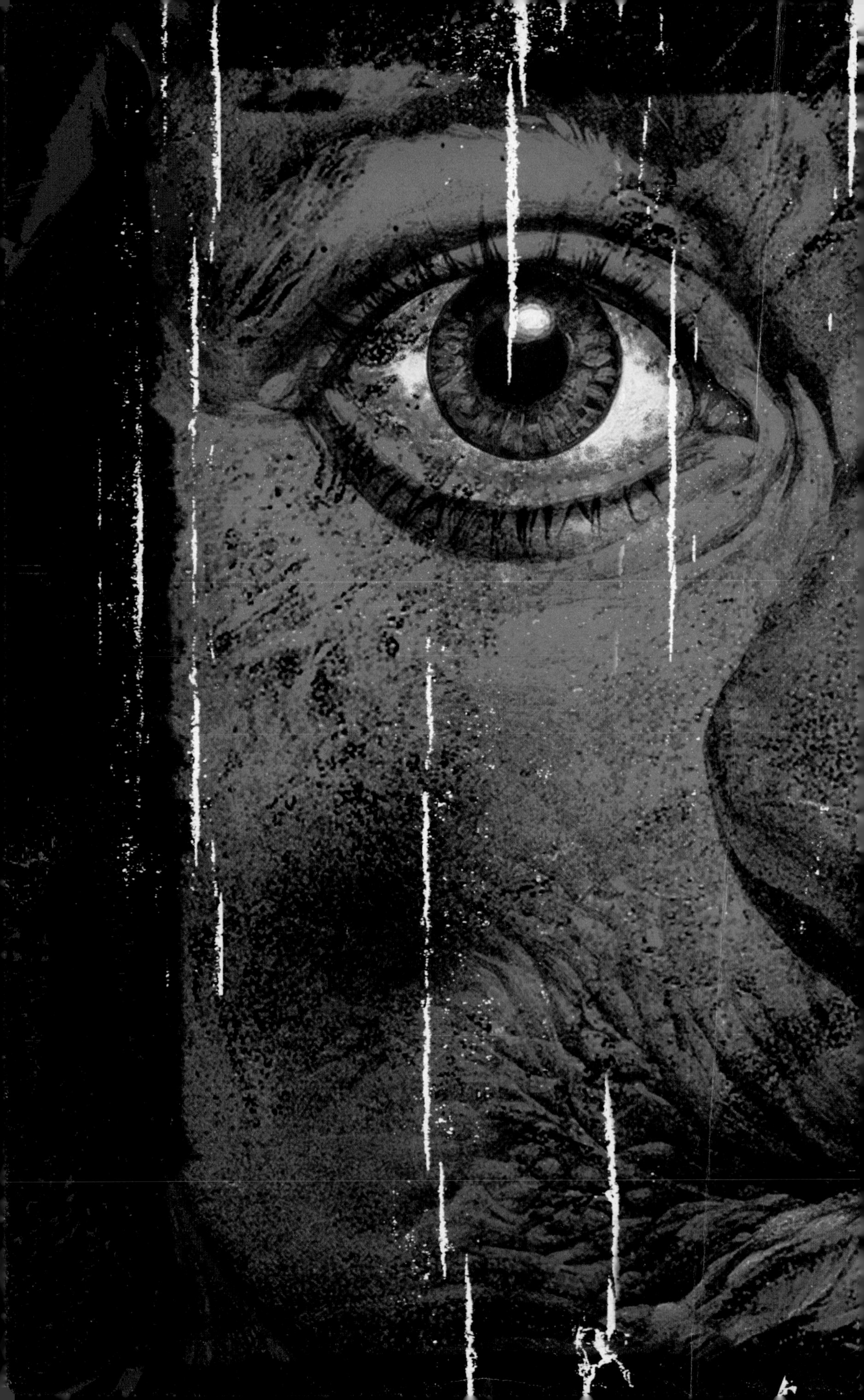

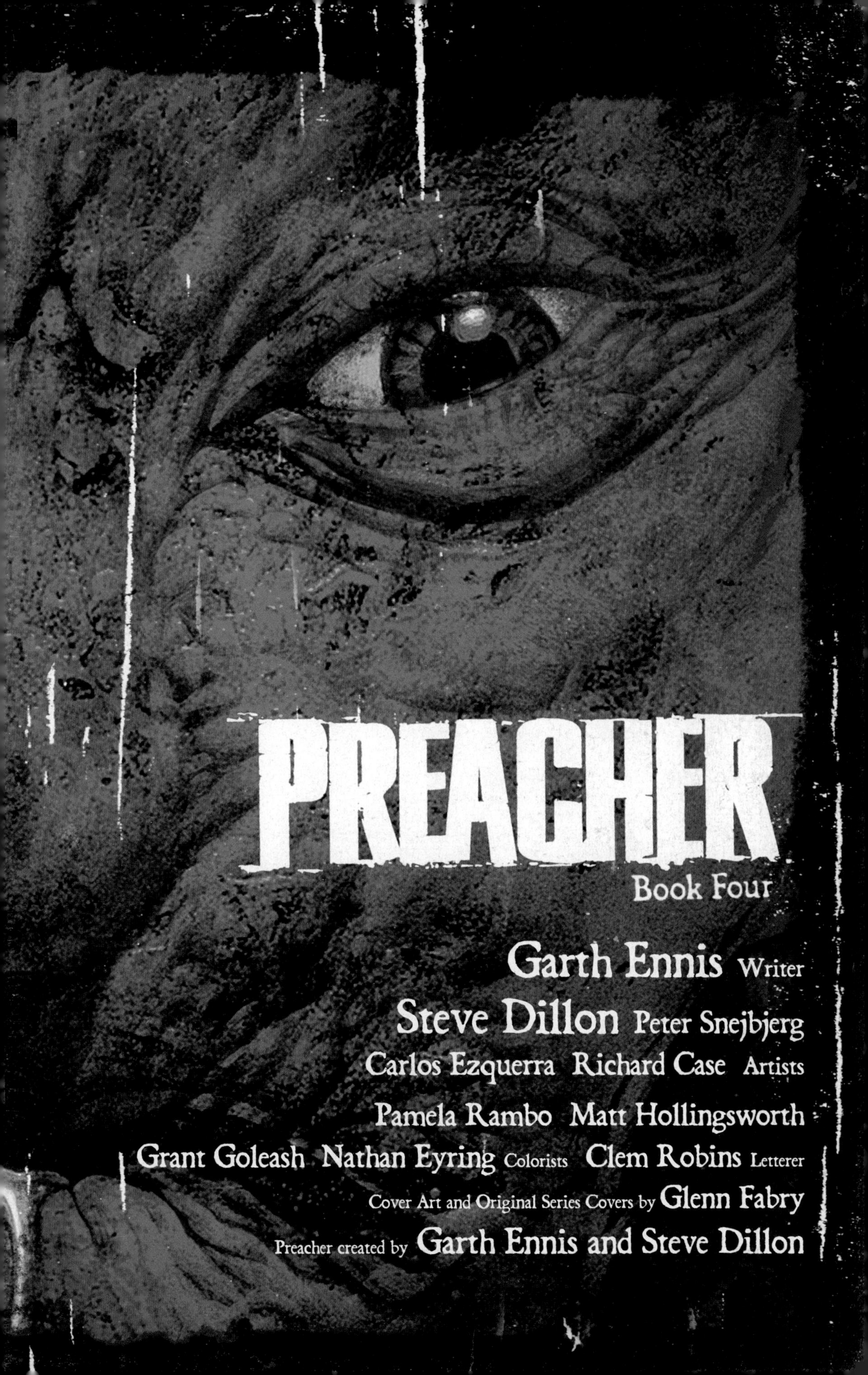

PREACHER

Book Four

Garth Ennis Writer

Steve Dillon Peter Snejbjerg

Carlos Ezquerra Richard Case Artists

Pamela Rambo Matt Hollingsworth

Grant Goleash Nathan Eyring Colorists Clem Robins Letterer

Cover Art and Original Series Covers by Glenn Fabry

Preacher created by Garth Ennis and Steve Dillon

Axel Alonso Julie Rottenberg Editors – Original Series Scott Nybakken Editor
Robbin Brosterman Design Director – Books Louis Prandi Publication Design

Shelly Bond Executive Editor – Vertigo Hank Kanalz Senior VP – Vertigo and Integrated Publishing

Diane Nelson President Dan DiDio and Jim Lee Co-Publishers Geoff Johns Chief Creative Officer
Amit Desai Senior VP – Marketing and Franchise Management Amy Genkins Senior VP – Business and Legal Affairs
Nairi Gardiner Senior VP – Finance Jeff Boison VP – Publishing Planning Mark Chiarello VP – Art Direction and Design
John Cunningham VP – Marketing Terri Cunningham VP – Editorial Administration Larry Ganem VP – Talent Relations and Services
Alison Gill Senior VP – Manufacturing and Operations Jay Kogan VP – Business and Legal Affairs, Publishing Jack Mahan VP – Business Affairs, Talent
Nick Napolitano VP – Manufacturing Administration Sue Pohja VP – Book Sales Fred Ruiz VP – Manufacturing Operations
Courtney Simmons Senior VP – Publicity Bob Wayne Senior VP – Sales

PREACHER BOOK FOUR

Library of Congress Cataloging-in-Publication Data

Ennis, Garth, author.
  Preacher, book four / writer, Garth Ennis ; artist, Steve Dillon.
    pages cm
  ISBN 978-1-4012-3094-4 (paperback)
  1. Custer, Jesse (Fictitious character)—Comic books, strips, etc. 2. Clergy—Comic books, strips, etc. 3. Vigilantes—Comic books, strips, etc. 4. Graphic novels. I. Dillon,
Steve, illustrator. II. Title. III. Title: Preacher. Book 4.
  PN6727.E56P735 2014
  741.5'973—dc23
                              2014011931

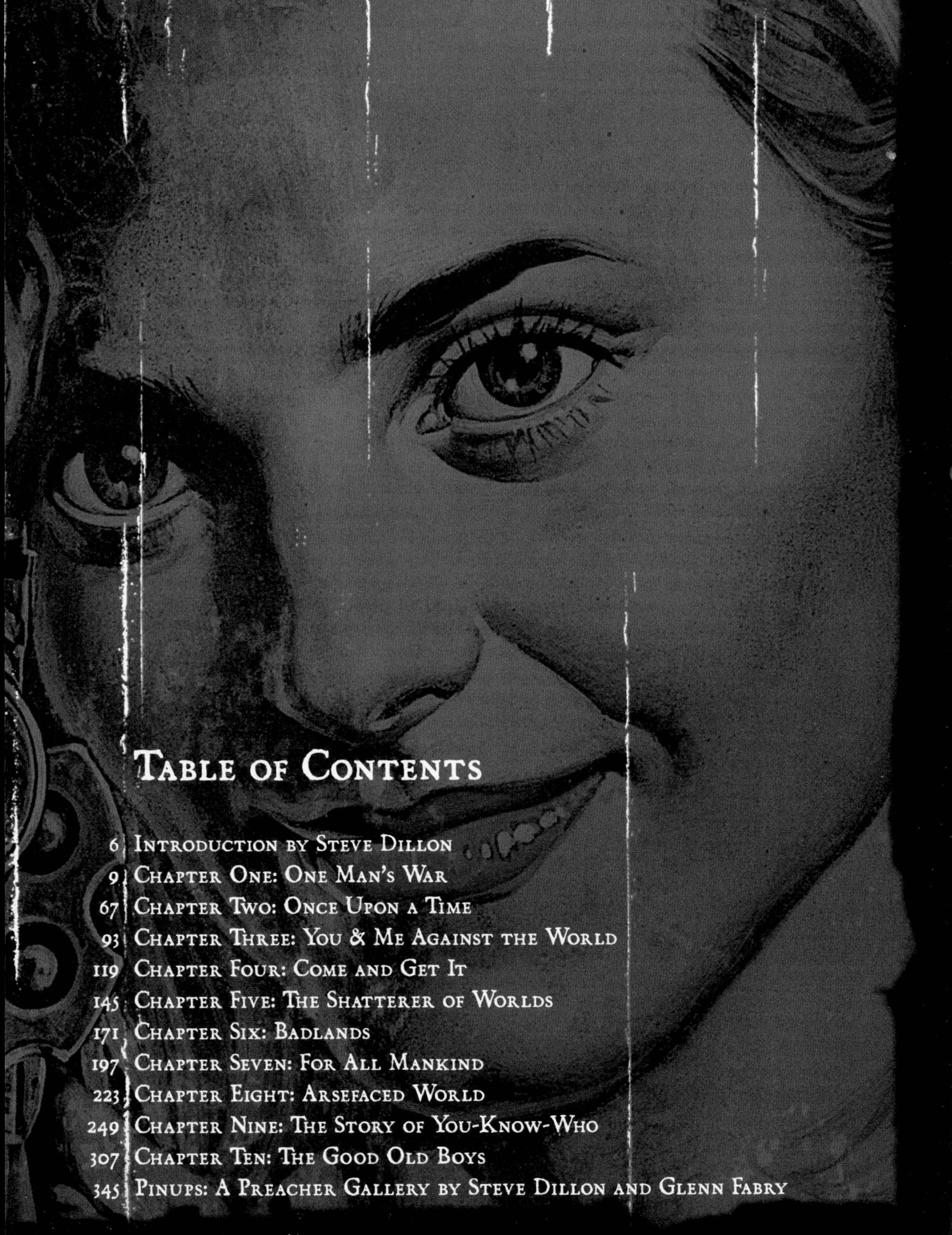

Table of Contents

Well, here we go. My first PREACHER introduction. My first chance, outside of interviews, to say something about the story and characters that lived with me for seven years of my life. When I drew the final lines in the final panel it was a bittersweet moment. I had that feeling of satisfaction that you get from completing an epic journey that had many ups and downs, but there was also a sadness of the sort that comes from turning to your traveling companions and saying, "Well... It's been nice knowing you. Take care." It was strange to think I'd never draw those guys again (except, maybe, as convention sketches), but I accepted that the story had been told. The beginning, the middle and the end were all there and nothing more needed to be said.

Speaking of the beginning, it was a strange time for me. My family and I had just moved back to England after spending a number of years in Ireland. There were four of us living in a small rented house while we waited to complete the deal on the house we wanted to buy. Just to make things more interesting, my wife was also heavily pregnant with my youngest son, Jamie, and I had to set up some sort of drawing space in a room no bigger than a large cupboard so I could start work on my and Garth's new project, PREACHER.

As I worked on that first issue my mind was swinging back and forth between "This is going to be really cool — the best thing we've ever done together!" and "Nobody's going to get it — it's going to bomb!" The combination of the upheaval in my private life and my worries that the thing I was working on might be cancelled in pretty short order due to controversy and/or bad sales made the weeks before the book hit the shops less than relaxed. Essentially, I was waiting on two births, that of my son and that of PREACHER. While one was, obviously, more important than the other (my wife would have done me some serious damage at the time if she had thought that I was comparing the two *at all*), both were nail-biting affairs in their own way and, thankfully, both ended up going pretty well.

As I write this, Jamie is a strapping sixteen-year-old. He's taller and broader than me (broader in a good, athletic way, as opposed to broader in a forty-something, too-many-beers way like myself), he's doing really well at school and he's playing rugby of a pretty high standard. Those PREACHER guys seem to be doing pretty well too. The collections have stayed in print and still seem to be popular. We now have proper, grown-up, hardback editions and a whole new generation of readers following the trials and tribulations of Jesse, Tulip, Cassidy, Arseface, Starr et al. When you've been so close to something it's hard to stand back and analyze it objectively, but as it's been nearly ten years since I drew that last panel, I might have a bit of a chance.

The journey that these characters make is a long and arduous one, with many twists and turns, and through it all Garth deals with some pretty eternal themes — love, friendship, loyalty, betrayal, honor, and the question of how far you should go in the pursuit of what you believe to be right. While the stories are at times shocking, sometimes surreal, and often hilarious, these relatively sober themes make up the core of the tale. Even though we do some terrible things to them, Garth and I have always had a genuine fondness for all the main characters in PREACHER, and I hope that comes through to the reader. I still miss those guys, and I hope you enjoy following their stories as much as we enjoyed telling them.

Now to the volume in your hands. When you've designed and worked on a set of characters for a long time it's always interesting to see somebody else's take on them. In an ideal world I would have illustrated everything involved in the PREACHER saga, but because of time constraints it was just not possible for me to draw the regular title as well as all the specials. That said, I could not have asked for a better bunch of guys to step in and do the job. Richard Case, Peter Snejbjerg and Carlos Ezquerra are all artists with very individual and distinctive styles that work perfectly for the stories they were asked to draw. I've shared quite a few beers with Richard and Peter over the years and they are top blokes. While I have only met Carlos briefly, I can assure you that he is a decent chap of the highest order and a true legend of British comics. It was a real treat to have these great artists involved with PREACHER.

Writing this has made me go a bit misty-eyed with nostalgia. PREACHER took up a large chunk of my life, but it did more for me than just pay the bills. If I'm going to be remembered for anything in my career, I'm happy for it to be the fact that I was the lucky bloke that got to work with Garth on telling the tale of Jesse Custer.

Cheers!

— Steve Dillon
February 2011

PREACHER

Book Four

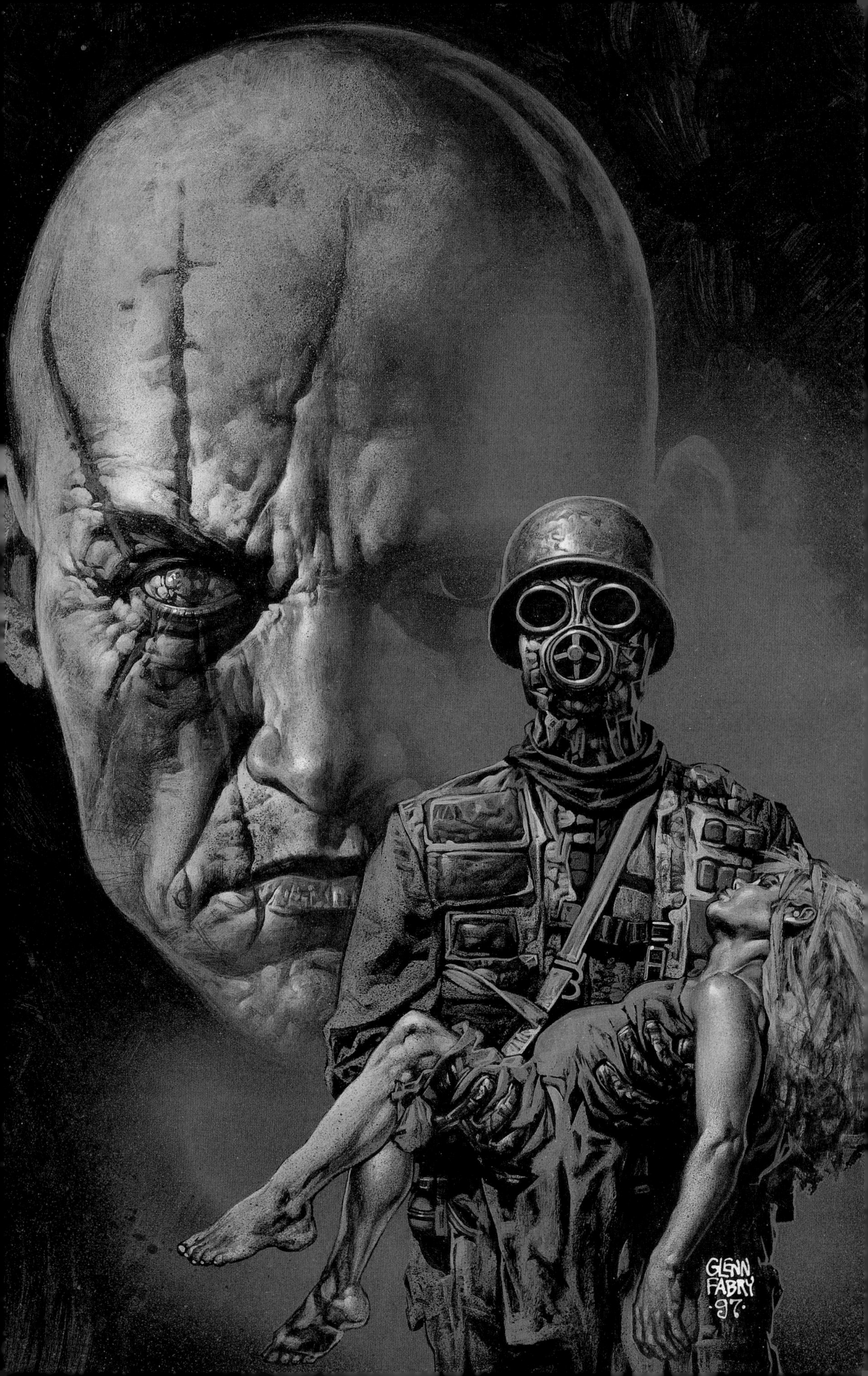
GLENN FABRY ·97·

"So you have become a monster in order to save the world."

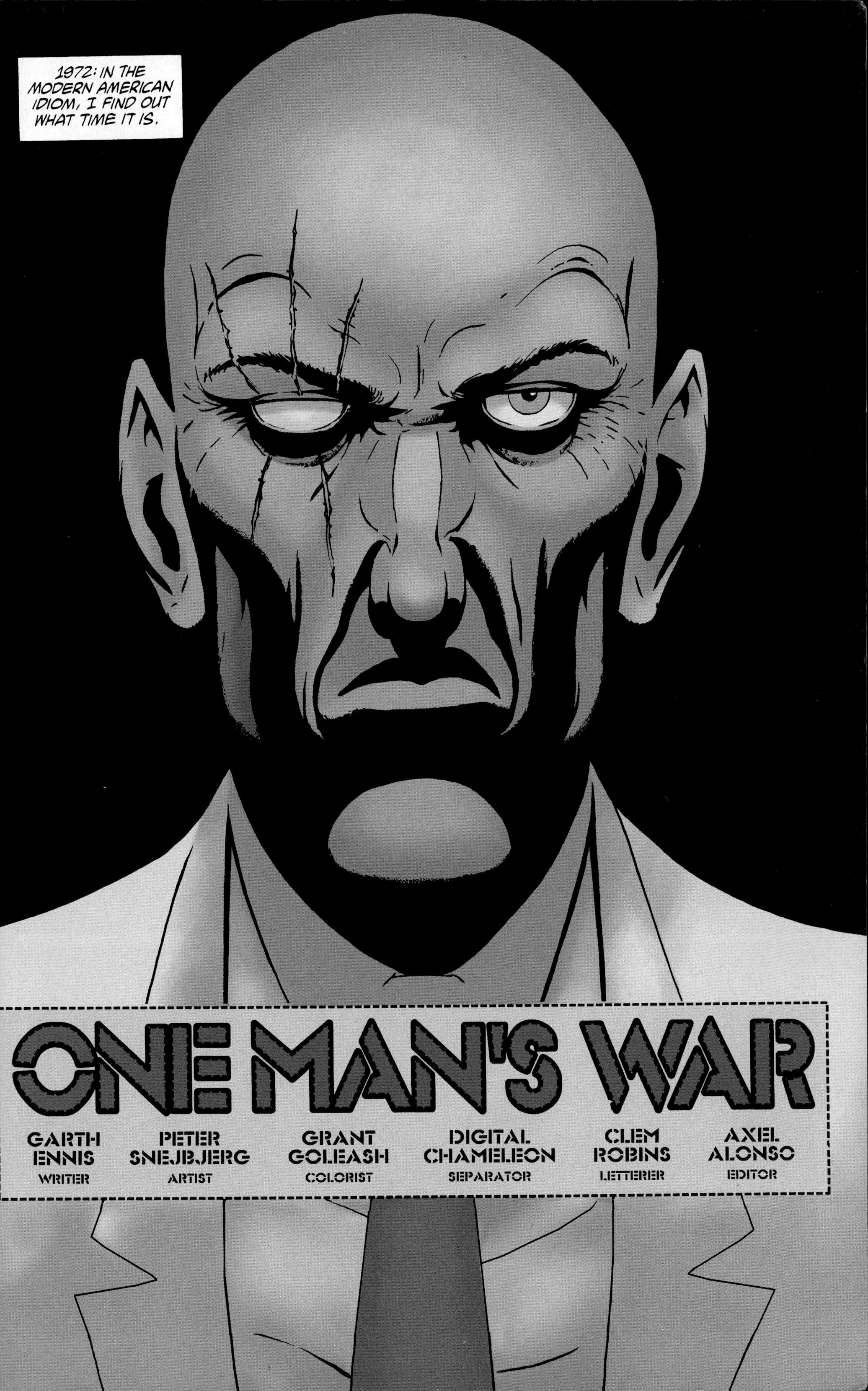
1972: IN THE MODERN AMERICAN IDIOM, I FIND OUT WHAT TIME IT IS.
ONE MAN'S WAR
GARTH ENNIS WRITER
PETER SNEJBJERG ARTIST
GRANT GOLEASH COLORIST
DIGITAL CHAMELEON SEPARATOR
CLEM ROBINS LETTERER
AXEL ALONSO EDITOR

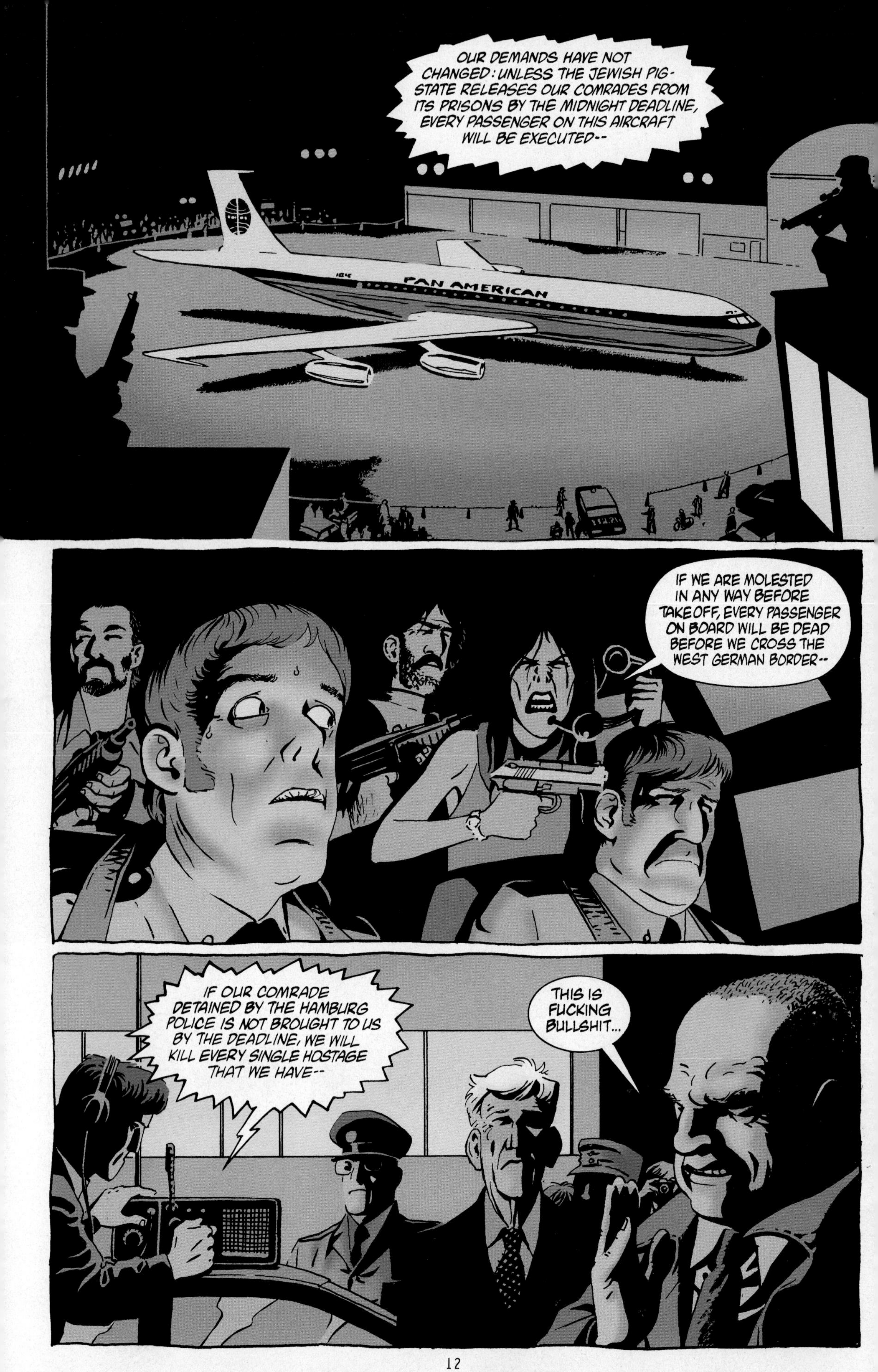

OUR DEMANDS HAVE NOT CHANGED: UNLESS THE JEWISH PIG-STATE RELEASES OUR COMRADES FROM ITS PRISONS BY THE MIDNIGHT DEADLINE, EVERY PASSENGER ON THIS AIRCRAFT WILL BE EXECUTED--
PAN AMERICAN
IF WE ARE MOLESTED IN ANY WAY BEFORE TAKEOFF, EVERY PASSENGER ON BOARD WILL BE DEAD BEFORE WE CROSS THE WEST GERMAN BORDER--
IF OUR COMRADE DETAINED BY THE HAMBURG POLICE IS NOT BROUGHT TO US BY THE DEADLINE, WE WILL KILL EVERY SINGLE HOSTAGE THAT WE HAVE--
THIS IS FUCKING BULLSHIT...

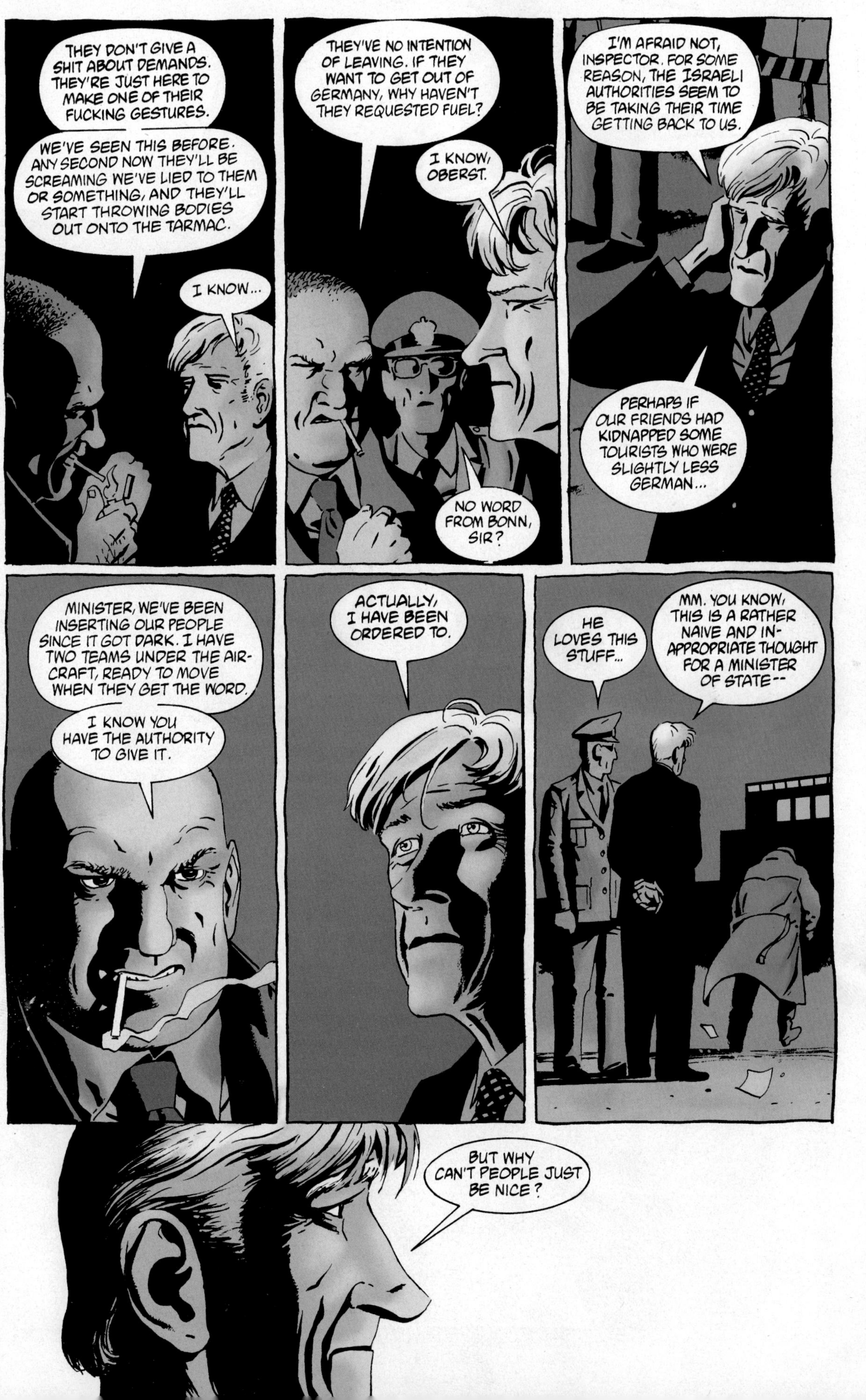
THEY DON'T GIVE A SHIT ABOUT DEMANDS. THEY'RE JUST HERE TO MAKE ONE OF THEIR FUCKING GESTURES.
WE'VE SEEN THIS BEFORE. ANY SECOND NOW THEY'LL BE SCREAMING WE'VE LIED TO THEM OR SOMETHING, AND THEY'LL START THROWING BODIES OUT ONTO THE TARMAC.
I KNOW...
THEY'VE NO INTENTION OF LEAVING. IF THEY WANT TO GET OUT OF GERMANY, WHY HAVEN'T THEY REQUESTED FUEL?
I KNOW, OBERST.
NO WORD FROM BONN, SIR?
I'M AFRAID NOT, INSPECTOR. FOR SOME REASON, THE ISRAELI AUTHORITIES SEEM TO BE TAKING THEIR TIME GETTING BACK TO US.
PERHAPS IF OUR FRIENDS HAD KIDNAPPED SOME TOURISTS WHO WERE SLIGHTLY LESS GERMAN...
MINISTER, WE'VE BEEN INSERTING OUR PEOPLE SINCE IT GOT DARK. I HAVE TWO TEAMS UNDER THE AIR-CRAFT, READY TO MOVE WHEN THEY GET THE WORD.
I KNOW YOU HAVE THE AUTHORITY TO GIVE IT.
ACTUALLY, I HAVE BEEN ORDERED TO.
HE LOVES THIS STUFF...
MM. YOU KNOW, THIS IS A RATHER NAIVE AND IN-APPROPRIATE THOUGHT FOR A MINISTER OF STATE--
BUT WHY CAN'T PEOPLE JUST BE NICE?

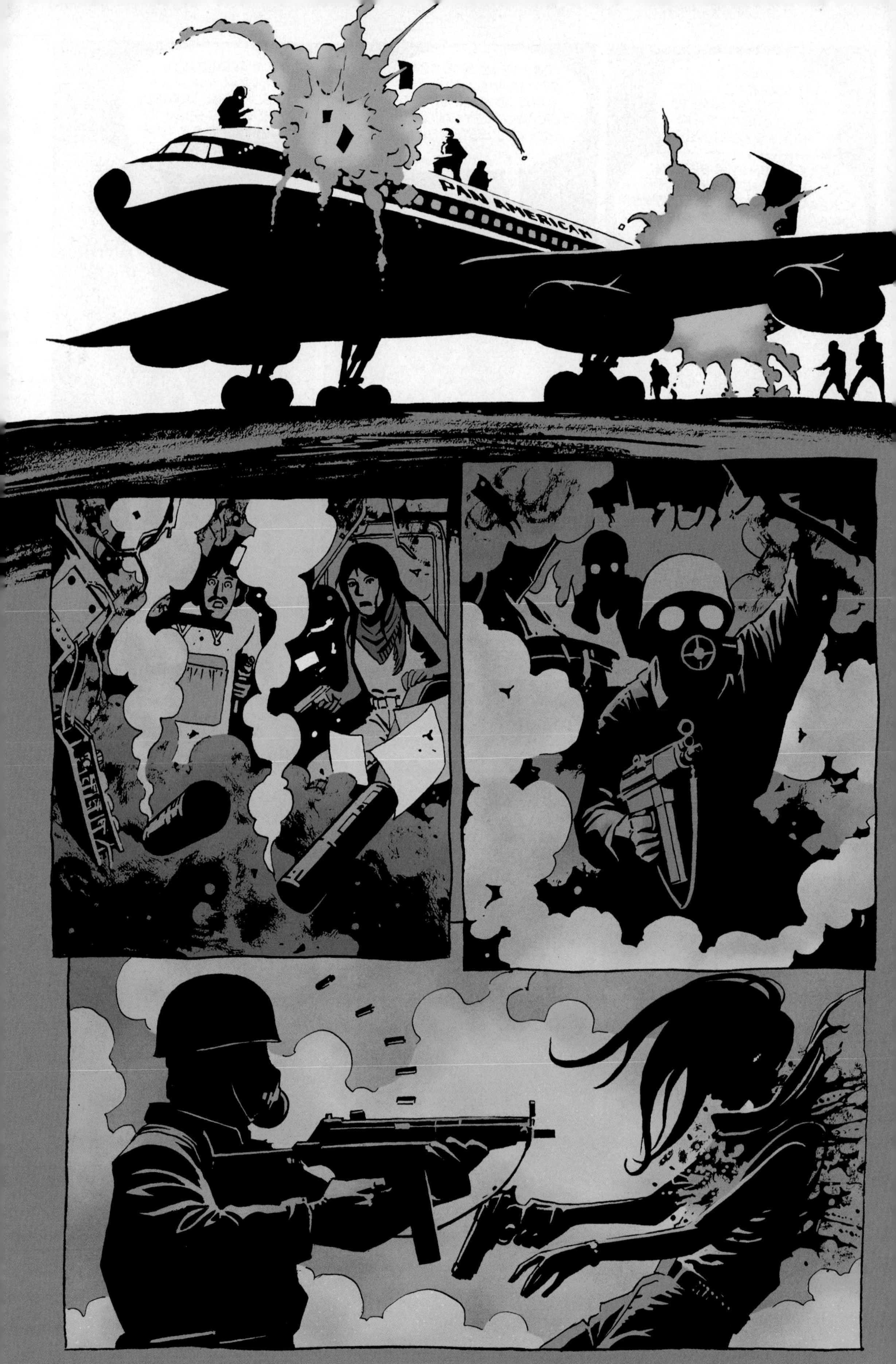
PAN AMERICAN

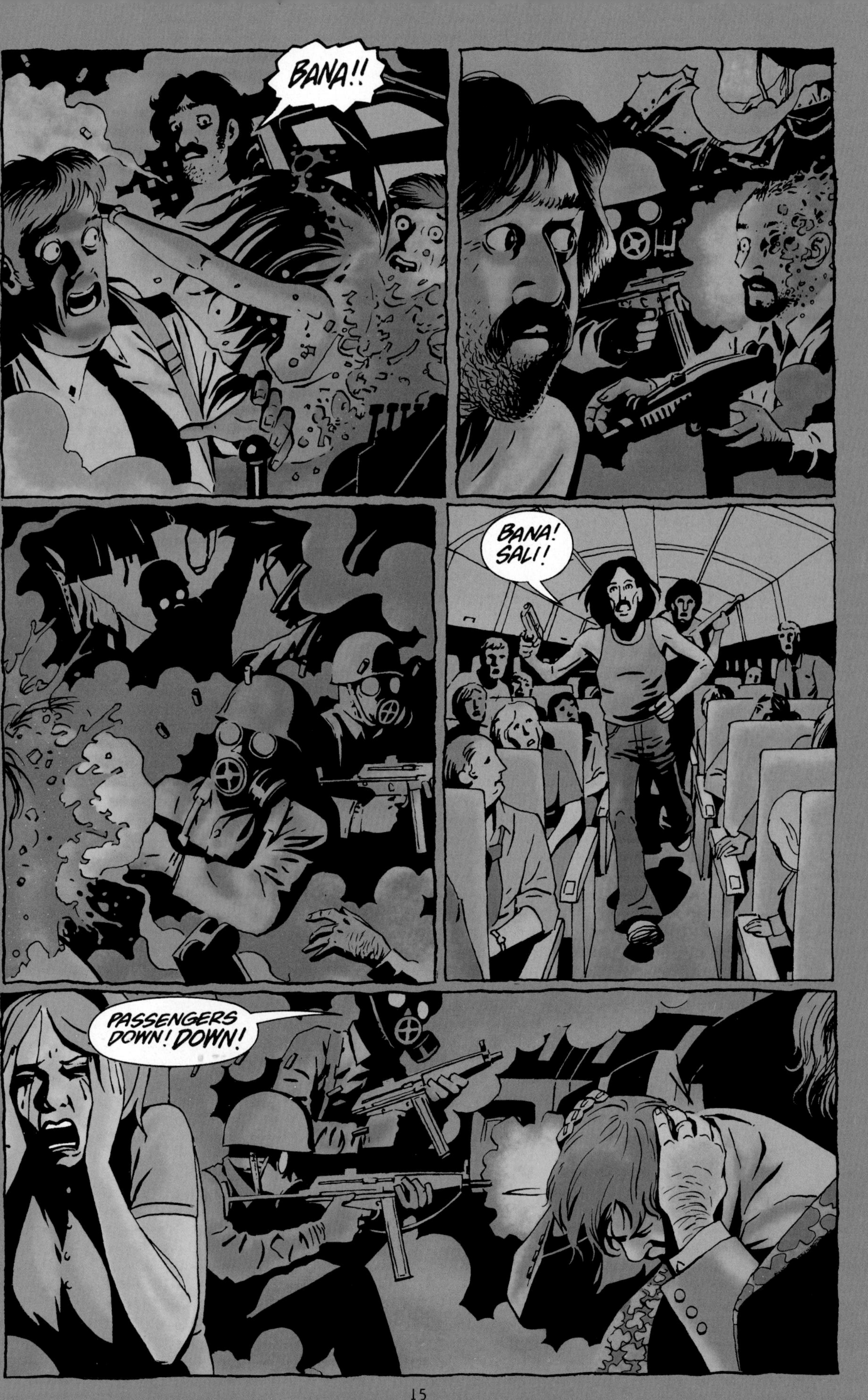
BANA!!
BANA! SALI!
PASSENGERS DOWN! DOWN!

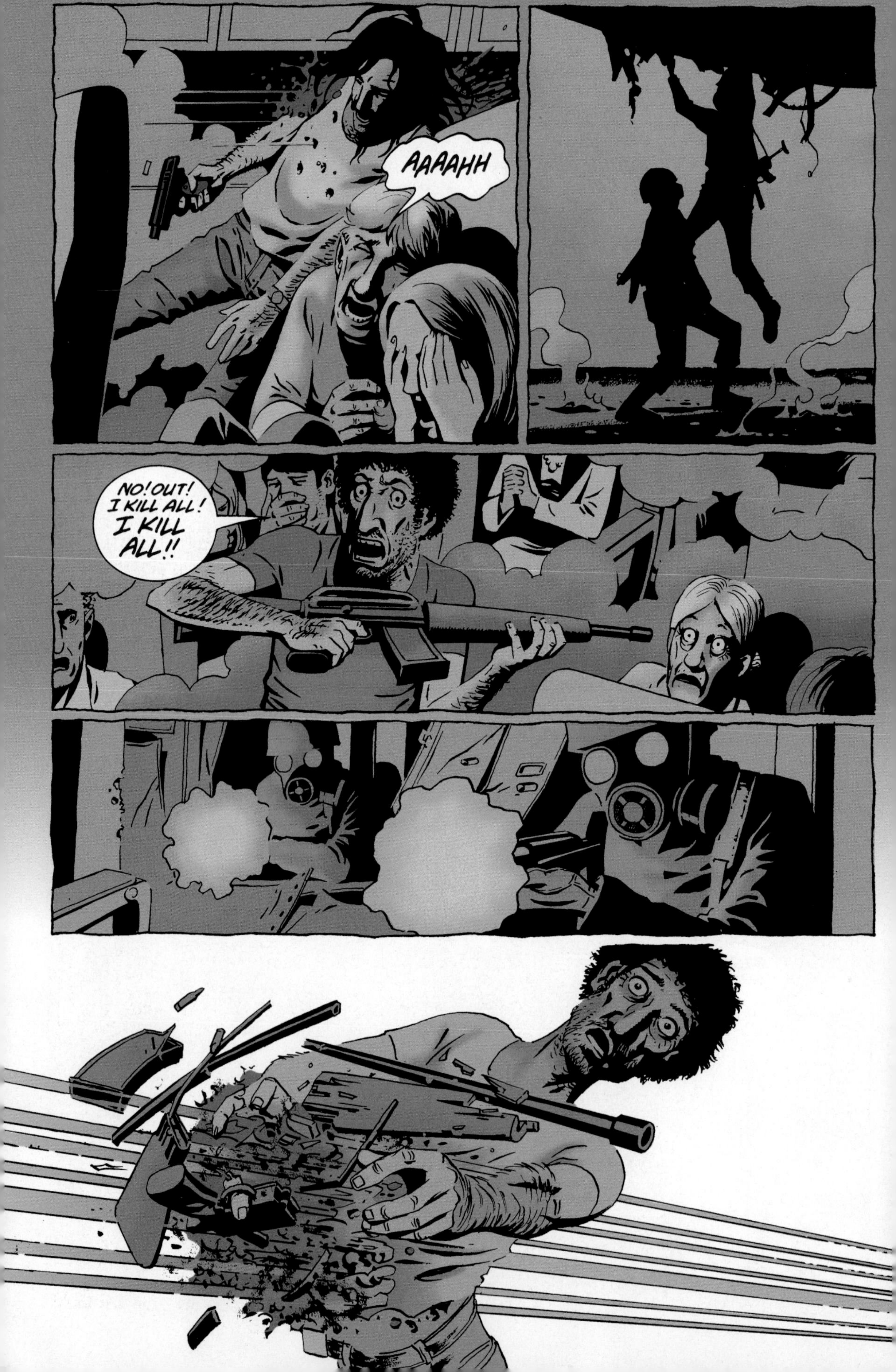
AAAAHH
NO! OUT! I KILL ALL! I KILL ALL!!

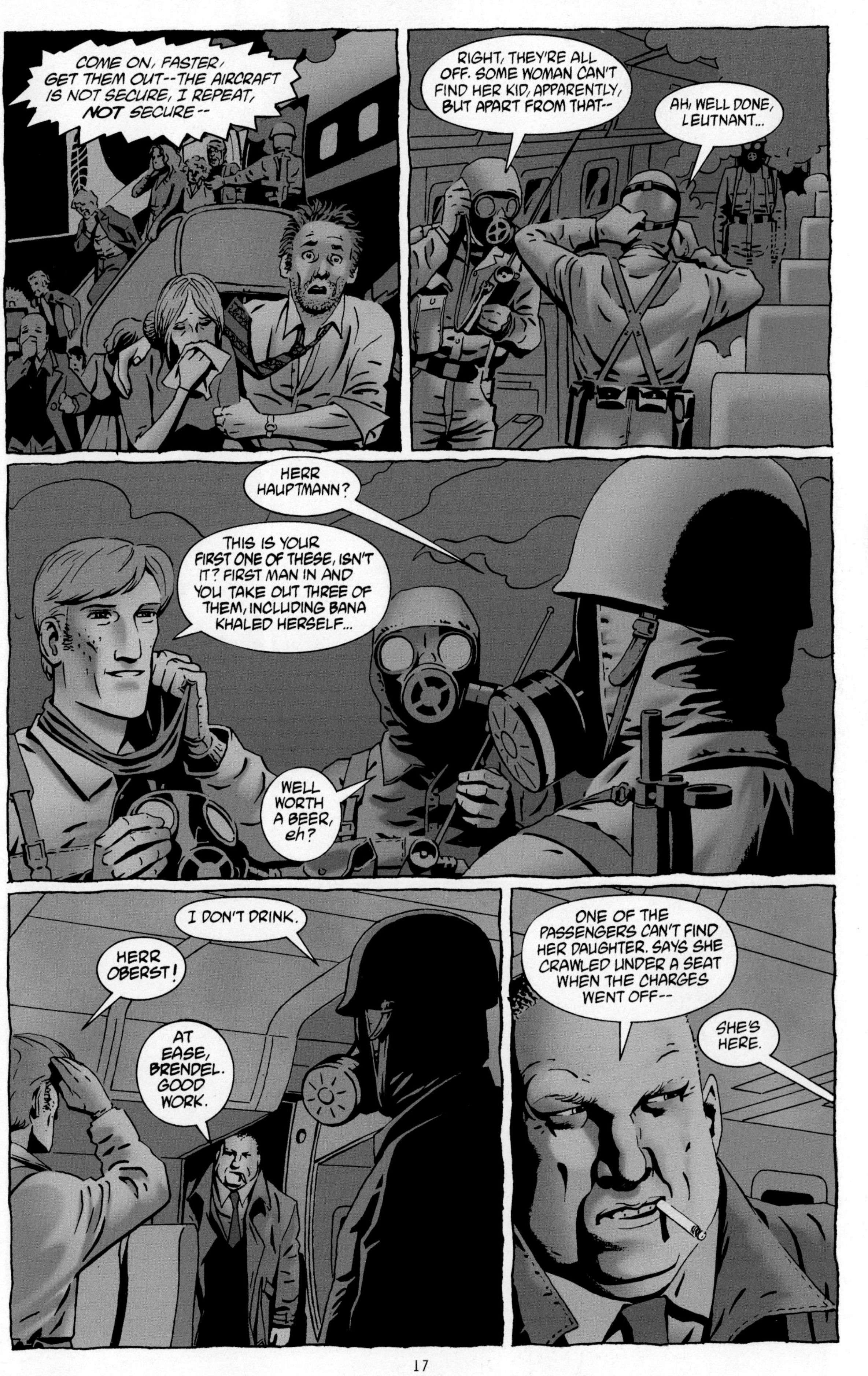
COME ON, FASTER, GET THEM OUT--THE AIRCRAFT IS NOT SECURE, I REPEAT, NOT SECURE--
RIGHT, THEY'RE ALL OFF. SOME WOMAN CAN'T FIND HER KID, APPARENTLY, BUT APART FROM THAT--
AH, WELL DONE, LEUTNANT...
HERR HAUPTMANN?
THIS IS YOUR FIRST ONE OF THESE, ISN'T IT? FIRST MAN IN AND YOU TAKE OUT THREE OF THEM, INCLUDING BANA KHALED HERSELF...
WELL WORTH A BEER, eh?
I DON'T DRINK.
HERR OBERST!
AT EASE, BRENDEL. GOOD WORK.
ONE OF THE PASSENGERS CAN'T FIND HER DAUGHTER. SAYS SHE CRAWLED UNDER A SEAT WHEN THE CHARGES WENT OFF--
SHE'S HERE.

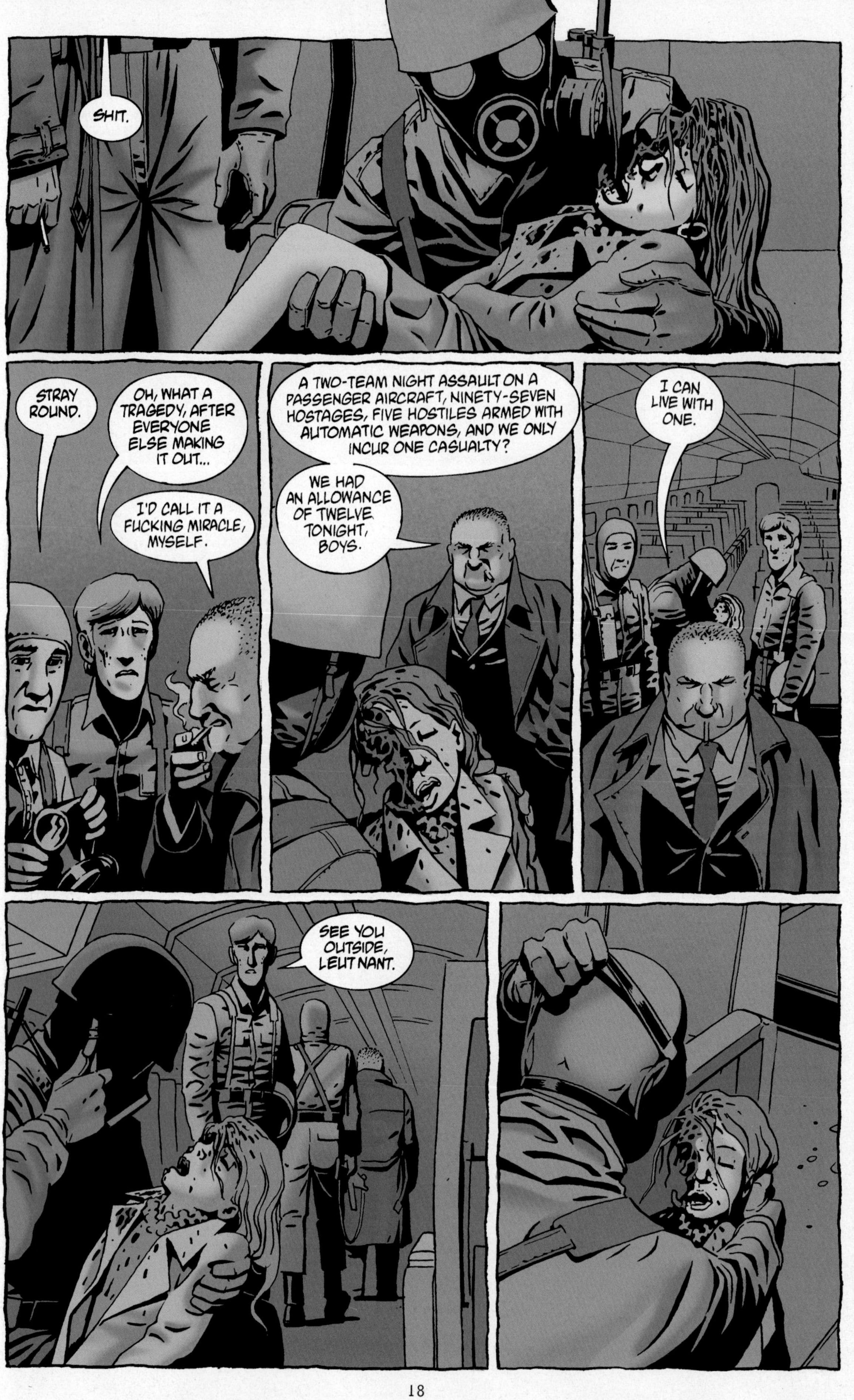
SHIT.
STRAY ROUND.
OH, WHAT A TRAGEDY, AFTER EVERYONE ELSE MAKING IT OUT...
I'D CALL IT A FUCKING MIRACLE, MYSELF.
A TWO-TEAM NIGHT ASSAULT ON A PASSENGER AIRCRAFT, NINETY-SEVEN HOSTAGES, FIVE HOSTILES ARMED WITH AUTOMATIC WEAPONS, AND WE ONLY INCUR ONE CASUALTY?
WE HAD AN ALLOWANCE OF TWELVE TONIGHT, BOYS.
I CAN LIVE WITH ONE.
SEE YOU OUTSIDE, LEUTNANT.

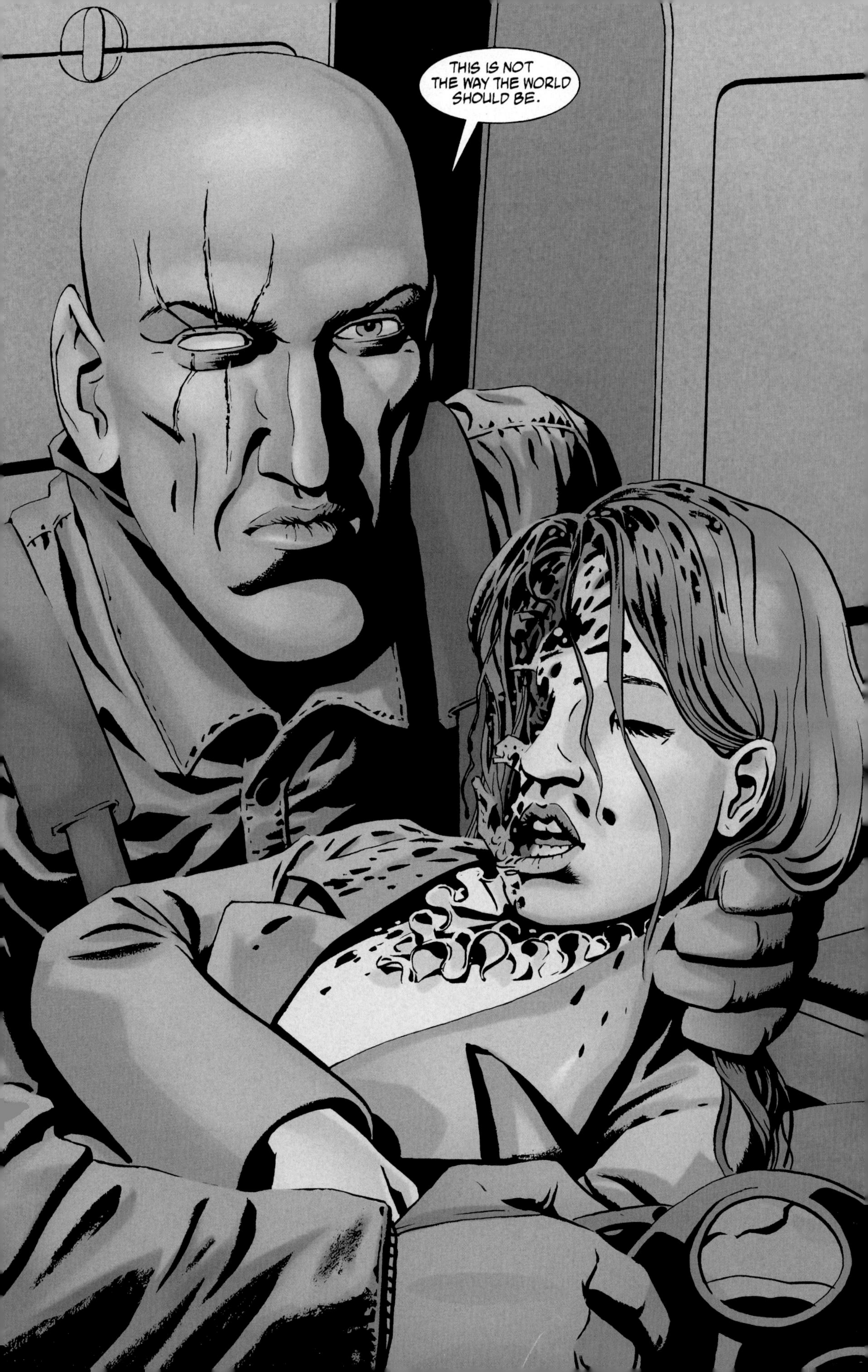
THIS IS NOT THE WAY THE WORLD SHOULD BE.

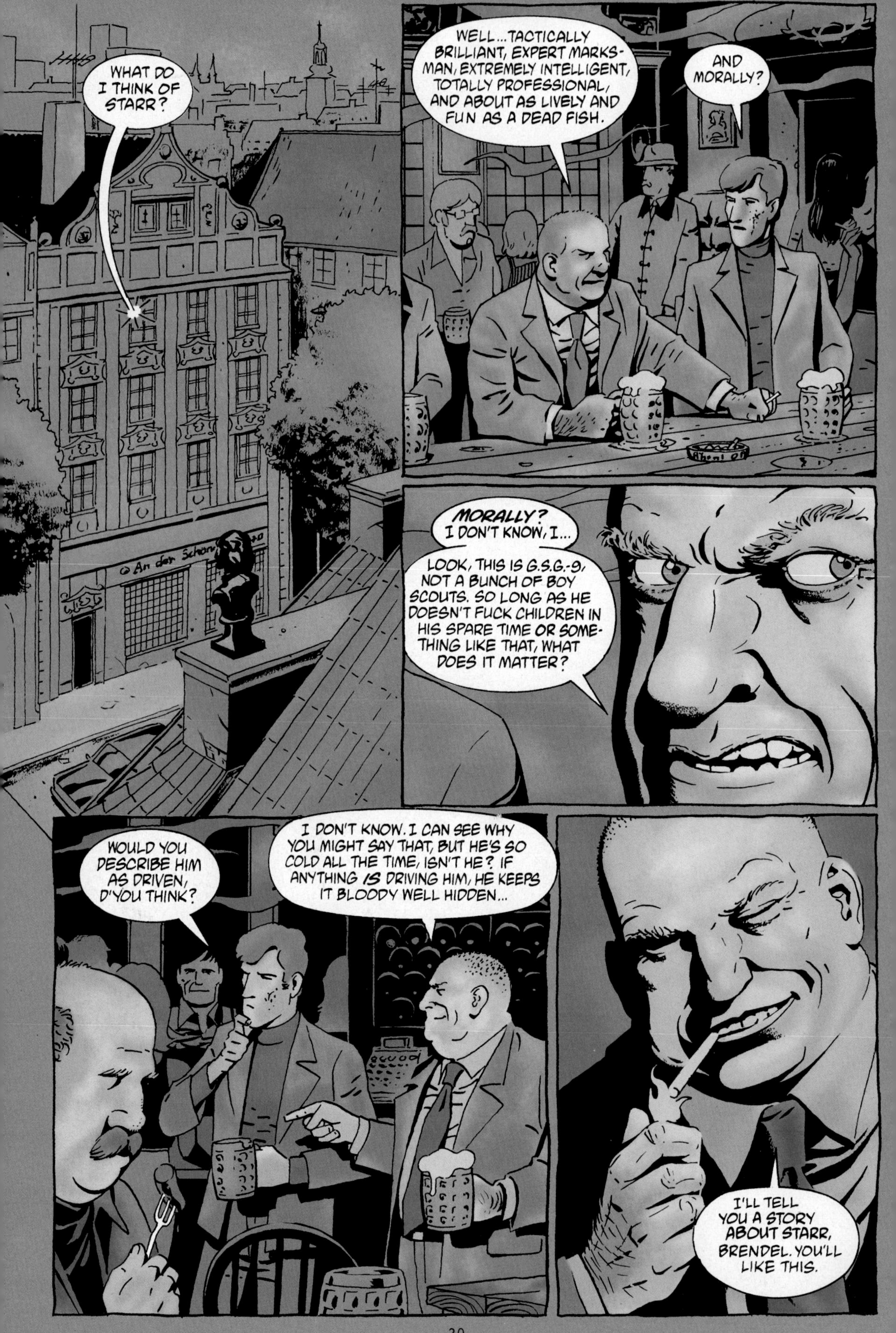
WHAT DO I THINK OF STARR?
WELL... TACTICALLY BRILLIANT, EXPERT MARKSMAN, EXTREMELY INTELLIGENT, TOTALLY PROFESSIONAL, AND ABOUT AS LIVELY AND FUN AS A DEAD FISH.
AND MORALLY?
MORALLY? I DON'T KNOW, I...
LOOK, THIS IS G.S.G.-9, NOT A BUNCH OF BOY SCOUTS. SO LONG AS HE DOESN'T FUCK CHILDREN IN HIS SPARE TIME OR SOMETHING LIKE THAT, WHAT DOES IT MATTER?
WOULD YOU DESCRIBE HIM AS DRIVEN, D'YOU THINK?
I DON'T KNOW. I CAN SEE WHY YOU MIGHT SAY THAT, BUT HE'S SO COLD ALL THE TIME, ISN'T HE? IF ANYTHING IS DRIVING HIM, HE KEEPS IT BLOODY WELL HIDDEN...
I'LL TELL YOU A STORY ABOUT STARR, BRENDEL. YOU'LL LIKE THIS.

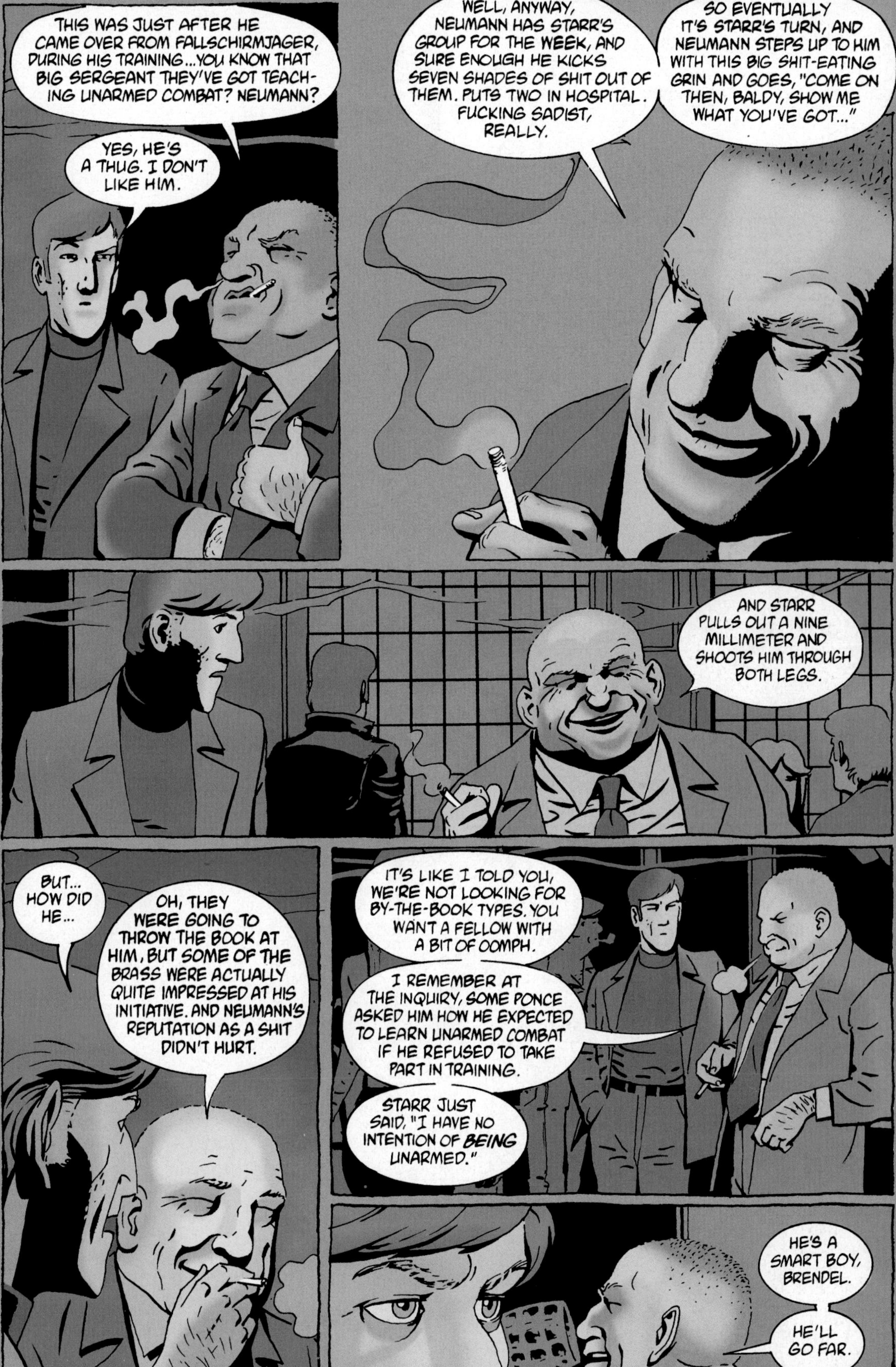
THIS WAS JUST AFTER HE CAME OVER FROM FALLSCHIRMJAGER, DURING HIS TRAINING... YOU KNOW THAT BIG SERGEANT THEY'VE GOT TEACHING UNARMED COMBAT? NEUMANN?
YES, HE'S A THUG. I DON'T LIKE HIM.
WELL, ANYWAY, NEUMANN HAS STARR'S GROUP FOR THE WEEK, AND SURE ENOUGH HE KICKS SEVEN SHADES OF SHIT OUT OF THEM. PUTS TWO IN HOSPITAL. FUCKING SADIST, REALLY.
SO EVENTUALLY IT'S STARR'S TURN, AND NEUMANN STEPS UP TO HIM WITH THIS BIG SHIT-EATING GRIN AND GOES, "COME ON THEN, BALDY, SHOW ME WHAT YOU'VE GOT..."
AND STARR PULLS OUT A NINE MILLIMETER AND SHOOTS HIM THROUGH BOTH LEGS.
BUT... HOW DID HE...
OH, THEY WERE GOING TO THROW THE BOOK AT HIM, BUT SOME OF THE BRASS WERE ACTUALLY QUITE IMPRESSED AT HIS INITIATIVE. AND NEUMANN'S REPUTATION AS A SHIT DIDN'T HURT.
IT'S LIKE I TOLD YOU, WE'RE NOT LOOKING FOR BY-THE-BOOK TYPES. YOU WANT A FELLOW WITH A BIT OF OOMPH.
I REMEMBER AT THE INQUIRY, SOME PONCE ASKED HIM HOW HE EXPECTED TO LEARN UNARMED COMBAT IF HE REFUSED TO TAKE PART IN TRAINING.
STARR JUST SAID, "I HAVE NO INTENTION OF *BEING* UNARMED."
HE'S A SMART BOY, BRENDEL.
HE'LL GO FAR.

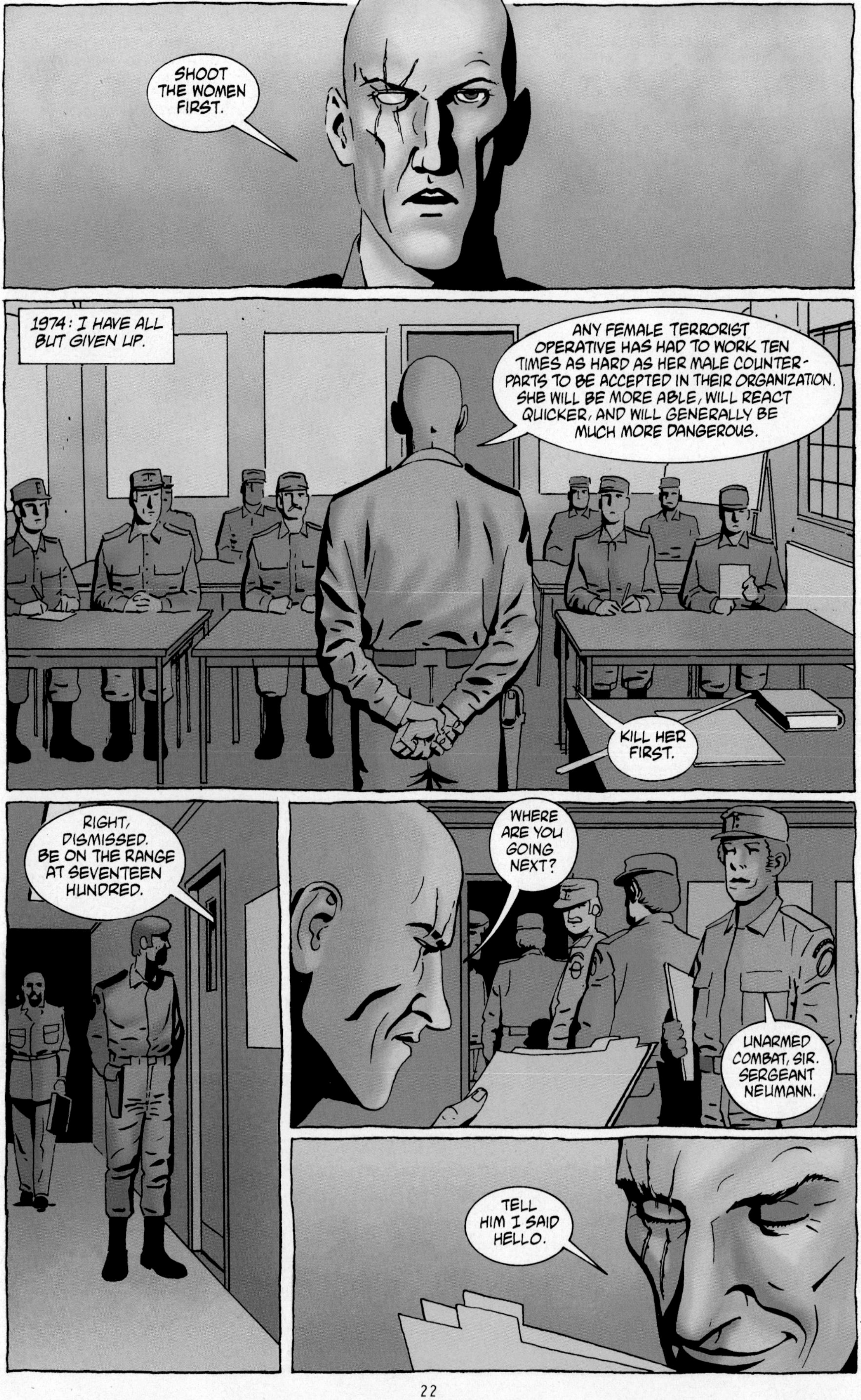
SHOOT THE WOMEN FIRST.
1974: I HAVE ALL BUT GIVEN UP.
ANY FEMALE TERRORIST OPERATIVE HAS HAD TO WORK TEN TIMES AS HARD AS HER MALE COUNTER-PARTS TO BE ACCEPTED IN THEIR ORGANIZATION. SHE WILL BE MORE ABLE, WILL REACT QUICKER, AND WILL GENERALLY BE MUCH MORE DANGEROUS.
KILL HER FIRST.
RIGHT, DISMISSED. BE ON THE RANGE AT SEVENTEEN HUNDRED.
WHERE ARE YOU GOING NEXT?
UNARMED COMBAT, SIR. SERGEANT NEUMANN.
TELL HIM I SAID HELLO.

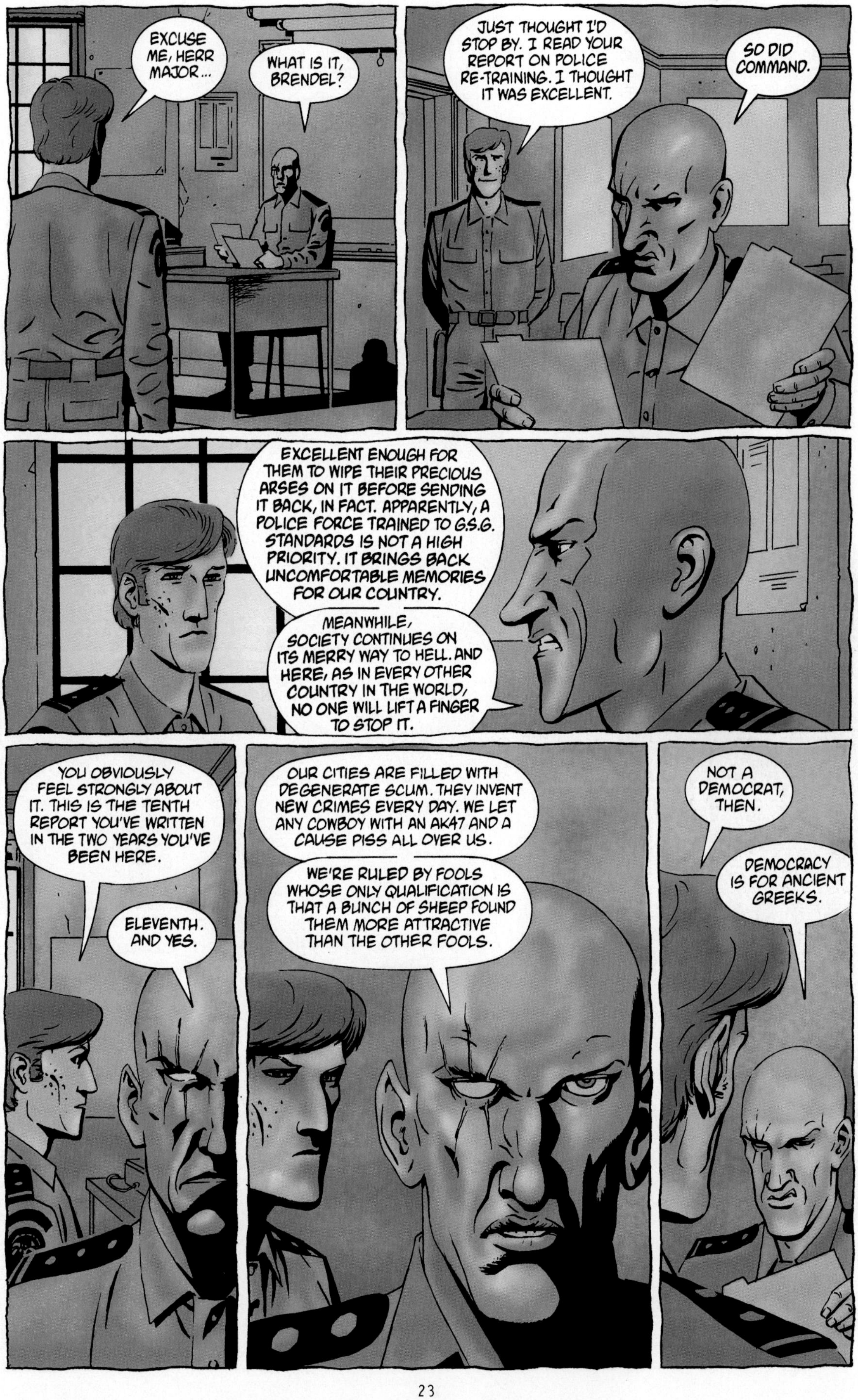
EXCUSE ME, HERR MAJOR...
WHAT IS IT, BRENDEL?
JUST THOUGHT I'D STOP BY. I READ YOUR REPORT ON POLICE RE-TRAINING. I THOUGHT IT WAS EXCELLENT.
SO DID COMMAND.
EXCELLENT ENOUGH FOR THEM TO WIPE THEIR PRECIOUS ARSES ON IT BEFORE SENDING IT BACK, IN FACT. APPARENTLY, A POLICE FORCE TRAINED TO G.S.G. STANDARDS IS NOT A HIGH PRIORITY. IT BRINGS BACK UNCOMFORTABLE MEMORIES FOR OUR COUNTRY.
MEANWHILE, SOCIETY CONTINUES ON ITS MERRY WAY TO HELL. AND HERE, AS IN EVERY OTHER COUNTRY IN THE WORLD, NO ONE WILL LIFT A FINGER TO STOP IT.
YOU OBVIOUSLY FEEL STRONGLY ABOUT IT. THIS IS THE TENTH REPORT YOU'VE WRITTEN IN THE TWO YEARS YOU'VE BEEN HERE.
ELEVENTH. AND YES.
OUR CITIES ARE FILLED WITH DEGENERATE SCUM. THEY INVENT NEW CRIMES EVERY DAY. WE LET ANY COWBOY WITH AN AK47 AND A CAUSE PISS ALL OVER US.
WE'RE RULED BY FOOLS WHOSE ONLY QUALIFICATION IS THAT A BUNCH OF SHEEP FOUND THEM MORE ATTRACTIVE THAN THE OTHER FOOLS.
NOT A DEMOCRAT, THEN.
DEMOCRACY IS FOR ANCIENT GREEKS.

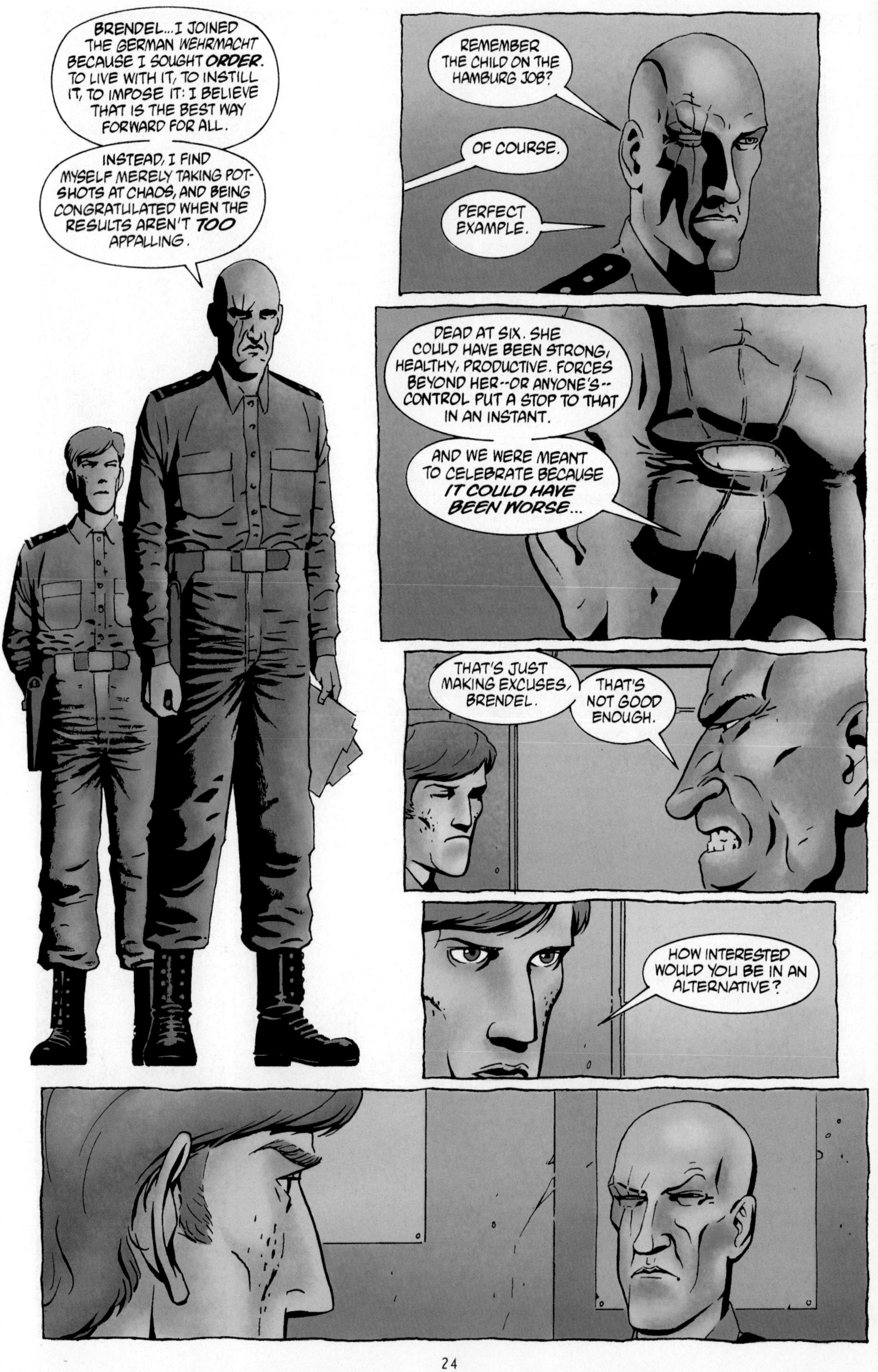
BRENDEL... I JOINED THE GERMAN WEHRMACHT BECAUSE I SOUGHT ORDER. TO LIVE WITH IT, TO INSTILL IT, TO IMPOSE IT: I BELIEVE THAT IS THE BEST WAY FORWARD FOR ALL.
INSTEAD, I FIND MYSELF MERELY TAKING POT-SHOTS AT CHAOS, AND BEING CONGRATULATED WHEN THE RESULTS AREN'T TOO APPALLING.
REMEMBER THE CHILD ON THE HAMBURG JOB?
OF COURSE.
PERFECT EXAMPLE.
DEAD AT SIX. SHE COULD HAVE BEEN STRONG, HEALTHY, PRODUCTIVE. FORCES BEYOND HER--OR ANYONE'S--CONTROL PUT A STOP TO THAT IN AN INSTANT.
AND WE WERE MEANT TO CELEBRATE BECAUSE IT COULD HAVE BEEN WORSE...
THAT'S JUST MAKING EXCUSES, BRENDEL.
THAT'S NOT GOOD ENOUGH.
HOW INTERESTED WOULD YOU BE IN AN ALTERNATIVE?

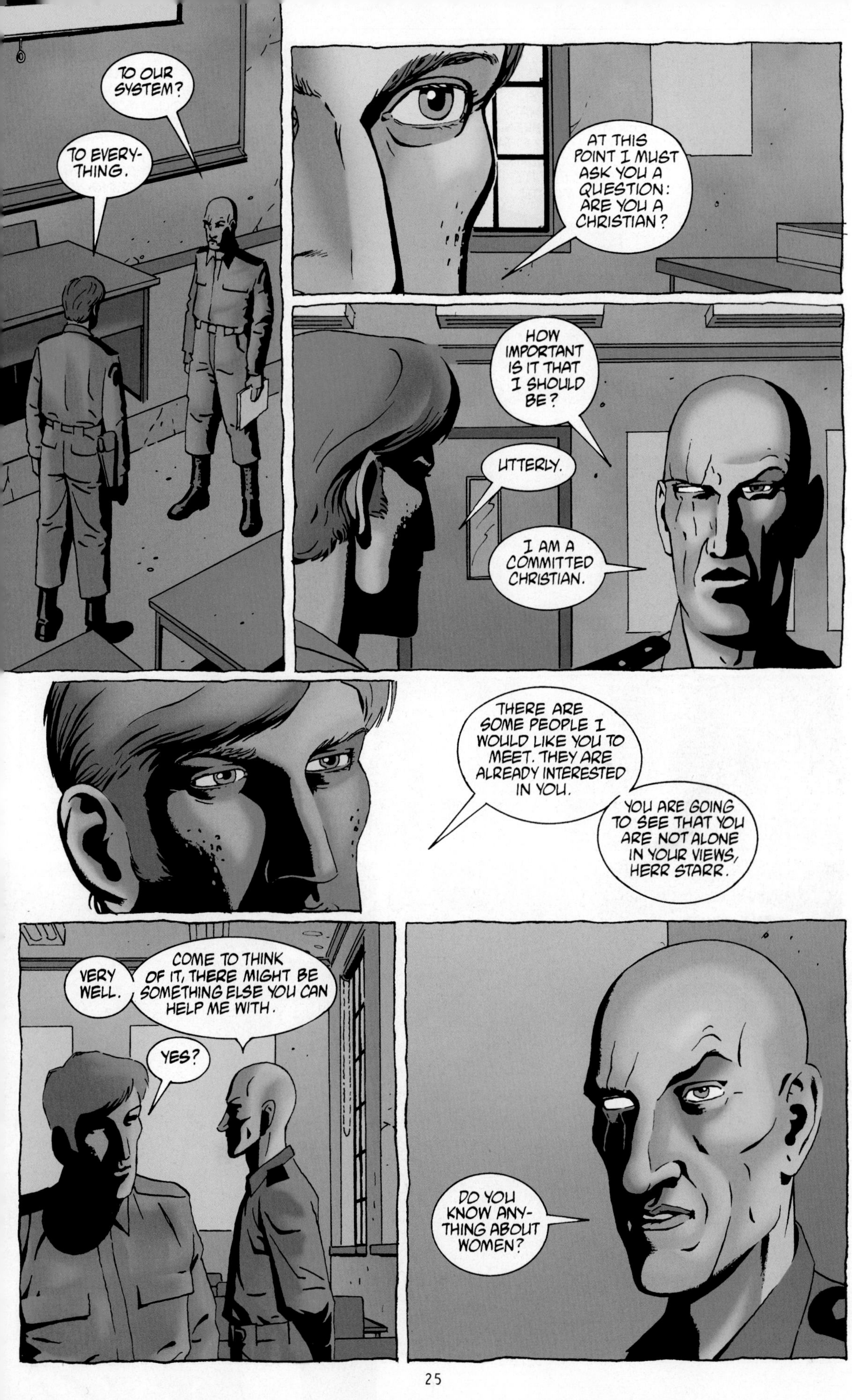
TO OUR SYSTEM?
TO EVERY-THING.
AT THIS POINT I MUST ASK YOU A QUESTION: ARE YOU A CHRISTIAN?
HOW IMPORTANT IS IT THAT I SHOULD BE?
UTTERLY.
I AM A COMMITTED CHRISTIAN.
THERE ARE SOME PEOPLE I WOULD LIKE YOU TO MEET. THEY ARE ALREADY INTERESTED IN YOU.
YOU ARE GOING TO SEE THAT YOU ARE NOT ALONE IN YOUR VIEWS, HERR STARR.
VERY WELL.
COME TO THINK OF IT, THERE MIGHT BE SOMETHING ELSE YOU CAN HELP ME WITH.
YES?
DO YOU KNOW ANY-THING ABOUT WOMEN?

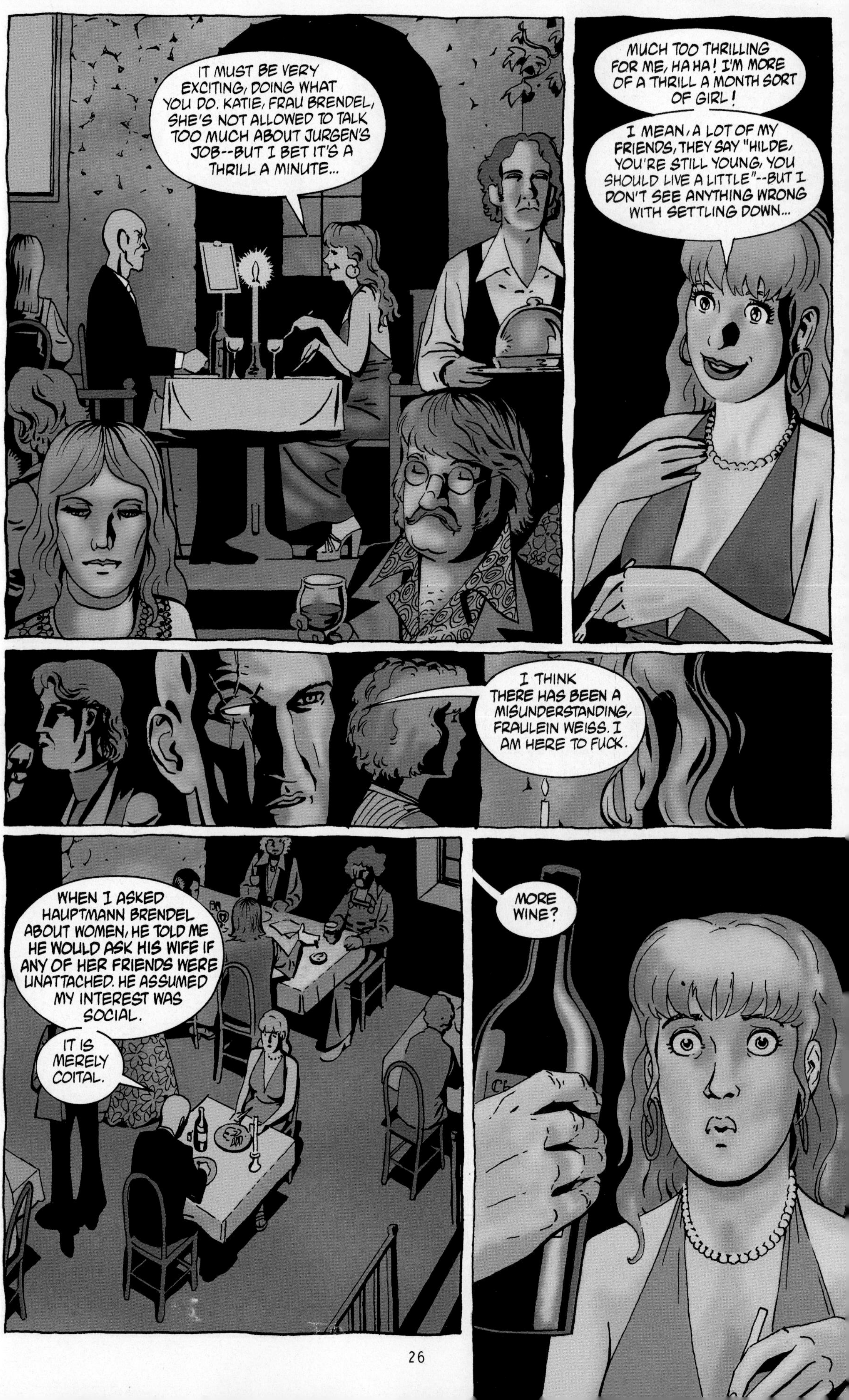
IT MUST BE VERY EXCITING, DOING WHAT YOU DO. KATIE, FRAU BRENDEL, SHE'S NOT ALLOWED TO TALK TOO MUCH ABOUT JURGEN'S JOB--BUT I BET IT'S A THRILL A MINUTE...
MUCH TOO THRILLING FOR ME, HA HA! I'M MORE OF A THRILL A MONTH SORT OF GIRL!
I MEAN, A LOT OF MY FRIENDS, THEY SAY "HILDE, YOU'RE STILL YOUNG, YOU SHOULD LIVE A LITTLE"--BUT I DON'T SEE ANYTHING WRONG WITH SETTLING DOWN...
I THINK THERE HAS BEEN A MISUNDERSTANDING, FRAULEIN WEISS. I AM HERE TO FUCK.
WHEN I ASKED HAUPTMANN BRENDEL ABOUT WOMEN, HE TOLD ME HE WOULD ASK HIS WIFE IF ANY OF HER FRIENDS WERE UNATTACHED. HE ASSUMED MY INTEREST WAS SOCIAL.
IT IS MERELY COITAL.
MORE WINE?

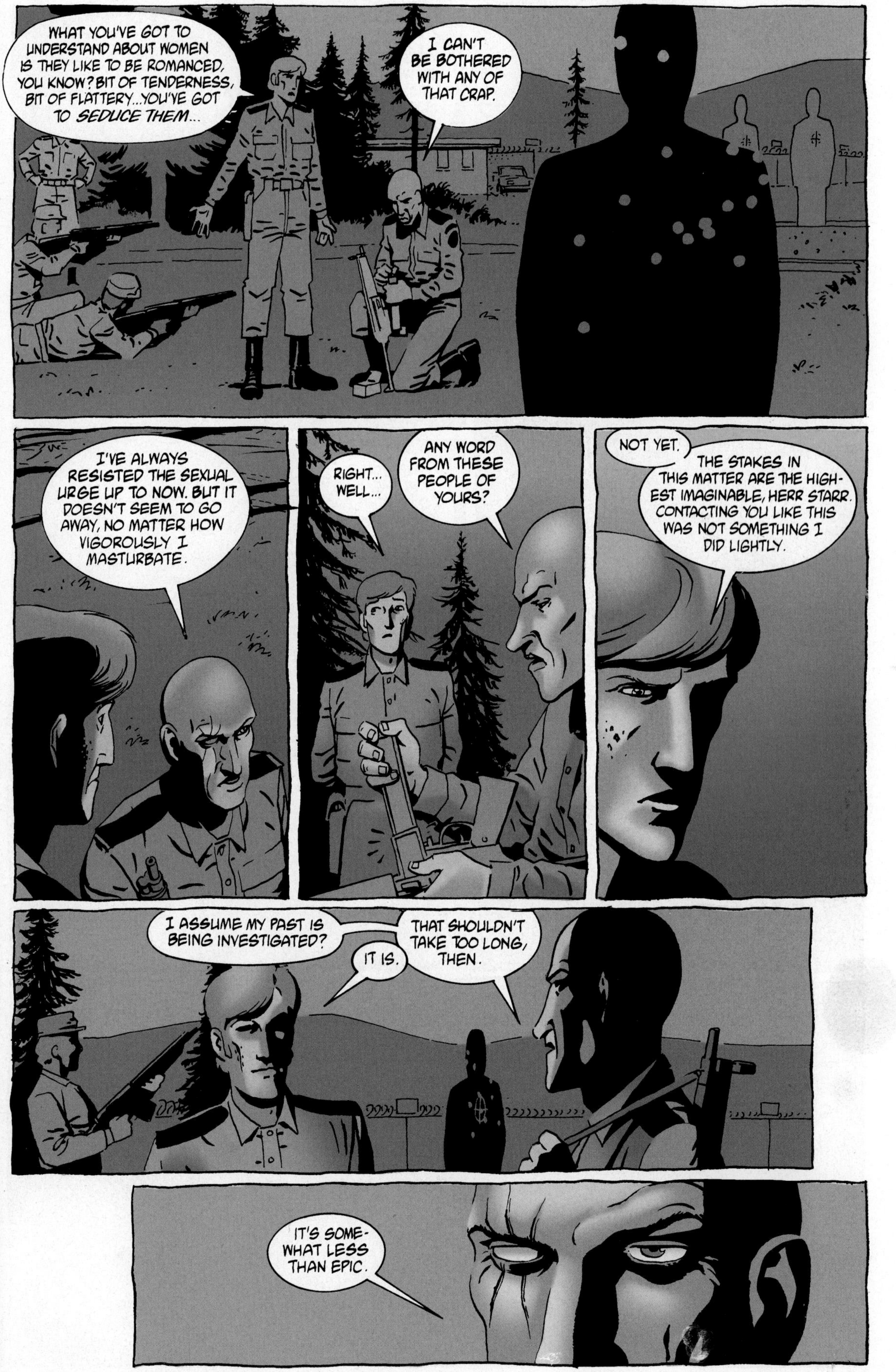
WHAT YOU'VE GOT TO UNDERSTAND ABOUT WOMEN IS THEY LIKE TO BE ROMANCED, YOU KNOW? BIT OF TENDERNESS, BIT OF FLATTERY...YOU'VE GOT TO SEDUCE THEM...
I CAN'T BE BOTHERED WITH ANY OF THAT CRAP.
I'VE ALWAYS RESISTED THE SEXUAL URGE UP TO NOW. BUT IT DOESN'T SEEM TO GO AWAY, NO MATTER HOW VIGOROUSLY I MASTURBATE.
RIGHT... WELL...
ANY WORD FROM THESE PEOPLE OF YOURS?
NOT YET.
THE STAKES IN THIS MATTER ARE THE HIGHEST IMAGINABLE, HERR STARR. CONTACTING YOU LIKE THIS WAS NOT SOMETHING I DID LIGHTLY.
I ASSUME MY PAST IS BEING INVESTIGATED?
IT IS.
THAT SHOULDN'T TAKE TOO LONG, THEN.
IT'S SOMEWHAT LESS THAN EPIC.

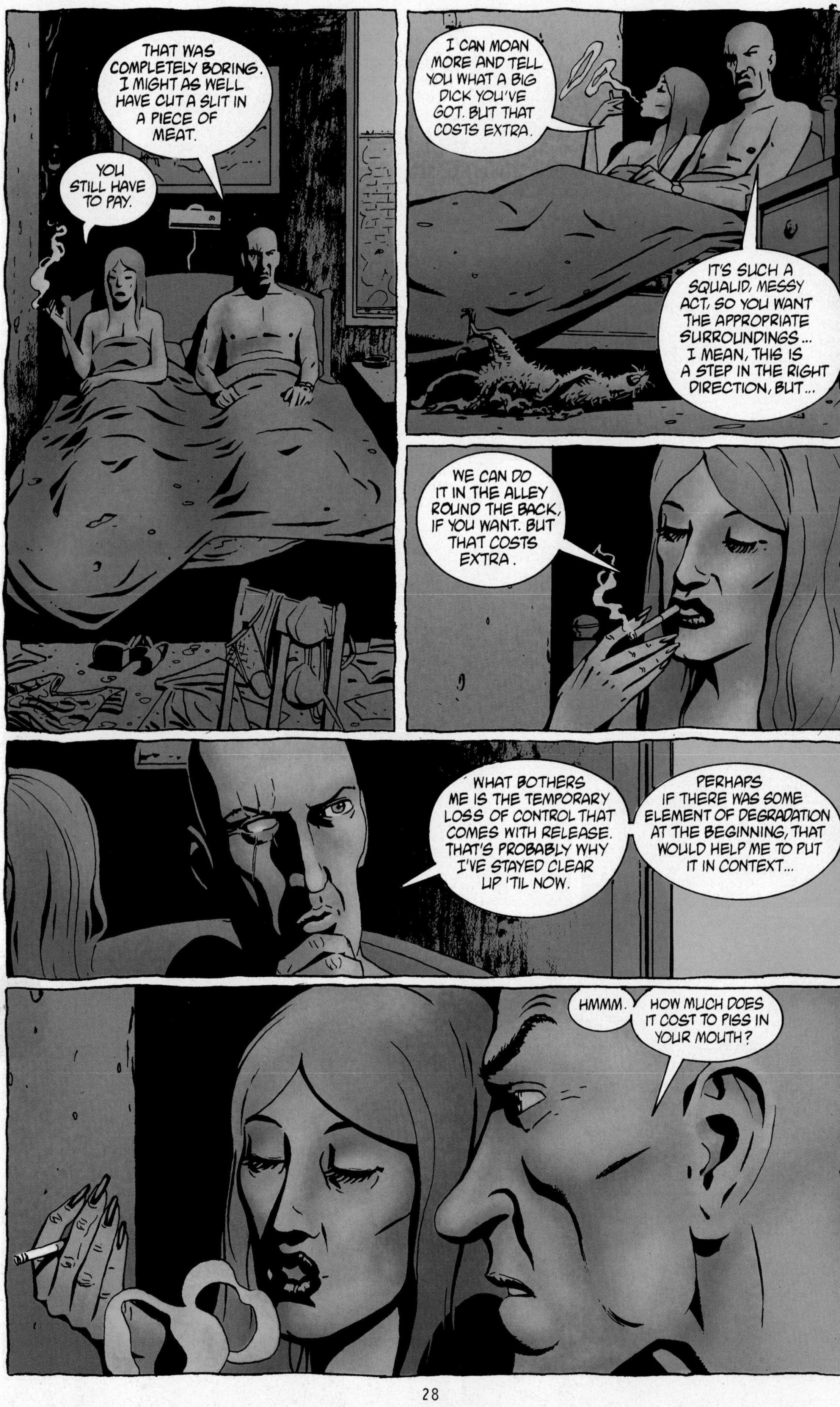
THAT WAS COMPLETELY BORING. I MIGHT AS WELL HAVE CUT A SLIT IN A PIECE OF MEAT.
YOU STILL HAVE TO PAY.
I CAN MOAN MORE AND TELL YOU WHAT A BIG DICK YOU'VE GOT. BUT THAT COSTS EXTRA.
IT'S SUCH A SQUALID, MESSY ACT, SO YOU WANT THE APPROPRIATE SURROUNDINGS... I MEAN, THIS IS A STEP IN THE RIGHT DIRECTION, BUT...
WE CAN DO IT IN THE ALLEY ROUND THE BACK, IF YOU WANT. BUT THAT COSTS EXTRA.
WHAT BOTHERS ME IS THE TEMPORARY LOSS OF CONTROL THAT COMES WITH RELEASE. THAT'S PROBABLY WHY I'VE STAYED CLEAR UP 'TIL NOW.
PERHAPS IF THERE WAS SOME ELEMENT OF DEGRADATION AT THE BEGINNING, THAT WOULD HELP ME TO PUT IT IN CONTEXT...
HMMM.
HOW MUCH DOES IT COST TO PISS IN YOUR MOUTH?

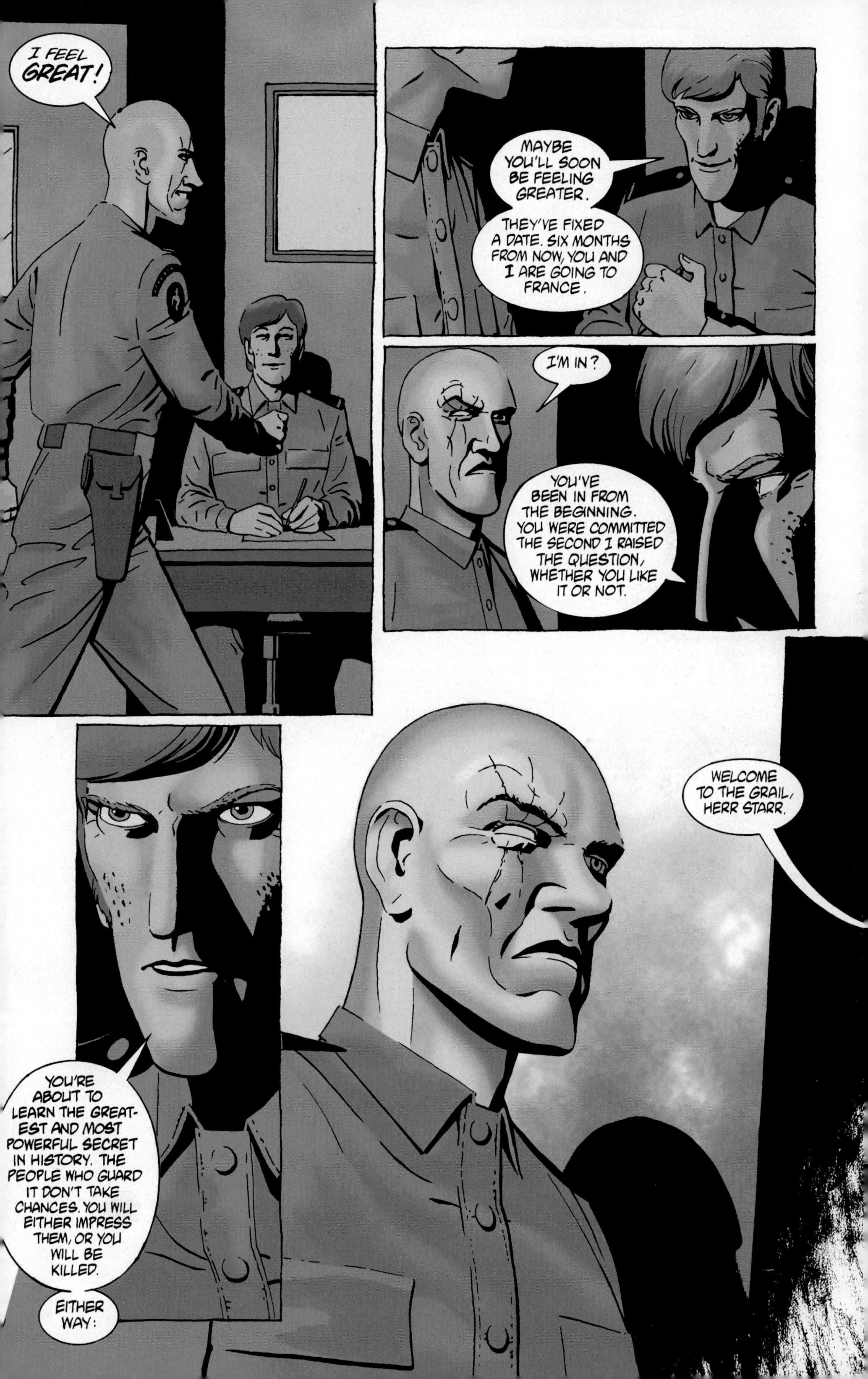
I FEEL GREAT!
MAYBE YOU'LL SOON BE FEELING GREATER.
THEY'VE FIXED A DATE. SIX MONTHS FROM NOW, YOU AND I ARE GOING TO FRANCE.
I'M IN?
YOU'VE BEEN IN FROM THE BEGINNING. YOU WERE COMMITTED THE SECOND I RAISED THE QUESTION, WHETHER YOU LIKE IT OR NOT.
YOU'RE ABOUT TO LEARN THE GREAT-EST AND MOST POWERFUL SECRET IN HISTORY. THE PEOPLE WHO GUARD IT DON'T TAKE CHANCES. YOU WILL EITHER IMPRESS THEM, OR YOU WILL BE KILLED.
EITHER WAY:
WELCOME TO THE GRAIL, HERR STARR.

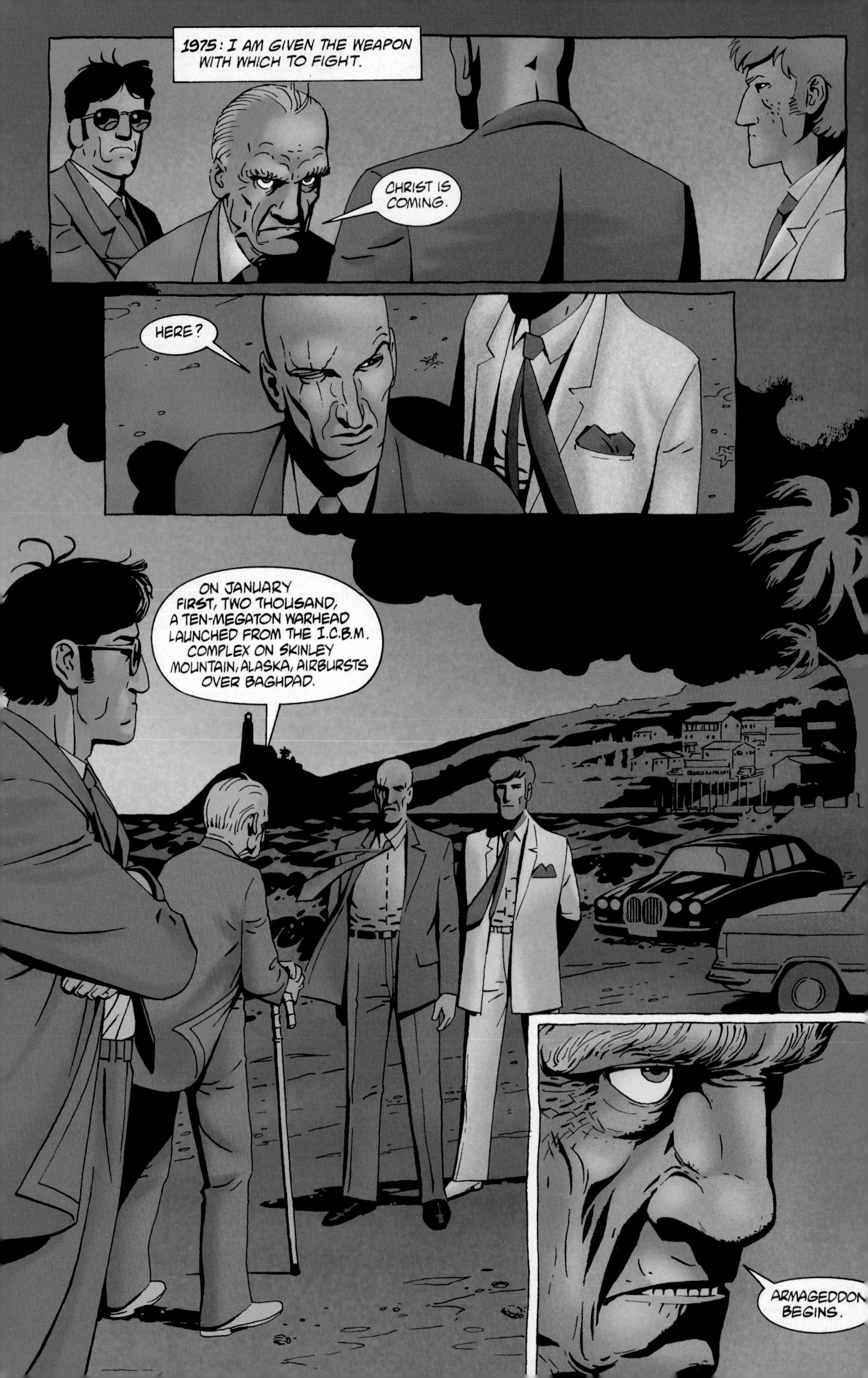
1975: I AM GIVEN THE WEAPON WITH WHICH TO FIGHT.
CHRIST IS COMING.
HERE?
ON JANUARY FIRST, TWO THOUSAND, A TEN-MEGATON WARHEAD LAUNCHED FROM THE I.C.B.M. COMPLEX ON SKINLEY MOUNTAIN, ALASKA, AIRBURSTS OVER BAGHDAD.
ARMAGEDDON BEGINS.

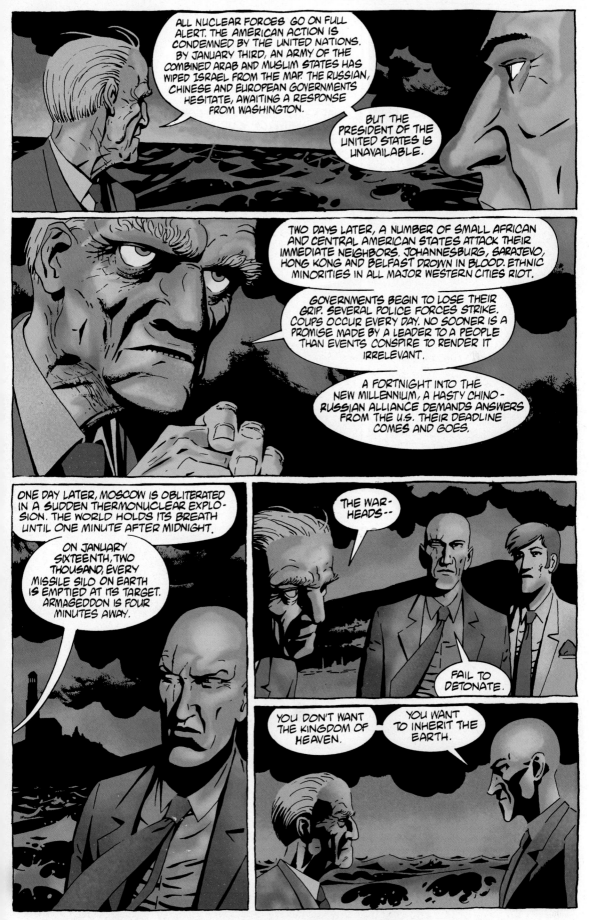

ALL NUCLEAR FORCES GO ON FULL ALERT. THE AMERICAN ACTION IS CONDEMNED BY THE UNITED NATIONS. BY JANUARY THIRD, AN ARMY OF THE COMBINED ARAB AND MUSLIM STATES HAS WIPED ISRAEL FROM THE MAP. THE RUSSIAN, CHINESE AND EUROPEAN GOVERNMENTS HESITATE, AWAITING A RESPONSE FROM WASHINGTON.

BUT THE PRESIDENT OF THE UNITED STATES IS UNAVAILABLE.

TWO DAYS LATER, A NUMBER OF SMALL AFRICAN AND CENTRAL AMERICAN STATES ATTACK THEIR IMMEDIATE NEIGHBORS. JOHANNESBURG, SARAJEVO, HONG KONG AND BELFAST DROWN IN BLOOD. ETHNIC MINORITIES IN ALL MAJOR WESTERN CITIES RIOT.

GOVERNMENTS BEGIN TO LOSE THEIR GRIP. SEVERAL POLICE FORCES STRIKE. COUPS OCCUR EVERY DAY. NO SOONER IS A PROMISE MADE BY A LEADER TO A PEOPLE THAN EVENTS CONSPIRE TO RENDER IT IRRELEVANT.

A FORTNIGHT INTO THE NEW MILLENNIUM, A HASTY CHINO-RUSSIAN ALLIANCE DEMANDS ANSWERS FROM THE U.S. THEIR DEADLINE COMES AND GOES.

ONE DAY LATER, MOSCOW IS OBLITERATED IN A SUDDEN THERMONUCLEAR EXPLOSION. THE WORLD HOLDS ITS BREATH UNTIL ONE MINUTE AFTER MIDNIGHT.

ON JANUARY SIXTEENTH, TWO THOUSAND, EVERY MISSILE SILO ON EARTH IS EMPTIED AT ITS TARGET. ARMAGEDDON IS FOUR MINUTES AWAY.

THE WAR-HEADS--

FAIL TO DETONATE.

YOU DON'T WANT THE KINGDOM OF HEAVEN.

YOU WANT TO INHERIT THE EARTH.

31

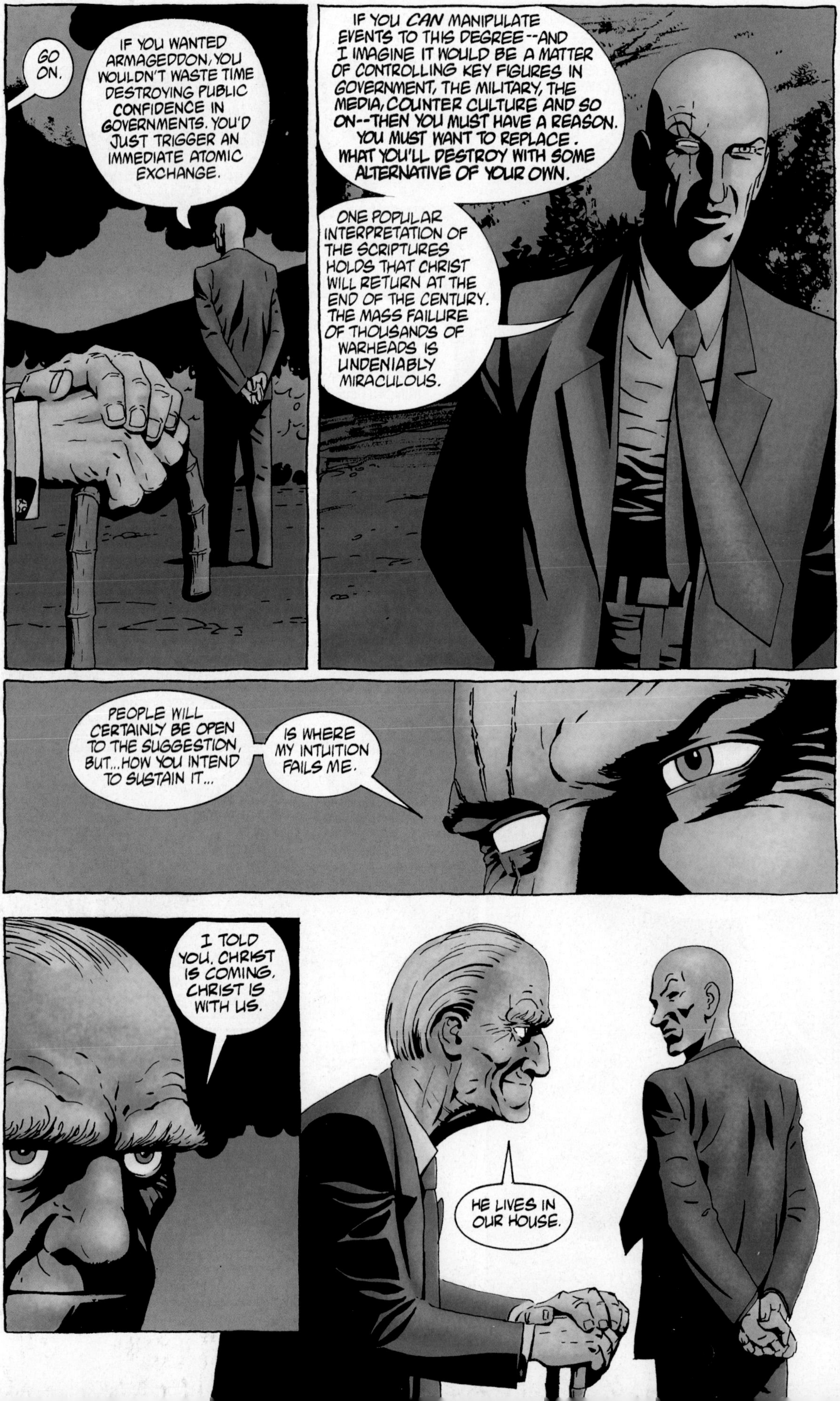
GO ON.
IF YOU WANTED ARMAGEDDON, YOU WOULDN'T WASTE TIME DESTROYING PUBLIC CONFIDENCE IN GOVERNMENTS. YOU'D JUST TRIGGER AN IMMEDIATE ATOMIC EXCHANGE.
IF YOU CAN MANIPULATE EVENTS TO THIS DEGREE--AND I IMAGINE IT WOULD BE A MATTER OF CONTROLLING KEY FIGURES IN GOVERNMENT, THE MILITARY, THE MEDIA, COUNTER CULTURE AND SO ON--THEN YOU MUST HAVE A REASON. YOU MUST WANT TO REPLACE . WHAT YOU'LL DESTROY WITH SOME ALTERNATIVE OF YOUR OWN.
ONE POPULAR INTERPRETATION OF THE SCRIPTURES HOLDS THAT CHRIST WILL RETURN AT THE END OF THE CENTURY. THE MASS FAILURE OF THOUSANDS OF WARHEADS IS UNDENIABLY MIRACULOUS.
PEOPLE WILL CERTAINLY BE OPEN TO THE SUGGESTION, BUT...HOW YOU INTEND TO SUSTAIN IT...
IS WHERE MY INTUITION FAILS ME.
I TOLD YOU. CHRIST IS COMING. CHRIST IS WITH US.
HE LIVES IN OUR HOUSE.

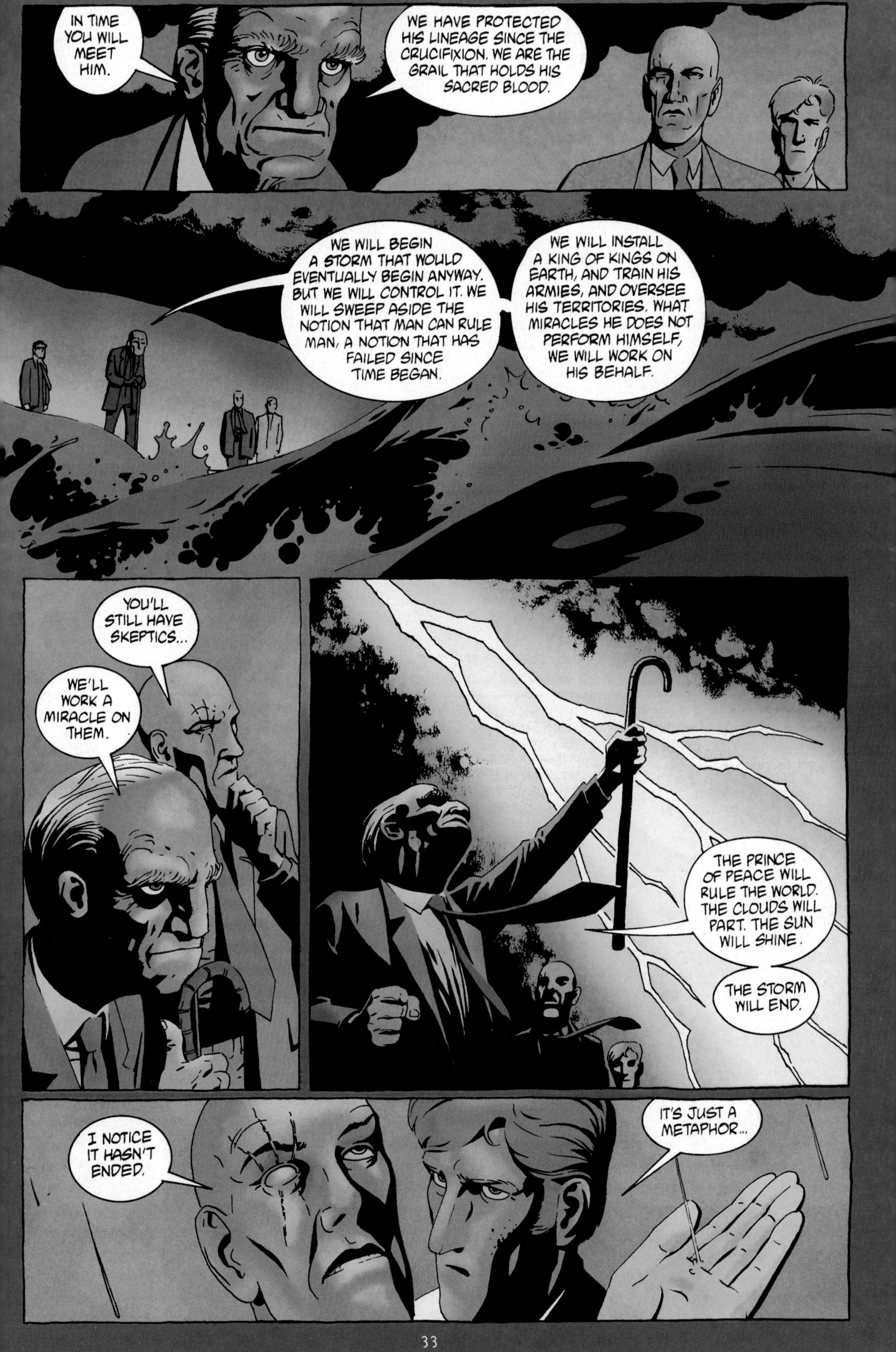
IN TIME YOU WILL MEET HIM.
WE HAVE PROTECTED HIS LINEAGE SINCE THE CRUCIFIXION. WE ARE THE GRAIL THAT HOLDS HIS SACRED BLOOD.
WE WILL BEGIN A STORM THAT WOULD EVENTUALLY BEGIN ANYWAY. BUT WE WILL CONTROL IT. WE WILL SWEEP ASIDE THE NOTION THAT MAN CAN RULE MAN, A NOTION THAT HAS FAILED SINCE TIME BEGAN.
WE WILL INSTALL A KING OF KINGS ON EARTH, AND TRAIN HIS ARMIES, AND OVERSEE HIS TERRITORIES. WHAT MIRACLES HE DOES NOT PERFORM HIMSELF, WE WILL WORK ON HIS BEHALF.
YOU'LL STILL HAVE SKEPTICS...
WE'LL WORK A MIRACLE ON THEM.
THE PRINCE OF PEACE WILL RULE THE WORLD. THE CLOUDS WILL PART. THE SUN WILL SHINE.
THE STORM WILL END.
I NOTICE IT HASN'T ENDED.
IT'S JUST A METAPHOR...

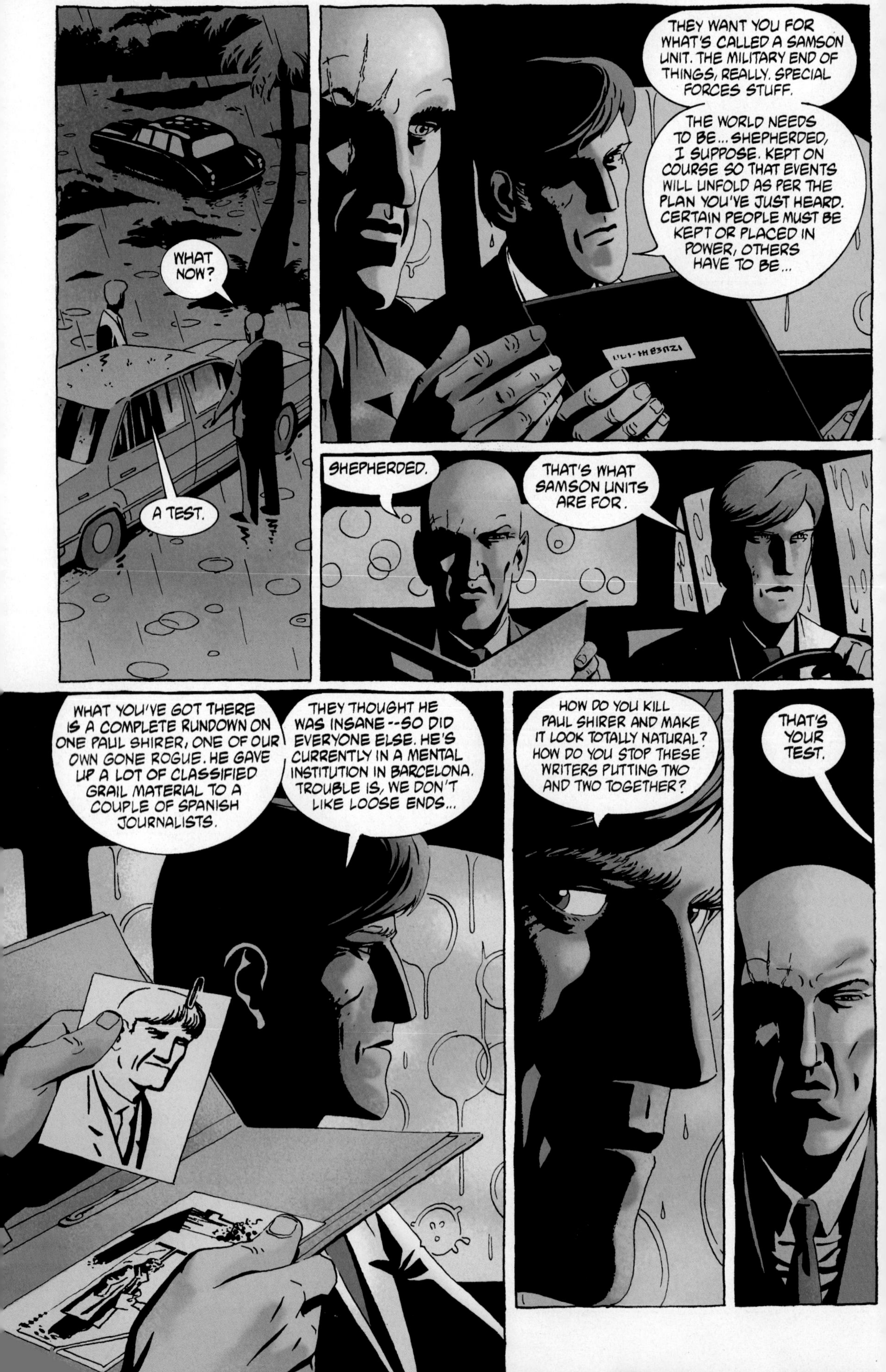

WHAT NOW?
A TEST.
THEY WANT YOU FOR WHAT'S CALLED A SAMSON UNIT. THE MILITARY END OF THINGS, REALLY. SPECIAL FORCES STUFF.
THE WORLD NEEDS TO BE... SHEPHERDED, I SUPPOSE. KEPT ON COURSE SO THAT EVENTS WILL UNFOLD AS PER THE PLAN YOU'VE JUST HEARD. CERTAIN PEOPLE MUST BE KEPT OR PLACED IN POWER, OTHERS HAVE TO BE...
SHEPHERDED.
THAT'S WHAT SAMSON UNITS ARE FOR.
WHAT YOU'VE GOT THERE IS A COMPLETE RUNDOWN ON ONE PAUL SHIRER, ONE OF OUR OWN GONE ROGUE. HE GAVE UP A LOT OF CLASSIFIED GRAIL MATERIAL TO A COUPLE OF SPANISH JOURNALISTS.
THEY THOUGHT HE WAS INSANE--SO DID EVERYONE ELSE. HE'S CURRENTLY IN A MENTAL INSTITUTION IN BARCELONA. TROUBLE IS, WE DON'T LIKE LOOSE ENDS...
HOW DO YOU KILL PAUL SHIRER AND MAKE IT LOOK TOTALLY NATURAL? HOW DO YOU STOP THESE WRITERS PUTTING TWO AND TWO TOGETHER?
THAT'S YOUR TEST.

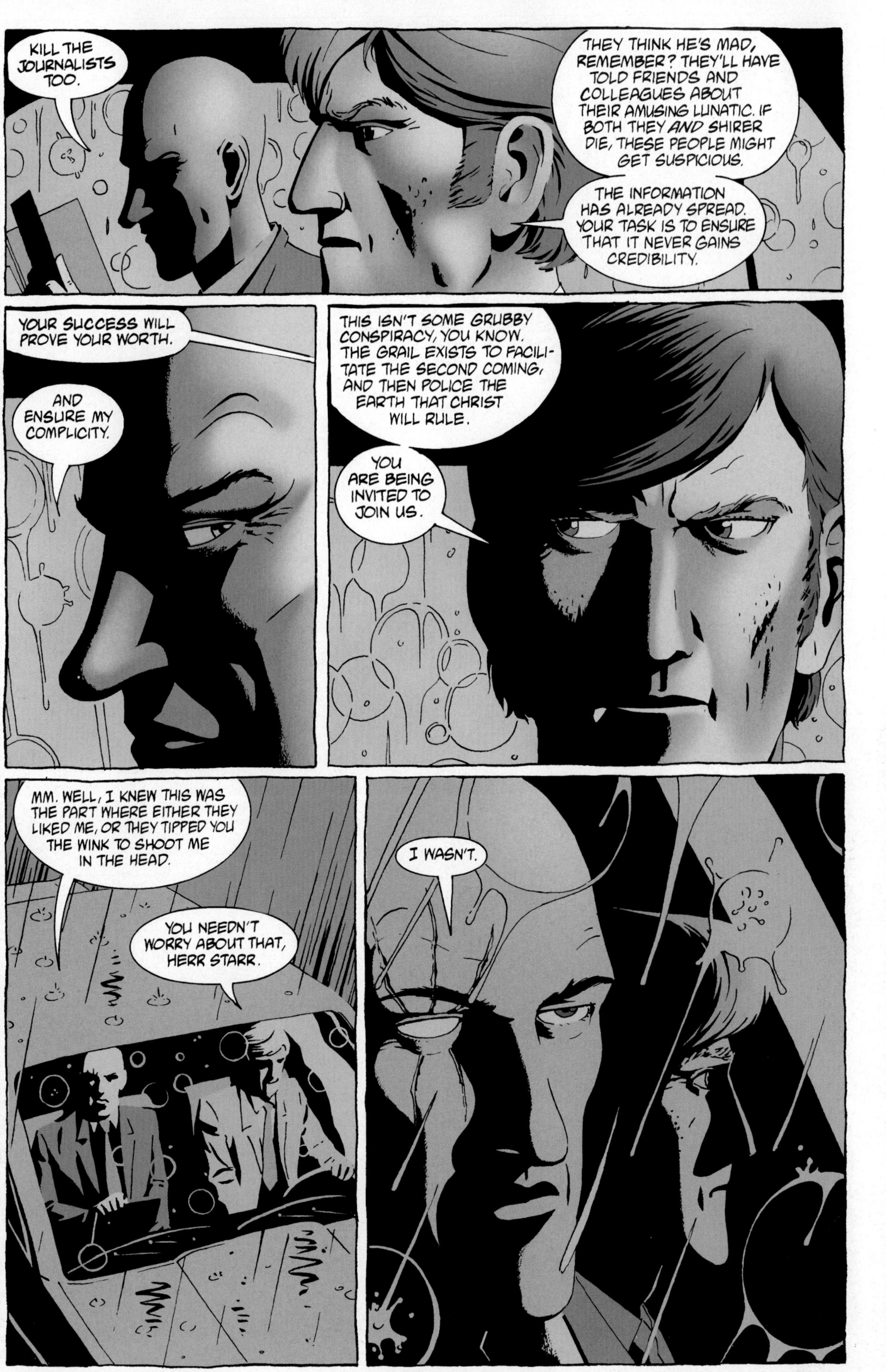
KILL THE JOURNALISTS TOO.
THEY THINK HE'S MAD, REMEMBER? THEY'LL HAVE TOLD FRIENDS AND COLLEAGUES ABOUT THEIR AMUSING LUNATIC. IF BOTH THEY *AND* SHIRER DIE, THESE PEOPLE MIGHT GET SUSPICIOUS.
THE INFORMATION HAS ALREADY SPREAD. YOUR TASK IS TO ENSURE THAT IT NEVER GAINS CREDIBILITY.
YOUR SUCCESS WILL PROVE YOUR WORTH.
AND ENSURE MY COMPLICITY.
THIS ISN'T SOME GRUBBY CONSPIRACY, YOU KNOW. THE GRAIL EXISTS TO FACILITATE THE SECOND COMING, AND THEN POLICE THE EARTH THAT CHRIST WILL RULE.
YOU ARE BEING INVITED TO JOIN US.
MM. WELL, I KNEW THIS WAS THE PART WHERE EITHER THEY LIKED ME, OR THEY TIPPED YOU THE WINK TO SHOOT ME IN THE HEAD.
YOU NEEDN'T WORRY ABOUT THAT, HERR STARR.
I WASN'T.

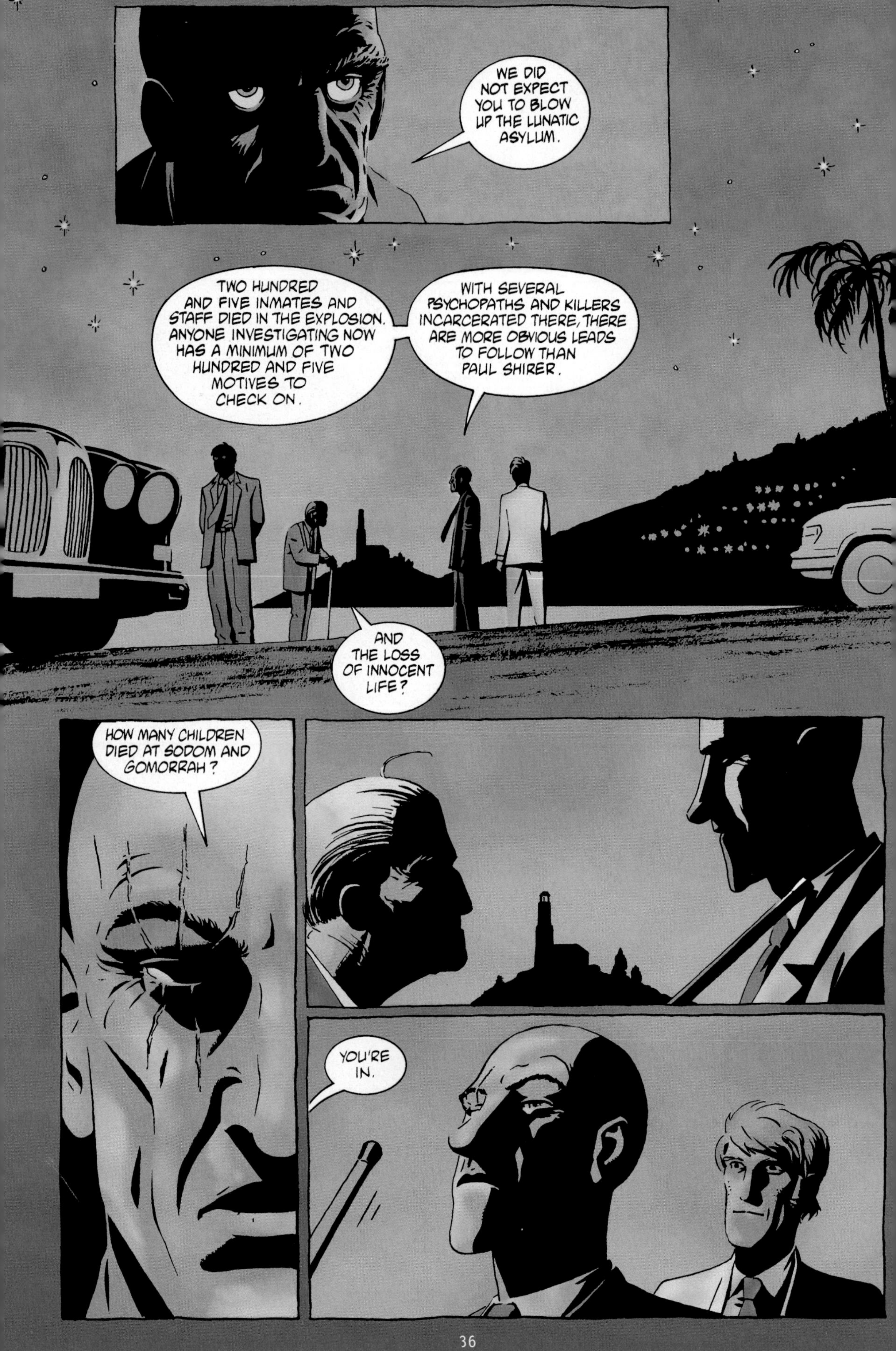
WE DID NOT EXPECT YOU TO BLOW UP THE LUNATIC ASYLUM.
TWO HUNDRED AND FIVE INMATES AND STAFF DIED IN THE EXPLOSION. ANYONE INVESTIGATING NOW HAS A MINIMUM OF TWO HUNDRED AND FIVE MOTIVES TO CHECK ON.
WITH SEVERAL PSYCHOPATHS AND KILLERS INCARCERATED THERE, THERE ARE MORE OBVIOUS LEADS TO FOLLOW THAN PAUL SHIRER.
AND THE LOSS OF INNOCENT LIFE?
HOW MANY CHILDREN DIED AT SODOM AND GOMORRAH?
YOU'RE IN.

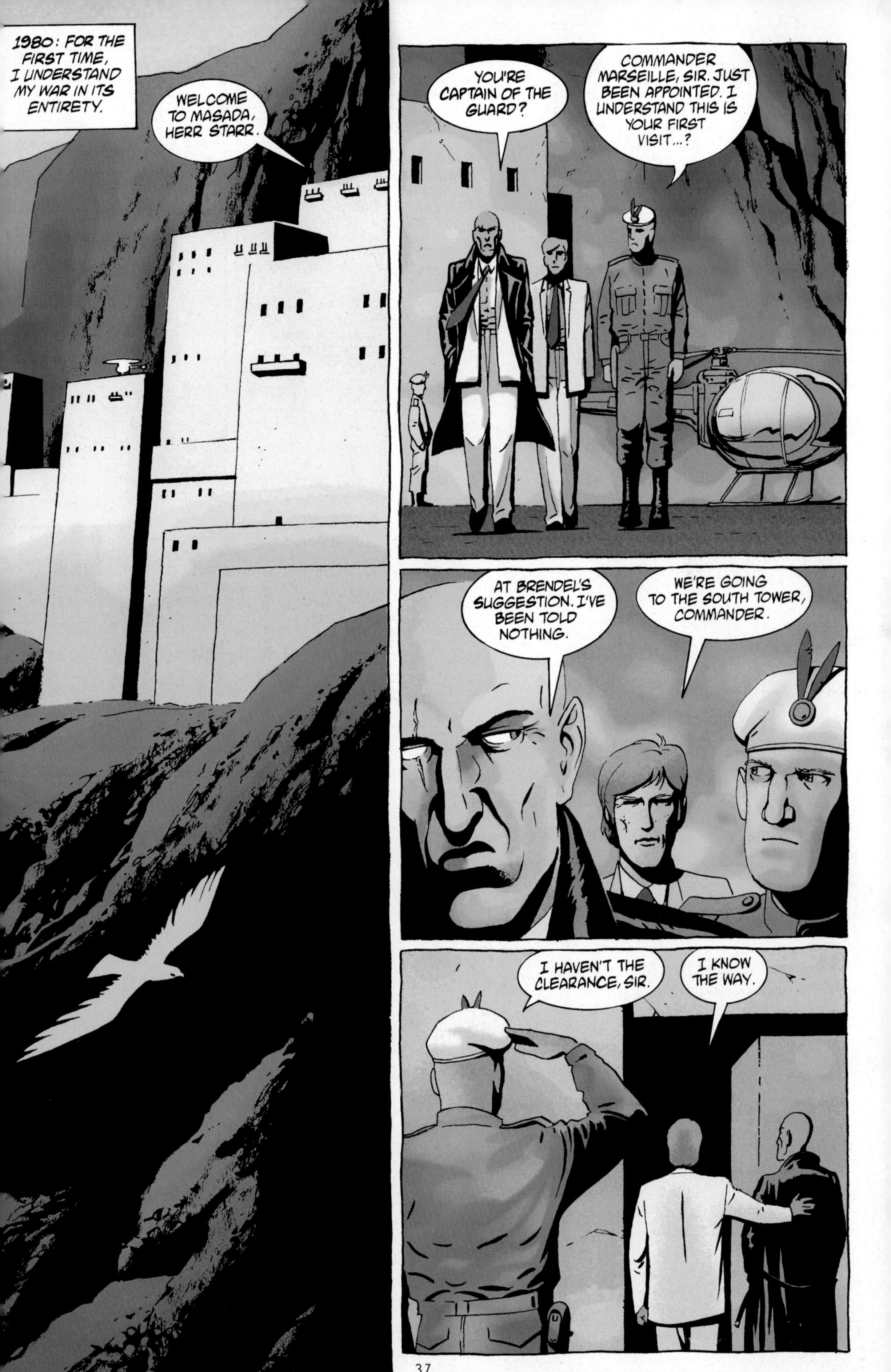

1980: FOR THE FIRST TIME, I UNDERSTAND MY WAR IN ITS ENTIRETY.
WELCOME TO MASADA, HERR STARR.
YOU'RE CAPTAIN OF THE GUARD?
COMMANDER MARSEILLE, SIR. JUST BEEN APPOINTED. I UNDERSTAND THIS IS YOUR FIRST VISIT...?
AT BRENDEL'S SUGGESTION. I'VE BEEN TOLD NOTHING.
WE'RE GOING TO THE SOUTH TOWER, COMMANDER.
I HAVEN'T THE CLEARANCE, SIR.
I KNOW THE WAY.

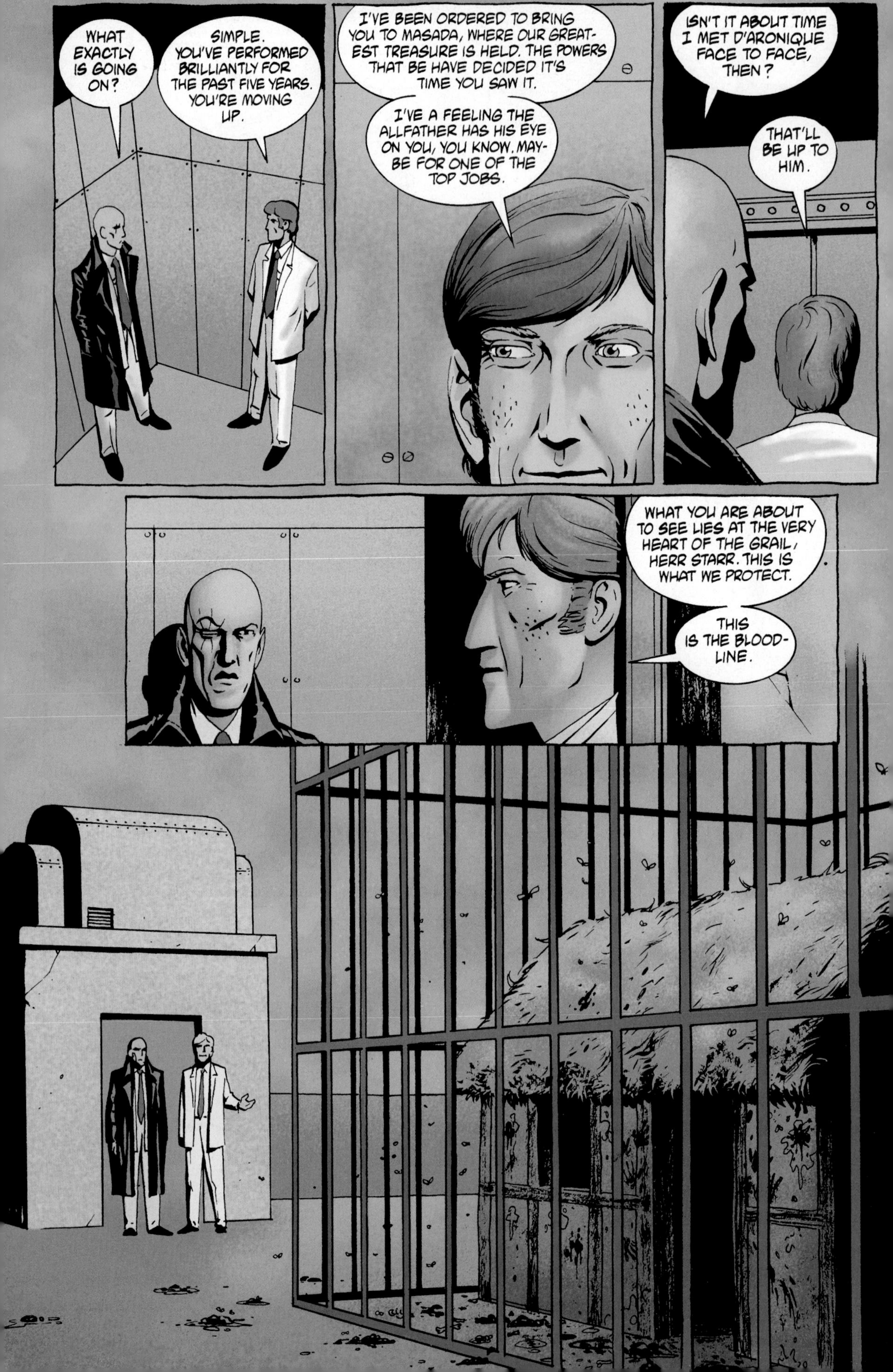
WHAT EXACTLY IS GOING ON?
SIMPLE. YOU'VE PERFORMED BRILLIANTLY FOR THE PAST FIVE YEARS. YOU'RE MOVING UP.
I'VE BEEN ORDERED TO BRING YOU TO MASADA, WHERE OUR GREAT-EST TREASURE IS HELD. THE POWERS THAT BE HAVE DECIDED IT'S TIME YOU SAW IT.
I'VE A FEELING THE ALLFATHER HAS HIS EYE ON YOU, YOU KNOW. MAY-BE FOR ONE OF THE TOP JOBS.
ISN'T IT ABOUT TIME I MET D'ARONIQUE FACE TO FACE, THEN?
THAT'LL BE UP TO HIM.
WHAT YOU ARE ABOUT TO SEE LIES AT THE VERY HEART OF THE GRAIL, HERR STARR. THIS IS WHAT WE PROTECT.
THIS IS THE BLOOD-LINE.

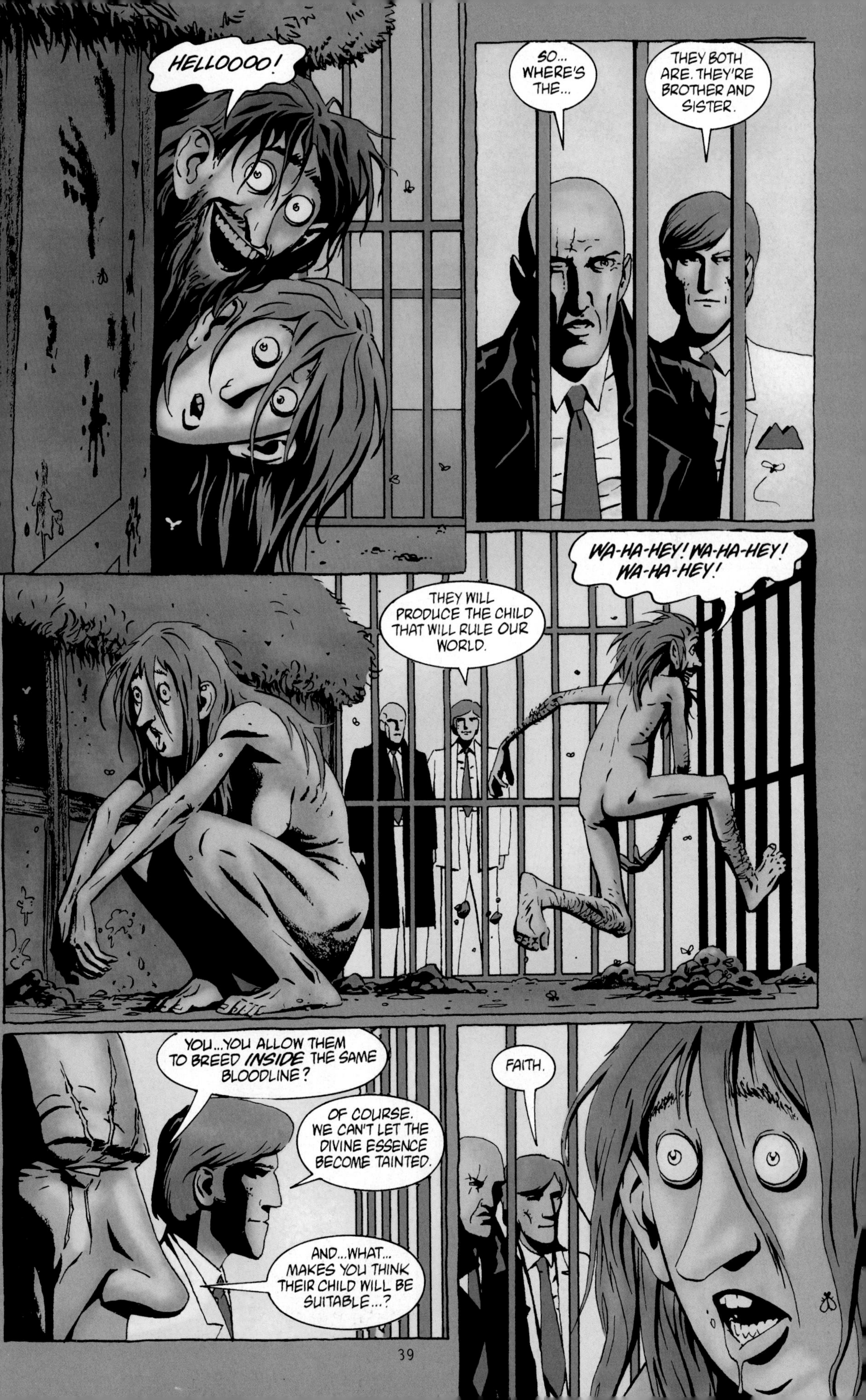
HELLOOOO!
SO... WHERE'S THE...
THEY BOTH ARE. THEY'RE BROTHER AND SISTER.
THEY WILL PRODUCE THE CHILD THAT WILL RULE OUR WORLD.
WA-HA-HEY! WA-HA-HEY! WA-HA-HEY!
YOU...YOU ALLOW THEM TO BREED INSIDE THE SAME BLOODLINE?
OF COURSE. WE CAN'T LET THE DIVINE ESSENCE BECOME TAINTED.
AND...WHAT... MAKES YOU THINK THEIR CHILD WILL BE SUITABLE...?
FAITH.

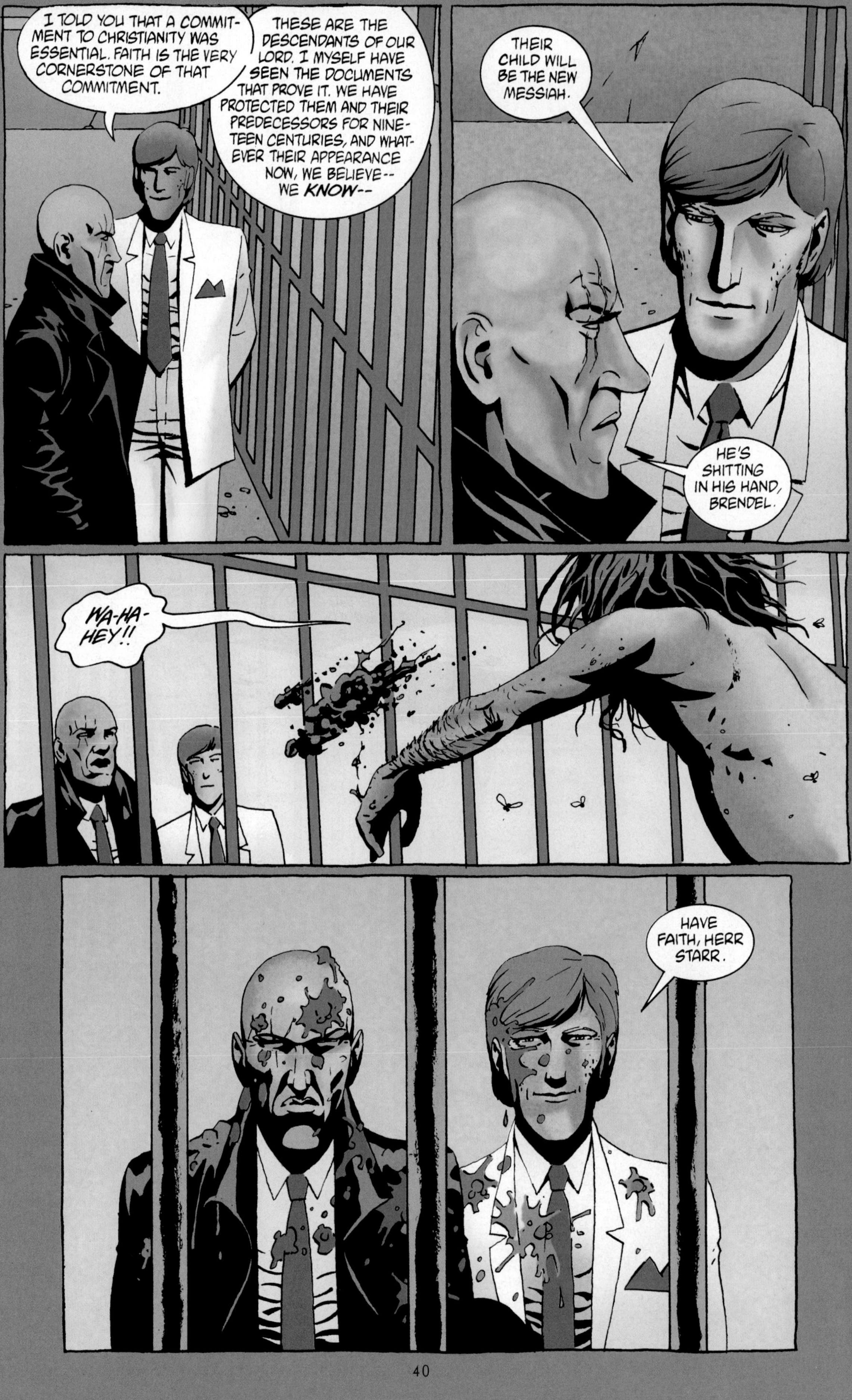
I TOLD YOU THAT A COMMITMENT TO CHRISTIANITY WAS ESSENTIAL. FAITH IS THE VERY CORNERSTONE OF THAT COMMITMENT.
THESE ARE THE DESCENDANTS OF OUR LORD. I MYSELF HAVE SEEN THE DOCUMENTS THAT PROVE IT. WE HAVE PROTECTED THEM AND THEIR PREDECESSORS FOR NINETEEN CENTURIES, AND WHATEVER THEIR APPEARANCE NOW, WE BELIEVE-- WE *KNOW*--
THEIR CHILD WILL BE THE NEW MESSIAH.
HE'S SHITTING IN HIS HAND, BRENDEL.
WA-HA-HEY!!
HAVE FAITH, HERR STARR.

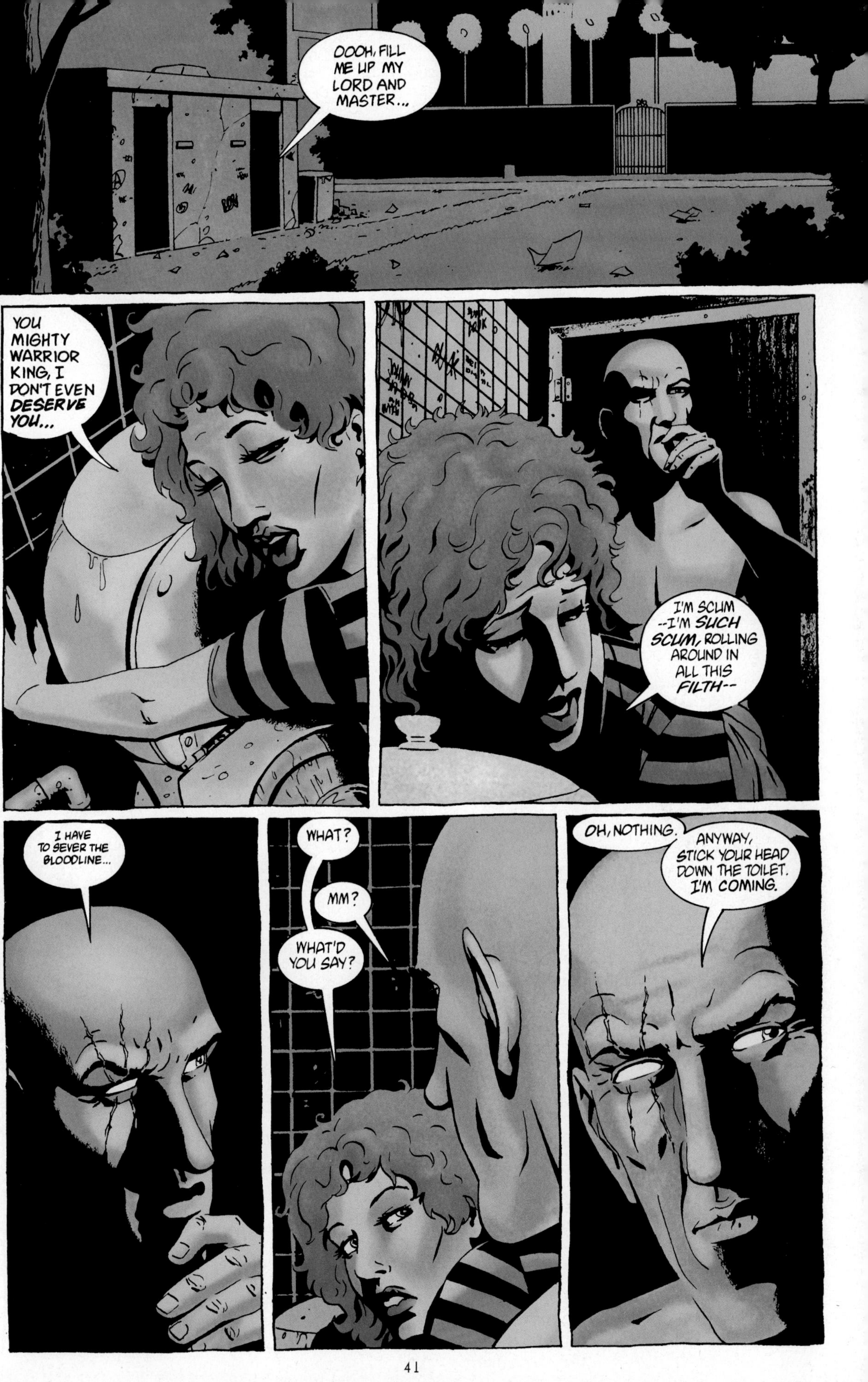
OOOH, FILL ME UP MY LORD AND MASTER...
YOU MIGHTY WARRIOR KING, I DON'T EVEN *DESERVE* YOU...
I'M SCUM --I'M *SUCH SCUM*, ROLLING AROUND IN ALL THIS *FILTH*--
I HAVE TO SEVER THE BLOODLINE...
WHAT?
MM?
WHAT'D YOU SAY?
OH, NOTHING.
ANYWAY, STICK YOUR HEAD DOWN THE TOILET. I'M COMING.

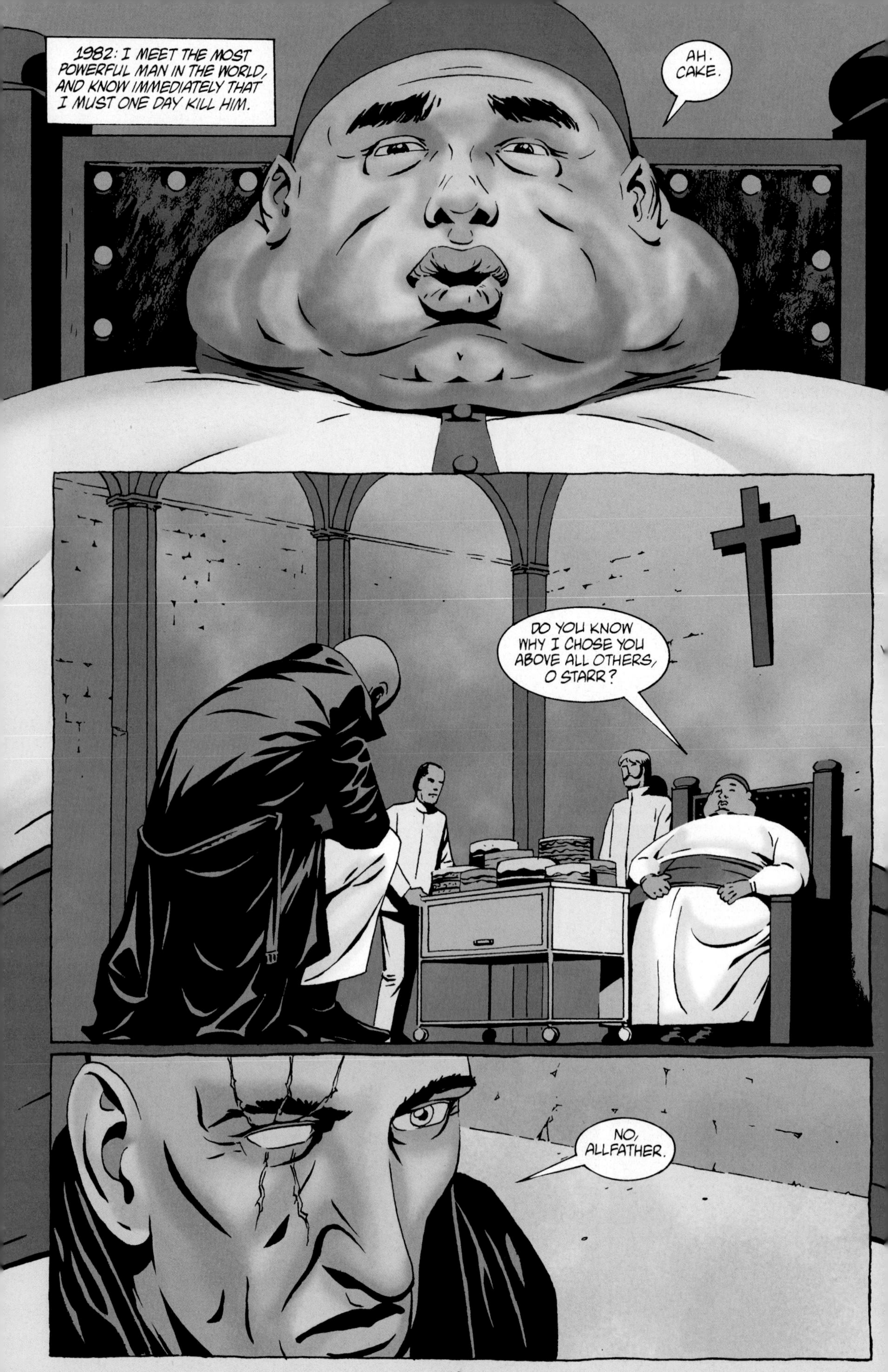
1982: I MEET THE MOST POWERFUL MAN IN THE WORLD, AND KNOW IMMEDIATELY THAT I MUST ONE DAY KILL HIM.
AH. CAKE.
DO YOU KNOW WHY I CHOSE YOU ABOVE ALL OTHERS, O STARR?
NO, ALLFATHER.

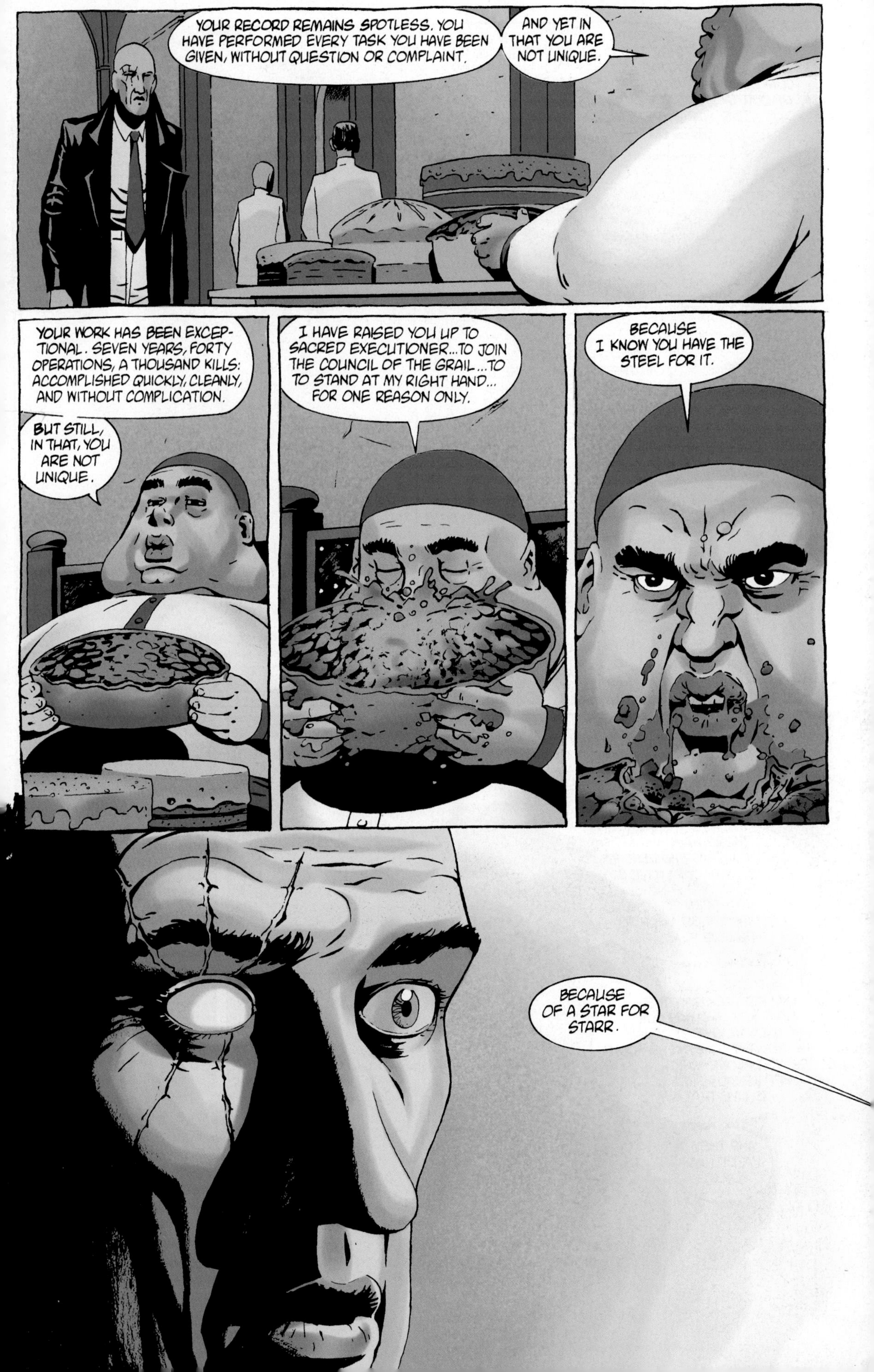
YOUR RECORD REMAINS SPOTLESS. YOU HAVE PERFORMED EVERY TASK YOU HAVE BEEN GIVEN, WITHOUT QUESTION OR COMPLAINT.
AND YET IN THAT YOU ARE NOT UNIQUE.
YOUR WORK HAS BEEN EXCEPTIONAL. SEVEN YEARS, FORTY OPERATIONS, A THOUSAND KILLS: ACCOMPLISHED QUICKLY, CLEANLY, AND WITHOUT COMPLICATION.
BUT STILL, IN THAT, YOU ARE NOT UNIQUE.
I HAVE RAISED YOU UP TO SACRED EXECUTIONER...TO JOIN THE COUNCIL OF THE GRAIL...TO TO STAND AT MY RIGHT HAND... FOR ONE REASON ONLY.
BECAUSE I KNOW YOU HAVE THE STEEL FOR IT.
BECAUSE OF A STAR FOR STARR.

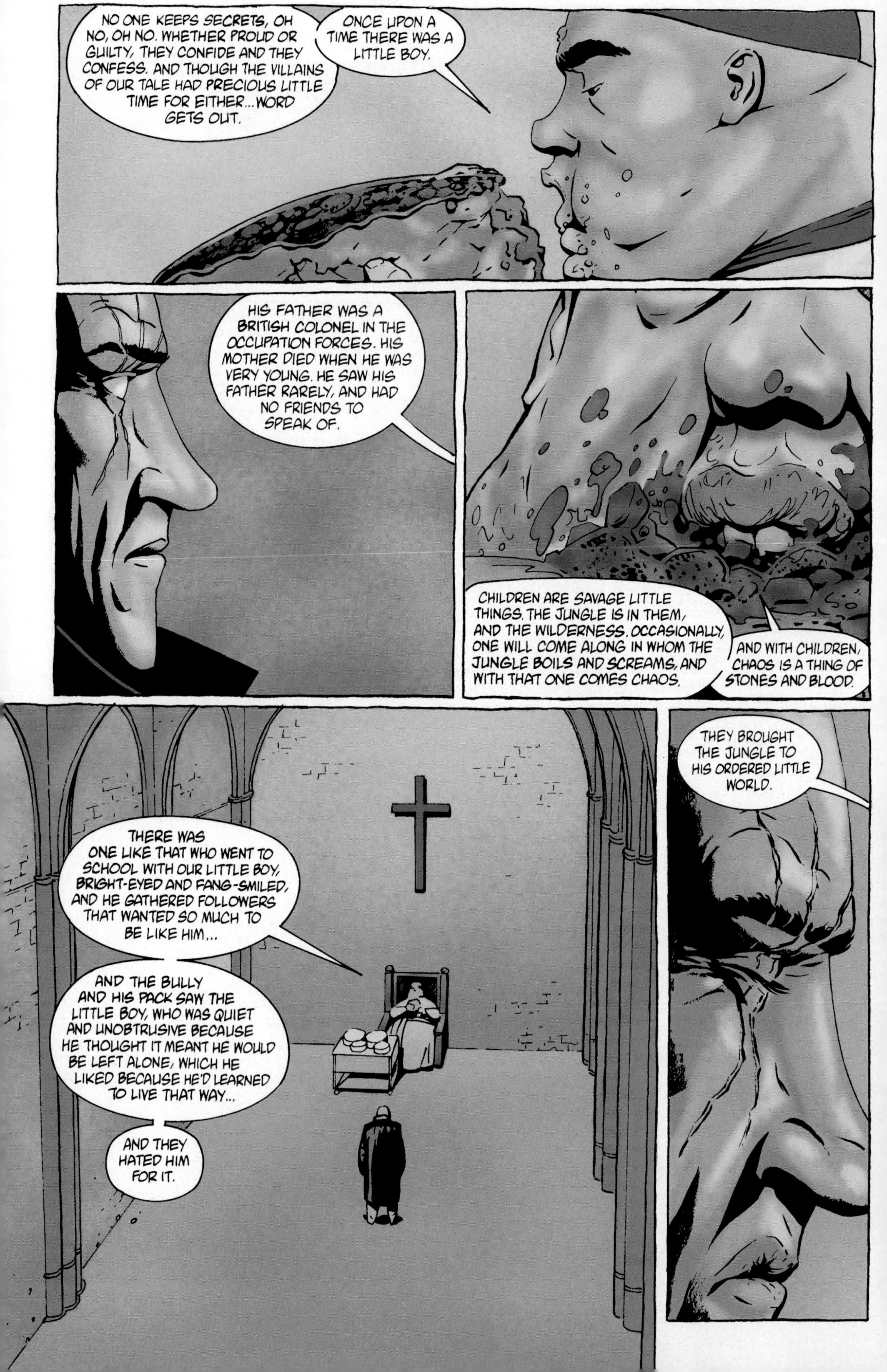
NO ONE KEEPS SECRETS, OH NO, OH NO. WHETHER PROUD OR GUILTY, THEY CONFIDE AND THEY CONFESS. AND THOUGH THE VILLAINS OF OUR TALE HAD PRECIOUS LITTLE TIME FOR EITHER... WORD GETS OUT.
ONCE UPON A TIME THERE WAS A LITTLE BOY.
HIS FATHER WAS A BRITISH COLONEL IN THE OCCUPATION FORCES. HIS MOTHER DIED WHEN HE WAS VERY YOUNG. HE SAW HIS FATHER RARELY, AND HAD NO FRIENDS TO SPEAK OF.
CHILDREN ARE SAVAGE LITTLE THINGS. THE JUNGLE IS IN THEM, AND THE WILDERNESS. OCCASIONALLY, ONE WILL COME ALONG IN WHOM THE JUNGLE BOILS AND SCREAMS, AND WITH THAT ONE COMES CHAOS.
AND WITH CHILDREN, CHAOS IS A THING OF STONES AND BLOOD.
THERE WAS ONE LIKE THAT WHO WENT TO SCHOOL WITH OUR LITTLE BOY, BRIGHT-EYED AND FANG-SMILED, AND HE GATHERED FOLLOWERS THAT WANTED SO MUCH TO BE LIKE HIM...
AND THE BULLY AND HIS PACK SAW THE LITTLE BOY, WHO WAS QUIET AND UNOBTRUSIVE BECAUSE HE THOUGHT IT MEANT HE WOULD BE LEFT ALONE, WHICH HE LIKED BECAUSE HE'D LEARNED TO LIVE THAT WAY...
AND THEY HATED HIM FOR IT.
THEY BROUGHT THE JUNGLE TO HIS ORDERED LITTLE WORLD.

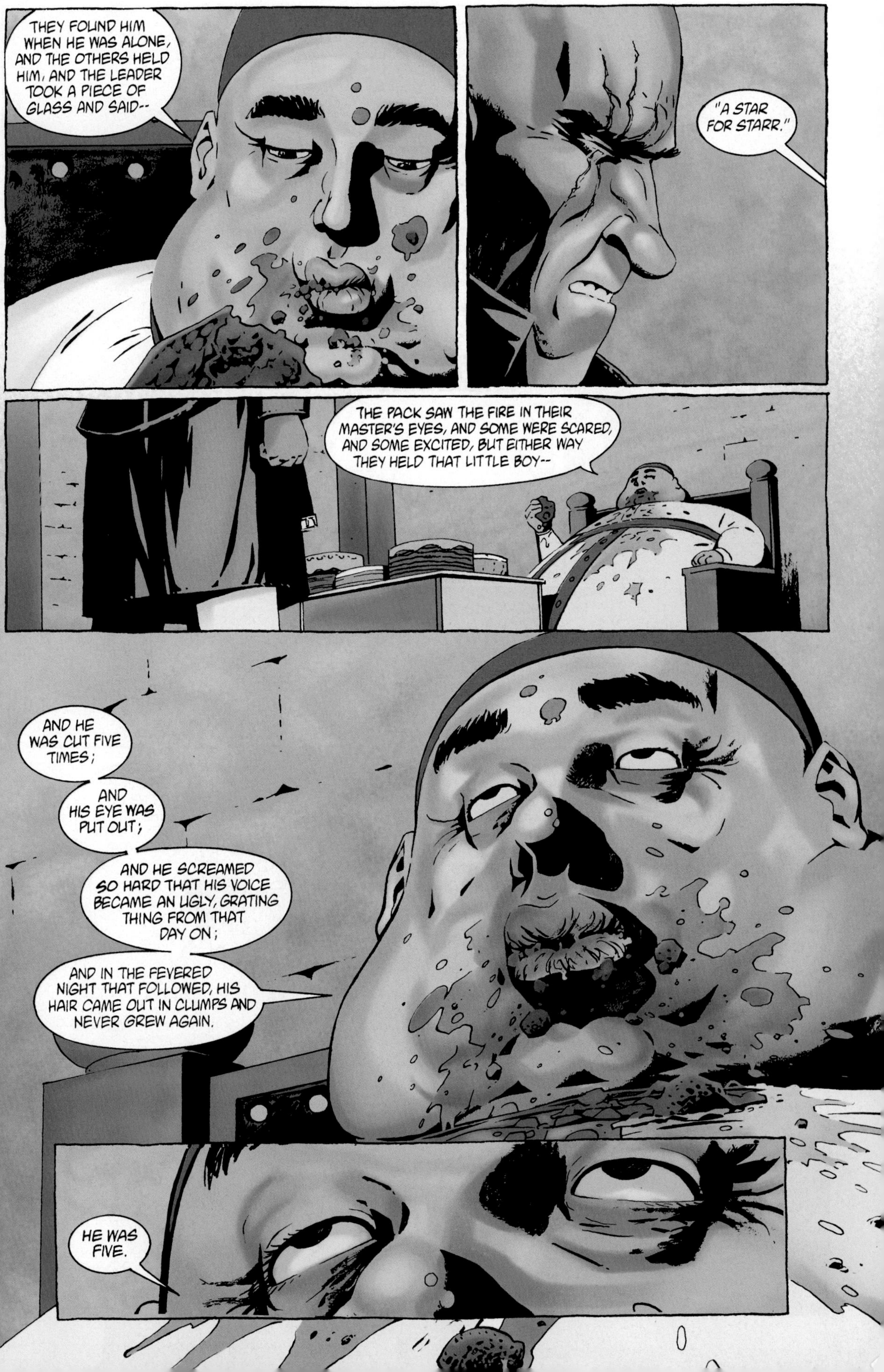
THEY FOUND HIM WHEN HE WAS ALONE, AND THE OTHERS HELD HIM, AND THE LEADER TOOK A PIECE OF GLASS AND SAID--
"A STAR FOR STARR."
THE PACK SAW THE FIRE IN THEIR MASTER'S EYES, AND SOME WERE SCARED, AND SOME EXCITED, BUT EITHER WAY THEY HELD THAT LITTLE BOY--
AND HE WAS CUT FIVE TIMES;
AND HIS EYE WAS PUT OUT;
AND HE SCREAMED SO HARD THAT HIS VOICE BECAME AN UGLY, GRATING THING FROM THAT DAY ON;
AND IN THE FEVERED NIGHT THAT FOLLOWED, HIS HAIR CAME OUT IN CLUMPS AND NEVER GREW AGAIN.
HE WAS FIVE.

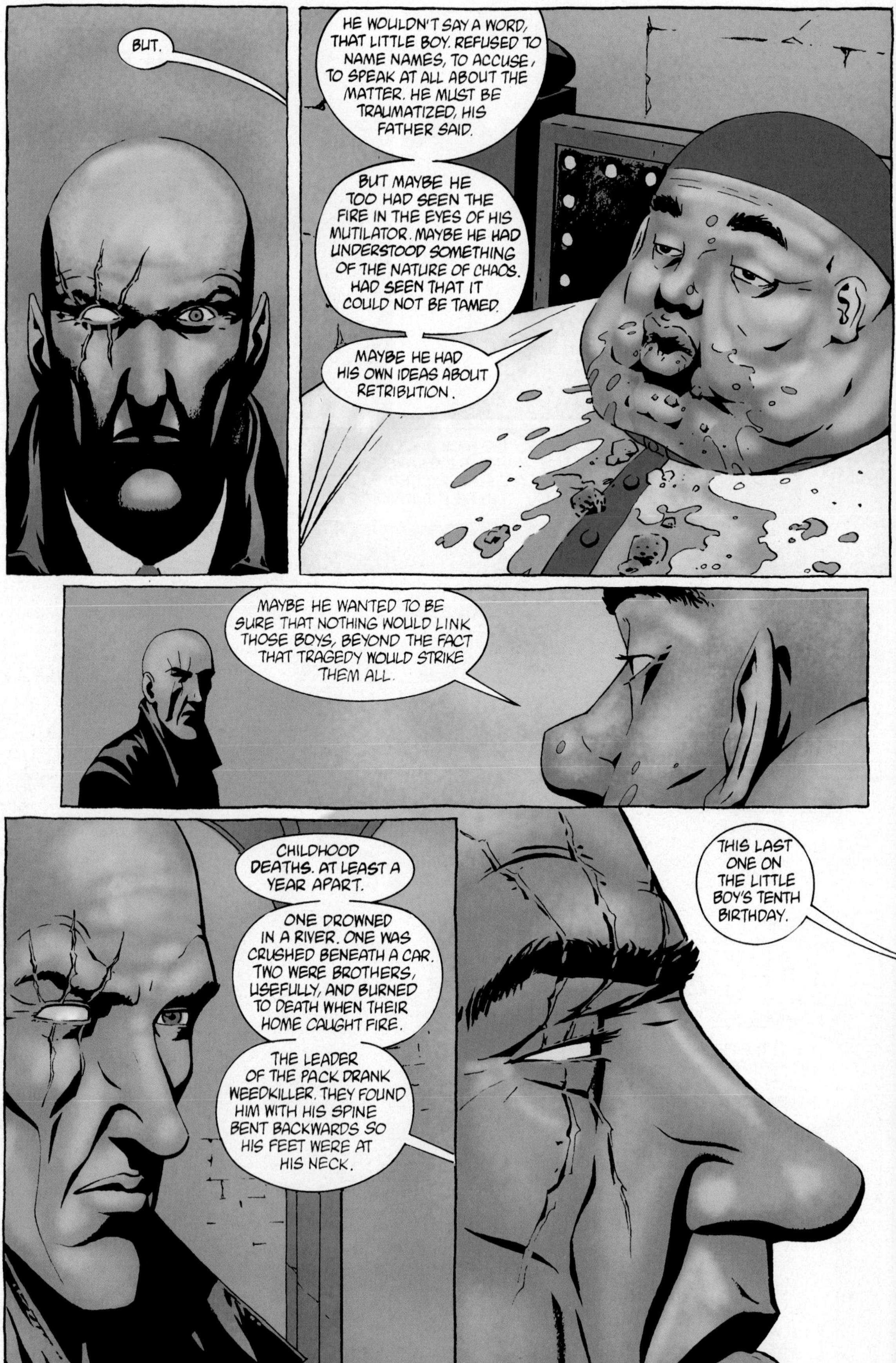
BUT.
HE WOULDN'T SAY A WORD, THAT LITTLE BOY. REFUSED TO NAME NAMES, TO ACCUSE, TO SPEAK AT ALL ABOUT THE MATTER. HE MUST BE TRAUMATIZED, HIS FATHER SAID.
BUT MAYBE HE TOO HAD SEEN THE FIRE IN THE EYES OF HIS MUTILATOR. MAYBE HE HAD UNDERSTOOD SOMETHING OF THE NATURE OF CHAOS. HAD SEEN THAT IT COULD NOT BE TAMED.
MAYBE HE HAD HIS OWN IDEAS ABOUT RETRIBUTION.
MAYBE HE WANTED TO BE SURE THAT NOTHING WOULD LINK THOSE BOYS, BEYOND THE FACT THAT TRAGEDY WOULD STRIKE THEM ALL.
CHILDHOOD DEATHS. AT LEAST A YEAR APART.
ONE DROWNED IN A RIVER. ONE WAS CRUSHED BENEATH A CAR. TWO WERE BROTHERS, USEFULLY, AND BURNED TO DEATH WHEN THEIR HOME CAUGHT FIRE.
THE LEADER OF THE PACK DRANK WEEDKILLER. THEY FOUND HIM WITH HIS SPINE BENT BACKWARDS SO HIS FEET WERE AT HIS NECK.
THIS LAST ONE ON THE LITTLE BOY'S TENTH BIRTHDAY.

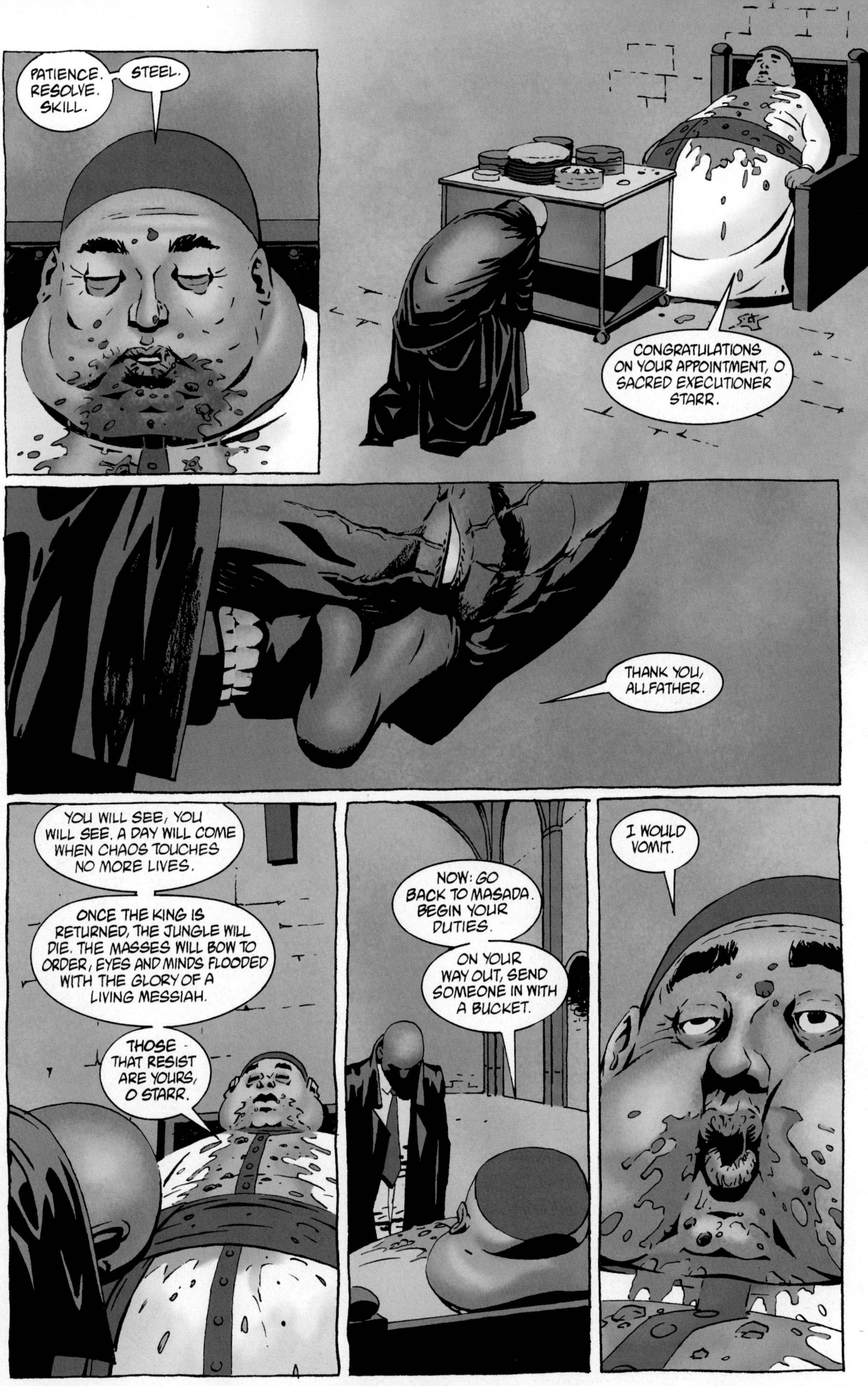

PATIENCE. RESOLVE. SKILL.
STEEL.
CONGRATULATIONS ON YOUR APPOINTMENT, O SACRED EXECUTIONER STARR.
THANK YOU, ALLFATHER.
YOU WILL SEE, YOU WILL SEE. A DAY WILL COME WHEN CHAOS TOUCHES NO MORE LIVES.
ONCE THE KING IS RETURNED, THE JUNGLE WILL DIE. THE MASSES WILL BOW TO ORDER, EYES AND MINDS FLOODED WITH THE GLORY OF A LIVING MESSIAH.
THOSE THAT RESIST ARE YOURS, O STARR.
NOW: GO BACK TO MASADA. BEGIN YOUR DUTIES.
ON YOUR WAY OUT, SEND SOMEONE IN WITH A BUCKET.
I WOULD VOMIT.

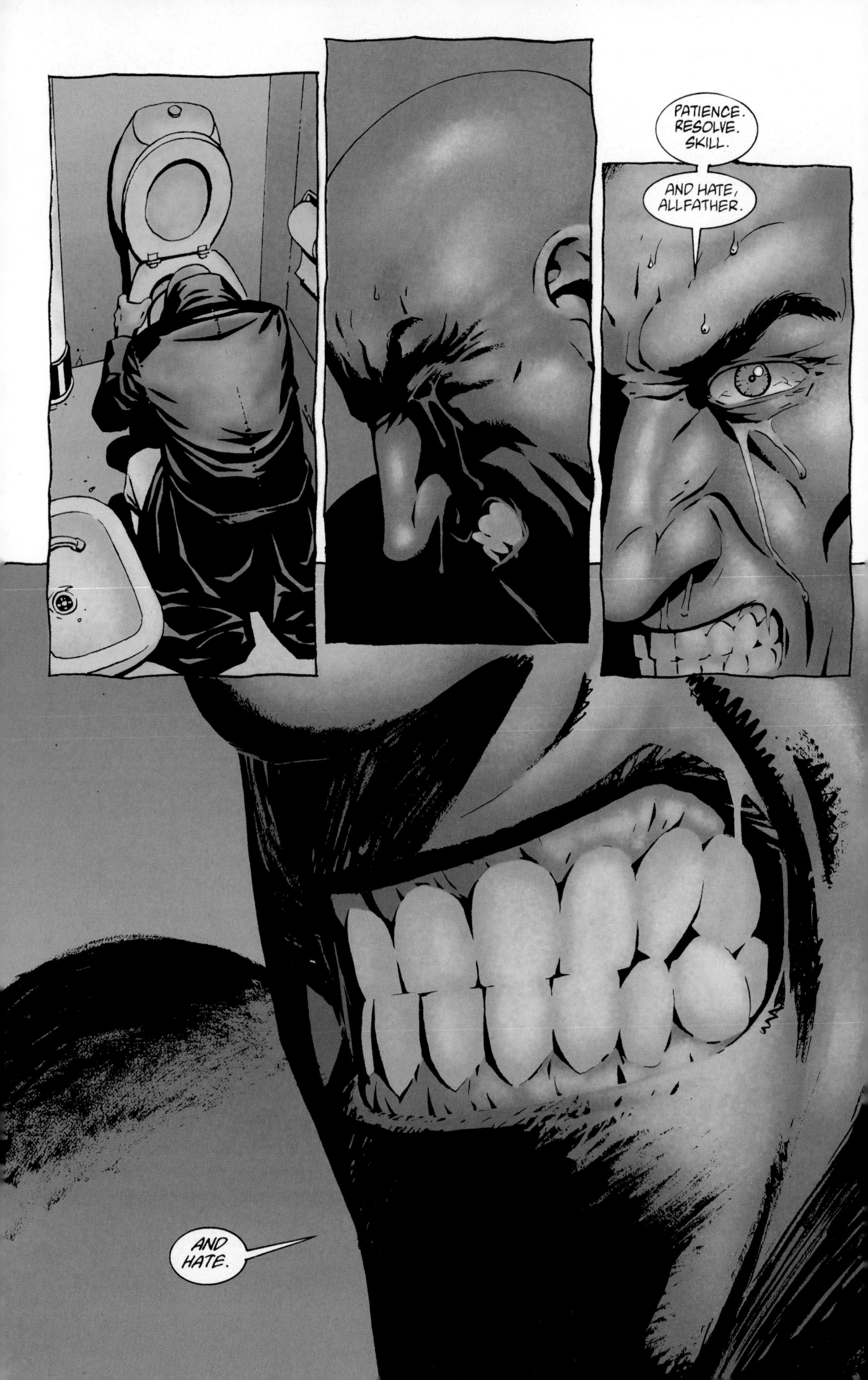
PATIENCE. RESOLVE. SKILL.
AND HATE, ALLFATHER.
AND HATE.

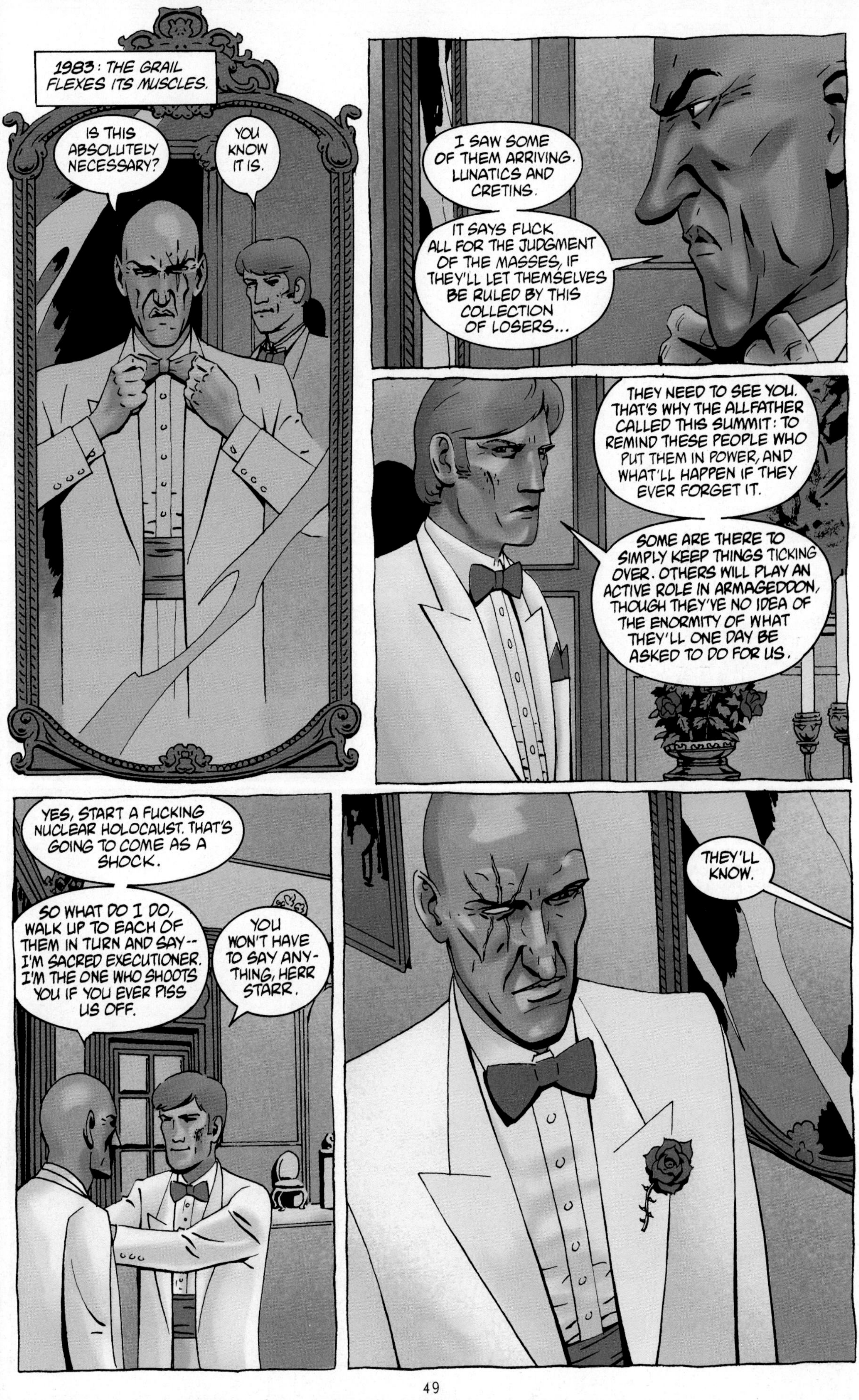
1983: THE GRAIL FLEXES ITS MUSCLES.
IS THIS ABSOLUTELY NECESSARY?
YOU KNOW IT IS.
I SAW SOME OF THEM ARRIVING. LUNATICS AND CRETINS.
IT SAYS FUCK ALL FOR THE JUDGMENT OF THE MASSES, IF THEY'LL LET THEMSELVES BE RULED BY THIS COLLECTION OF LOSERS...
THEY NEED TO SEE YOU. THAT'S WHY THE ALLFATHER CALLED THIS SUMMIT: TO REMIND THESE PEOPLE WHO PUT THEM IN POWER, AND WHAT'LL HAPPEN IF THEY EVER FORGET IT.
SOME ARE THERE TO SIMPLY KEEP THINGS TICKING OVER. OTHERS WILL PLAY AN ACTIVE ROLE IN ARMAGEDDON, THOUGH THEY'VE NO IDEA OF THE ENORMITY OF WHAT THEY'LL ONE DAY BE ASKED TO DO FOR US.
YES, START A FUCKING NUCLEAR HOLOCAUST. THAT'S GOING TO COME AS A SHOCK.
SO WHAT DO I DO, WALK UP TO EACH OF THEM IN TURN AND SAY-- I'M SACRED EXECUTIONER. I'M THE ONE WHO SHOOTS YOU IF YOU EVER PISS US OFF.
YOU WON'T HAVE TO SAY ANY-THING, HERR STARR.
THEY'LL KNOW.

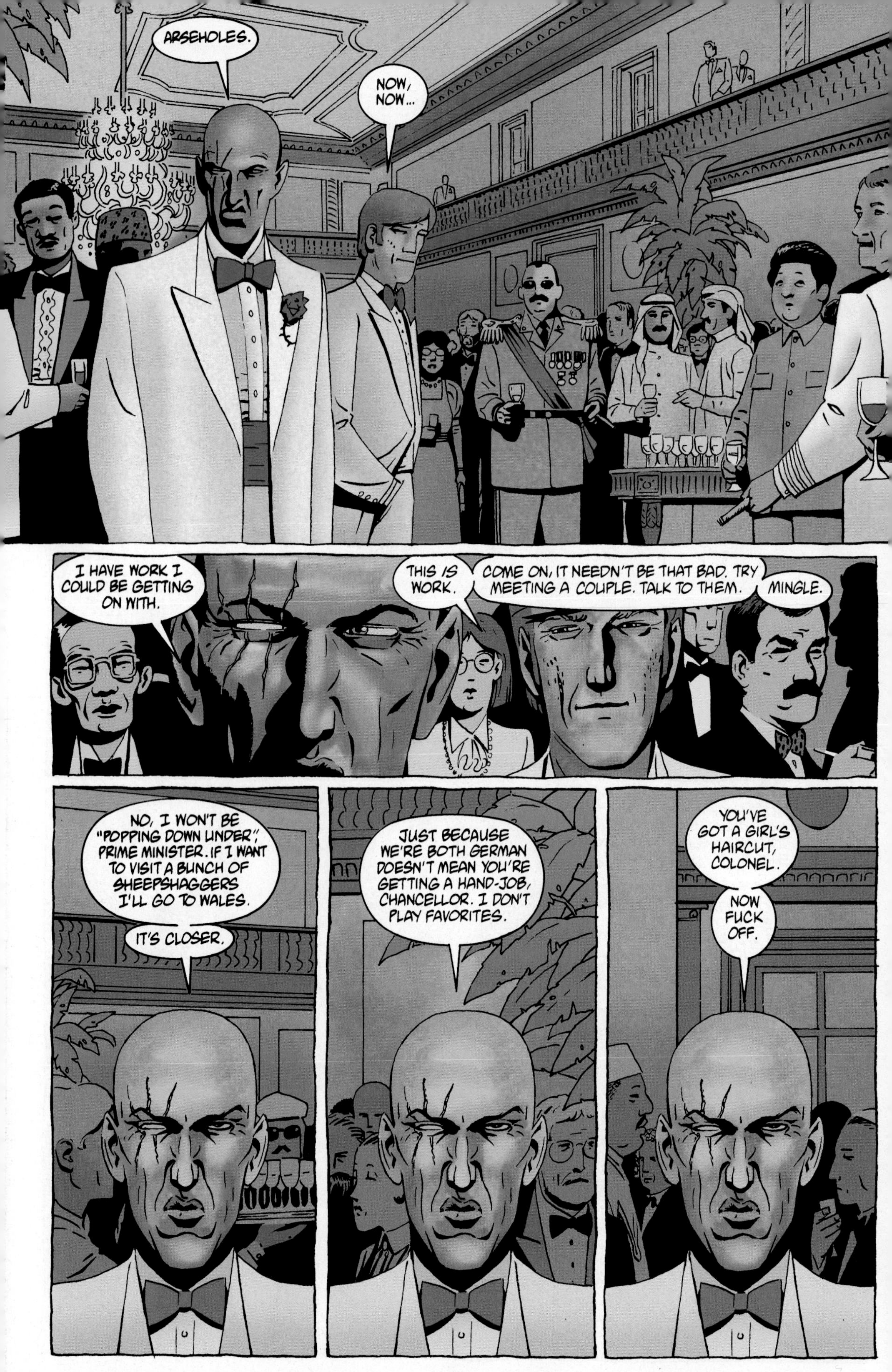
ARSEHOLES.
NOW, NOW...
I HAVE WORK I COULD BE GETTING ON WITH.
THIS *IS* WORK.
COME ON, IT NEEDN'T BE THAT BAD. TRY MEETING A COUPLE. TALK TO THEM.
MINGLE.
NO, I WON'T BE "POPPING DOWN UNDER", PRIME MINISTER. IF I WANT TO VISIT A BUNCH OF SHEEPSHAGGERS I'LL GO TO WALES.
IT'S CLOSER.
JUST BECAUSE WE'RE BOTH GERMAN DOESN'T MEAN YOU'RE GETTING A HAND-JOB, CHANCELLOR. I DON'T PLAY FAVORITES.
YOU'VE GOT A GIRL'S HAIRCUT, COLONEL.
NOW FUCK OFF.

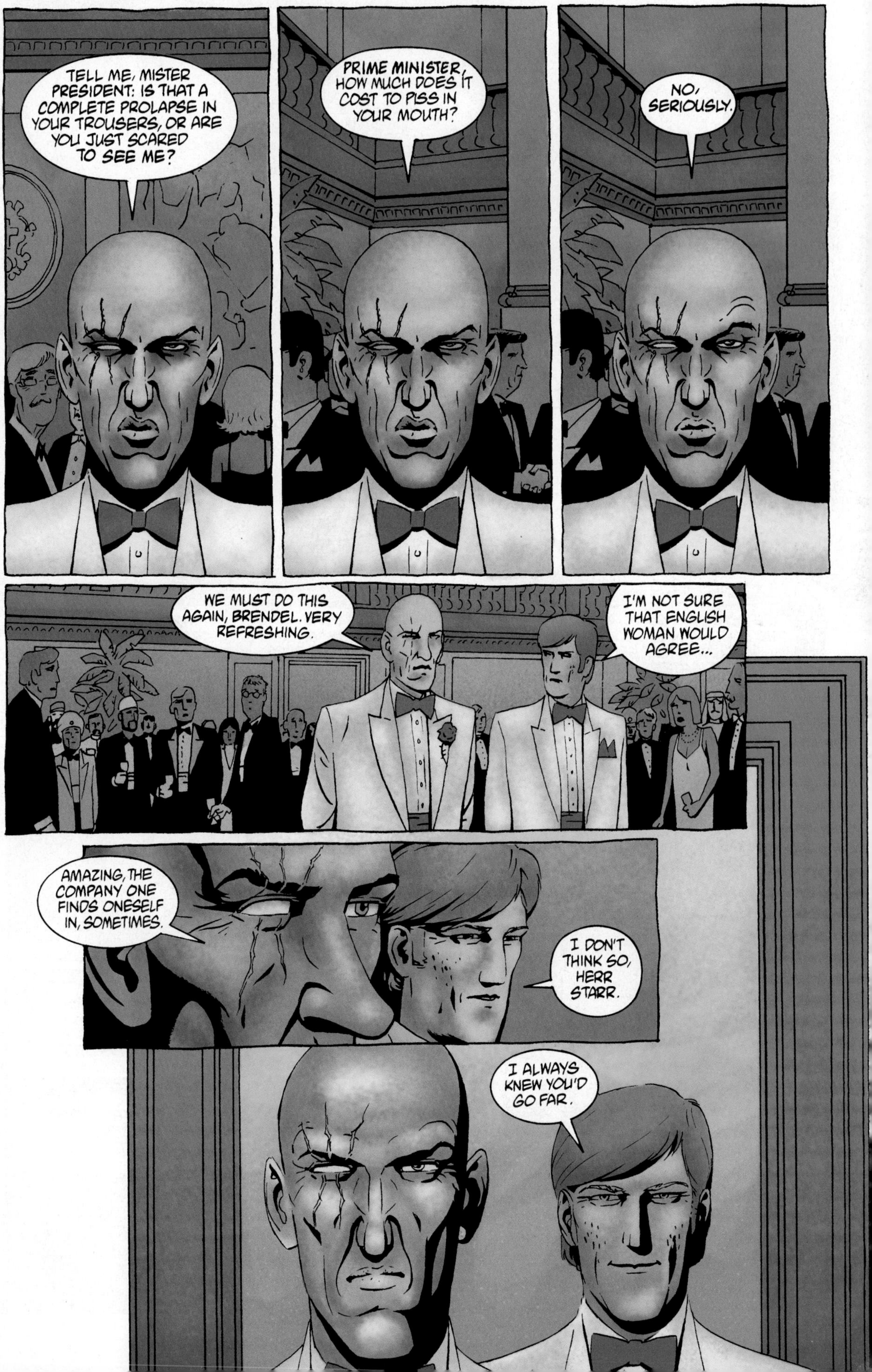
TELL ME, MISTER PRESIDENT: IS THAT A COMPLETE PROLAPSE IN YOUR TROUSERS, OR ARE YOU JUST SCARED TO SEE ME?
PRIME MINISTER, HOW MUCH DOES IT COST TO PISS IN YOUR MOUTH?
NO, SERIOUSLY.
WE MUST DO THIS AGAIN, BRENDEL. VERY REFRESHING.
I'M NOT SURE THAT ENGLISH WOMAN WOULD AGREE...
AMAZING, THE COMPANY ONE FINDS ONESELF IN, SOMETIMES.
I DON'T THINK SO, HERR STARR.
I ALWAYS KNEW YOU'D GO FAR.

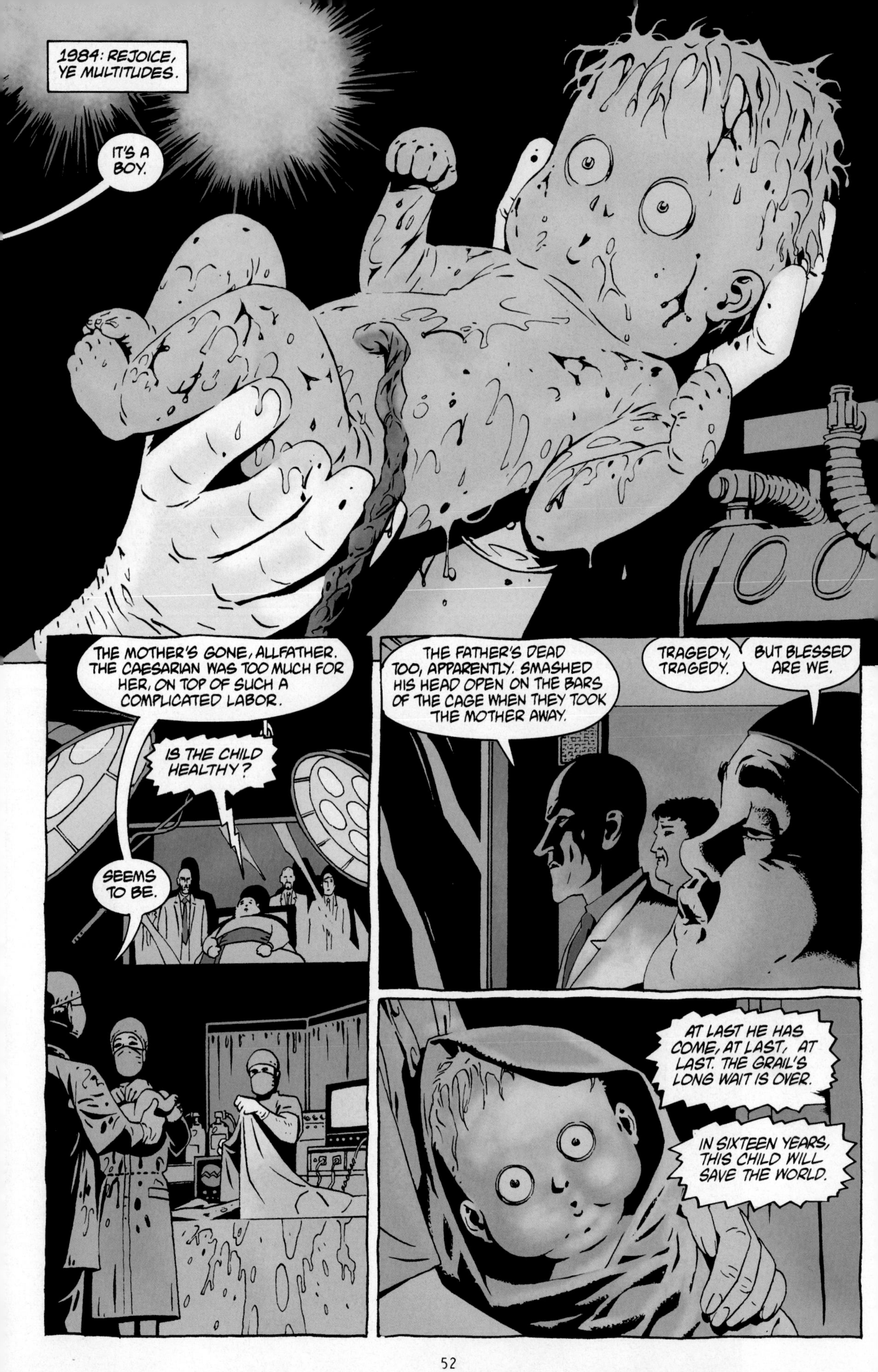
1984: REJOICE, YE MULTITUDES.
IT'S A BOY.
THE MOTHER'S GONE, ALLFATHER. THE CAESARIAN WAS TOO MUCH FOR HER, ON TOP OF SUCH A COMPLICATED LABOR.
IS THE CHILD HEALTHY?
SEEMS TO BE.
THE FATHER'S DEAD TOO, APPARENTLY. SMASHED HIS HEAD OPEN ON THE BARS OF THE CAGE WHEN THEY TOOK THE MOTHER AWAY.
TRAGEDY, TRAGEDY.
BUT BLESSED ARE WE.
AT LAST HE HAS COME, AT LAST, AT LAST. THE GRAIL'S LONG WAIT IS OVER.
IN SIXTEEN YEARS, THIS CHILD WILL SAVE THE WORLD.

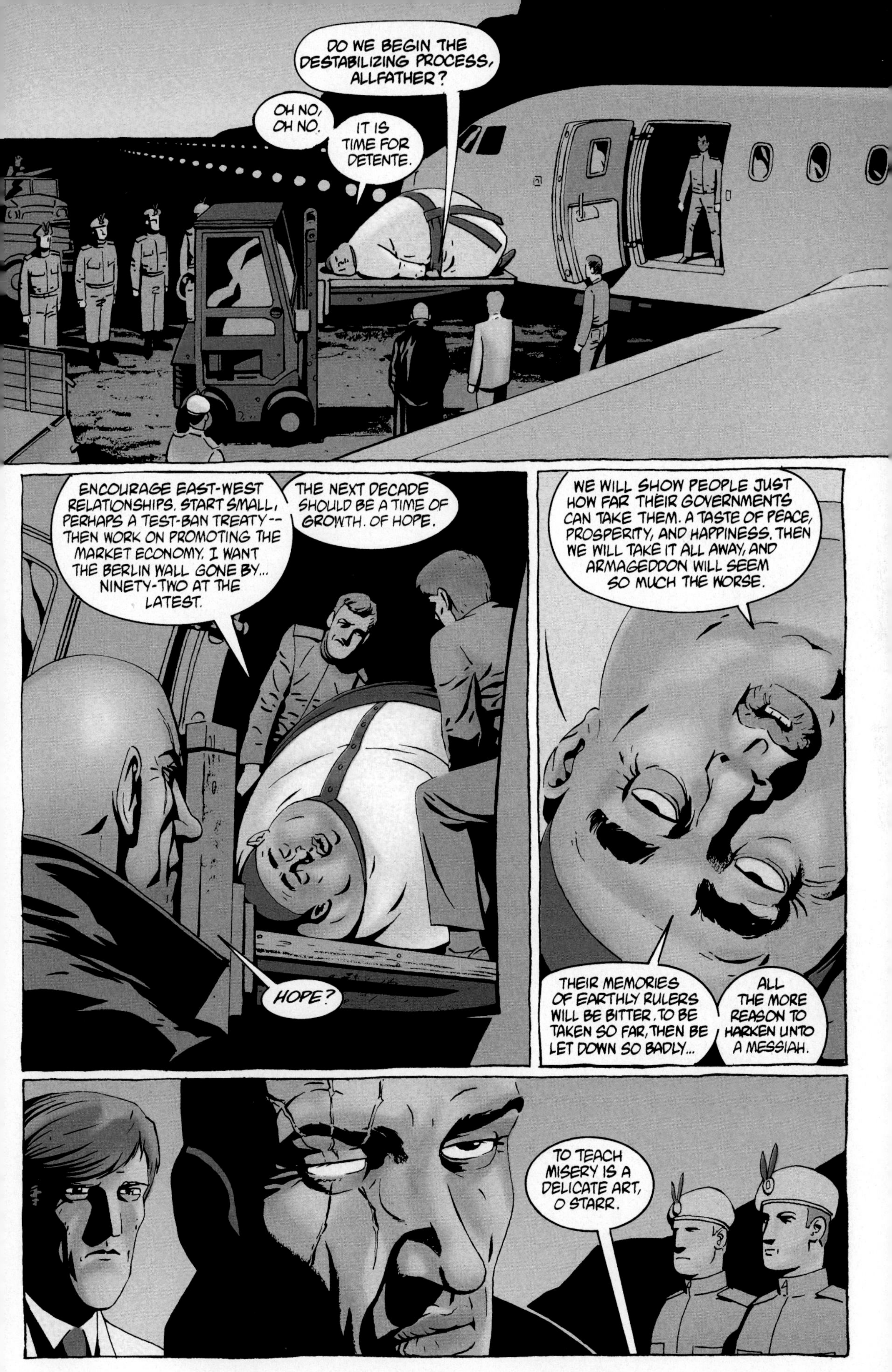
DO WE BEGIN THE DESTABILIZING PROCESS, ALLFATHER?
OH NO, OH NO.
IT IS TIME FOR DETENTE.
ENCOURAGE EAST-WEST RELATIONSHIPS. START SMALL, PERHAPS A TEST-BAN TREATY--THEN WORK ON PROMOTING THE MARKET ECONOMY. I WANT THE BERLIN WALL GONE BY... NINETY-TWO AT THE LATEST.
THE NEXT DECADE SHOULD BE A TIME OF GROWTH. OF HOPE.
HOPE?
WE WILL SHOW PEOPLE JUST HOW FAR THEIR GOVERNMENTS CAN TAKE THEM. A TASTE OF PEACE, PROSPERITY, AND HAPPINESS. THEN WE WILL TAKE IT ALL AWAY, AND ARMAGEDDON WILL SEEM SO MUCH THE WORSE.
THEIR MEMORIES OF EARTHLY RULERS WILL BE BITTER. TO BE TAKEN SO FAR, THEN BE LET DOWN SO BADLY...
ALL THE MORE REASON TO HARKEN UNTO A MESSIAH.
TO TEACH MISERY IS A DELICATE ART, O STARR.

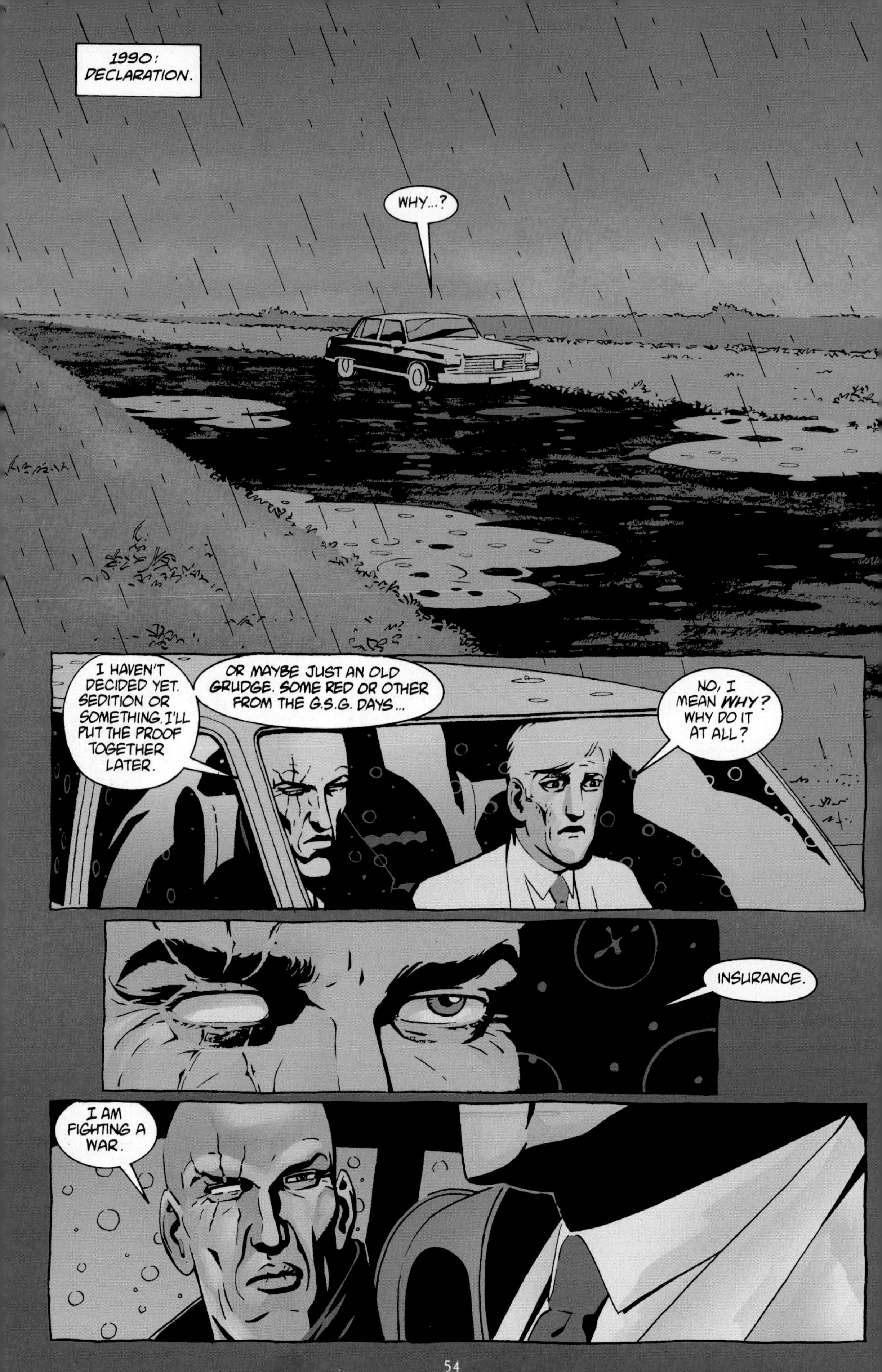
1990: DECLARATION.
WHY...?
I HAVEN'T DECIDED YET. SEDITION OR SOMETHING. I'LL PUT THE PROOF TOGETHER LATER.
OR MAYBE JUST AN OLD GRUDGE. SOME RED OR OTHER FROM THE G.S.G. DAYS...
NO, I MEAN WHY? WHY DO IT AT ALL?
INSURANCE.
I AM FIGHTING A WAR.

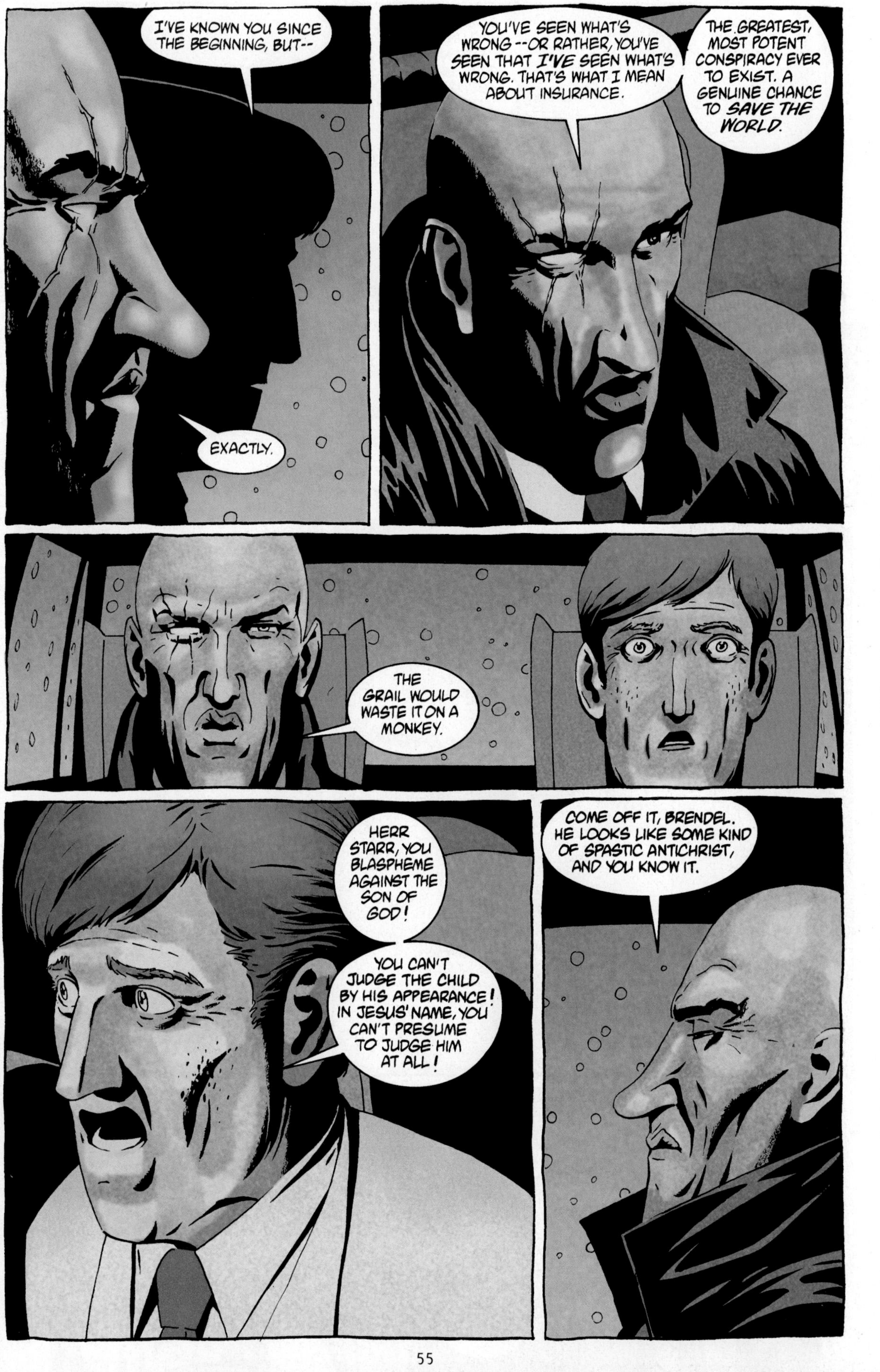
I'VE KNOWN YOU SINCE THE BEGINNING, BUT--
EXACTLY.
YOU'VE SEEN WHAT'S WRONG --OR RATHER, YOU'VE SEEN THAT I'VE SEEN WHAT'S WRONG. THAT'S WHAT I MEAN ABOUT INSURANCE.
THE GREATEST, MOST POTENT CONSPIRACY EVER TO EXIST. A GENUINE CHANCE TO SAVE THE WORLD.
THE GRAIL WOULD WASTE IT ON A MONKEY.
HERR STARR, YOU BLASPHEME AGAINST THE SON OF GOD!
YOU CAN'T JUDGE THE CHILD BY HIS APPEARANCE! IN JESUS' NAME, YOU CAN'T PRESUME TO JUDGE HIM AT ALL!
COME OFF IT, BRENDEL. HE LOOKS LIKE SOME KIND OF SPASTIC ANTICHRIST, AND YOU KNOW IT.

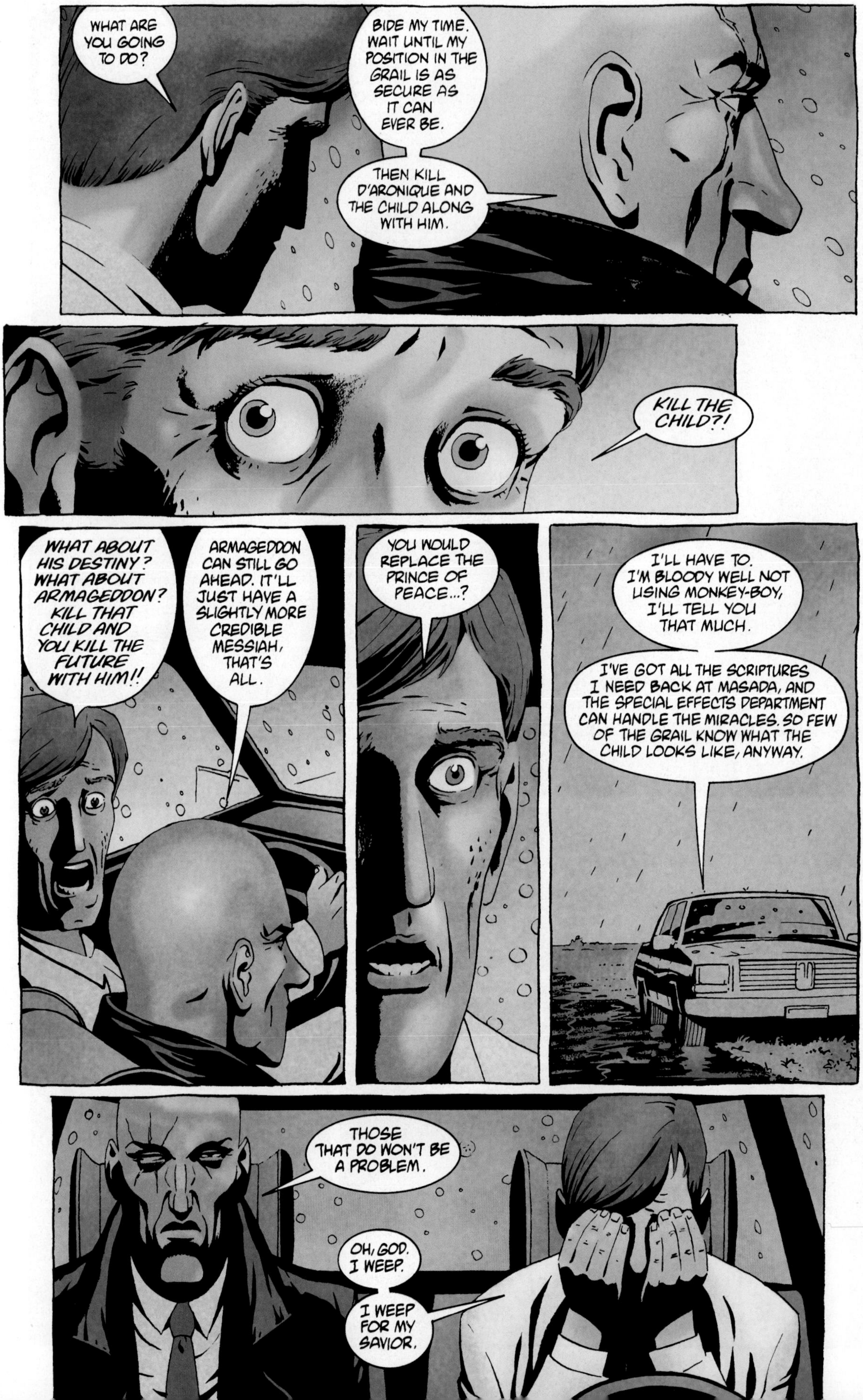
WHAT ARE YOU GOING TO DO?
BIDE MY TIME. WAIT UNTIL MY POSITION IN THE GRAIL IS AS SECURE AS IT CAN EVER BE.
THEN KILL D'ARONIQUE AND THE CHILD ALONG WITH HIM.
KILL THE CHILD?!
WHAT ABOUT HIS DESTINY? WHAT ABOUT ARMAGEDDON? KILL THAT CHILD AND YOU KILL THE FUTURE WITH HIM!!
ARMAGEDDON CAN STILL GO AHEAD. IT'LL JUST HAVE A SLIGHTLY MORE CREDIBLE MESSIAH, THAT'S ALL.
YOU WOULD REPLACE THE PRINCE OF PEACE...?
I'LL HAVE TO. I'M BLOODY WELL NOT USING MONKEY-BOY, I'LL TELL YOU THAT MUCH.
I'VE GOT ALL THE SCRIPTURES I NEED BACK AT MASADA, AND THE SPECIAL EFFECTS DEPARTMENT CAN HANDLE THE MIRACLES. SO FEW OF THE GRAIL KNOW WHAT THE CHILD LOOKS LIKE, ANYWAY.
THOSE THAT DO WON'T BE A PROBLEM.
OH, GOD. I WEEP.
I WEEP FOR MY SAVIOR.

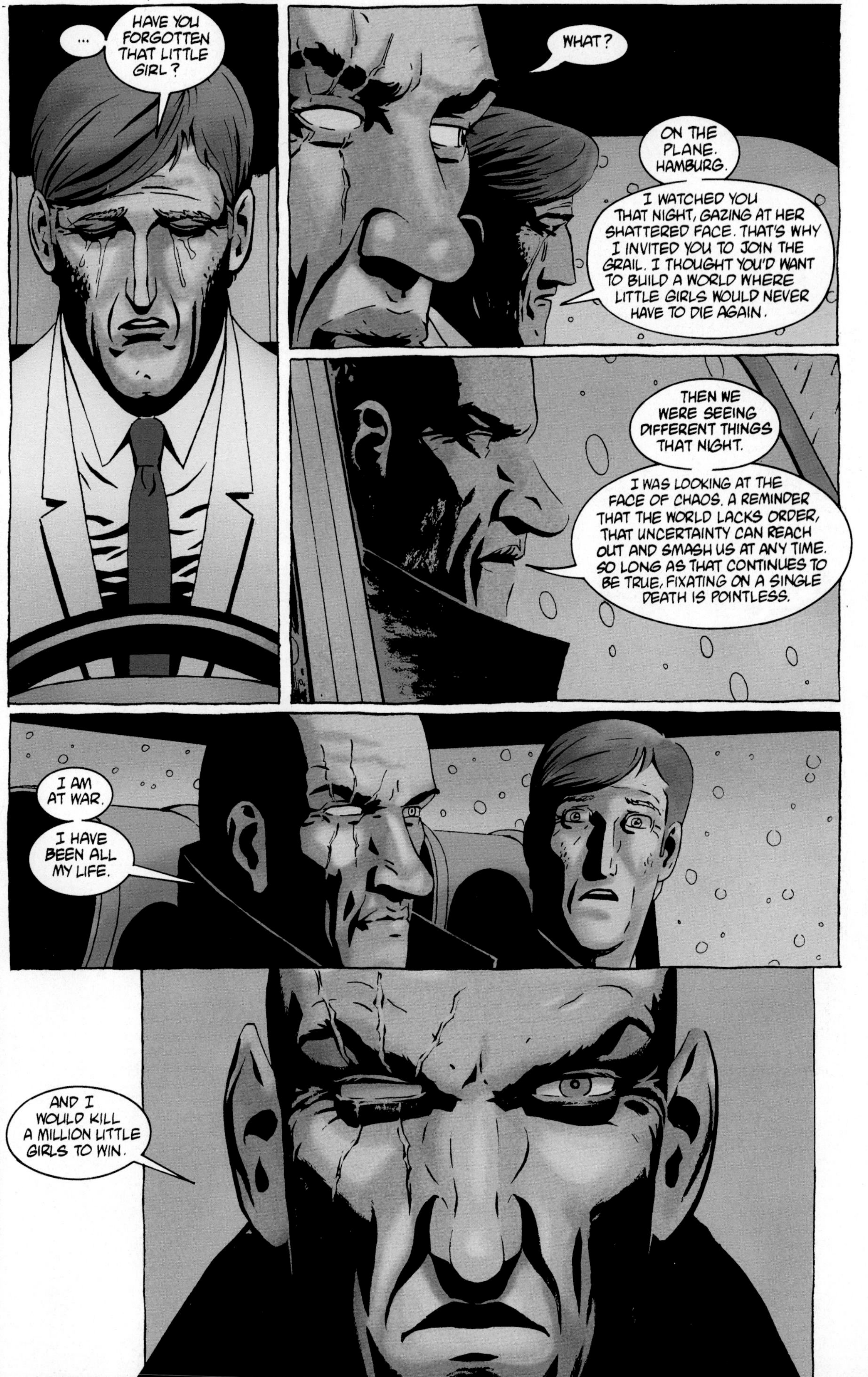
...
HAVE YOU FORGOTTEN THAT LITTLE GIRL?
WHAT?
ON THE PLANE. HAMBURG.
I WATCHED YOU THAT NIGHT, GAZING AT HER SHATTERED FACE. THAT'S WHY I INVITED YOU TO JOIN THE GRAIL. I THOUGHT YOU'D WANT TO BUILD A WORLD WHERE LITTLE GIRLS WOULD NEVER HAVE TO DIE AGAIN.
THEN WE WERE SEEING DIFFERENT THINGS THAT NIGHT.
I WAS LOOKING AT THE FACE OF CHAOS. A REMINDER THAT THE WORLD LACKS ORDER, THAT UNCERTAINTY CAN REACH OUT AND SMASH US AT ANY TIME. SO LONG AS THAT CONTINUES TO BE TRUE, FIXATING ON A SINGLE DEATH IS POINTLESS.
I AM AT WAR.
I HAVE BEEN ALL MY LIFE.
AND I WOULD KILL A MILLION LITTLE GIRLS TO WIN.

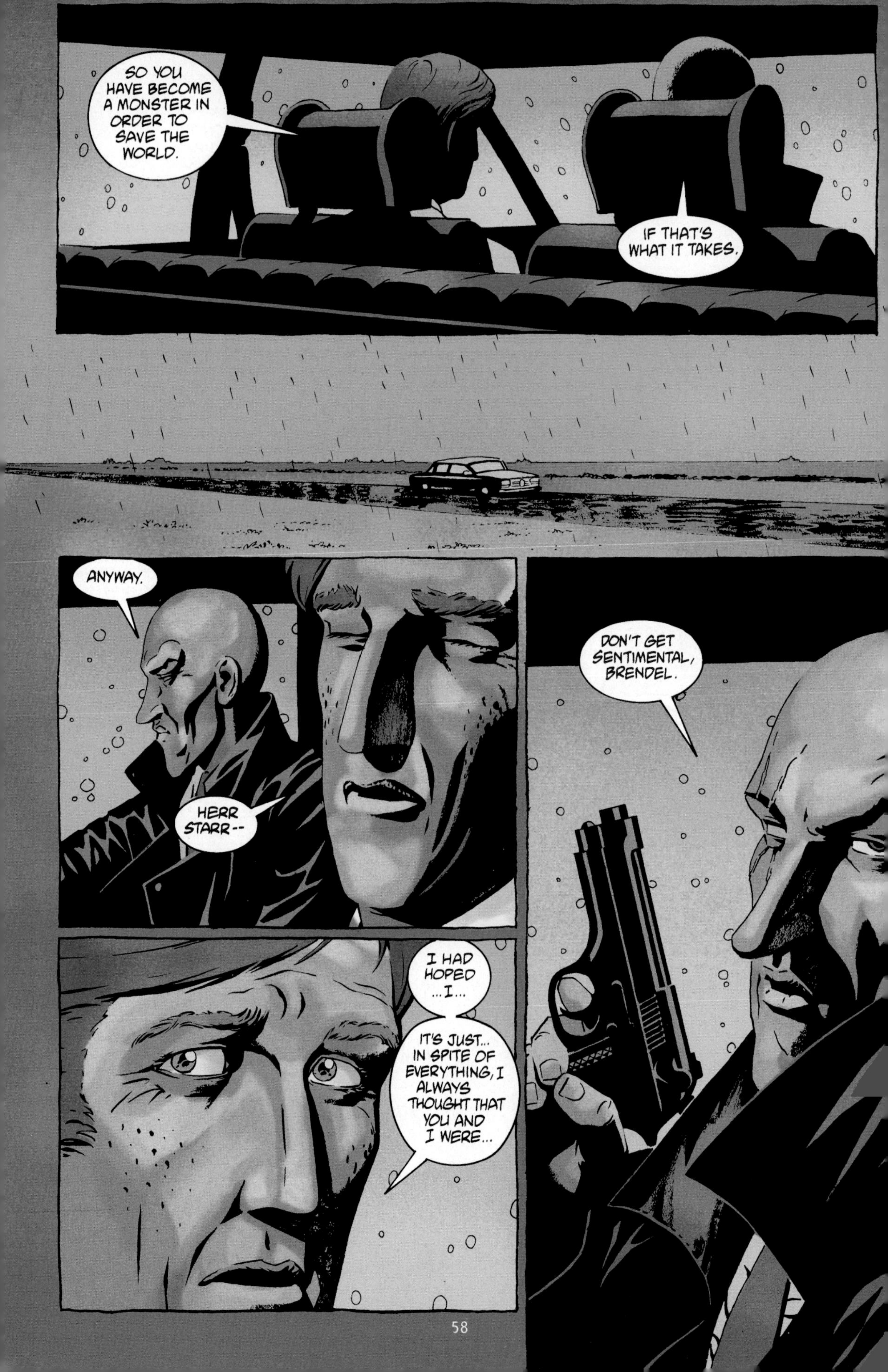
SO YOU HAVE BECOME A MONSTER IN ORDER TO SAVE THE WORLD.
IF THAT'S WHAT IT TAKES.
ANYWAY.
HERR STARR--
I HAD HOPED ...I...
IT'S JUST... IN SPITE OF EVERYTHING, I ALWAYS THOUGHT THAT YOU AND I WERE...
DON'T GET SENTIMENTAL, BRENDEL.

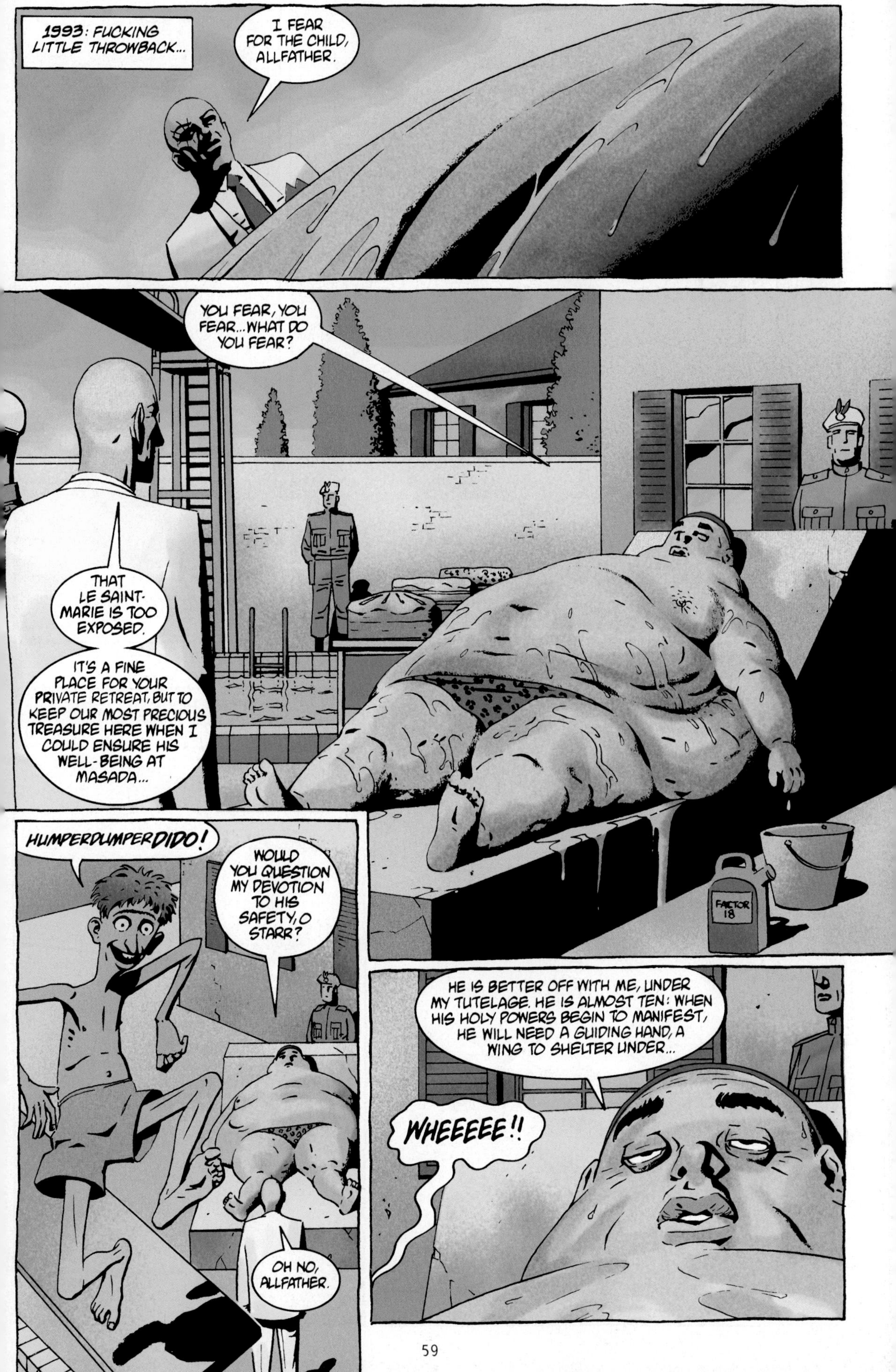
1993: FUCKING LITTLE THROWBACK...
I FEAR FOR THE CHILD, ALLFATHER.
YOU FEAR, YOU FEAR...WHAT DO YOU FEAR?
THAT LE SAINT-MARIE IS TOO EXPOSED.
IT'S A FINE PLACE FOR YOUR PRIVATE RETREAT, BUT TO KEEP OUR MOST PRECIOUS TREASURE HERE WHEN I COULD ENSURE HIS WELL-BEING AT MASADA...
FACTOR 18
HUMPERDUMPERDIDO!
WOULD YOU QUESTION MY DEVOTION TO HIS SAFETY, O STARR?
OH NO, ALLFATHER.
HE IS BETTER OFF WITH ME, UNDER MY TUTELAGE. HE IS ALMOST TEN: WHEN HIS HOLY POWERS BEGIN TO MANIFEST, HE WILL NEED A GUIDING HAND, A WING TO SHELTER UNDER...
WHEEEEE!!

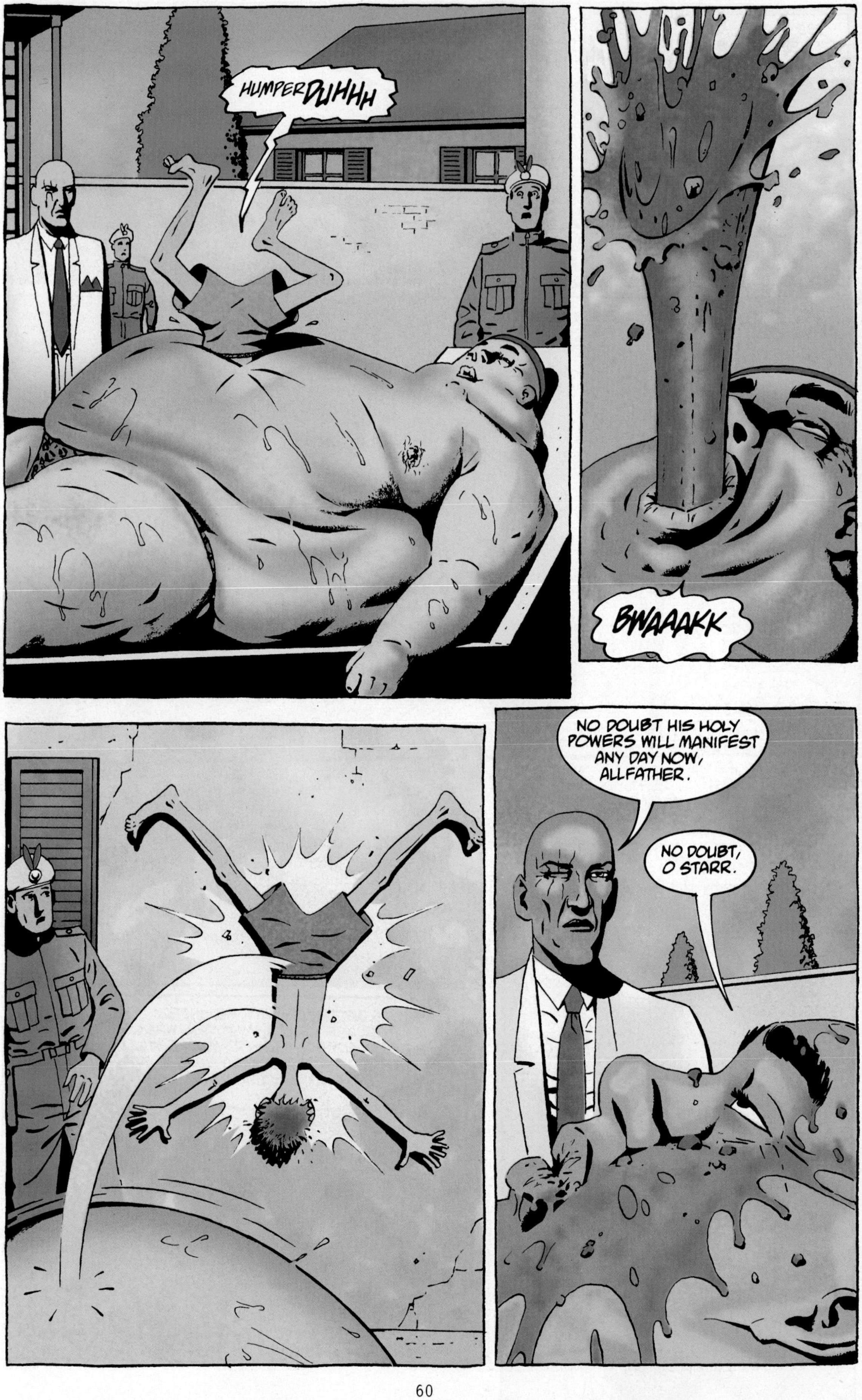
HUMPERDUHHH
BWAAAKK
NO DOUBT HIS HOLY POWERS WILL MANIFEST ANY DAY NOW, ALLFATHER.
NO DOUBT, O STARR.

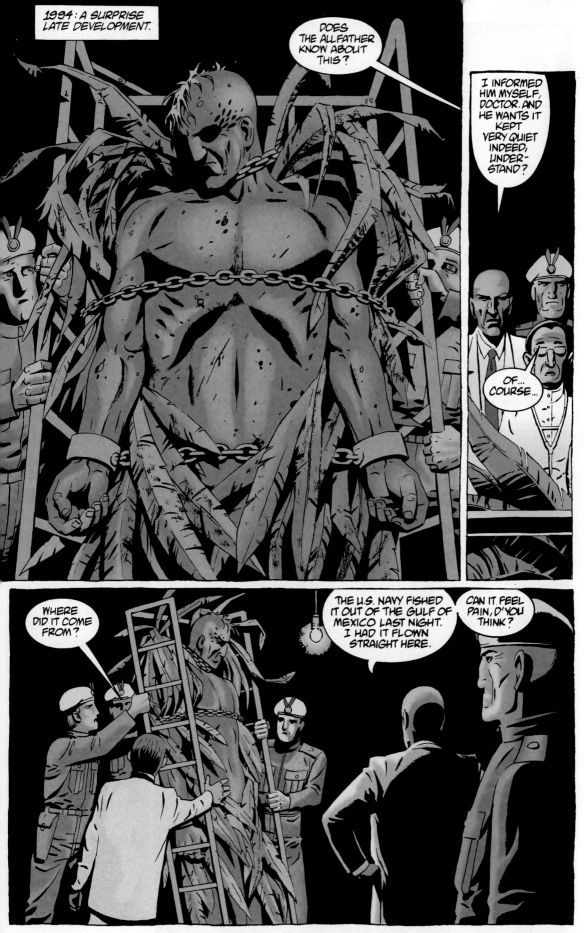

1994: A SURPRISE LATE DEVELOPMENT.

DOES THE ALLFATHER KNOW ABOUT THIS?

I INFORMED HIM MYSELF, DOCTOR. AND HE WANTS IT KEPT VERY QUIET INDEED, UNDERSTAND?

OF... COURSE...

WHERE DID IT COME FROM?

THE U.S. NAVY FISHED IT OUT OF THE GULF OF MEXICO LAST NIGHT. I HAD IT FLOWN STRAIGHT HERE.

CAN IT FEEL PAIN, D'YOU THINK?

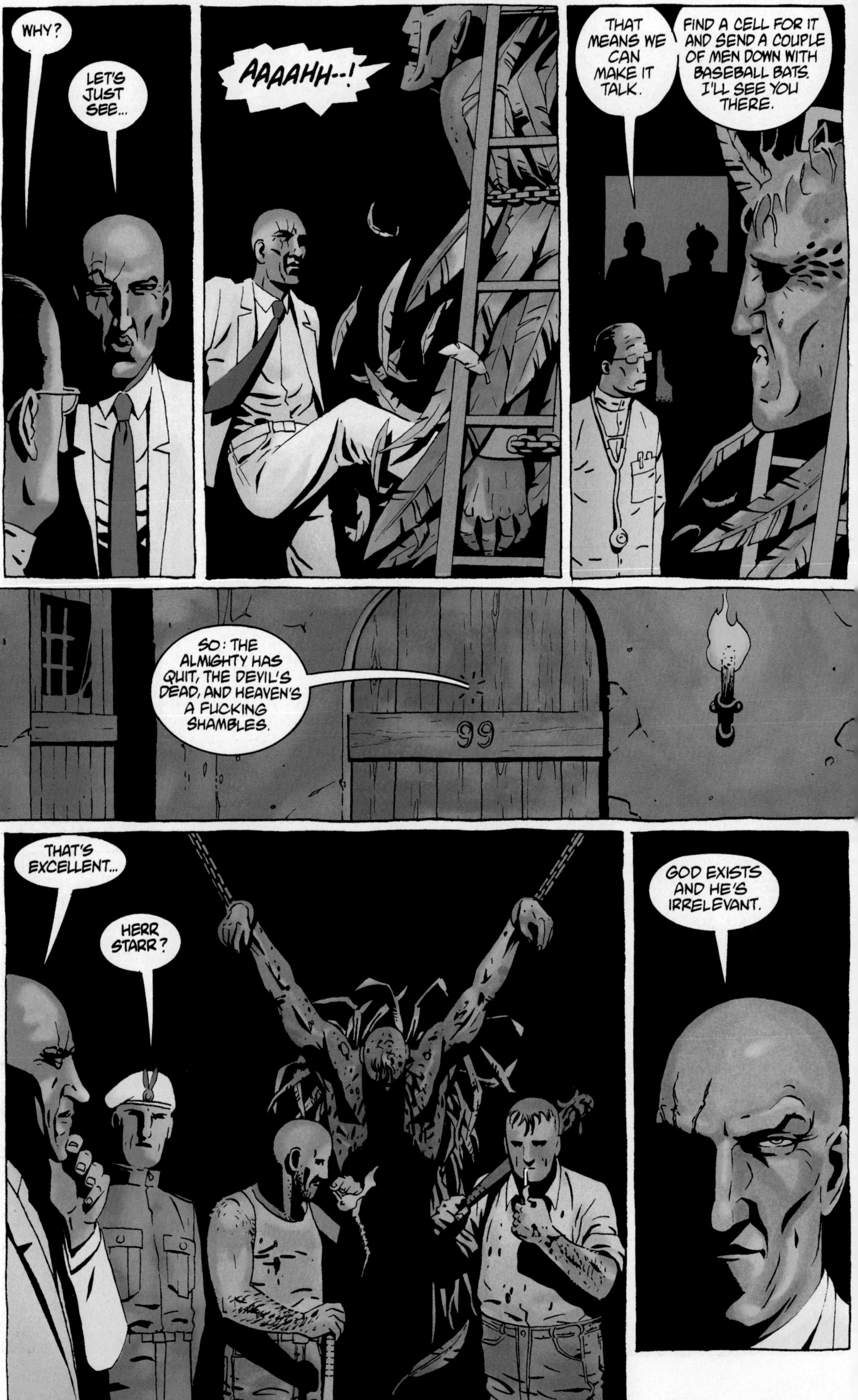
WHY?
LET'S JUST SEE...
AAAAHH--!
THAT MEANS WE CAN MAKE IT TALK.
FIND A CELL FOR IT AND SEND A COUPLE OF MEN DOWN WITH BASEBALL BATS. I'LL SEE YOU THERE.
SO: THE ALMIGHTY HAS QUIT, THE DEVIL'S DEAD, AND HEAVEN'S A FUCKING SHAMBLES.
99
THAT'S EXCELLENT...
HERR STARR?
GOD EXISTS AND HE'S IRRELEVANT.

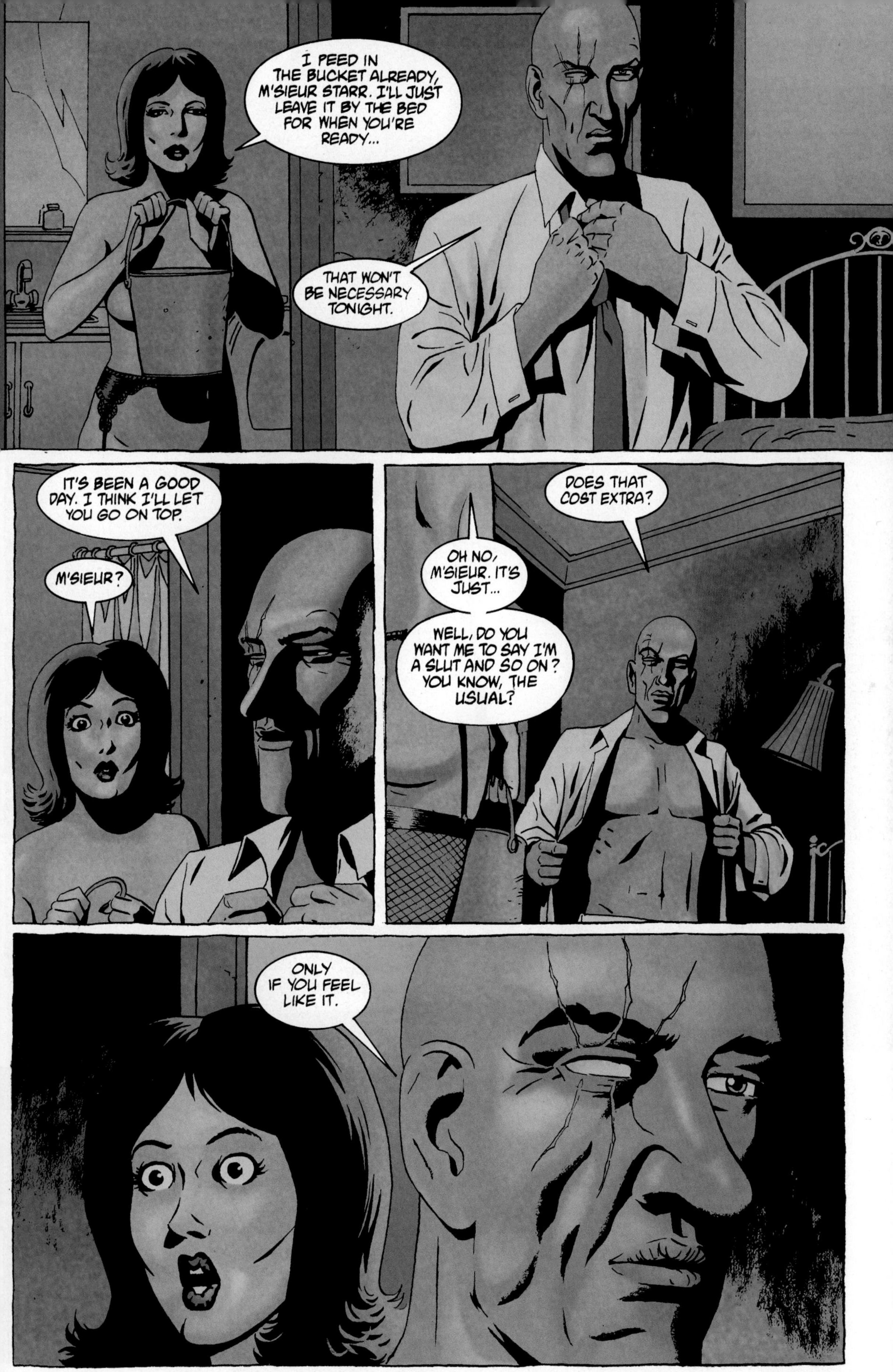
I PEED IN THE BUCKET ALREADY, M'SIEUR STARR. I'LL JUST LEAVE IT BY THE BED FOR WHEN YOU'RE READY...
THAT WON'T BE NECESSARY TONIGHT.
IT'S BEEN A GOOD DAY. I THINK I'LL LET YOU GO ON TOP.
M'SIEUR?
DOES THAT COST EXTRA?
OH NO, M'SIEUR. IT'S JUST...
WELL, DO YOU WANT ME TO SAY I'M A SLUT AND SO ON? YOU KNOW, THE USUAL?
ONLY IF YOU FEEL LIKE IT.

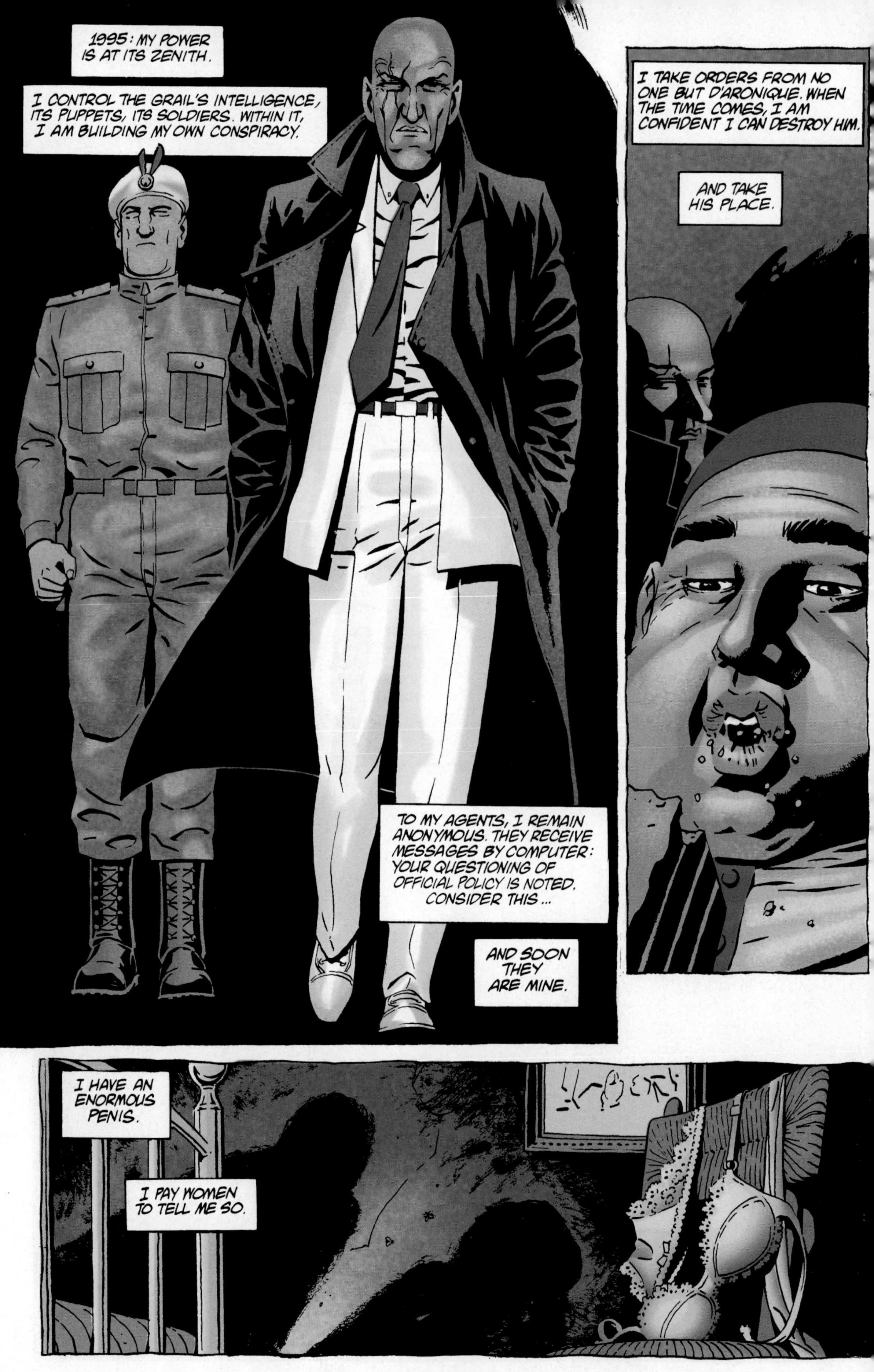

1995: MY POWER IS AT ITS ZENITH.
I CONTROL THE GRAIL'S INTELLIGENCE, ITS PUPPETS, ITS SOLDIERS. WITHIN IT, I AM BUILDING MY OWN CONSPIRACY.
TO MY AGENTS, I REMAIN ANONYMOUS. THEY RECEIVE MESSAGES BY COMPUTER: YOUR QUESTIONING OF OFFICIAL POLICY IS NOTED. CONSIDER THIS ...
AND SOON THEY ARE MINE.
I TAKE ORDERS FROM NO ONE BUT D'ARONIQUE. WHEN THE TIME COMES, I AM CONFIDENT I CAN DESTROY HIM.
AND TAKE HIS PLACE.
I HAVE AN ENORMOUS PENIS.
I PAY WOMEN TO TELL ME SO.

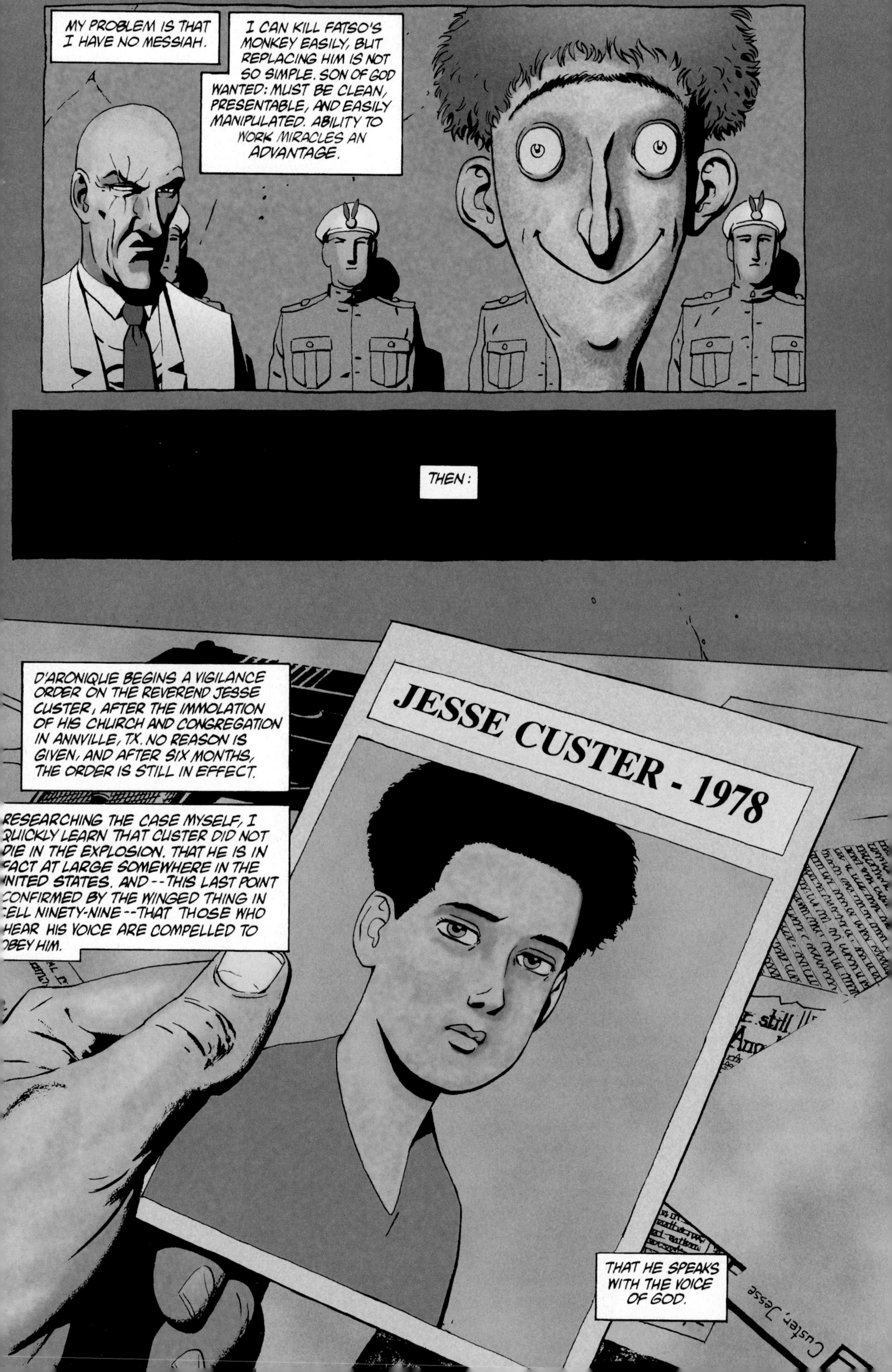
MY PROBLEM IS THAT I HAVE NO MESSIAH.
I CAN KILL FATSO'S MONKEY EASILY, BUT REPLACING HIM IS NOT SO SIMPLE. SON OF GOD WANTED: MUST BE CLEAN, PRESENTABLE, AND EASILY MANIPULATED. ABILITY TO WORK MIRACLES AN ADVANTAGE.
THEN:
D'ARONIQUE BEGINS A VIGILANCE ORDER ON THE REVEREND JESSE CUSTER, AFTER THE IMMOLATION OF HIS CHURCH AND CONGREGATION IN ANNVILLE, TX. NO REASON IS GIVEN, AND AFTER SIX MONTHS, THE ORDER IS STILL IN EFFECT.
JESSE CUSTER - 1978
RESEARCHING THE CASE MYSELF, I QUICKLY LEARN THAT CUSTER DID NOT IE IN THE EXPLOSION. THAT HE IS IN ACT AT LARGE SOMEWHERE IN THE NITED STATES. AND--THIS LAST POINT ONFIRMED BY THE WINGED THING IN ELL NINETY-NINE--THAT THOSE WHO HEAR HIS VOICE ARE COMPELLED TO BEY HIM.
THAT HE SPEAKS WITH THE VOICE OF GOD.
Custer, Jesse

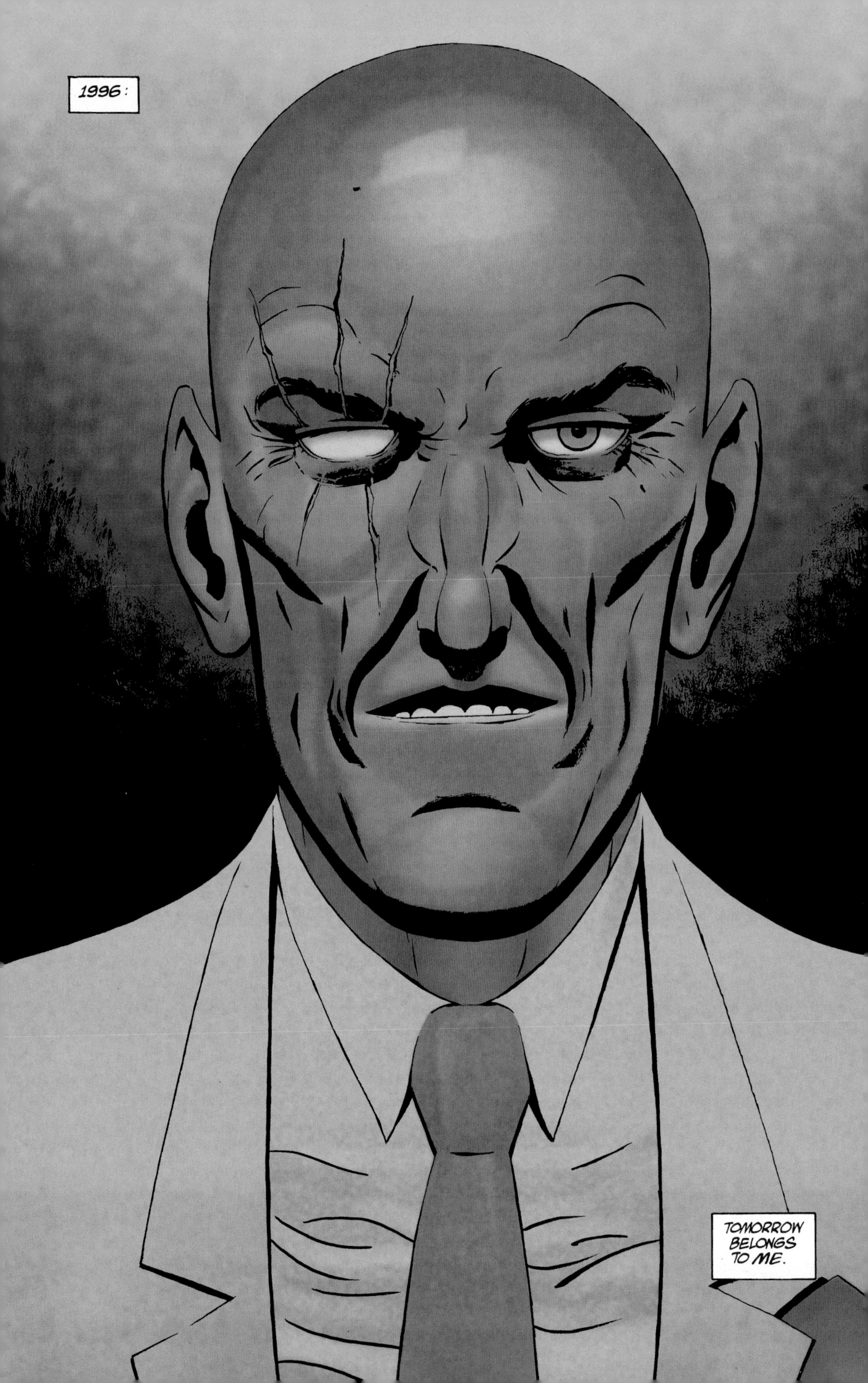
1996:
TOMORROW BELONGS TO ME.

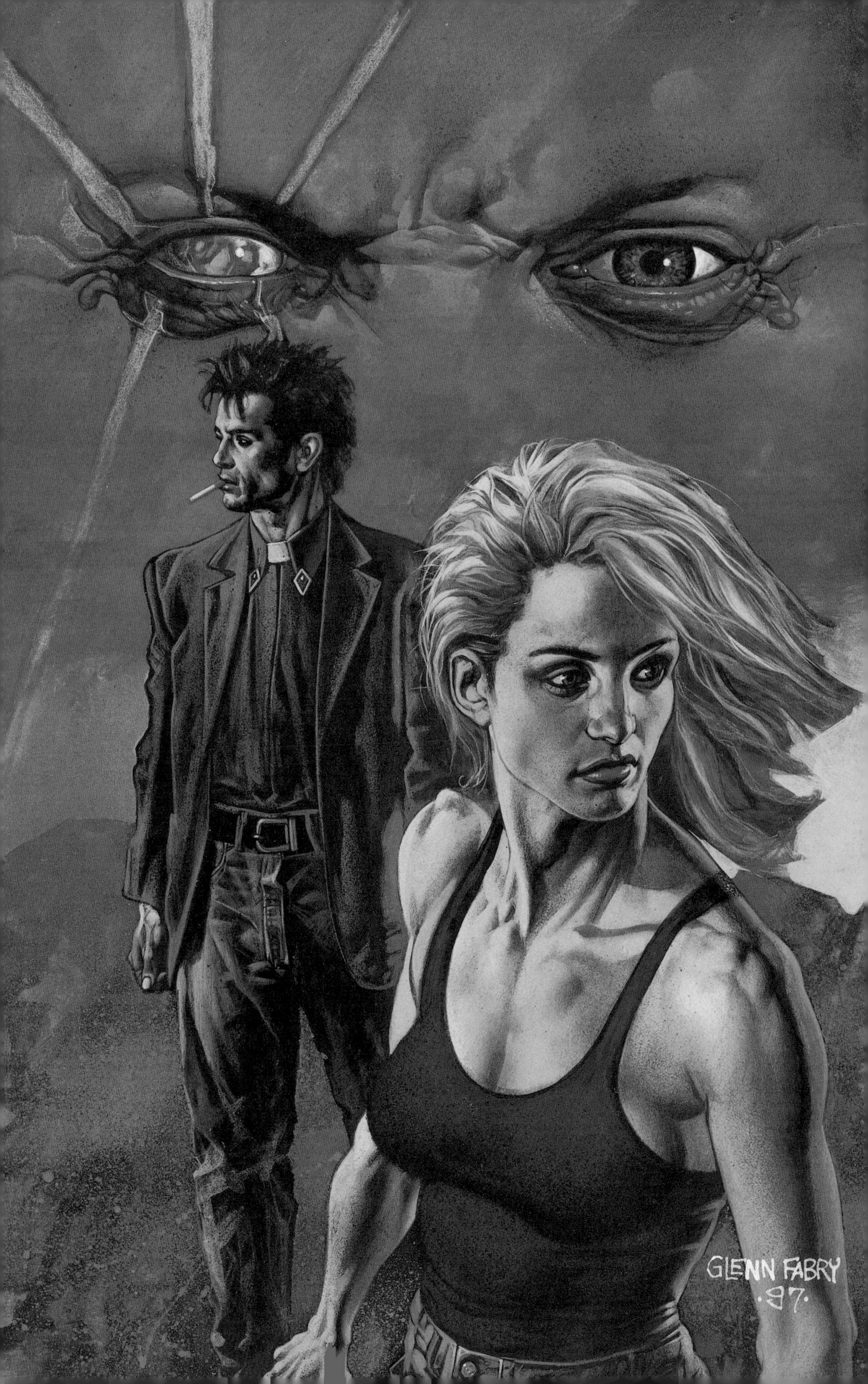
GLENN FABRY
·97·

"Different Custer. He was the dumb one liked gettin' his ass kicked."

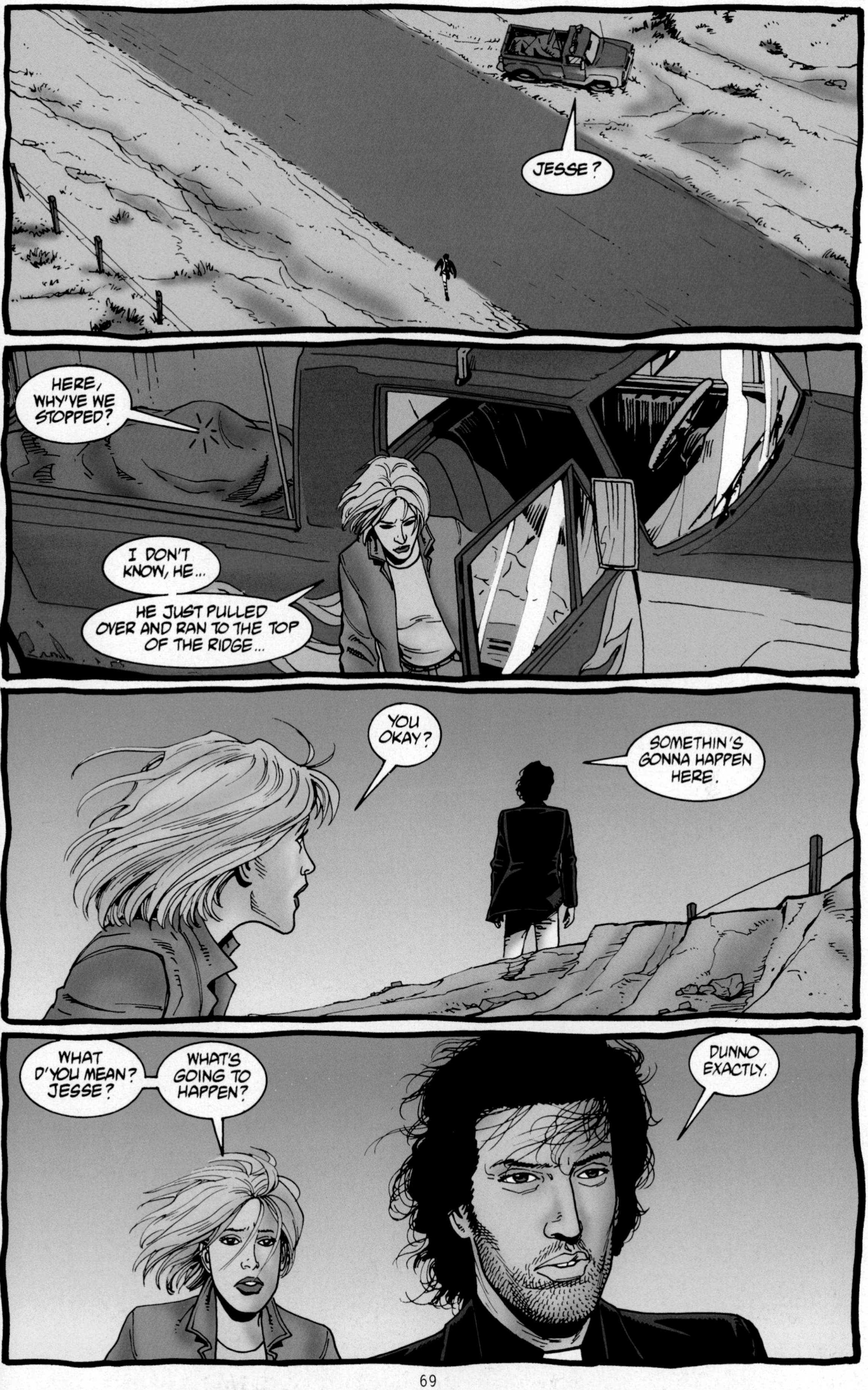
JESSE?
HERE, WHY'VE WE STOPPED?
I DON'T KNOW, HE...
HE JUST PULLED OVER AND RAN TO THE TOP OF THE RIDGE...
YOU OKAY?
SOMETHIN'S GONNA HAPPEN HERE.
WHAT D'YOU MEAN? JESSE?
WHAT'S GOING TO HAPPEN?
DUNNO EXACTLY.

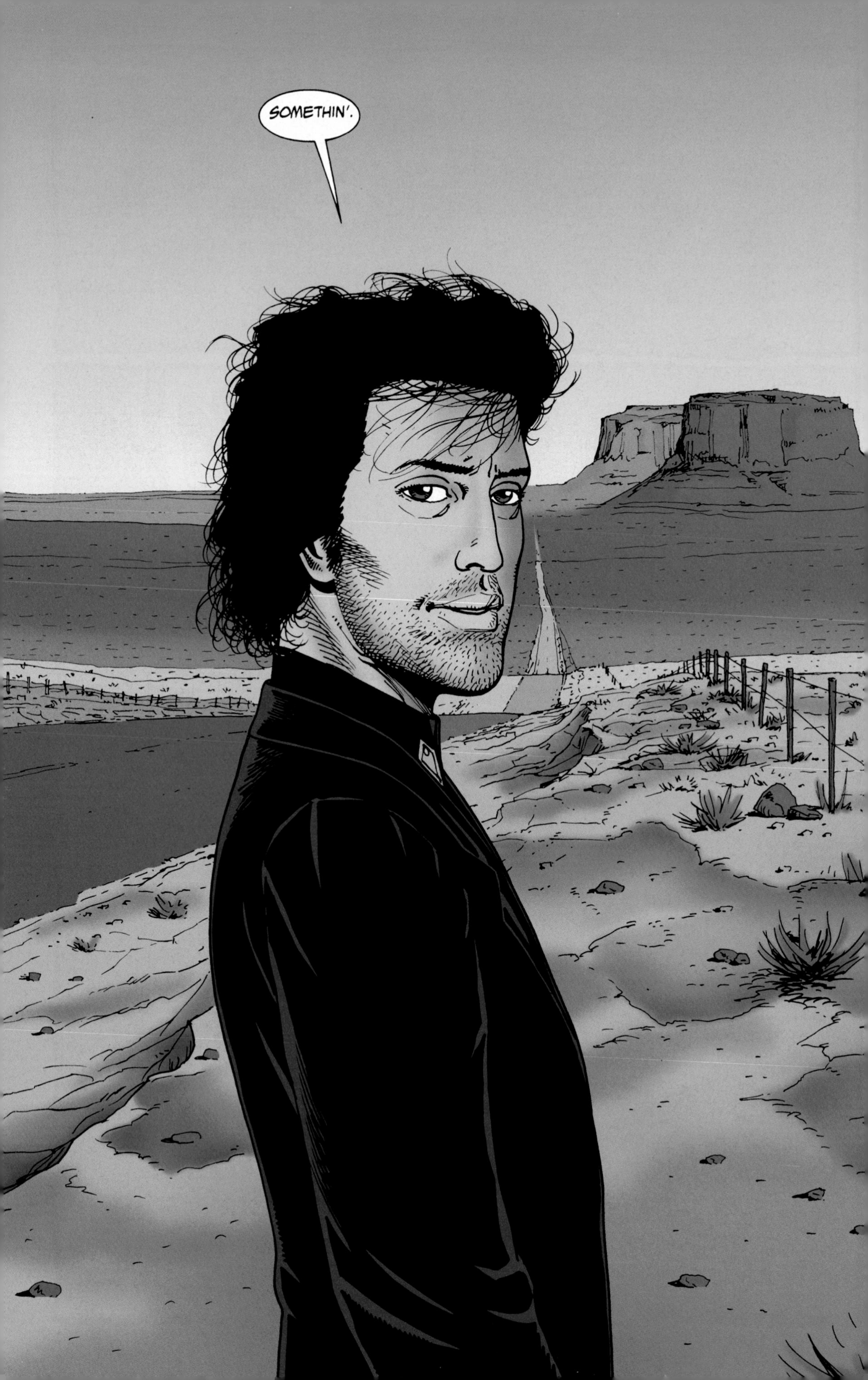
SOMETHIN'.

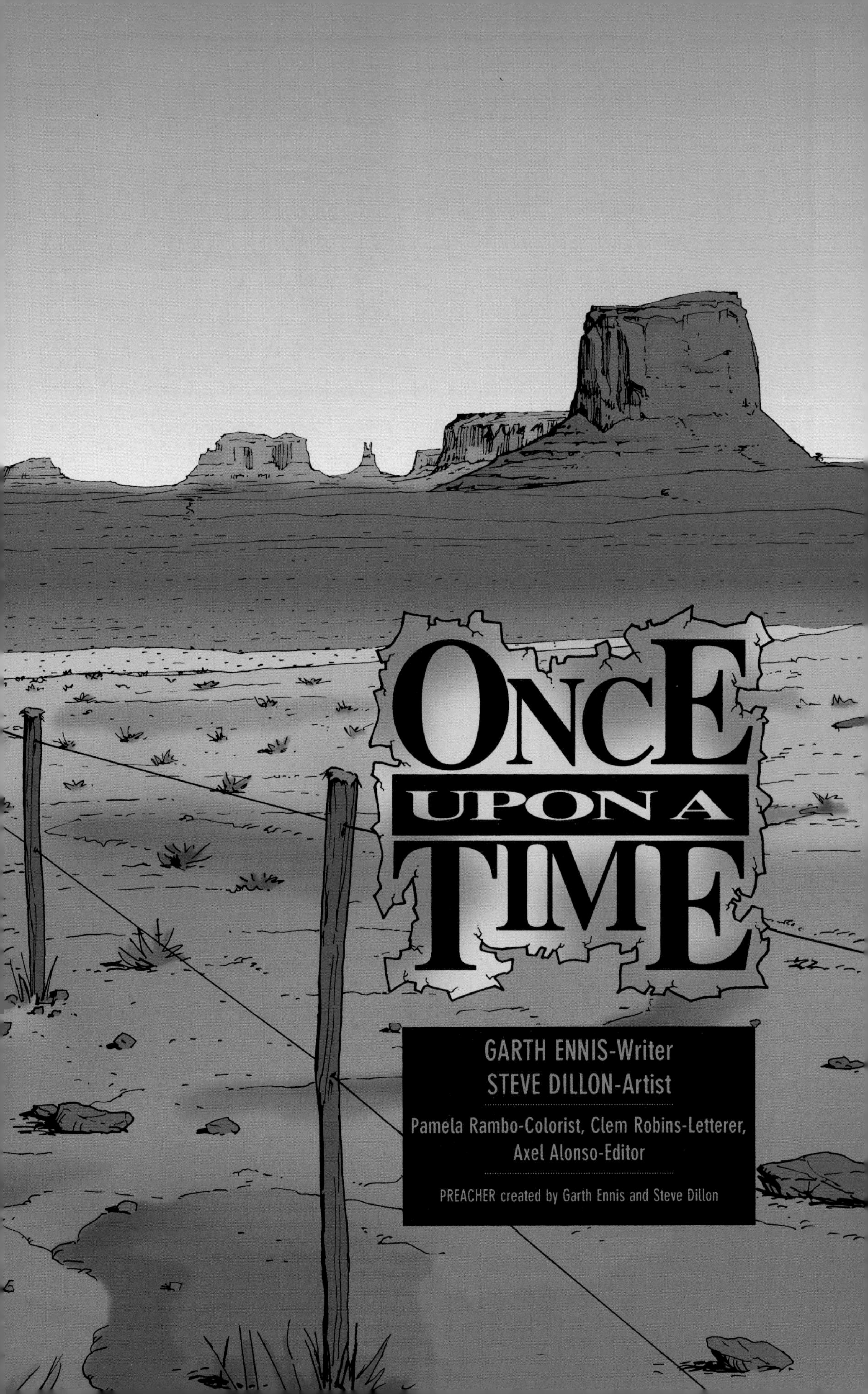
ONCE
UPON A
TIME
GARTH ENNIS-Writer
STEVE DILLON-Artist
Pamela Rambo-Colorist, Clem Robins-Letterer,
Axel Alonso-Editor
PREACHER created by Garth Ennis and Steve Dillon

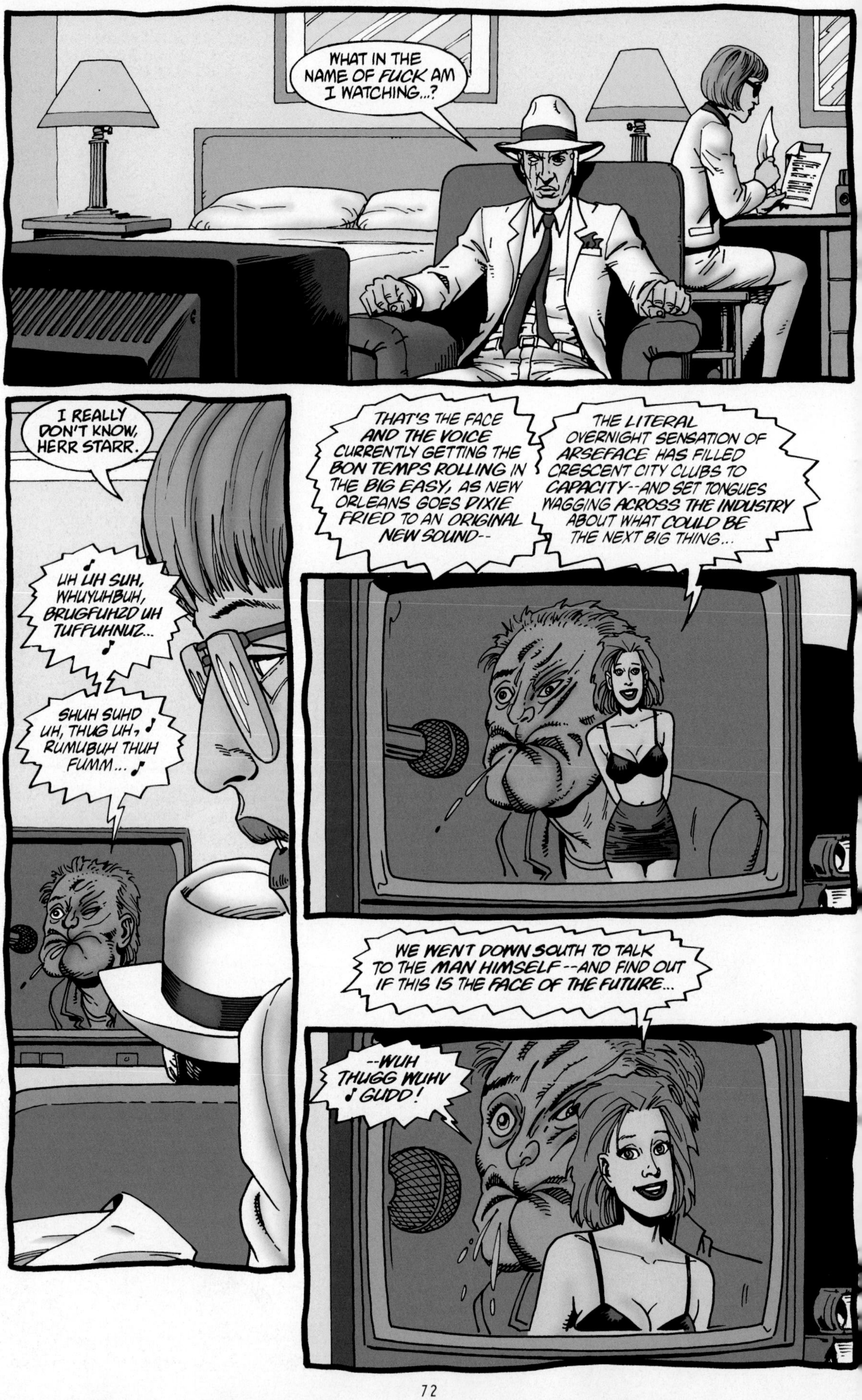
WHAT IN THE NAME OF FUCK AM I WATCHING...?
I REALLY DON'T KNOW, HERR STARR.
UH UH SUH, WHUYUHBUH, BRUGFUHZD UH TUFFUHNUZ...
SHUH SUHD UH, THUG UH, RUMUBUH THUH FUMM...
THAT'S THE FACE AND THE VOICE CURRENTLY GETTING THE BON TEMPS ROLLING IN THE BIG EASY, AS NEW ORLEANS GOES DIXIE FRIED TO AN ORIGINAL NEW SOUND--
THE LITERAL OVERNIGHT SENSATION OF ARSEFACE HAS FILLED CRESCENT CITY CLUBS TO CAPACITY--AND SET TONGUES WAGGING ACROSS THE INDUSTRY ABOUT WHAT COULD BE THE NEXT BIG THING...
WE WENT DOWN SOUTH TO TALK TO THE MAN HIMSELF--AND FIND OUT IF THIS IS THE FACE OF THE FUTURE...
--WUH THUGG WUHV GUDD!

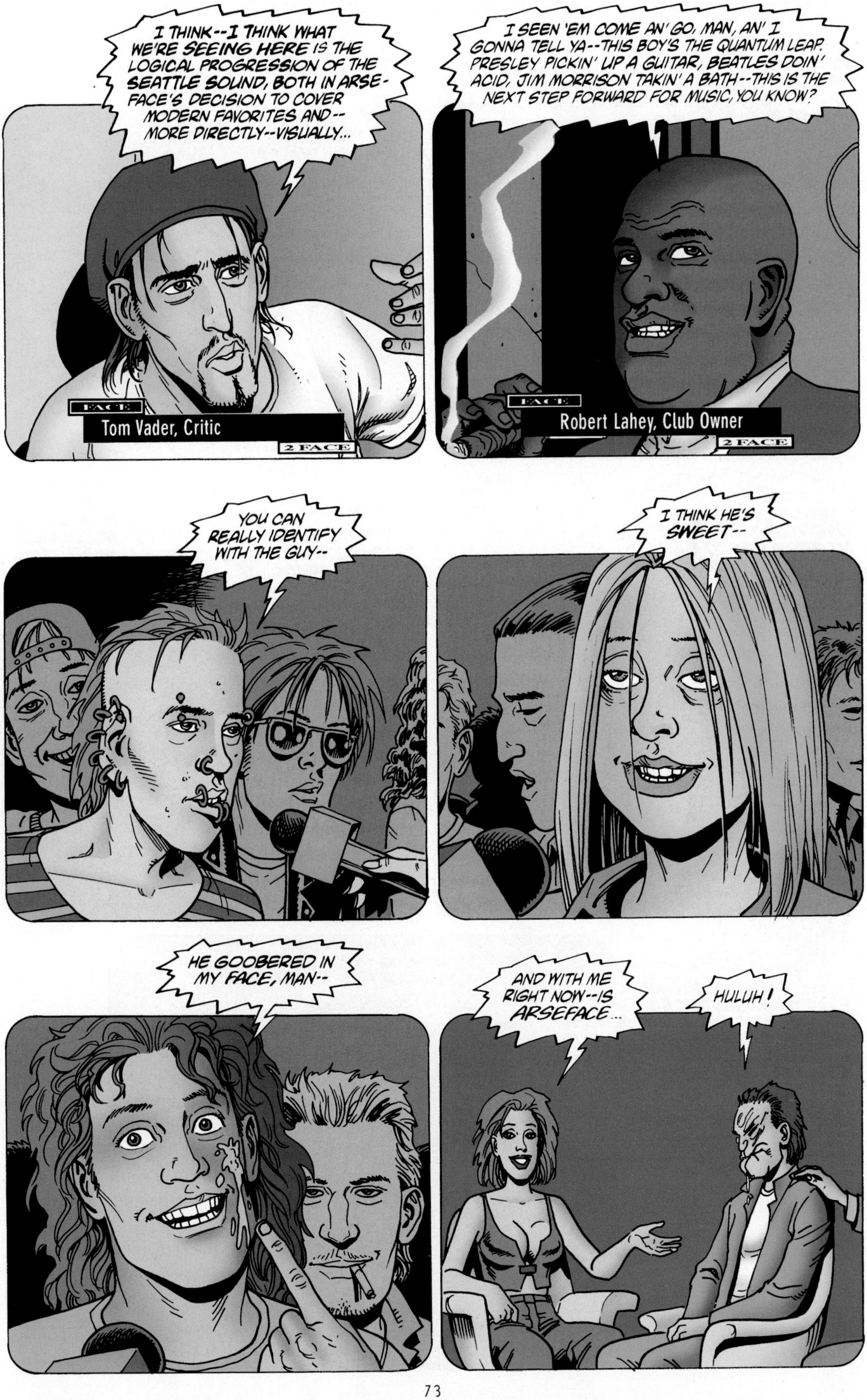
I THINK--I THINK WHAT WE'RE SEEING HERE IS THE LOGICAL PROGRESSION OF THE SEATTLE SOUND, BOTH IN ARSE-FACE'S DECISION TO COVER MODERN FAVORITES AND--MORE DIRECTLY--VISUALLY...
FACE
Tom Vader, Critic
2 FACE
I SEEN 'EM COME AN' GO, MAN, AN' I GONNA TELL YA--THIS BOY'S THE QUANTUM LEAP. PRESLEY PICKIN' UP A GUITAR, BEATLES DOIN' ACID, JIM MORRISON TAKIN' A BATH--THIS IS THE NEXT STEP FORWARD FOR MUSIC, YOU KNOW?
FACE
Robert Lahey, Club Owner
2 FACE
YOU CAN REALLY IDENTIFY WITH THE GUY--
I THINK HE'S SWEET--
HE GOOBERED IN MY FACE, MAN--
AND WITH ME RIGHT NOW--IS ARSEFACE...
HULUH!

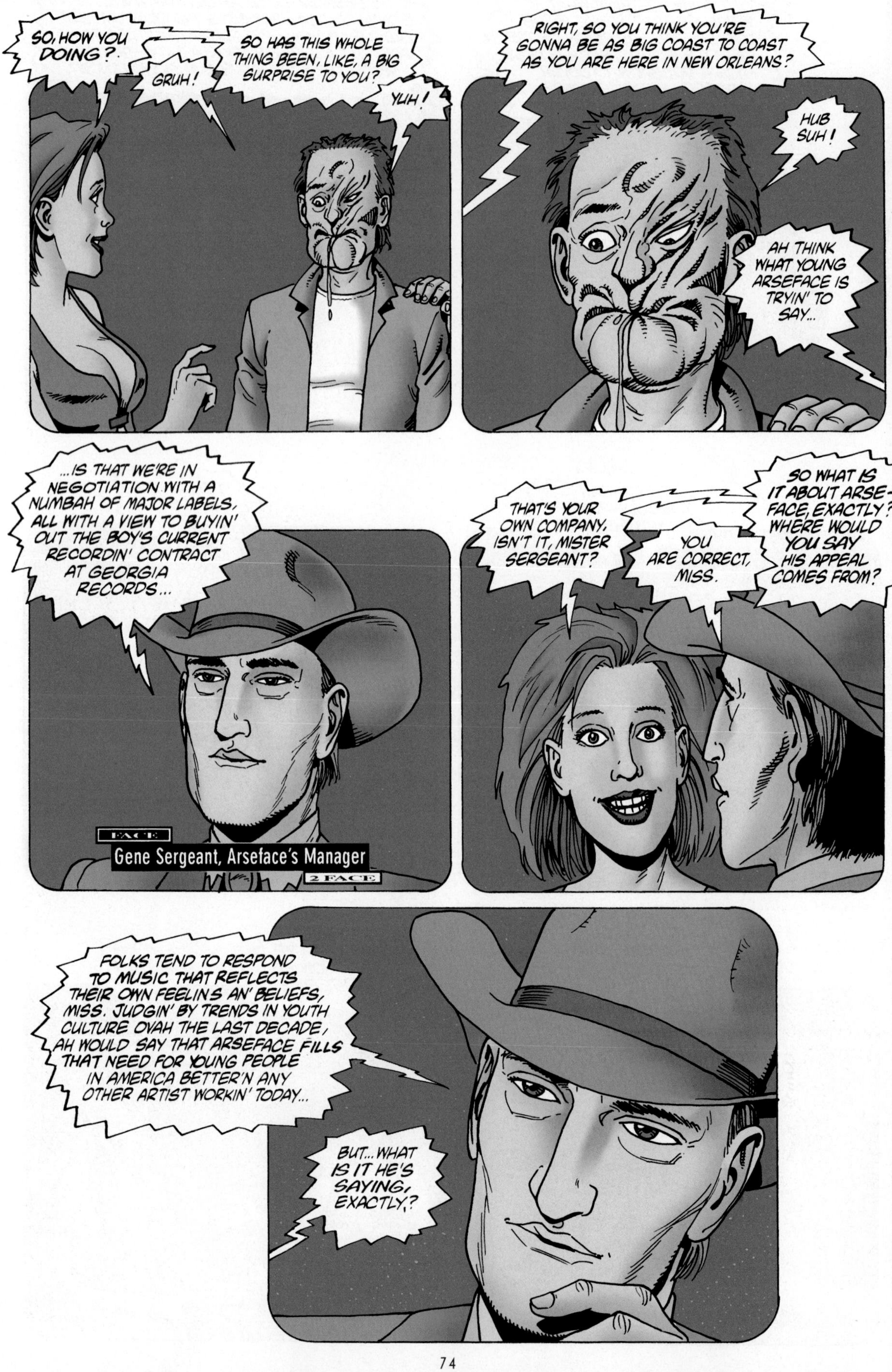
SO, HOW YOU DOING?
GRUH!
SO HAS THIS WHOLE THING BEEN, LIKE, A BIG SURPRISE TO YOU?
YUH!
RIGHT, SO YOU THINK YOU'RE GONNA BE AS BIG COAST TO COAST AS YOU ARE HERE IN NEW ORLEANS?
HUB SUH!
AH THINK WHAT YOUNG ARSEFACE IS TRYIN' TO SAY...
...IS THAT WE'RE IN NEGOTIATION WITH A NUMBAH OF MAJOR LABELS, ALL WITH A VIEW TO BUYIN' OUT THE BOY'S CURRENT RECORDIN' CONTRACT AT GEORGIA RECORDS...
FACE
Gene Sergeant, Arseface's Manager
2 FACE
THAT'S YOUR OWN COMPANY, ISN'T IT, MISTER SERGEANT?
YOU ARE CORRECT, MISS.
SO WHAT IS IT ABOUT ARSEFACE, EXACTLY? WHERE WOULD YOU SAY HIS APPEAL COMES FROM?
FOLKS TEND TO RESPOND TO MUSIC THAT REFLECTS THEIR OWN FEELIN'S AN' BELIEFS, MISS. JUDGIN' BY TRENDS IN YOUTH CULTURE OVAH THE LAST DECADE, AH WOULD SAY THAT ARSEFACE FILLS THAT NEED FOR YOUNG PEOPLE IN AMERICA BETTER'N ANY OTHER ARTIST WORKIN' TODAY...
BUT...WHAT IS IT HE'S SAYING, EXACTLY?

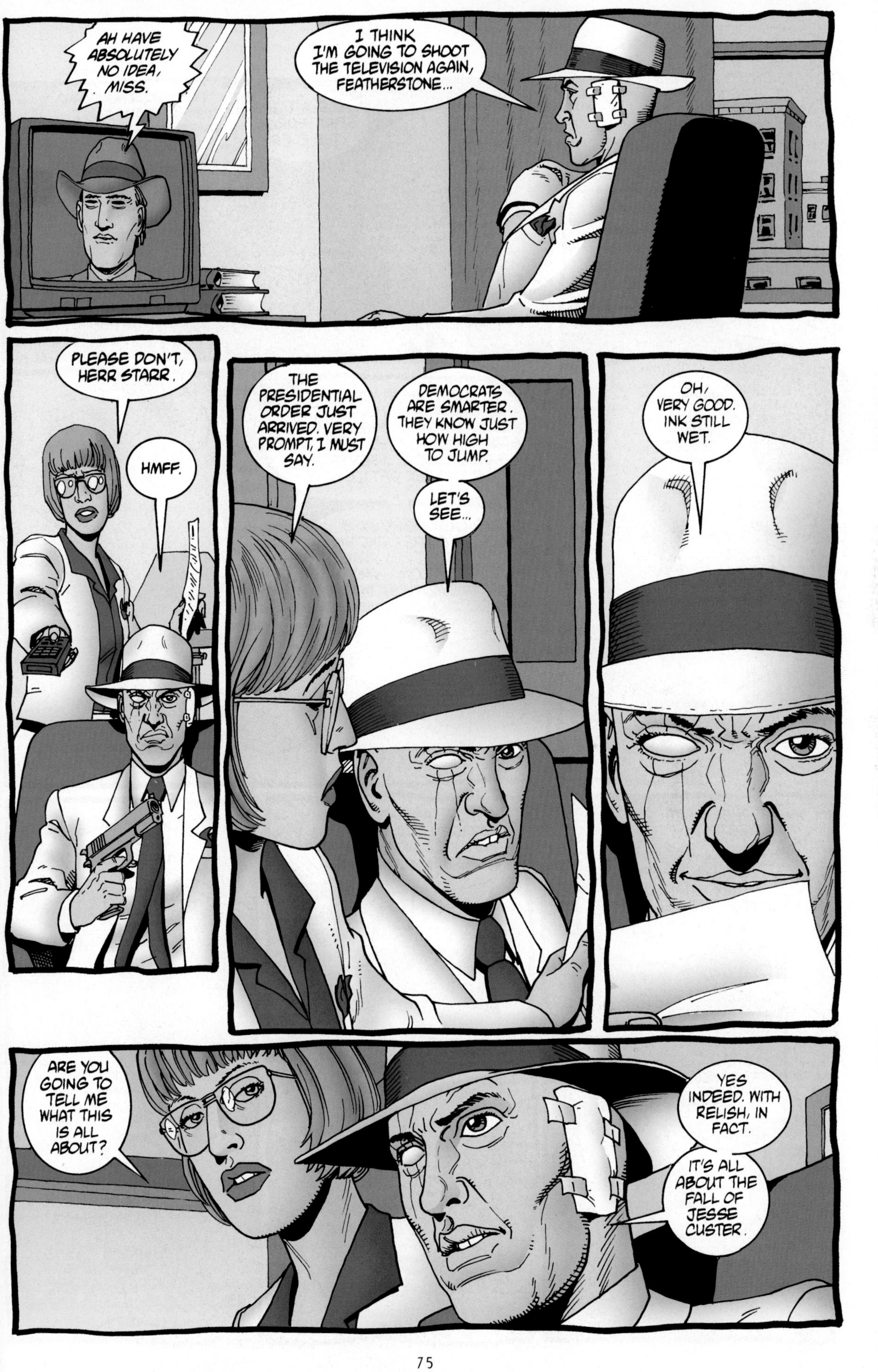
AH HAVE ABSOLUTELY NO IDEA, MISS.
I THINK I'M GOING TO SHOOT THE TELEVISION AGAIN, FEATHERSTONE...
PLEASE DON'T, HERR STARR.
HMFF.
THE PRESIDENTIAL ORDER JUST ARRIVED. VERY PROMPT, I MUST SAY.
DEMOCRATS ARE SMARTER. THEY KNOW JUST HOW HIGH TO JUMP.
LET'S SEE...
OH, VERY GOOD. INK STILL WET.
ARE YOU GOING TO TELL ME WHAT THIS IS ALL ABOUT?
YES INDEED. WITH RELISH, IN FACT.
IT'S ALL ABOUT THE FALL OF JESSE CUSTER.

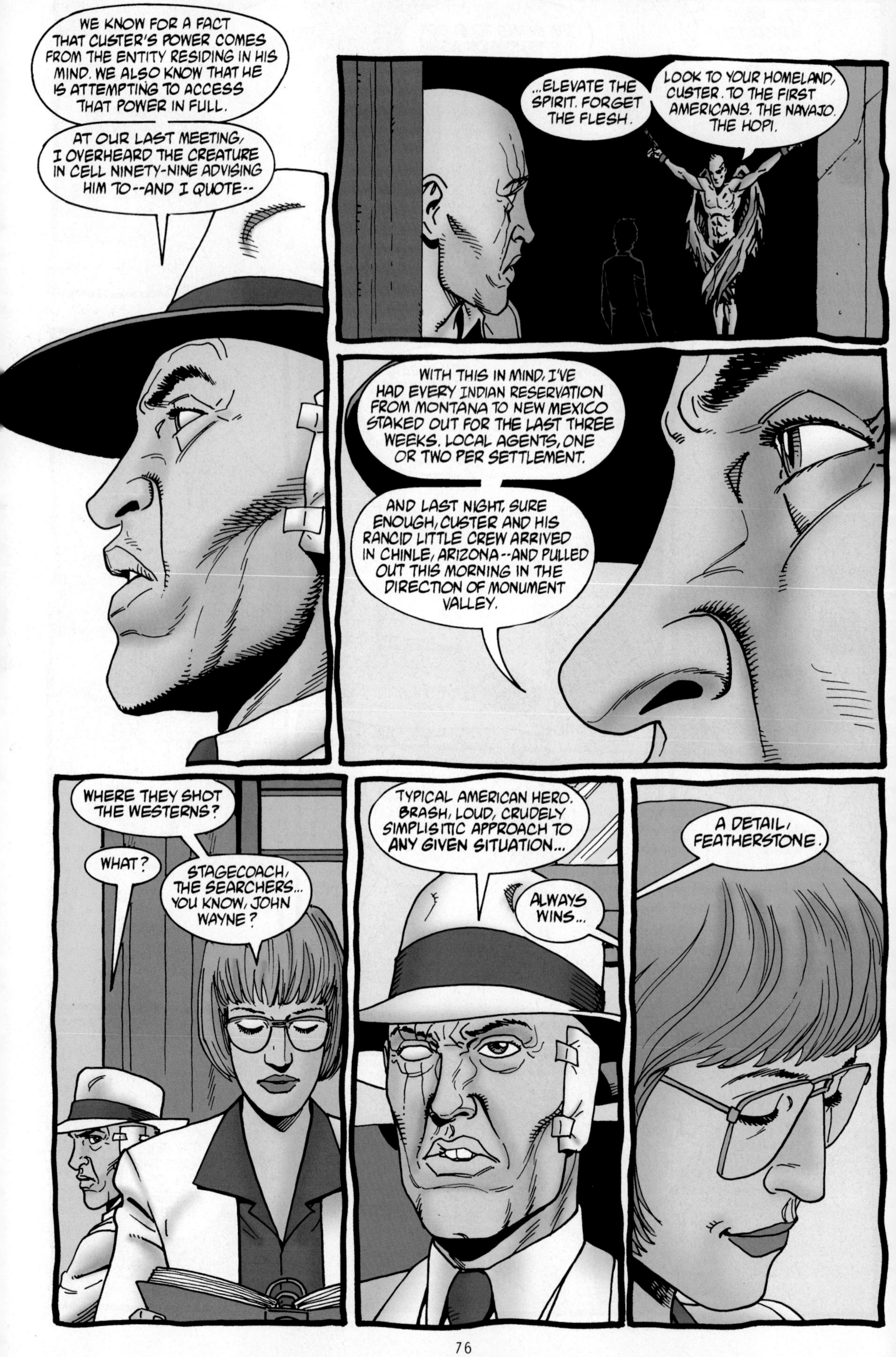
WE KNOW FOR A FACT THAT CUSTER'S POWER COMES FROM THE ENTITY RESIDING IN HIS MIND. WE ALSO KNOW THAT HE IS ATTEMPTING TO ACCESS THAT POWER IN FULL.
AT OUR LAST MEETING, I OVERHEARD THE CREATURE IN CELL NINETY-NINE ADVISING HIM TO--AND I QUOTE--
...ELEVATE THE SPIRIT. FORGET THE FLESH.
LOOK TO YOUR HOMELAND, CUSTER. TO THE FIRST AMERICANS. THE NAVAJO. THE HOPI.
WITH THIS IN MIND, I'VE HAD EVERY INDIAN RESERVATION FROM MONTANA TO NEW MEXICO STAKED OUT FOR THE LAST THREE WEEKS. LOCAL AGENTS, ONE OR TWO PER SETTLEMENT.
AND LAST NIGHT, SURE ENOUGH, CUSTER AND HIS RANCID LITTLE CREW ARRIVED IN CHINLE, ARIZONA--AND PULLED OUT THIS MORNING IN THE DIRECTION OF MONUMENT VALLEY.
WHERE THEY SHOT THE WESTERNS?
WHAT?
STAGECOACH, THE SEARCHERS... YOU KNOW, JOHN WAYNE?
TYPICAL AMERICAN HERO. BRASH, LOUD, CRUDELY SIMPLISITIC APPROACH TO ANY GIVEN SITUATION...
ALWAYS WINS...
A DETAIL, FEATHERSTONE.

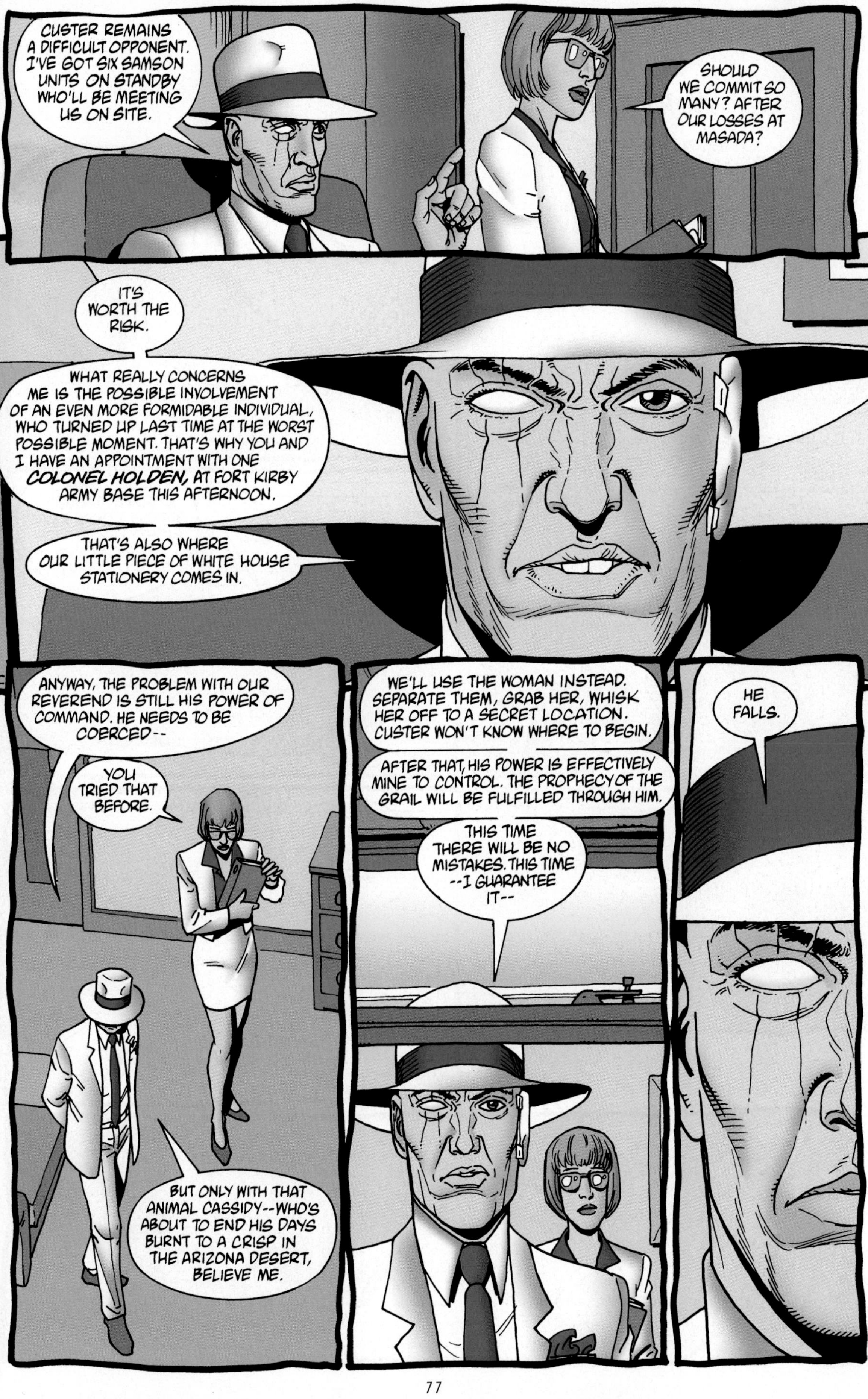
CUSTER REMAINS A DIFFICULT OPPONENT. I'VE GOT SIX SAMSON UNITS ON STANDBY WHO'LL BE MEETING US ON SITE.
SHOULD WE COMMIT SO MANY? AFTER OUR LOSSES AT MASADA?
IT'S WORTH THE RISK.
WHAT REALLY CONCERNS ME IS THE POSSIBLE INVOLVEMENT OF AN EVEN MORE FORMIDABLE INDIVIDUAL, WHO TURNED UP LAST TIME AT THE WORST POSSIBLE MOMENT. THAT'S WHY YOU AND I HAVE AN APPOINTMENT WITH ONE COLONEL HOLDEN, AT FORT KIRBY ARMY BASE THIS AFTERNOON.
THAT'S ALSO WHERE OUR LITTLE PIECE OF WHITE HOUSE STATIONERY COMES IN.
ANYWAY, THE PROBLEM WITH OUR REVEREND IS STILL HIS POWER OF COMMAND. HE NEEDS TO BE COERCED--
YOU TRIED THAT BEFORE.
BUT ONLY WITH THAT ANIMAL CASSIDY--WHO'S ABOUT TO END HIS DAYS BURNT TO A CRISP IN THE ARIZONA DESERT, BELIEVE ME.
WE'LL USE THE WOMAN INSTEAD. SEPARATE THEM, GRAB HER, WHISK HER OFF TO A SECRET LOCATION. CUSTER WON'T KNOW WHERE TO BEGIN.
AFTER THAT, HIS POWER IS EFFECTIVELY MINE TO CONTROL. THE PROPHECY OF THE GRAIL WILL BE FULFILLED THROUGH HIM.
THIS TIME THERE WILL BE NO MISTAKES. THIS TIME --I GUARANTEE IT--
HE FALLS.

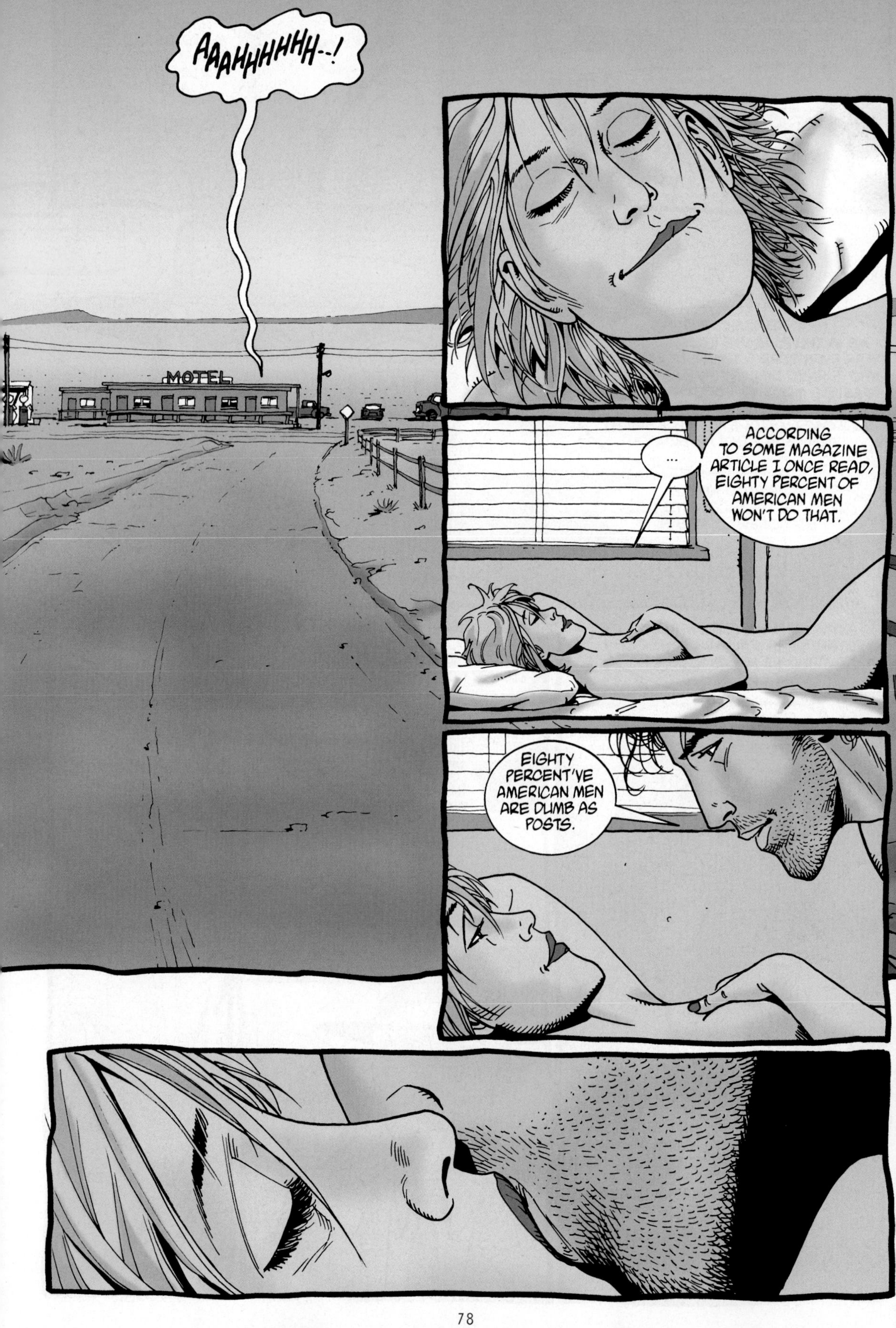
AAAHHHHHH--!
MOTEL
...
ACCORDING TO SOME MAGAZINE ARTICLE I ONCE READ, EIGHTY PERCENT OF AMERICAN MEN WON'T DO THAT.
EIGHTY PERCENT'YE AMERICAN MEN ARE DUMB AS POSTS.

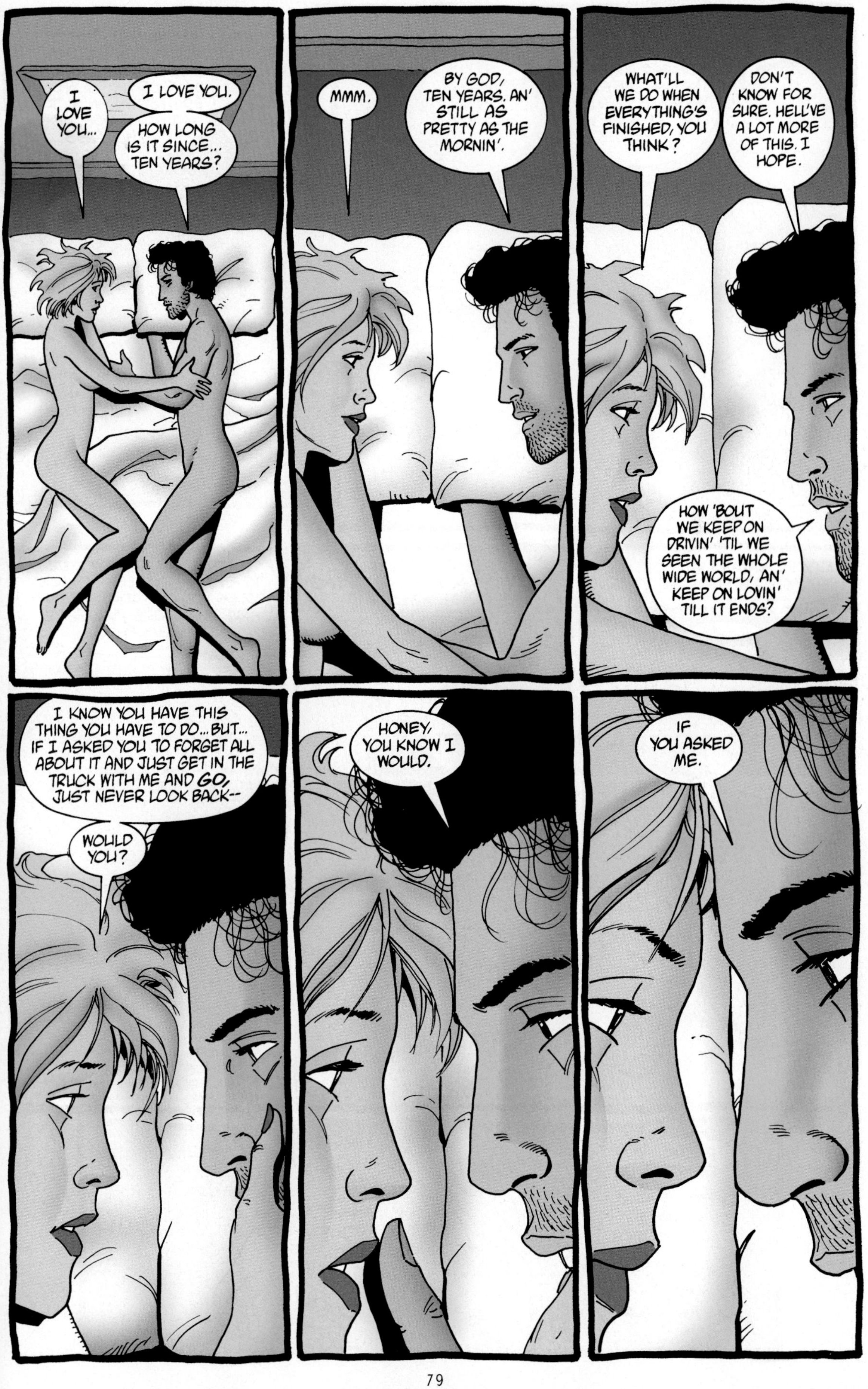
I LOVE YOU...
I LOVE YOU.
HOW LONG IS IT SINCE... TEN YEARS?
MMM.
BY GOD, TEN YEARS. AN' STILL AS PRETTY AS THE MORNIN'.
WHAT'LL WE DO WHEN EVERYTHING'S FINISHED, YOU THINK?
DON'T KNOW FOR SURE. HELL'VE A LOT MORE OF THIS. I HOPE.
HOW 'BOUT WE KEEP ON DRIVIN' 'TIL WE SEEN THE WHOLE WIDE WORLD, AN' KEEP ON LOVIN' TILL IT ENDS?
I KNOW YOU HAVE THIS THING YOU HAVE TO DO... BUT... IF I ASKED YOU TO FORGET ALL ABOUT IT AND JUST GET IN THE TRUCK WITH ME AND GO, JUST NEVER LOOK BACK--
WOULD YOU?
HONEY, YOU KNOW I WOULD.
IF YOU ASKED ME.

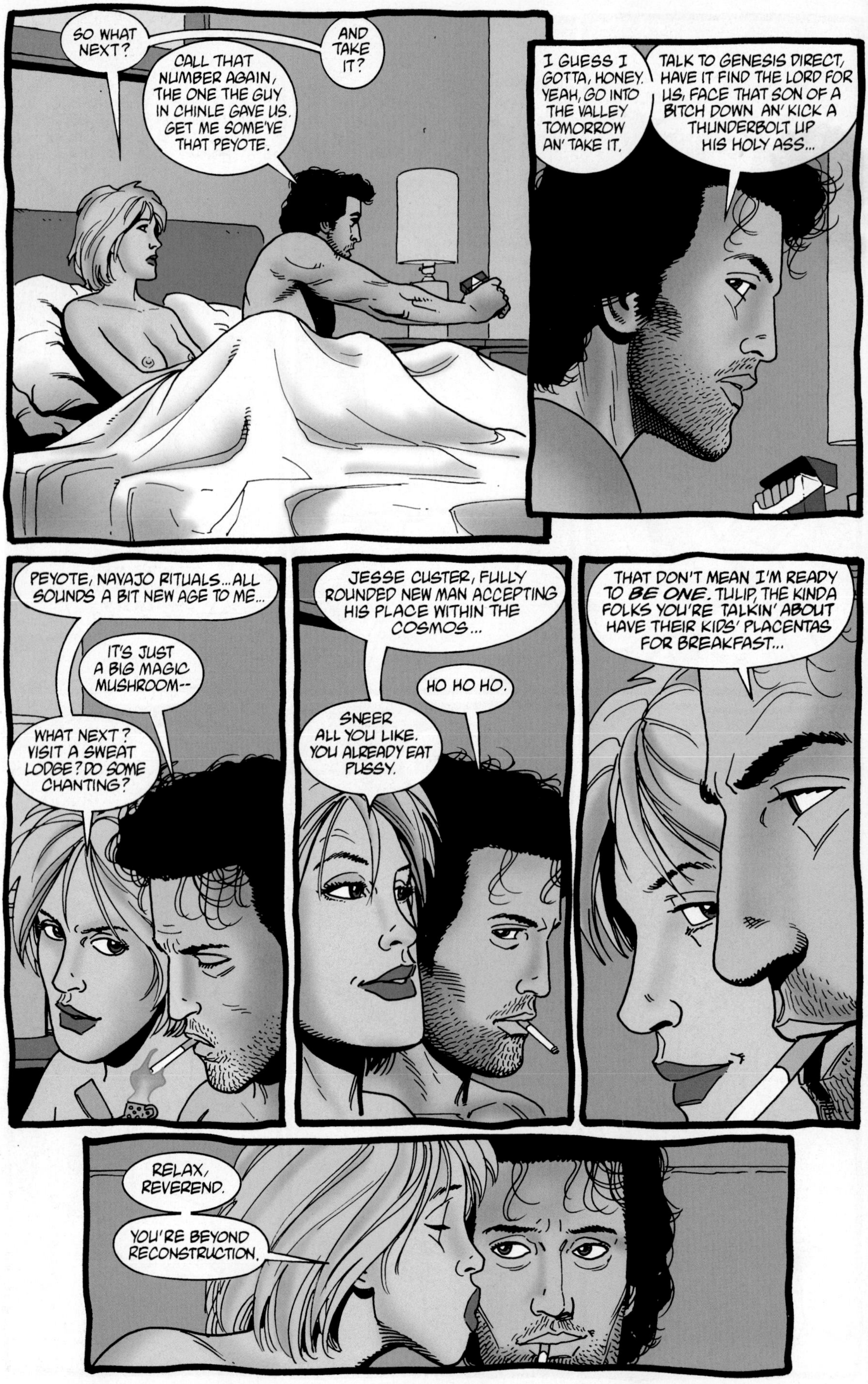
SO WHAT NEXT?
AND TAKE IT?
CALL THAT NUMBER AGAIN, THE ONE THE GUY IN CHINLE GAVE US. GET ME SOME'VE THAT PEYOTE.
I GUESS I GOTTA, HONEY. YEAH, GO INTO THE VALLEY TOMORROW AN' TAKE IT.
TALK TO GENESIS DIRECT, HAVE IT FIND THE LORD FOR US, FACE THAT SON OF A BITCH DOWN AN' KICK A THUNDERBOLT UP HIS HOLY ASS...
PEYOTE, NAVAJO RITUALS...ALL SOUNDS A BIT NEW AGE TO ME...
IT'S JUST A BIG MAGIC MUSHROOM--
WHAT NEXT? VISIT A SWEAT LODGE? DO SOME CHANTING?
JESSE CUSTER, FULLY ROUNDED NEW MAN ACCEPTING HIS PLACE WITHIN THE COSMOS...
HO HO HO.
SNEER ALL YOU LIKE. YOU ALREADY EAT PUSSY.
THAT DON'T MEAN I'M READY TO ***BE ONE.*** TULIP, THE KINDA FOLKS YOU'RE TALKIN' ABOUT HAVE THEIR KIDS' PLACENTAS FOR BREAKFAST...
RELAX, REVEREND.
YOU'RE BEYOND RECONSTRUCTION.

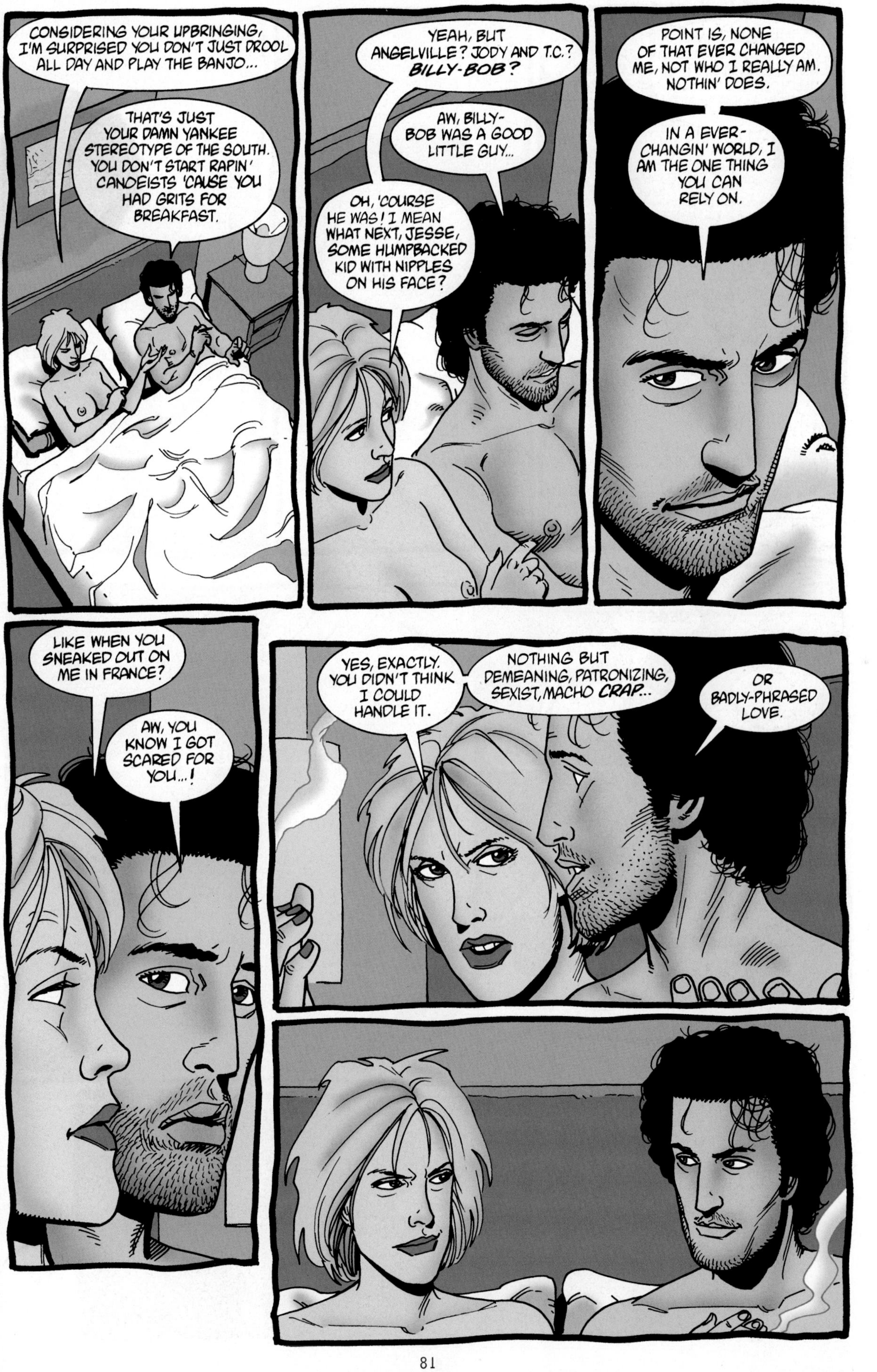
CONSIDERING YOUR UPBRINGING, I'M SURPRISED YOU DON'T JUST DROOL ALL DAY AND PLAY THE BANJO...
THAT'S JUST YOUR DAMN YANKEE STEREOTYPE OF THE SOUTH. YOU DON'T START RAPIN' CANOEISTS 'CAUSE YOU HAD GRITS FOR BREAKFAST.
YEAH, BUT ANGELVILLE? JODY AND T.C.? BILLY-BOB?
AW, BILLY-BOB WAS A GOOD LITTLE GUY...
OH, 'COURSE HE WAS! I MEAN WHAT NEXT, JESSE, SOME HUMPBACKED KID WITH NIPPLES ON HIS FACE?
POINT IS, NONE OF THAT EVER CHANGED ME, NOT WHO I REALLY AM. NOTHIN' DOES.
IN A EVER-CHANGIN' WORLD, I AM THE ONE THING YOU CAN RELY ON.
LIKE WHEN YOU SNEAKED OUT ON ME IN FRANCE?
AW, YOU KNOW I GOT SCARED FOR YOU...!
YES, EXACTLY. YOU DIDN'T THINK I COULD HANDLE IT.
NOTHING BUT DEMEANING, PATRONIZING, SEXIST, MACHO CRAP...
OR BADLY-PHRASED LOVE.

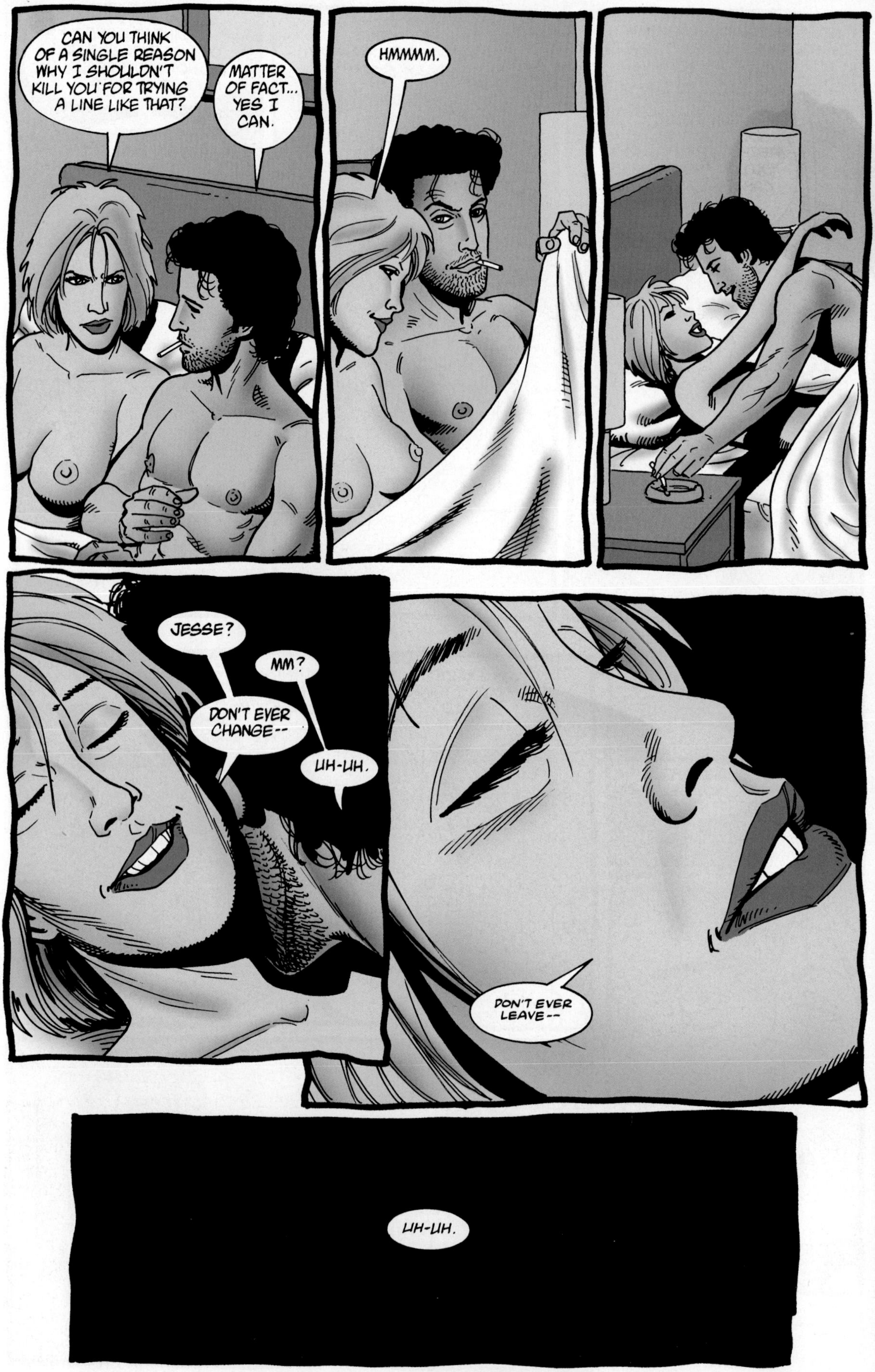
CAN YOU THINK OF A SINGLE REASON WHY I SHOULDN'T KILL YOU FOR TRYING A LINE LIKE THAT?
MATTER OF FACT... YES I CAN.
HMMMM.
JESSE?
MM?
DON'T EVER CHANGE--
UH-UH.
DON'T EVER LEAVE--
UH-UH.

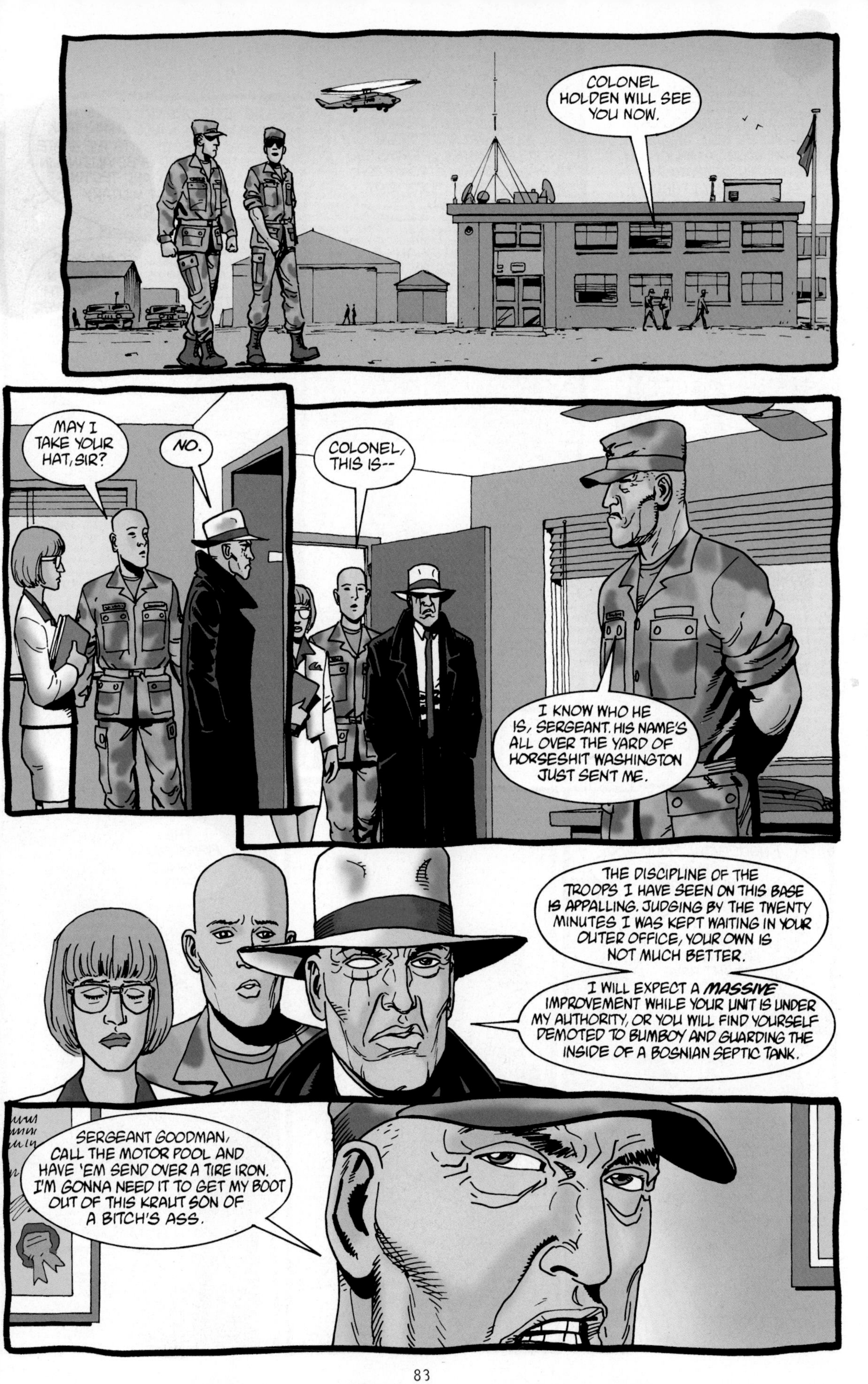
COLONEL HOLDEN WILL SEE YOU NOW.
MAY I TAKE YOUR HAT, SIR?
NO.
COLONEL, THIS IS--
I KNOW WHO HE IS, SERGEANT. HIS NAME'S ALL OVER THE YARD OF HORSESHIT WASHINGTON JUST SENT ME.
THE DISCIPLINE OF THE TROOPS I HAVE SEEN ON THIS BASE IS APPALLING. JUDGING BY THE TWENTY MINUTES I WAS KEPT WAITING IN YOUR OUTER OFFICE, YOUR OWN IS NOT MUCH BETTER.
I WILL EXPECT A MASSIVE IMPROVEMENT WHILE YOUR UNIT IS UNDER MY AUTHORITY, OR YOU WILL FIND YOURSELF DEMOTED TO BUMBOY AND GUARDING THE INSIDE OF A BOSNIAN SEPTIC TANK.
SERGEANT GOODMAN, CALL THE MOTOR POOL AND HAVE 'EM SEND OVER A TIRE IRON. I'M GONNA NEED IT TO GET MY BOOT OUT OF THIS KRAUT SON OF A BITCH'S ASS.

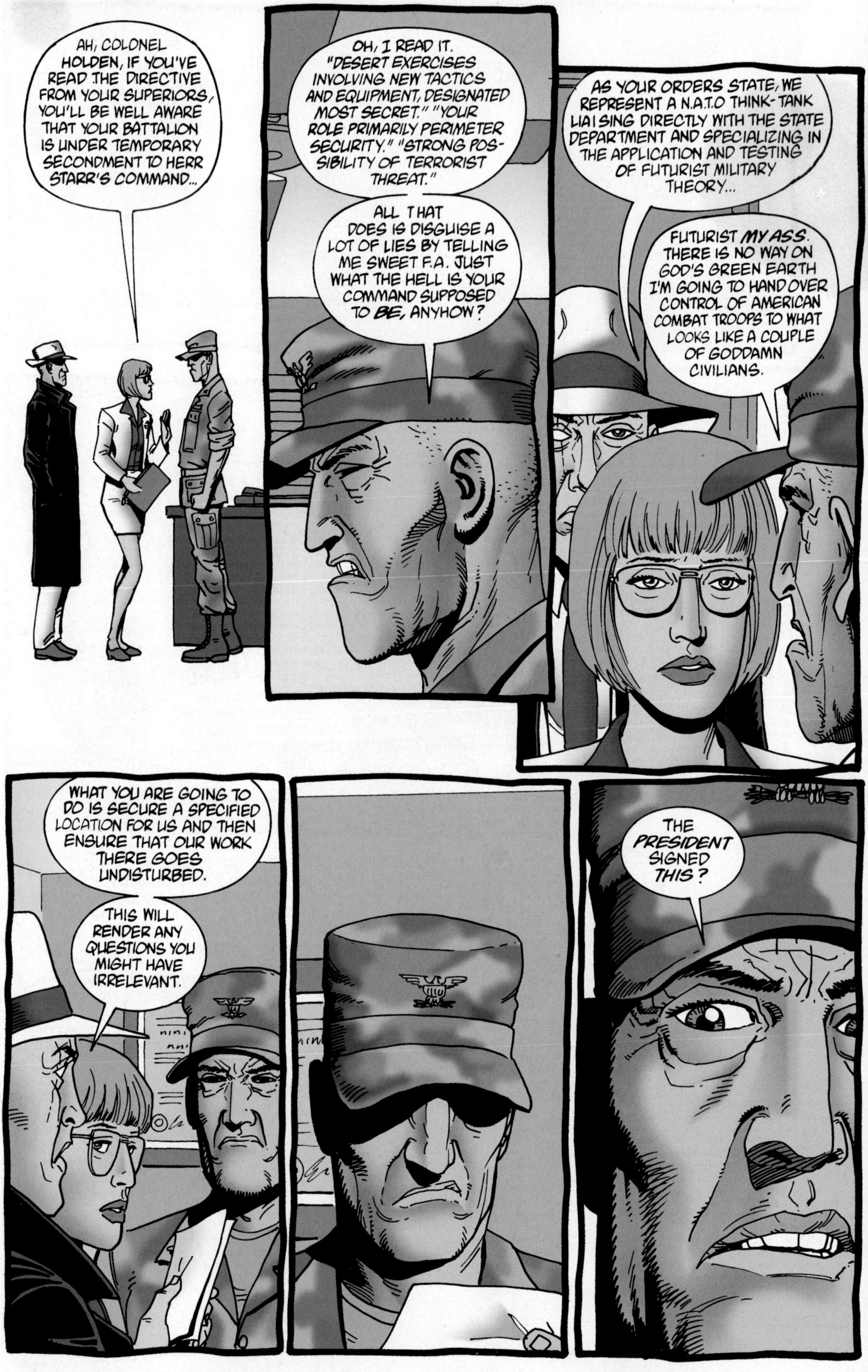
AH, COLONEL HOLDEN, IF YOU'VE READ THE DIRECTIVE FROM YOUR SUPERIORS, YOU'LL BE WELL AWARE THAT YOUR BATTALION IS UNDER TEMPORARY SECONDMENT TO HERR STARR'S COMMAND...
OH, I READ IT. "DESERT EXERCISES INVOLVING NEW TACTICS AND EQUIPMENT, DESIGNATED MOST SECRET." "YOUR ROLE PRIMARILY PERIMETER SECURITY." "STRONG POSSIBILITY OF TERRORIST THREAT."
ALL THAT DOES IS DISGUISE A LOT OF LIES BY TELLING ME SWEET F.A. JUST WHAT THE HELL IS YOUR COMMAND SUPPOSED TO BE, ANYHOW?
AS YOUR ORDERS STATE, WE REPRESENT A N.A.T.O THINK-TANK LIAISING DIRECTLY WITH THE STATE DEPARTMENT AND SPECIALIZING IN THE APPLICATION AND TESTING OF FUTURIST MILITARY THEORY...
FUTURIST MY ASS. THERE IS NO WAY ON GOD'S GREEN EARTH I'M GOING TO HAND OVER CONTROL OF AMERICAN COMBAT TROOPS TO WHAT LOOKS LIKE A COUPLE OF GODDAMN CIVILIANS.
WHAT YOU ARE GOING TO DO IS SECURE A SPECIFIED LOCATION FOR US AND THEN ENSURE THAT OUR WORK THERE GOES UNDISTURBED.
THIS WILL RENDER ANY QUESTIONS YOU MIGHT HAVE IRRELEVANT.
THE PRESIDENT SIGNED THIS?

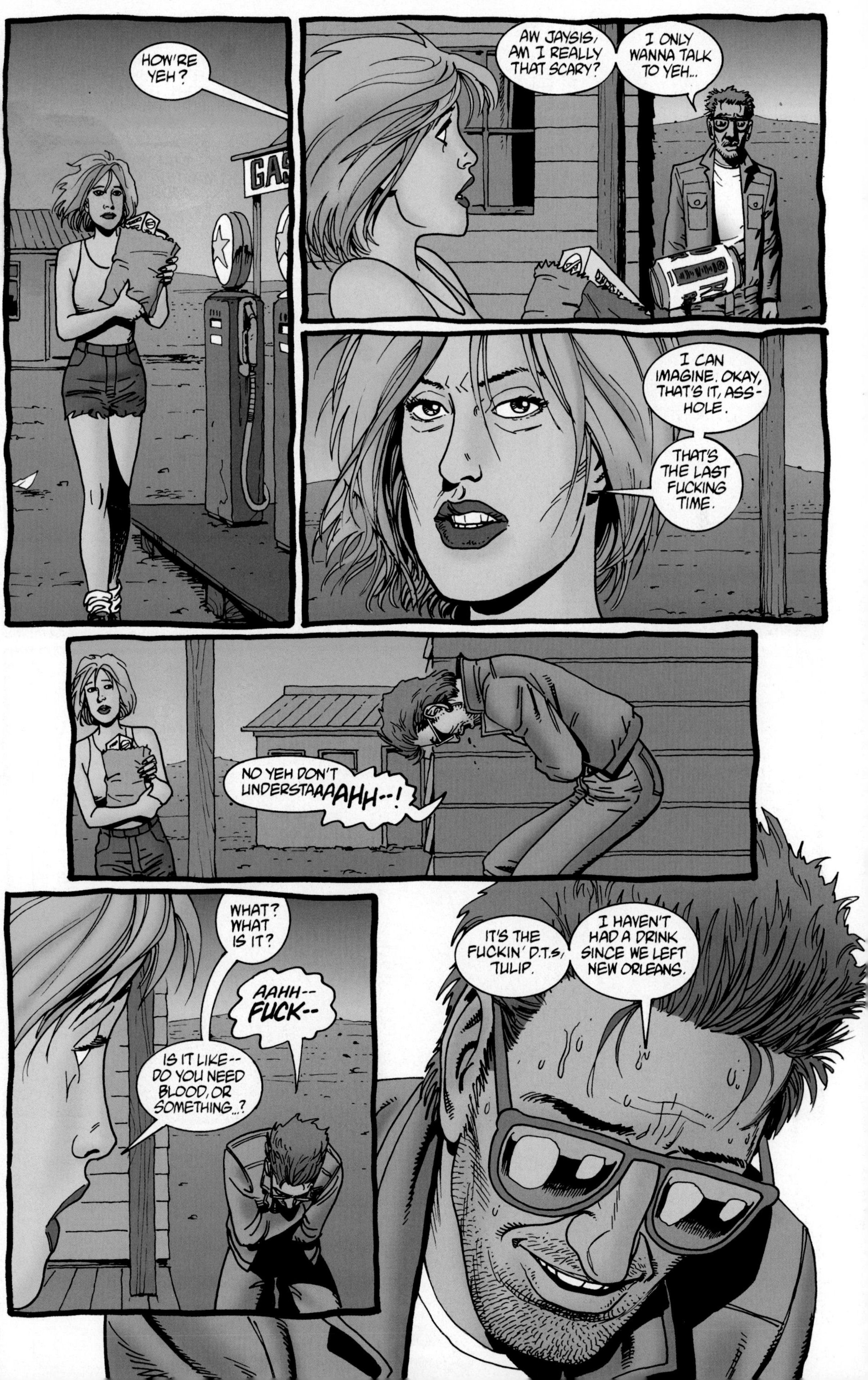
HOW'RE YEH?
AW JAYSIS, AM I REALLY THAT SCARY?
I ONLY WANNA TALK TO YEH...
I CAN IMAGINE. OKAY, THAT'S IT, ASS-HOLE.
THAT'S THE LAST FUCKING TIME.
NO YEH DON'T UNDERSTAAAAHH--!
WHAT? WHAT IS IT?
AAHH-- FUCK--
IS IT LIKE-- DO YOU NEED BLOOD, OR SOMETHING...?
IT'S THE FUCKIN' D.T.S, TULIP.
I HAVEN'T HAD A DRINK SINCE WE LEFT NEW ORLEANS.
GAS

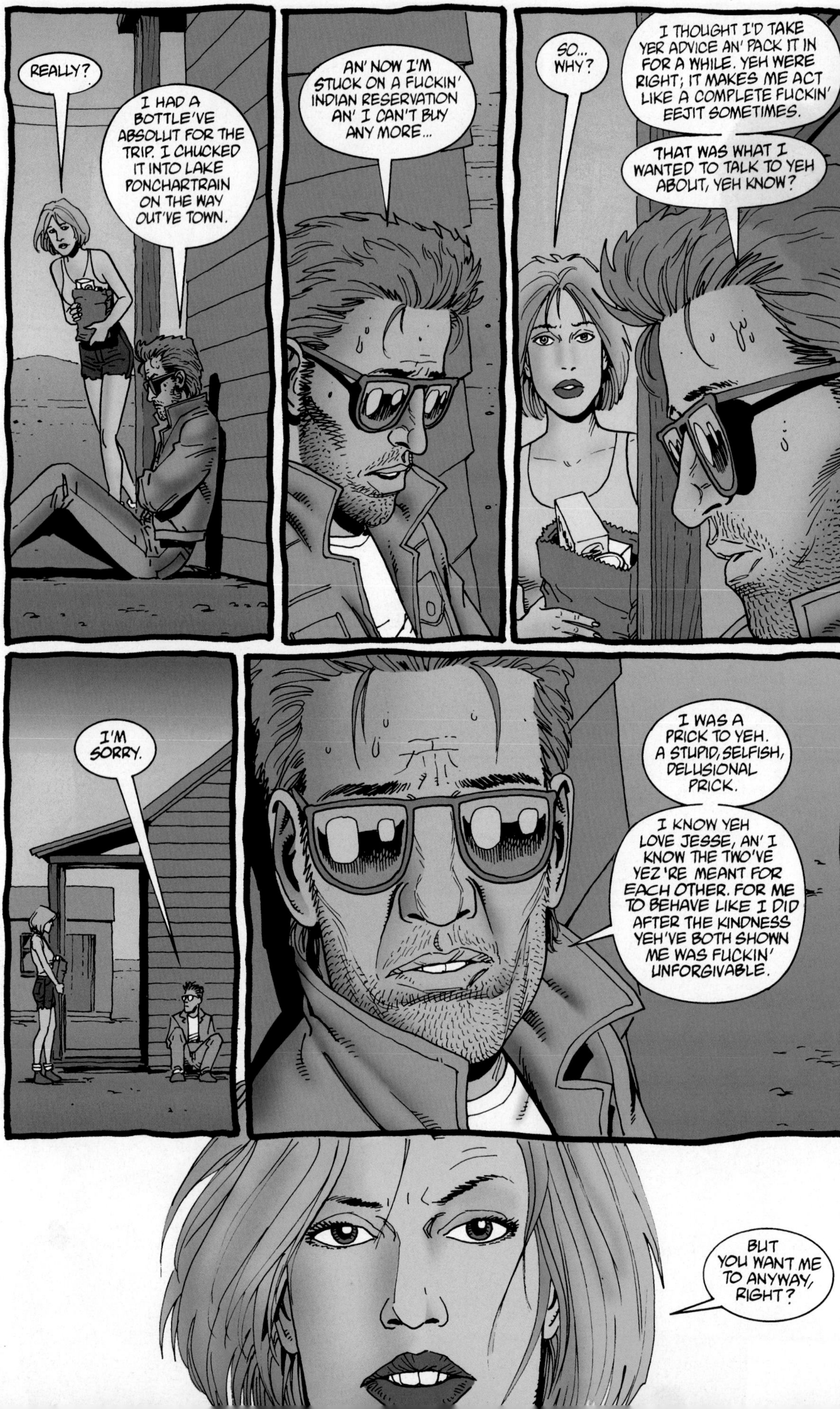
REALLY?
I HAD A BOTTLE'VE ABSOLUT FOR THE TRIP. I CHUCKED IT INTO LAKE PONCHARTRAIN ON THE WAY OUT'VE TOWN.
AN' NOW I'M STUCK ON A FUCKIN' INDIAN RESERVATION AN' I CAN'T BUY ANY MORE...
SO... WHY?
I THOUGHT I'D TAKE YER ADVICE AN' PACK IT IN FOR A WHILE. YEH WERE RIGHT; IT MAKES ME ACT LIKE A COMPLETE FUCKIN' EEJIT SOMETIMES.
THAT WAS WHAT I WANTED TO TALK TO YEH ABOUT, YEH KNOW?
I'M SORRY.
I WAS A PRICK TO YEH. A STUPID, SELFISH, DELUSIONAL PRICK.
I KNOW YEH LOVE JESSE, AN' I KNOW THE TWO'VE YEZ'RE MEANT FOR EACH OTHER. FOR ME TO BEHAVE LIKE I DID AFTER THE KINDNESS YEH'VE BOTH SHOWN ME WAS FUCKIN' UNFORGIVABLE.
BUT YOU WANT ME TO ANYWAY, RIGHT?

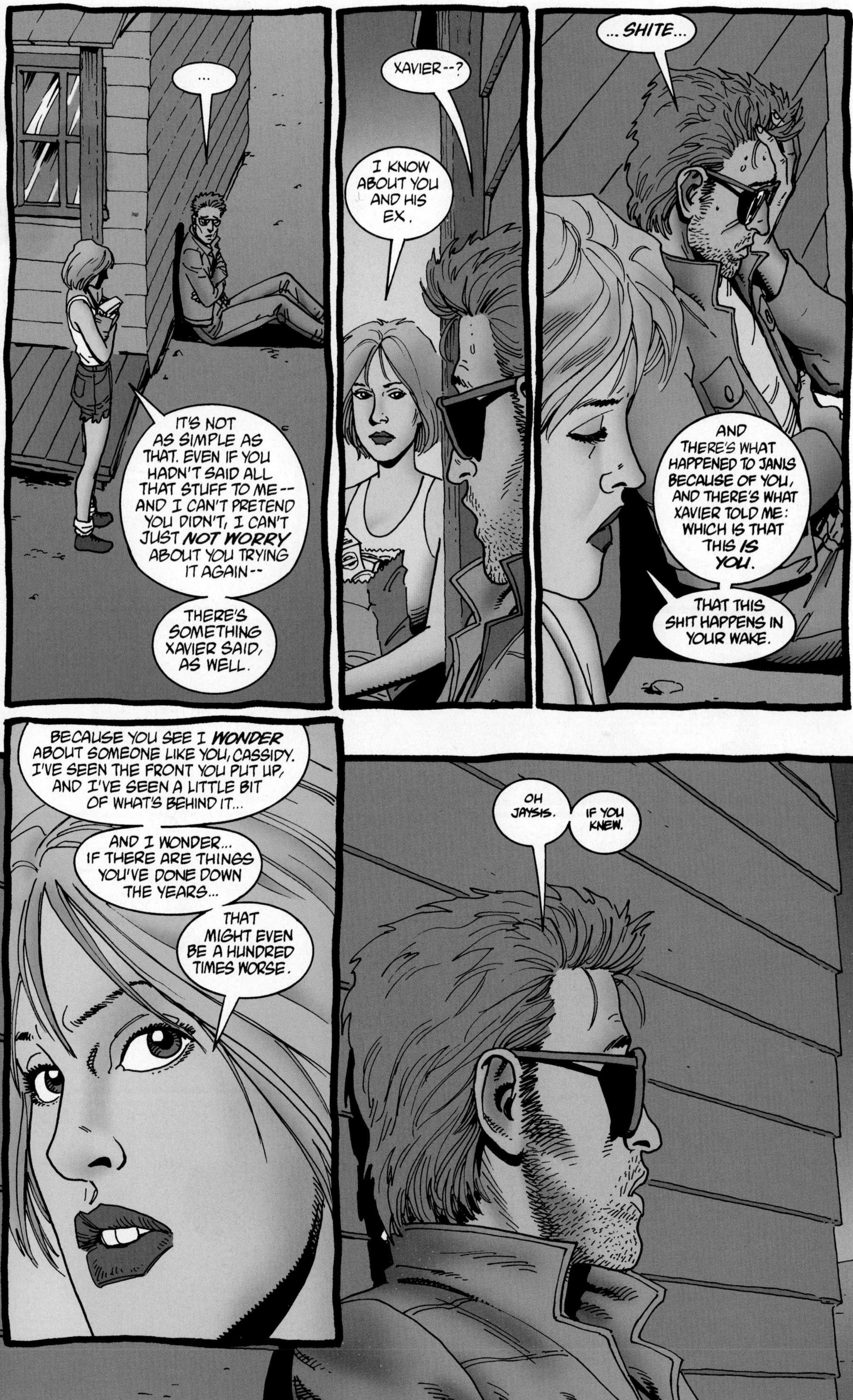
...
IT'S NOT AS SIMPLE AS THAT. EVEN IF YOU HADN'T SAID ALL THAT STUFF TO ME -- AND I CAN'T PRETEND YOU DIDN'T, I CAN'T JUST **NOT WORRY** ABOUT YOU TRYING IT AGAIN --
THERE'S SOMETHING XAVIER SAID, AS WELL.
XAVIER --?
I KNOW ABOUT YOU AND HIS EX.
... SHITE ...
AND THERE'S WHAT HAPPENED TO JANIS BECAUSE OF YOU, AND THERE'S WHAT XAVIER TOLD ME: WHICH IS THAT THIS ***IS YOU***.
THAT THIS SHIT HAPPENS IN YOUR WAKE.
BECAUSE YOU SEE I ***WONDER*** ABOUT SOMEONE LIKE YOU, CASSIDY. I'VE SEEN THE FRONT YOU PUT UP, AND I'VE SEEN A LITTLE BIT OF WHAT'S BEHIND IT...
AND I WONDER... IF THERE ARE THINGS YOU'VE DONE DOWN THE YEARS...
THAT MIGHT EVEN BE A HUNDRED TIMES WORSE.
OH JAYSIS.
IF YOU KNEW.

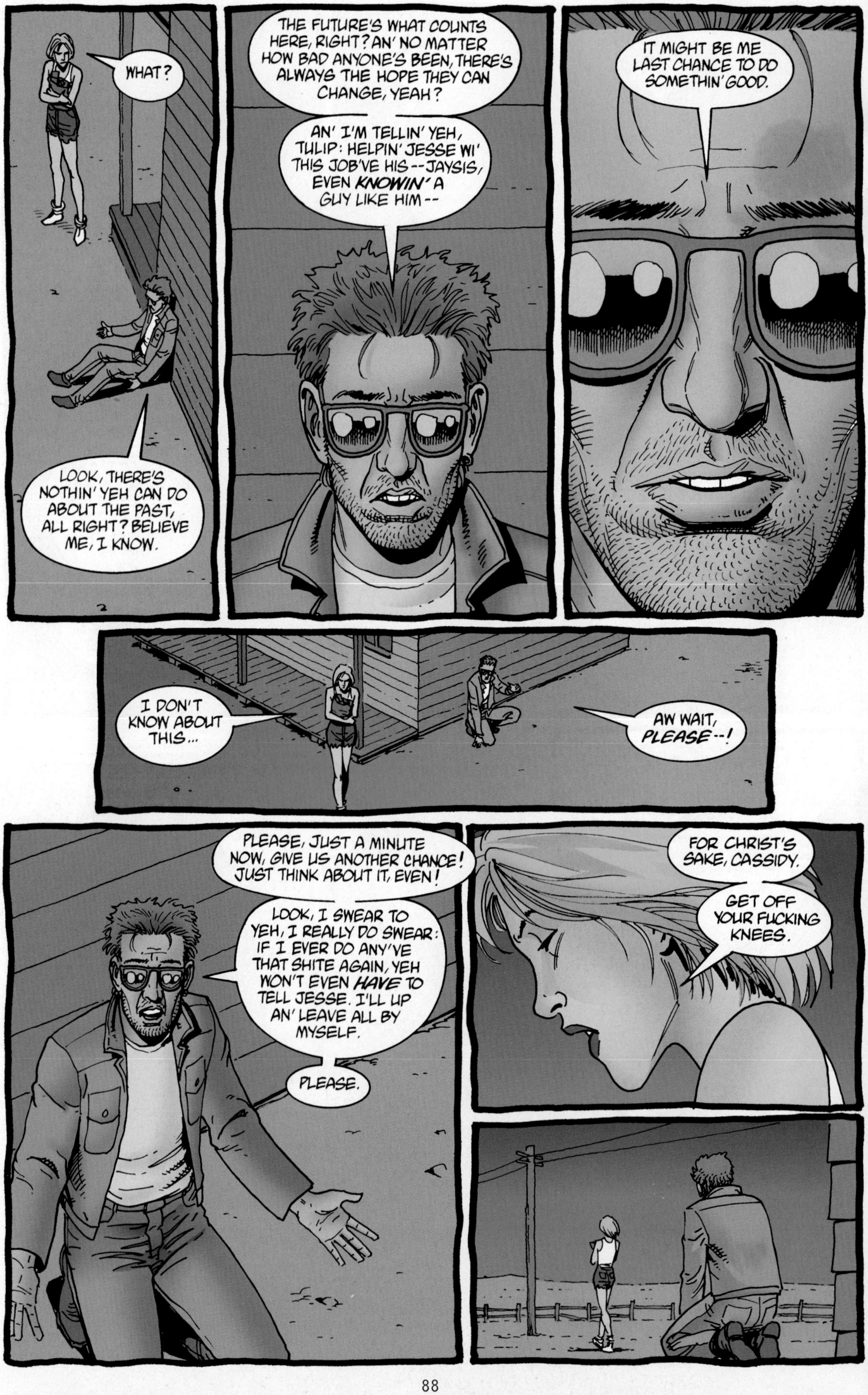
WHAT?
LOOK, THERE'S NOTHIN' YEH CAN DO ABOUT THE PAST, ALL RIGHT? BELIEVE ME, I KNOW.
THE FUTURE'S WHAT COUNTS HERE, RIGHT? AN' NO MATTER HOW BAD ANYONE'S BEEN, THERE'S ALWAYS THE HOPE THEY CAN CHANGE, YEAH?
AN' I'M TELLIN' YEH, TULIP: HELPIN' JESSE WI' THIS JOB'VE HIS--JAYSIS, EVEN *KNOWIN'* A GUY LIKE HIM--
IT MIGHT BE ME LAST CHANCE TO DO SOMETHIN' GOOD.
I DON'T KNOW ABOUT THIS...
AW WAIT, *PLEASE*--!
PLEASE, JUST A MINUTE NOW, GIVE US ANOTHER CHANCE! JUST THINK ABOUT IT, EVEN!
LOOK, I SWEAR TO YEH, I REALLY DO SWEAR: IF I EVER DO ANY'VE THAT SHITE AGAIN, YEH WON'T EVEN *HAVE* TO TELL JESSE. I'LL UP AN' LEAVE ALL BY MYSELF.
PLEASE.
FOR CHRIST'S SAKE, CASSIDY.
GET OFF YOUR FUCKING KNEES.

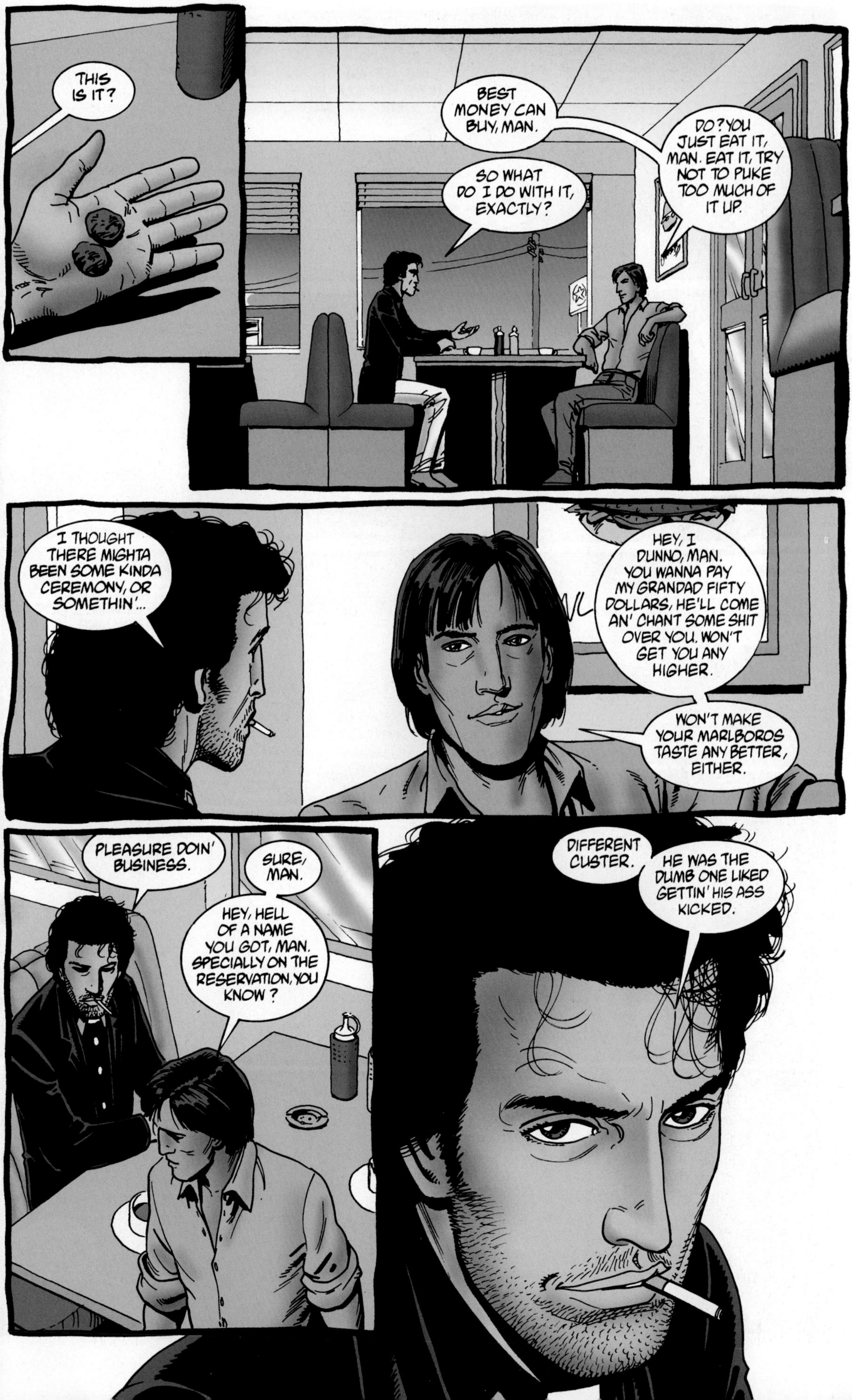
THIS IS IT?
BEST MONEY CAN BUY, MAN.
SO WHAT DO I DO WITH IT, EXACTLY?
DO? YOU JUST EAT IT, MAN. EAT IT, TRY NOT TO PUKE TOO MUCH OF IT UP.
I THOUGHT THERE MIGHTA BEEN SOME KINDA CEREMONY, OR SOMETHIN'...
HEY, I DUNNO, MAN. YOU WANNA PAY MY GRANDAD FIFTY DOLLARS, HE'LL COME AN' CHANT SOME SHIT OVER YOU. WON'T GET YOU ANY HIGHER.
WON'T MAKE YOUR MARLBOROS TASTE ANY BETTER, EITHER.
PLEASURE DOIN' BUSINESS.
SURE, MAN.
HEY, HELL OF A NAME YOU GOT, MAN. SPECIALLY ON THE RESERVATION, YOU KNOW?
DIFFERENT CUSTER.
HE WAS THE DUMB ONE LIKED GETTIN' HIS ASS KICKED.

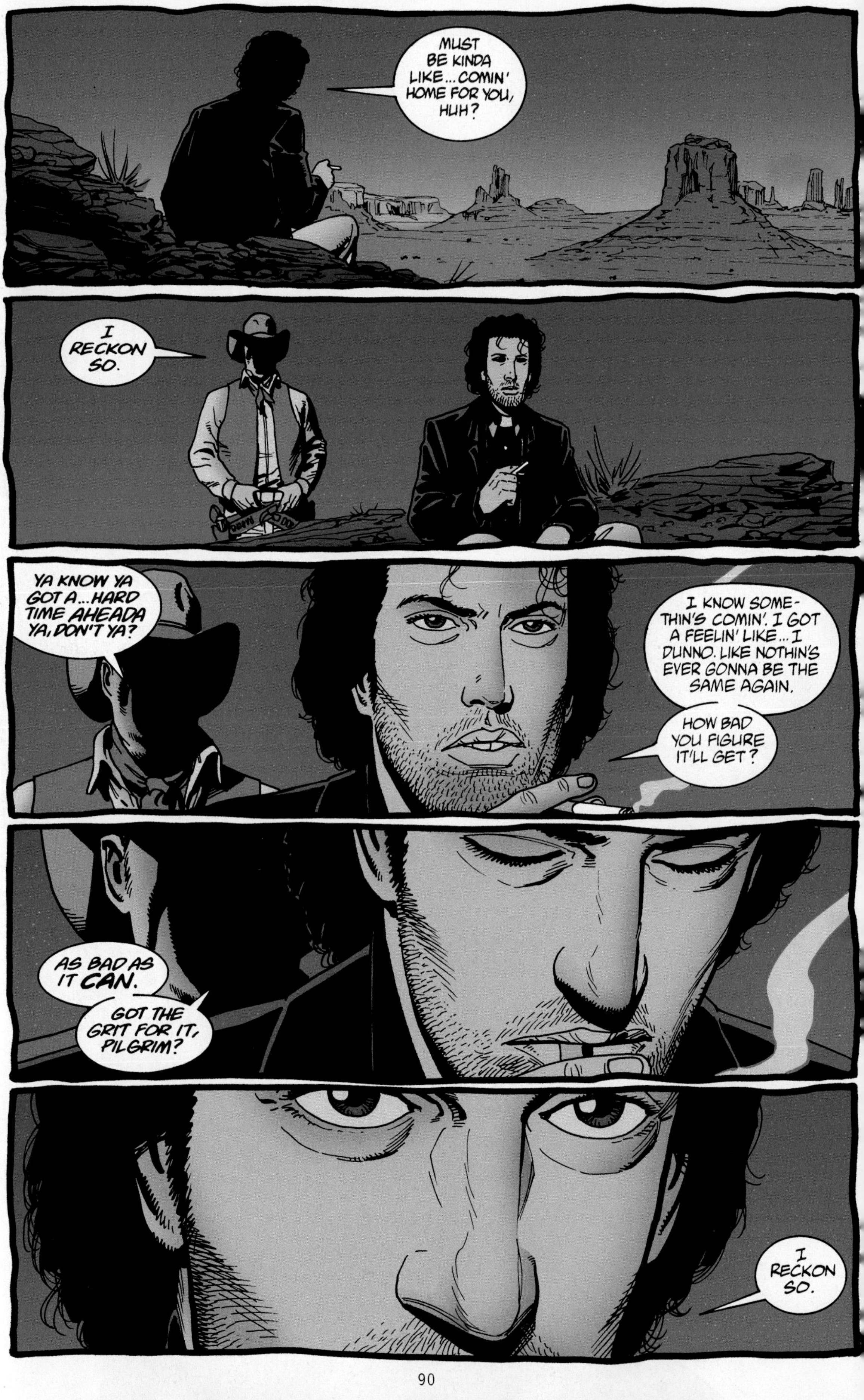
MUST BE KINDA LIKE... COMIN' HOME FOR YOU, HUH?
I RECKON SO.
YA KNOW YA GOT A... HARD TIME AHEADA YA, DON'T YA?
I KNOW SOME-THIN'S COMIN'. I GOT A FEELIN' LIKE... I DUNNO. LIKE NOTHIN'S EVER GONNA BE THE SAME AGAIN.
HOW BAD YOU FIGURE IT'LL GET?
AS BAD AS IT CAN.
GOT THE GRIT FOR IT, PILGRIM?
I RECKON SO.

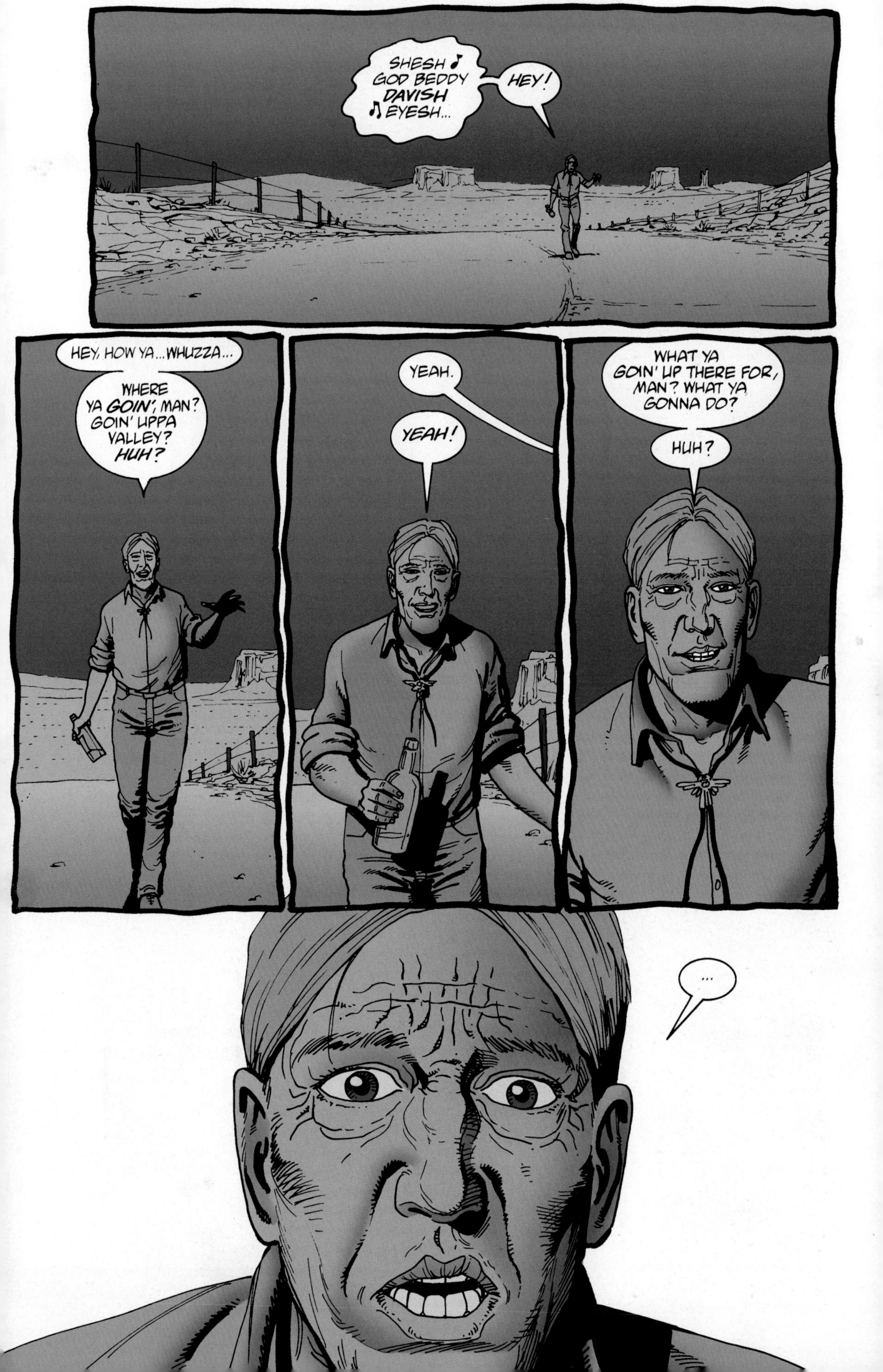
SHESH ♪ GOD BEDDY DAVISH ♫ EYESH...
HEY!
HEY, HOW YA... WHUZZA...
WHERE YA GOIN', MAN? GOIN' UPPA VALLEY? HUH?
YEAH.
YEAH!
WHAT YA GOIN' UP THERE FOR, MAN? WHAT YA GONNA DO?
HUH?
...

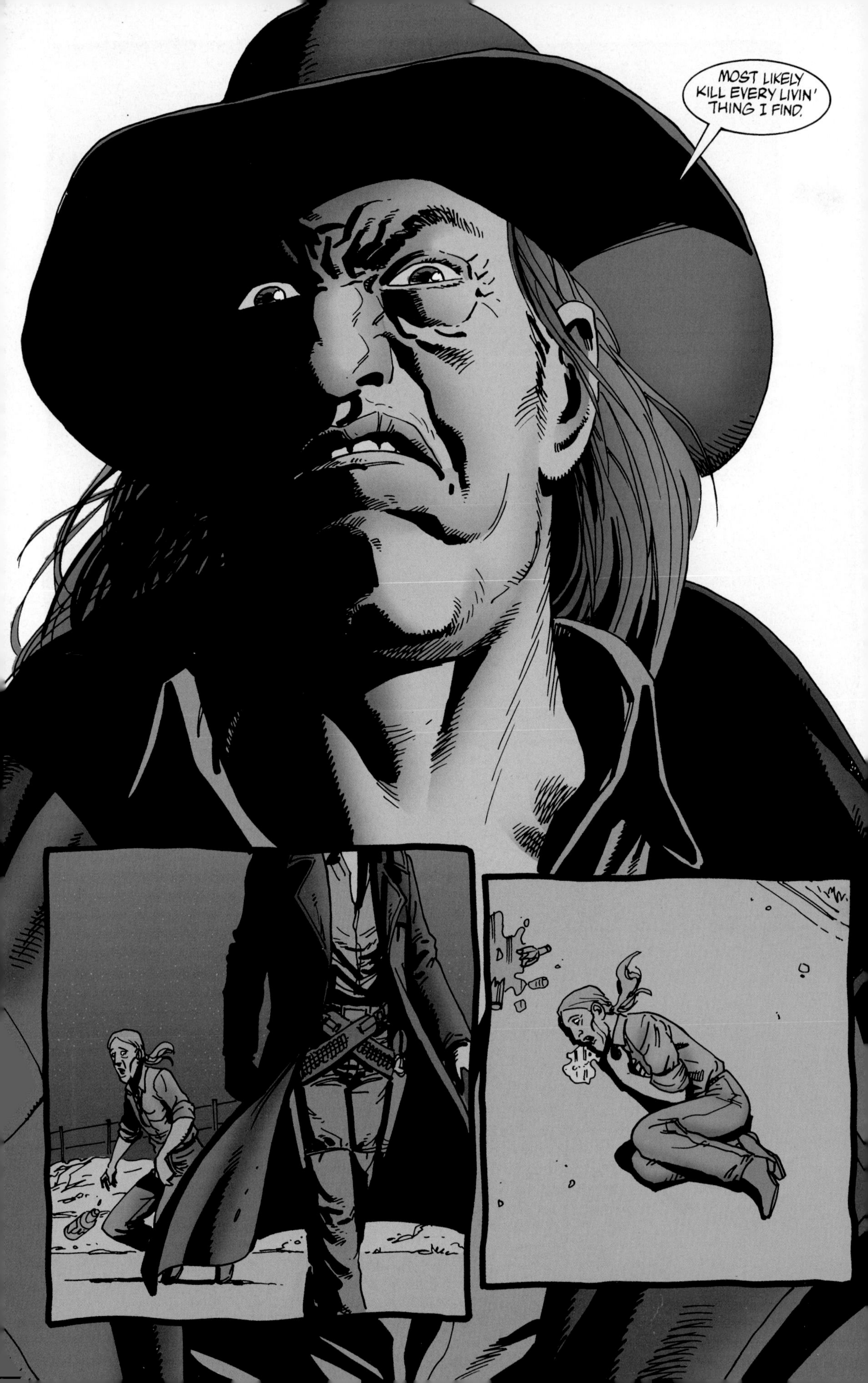
MOST LIKELY KILL EVERY LIVIN' THING I FIND.

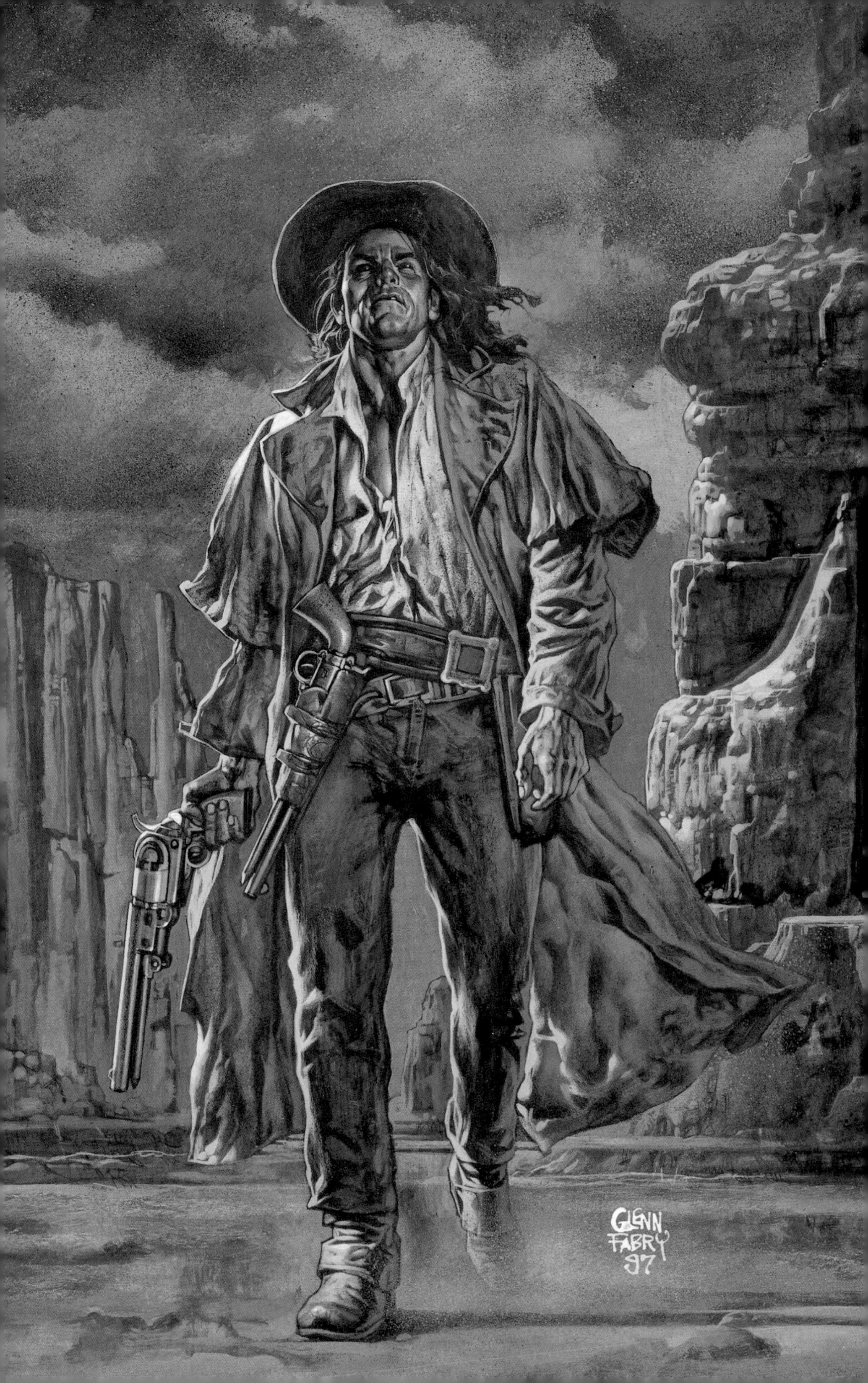
GLENN
FABRY
97

"There's not a country on this Earth
wasn't born outta blood an' killin'."

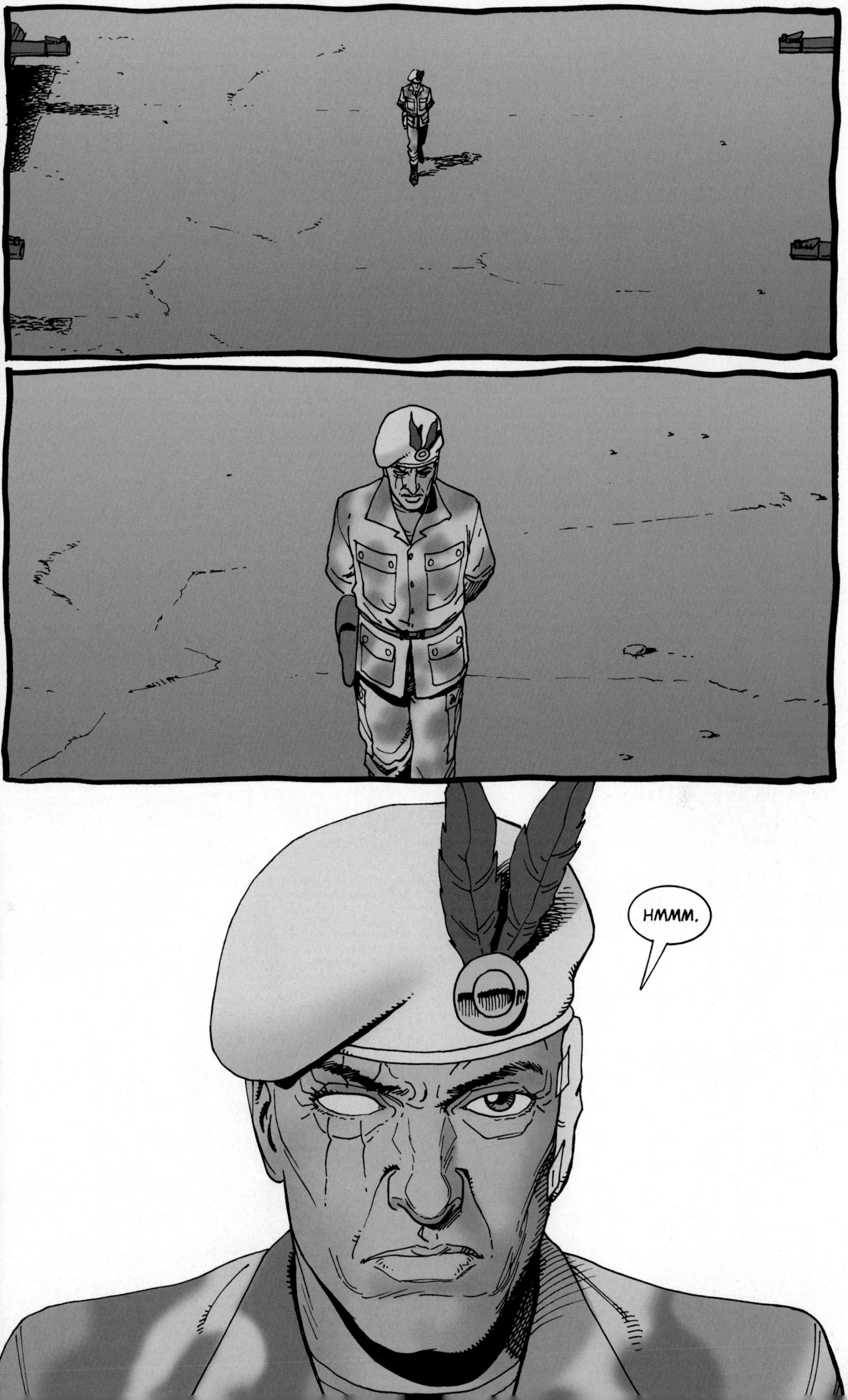
HMMM.

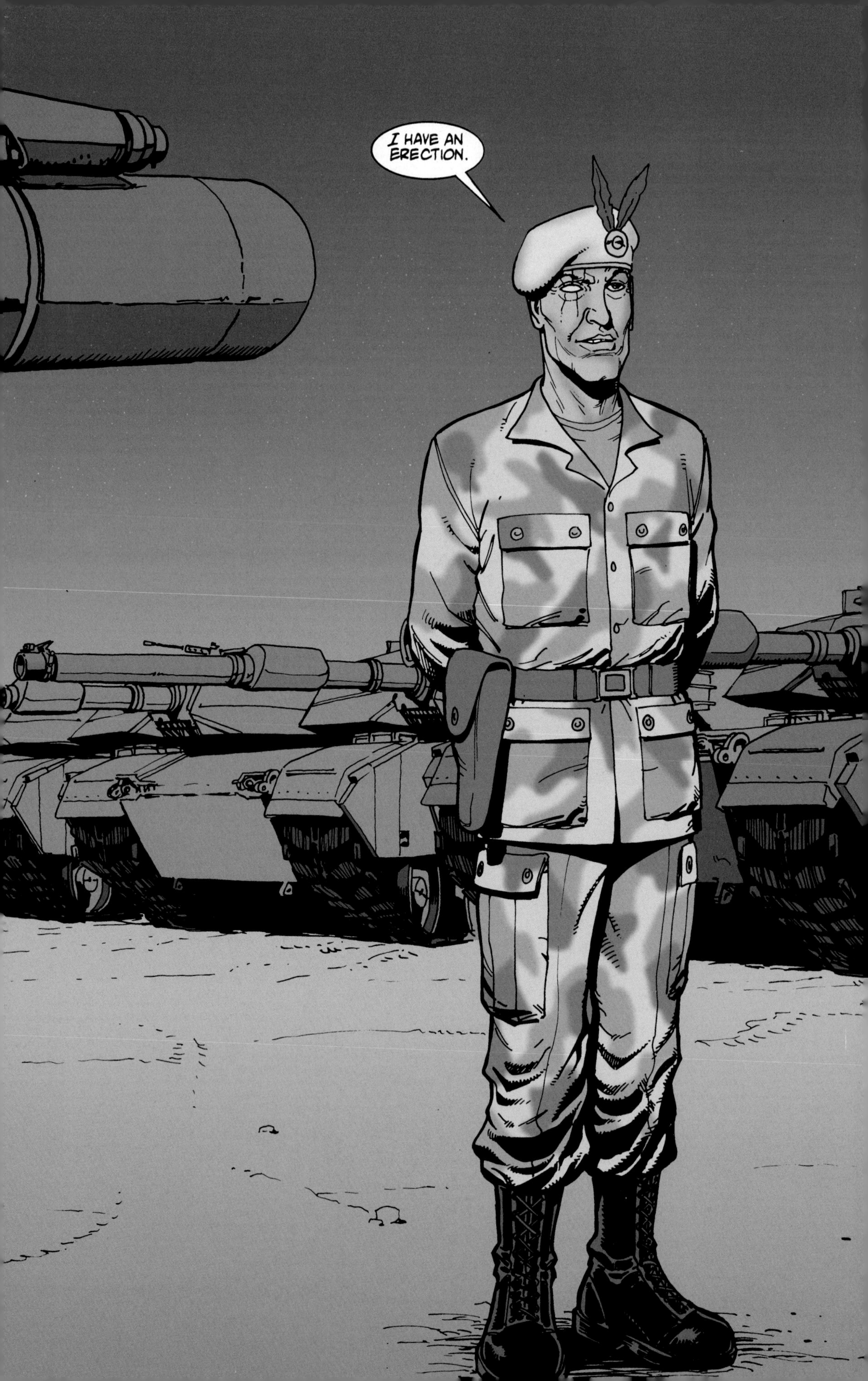
I HAVE AN ERECTION.

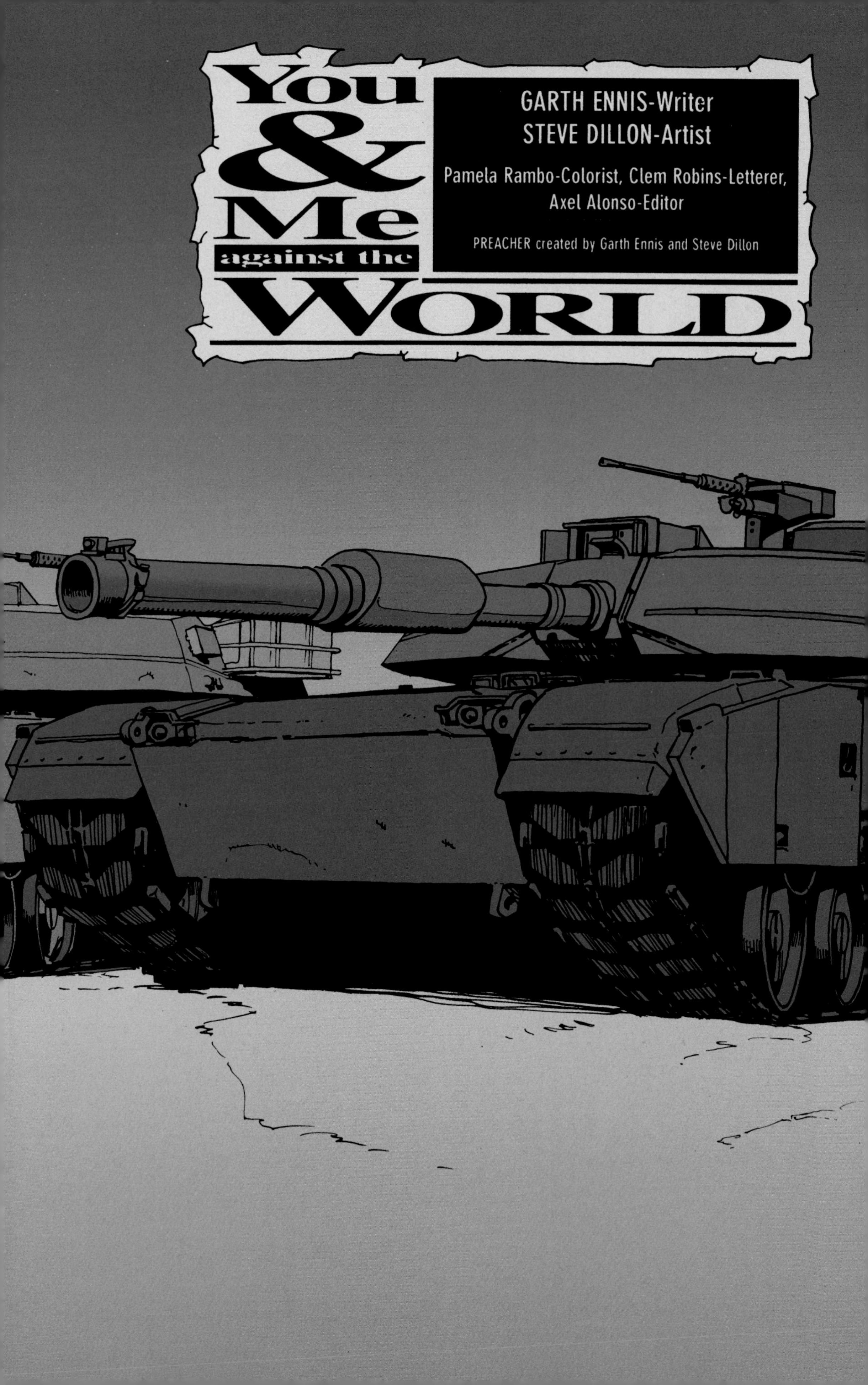
You & Me against the WORLD
GARTH ENNIS-Writer
STEVE DILLON-Artist
Pamela Rambo-Colorist, Clem Robins-Letterer,
Axel Alonso-Editor
PREACHER created by Garth Ennis and Steve Dillon

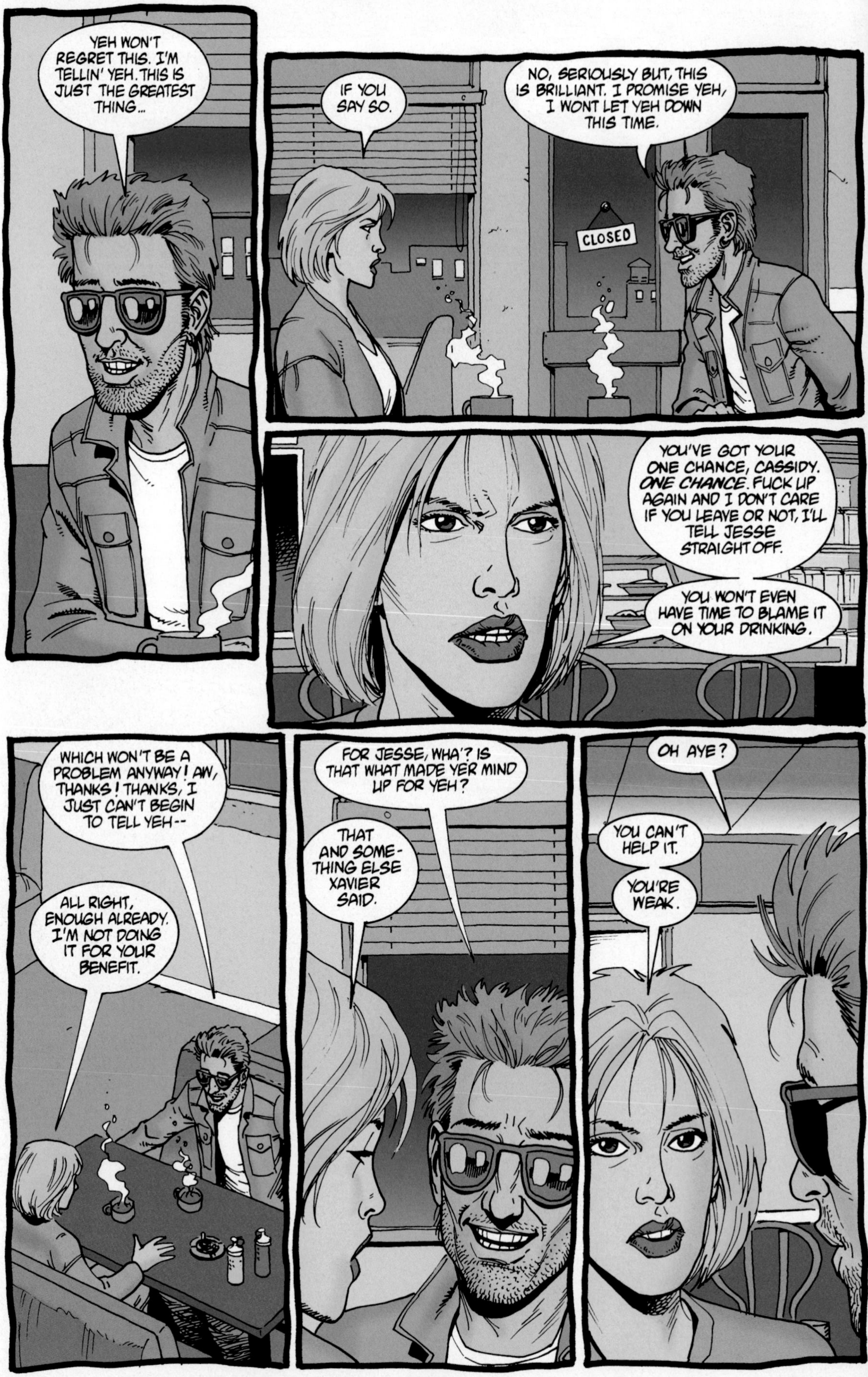
YEH WON'T REGRET THIS. I'M TELLIN' YEH. THIS IS JUST THE GREATEST THING...
IF YOU SAY SO.
NO, SERIOUSLY BUT, THIS IS BRILLIANT. I PROMISE YEH, I WONT LET YEH DOWN THIS TIME.
CLOSED
YOU'VE GOT YOUR ONE CHANCE, CASSIDY. *ONE CHANCE*. FUCK UP AGAIN AND I DON'T CARE IF YOU LEAVE OR NOT, I'LL TELL JESSE STRAIGHT OFF.
YOU WON'T EVEN HAVE TIME TO BLAME IT ON YOUR DRINKING.
WHICH WON'T BE A PROBLEM ANYWAY! AW, THANKS! THANKS, I JUST CAN'T BEGIN TO TELL YEH--
ALL RIGHT, ENOUGH ALREADY. I'M NOT DOING IT FOR YOUR BENEFIT.
FOR JESSE, WHA'? IS THAT WHAT MADE YER MIND UP FOR YEH?
THAT AND SOME-THING ELSE XAVIER SAID.
OH AYE?
YOU CAN'T HELP IT.
YOU'RE WEAK.

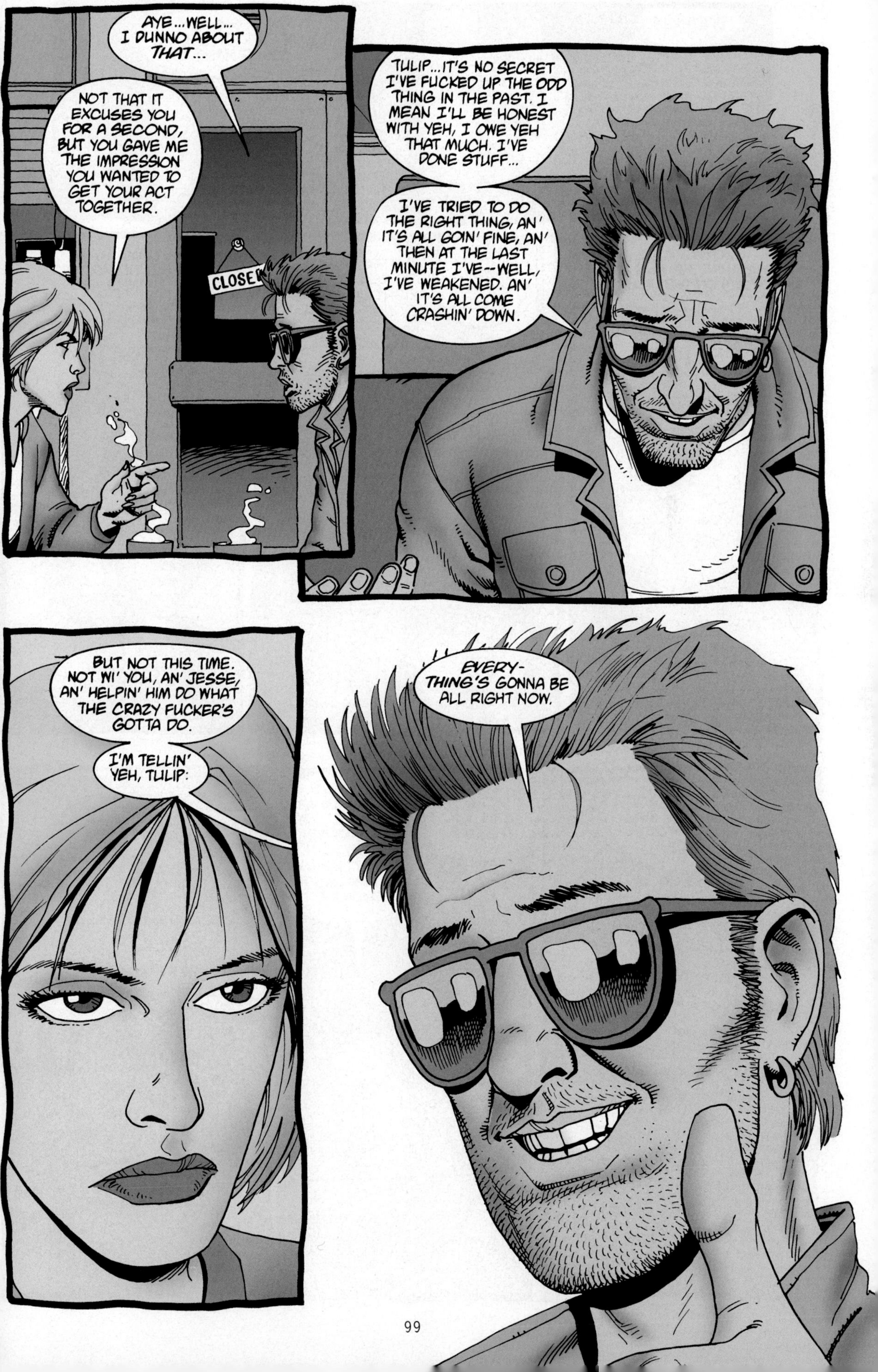
NOT THAT IT EXCUSES YOU FOR A SECOND, BUT YOU GAVE ME THE IMPRESSION YOU WANTED TO GET YOUR ACT TOGETHER.
AYE...WELL... I DUNNO ABOUT THAT...
CLOSED
TULIP...IT'S NO SECRET I'VE FUCKED UP THE ODD THING IN THE PAST. I MEAN I'LL BE HONEST WITH YEH, I OWE YEH THAT MUCH. I'VE DONE STUFF...
I'VE TRIED TO DO THE RIGHT THING, AN' IT'S ALL GOIN' FINE, AN' THEN AT THE LAST MINUTE I'VE--WELL, I'VE WEAKENED. AN' IT'S ALL COME CRASHIN' DOWN.
BUT NOT THIS TIME. NOT WI' YOU, AN' JESSE, AN' HELPIN' HIM DO WHAT THE CRAZY FUCKER'S GOTTA DO.
I'M TELLIN' YEH, TULIP:
EVERYTHING'S GONNA BE ALL RIGHT NOW.

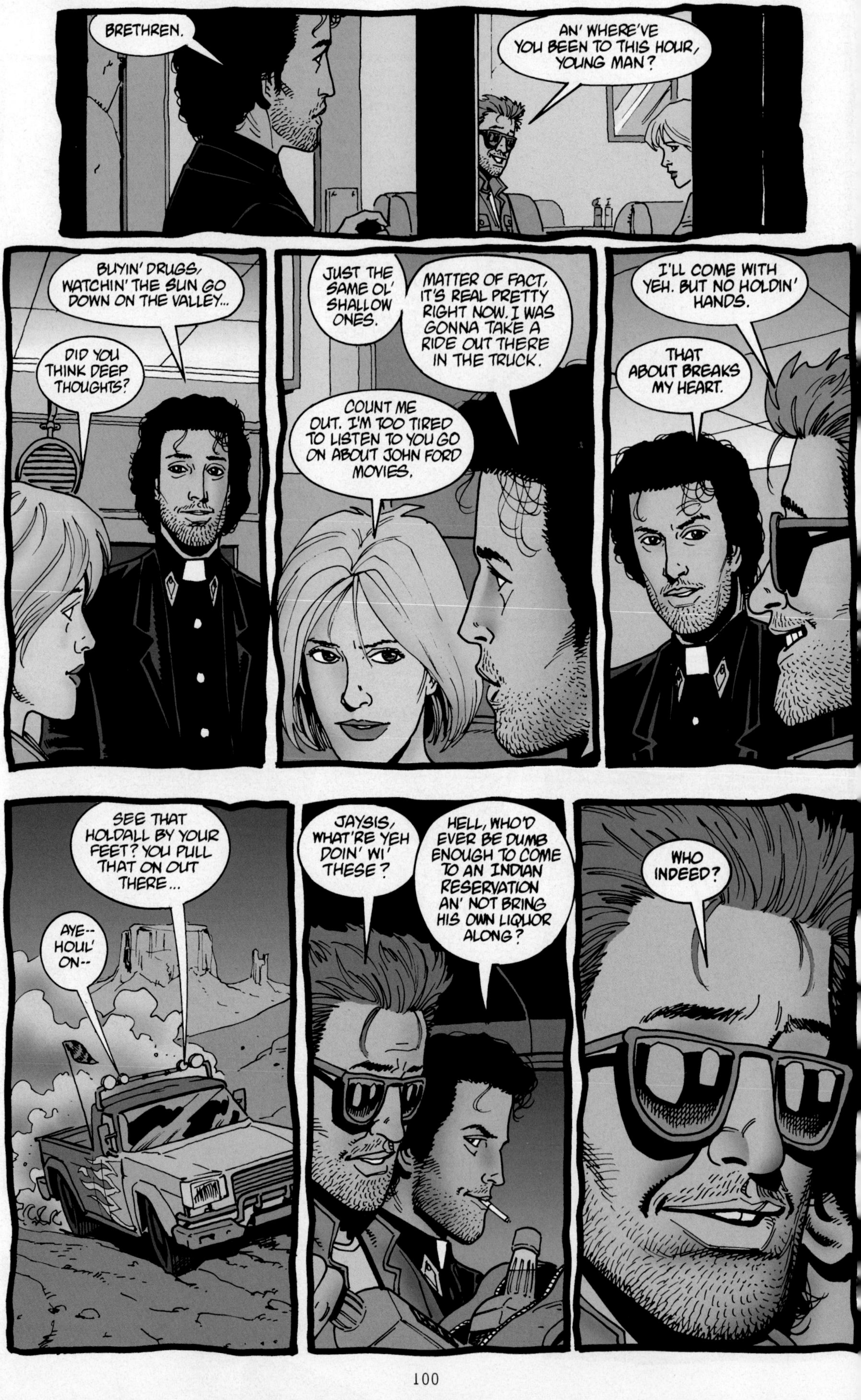
BRETHREN.
AN' WHERE'VE YOU BEEN TO THIS HOUR, YOUNG MAN?
BUYIN' DRUGS, WATCHIN' THE SUN GO DOWN ON THE VALLEY...
DID YOU THINK DEEP THOUGHTS?
JUST THE SAME OL' SHALLOW ONES.
MATTER OF FACT, IT'S REAL PRETTY RIGHT NOW. I WAS GONNA TAKE A RIDE OUT THERE IN THE TRUCK.
COUNT ME OUT. I'M TOO TIRED TO LISTEN TO YOU GO ON ABOUT JOHN FORD MOVIES.
I'LL COME WITH YEH. BUT NO HOLDIN' HANDS.
THAT ABOUT BREAKS MY HEART.
SEE THAT HOLDALL BY YOUR FEET? YOU PULL THAT ON OUT THERE...
AYE-- HOUL' ON--
JAYSIS, WHAT'RE YEH DOIN' WI' THESE?
HELL, WHO'D EVER BE DUMB ENOUGH TO COME TO AN INDIAN RESERVATION AN' NOT BRING HIS OWN LIQUOR ALONG?
WHO INDEED?

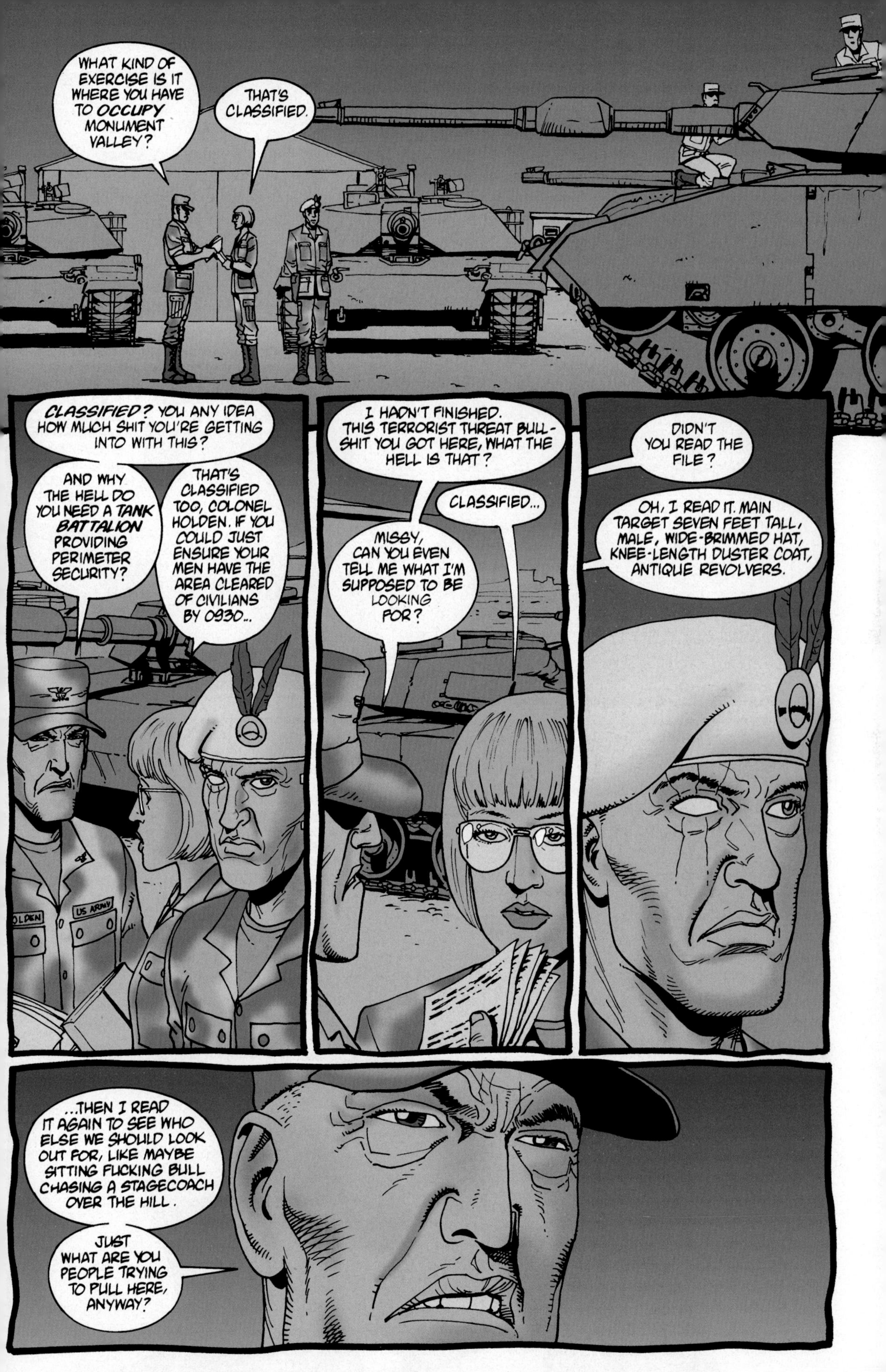
WHAT KIND OF EXERCISE IS IT WHERE YOU HAVE TO OCCUPY MONUMENT VALLEY?
THAT'S CLASSIFIED.
CLASSIFIED? YOU ANY IDEA HOW MUCH SHIT YOU'RE GETTING INTO WITH THIS?
AND WHY THE HELL DO YOU NEED A TANK BATTALION PROVIDING PERIMETER SECURITY?
THAT'S CLASSIFIED TOO, COLONEL HOLDEN. IF YOU COULD JUST ENSURE YOUR MEN HAVE THE AREA CLEARED OF CIVILIANS BY 0930...
HOLDEN
US ARMY
I HADN'T FINISHED. THIS TERRORIST THREAT BULLSHIT YOU GOT HERE, WHAT THE HELL IS THAT?
CLASSIFIED...
MISSY, CAN YOU EVEN TELL ME WHAT I'M SUPPOSED TO BE LOOKING FOR?
DIDN'T YOU READ THE FILE?
OH, I READ IT. MAIN TARGET SEVEN FEET TALL, MALE, WIDE-BRIMMED HAT, KNEE-LENGTH DUSTER COAT, ANTIQUE REVOLVERS.
...THEN I READ IT AGAIN TO SEE WHO ELSE WE SHOULD LOOK OUT FOR, LIKE MAYBE SITTING FUCKING BULL CHASING A STAGECOACH OVER THE HILL.
JUST WHAT ARE YOU PEOPLE TRYING TO PULL HERE, ANYWAY?

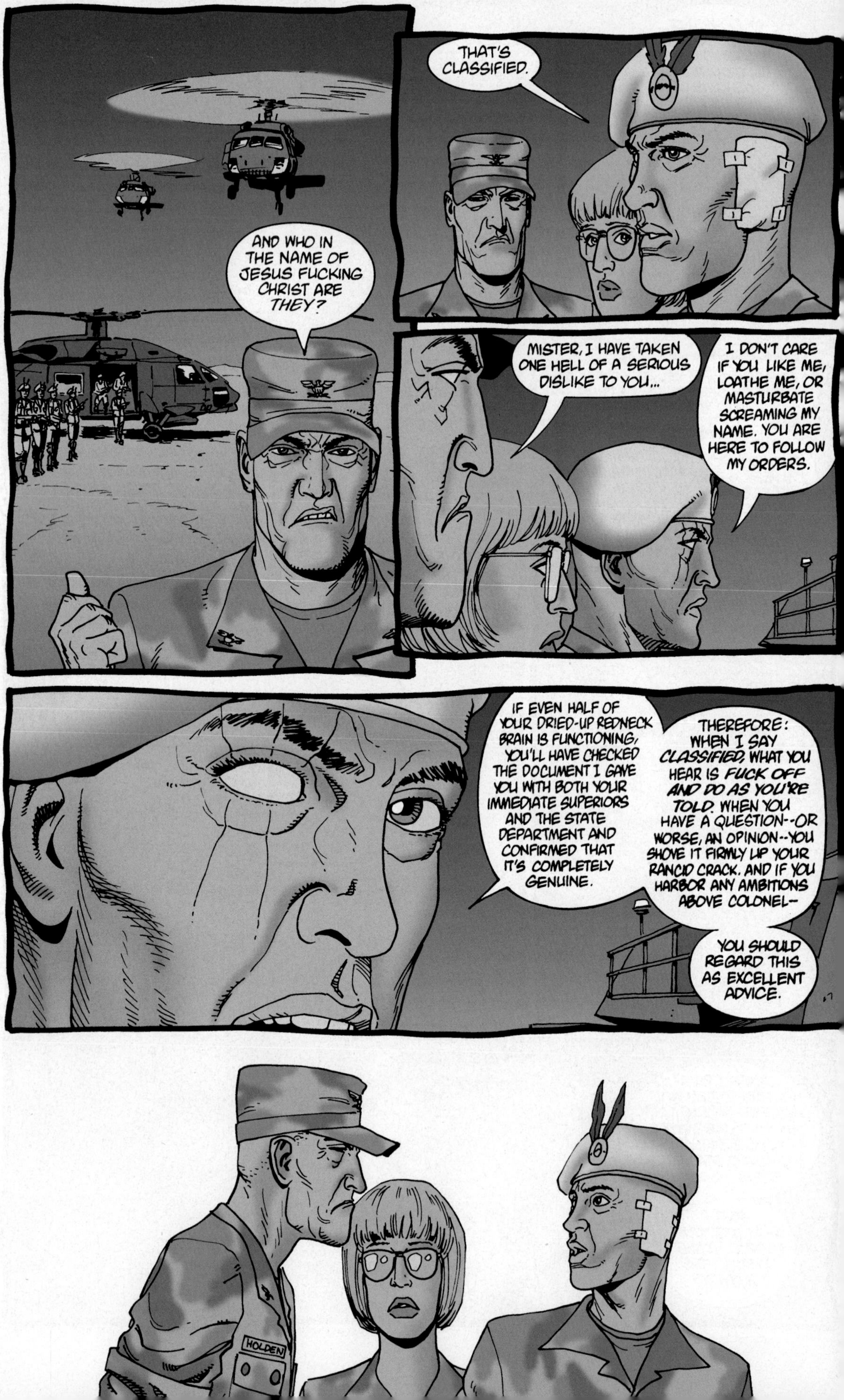
AND WHO IN THE NAME OF JESUS FUCKING CHRIST ARE THEY?
THAT'S CLASSIFIED.
MISTER, I HAVE TAKEN ONE HELL OF A SERIOUS DISLIKE TO YOU...
I DON'T CARE IF YOU LIKE ME, LOATHE ME, OR MASTURBATE SCREAMING MY NAME. YOU ARE HERE TO FOLLOW MY ORDERS.
IF EVEN HALF OF YOUR DRIED-UP REDNECK BRAIN IS FUNCTIONING, YOU'LL HAVE CHECKED THE DOCUMENT I GAVE YOU WITH BOTH YOUR IMMEDIATE SUPERIORS AND THE STATE DEPARTMENT AND CONFIRMED THAT IT'S COMPLETELY GENUINE.
THEREFORE: WHEN I SAY CLASSIFIED, WHAT YOU HEAR IS FUCK OFF AND DO AS YOU'RE TOLD. WHEN YOU HAVE A QUESTION--OR WORSE, AN OPINION--YOU SHOVE IT FIRMLY UP YOUR RANCID CRACK. AND IF YOU HARBOR ANY AMBITIONS ABOVE COLONEL-
YOU SHOULD REGARD THIS AS EXCELLENT ADVICE.
HOLDEN

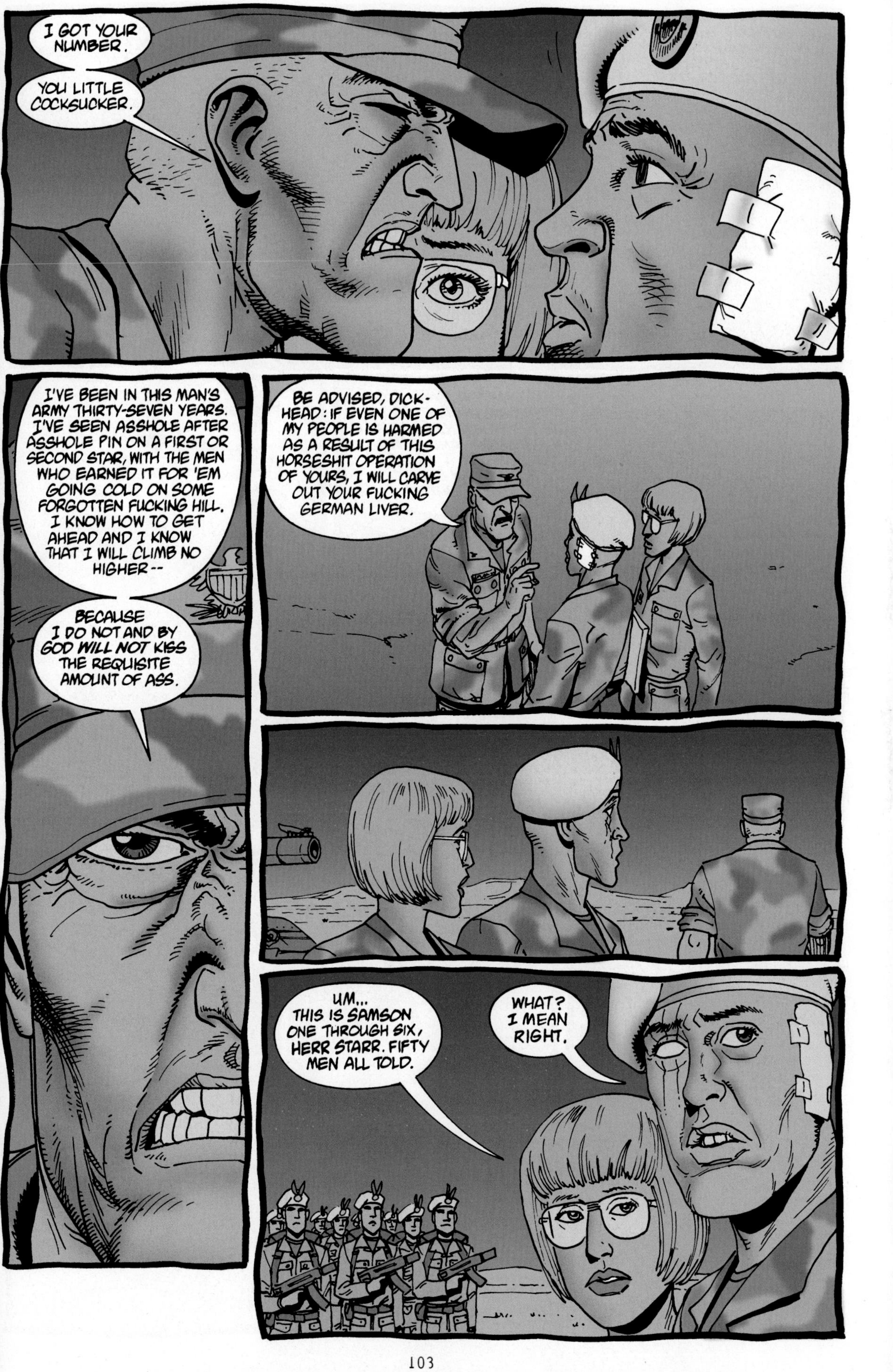
I GOT YOUR NUMBER.
YOU LITTLE COCKSUCKER.
I'VE BEEN IN THIS MAN'S ARMY THIRTY-SEVEN YEARS. I'VE SEEN ASSHOLE AFTER ASSHOLE PIN ON A FIRST OR SECOND STAR, WITH THE MEN WHO EARNED IT FOR 'EM GOING COLD ON SOME FORGOTTEN FUCKING HILL. I KNOW HOW TO GET AHEAD AND I KNOW THAT I WILL CLIMB NO HIGHER--
BECAUSE I DO NOT AND BY GOD *WILL NOT* KISS THE REQUISITE AMOUNT OF ASS.
BE ADVISED, DICK-HEAD: IF EVEN ONE OF MY PEOPLE IS HARMED AS A RESULT OF THIS HORSESHIT OPERATION OF YOURS, I WILL CARVE OUT YOUR FUCKING GERMAN LIVER.
UM... THIS IS SAMSON ONE THROUGH SIX, HERR STARR. FIFTY MEN ALL TOLD.
WHAT? I MEAN RIGHT.

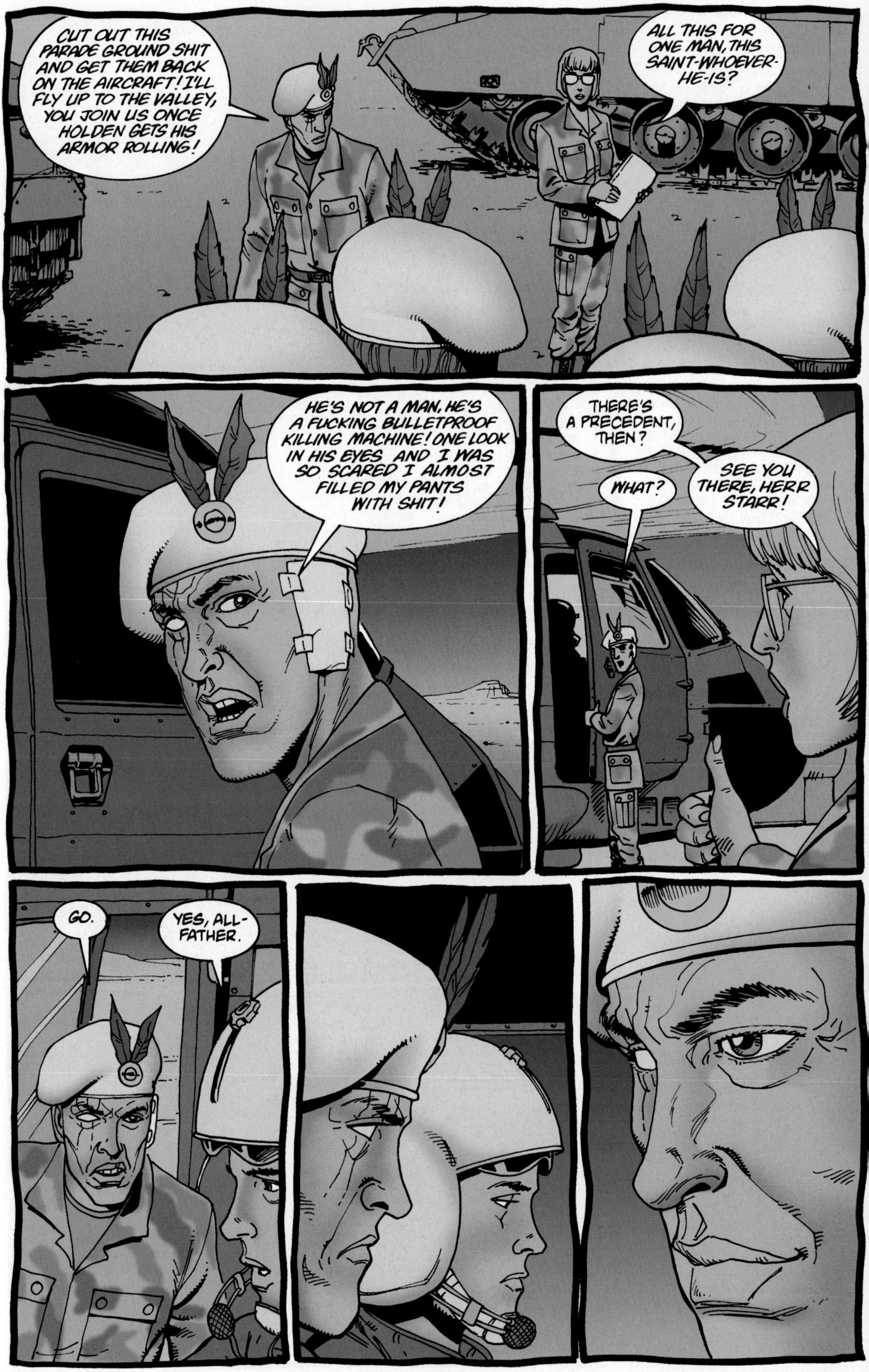
CUT OUT THIS PARADE GROUND SHIT AND GET THEM BACK ON THE AIRCRAFT! I'LL FLY UP TO THE VALLEY, YOU JOIN US ONCE HOLDEN GETS HIS ARMOR ROLLING!
ALL THIS FOR ONE MAN, THIS SAINT-WHOEVER-HE-IS?
HE'S NOT A MAN, HE'S A FUCKING BULLETPROOF KILLING MACHINE! ONE LOOK IN HIS EYES AND I WAS SO SCARED I ALMOST FILLED MY PANTS WITH SHIT!
THERE'S A PRECEDENT, THEN?
WHAT?
SEE YOU THERE, HERR STARR!
GO.
YES, ALL-FATHER.

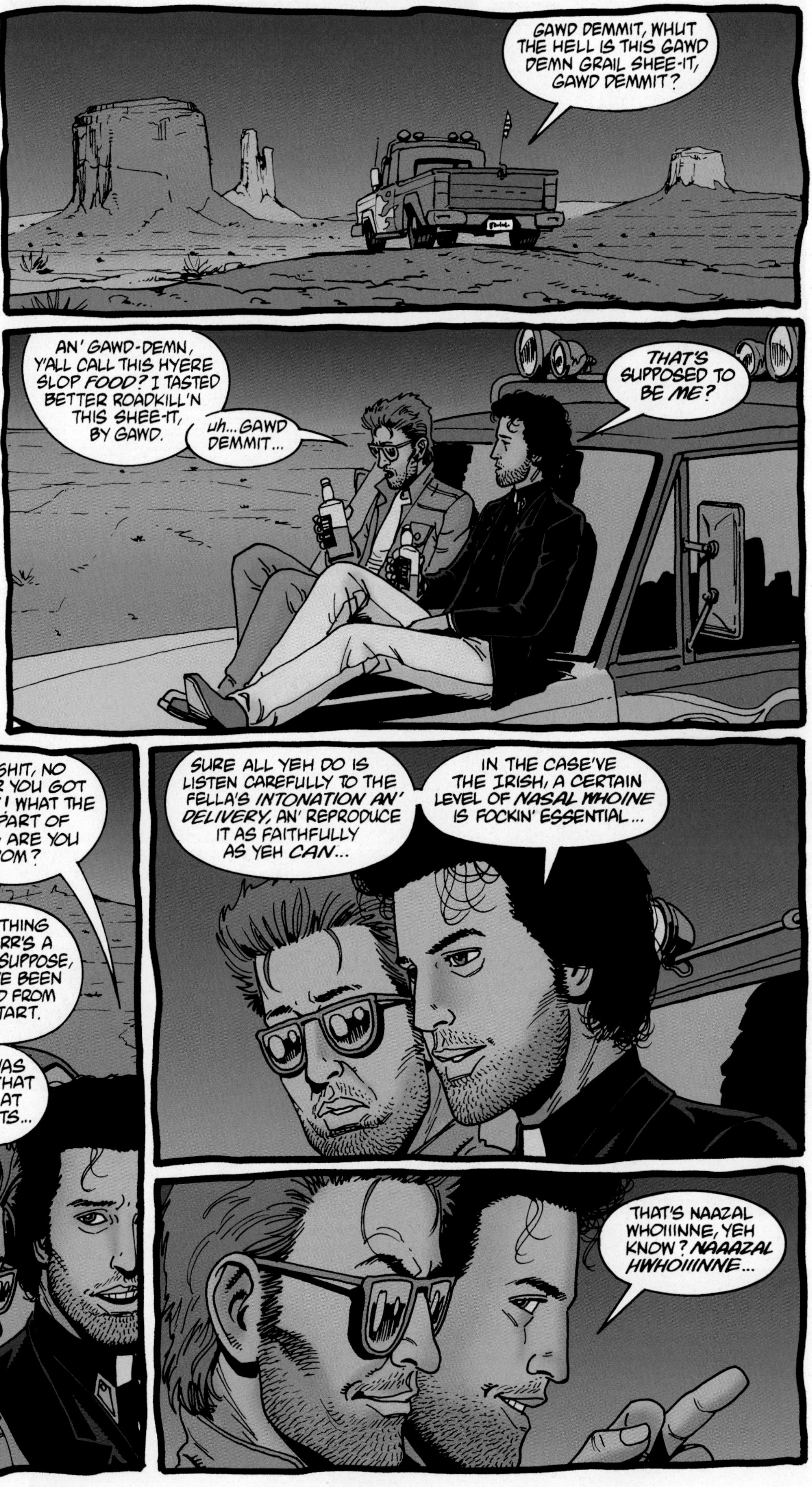
GAWD DEMMIT, WHUT THE HELL IS THIS GAWD DEMN GRAIL SHEE-IT, GAWD DEMMIT?
AN' GAWD-DEMN, Y'ALL CALL THIS HYERE SLOP FOOD? I TASTED BETTER ROADKILL'N THIS SHEE-IT, BY GAWD.
uh...GAWD DEMMIT...
THAT'S SUPPOSED TO BE ME?
HOLY SHIT, NO WONDER YOU GOT CAUGHT! WHAT THE FUCK PART OF TEXAS ARE YOU FROM?
GOOD THING OUL' STARR'S A JERRY, I SUPPOSE, OR I'D'VE BEEN FUCKED FROM THE START.
AH, I WAS NEVER THAT GREAT AT ACCENTS...
SURE ALL YEH DO IS LISTEN CAREFULLY TO THE FELLA'S INTONATION AN' DELIVERY, AN' REPRODUCE IT AS FAITHFULLY AS YEH CAN...
IN THE CASE'VE THE IRISH, A CERTAIN LEVEL OF NASAL WHOINE IS FOCKIN' ESSENTIAL...
THAT'S NAAZAL WHOIIINNE, YEH KNOW? NAAAZAL HWHOIIINNE...

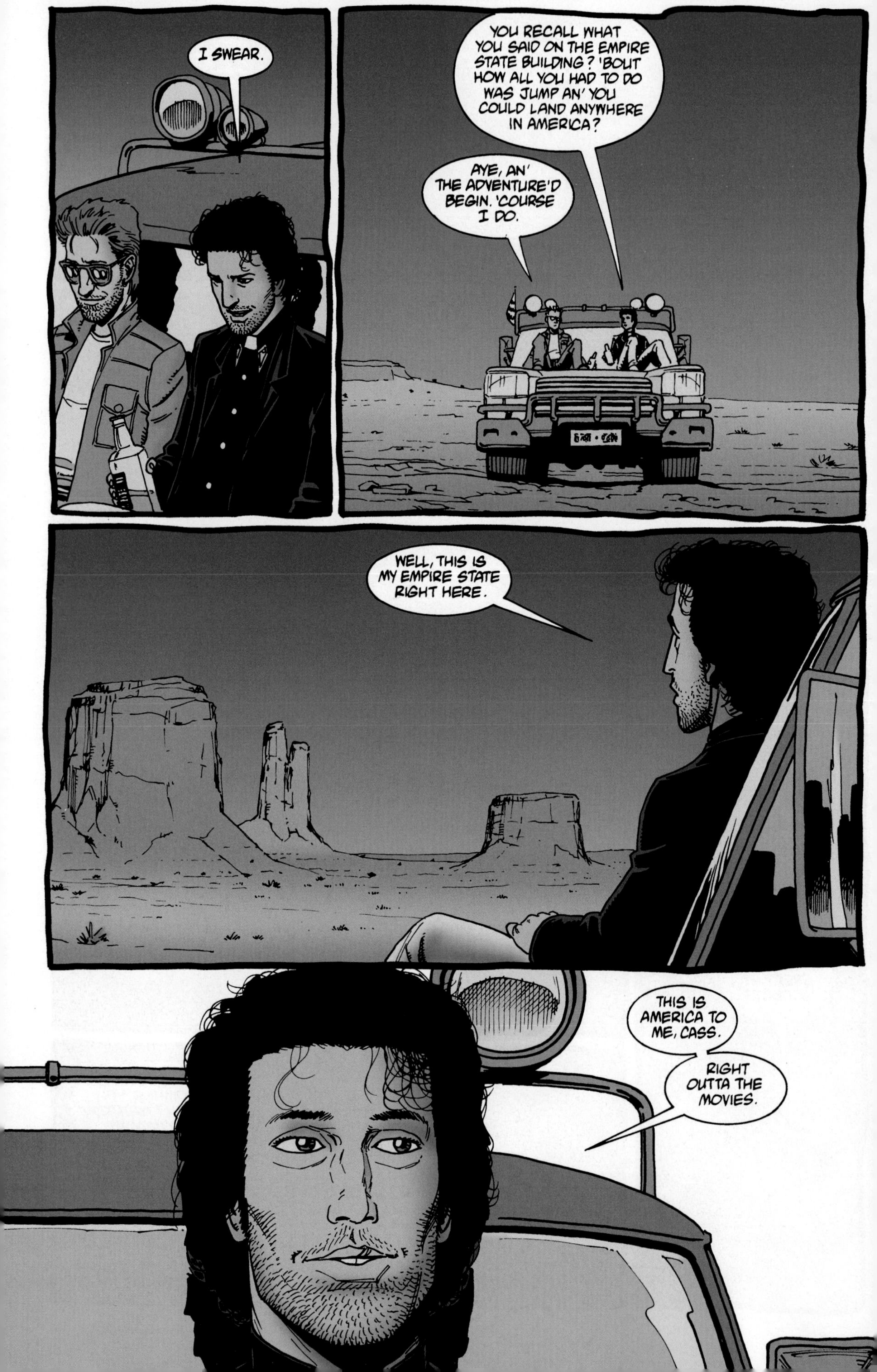
I SWEAR.
YOU RECALL WHAT YOU SAID ON THE EMPIRE STATE BUILDING? 'BOUT HOW ALL YOU HAD TO DO WAS JUMP AN' YOU COULD LAND ANYWHERE IN AMERICA?
AYE, AN' THE ADVENTURE'D BEGIN. 'COURSE I DO.
WELL, THIS IS MY EMPIRE STATE RIGHT HERE.
THIS IS AMERICA TO ME, CASS.
RIGHT OUTTA THE MOVIES.

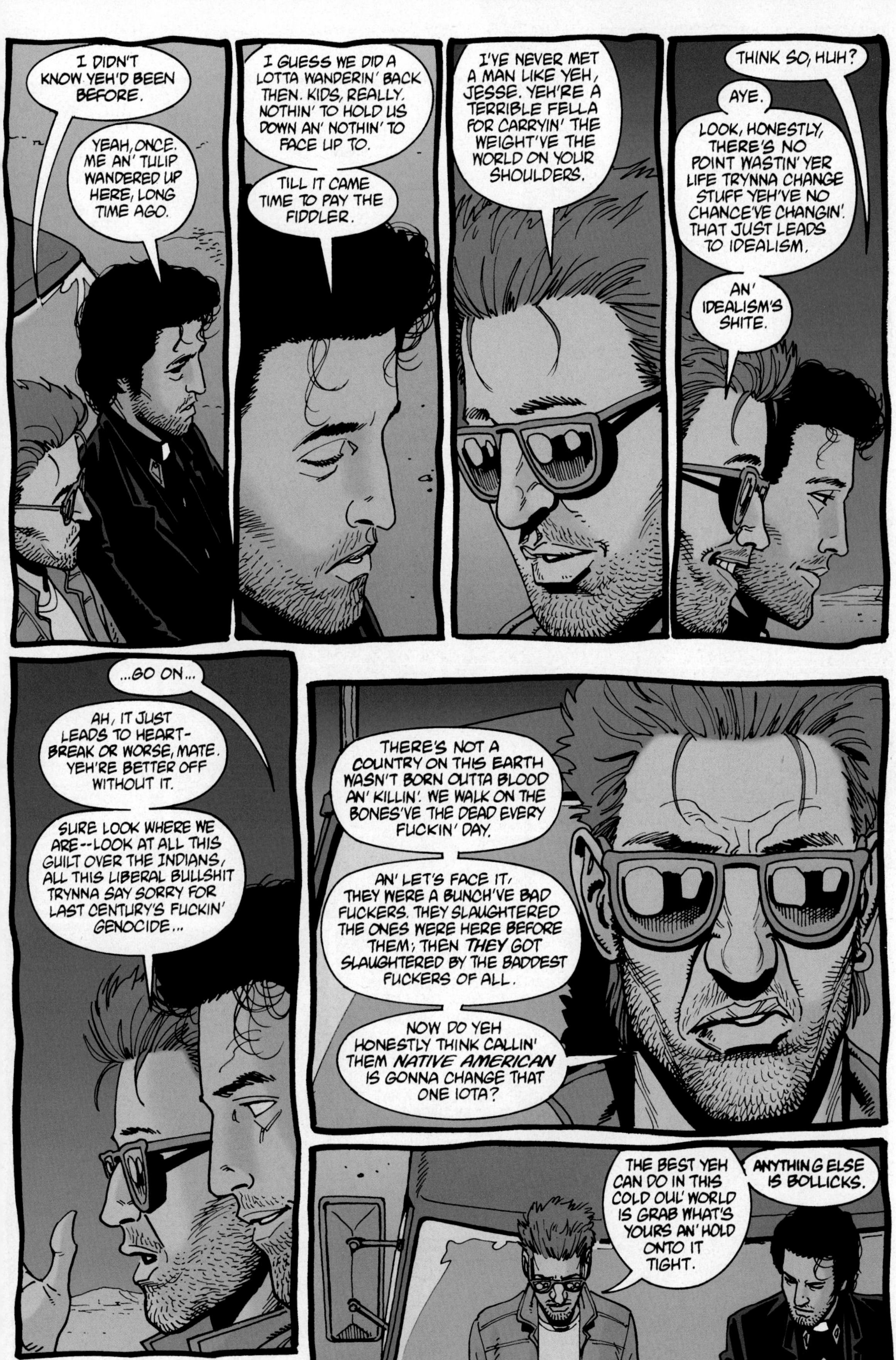
I DIDN'T KNOW YEH'D BEEN BEFORE.
YEAH, ONCE. ME AN' TULIP WANDERED UP HERE, LONG TIME AGO.
I GUESS WE DID A LOTTA WANDERIN' BACK THEN. KIDS, REALLY. NOTHIN' TO HOLD US DOWN AN' NOTHIN' TO FACE UP TO.
TILL IT CAME TIME TO PAY THE FIDDLER.
I'VE NEVER MET A MAN LIKE YEH, JESSE. YEH'RE A TERRIBLE FELLA FOR CARRYIN' THE WEIGHT'VE THE WORLD ON YOUR SHOULDERS.
THINK SO, HUH?
AYE.
LOOK, HONESTLY, THERE'S NO POINT WASTIN' YER LIFE TRYNNA CHANGE STUFF YEH'VE NO CHANCE'VE CHANGIN'. THAT JUST LEADS TO IDEALISM.
AN' IDEALISM'S SHITE.
...GO ON...
AH, IT JUST LEADS TO HEART-BREAK OR WORSE, MATE. YEH'RE BETTER OFF WITHOUT IT.
SURE LOOK WHERE WE ARE--LOOK AT ALL THIS GUILT OVER THE INDIANS, ALL THIS LIBERAL BULLSHIT TRYNNA SAY SORRY FOR LAST CENTURY'S FUCKIN' GENOCIDE...
THERE'S NOT A COUNTRY ON THIS EARTH WASN'T BORN OUTTA BLOOD AN' KILLIN'. WE WALK ON THE BONES'VE THE DEAD EVERY FUCKIN' DAY.
AN' LET'S FACE IT, THEY WERE A BUNCH'VE BAD FUCKERS. THEY SLAUGHTERED THE ONES WERE HERE BEFORE THEM; THEN *THEY* GOT SLAUGHTERED BY THE BADDEST FUCKERS OF ALL.
NOW DO YEH HONESTLY THINK CALLIN' THEM *NATIVE AMERICAN* IS GONNA CHANGE THAT ONE IOTA?
THE BEST YEH CAN DO IN THIS COLD OUL' WORLD IS GRAB WHAT'S YOURS AN' HOLD ONTO IT TIGHT.
ANYTHING ELSE IS BOLLICKS.

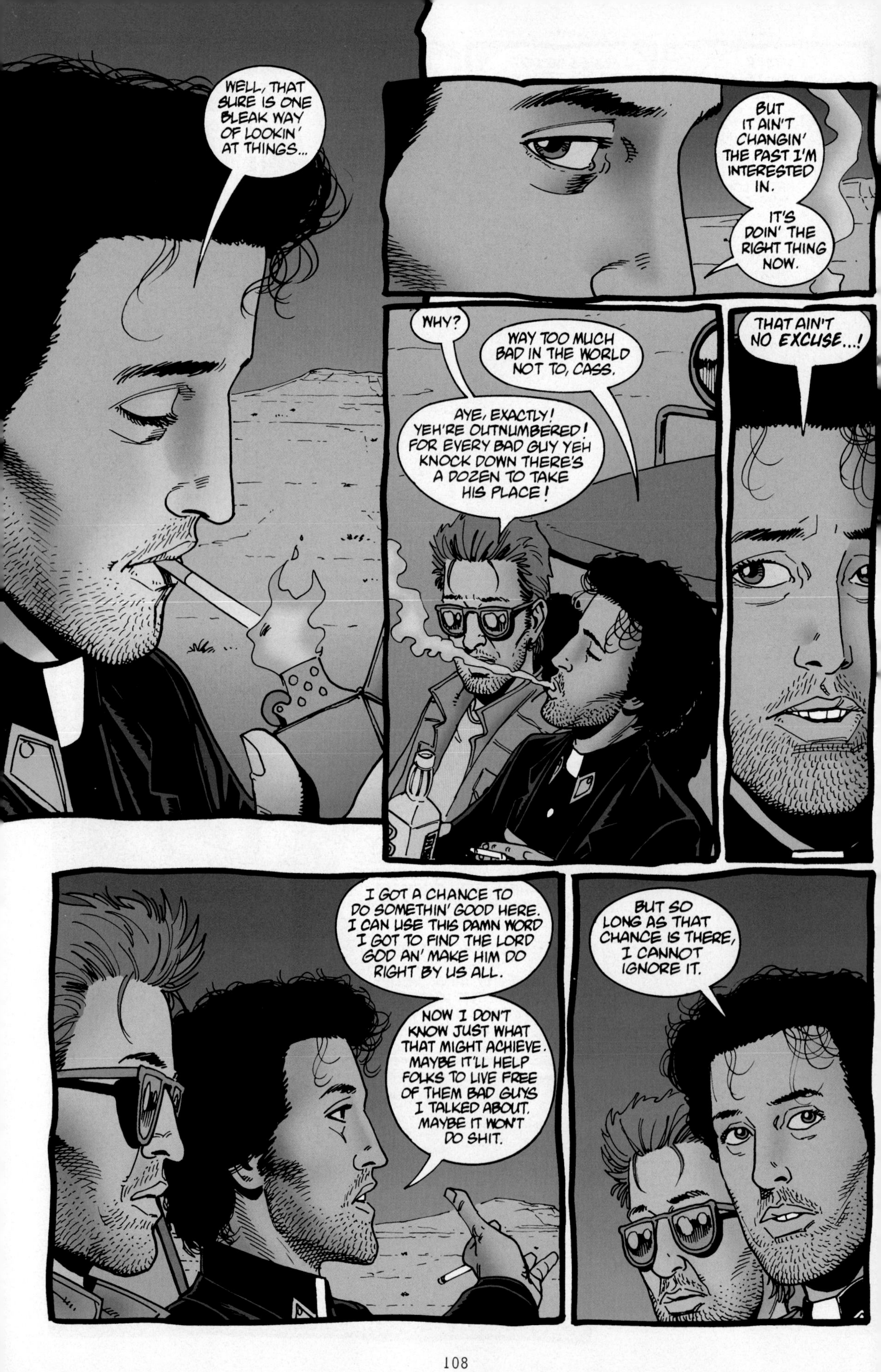
WELL, THAT SURE IS ONE BLEAK WAY OF LOOKIN' AT THINGS...
BUT IT AIN'T CHANGIN' THE PAST I'M INTERESTED IN.
IT'S DOIN' THE RIGHT THING NOW.
WHY?
WAY TOO MUCH BAD IN THE WORLD NOT TO, CASS.
AYE, EXACTLY! YEH'RE OUTNUMBERED! FOR EVERY BAD GUY YEH KNOCK DOWN THERE'S A DOZEN TO TAKE HIS PLACE!
THAT AIN'T NO EXCUSE...!
I GOT A CHANCE TO DO SOMETHIN' GOOD HERE. I CAN USE THIS DAMN WORD I GOT TO FIND THE LORD GOD AN' MAKE HIM DO RIGHT BY US ALL.
NOW I DON'T KNOW JUST WHAT THAT MIGHT ACHIEVE. MAYBE IT'LL HELP FOLKS TO LIVE FREE OF THEM BAD GUYS I TALKED ABOUT. MAYBE IT WON'T DO SHIT.
BUT SO LONG AS THAT CHANCE IS THERE, I CANNOT IGNORE IT.

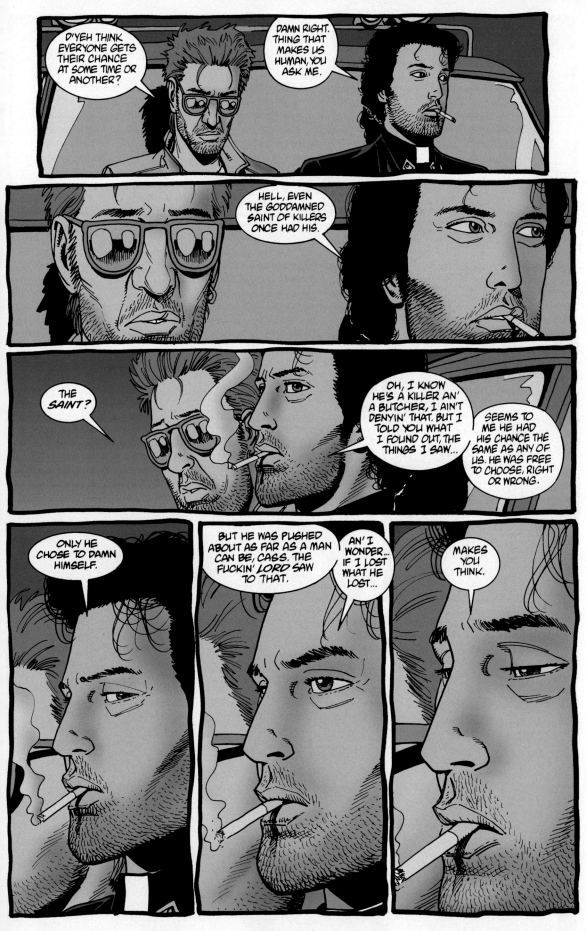

D'YEH THINK EVERYONE GETS THEIR CHANCE AT SOME TIME OR ANOTHER?

DAMN RIGHT. THING THAT MAKES US HUMAN, YOU ASK ME.

HELL, EVEN THE GODDAMNED SAINT OF KILLERS ONCE HAD HIS.

THE SAINT?

OH, I KNOW HE'S A KILLER AN' A BUTCHER, I AIN'T DENYIN' THAT. BUT I TOLD YOU WHAT I FOUND OUT, THE THINGS I SAW...

SEEMS TO ME HE HAD HIS CHANCE THE SAME AS ANY OF US. HE WAS FREE TO CHOOSE, RIGHT OR WRONG.

ONLY HE CHOSE TO DAMN HIMSELF.

BUT HE WAS PUSHED ABOUT AS FAR AS A MAN CAN BE, CASS. THE FUCKIN' LORD SAW TO THAT.

AN' I WONDER... IF I LOST WHAT HE LOST...

MAKES YOU THINK.

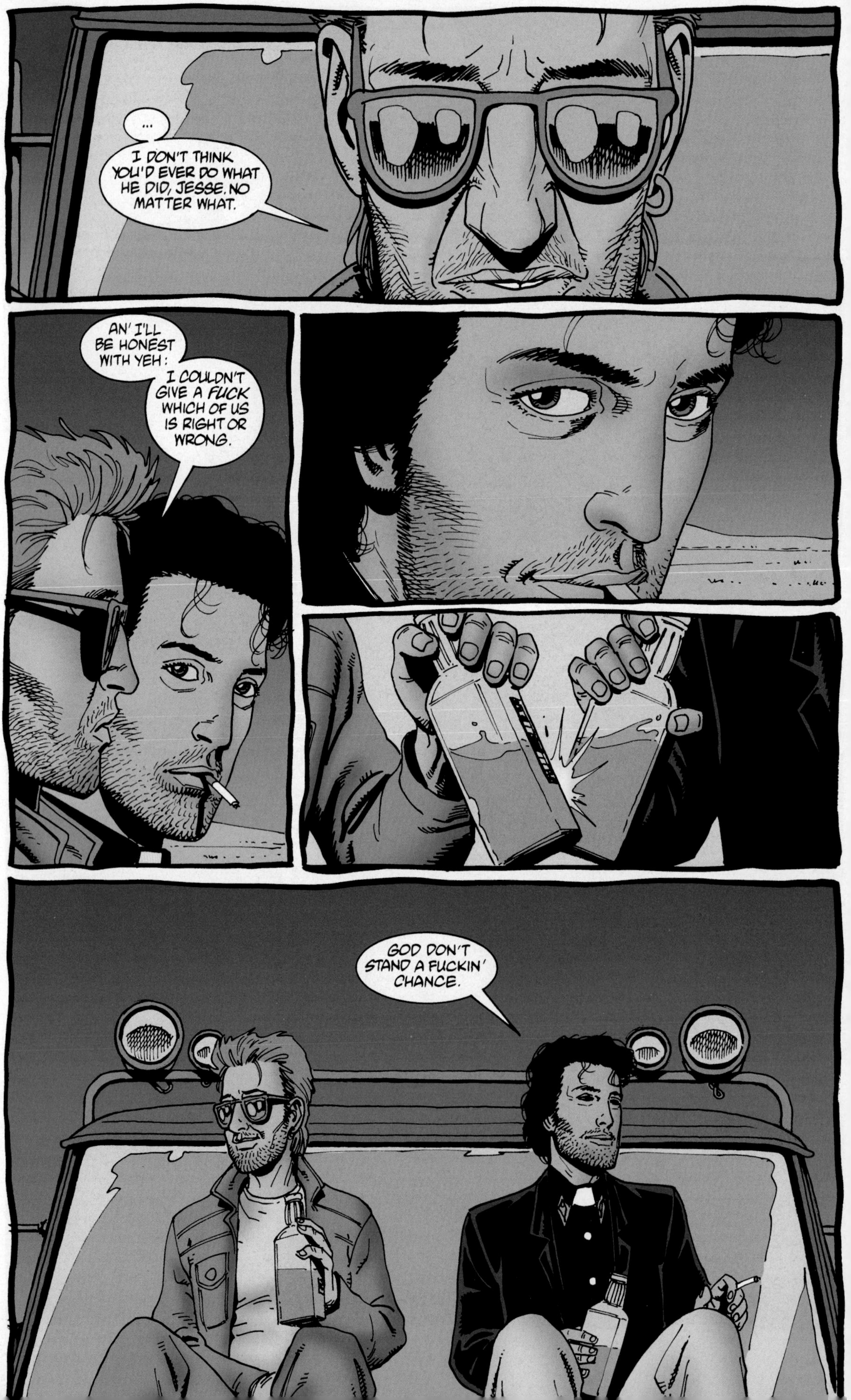
...
I DON'T THINK YOU'D EVER DO WHAT HE DID, JESSE. NO MATTER WHAT.
AN' I'LL BE HONEST WITH YEH:
I COULDN'T GIVE A *FUCK* WHICH OF US IS RIGHT OR WRONG.
GOD DON'T STAND A FUCKIN' CHANCE.

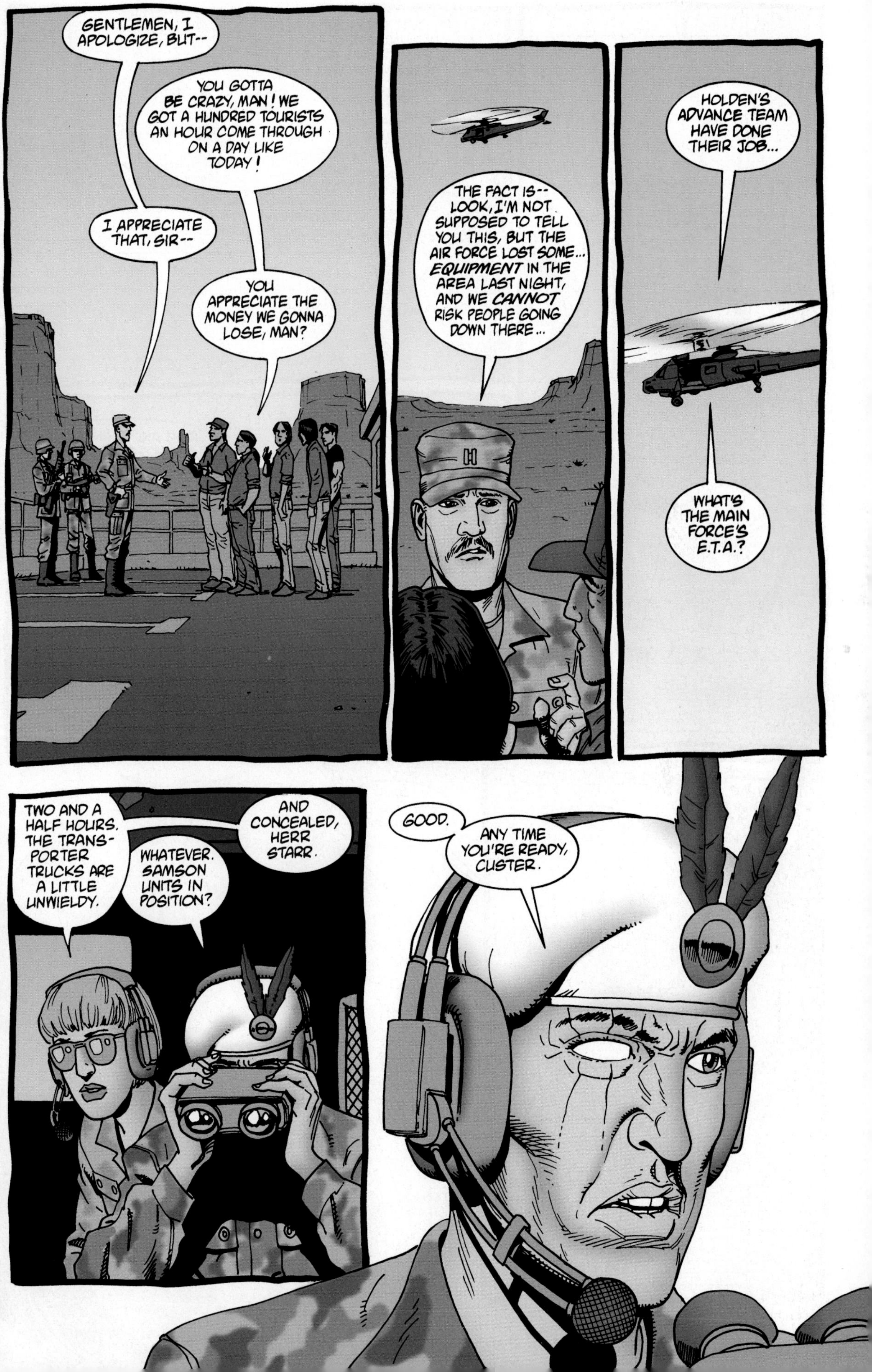
GENTLEMEN, I APOLOGIZE, BUT--
YOU GOTTA BE CRAZY, MAN! WE GOT A HUNDRED TOURISTS AN HOUR COME THROUGH ON A DAY LIKE TODAY!
I APPRECIATE THAT, SIR--
YOU APPRECIATE THE MONEY WE GONNA LOSE, MAN?
THE FACT IS-- LOOK, I'M NOT SUPPOSED TO TELL YOU THIS, BUT THE AIR FORCE LOST SOME... EQUIPMENT IN THE AREA LAST NIGHT, AND WE CANNOT RISK PEOPLE GOING DOWN THERE...
HOLDEN'S ADVANCE TEAM HAVE DONE THEIR JOB...
WHAT'S THE MAIN FORCE'S E.T.A.?
TWO AND A HALF HOURS. THE TRANS-PORTER TRUCKS ARE A LITTLE UNWIELDY.
WHATEVER. SAMSON UNITS IN POSITION?
AND CONCEALED, HERR STARR.
GOOD.
ANY TIME YOU'RE READY, CUSTER.

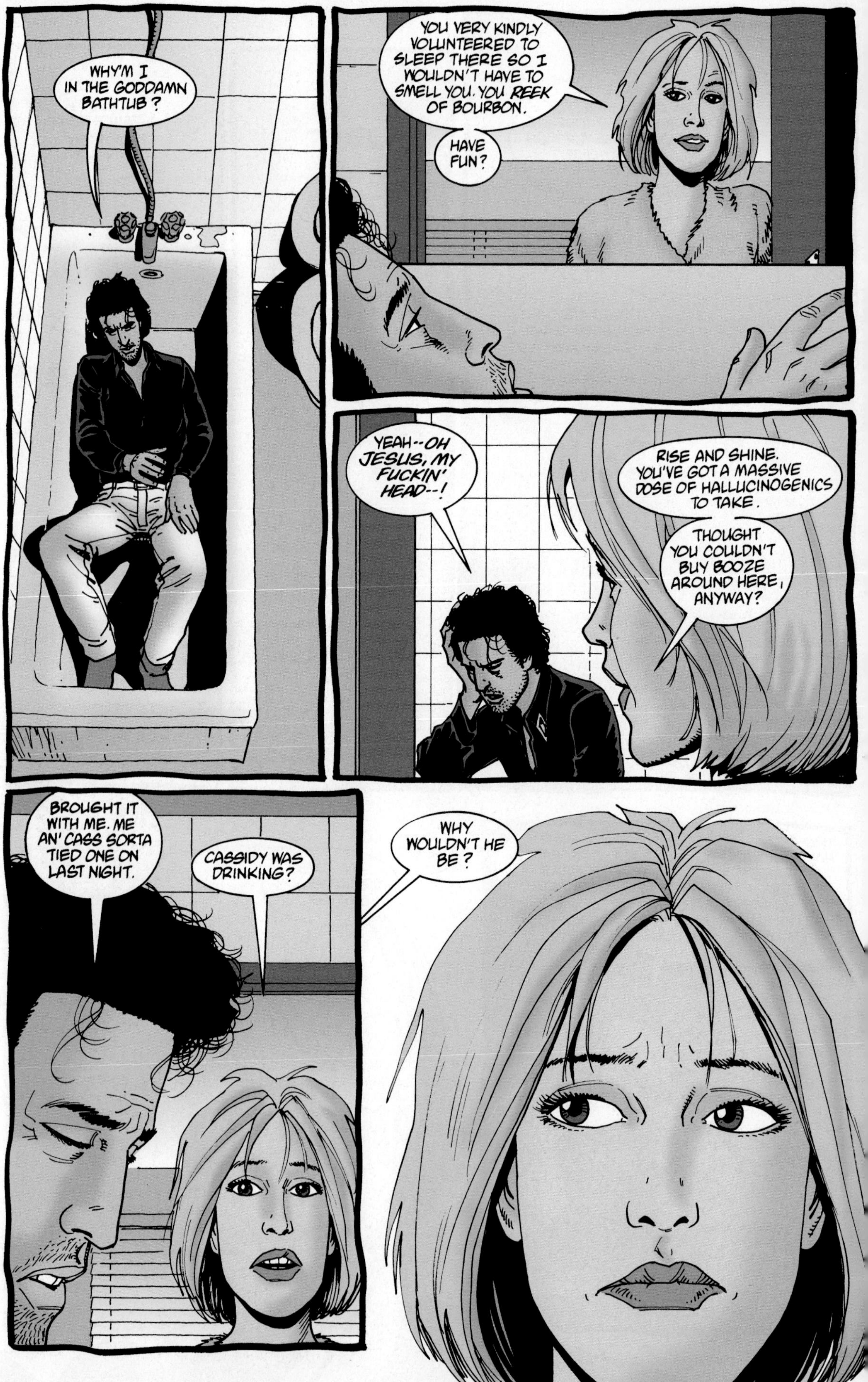
WHY'M I IN THE GODDAMN BATHTUB?
YOU VERY KINDLY VOLUNTEERED TO SLEEP THERE SO I WOULDN'T HAVE TO SMELL YOU. YOU REEK OF BOURBON.
HAVE FUN?
YEAH--OH JESUS, MY FUCKIN' HEAD--!
RISE AND SHINE. YOU'VE GOT A MASSIVE DOSE OF HALLUCINOGENICS TO TAKE.
THOUGHT YOU COULDN'T BUY BOOZE AROUND HERE, ANYWAY?
BROUGHT IT WITH ME. ME AN' CASS SORTA TIED ONE ON LAST NIGHT.
CASSIDY WAS DRINKING?
WHY WOULDN'T HE BE?

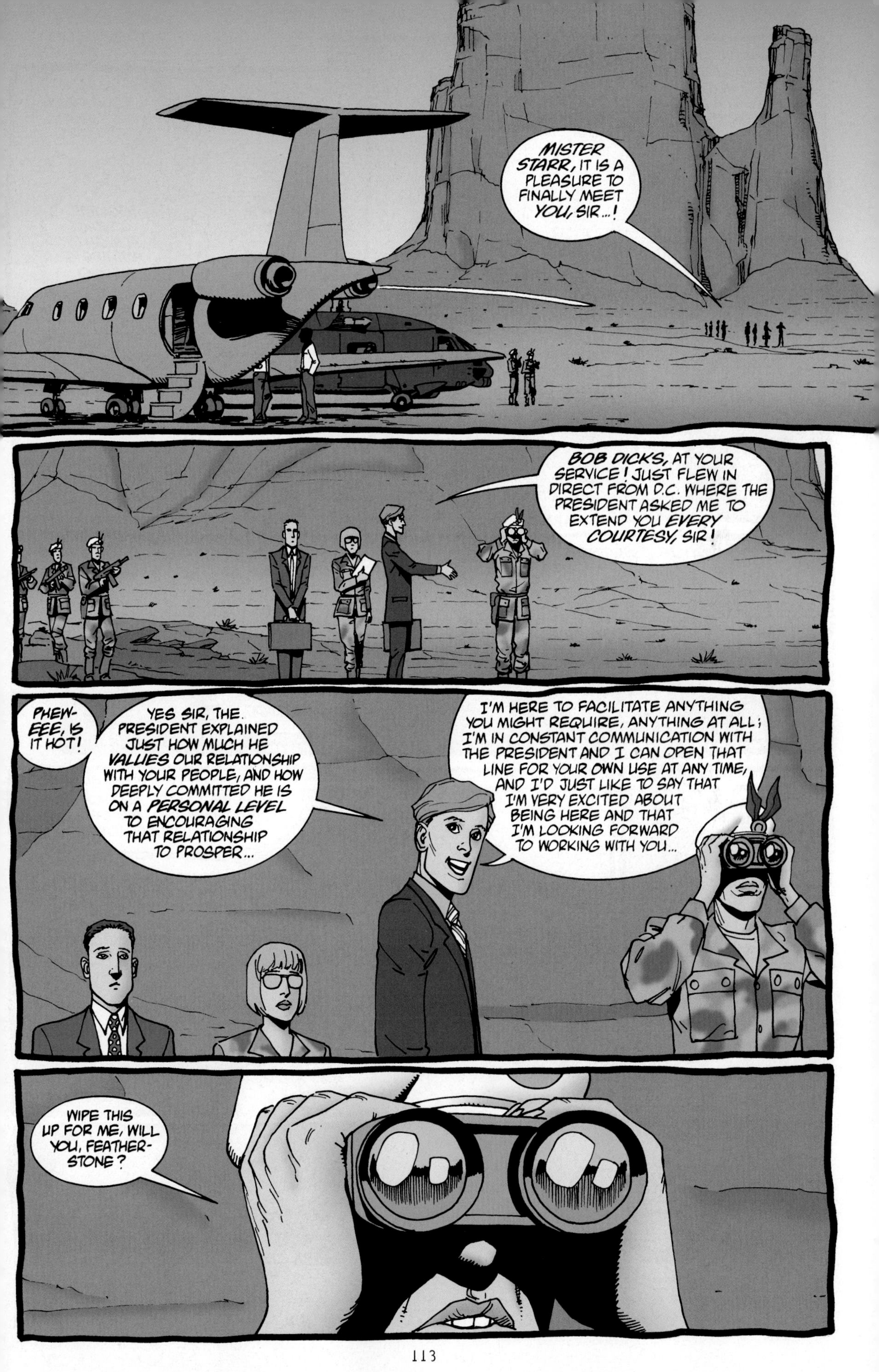
MISTER STARR, IT IS A PLEASURE TO FINALLY MEET YOU, SIR...!
BOB DICKS, AT YOUR SERVICE! JUST FLEW IN DIRECT FROM D.C. WHERE THE PRESIDENT ASKED ME TO EXTEND YOU EVERY COURTESY, SIR!
PHEW-EEE, IS IT HOT!
YES SIR, THE PRESIDENT EXPLAINED JUST HOW MUCH HE VALUES OUR RELATIONSHIP WITH YOUR PEOPLE, AND HOW DEEPLY COMMITTED HE IS ON A PERSONAL LEVEL TO ENCOURAGING THAT RELATIONSHIP TO PROSPER...
I'M HERE TO FACILITATE ANYTHING YOU MIGHT REQUIRE, ANYTHING AT ALL; I'M IN CONSTANT COMMUNICATION WITH THE PRESIDENT AND I CAN OPEN THAT LINE FOR YOUR OWN USE AT ANY TIME, AND I'D JUST LIKE TO SAY THAT I'M VERY EXCITED ABOUT BEING HERE AND THAT I'M LOOKING FORWARD TO WORKING WITH YOU...
WIPE THIS UP FOR ME, WILL YOU, FEATHER-STONE?

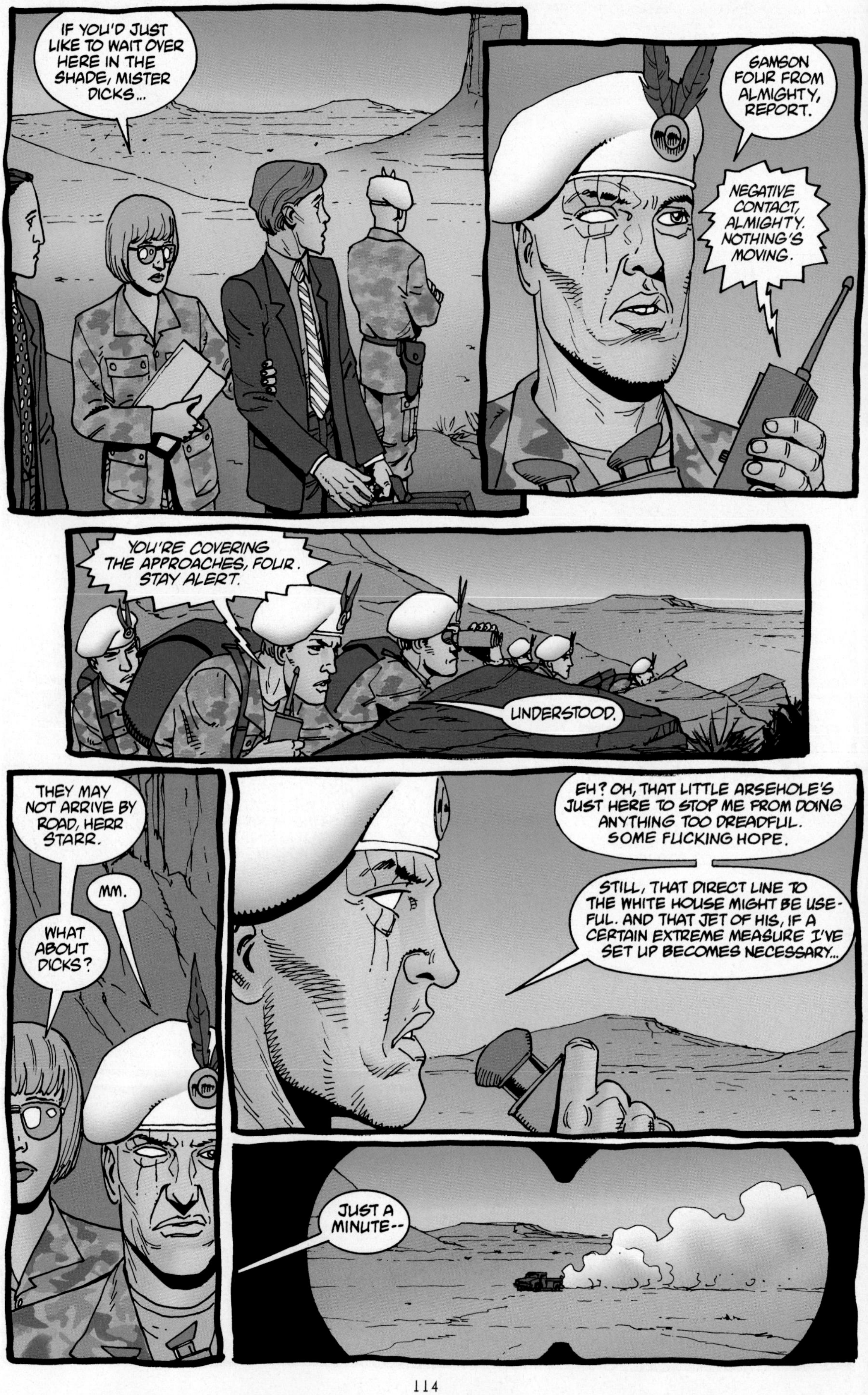
IF YOU'D JUST LIKE TO WAIT OVER HERE IN THE SHADE, MISTER DICKS...
SAMSON FOUR FROM ALMIGHTY, REPORT.
NEGATIVE CONTACT, ALMIGHTY. NOTHING'S MOVING.
YOU'RE COVERING THE APPROACHES, FOUR. STAY ALERT.
UNDERSTOOD.
THEY MAY NOT ARRIVE BY ROAD, HERR STARR.
MM.
WHAT ABOUT DICKS?
EH? OH, THAT LITTLE ARSEHOLE'S JUST HERE TO STOP ME FROM DOING ANYTHING TOO DREADFUL. SOME FUCKING HOPE.
STILL, THAT DIRECT LINE TO THE WHITE HOUSE MIGHT BE USE- FUL. AND THAT JET OF HIS, IF A CERTAIN EXTREME MEASURE I'VE SET UP BECOMES NECESSARY...
JUST A MINUTE--

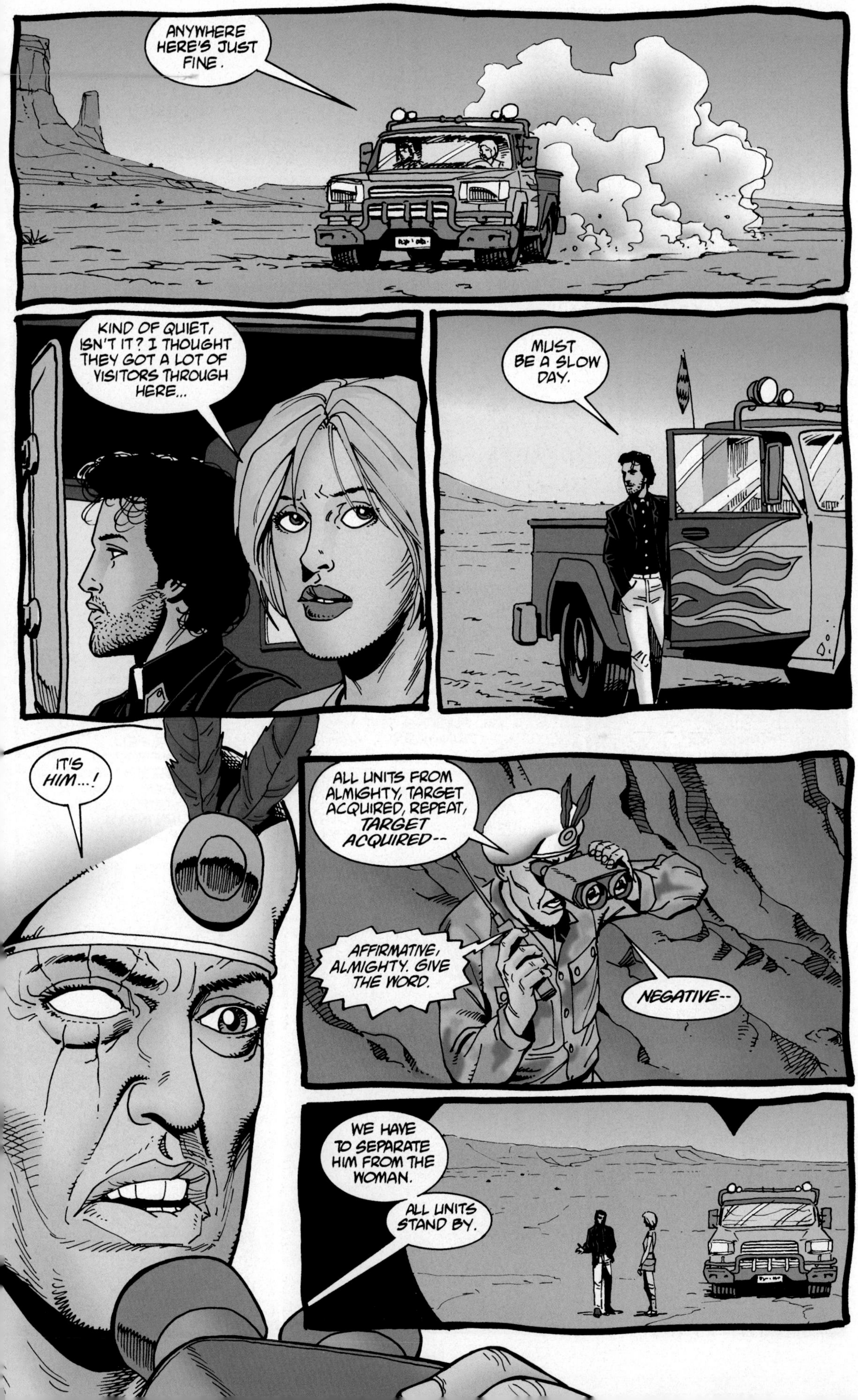
ANYWHERE HERE'S JUST FINE.
KIND OF QUIET, ISN'T IT? I THOUGHT THEY GOT A LOT OF VISITORS THROUGH HERE...
MUST BE A SLOW DAY.
IT'S HIM...!
ALL UNITS FROM ALMIGHTY, TARGET ACQUIRED, REPEAT, TARGET ACQUIRED--
AFFIRMATIVE, ALMIGHTY. GIVE THE WORD.
NEGATIVE--
WE HAVE TO SEPARATE HIM FROM THE WOMAN.
ALL UNITS STAND BY.

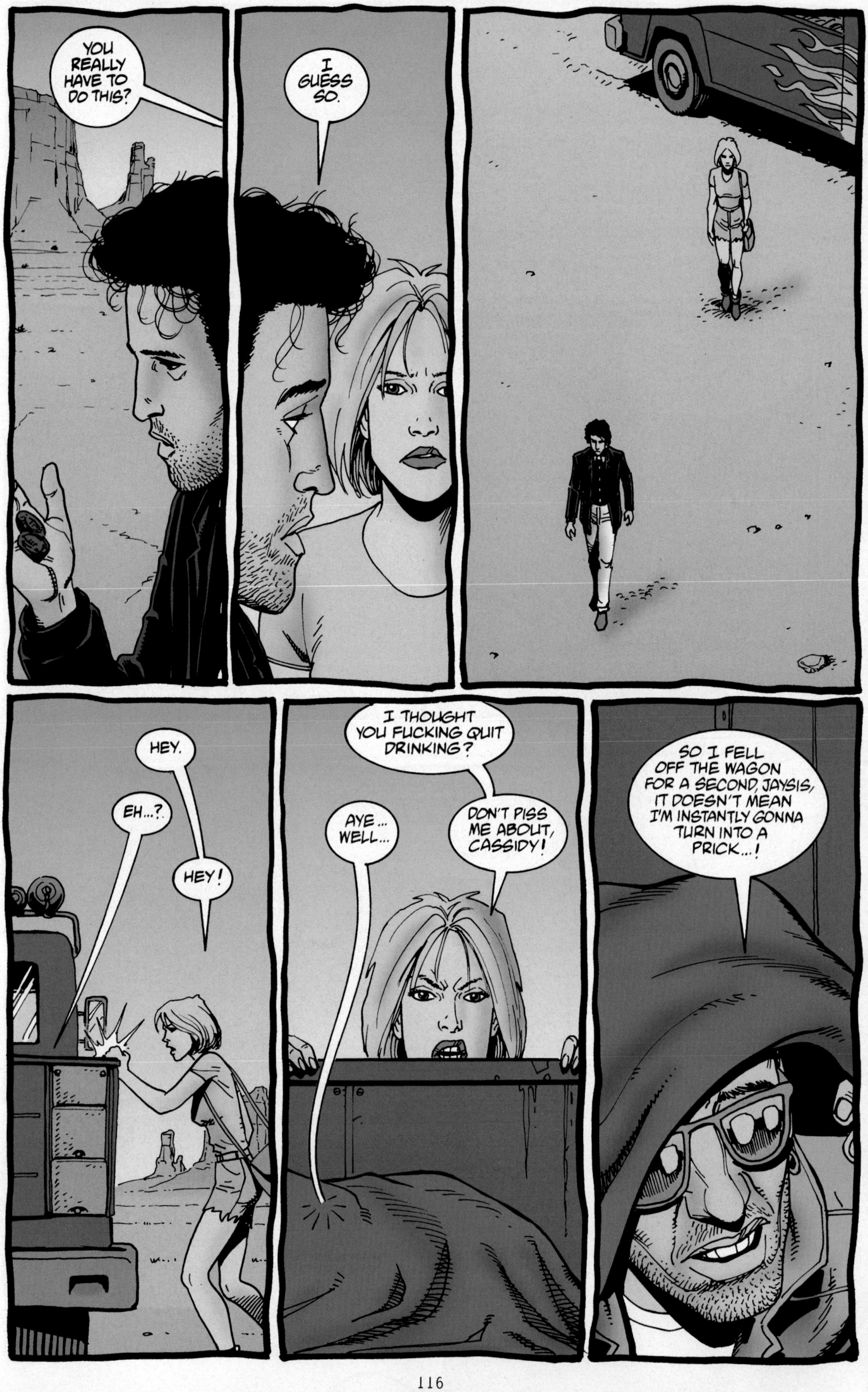
YOU REALLY HAVE TO DO THIS?
I GUESS SO.
HEY.
EH...?
HEY!
I THOUGHT YOU FUCKING QUIT DRINKING?
AYE... WELL...
DON'T PISS ME ABOUT, CASSIDY!
SO I FELL OFF THE WAGON FOR A SECOND, JAYSIS, IT DOESN'T MEAN I'M INSTANTLY GONNA TURN INTO A PRICK...!

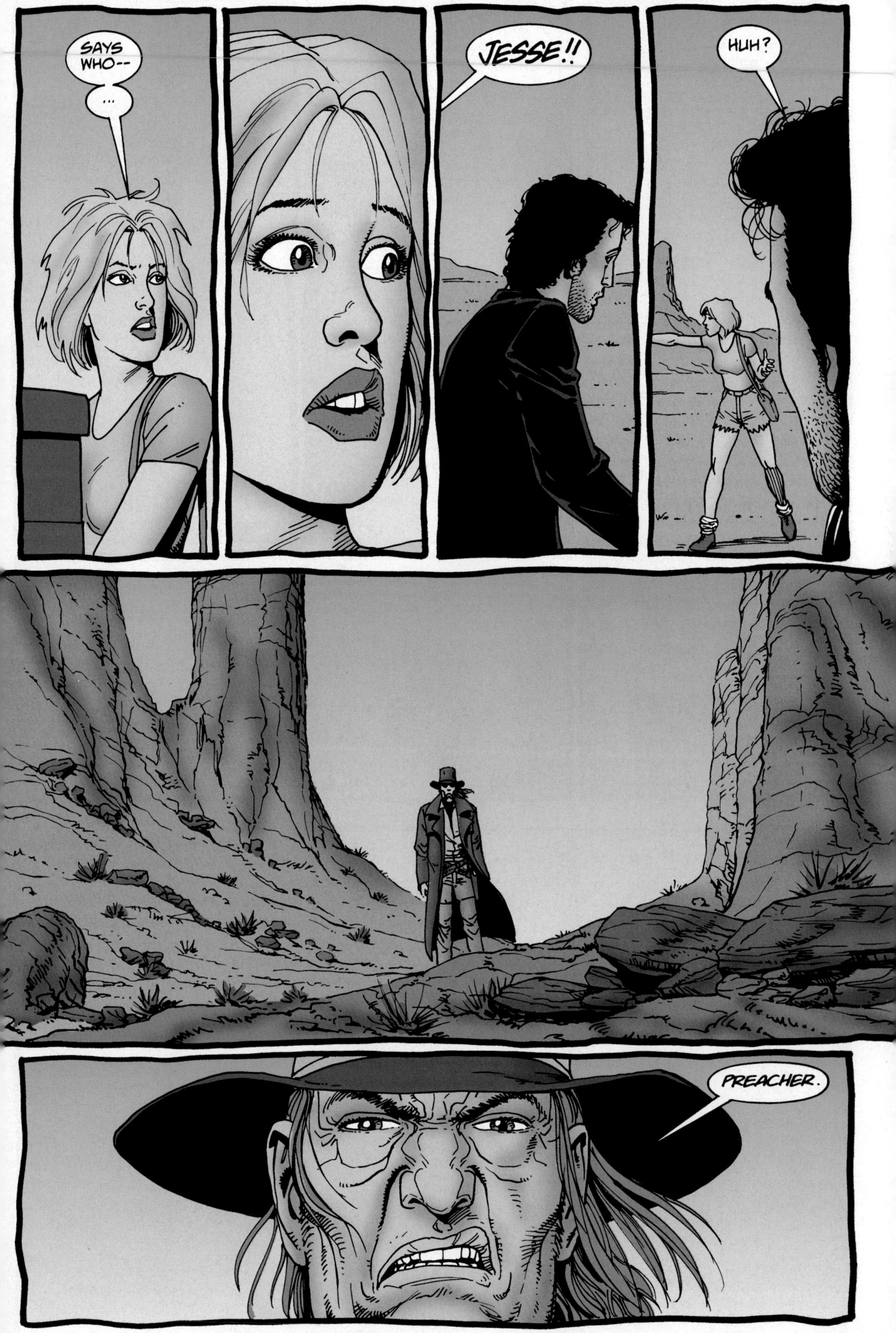
SAYS WHO--
...
JESSE!!
HUH?
PREACHER.

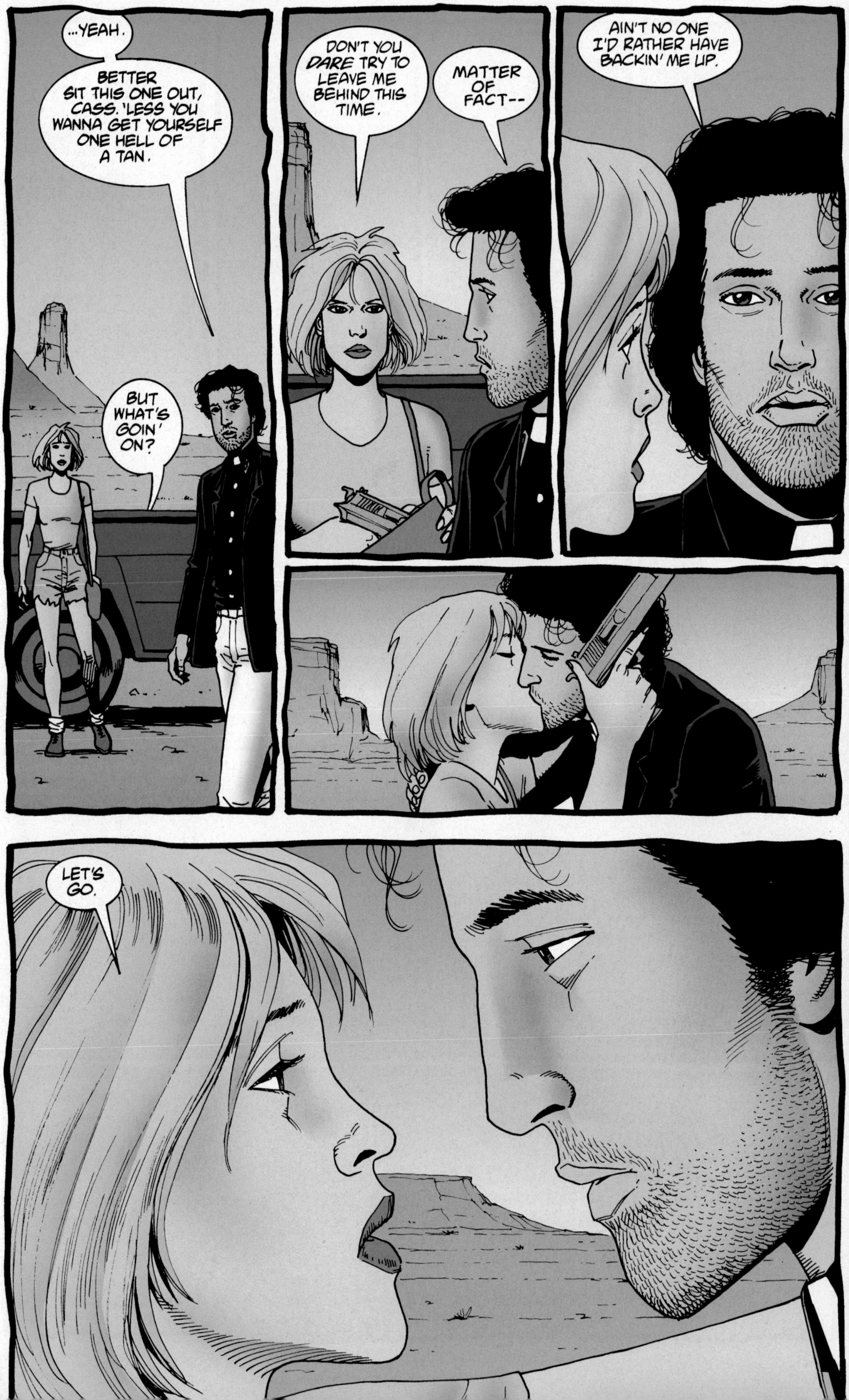
...YEAH.
BETTER SIT THIS ONE OUT, CASS. 'LESS YOU WANNA GET YOURSELF ONE HELL OF A TAN.
BUT WHAT'S GOIN' ON?
DON'T YOU DARE TRY TO LEAVE ME BEHIND THIS TIME.
MATTER OF FACT--
AIN'T NO ONE I'D RATHER HAVE BACKIN' ME UP.
LET'S GO.

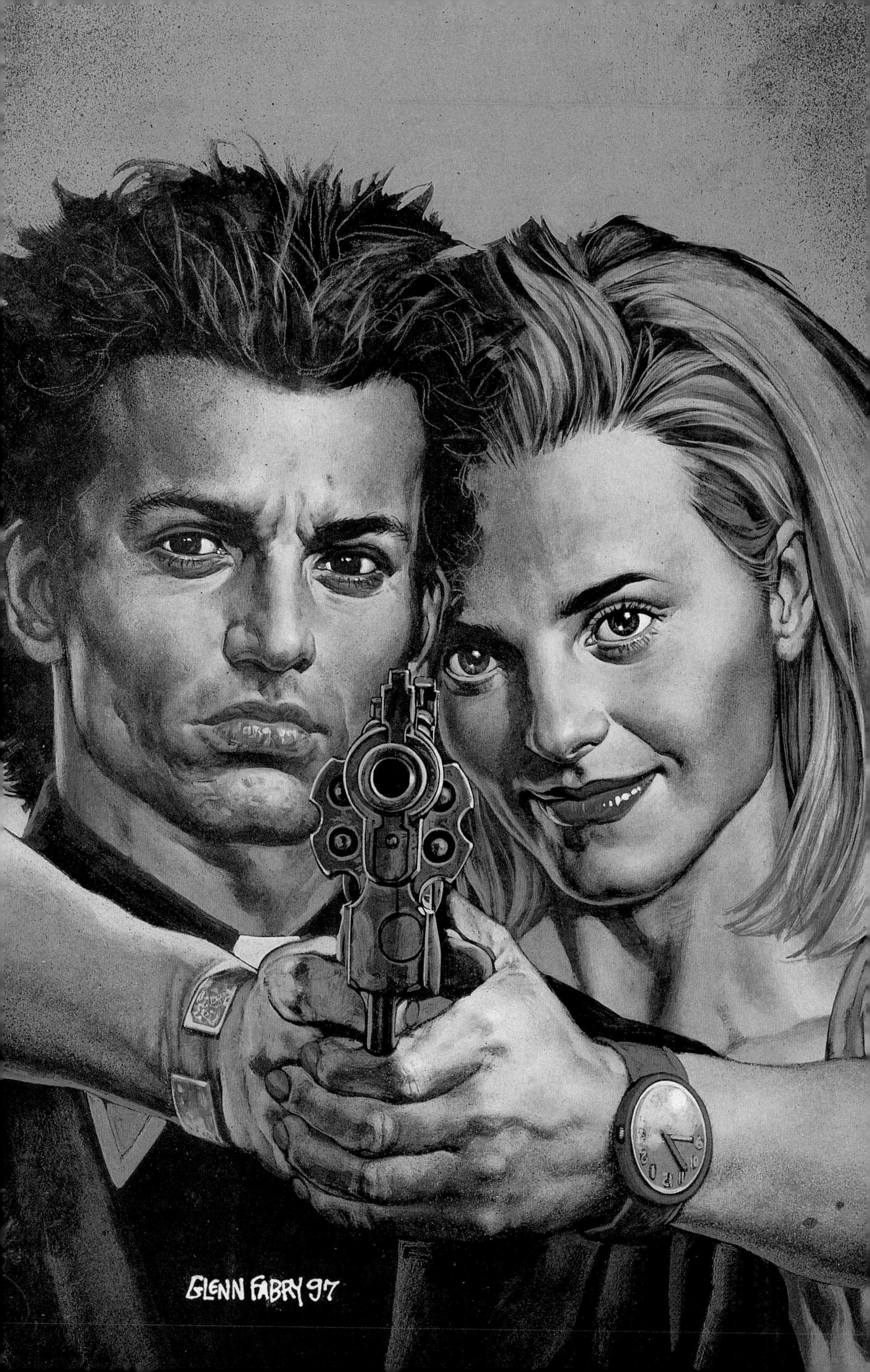
GLENN FABRY 97

"You been wronged, shit, we all been wronged by God!
We can't just walk away from it!"

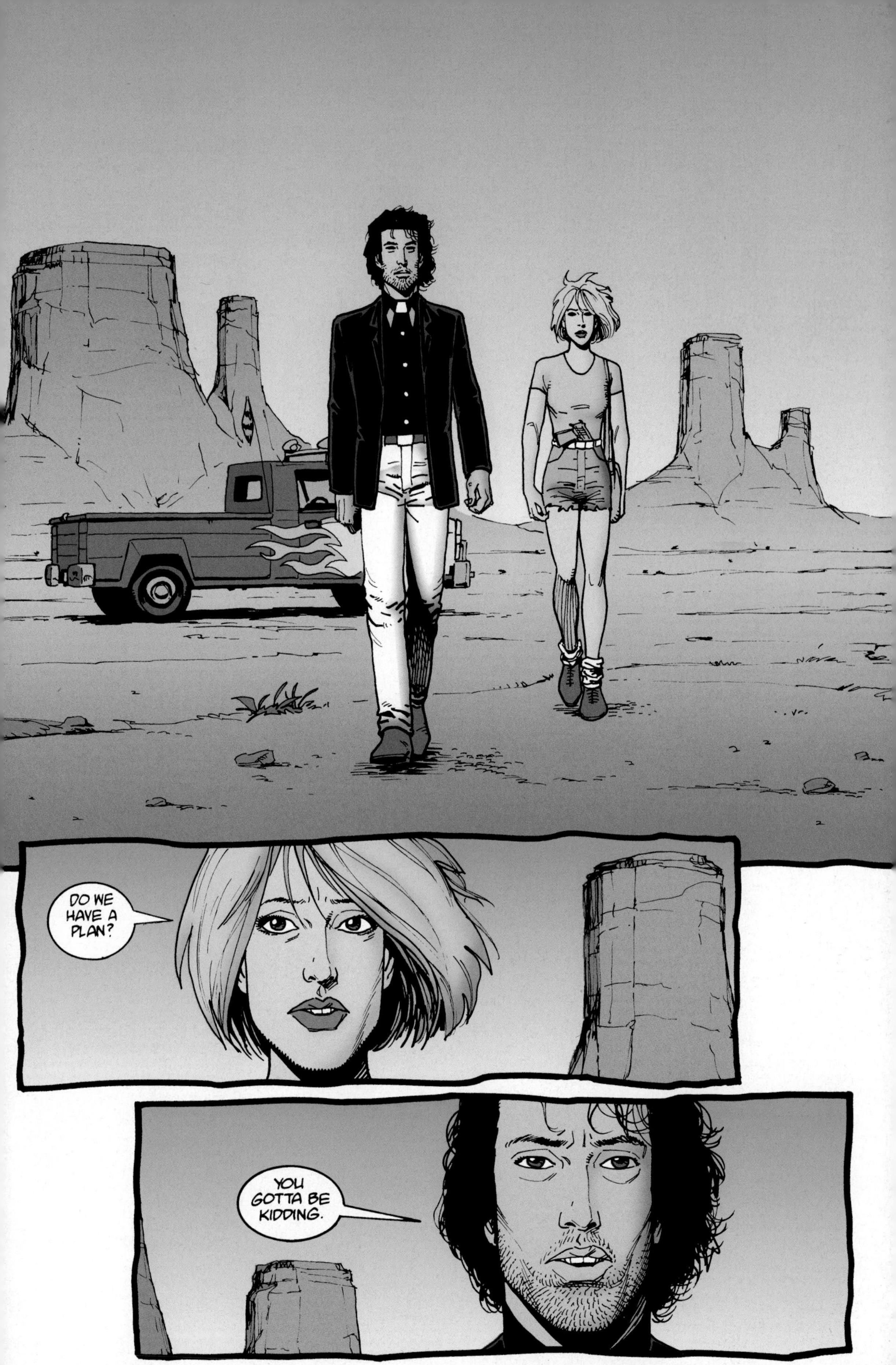
DO WE HAVE A PLAN?
YOU GOTTA BE KIDDING.

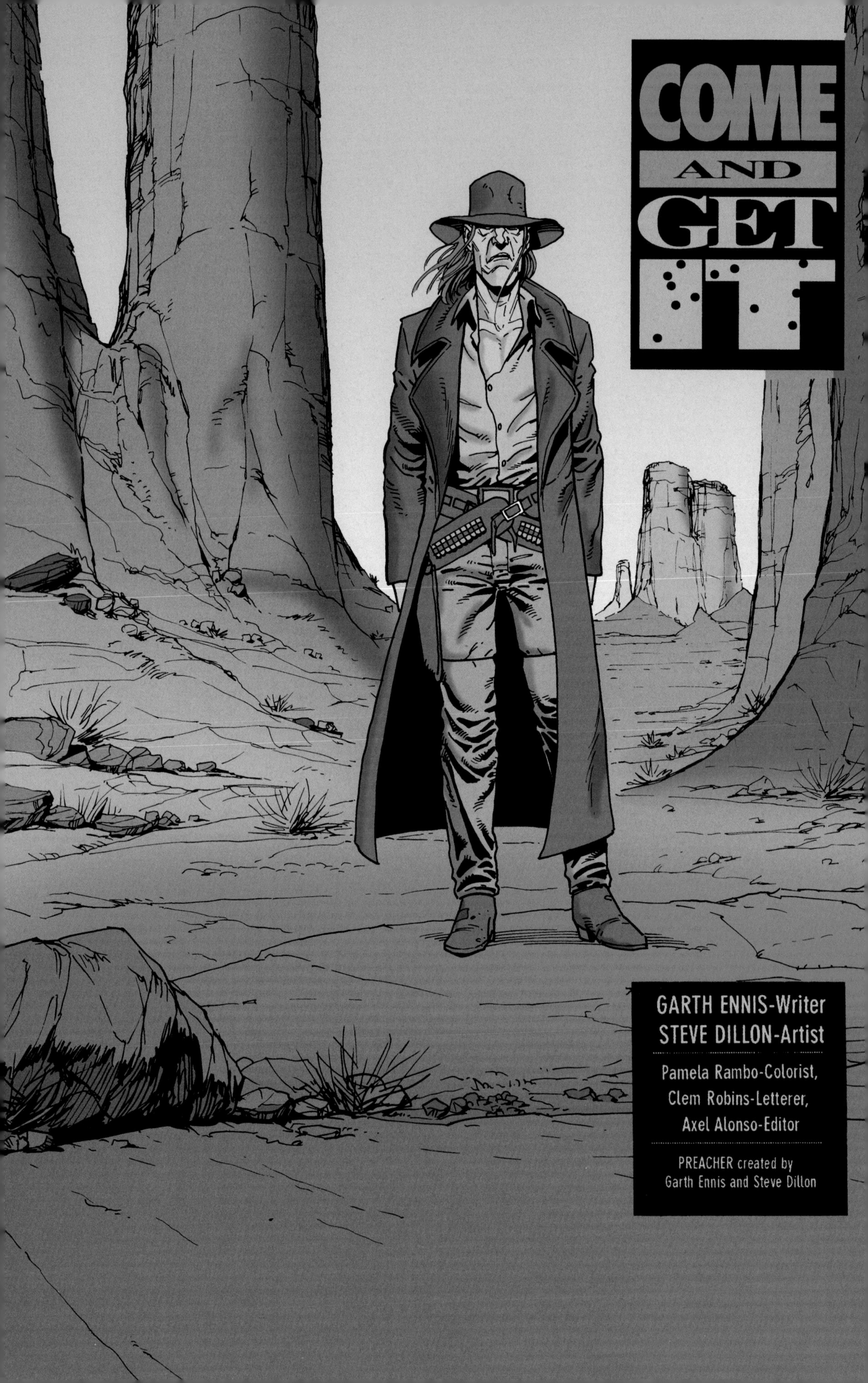

COME AND GET IT
GARTH ENNIS-Writer
STEVE DILLON-Artist
Pamela Rambo-Colorist,
Clem Robins-Letterer,
Axel Alonso-Editor
PREACHER created by
Garth Ennis and Steve Dillon

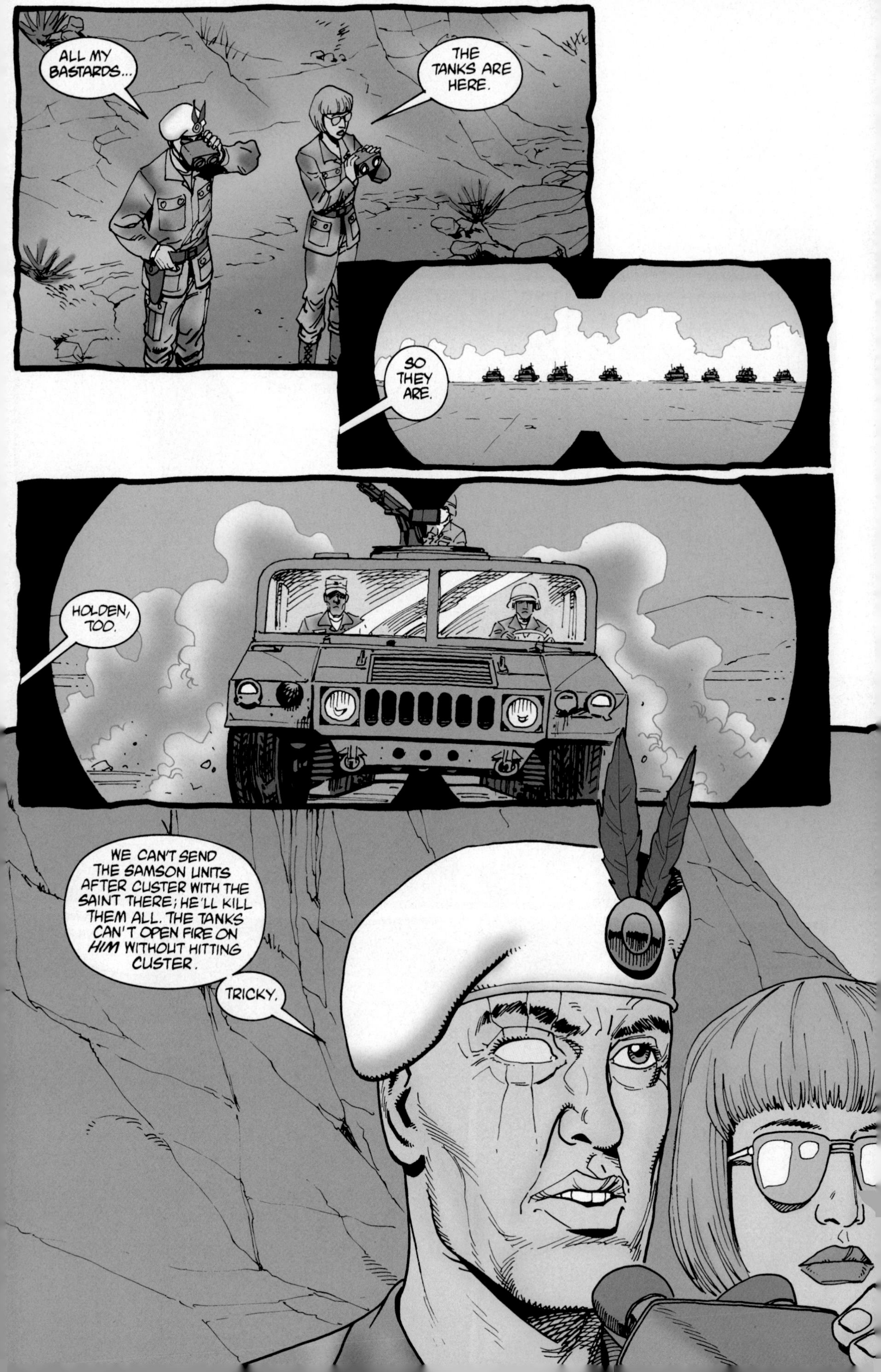
ALL MY BASTARDS...
THE TANKS ARE HERE.
SO THEY ARE.
HOLDEN, TOO.
WE CAN'T SEND THE SAMSON UNITS AFTER CUSTER WITH THE SAINT THERE; HE'LL KILL THEM ALL. THE TANKS CAN'T OPEN FIRE ON *HIM* WITHOUT HITTING CUSTER.
TRICKY.

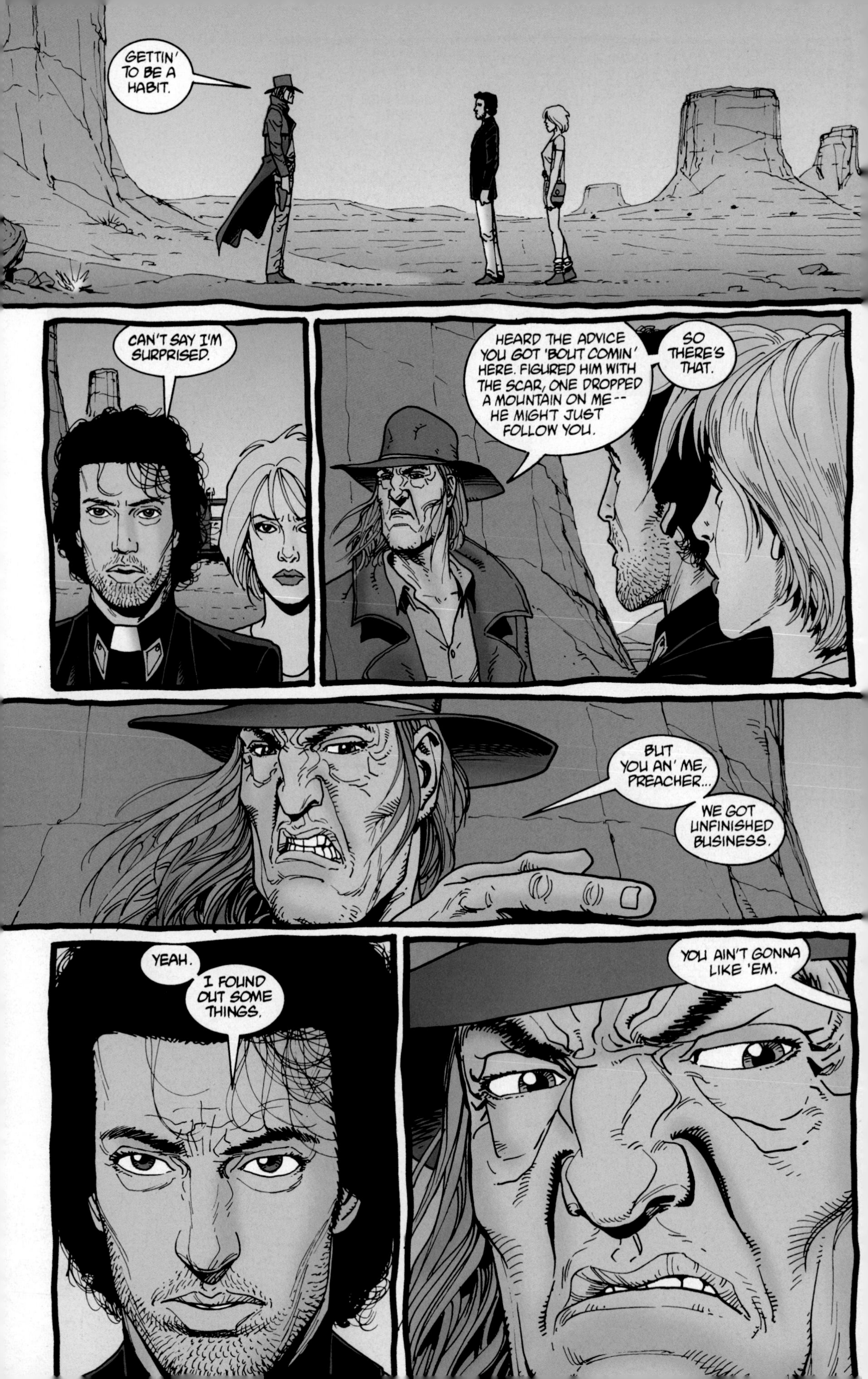
GETTIN' TO BE A HABIT.
CAN'T SAY I'M SURPRISED.
HEARD THE ADVICE YOU GOT 'BOUT COMIN' HERE. FIGURED HIM WITH THE SCAR, ONE DROPPED A MOUNTAIN ON ME-- HE MIGHT JUST FOLLOW YOU.
SO THERE'S THAT.
BUT YOU AN' ME, PREACHER...
WE GOT UNFINISHED BUSINESS.
YEAH.
I FOUND OUT SOME THINGS.
YOU AIN'T GONNA LIKE 'EM.

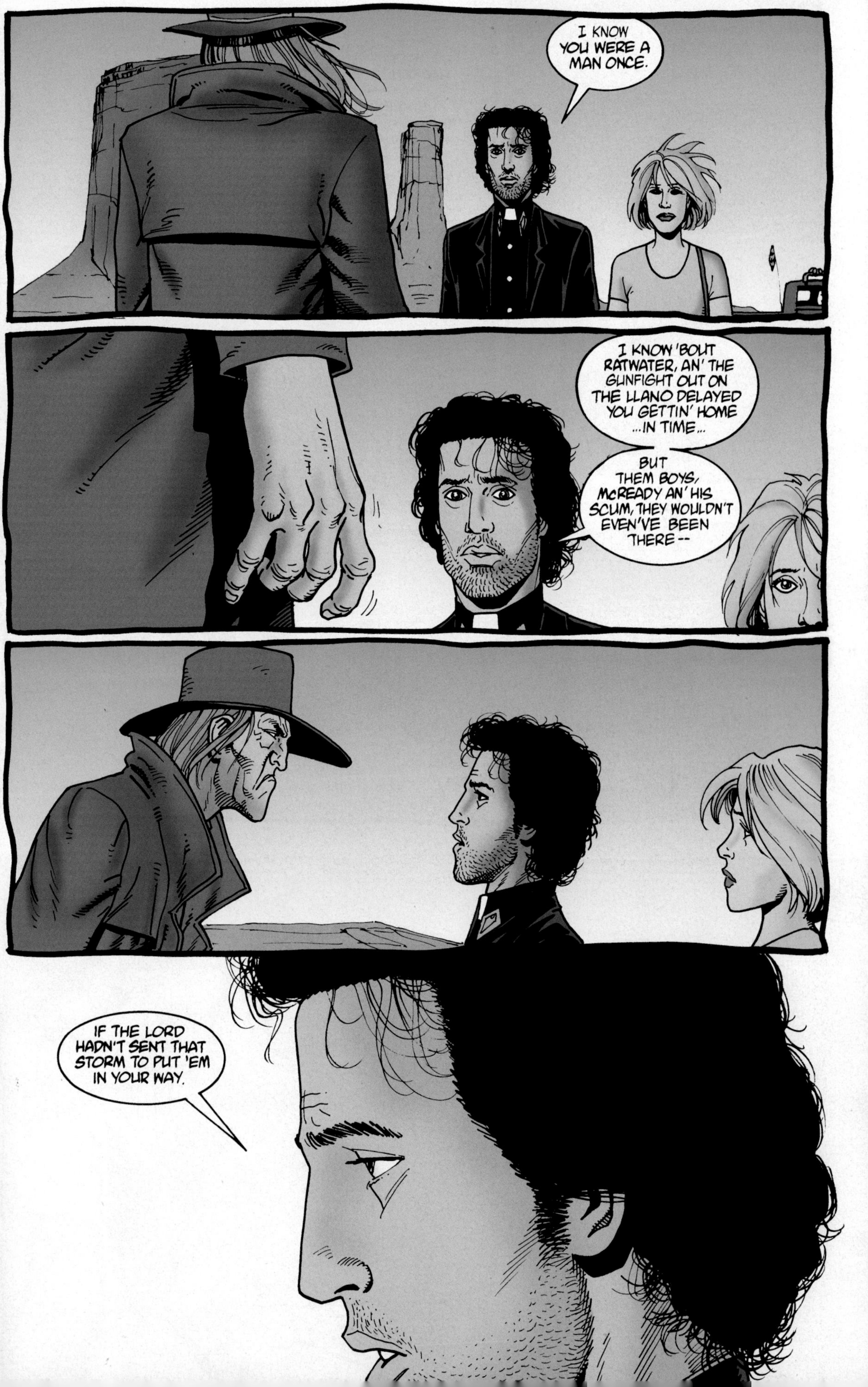
I KNOW YOU WERE A MAN ONCE.
I KNOW 'BOUT RATWATER, AN' THE GUNFIGHT OUT ON THE LLANO DELAYED YOU GETTIN' HOME ...IN TIME...
BUT THEM BOYS, McREADY AN' HIS SCUM, THEY WOULDN'T EVEN'VE BEEN THERE --
IF THE LORD HADN'T SENT THAT STORM TO PUT 'EM IN YOUR WAY.

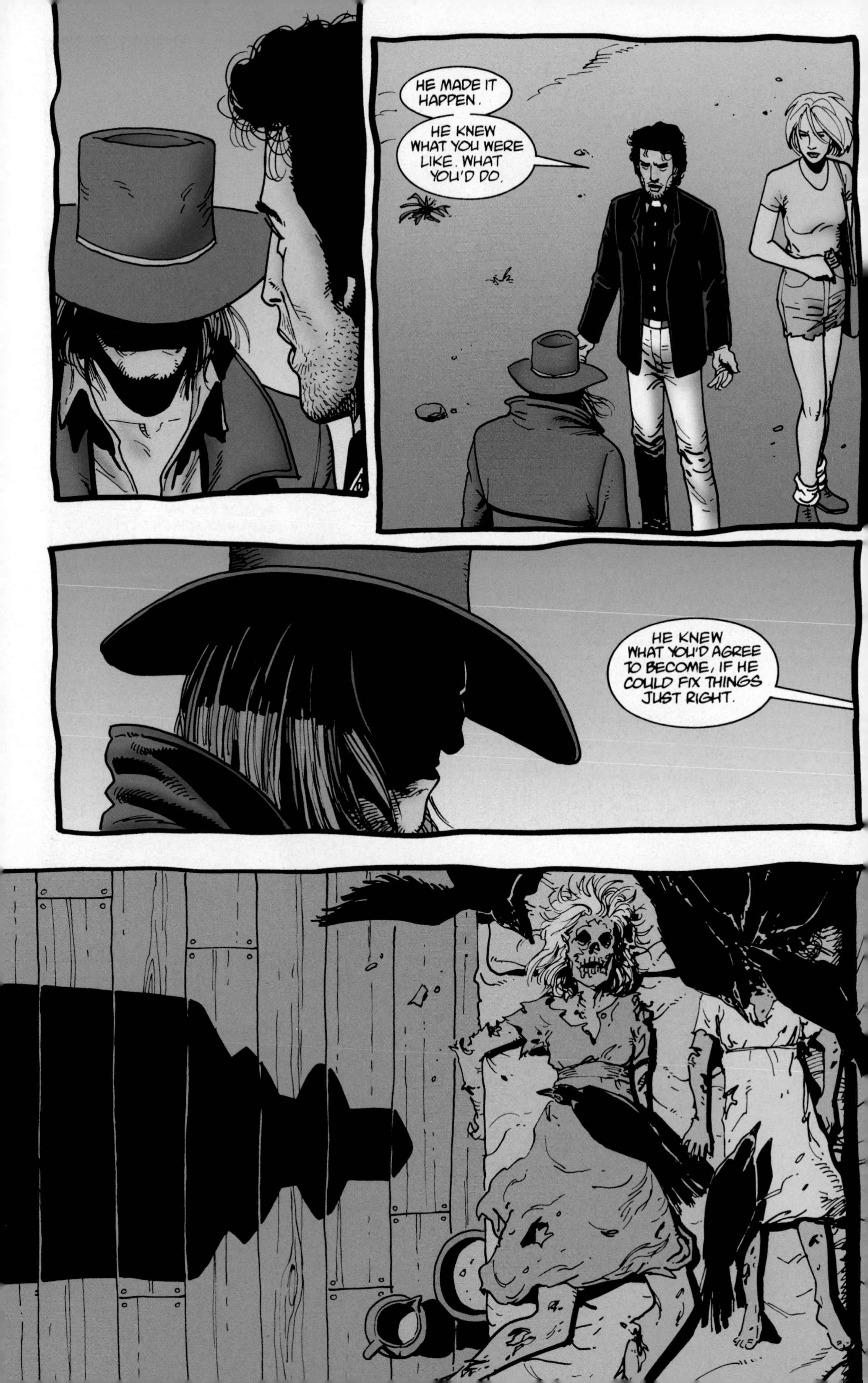
HE MADE IT HAPPEN.
HE KNEW WHAT YOU WERE LIKE. WHAT YOU'D DO.
HE KNEW WHAT YOU'D AGREE TO BECOME, IF HE COULD FIX THINGS JUST RIGHT.

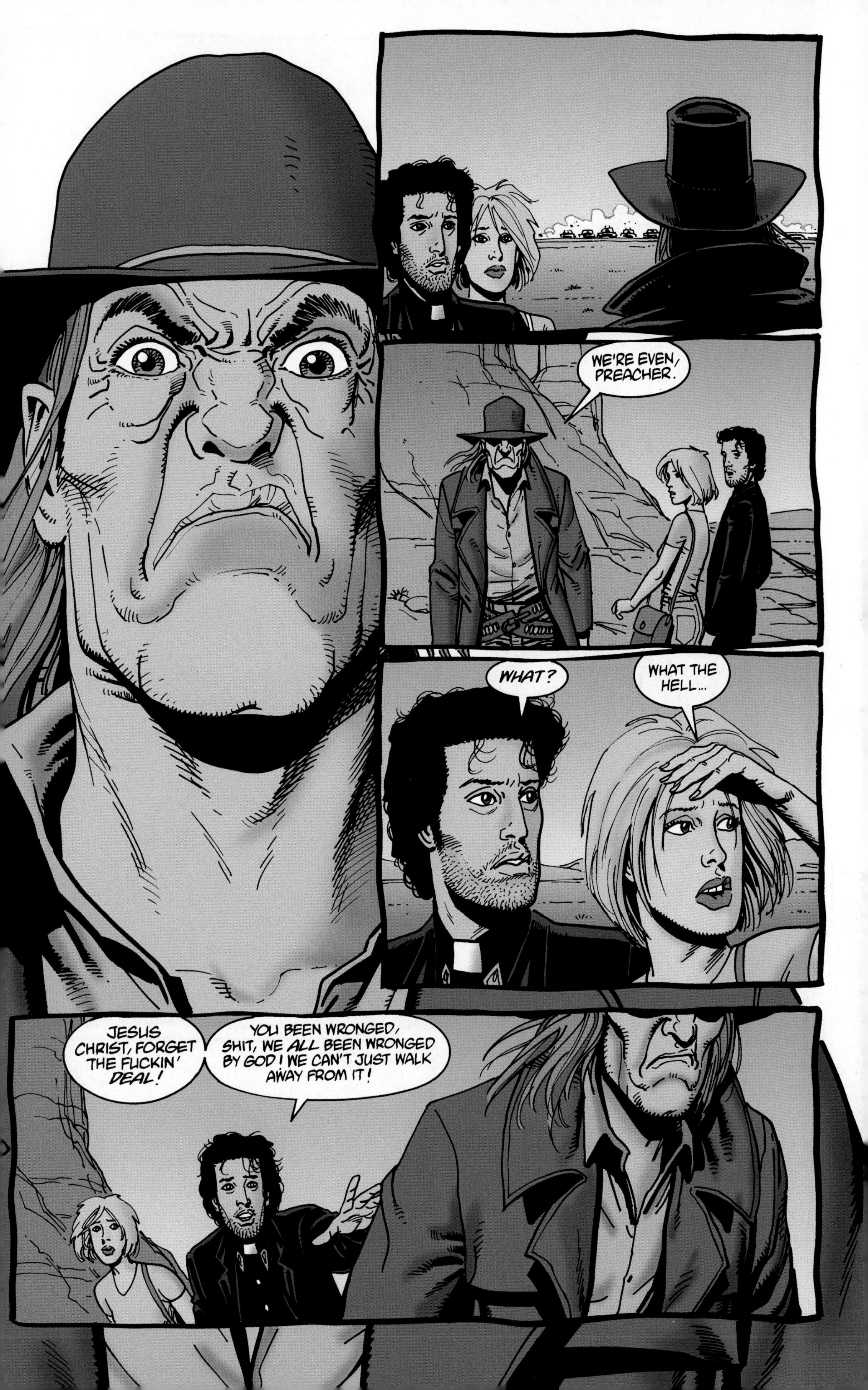
WE'RE EVEN, PREACHER.
WHAT?
WHAT THE HELL...
JESUS CHRIST, FORGET THE FUCKIN' DEAL!
YOU BEEN WRONGED, SHIT, WE ALL BEEN WRONGED BY GOD! WE CAN'T JUST WALK AWAY FROM IT!

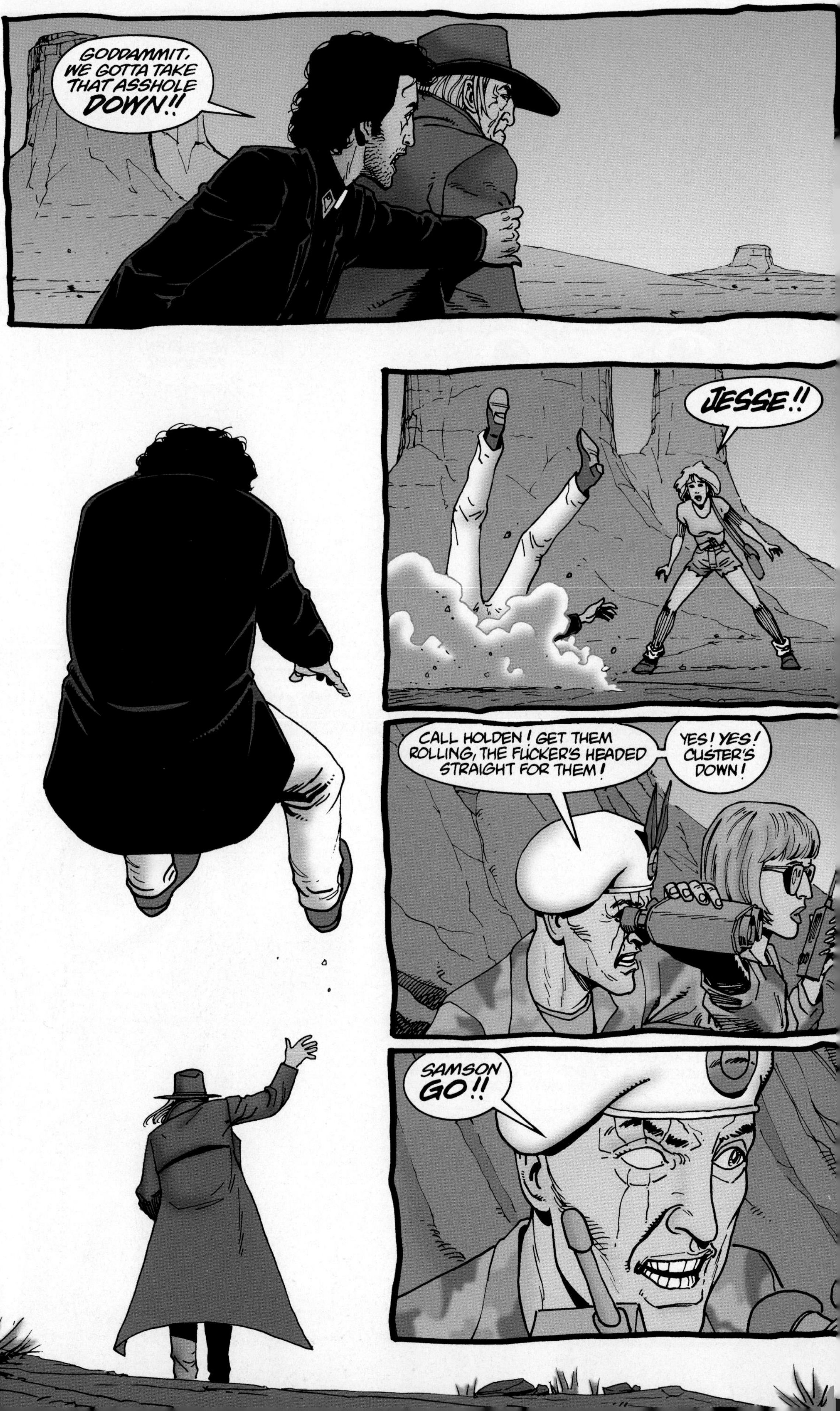
GODDAMMIT, WE GOTTA TAKE THAT ASSHOLE DOWN!!
JESSE!!
CALL HOLDEN! GET THEM ROLLING, THE FUCKER'S HEADED STRAIGHT FOR THEM!
YES! YES! CUSTER'S DOWN!
SAMSON GO!!

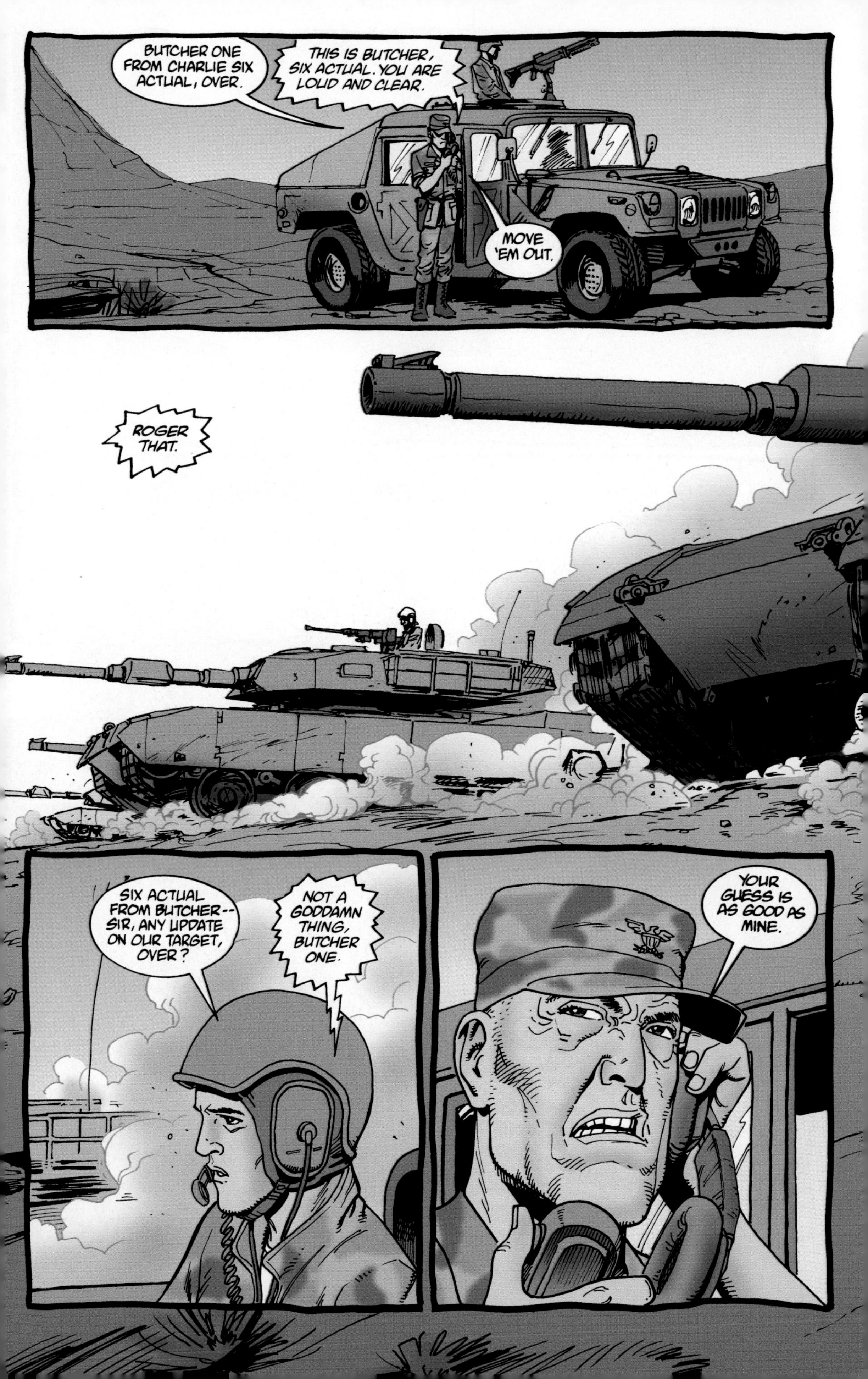
BUTCHER ONE FROM CHARLIE SIX ACTUAL, OVER.
THIS IS BUTCHER, SIX ACTUAL. YOU ARE LOUD AND CLEAR.
MOVE 'EM OUT.
ROGER THAT.
SIX ACTUAL FROM BUTCHER-- SIR, ANY UPDATE ON OUR TARGET, OVER?
NOT A GODDAMN THING, BUTCHER ONE.
YOUR GUESS IS AS GOOD AS MINE.

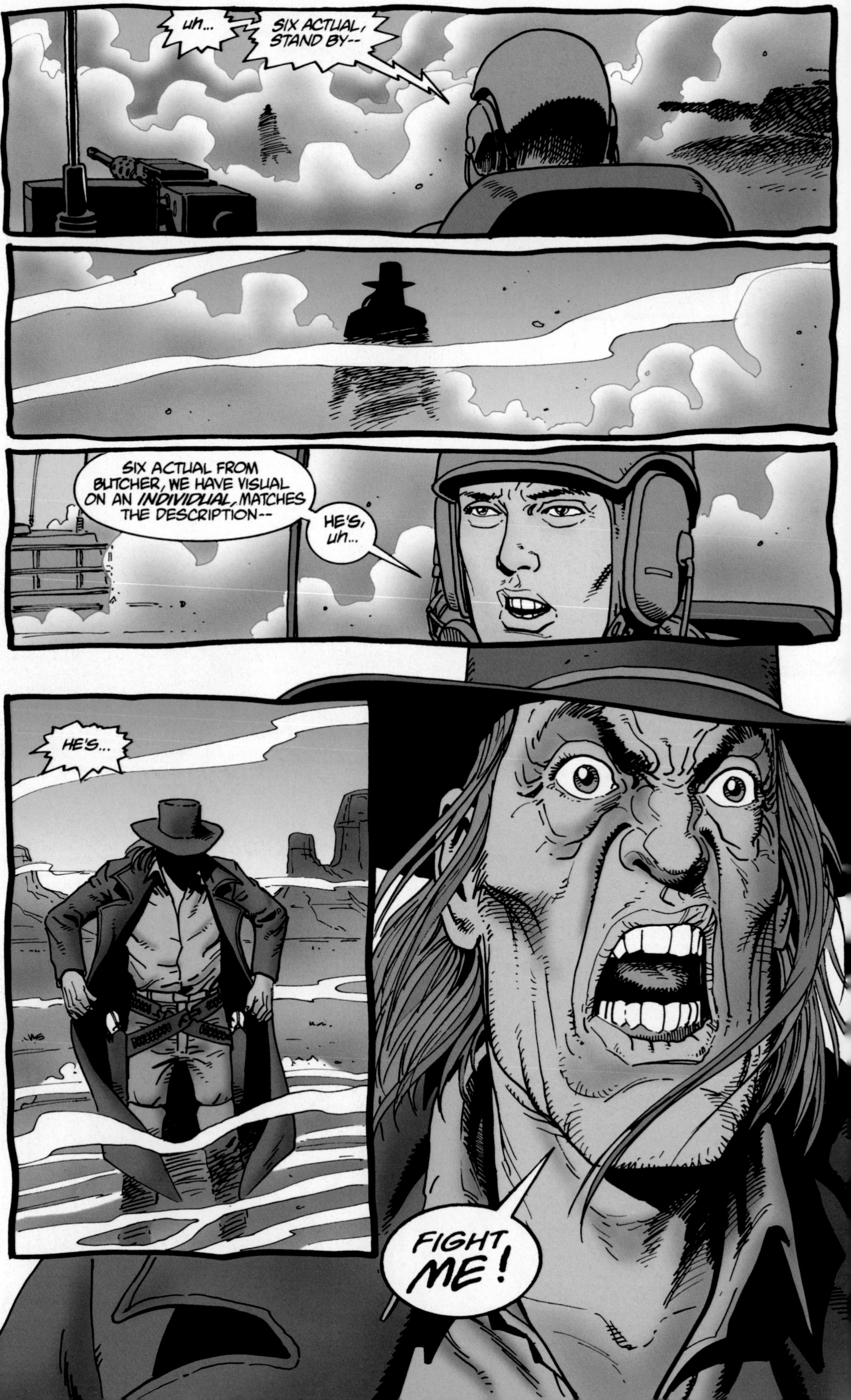
uh...
SIX ACTUAL, STAND BY--
SIX ACTUAL FROM BUTCHER, WE HAVE VISUAL ON AN *INDIVIDUAL*, MATCHES THE DESCRIPTION--
HE'S, uh...
HE'S...
FIGHT ME!

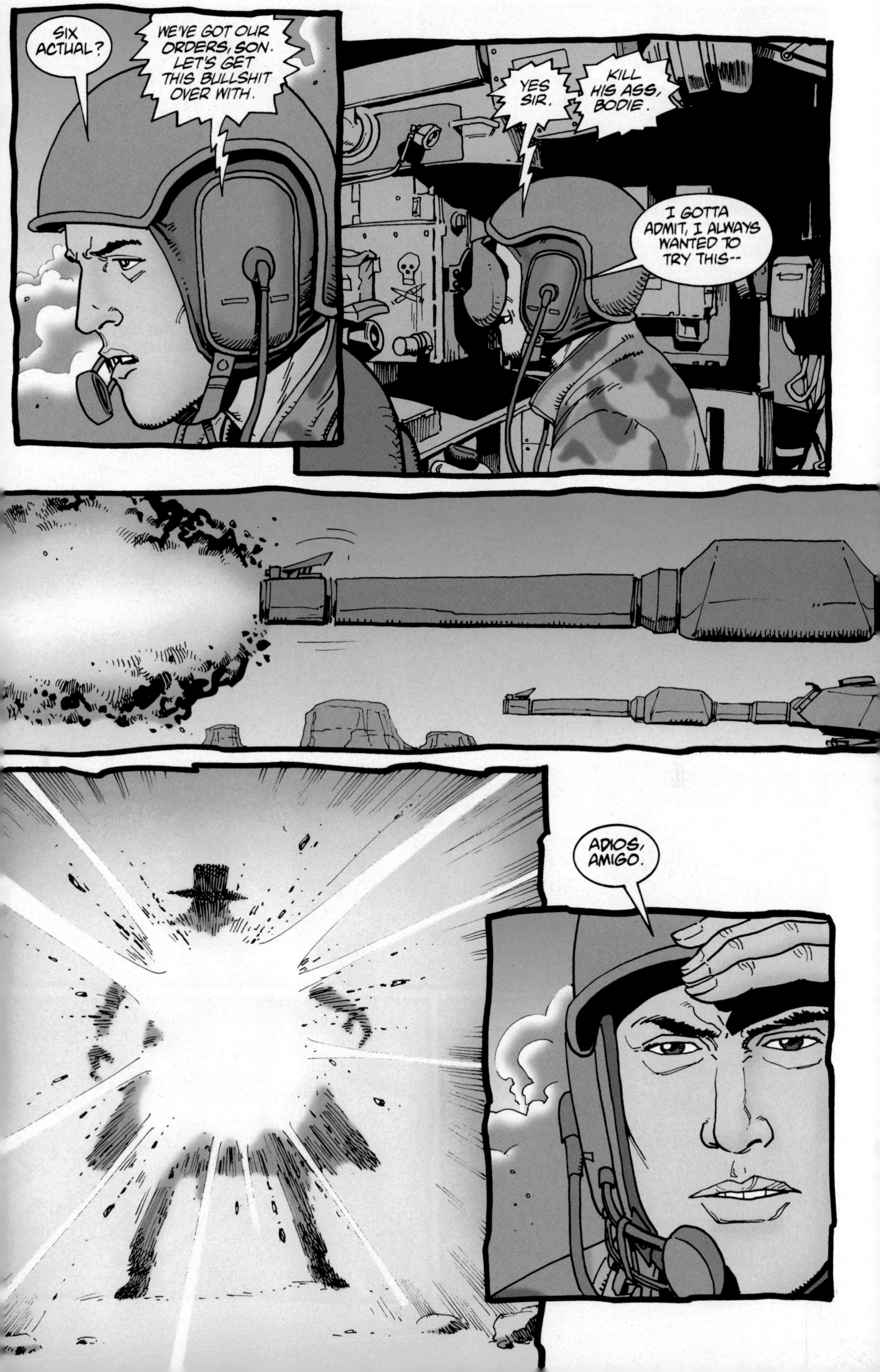
SIX ACTUAL?
WE'VE GOT OUR ORDERS, SON. LET'S GET THIS BULLSHIT OVER WITH.
YES SIR.
KILL HIS ASS, BODIE.
I GOTTA ADMIT, I ALWAYS WANTED TO TRY THIS--
ADIOS, AMIGO.

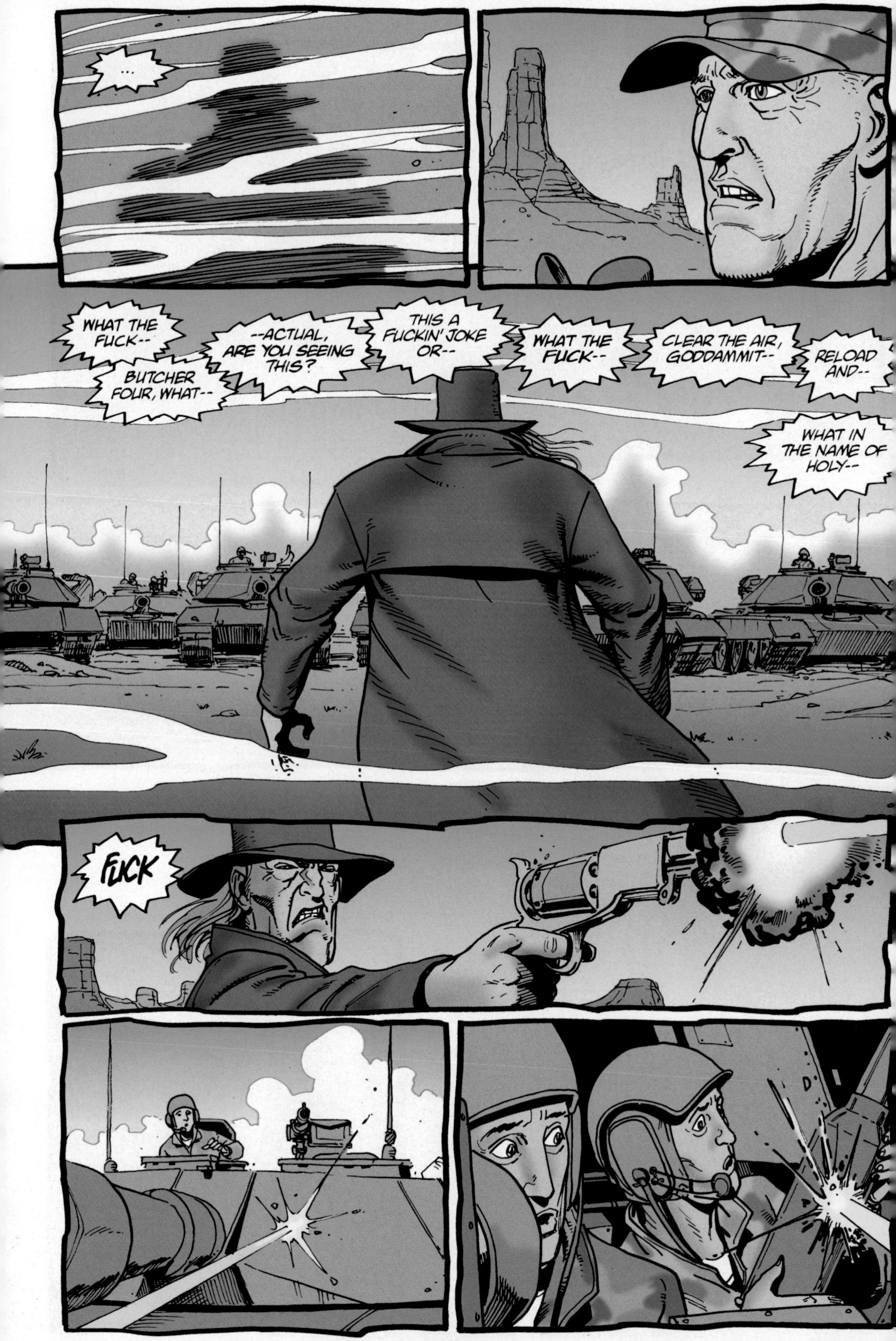
...
WHAT THE FUCK--
BUTCHER FOUR, WHAT--
--ACTUAL, ARE YOU SEEING THIS?
THIS A FUCKIN' JOKE OR--
WHAT THE FUCK--
CLEAR THE AIR, GODDAMMIT--
RELOAD AND--
WHAT IN THE NAME OF HOLY--
FUCK

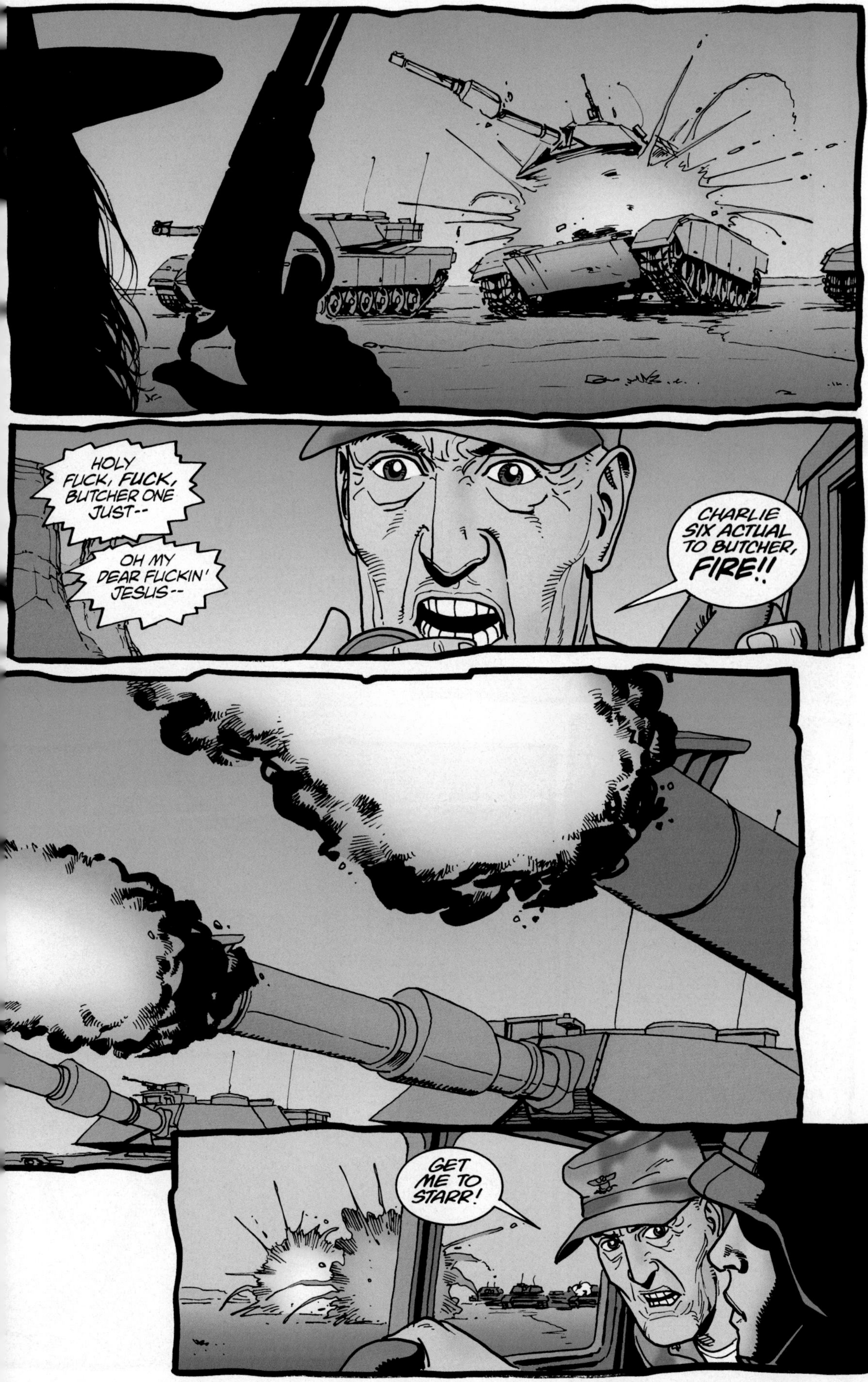
HOLY FUCK, FUCK, BUTCHER ONE JUST--
OH MY DEAR FUCKIN' JESUS--
CHARLIE SIX ACTUAL TO BUTCHER, FIRE!!
GET ME TO STARR!

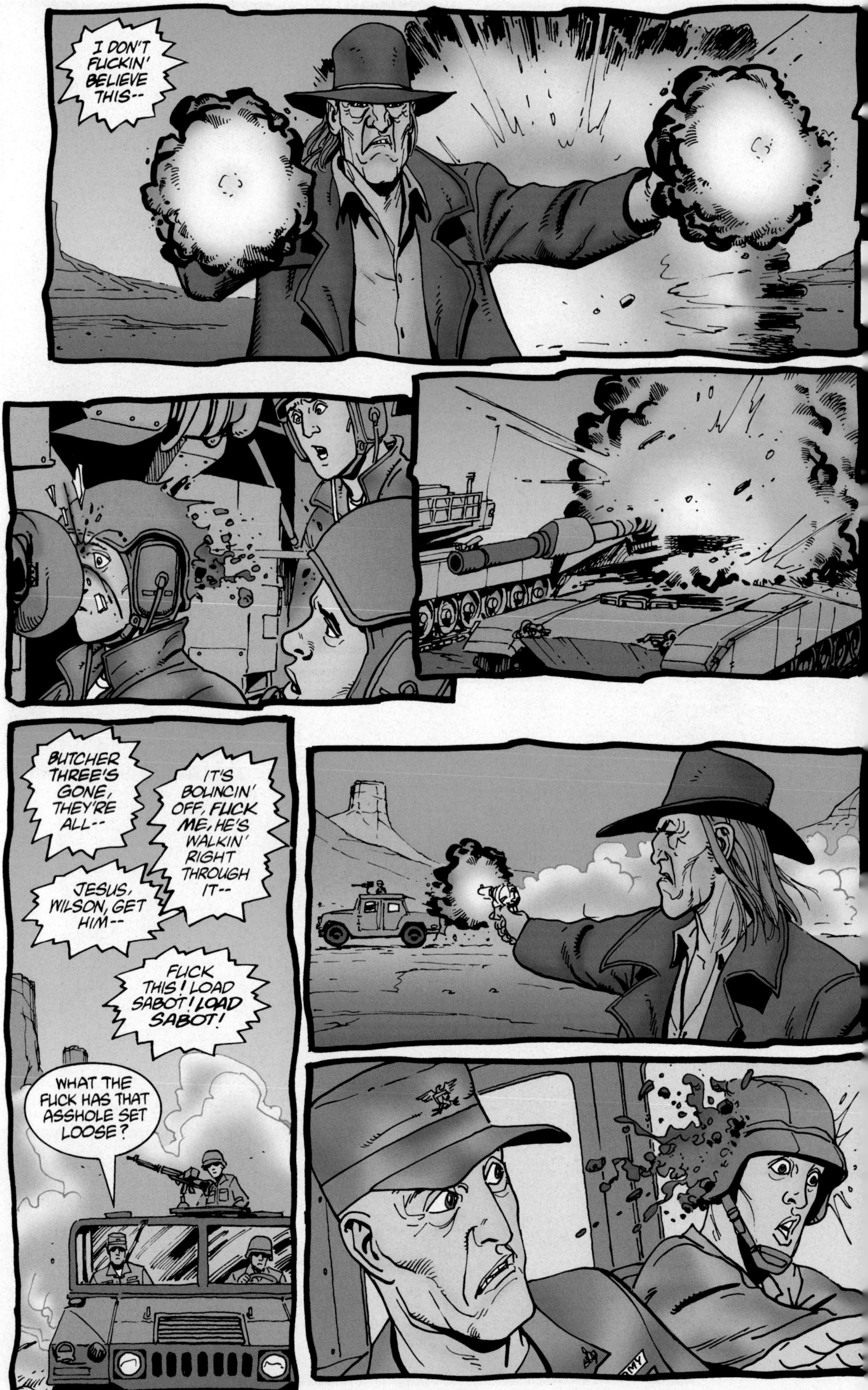
I DON'T FUCKIN' BELIEVE THIS--
BUTCHER THREE'S GONE, THEY'RE ALL--
IT'S BOUNCIN' OFF, FUCK ME, HE'S WALKIN' RIGHT THROUGH IT--
JESUS, WILSON, GET HIM--
FUCK THIS! LOAD SABOT! LOAD SABOT!
WHAT THE FUCK HAS THAT ASSHOLE SET LOOSE?

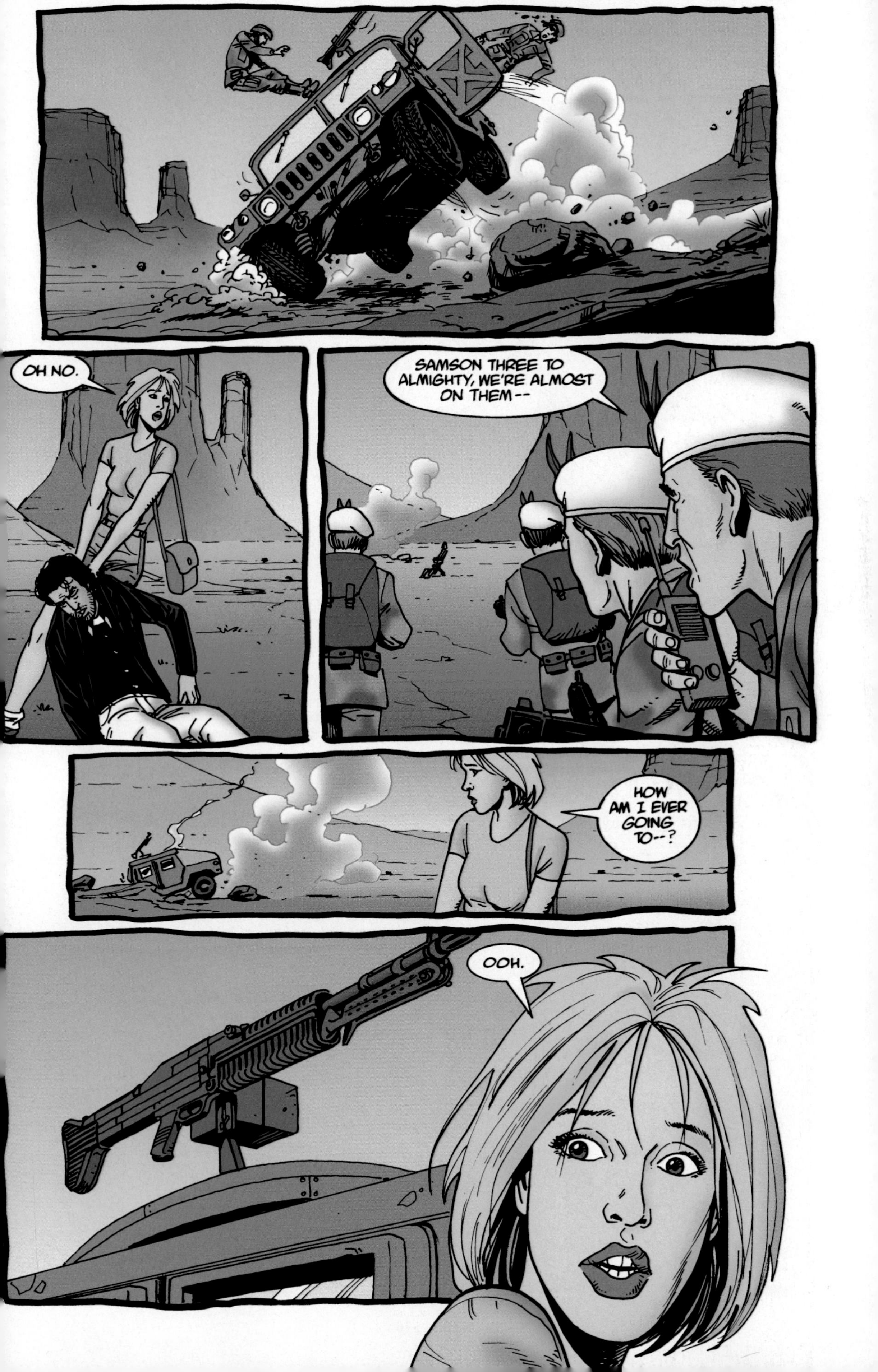
OH NO.
SAMSON THREE TO ALMIGHTY, WE'RE ALMOST ON THEM--
HOW AM I EVER GOING TO--?
OOH.

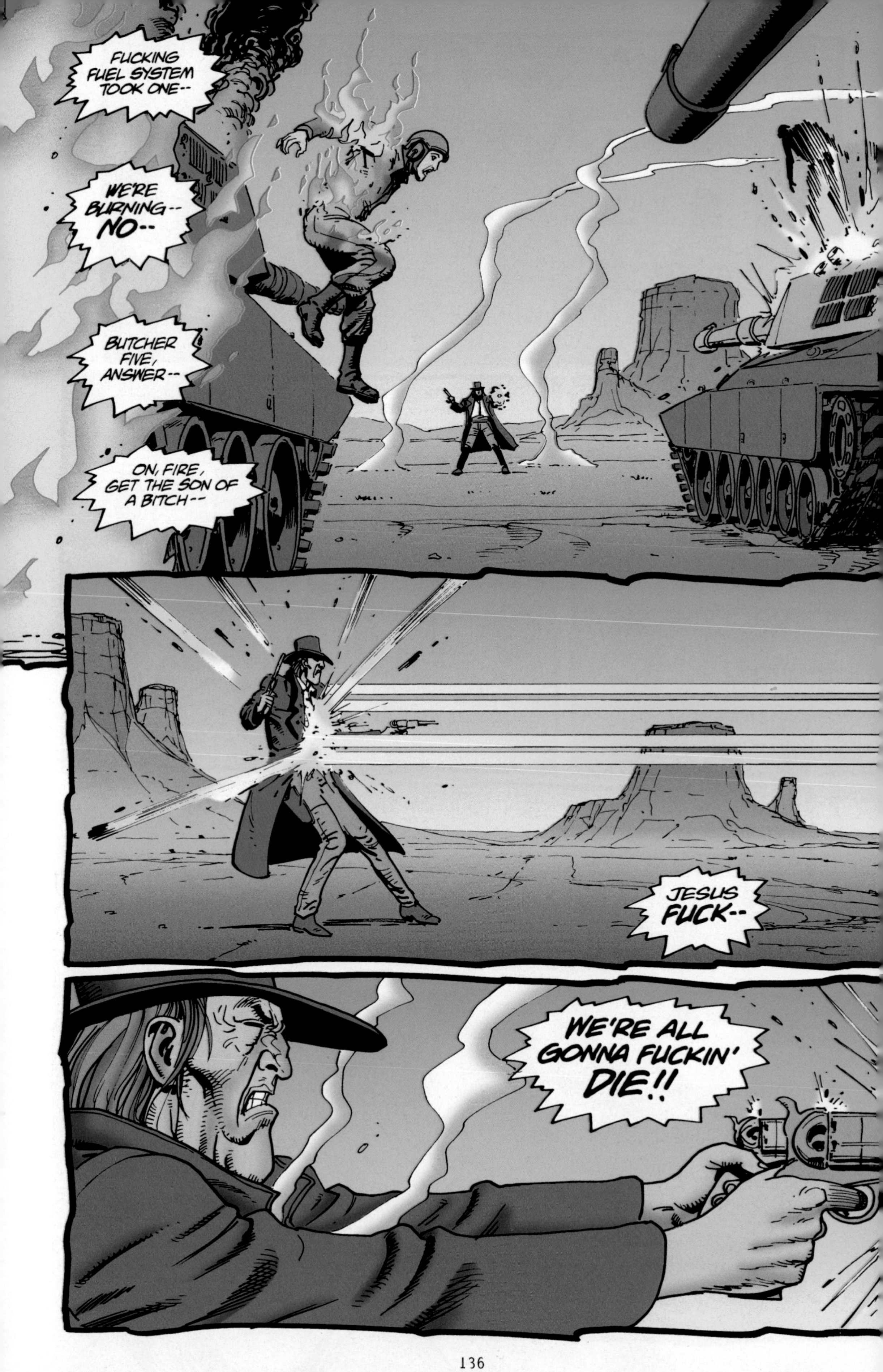
FUCKING FUEL SYSTEM TOOK ONE--
WE'RE BURNING-- NO--
BUTCHER FIVE, ANSWER--
ON, FIRE, GET THE SON OF A BITCH--
JESUS FUCK--
WE'RE ALL GONNA FUCKIN' DIE!!

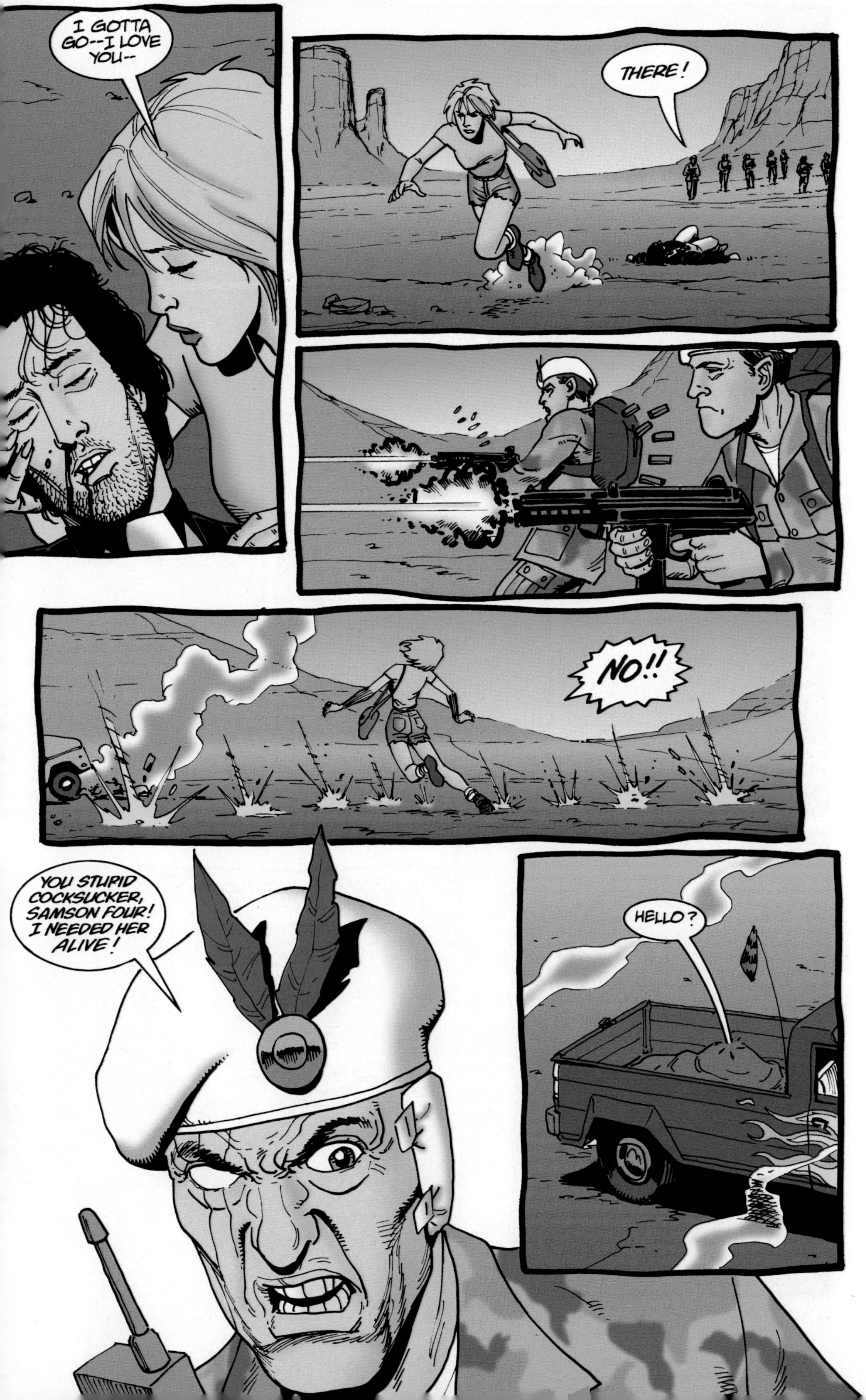
I GOTTA GO--I LOVE YOU--
THERE!
NO!!
YOU STUPID COCKSUCKER, SAMSON FOUR! I NEEDED HER ALIVE!
HELLO?

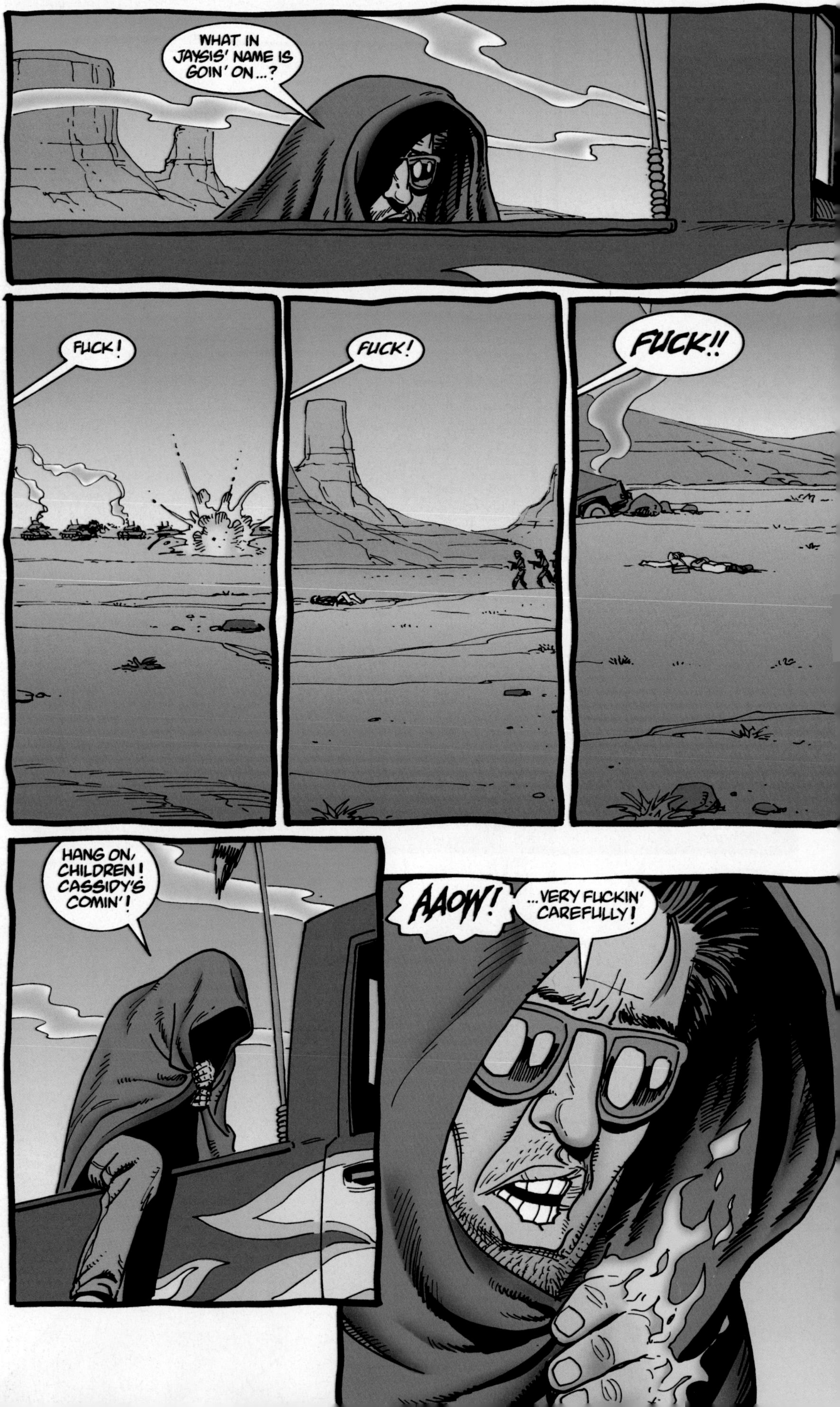
WHAT IN JAYSIS' NAME IS GOIN' ON...?
FUCK!
FUCK!
FUCK!!
HANG ON, CHILDREN! CASSIDY'S COMIN'!
AAOW!
...VERY FUCKIN' CAREFULLY!

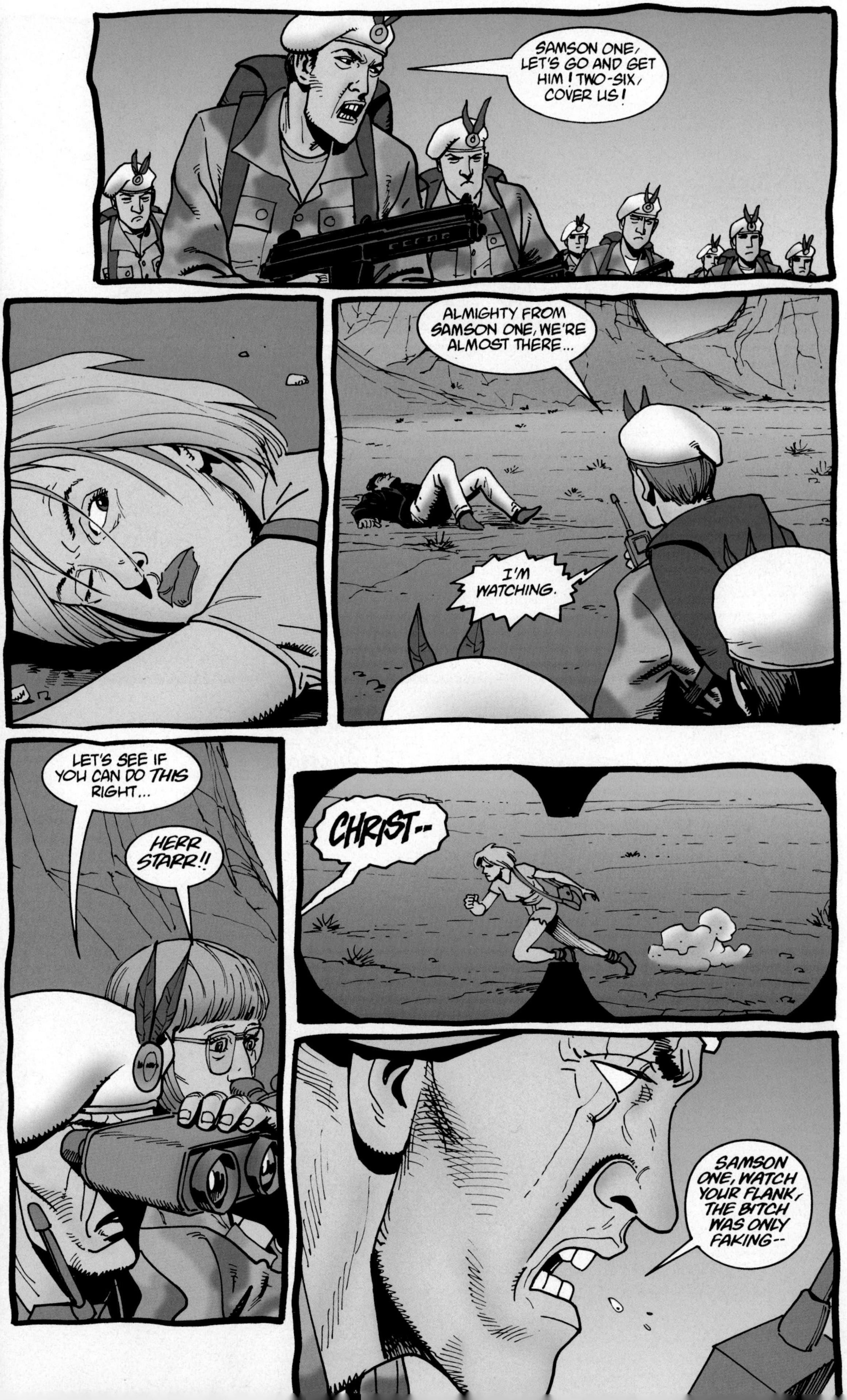
SAMSON ONE, LET'S GO AND GET HIM! TWO-SIX, COVER US!
ALMIGHTY FROM SAMSON ONE, WE'RE ALMOST THERE...
I'M WATCHING.
LET'S SEE IF YOU CAN DO THIS RIGHT...
HERR STARR!!
CHRIST--
SAMSON ONE, WATCH YOUR FLANK, THE BITCH WAS ONLY FAKING--

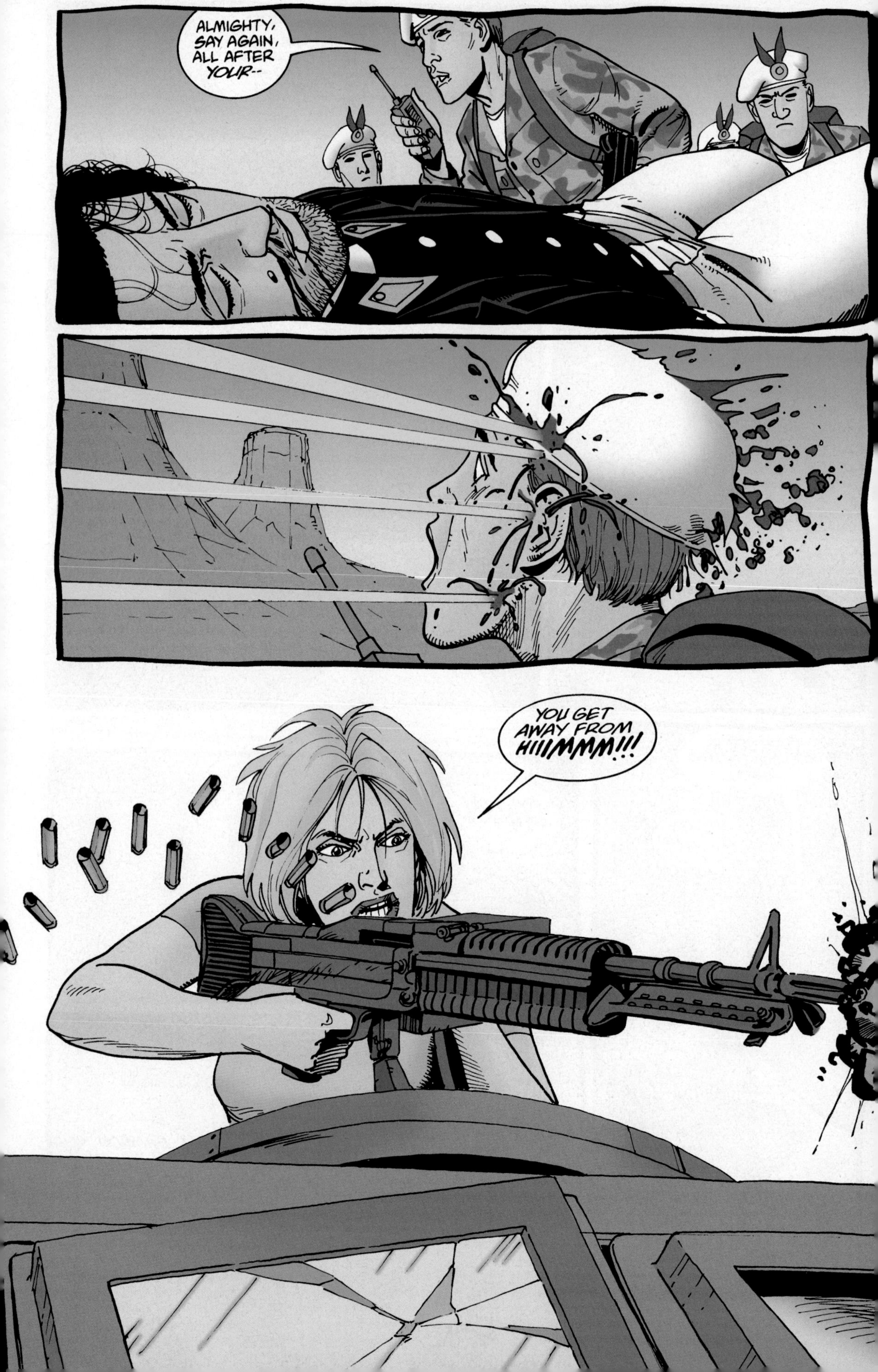
ALMIGHTY, SAY AGAIN, ALL AFTER YOUR--
YOU GET AWAY FROM HIIIMMM!!!

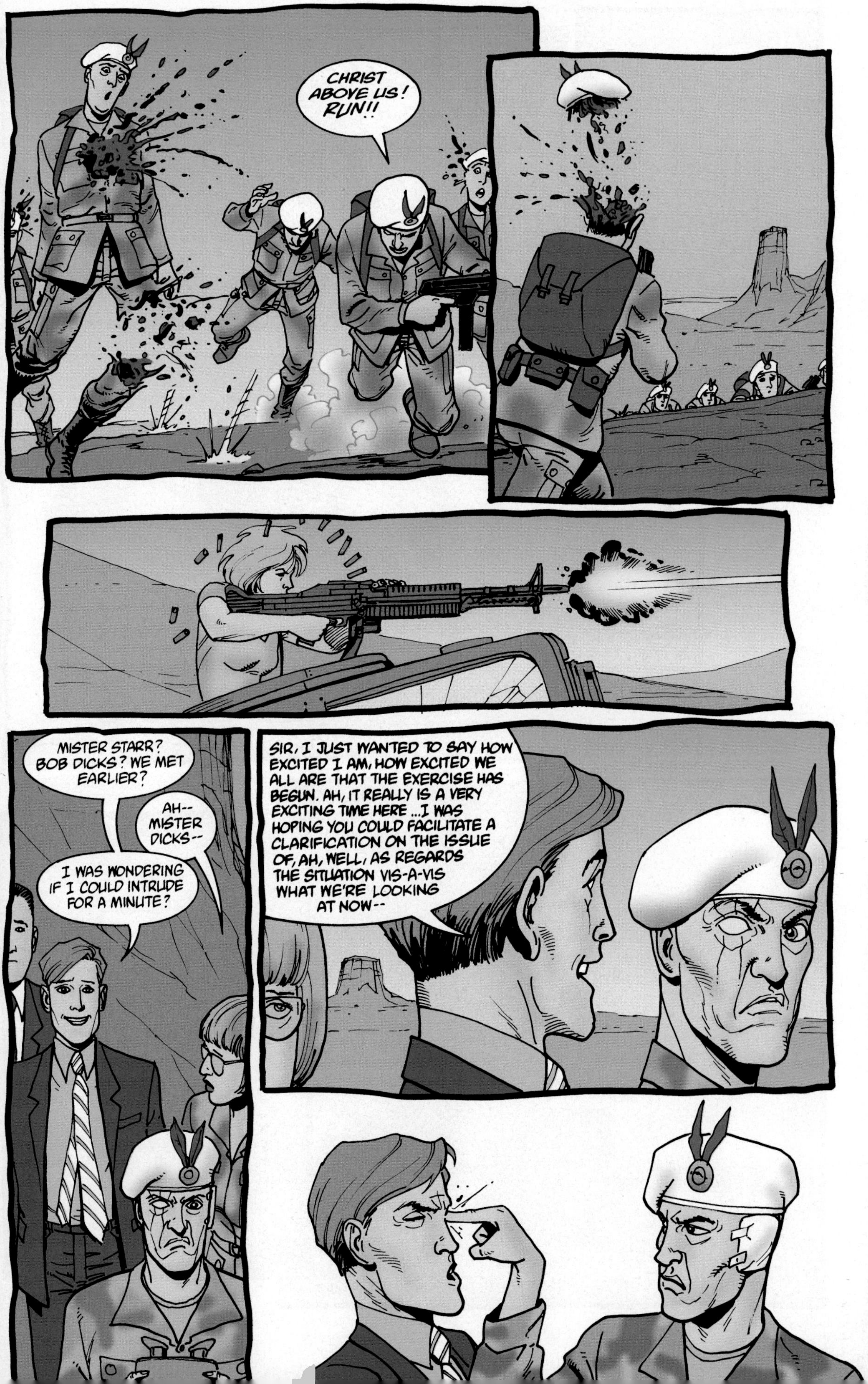
CHRIST ABOVE US! RUN!!
MISTER STARR? BOB DICKS? WE MET EARLIER?
AH-- MISTER DICKS--
I WAS WONDERING IF I COULD INTRUDE FOR A MINUTE?
SIR, I JUST WANTED TO SAY HOW EXCITED I AM, HOW EXCITED WE ALL ARE THAT THE EXERCISE HAS BEGUN. AH, IT REALLY IS A VERY EXCITING TIME HERE ...I WAS HOPING YOU COULD FACILITATE A CLARIFICATION ON THE ISSUE OF, AH, WELL, AS REGARDS THE SITUATION VIS-A-VIS WHAT WE'RE LOOKING AT NOW--

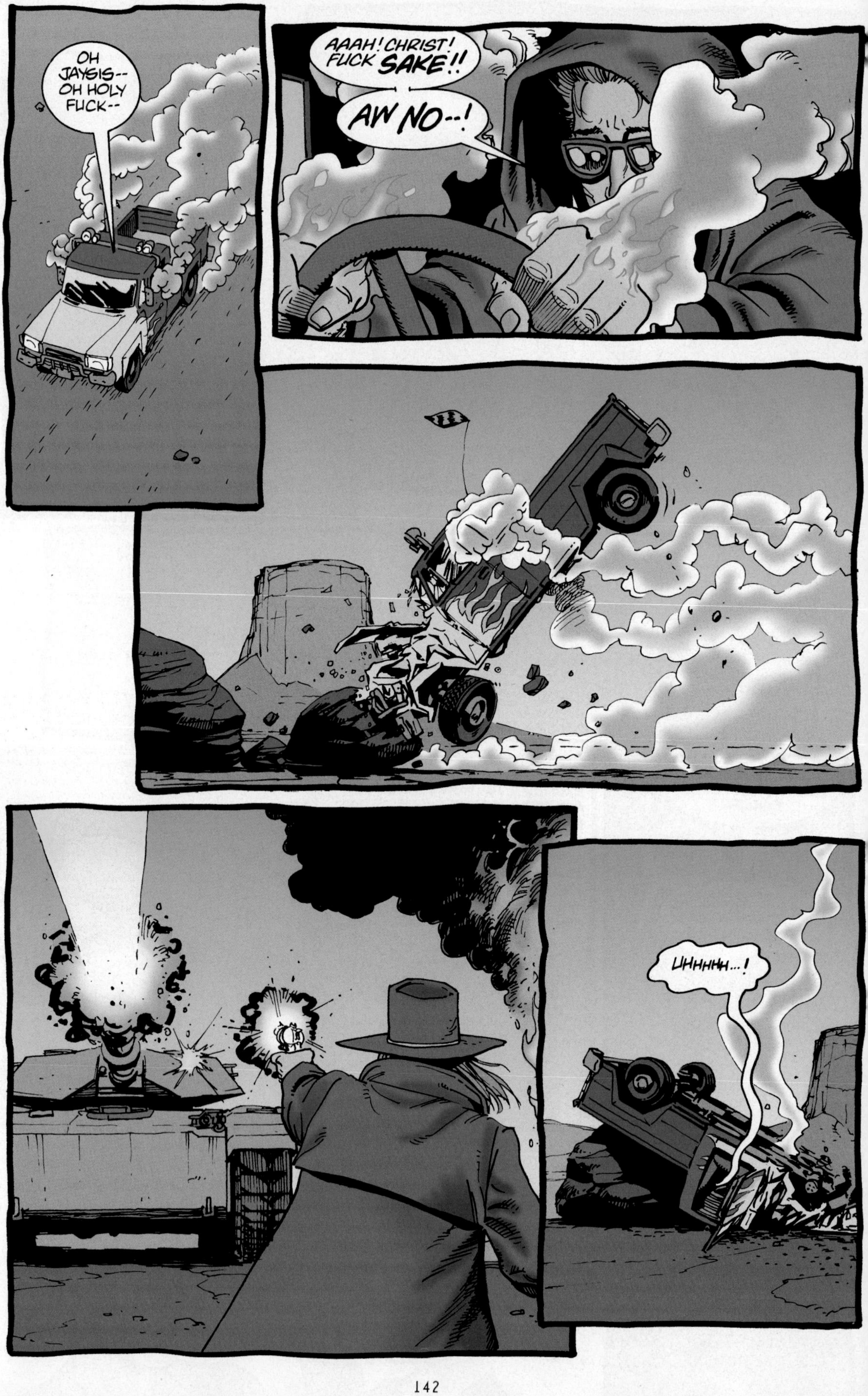
OH JAYSIS-- OH HOLY FUCK--
AAAH! CHRIST! FUCK SAKE!!
AW NO--!
UHHHHH...!

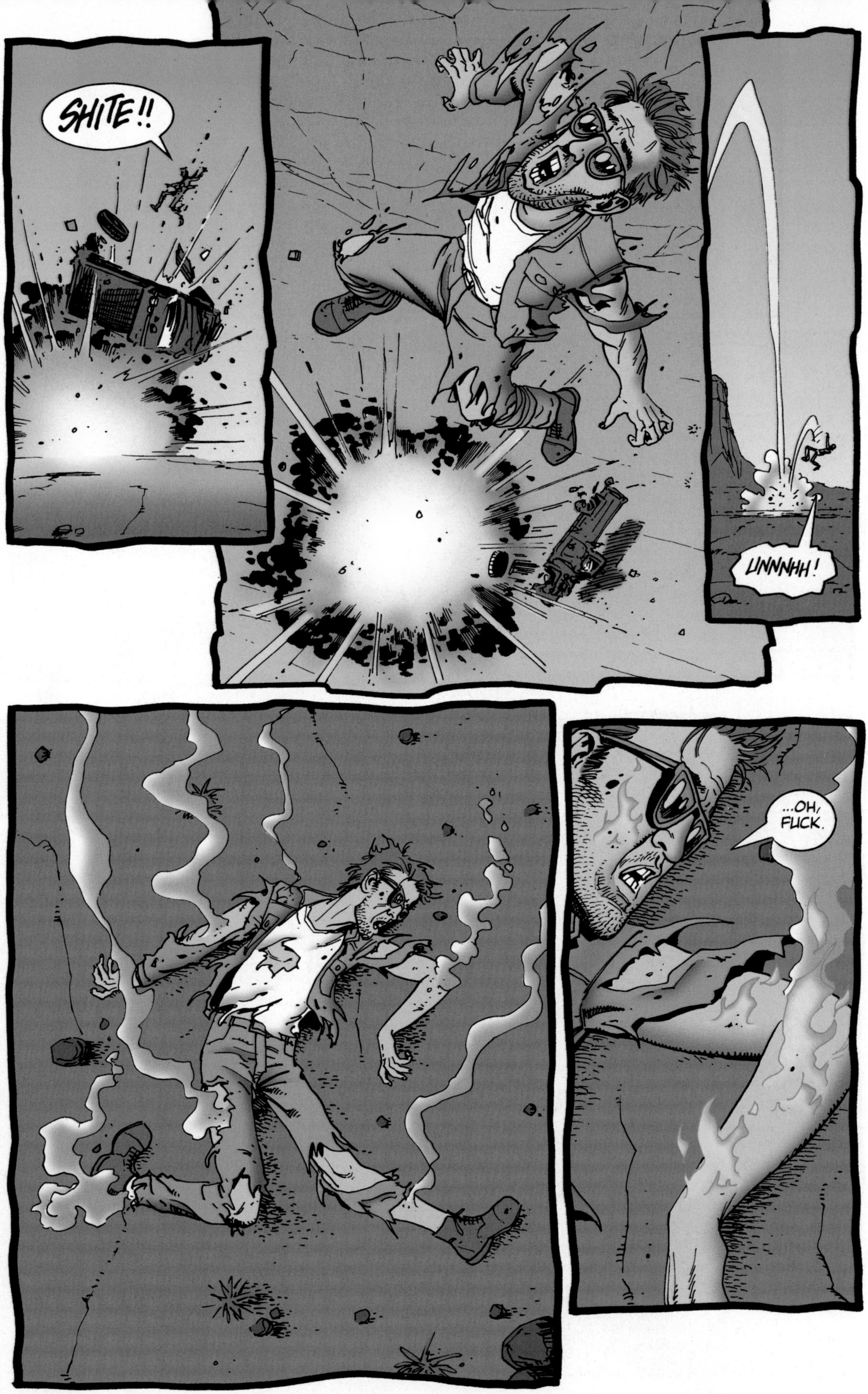
SHITE!!
UNNNHH!
...OH, FUCK.

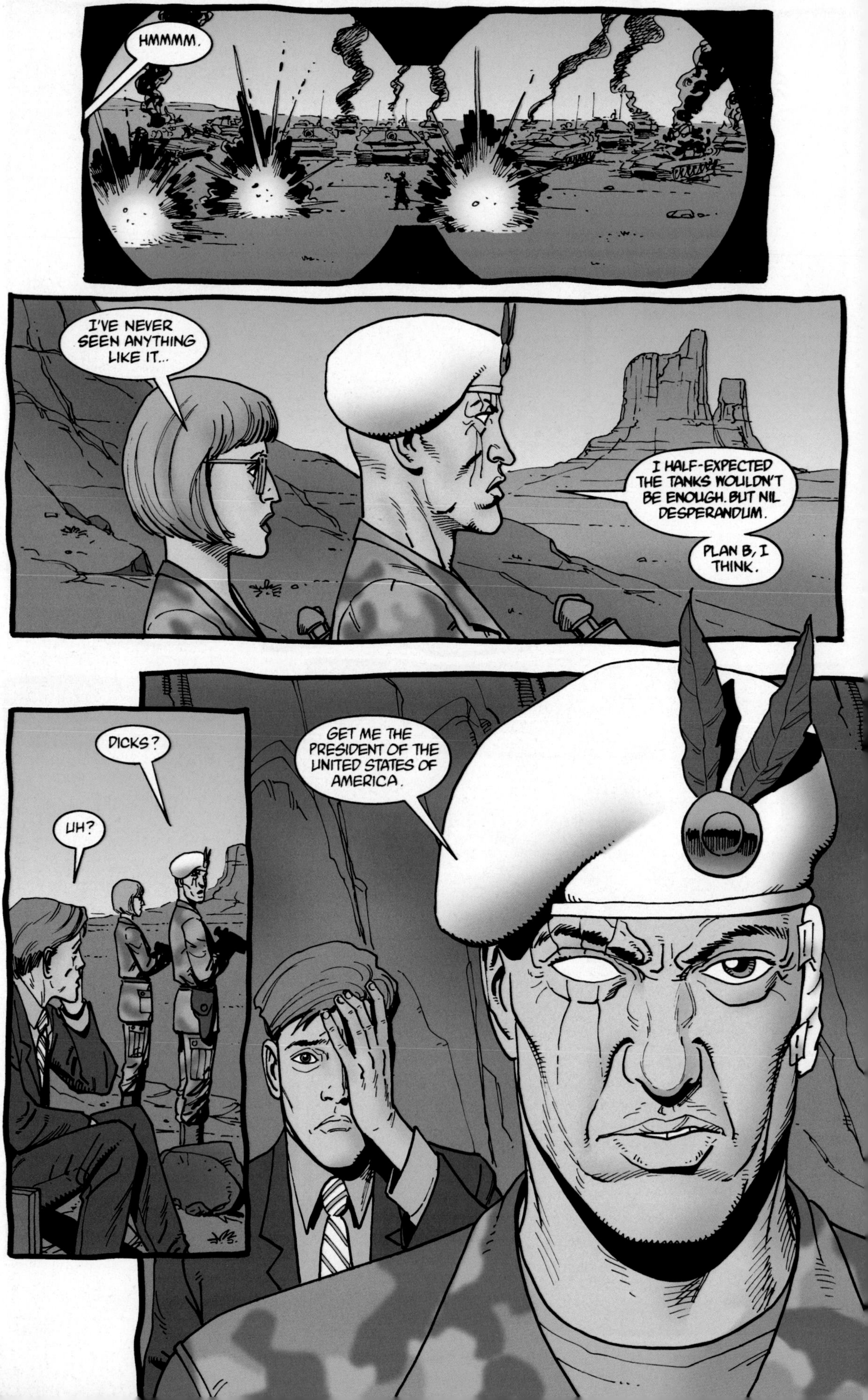
HMMMM.
I'VE NEVER SEEN ANYTHING LIKE IT...
I HALF-EXPECTED THE TANKS WOULDN'T BE ENOUGH. BUT NIL DESPERANDUM.
PLAN B, I THINK.
DICKS?
UH?
GET ME THE PRESIDENT OF THE UNITED STATES OF AMERICA.

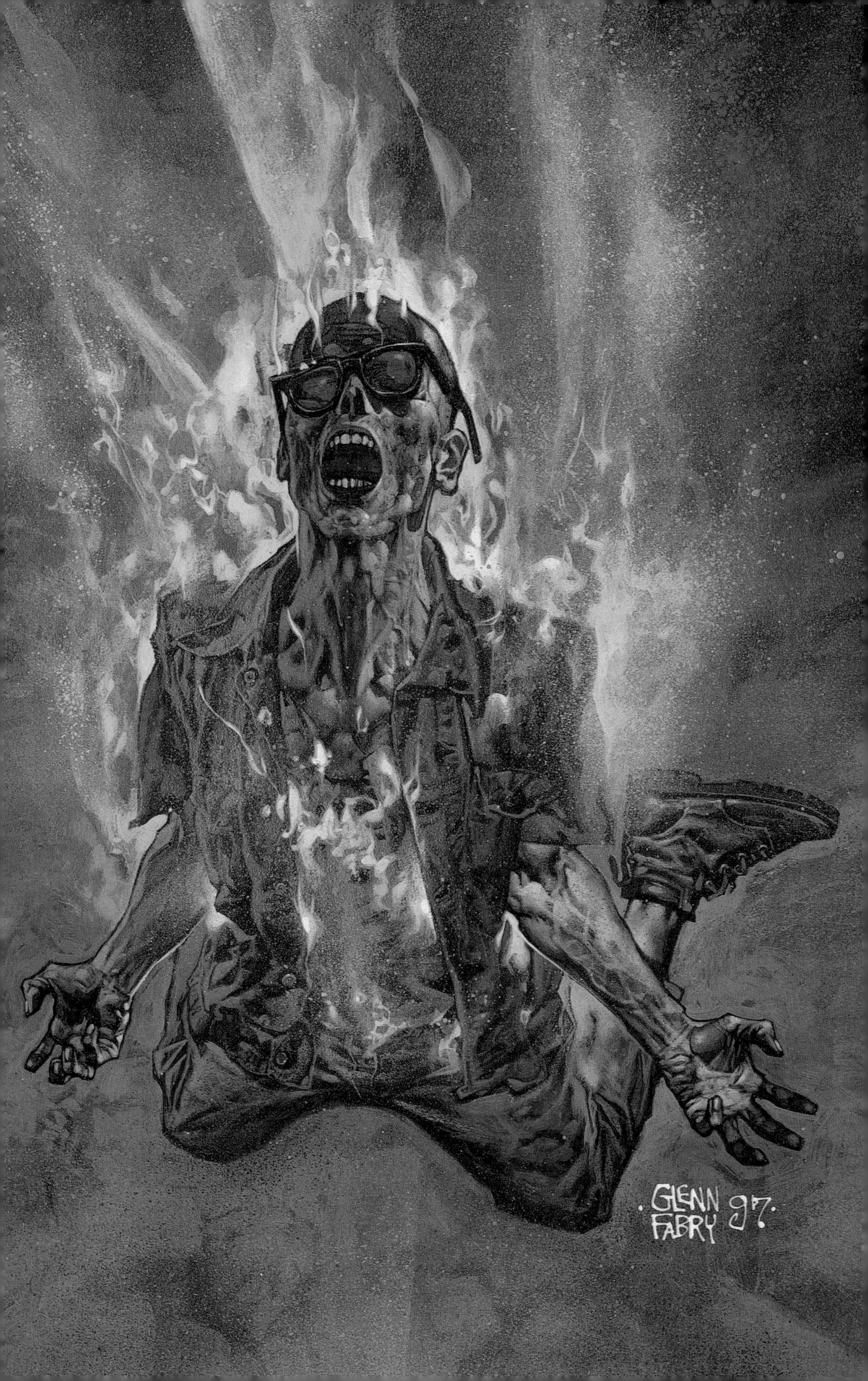
GLENN FABRY 97.

"You goddamned idiot, we don't both have to die!"

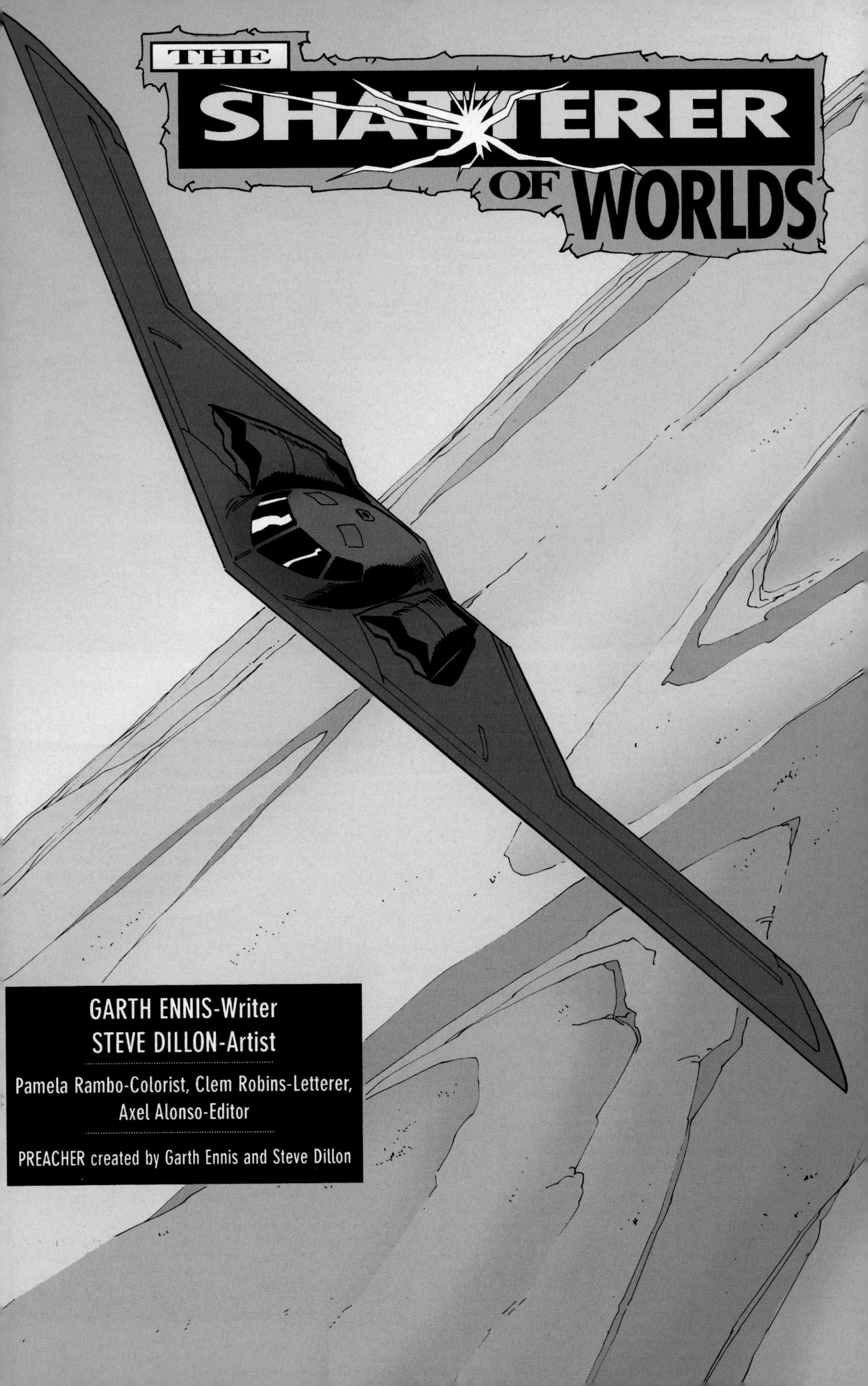
THE SHATTERER OF WORLDS
GARTH ENNIS-Writer
STEVE DILLON-Artist
Pamela Rambo-Colorist, Clem Robins-Letterer, Axel Alonso-Editor
PREACHER created by Garth Ennis and Steve Dillon

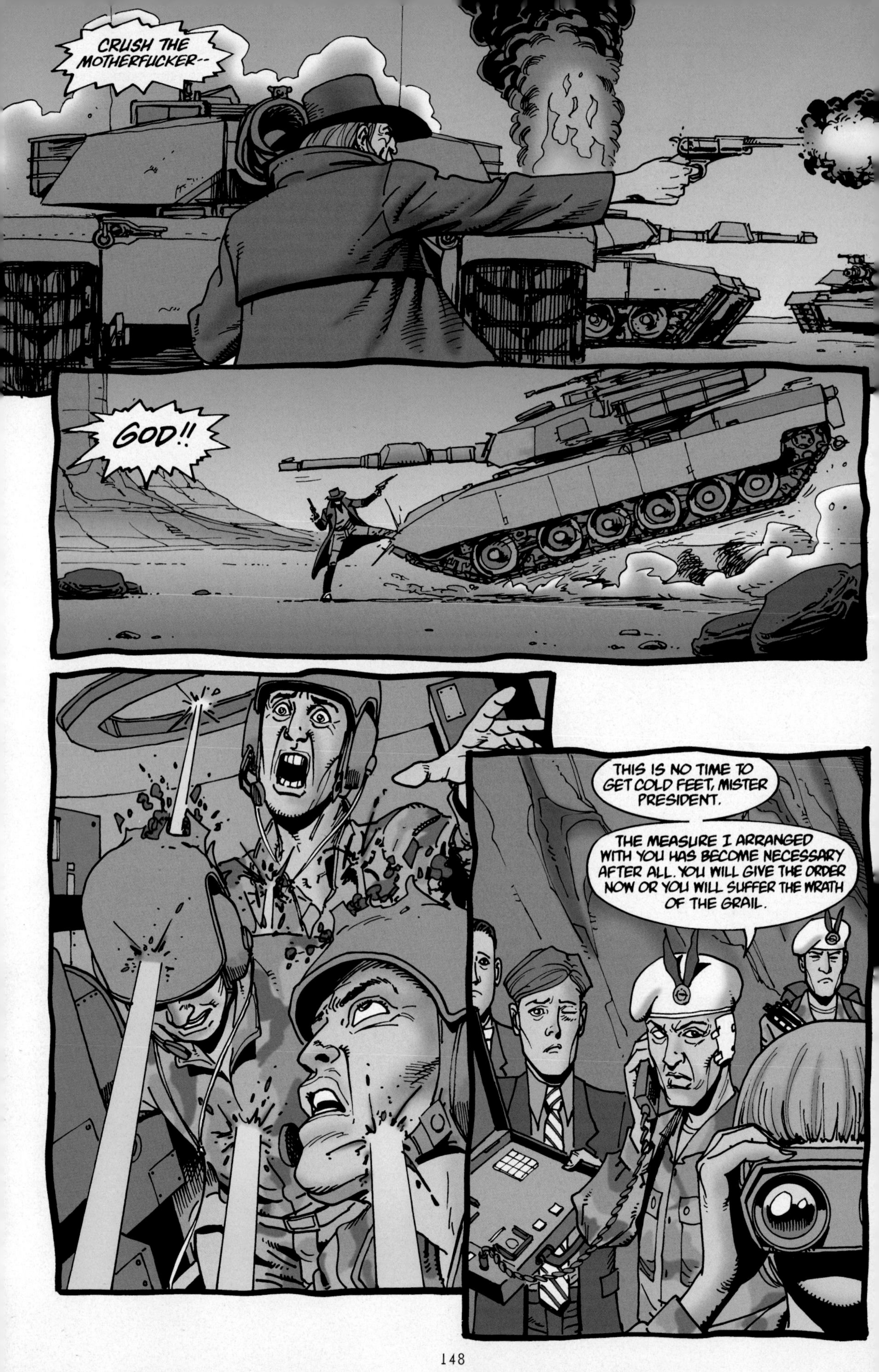
CRUSH THE MOTHERFUCKER--
GOD!!
THIS IS NO TIME TO GET COLD FEET, MISTER PRESIDENT.
THE MEASURE I ARRANGED WITH YOU HAS BECOME NECESSARY AFTER ALL. YOU WILL GIVE THE ORDER NOW OR YOU WILL SUFFER THE WRATH OF THE GRAIL.

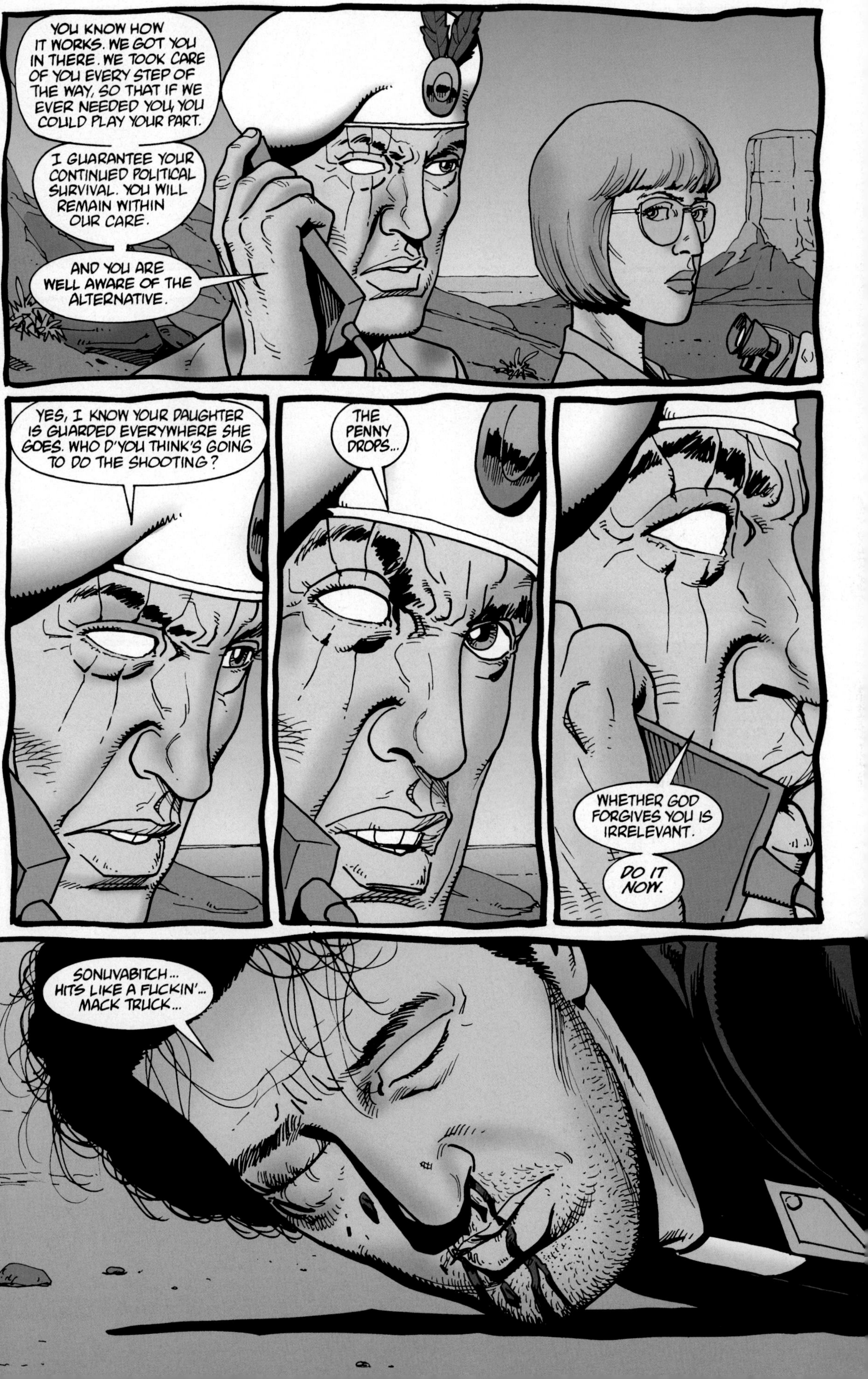
YOU KNOW HOW IT WORKS. WE GOT YOU IN THERE. WE TOOK CARE OF YOU EVERY STEP OF THE WAY, SO THAT IF WE EVER NEEDED YOU, YOU COULD PLAY YOUR PART.
I GUARANTEE YOUR CONTINUED POLITICAL SURVIVAL. YOU WILL REMAIN WITHIN OUR CARE.
AND YOU ARE WELL AWARE OF THE ALTERNATIVE.
YES, I KNOW YOUR DAUGHTER IS GUARDED EVERYWHERE SHE GOES. WHO D'YOU THINK'S GOING TO DO THE SHOOTING?
THE PENNY DROPS...
WHETHER GOD FORGIVES YOU IS IRRELEVANT.
DO IT NOW.
SONUVABITCH... HITS LIKE A FUCKIN'... MACK TRUCK...

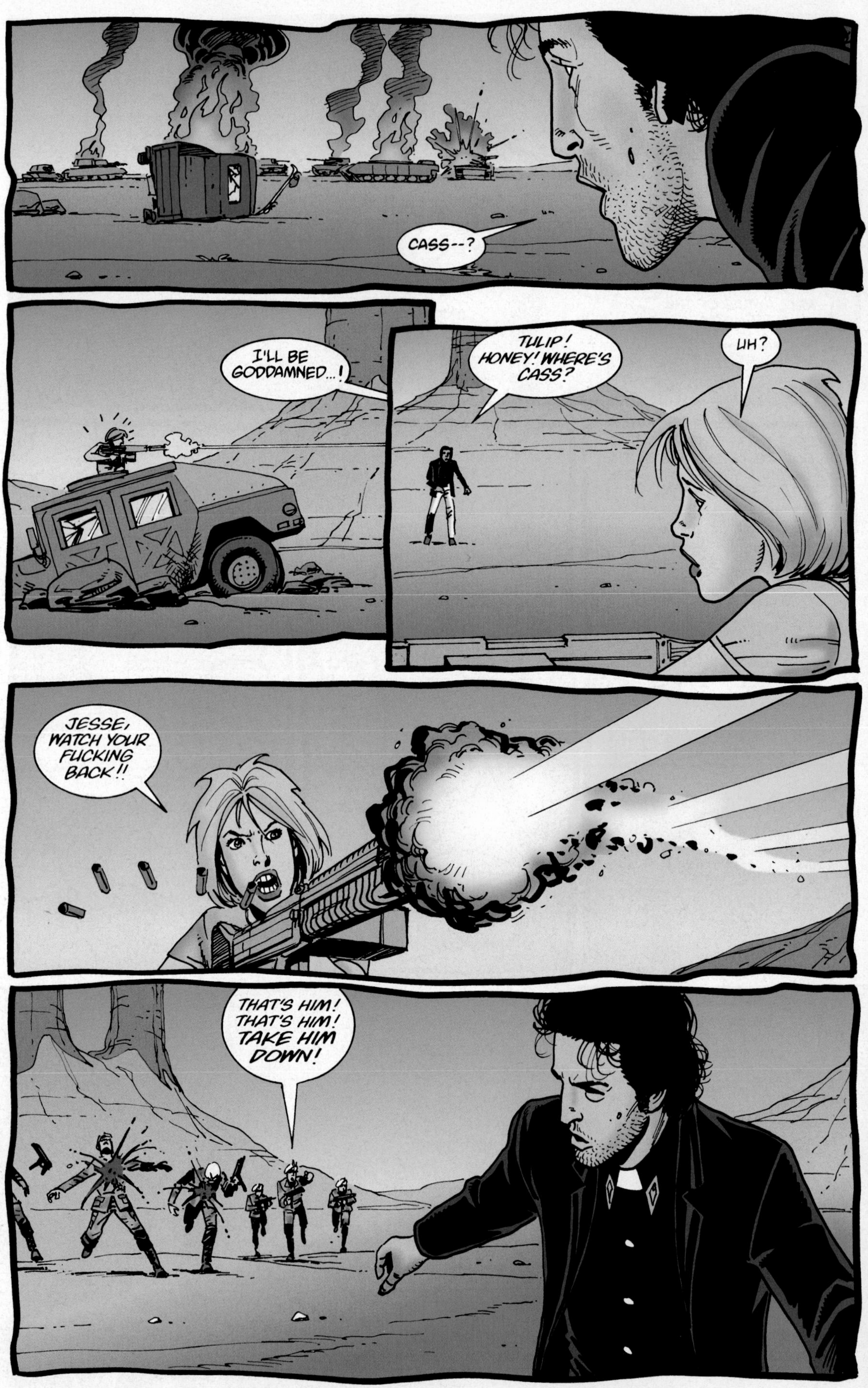
CASS--?
I'LL BE GODDAMNED...!
TULIP! HONEY! WHERE'S CASS?
UH?
JESSE, WATCH YOUR FUCKING BACK!!
THAT'S HIM! THAT'S HIM! TAKE HIM DOWN!

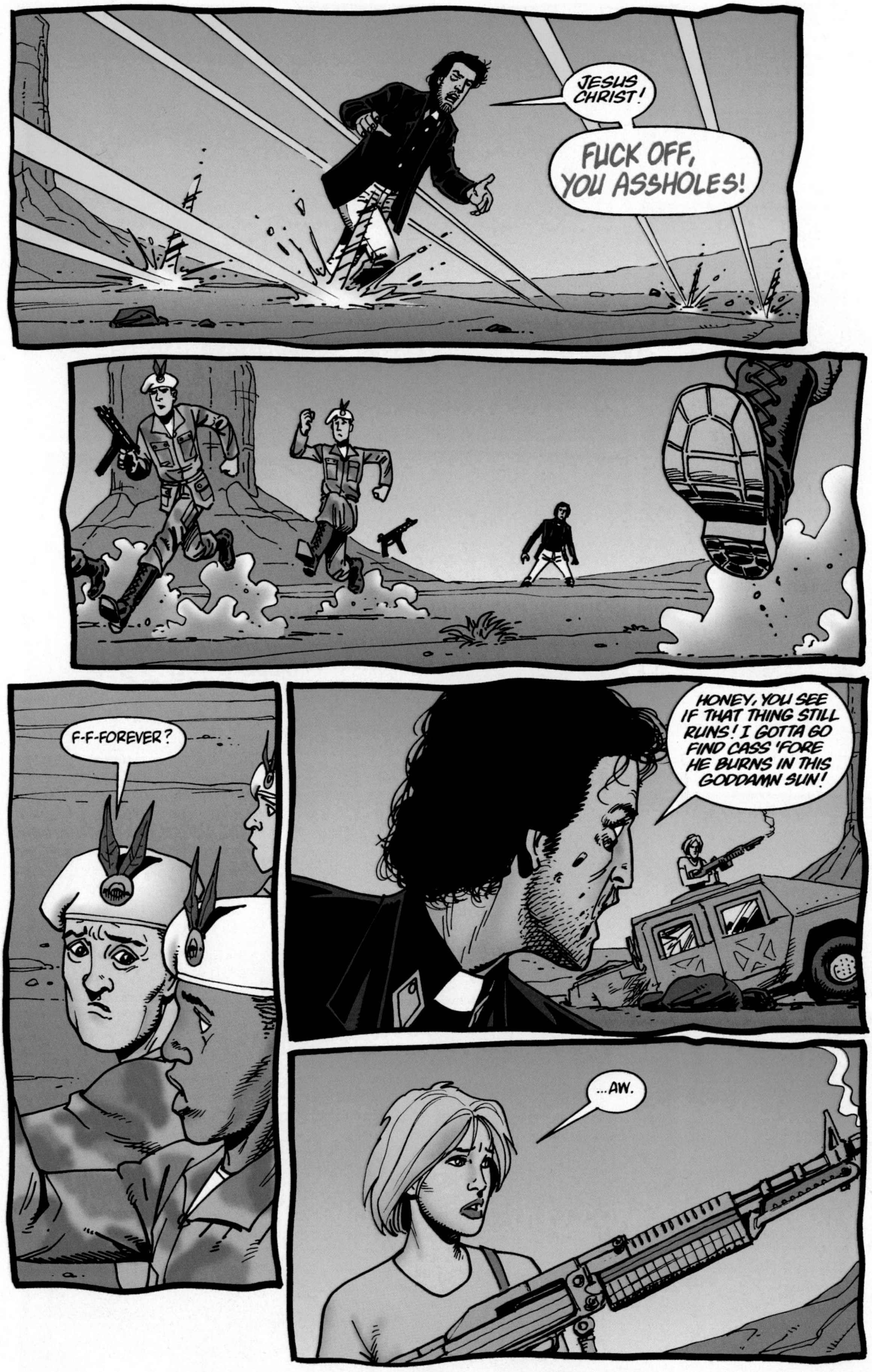
JESUS CHRIST!
FUCK OFF, YOU ASSHOLES!
F-F-FOREVER?
HONEY, YOU SEE IF THAT THING STILL RUNS! I GOTTA GO FIND CASS 'FORE HE BURNS IN THIS GODDAMN SUN!
...AW.

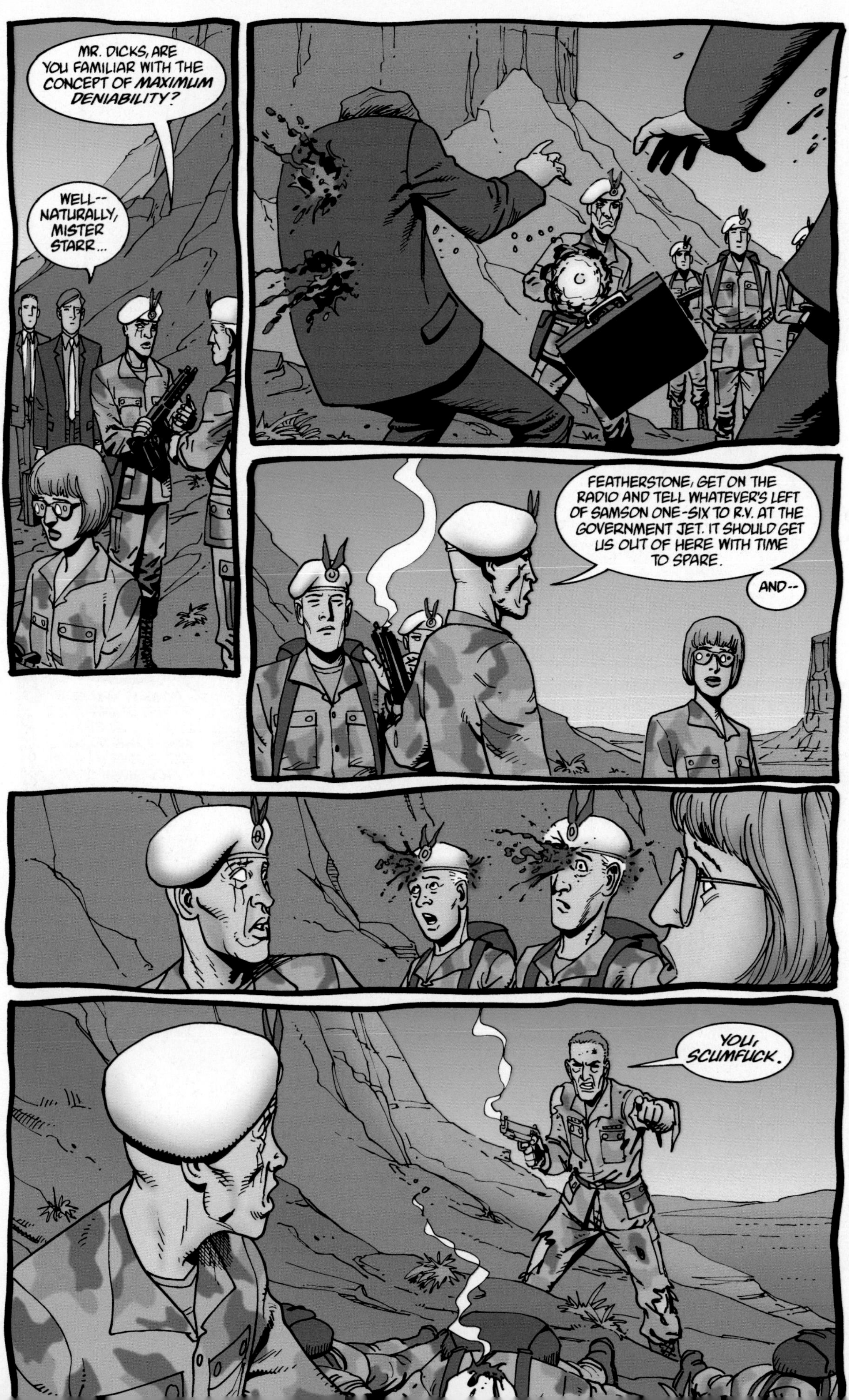
MR. DICKS, ARE YOU FAMILIAR WITH THE CONCEPT OF *MAXIMUM DENIABILITY?*
WELL-- NATURALLY, MISTER STARR...
FEATHERSTONE, GET ON THE RADIO AND TELL WHATEVER'S LEFT OF SAMSON ONE-SIX TO R.V. AT THE GOVERNMENT JET. IT SHOULD GET US OUT OF HERE WITH TIME TO SPARE.
AND--
YOU, SCUMFUCK.

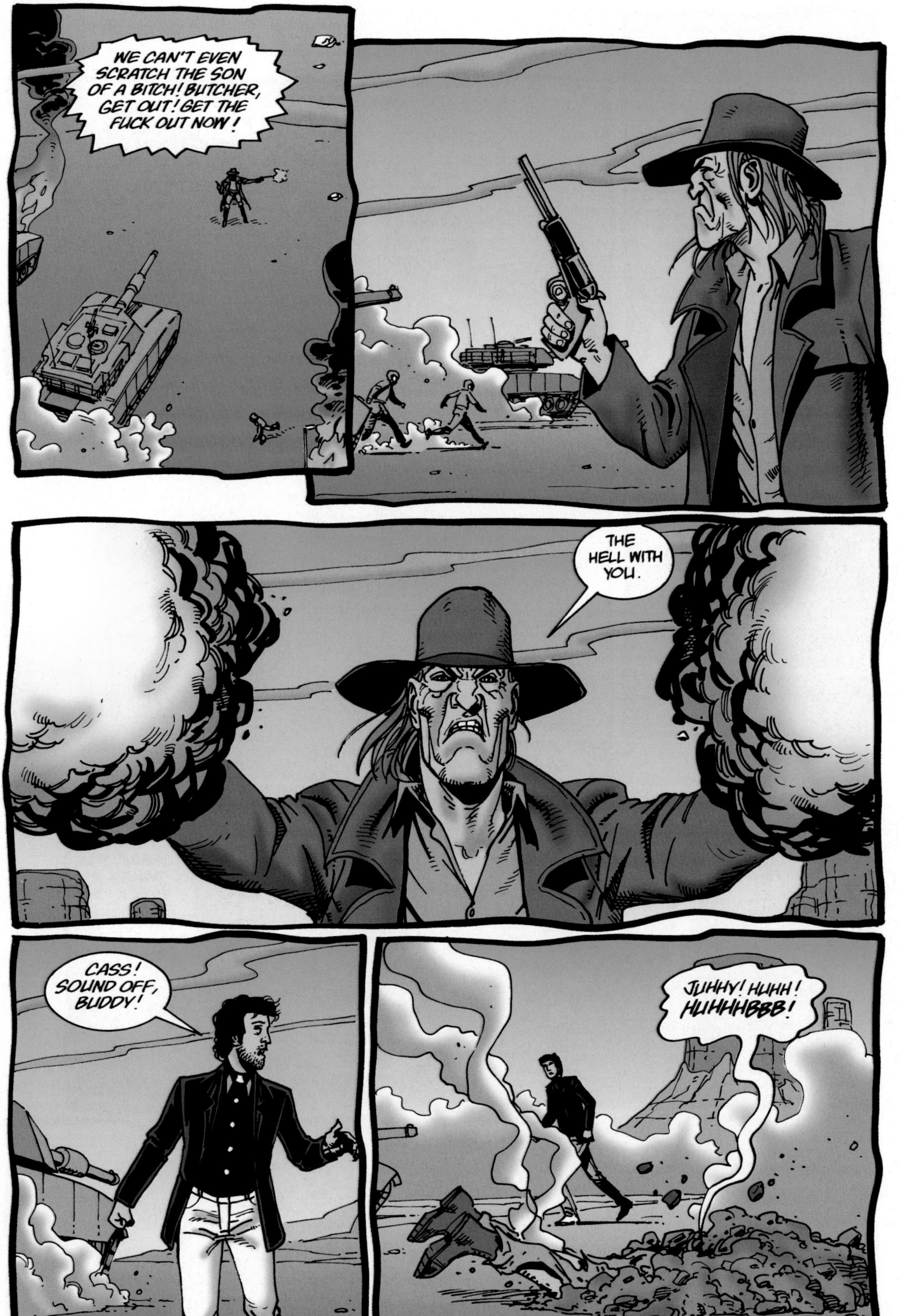
WE CAN'T EVEN SCRATCH THE SON OF A BITCH! BUTCHER, GET OUT! GET THE FUCK OUT NOW!
THE HELL WITH YOU.
CASS! SOUND OFF, BUDDY!
JUHHY! HUHH! HUHHHBBB!

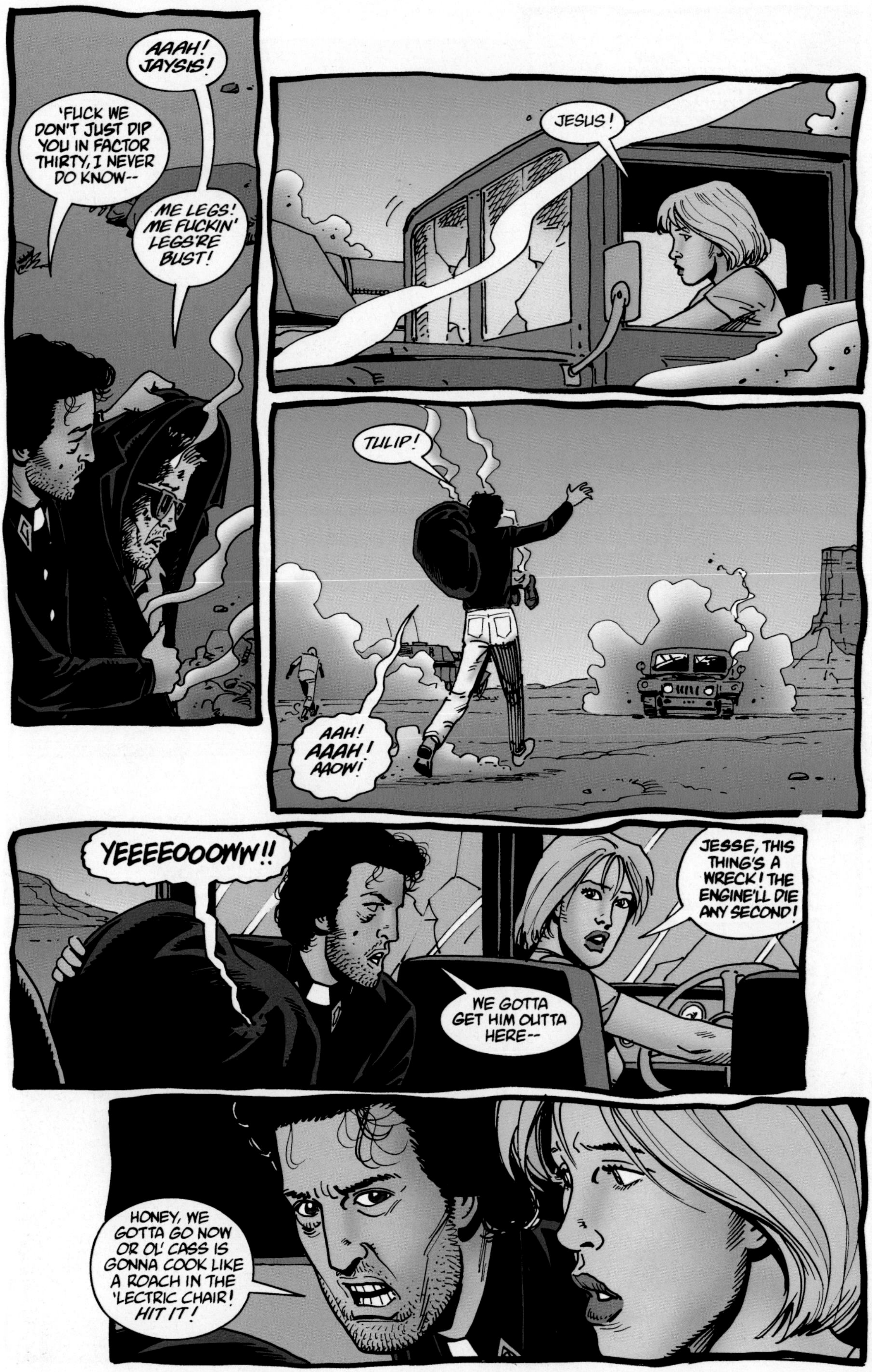

AAAH! JAYSIS!
'FUCK WE DON'T JUST DIP YOU IN FACTOR THIRTY, I NEVER DO KNOW--
ME LEGS! ME FUCKIN' LEGS'RE BUST!
JESUS!
TULIP!
AAH! AAAH! AAOW!
YEEEEOOOWW!!
JESSE, THIS THING'S A WRECK! THE ENGINE'LL DIE ANY SECOND!
WE GOTTA GET HIM OUTTA HERE--
HONEY, WE GOTTA GO NOW OR OL' CASS IS GONNA COOK LIKE A ROACH IN THE 'LECTRIC CHAIR! HIT IT!

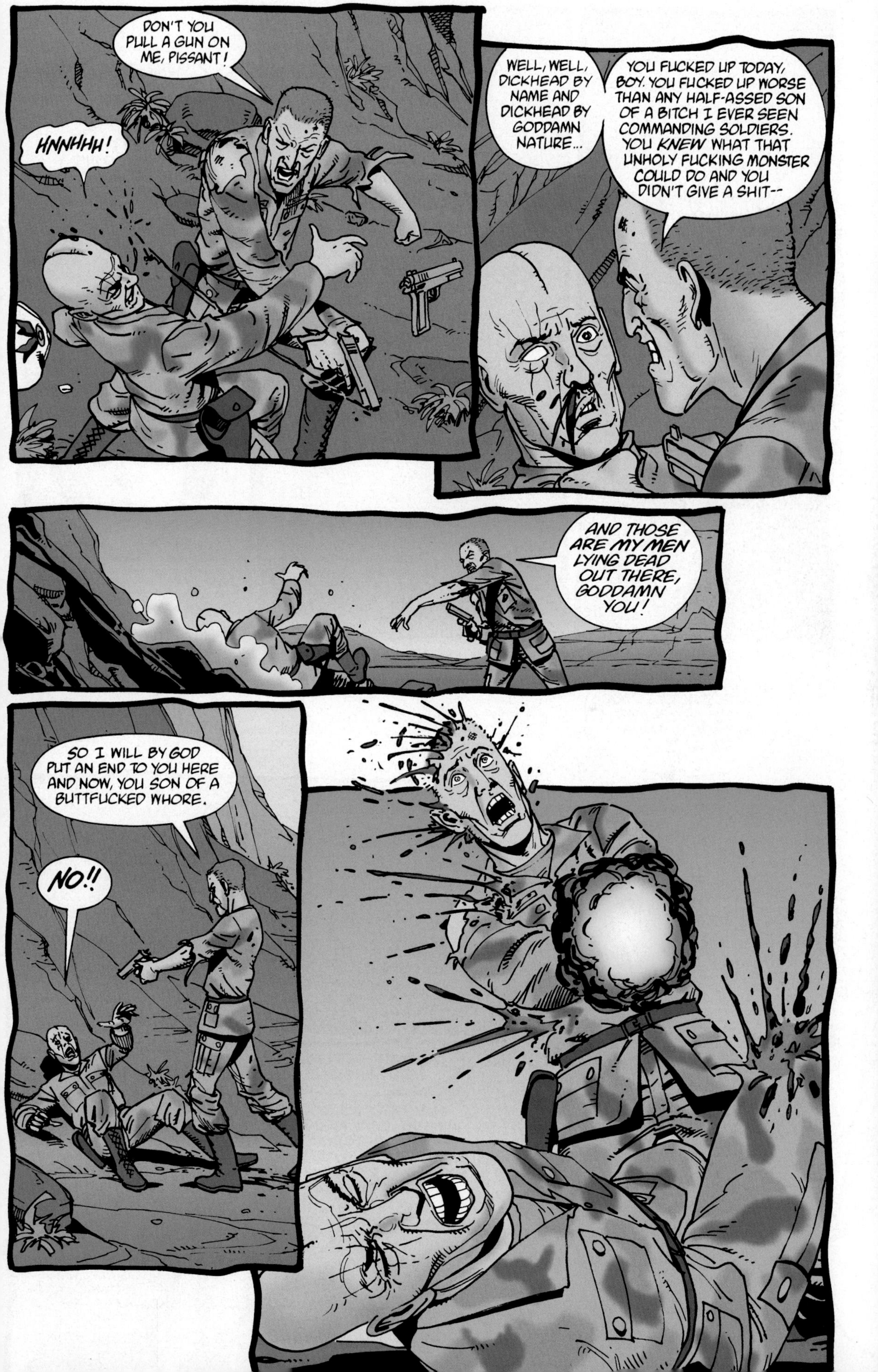
DON'T YOU PULL A GUN ON ME, PISSANT!
HNNHHH!
WELL, WELL, DICKHEAD BY NAME AND DICKHEAD BY GODDAMN NATURE...
YOU FUCKED UP TODAY, BOY. YOU FUCKED UP WORSE THAN ANY HALF-ASSED SON OF A BITCH I EVER SEEN COMMANDING SOLDIERS. YOU KNEW WHAT THAT UNHOLY FUCKING MONSTER COULD DO AND YOU DIDN'T GIVE A SHIT--
AND THOSE ARE MY MEN LYING DEAD OUT THERE, GODDAMN YOU!
SO I WILL BY GOD PUT AN END TO YOU HERE AND NOW, YOU SON OF A BUTTFUCKED WHORE.
NO!!

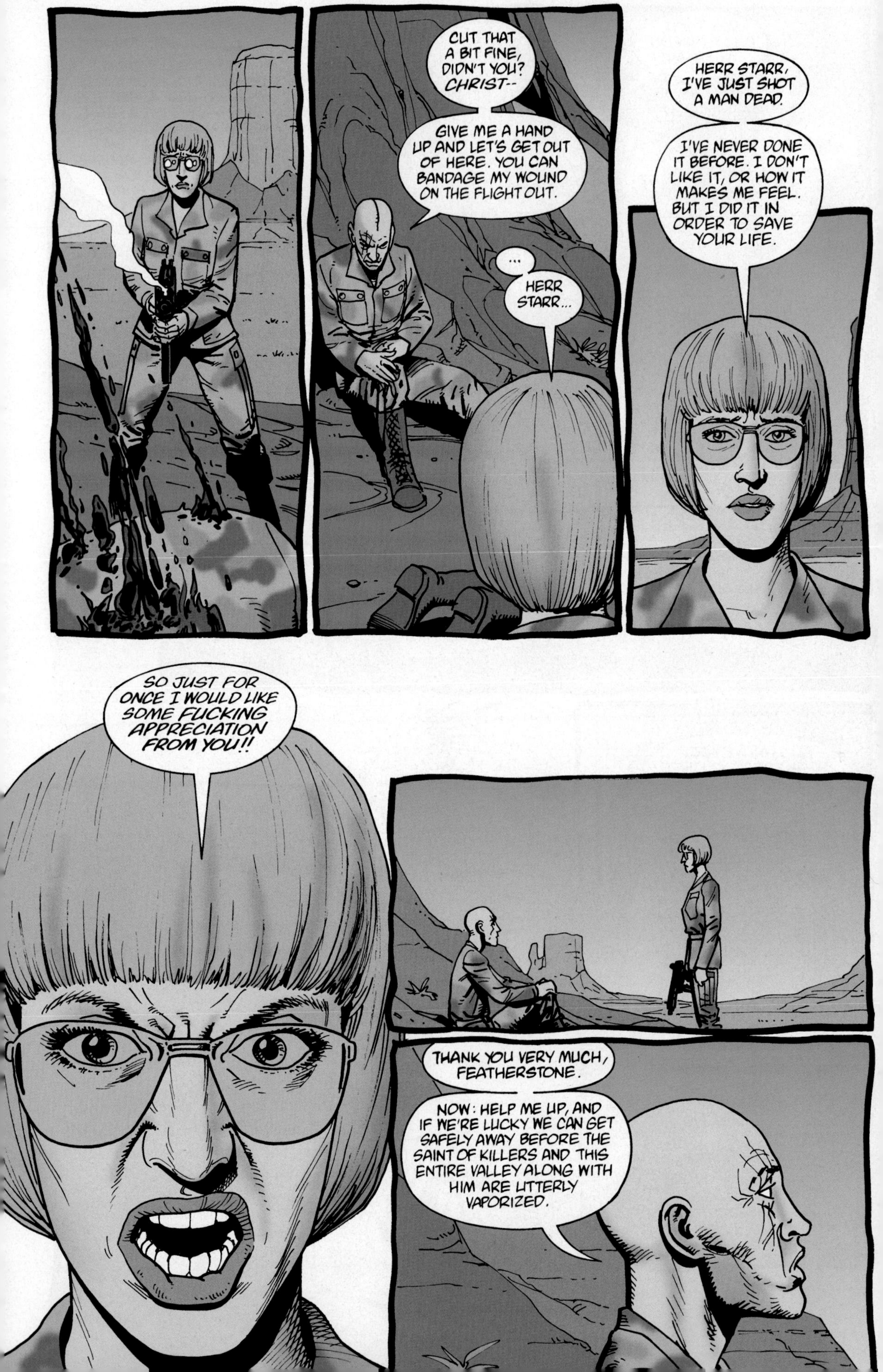
CUT THAT A BIT FINE, DIDN'T YOU? CHRIST--
GIVE ME A HAND UP AND LET'S GET OUT OF HERE. YOU CAN BANDAGE MY WOUND ON THE FLIGHT OUT.
...
HERR STARR...
HERR STARR, I'VE JUST SHOT A MAN DEAD.
I'VE NEVER DONE IT BEFORE. I DON'T LIKE IT, OR HOW IT MAKES ME FEEL. BUT I DID IT IN ORDER TO SAVE YOUR LIFE.
SO JUST FOR ONCE I WOULD LIKE SOME FUCKING APPRECIATION FROM YOU!!
THANK YOU VERY MUCH, FEATHERSTONE.
NOW: HELP ME UP, AND IF WE'RE LUCKY WE CAN GET SAFELY AWAY BEFORE THE SAINT OF KILLERS AND THIS ENTIRE VALLEY ALONG WITH HIM ARE UTTERLY VAPORIZED.

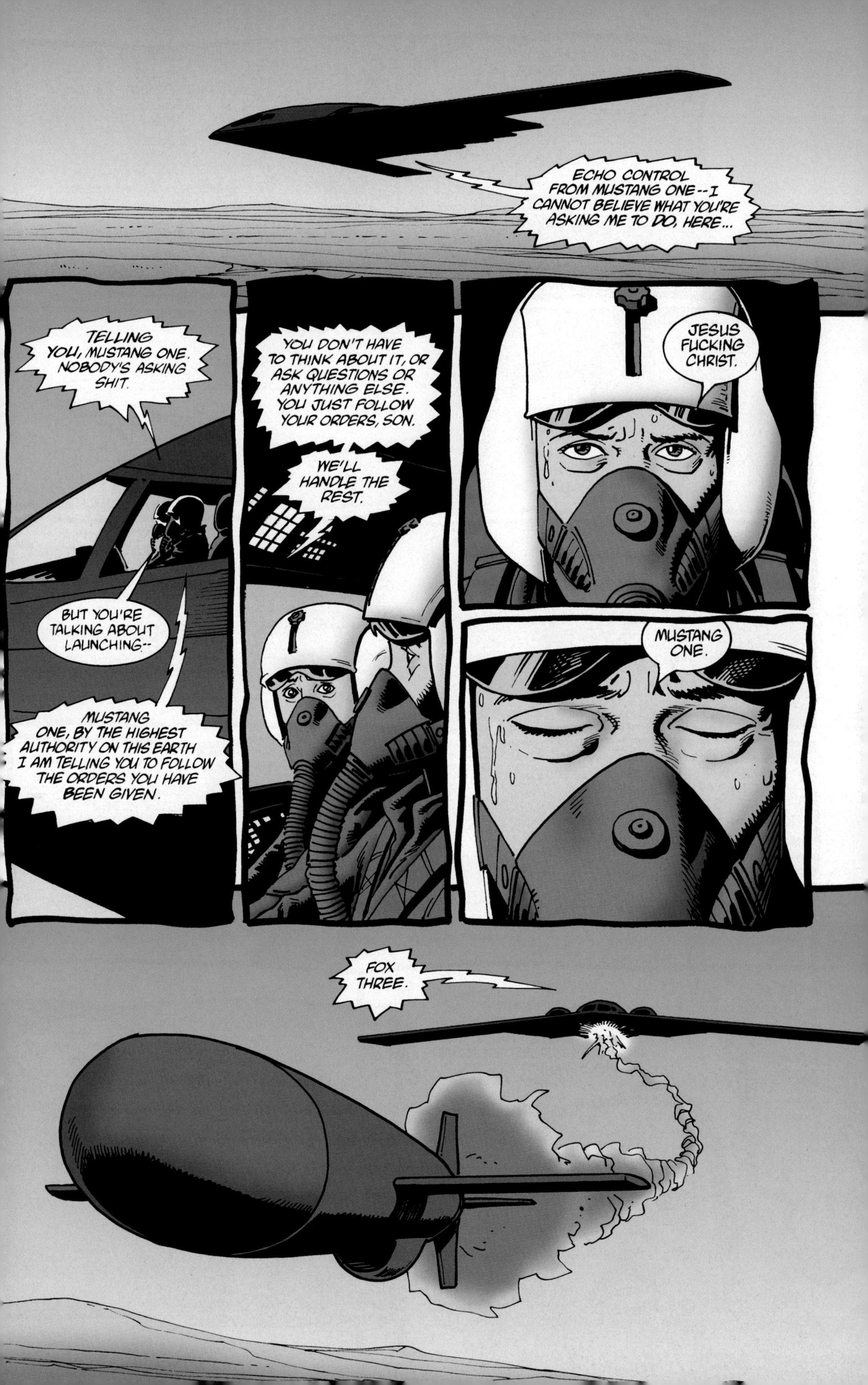
ECHO CONTROL FROM MUSTANG ONE--I CANNOT BELIEVE WHAT YOU'RE ASKING ME TO DO, HERE...
TELLING YOU, MUSTANG ONE. NOBODY'S ASKING SHIT.
BUT YOU'RE TALKING ABOUT LAUNCHING--
MUSTANG ONE, BY THE HIGHEST AUTHORITY ON THIS EARTH I AM TELLING YOU TO FOLLOW THE ORDERS YOU HAVE BEEN GIVEN.
YOU DON'T HAVE TO THINK ABOUT IT, OR ASK QUESTIONS OR ANYTHING ELSE. YOU JUST FOLLOW YOUR ORDERS, SON.
WE'LL HANDLE THE REST.
JESUS FUCKING CHRIST.
MUSTANG ONE.
FOX THREE.

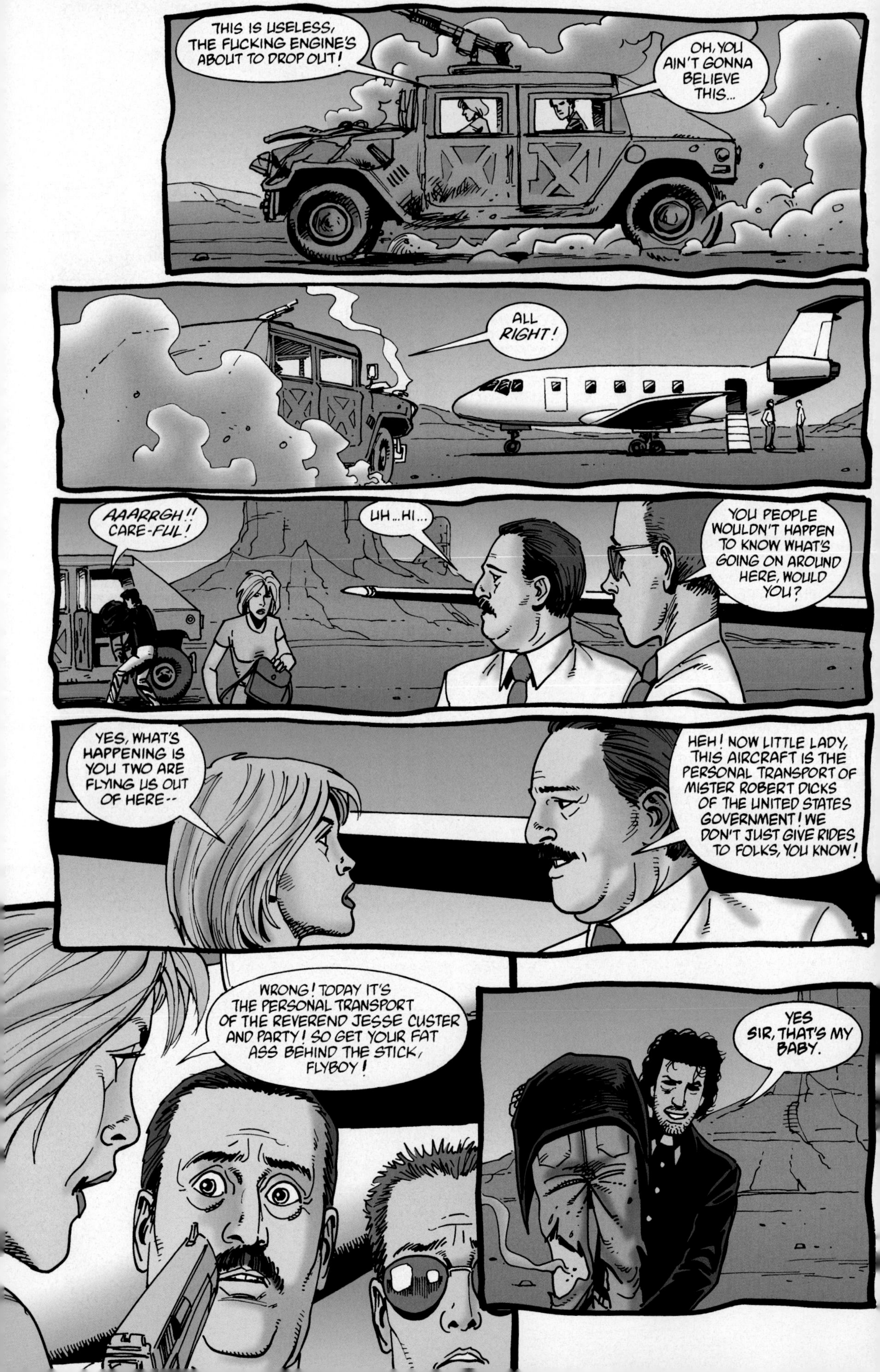
THIS IS USELESS, THE FUCKING ENGINE'S ABOUT TO DROP OUT!
OH, YOU AIN'T GONNA BELIEVE THIS...
ALL RIGHT!
AAARRGH!! CARE-FUL!
UH...HI...
YOU PEOPLE WOULDN'T HAPPEN TO KNOW WHAT'S GOING ON AROUND HERE, WOULD YOU?
YES, WHAT'S HAPPENING IS YOU TWO ARE FLYING US OUT OF HERE--
HEH! NOW LITTLE LADY, THIS AIRCRAFT IS THE PERSONAL TRANSPORT OF MISTER ROBERT DICKS OF THE UNITED STATES GOVERNMENT! WE DON'T JUST GIVE RIDES TO FOLKS, YOU KNOW!
WRONG! TODAY IT'S THE PERSONAL TRANSPORT OF THE REVEREND JESSE CUSTER AND PARTY! SO GET YOUR FAT ASS BEHIND THE STICK, FLYBOY!
YES SIR, THAT'S MY BABY.

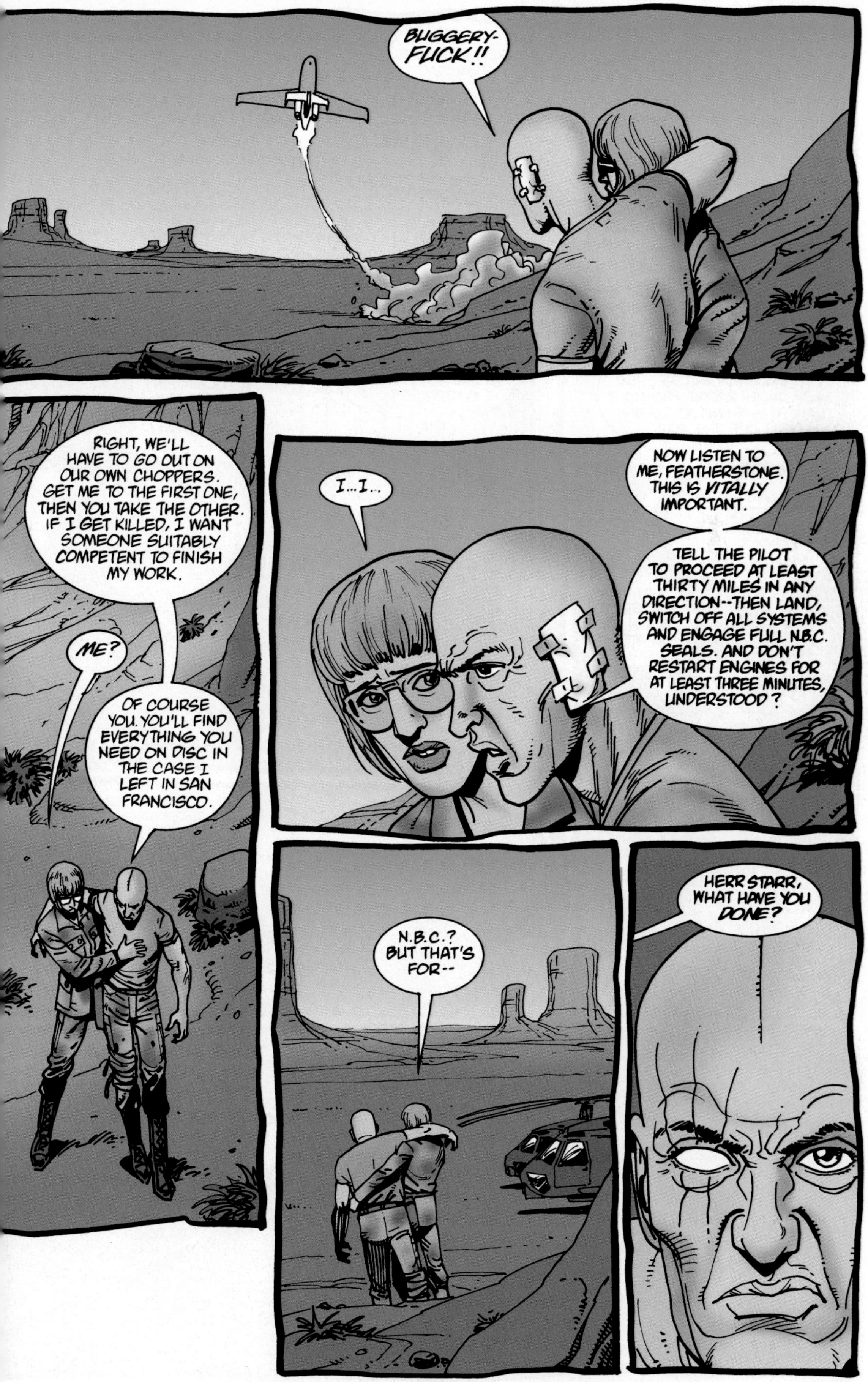
BUGGERY-FUCK!!
RIGHT, WE'LL HAVE TO GO OUT ON OUR OWN CHOPPERS. GET ME TO THE FIRST ONE, THEN YOU TAKE THE OTHER. IF I GET KILLED, I WANT SOMEONE SUITABLY COMPETENT TO FINISH MY WORK.
ME?
OF COURSE YOU. YOU'LL FIND EVERYTHING YOU NEED ON DISC IN THE CASE I LEFT IN SAN FRANCISCO.
I...I...
NOW LISTEN TO ME, FEATHERSTONE. THIS IS VITALLY IMPORTANT.
TELL THE PILOT TO PROCEED AT LEAST THIRTY MILES IN ANY DIRECTION--THEN LAND, SWITCH OFF ALL SYSTEMS AND ENGAGE FULL N.B.C. SEALS. AND DON'T RESTART ENGINES FOR AT LEAST THREE MINUTES, UNDERSTOOD?
N.B.C.? BUT THAT'S FOR--
HERR STARR, WHAT HAVE YOU DONE?

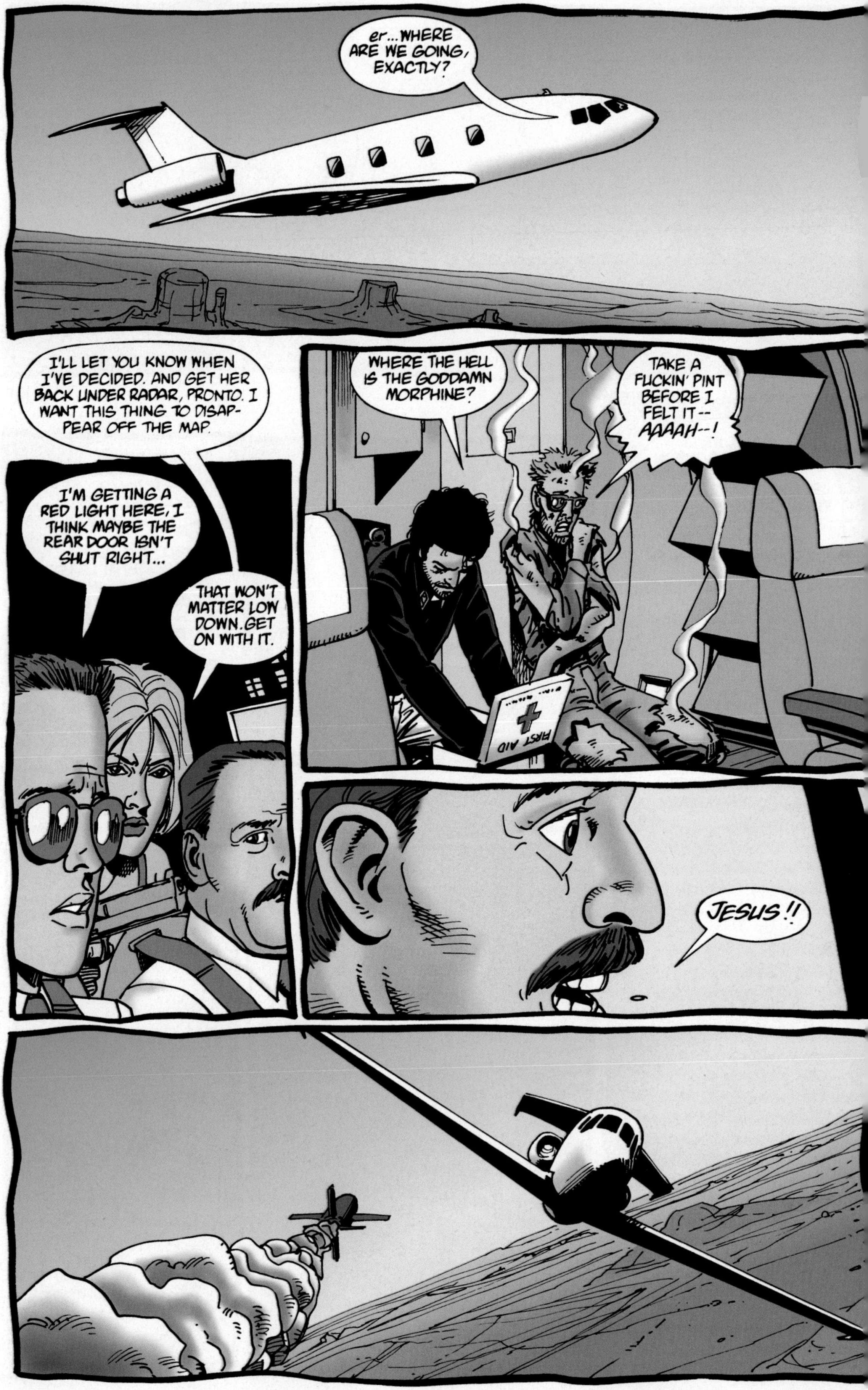
er... WHERE ARE WE GOING, EXACTLY?
I'LL LET YOU KNOW WHEN I'VE DECIDED. AND GET HER BACK UNDER RADAR, PRONTO. I WANT THIS THING TO DISAPPEAR OFF THE MAP.
I'M GETTING A RED LIGHT HERE, I THINK MAYBE THE REAR DOOR ISN'T SHUT RIGHT...
THAT WON'T MATTER LOW DOWN. GET ON WITH IT.
WHERE THE HELL IS THE GODDAMN MORPHINE?
TAKE A FUCKIN' PINT BEFORE I FELT IT-- AAAAH--!
FIRST AID
JESUS!!

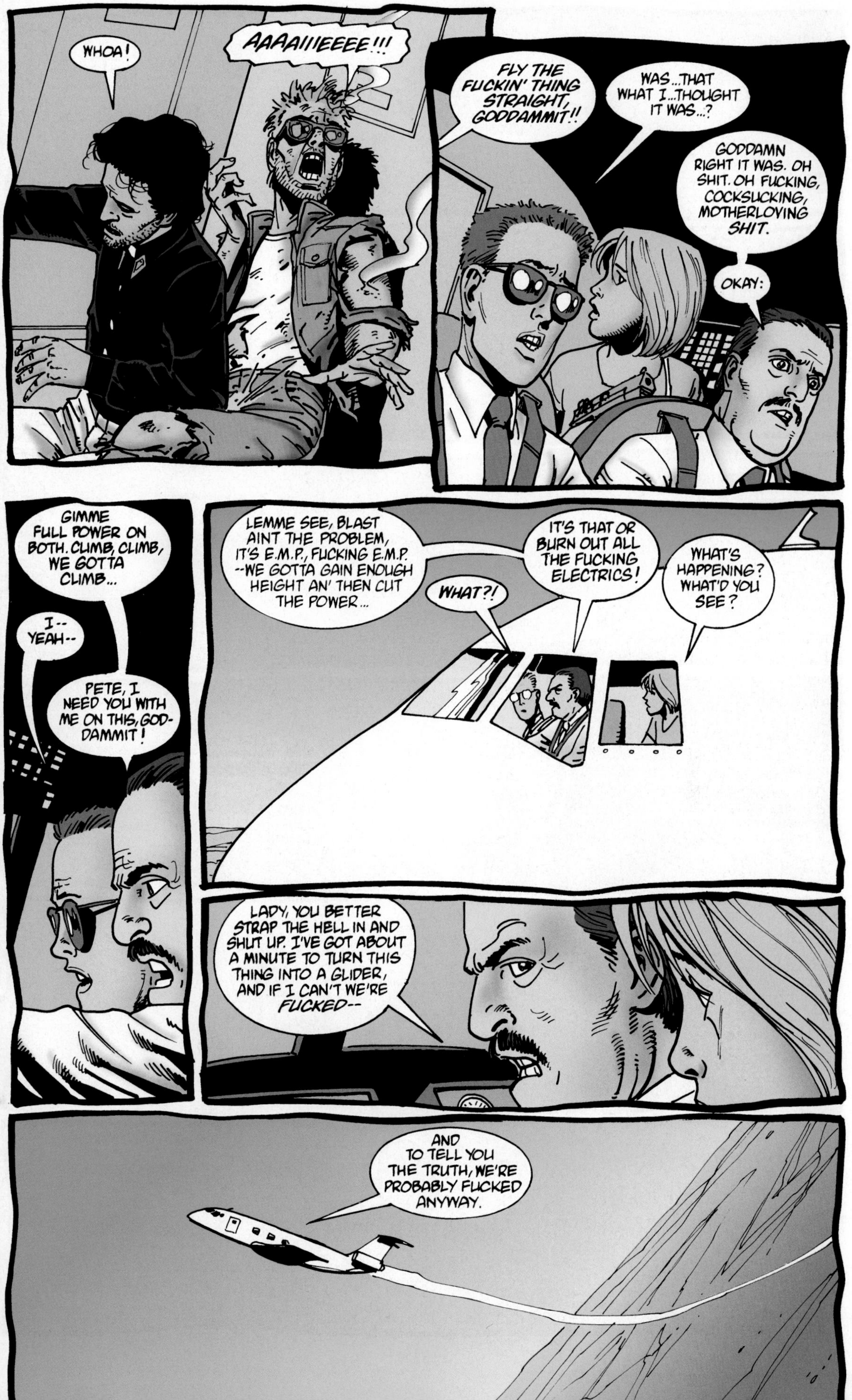
WHOA!
AAAAIIIEEEE!!!
FLY THE FUCKIN' THING STRAIGHT, GODDAMMIT!!
WAS...THAT WHAT I...THOUGHT IT WAS...?
GODDAMN RIGHT IT WAS. OH SHIT. OH FUCKING, COCKSUCKING, MOTHERLOVING SHIT.
OKAY:
GIMME FULL POWER ON BOTH. CLIMB, CLIMB, WE GOTTA CLIMB...
I-- YEAH--
PETE, I NEED YOU WITH ME ON THIS, GODDAMMIT!
LEMME SEE, BLAST AINT THE PROBLEM, IT'S E.M.P., FUCKING E.M.P. --WE GOTTA GAIN ENOUGH HEIGHT AN' THEN CUT THE POWER...
WHAT?!
IT'S THAT OR BURN OUT ALL THE FUCKING ELECTRICS!
WHAT'S HAPPENING? WHAT'D YOU SEE?
LADY, YOU BETTER STRAP THE HELL IN AND SHUT UP. I'VE GOT ABOUT A MINUTE TO TURN THIS THING INTO A GLIDER, AND IF I CAN'T WE'RE FUCKED--
AND TO TELL YOU THE TRUTH, WE'RE PROBABLY FUCKED ANYWAY.

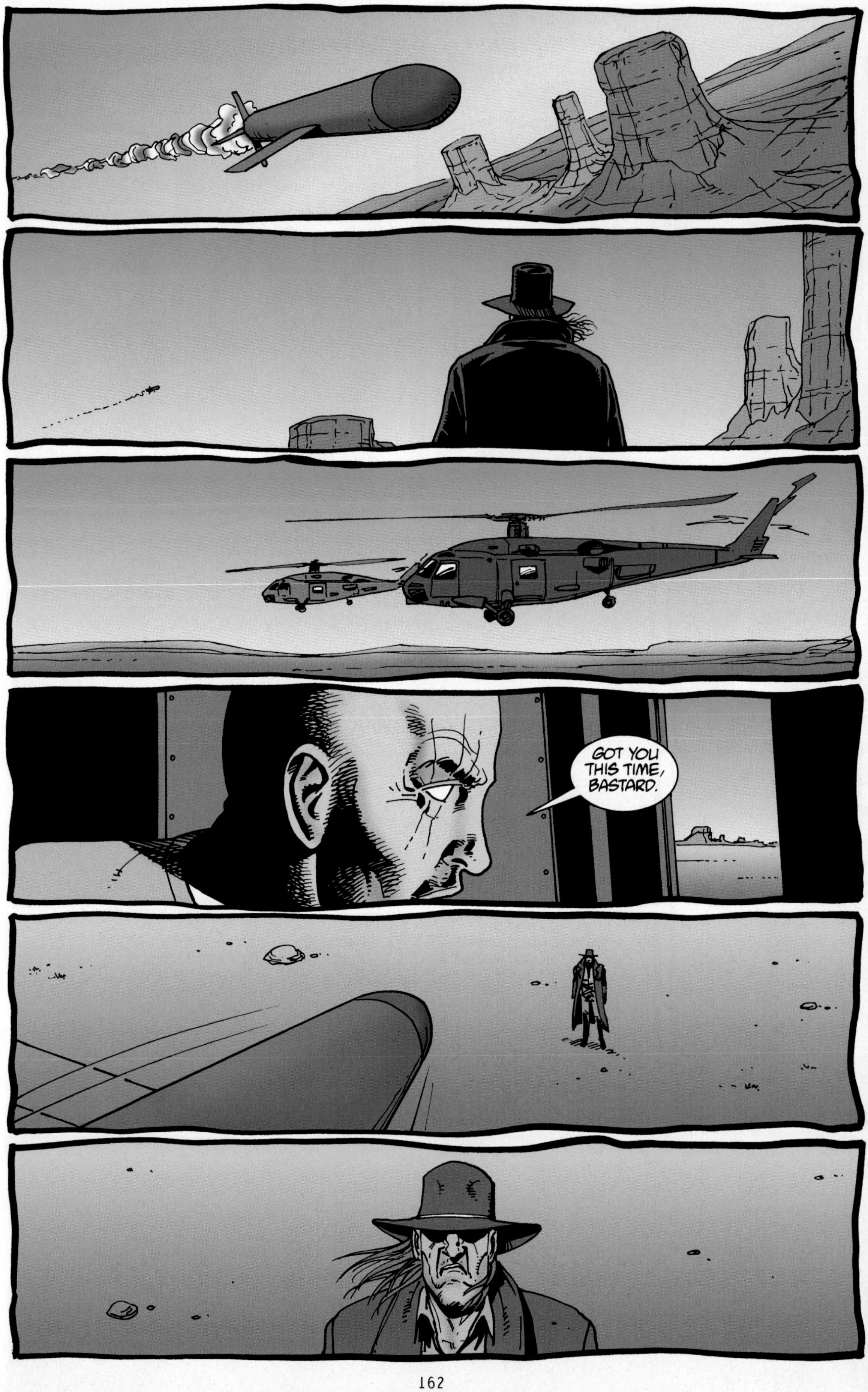
GOT YOU THIS TIME, BASTARD.

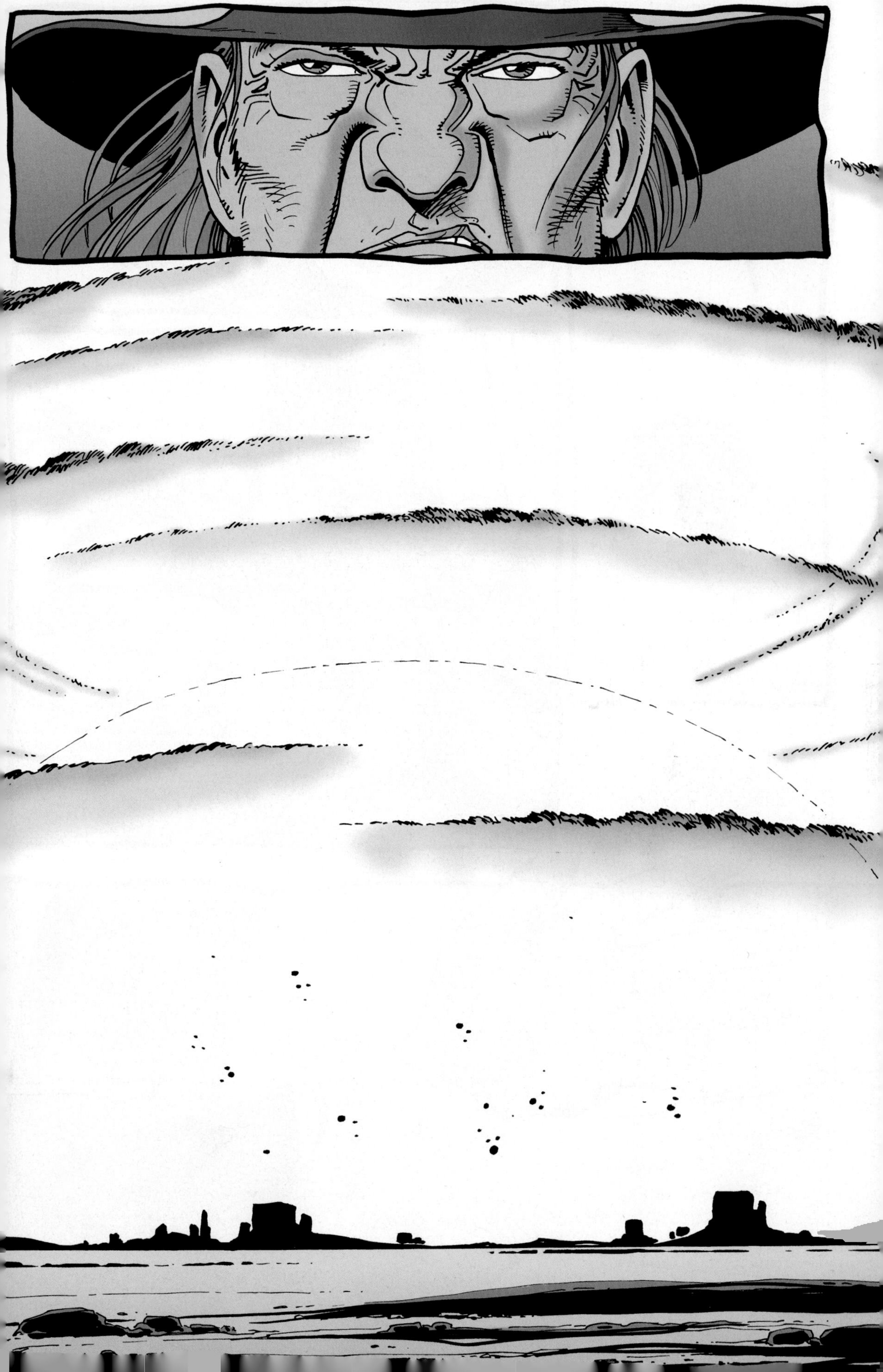

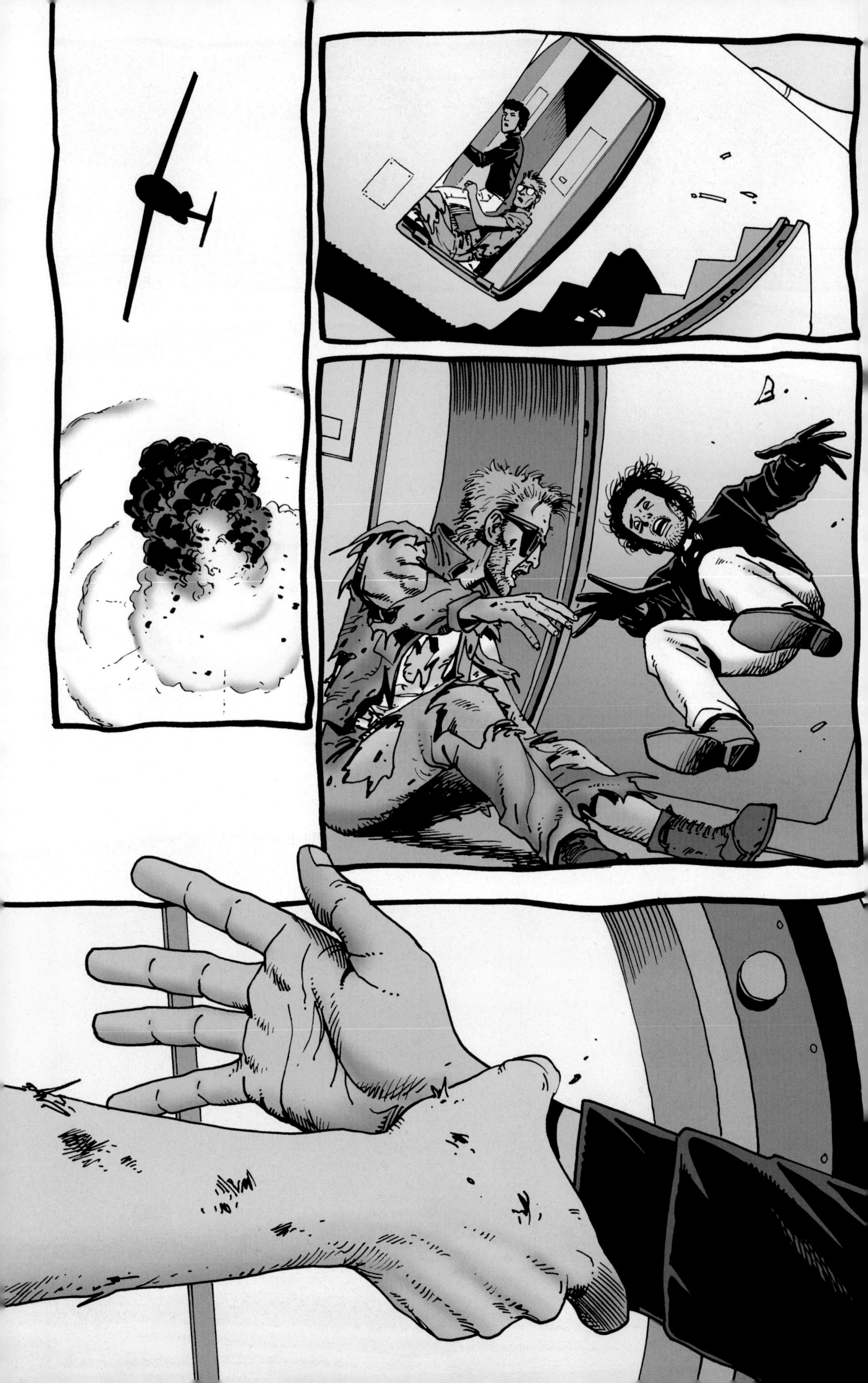

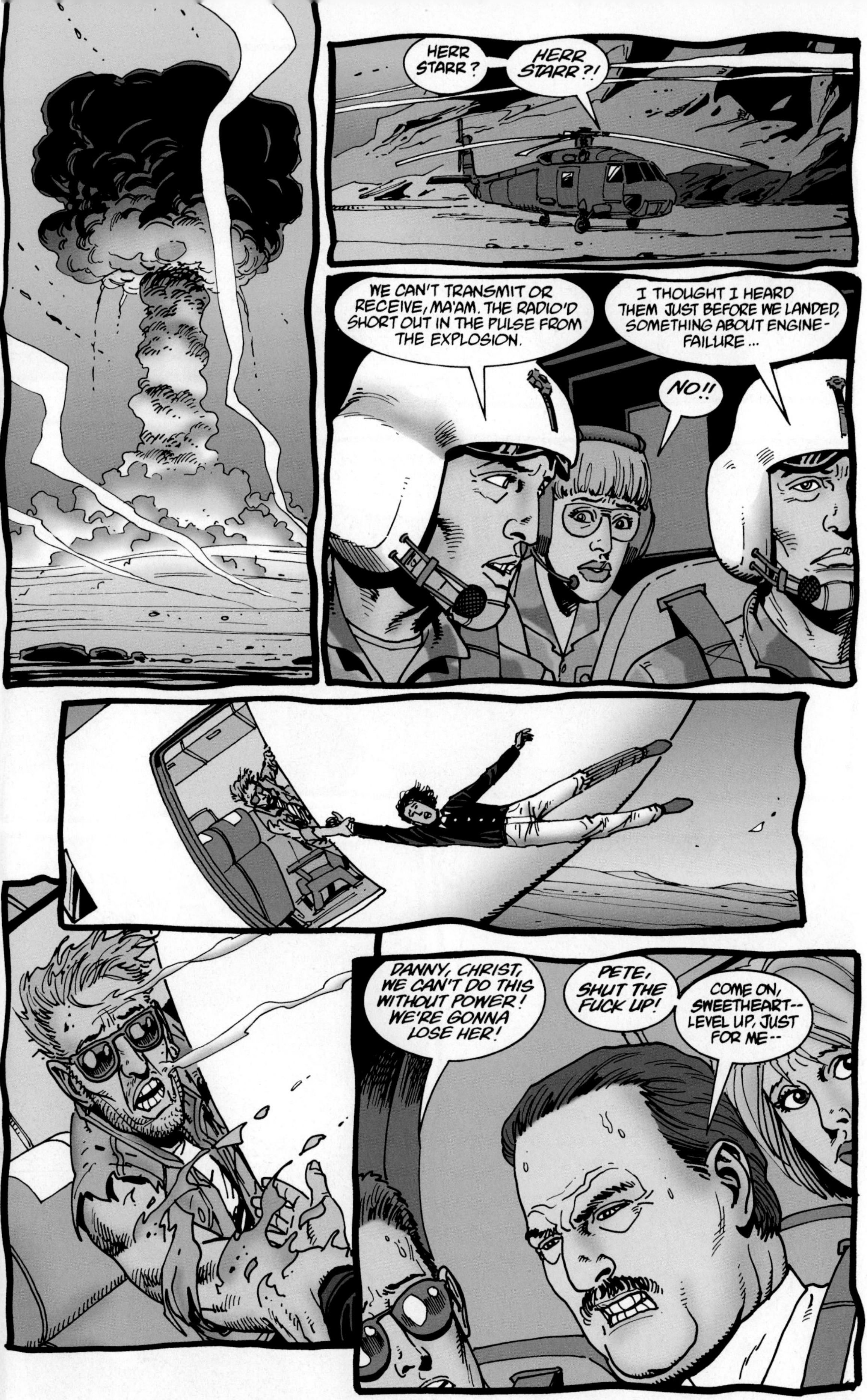
HERR STARR?
HERR STARR?!
WE CAN'T TRANSMIT OR RECEIVE, MA'AM. THE RADIO'D SHORT OUT IN THE PULSE FROM THE EXPLOSION.
I THOUGHT I HEARD THEM JUST BEFORE WE LANDED, SOMETHING ABOUT ENGINE-FAILURE ...
NO!!
DANNY, CHRIST, WE CAN'T DO THIS WITHOUT POWER! WE'RE GONNA LOSE HER!
PETE, SHUT THE FUCK UP!
COME ON, SWEETHEART-- LEVEL UP, JUST FOR ME--

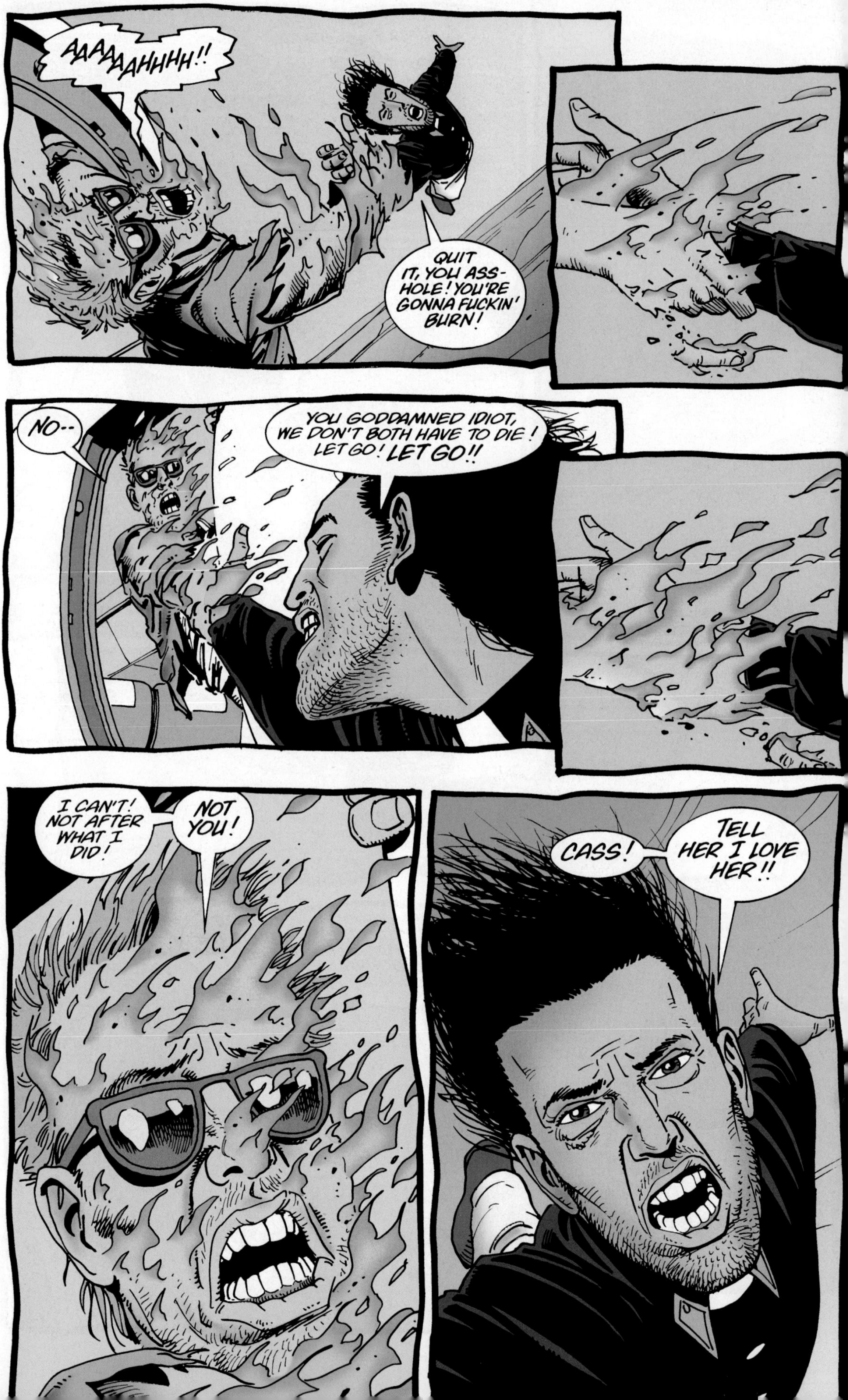
AAAAAAHHHH!!
QUIT IT, YOU ASS-HOLE! YOU'RE GONNA FUCKIN' BURN!
NO--
YOU GODDAMNED IDIOT, WE DON'T BOTH HAVE TO DIE! LET GO! LET GO!!
I CAN'T! NOT AFTER WHAT I DID!
NOT YOU!
CASS!
TELL HER I LOVE HER!!

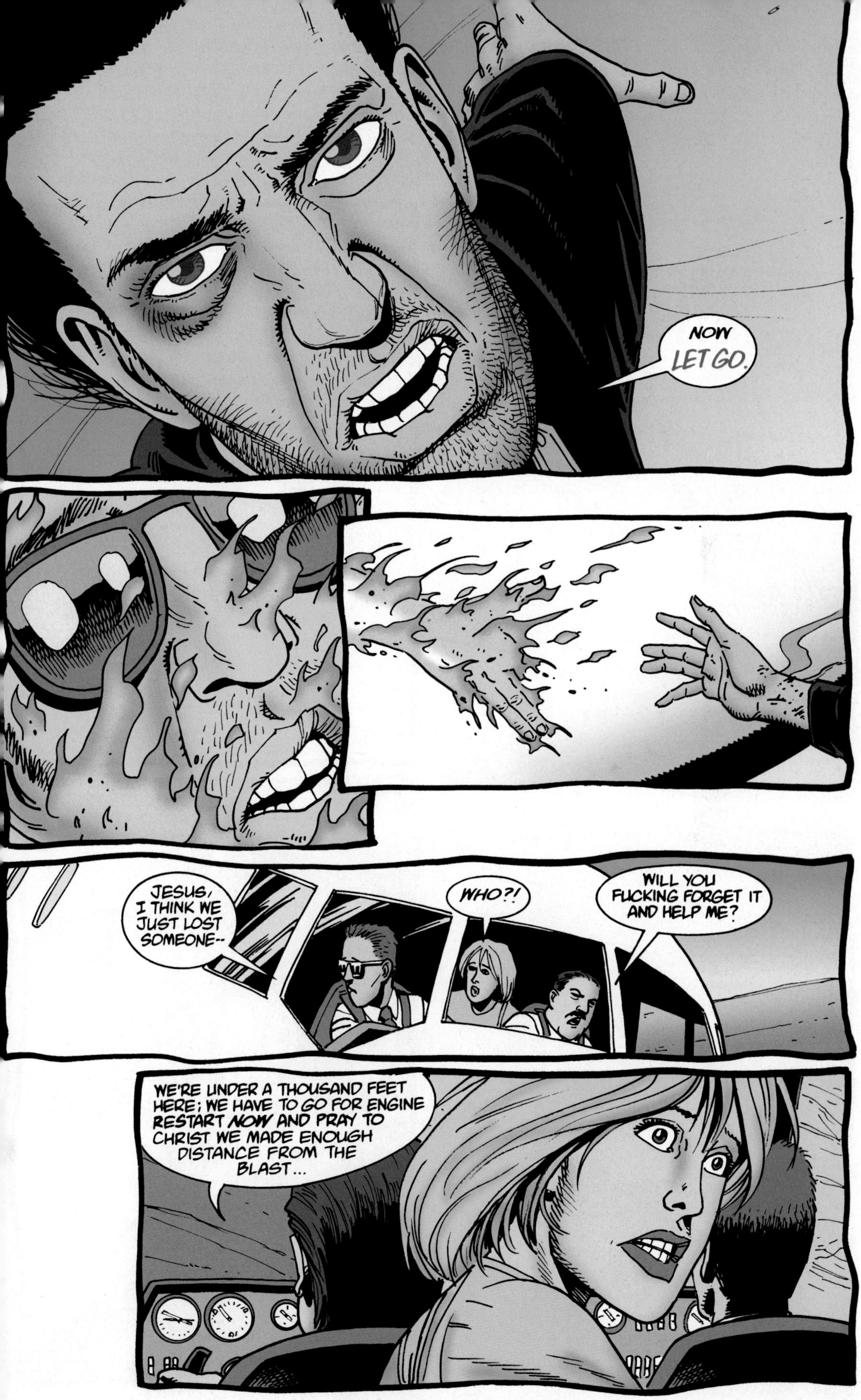
NOW LET GO.
JESUS, I THINK WE JUST LOST SOMEONE--
WHO?!
WILL YOU FUCKING FORGET IT AND HELP ME?
WE'RE UNDER A THOUSAND FEET HERE; WE HAVE TO GO FOR ENGINE RESTART NOW AND PRAY TO CHRIST WE MADE ENOUGH DISTANCE FROM THE BLAST...

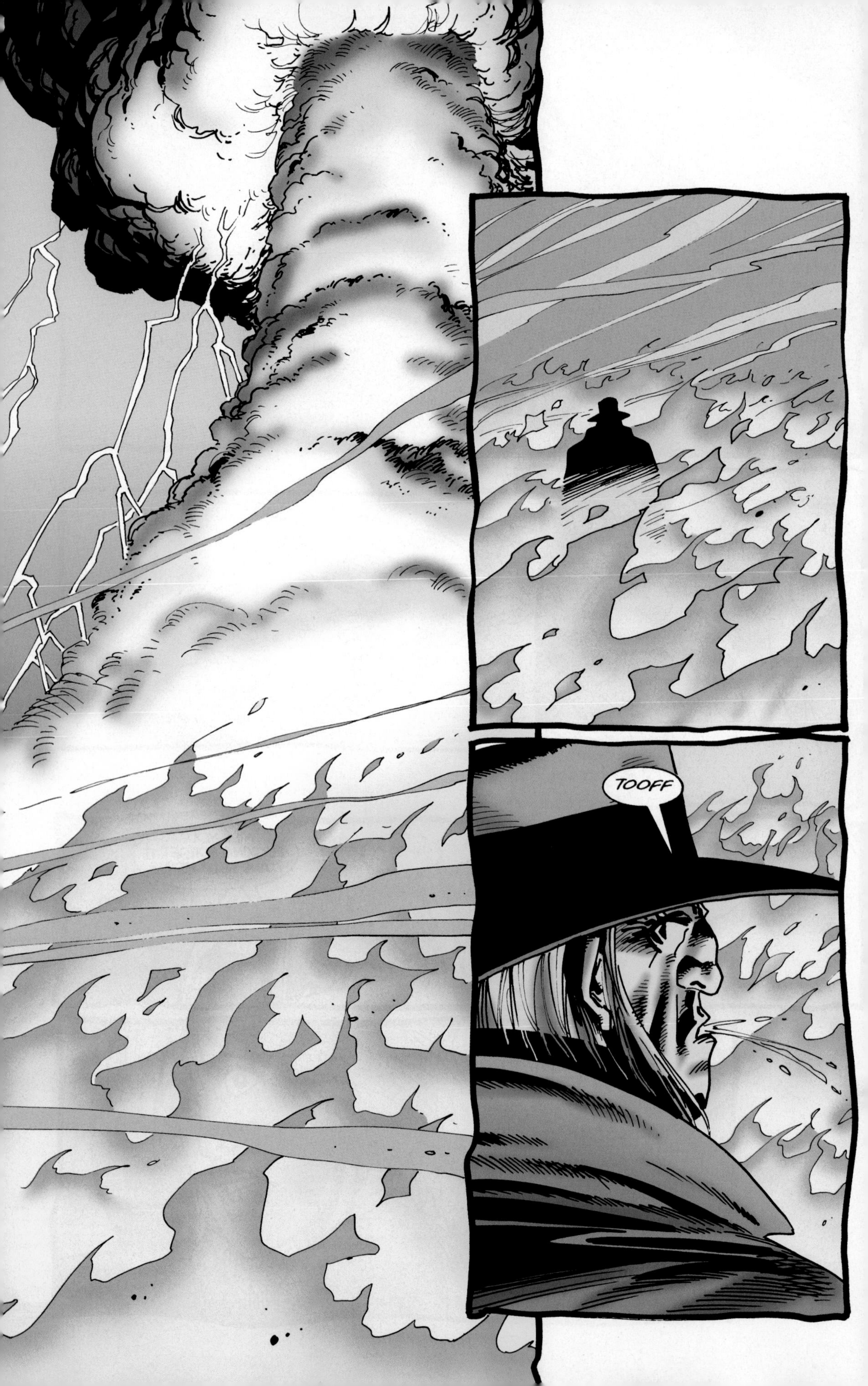
TOOFF

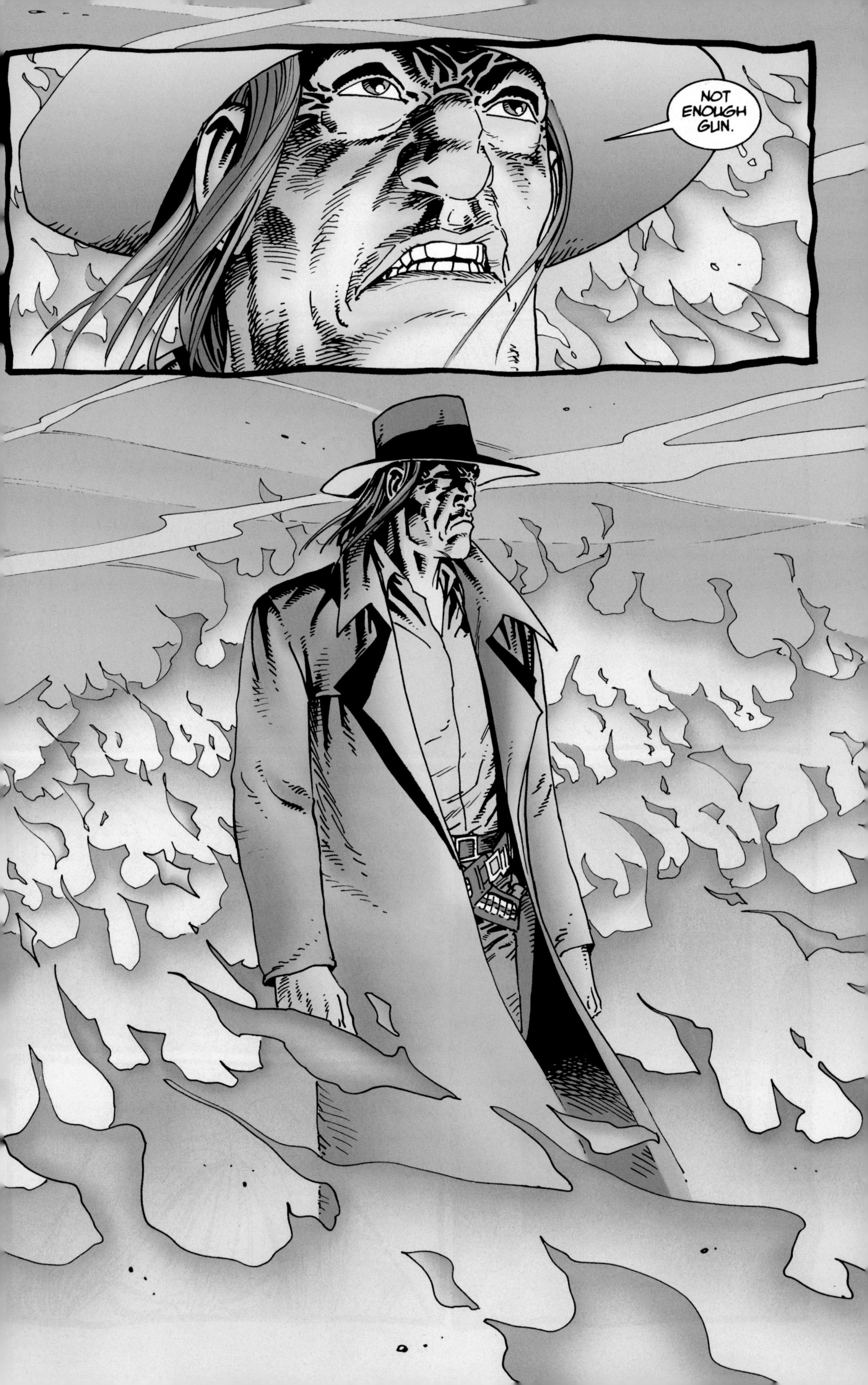
NOT ENOUGH GUN.

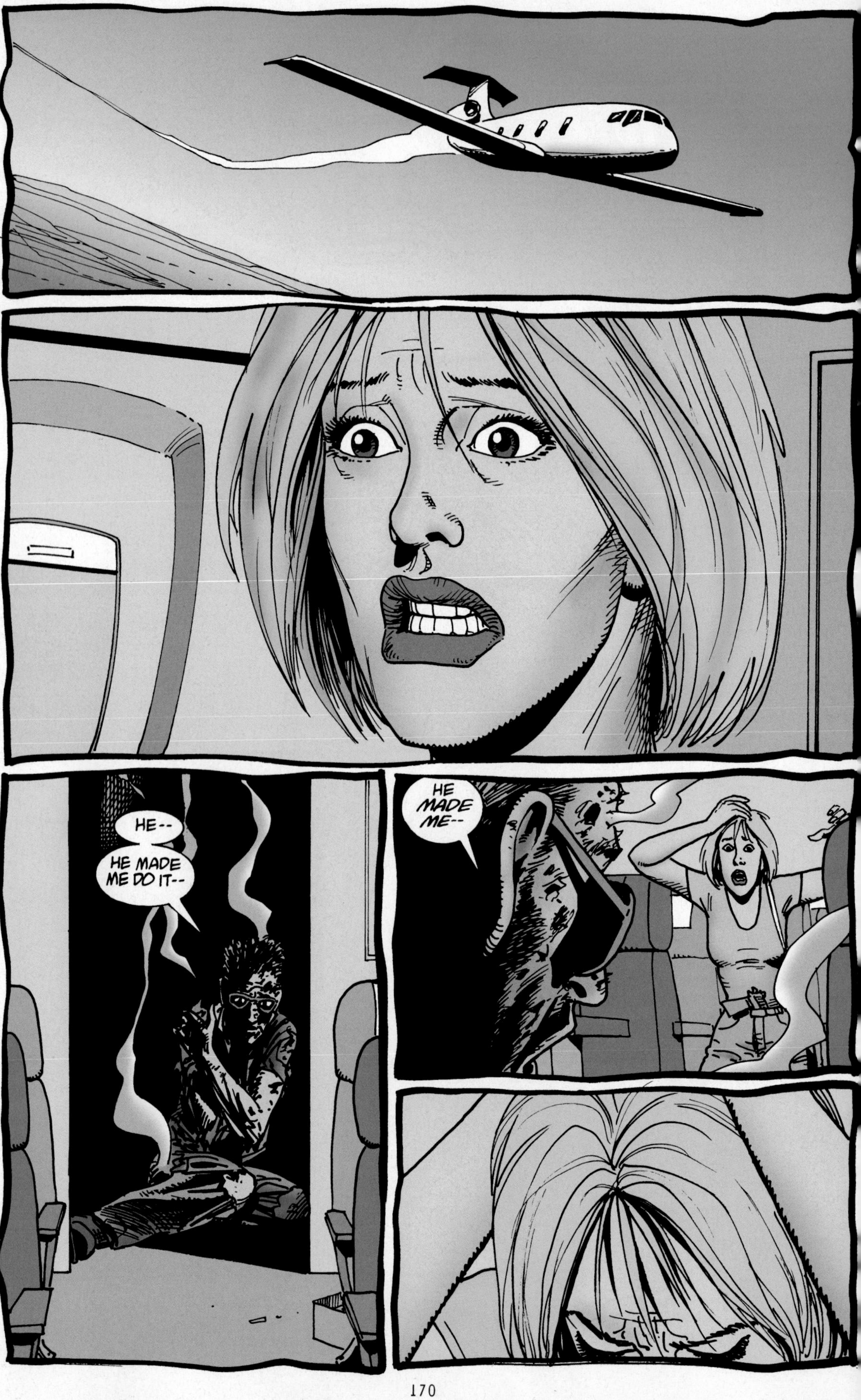
HE--
HE MADE ME DO IT--
HE MADE ME--

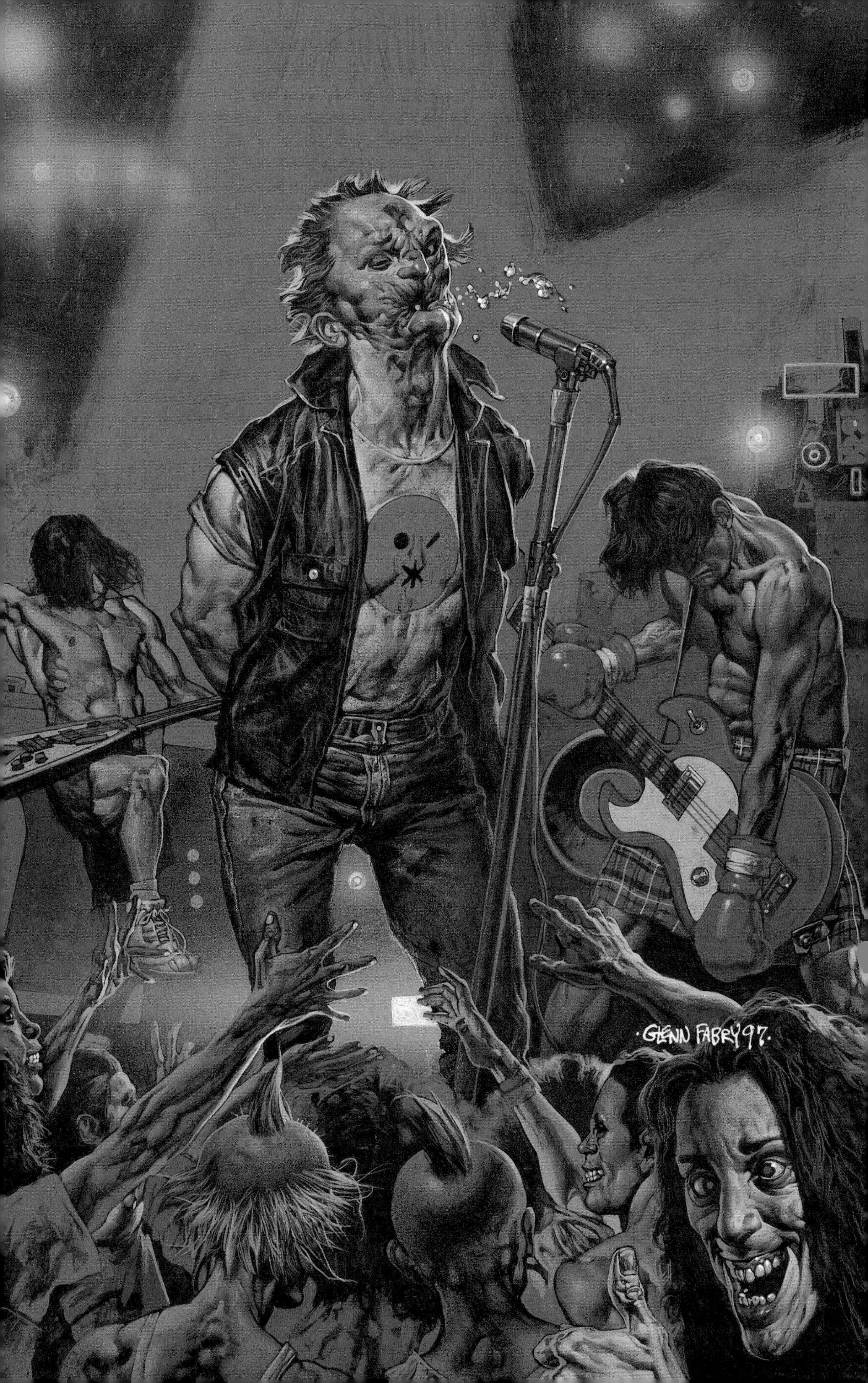
·GLENN FABRY 97·

"Okay, what about Arseface's alleged link
to an unidentified member of the Spice Girls?"

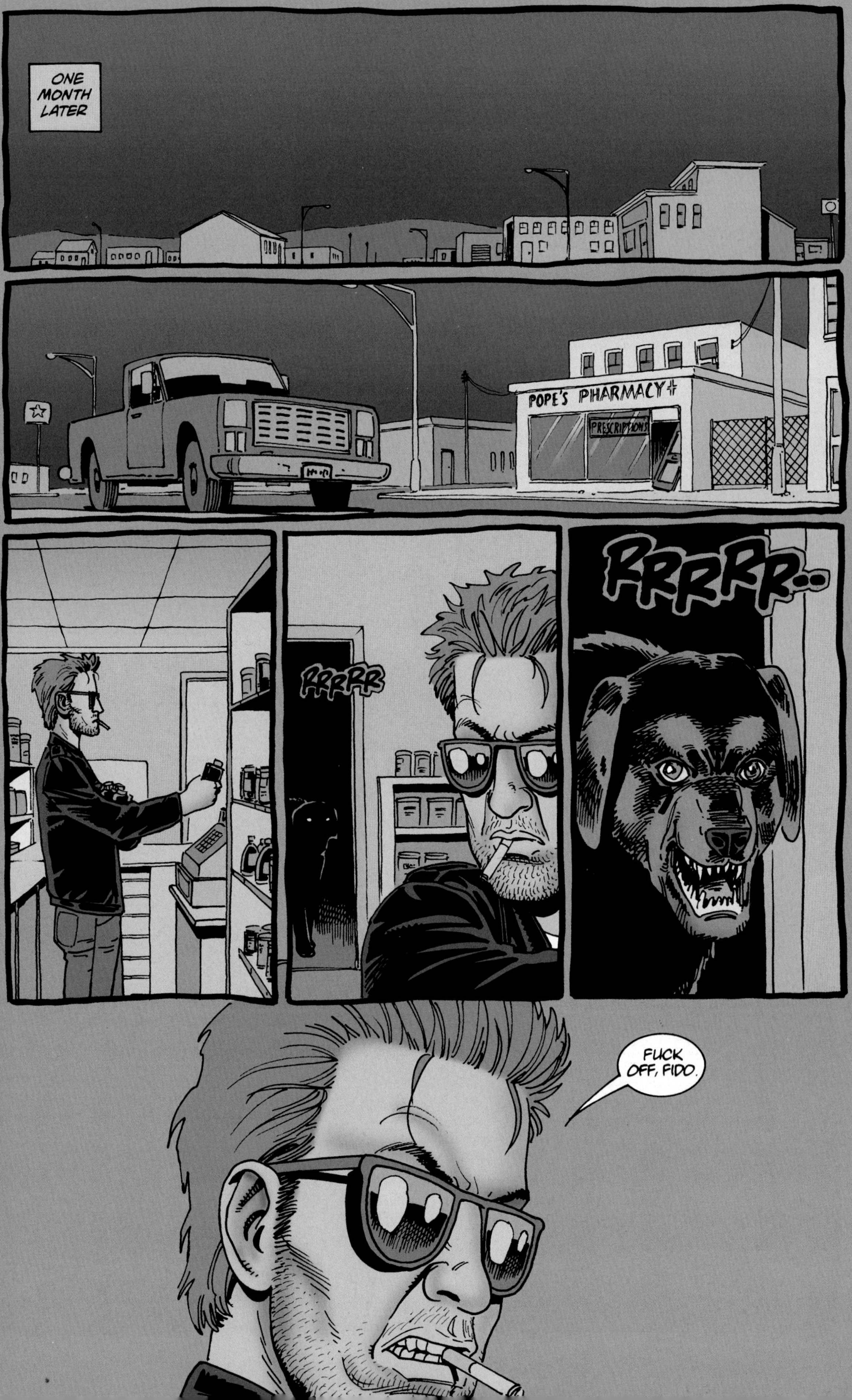
ONE MONTH LATER
POPE'S PHARMACY
PRESCRIPTIONS
RRRRR
RRRRR..
FUCK OFF, FIDO.

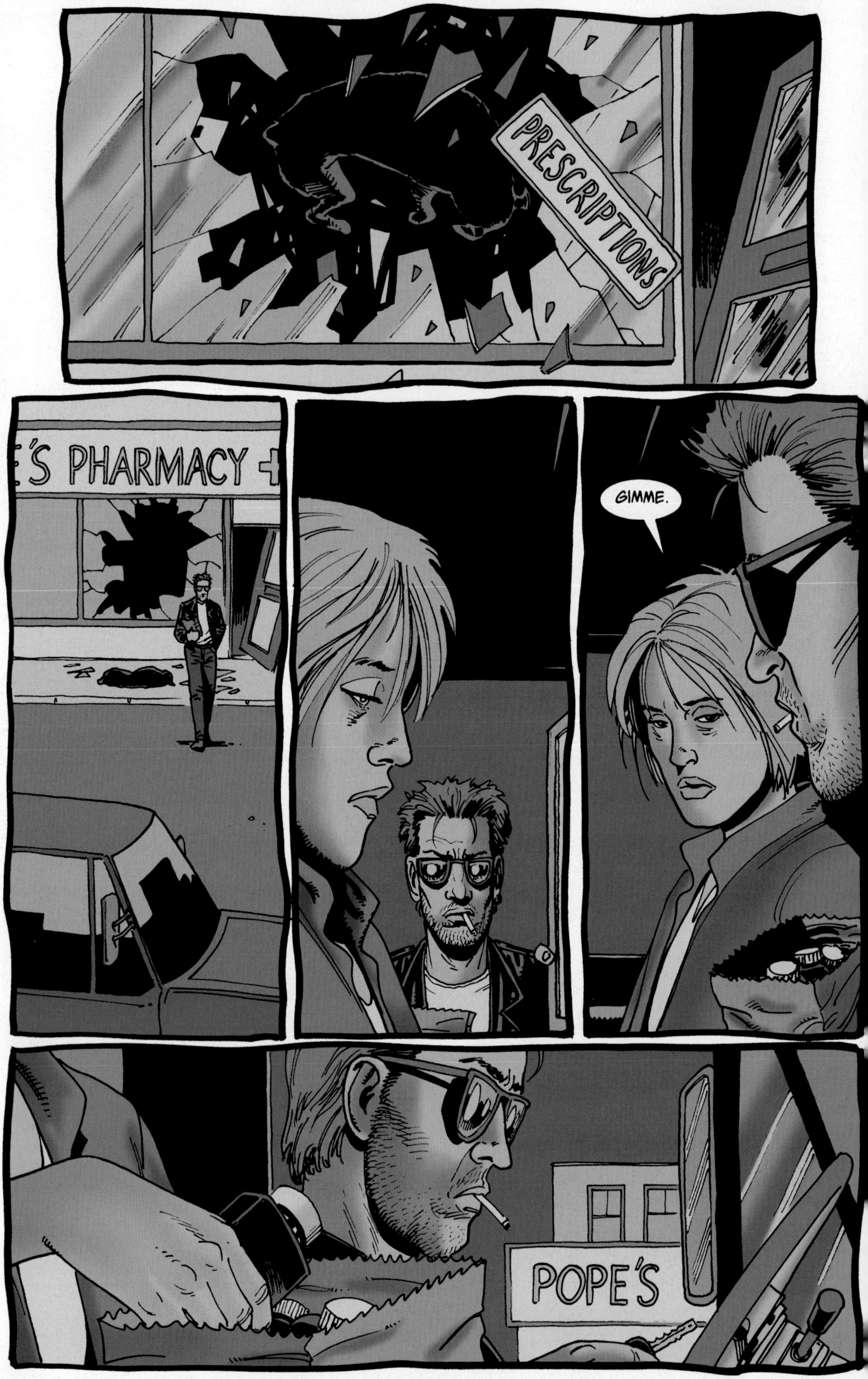
PRESCRIPTIONS
E'S PHARMACY
GIMME.
POPE'S

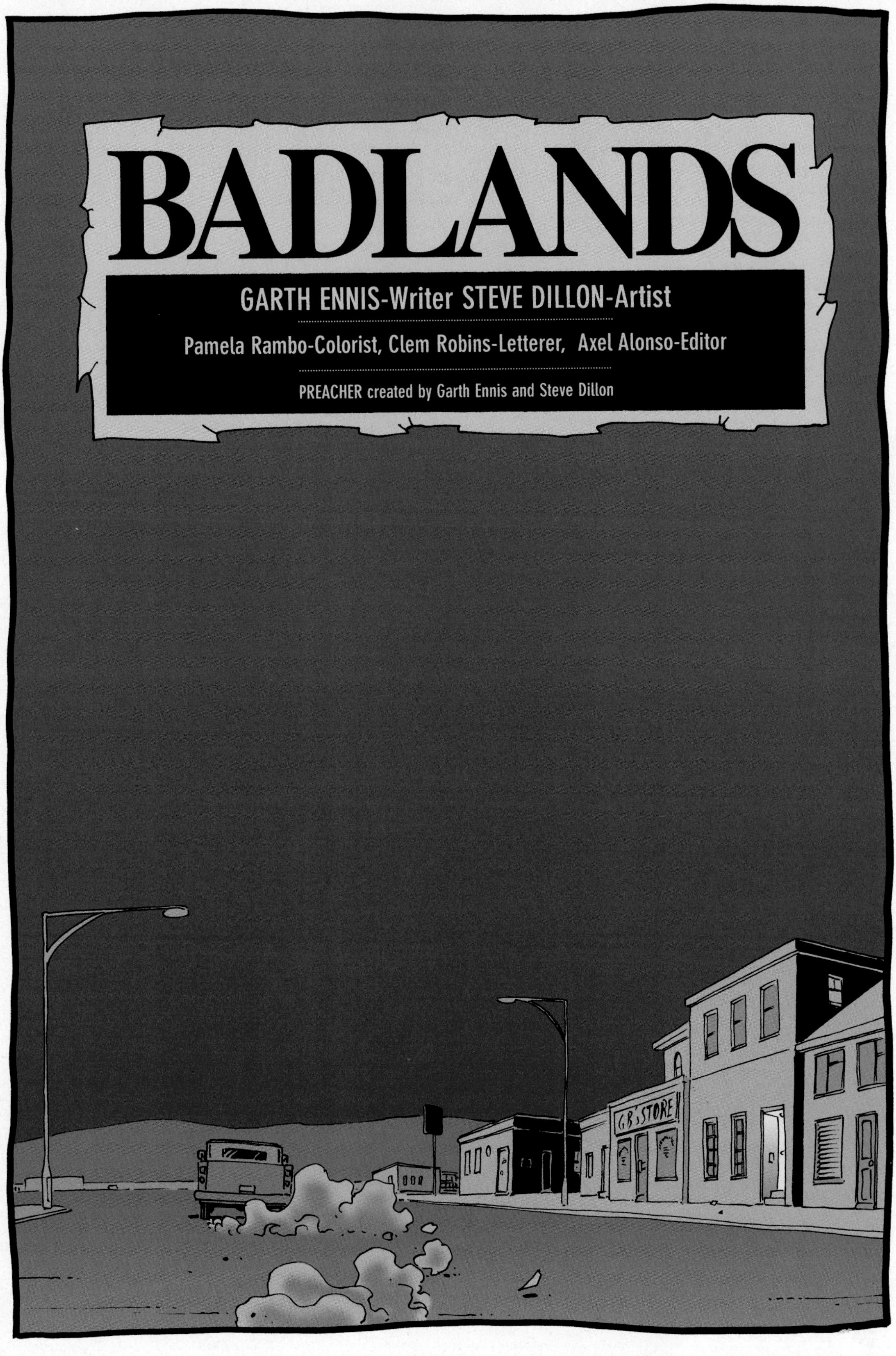
BADLANDS
GARTH ENNIS-Writer STEVE DILLON-Artist
Pamela Rambo-Colorist, Clem Robins-Letterer, Axel Alonso-Editor
PREACHER created by Garth Ennis and Steve Dillon
G.B.'s STORE

GOOD EVENING: I'M JEFF KING, LOOKING LONG AND HARD AT THE NEWS-- BEHIND THE NEWS.

TONIGHT: THE MONUMENT VALLEY TRAGEDY, THIRTY DAYS ON --WHAT HAS BEEN DONE? WHAT CAN BE DONE? WHAT WILL BE DONE?

JOIN ME: FOR A LONG HARD LOOK.

LONG HARD
LOOK

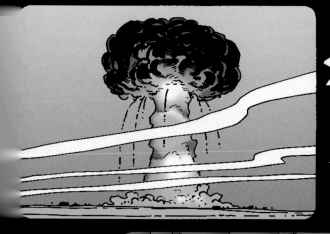

FRIDAY, JUNE THE TWENTY- THE DAY THEY'RE CALLING BAD NUCLEAR EXPLOSION RISES O VALLEY, ARIZONA. EIGHT HUNDR IN THE SURROUNDING AREA, M NATIVE AMERICAN NAVAJ DIE ALMOST IMMEDI

TWO THOUSAND MO ARE FATALLY IRRADIATED. T OF SO MANY LEGENDARY WE HAS BECOME A CANCER DEATH-BOWL.

NATIONAL AND INTERNATIONAL REACTION IS SWIFT: APPALLED HORROR. WHITE HOUSE DEPUTY PRESS SECRETARY WEAVER KENT IS FORCED TO RESIGN AFTER HIS "LOOK ON THE BRIGHT SIDE" ADDRESS--

WELL WHAT I MEA BY THAT IS, uh, RADIOA SPEAKING, WE'RE LOOK REMARKABLY LOW YIEL INITIAL TESTS INDICATE WINDS ARE CARRYING I NORTH INTO THE UNPO DESERT...

I MEAN LET'S FACE IMAGINE IF THIS HAD IN WASHINGTON,

THE PRESIDENT PROMISES SWIFT AND DECISIVE ACTION IN THE PURSUIT OF JUSTICE--BUT ITH NO GROUP CLAIMING RES- ONSIBILITY--NO CLUES AS TO METHOD OR MOTIVATION--NO EADS ON A DELIVERY VEHICLE OR THE ORIGIN OF THE DEVICE, EVEN NOW--

WHERE DO WE GO FROM HERE?

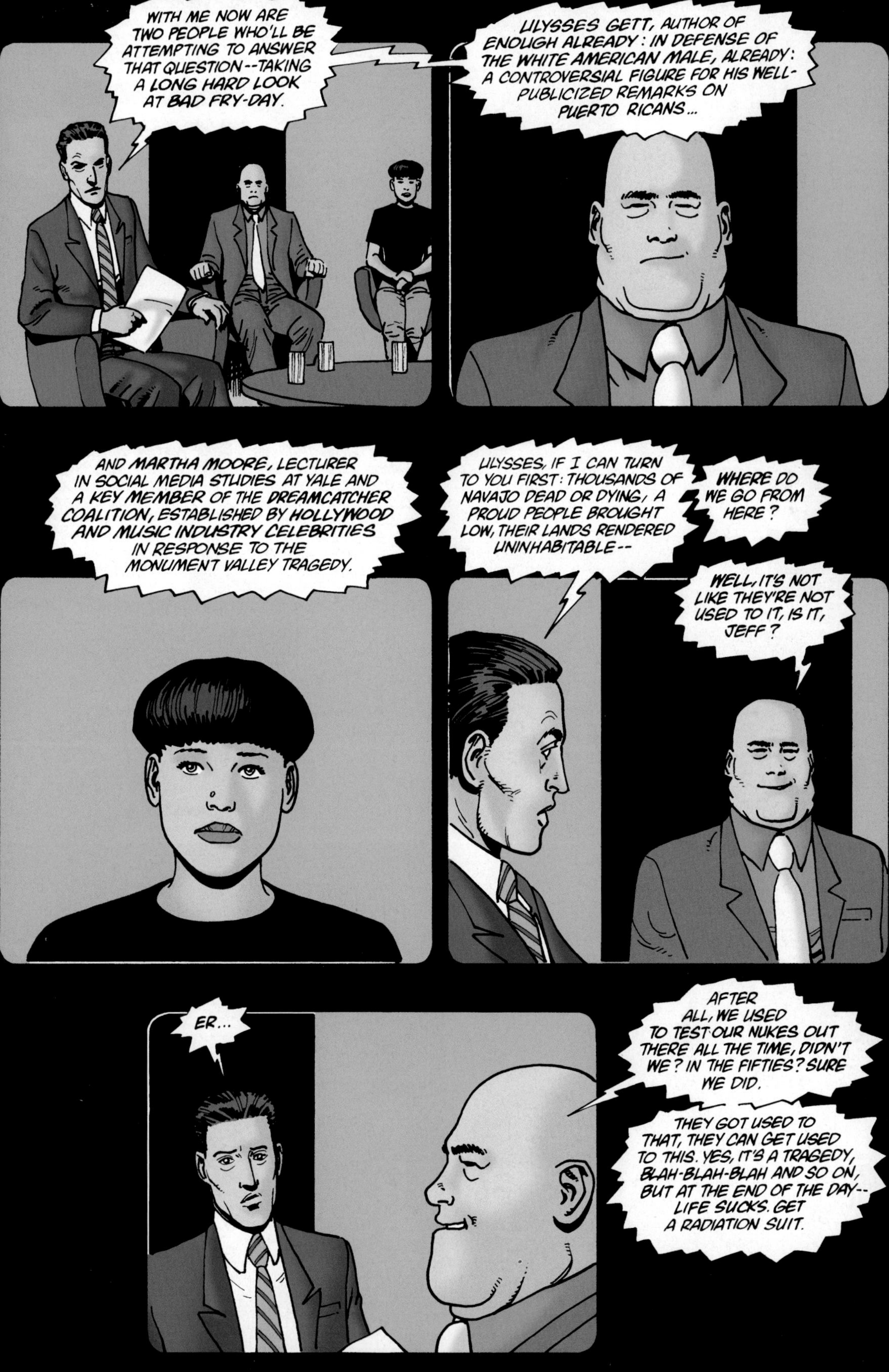
WITH ME NOW ARE TWO PEOPLE WHO'LL BE ATTEMPTING TO ANSWER THAT QUESTION--TAKING A LONG HARD LOOK AT BAD FRY-DAY.
ULYSSES GETT, AUTHOR OF ENOUGH ALREADY: IN DEFENSE OF THE WHITE AMERICAN MALE, ALREADY: A CONTROVERSIAL FIGURE FOR HIS WELL-PUBLICIZED REMARKS ON PUERTO RICANS...
AND MARTHA MOORE, LECTURER IN SOCIAL MEDIA STUDIES AT YALE AND A KEY MEMBER OF THE DREAMCATCHER COALITION, ESTABLISHED BY HOLLYWOOD AND MUSIC INDUSTRY CELEBRITIES IN RESPONSE TO THE MONUMENT VALLEY TRAGEDY.
ULYSSES, IF I CAN TURN TO YOU FIRST: THOUSANDS OF NAVAJO DEAD OR DYING, A PROUD PEOPLE BROUGHT LOW, THEIR LANDS RENDERED UNINHABITABLE--
WHERE DO WE GO FROM HERE?
WELL, IT'S NOT LIKE THEY'RE NOT USED TO IT, IS IT, JEFF?
ER...
AFTER ALL, WE USED TO TEST OUR NUKES OUT THERE ALL THE TIME, DIDN'T WE? IN THE FIFTIES? SURE WE DID.
THEY GOT USED TO THAT, THEY CAN GET USED TO THIS. YES, IT'S A TRAGEDY, BLAH-BLAH-BLAH AND SO ON, BUT AT THE END OF THE DAY--LIFE SUCKS. GET A RADIATION SUIT.

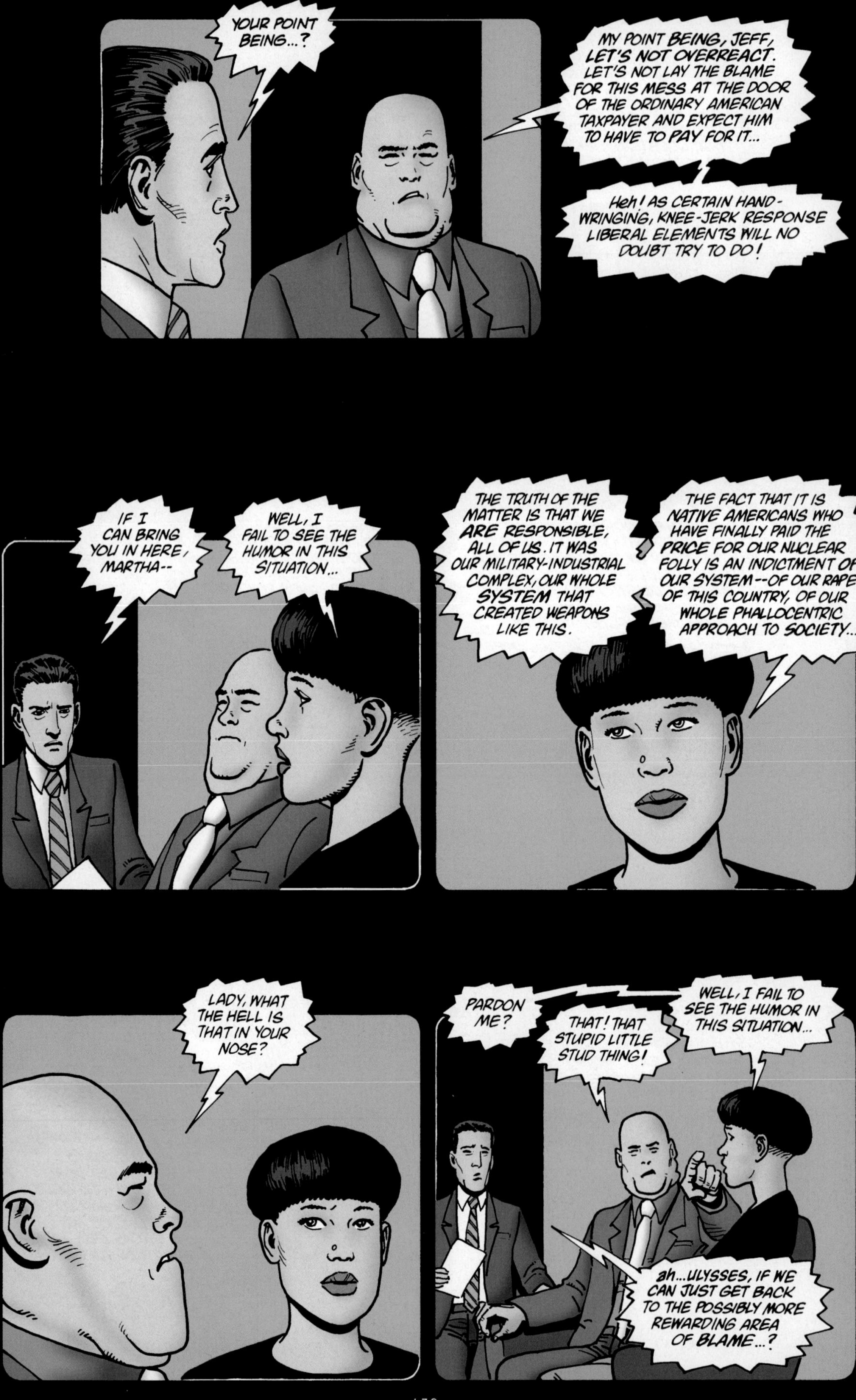
YOUR POINT BEING...?
MY POINT BEING, JEFF, LET'S NOT OVERREACT. LET'S NOT LAY THE BLAME FOR THIS MESS AT THE DOOR OF THE ORDINARY AMERICAN TAXPAYER AND EXPECT HIM TO HAVE TO PAY FOR IT...
Heh! AS CERTAIN HAND-WRINGING, KNEE-JERK RESPONSE LIBERAL ELEMENTS WILL NO DOUBT TRY TO DO!
IF I CAN BRING YOU IN HERE, MARTHA--
WELL, I FAIL TO SEE THE HUMOR IN THIS SITUATION...
THE TRUTH OF THE MATTER IS THAT WE ARE RESPONSIBLE, ALL OF US. IT WAS OUR MILITARY-INDUSTRIAL COMPLEX, OUR WHOLE SYSTEM THAT CREATED WEAPONS LIKE THIS.
THE FACT THAT IT IS NATIVE AMERICANS WHO HAVE FINALLY PAID THE PRICE FOR OUR NUCLEAR FOLLY IS AN INDICTMENT OF OUR SYSTEM--OF OUR RAPE OF THIS COUNTRY, OF OUR WHOLE PHALLOCENTRIC APPROACH TO SOCIETY...
LADY, WHAT THE HELL IS THAT IN YOUR NOSE?
PARDON ME?
THAT! THAT STUPID LITTLE STUD THING!
WELL, I FAIL TO SEE THE HUMOR IN THIS SITUATION...
ah...ULYSSES, IF WE CAN JUST GET BACK TO THE POSSIBLY MORE REWARDING AREA OF BLAME...?

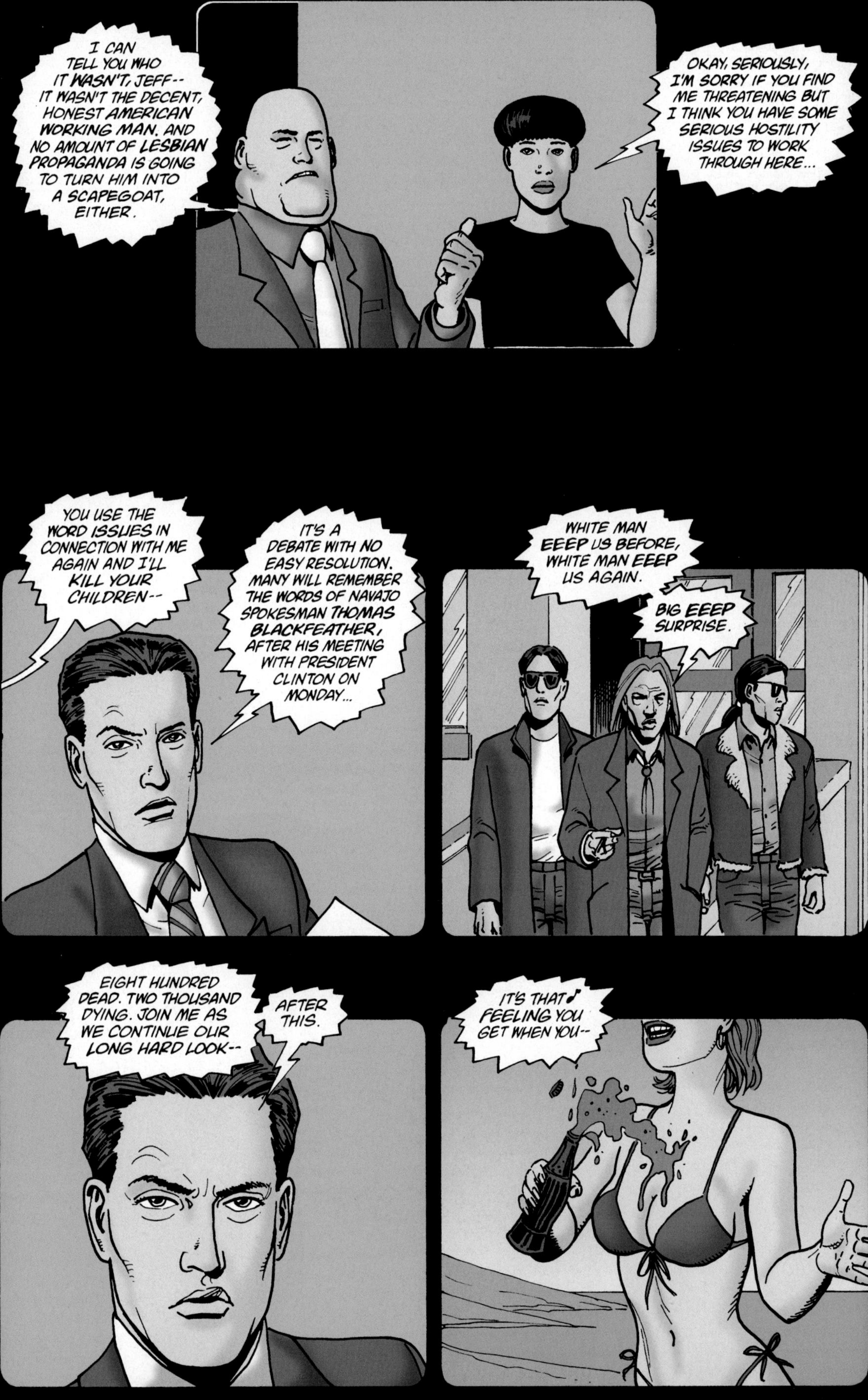
I CAN TELL YOU WHO IT WASN'T, JEFF-- IT WASN'T THE DECENT, HONEST AMERICAN WORKING MAN. AND NO AMOUNT OF LESBIAN PROPAGANDA IS GOING TO TURN HIM INTO A SCAPEGOAT, EITHER.
OKAY, SERIOUSLY, I'M SORRY IF YOU FIND ME THREATENING BUT I THINK YOU HAVE SOME SERIOUS HOSTILITY ISSUES TO WORK THROUGH HERE...
YOU USE THE WORD ISSUES IN CONNECTION WITH ME AGAIN AND I'LL KILL YOUR CHILDREN--
IT'S A DEBATE WITH NO EASY RESOLUTION. MANY WILL REMEMBER THE WORDS OF NAVAJO SPOKESMAN THOMAS BLACKFEATHER, AFTER HIS MEETING WITH PRESIDENT CLINTON ON MONDAY...
WHITE MAN EEEP US BEFORE, WHITE MAN EEEP US AGAIN.
BIG EEEP SURPRISE.
EIGHT HUNDRED DEAD. TWO THOUSAND DYING. JOIN ME AS WE CONTINUE OUR LONG HARD LOOK--
AFTER THIS.
IT'S THAT♪ FEELING YOU GET WHEN YOU--

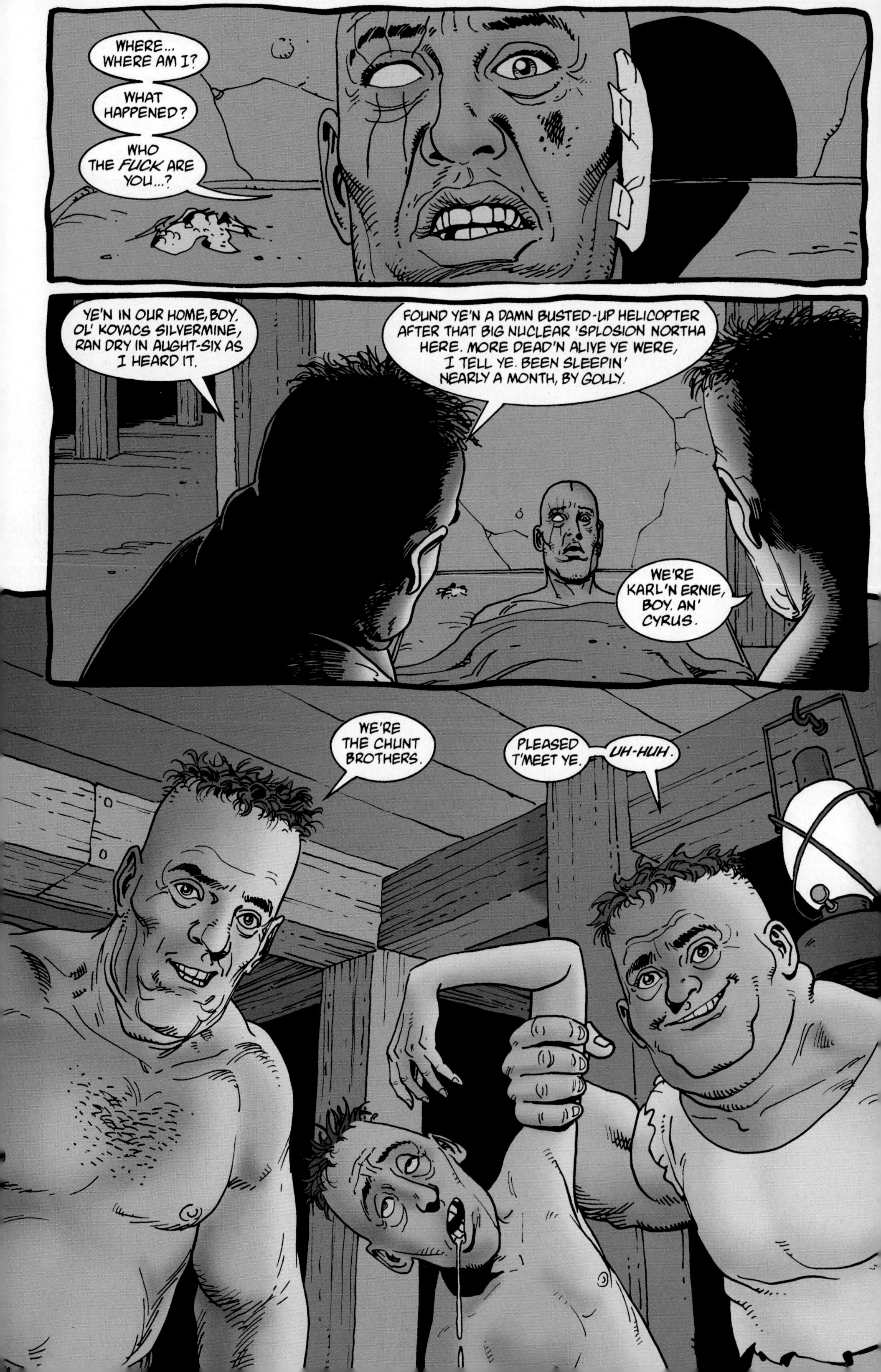
WHERE... WHERE AM I?
WHAT HAPPENED?
WHO THE *FUCK* ARE YOU...?
YE'N IN OUR HOME, BOY. OL' KOVACS SILVERMINE, RAN DRY IN AUGHT-SIX AS I HEARD IT.
FOUND YE'N A DAMN BUSTED-UP HELICOPTER AFTER THAT BIG NUCLEAR 'SPLOSION NORTHA HERE. MORE DEAD'N ALIVE YE WERE, I TELL YE. BEEN SLEEPIN' NEARLY A MONTH, BY GOLLY.
WE'RE KARL'N ERNIE, BOY. AN' CYRUS.
WE'RE THE CHUNT BROTHERS.
PLEASED T'MEET YE.
UH-HUH.

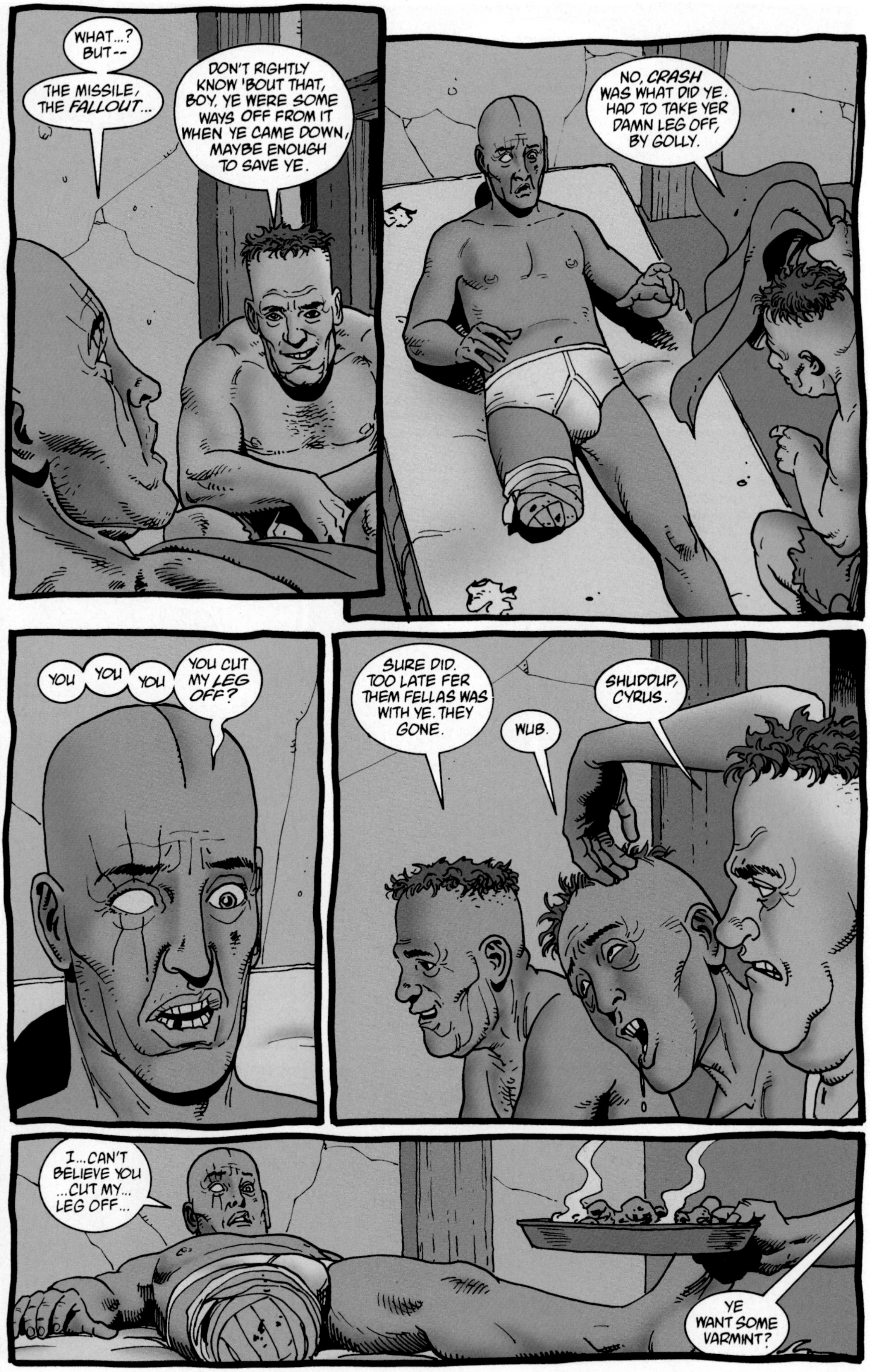
WHAT...? BUT--
THE MISSILE, THE *FALLOUT*...
DON'T RIGHTLY KNOW 'BOUT THAT, BOY. YE WERE SOME WAYS OFF FROM IT WHEN YE CAME DOWN, MAYBE ENOUGH TO SAVE YE.
NO, *CRASH* WAS WHAT DID YE. HAD TO TAKE YER DAMN LEG OFF, BY GOLLY.
YOU
YOU
YOU
YOU CUT MY *LEG* OFF?
SURE DID. TOO LATE FER THEM FELLAS WAS WITH YE. THEY GONE.
WUB.
SHUDDUP, CYRUS.
I...CAN'T BELIEVE YOU ...CUT MY... LEG OFF...
YE WANT SOME VARMINT?

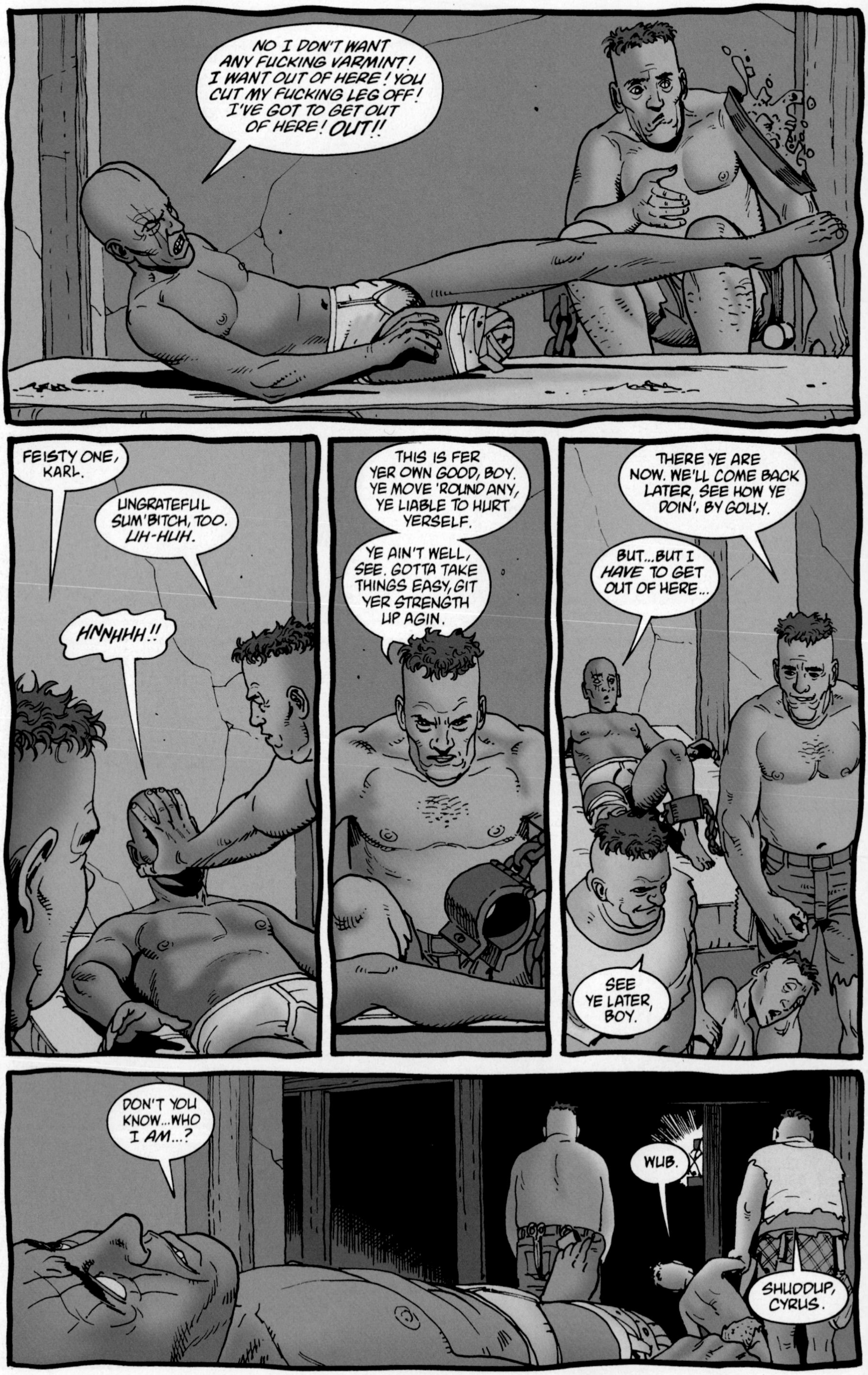
NO I DON'T WANT ANY FUCKING VARMINT! I WANT OUT OF HERE! YOU CUT MY FUCKING LEG OFF! I'VE GOT TO GET OUT OF HERE! OUT!!
FEISTY ONE, KARL.
UNGRATEFUL SUM'BITCH, TOO. UH-HUH.
HNHHH!!
THIS IS FER YER OWN GOOD, BOY. YE MOVE 'ROUND ANY, YE LIABLE TO HURT YERSELF.
YE AIN'T WELL, SEE. GOTTA TAKE THINGS EASY, GIT YER STRENGTH UP AGIN.
THERE YE ARE NOW. WE'LL COME BACK LATER, SEE HOW YE DOIN', BY GOLLY.
BUT...BUT I HAVE TO GET OUT OF HERE...
SEE YE LATER, BOY.
DON'T YOU KNOW...WHO I AM...?
WUB.
SHUDDUP, CYRUS.

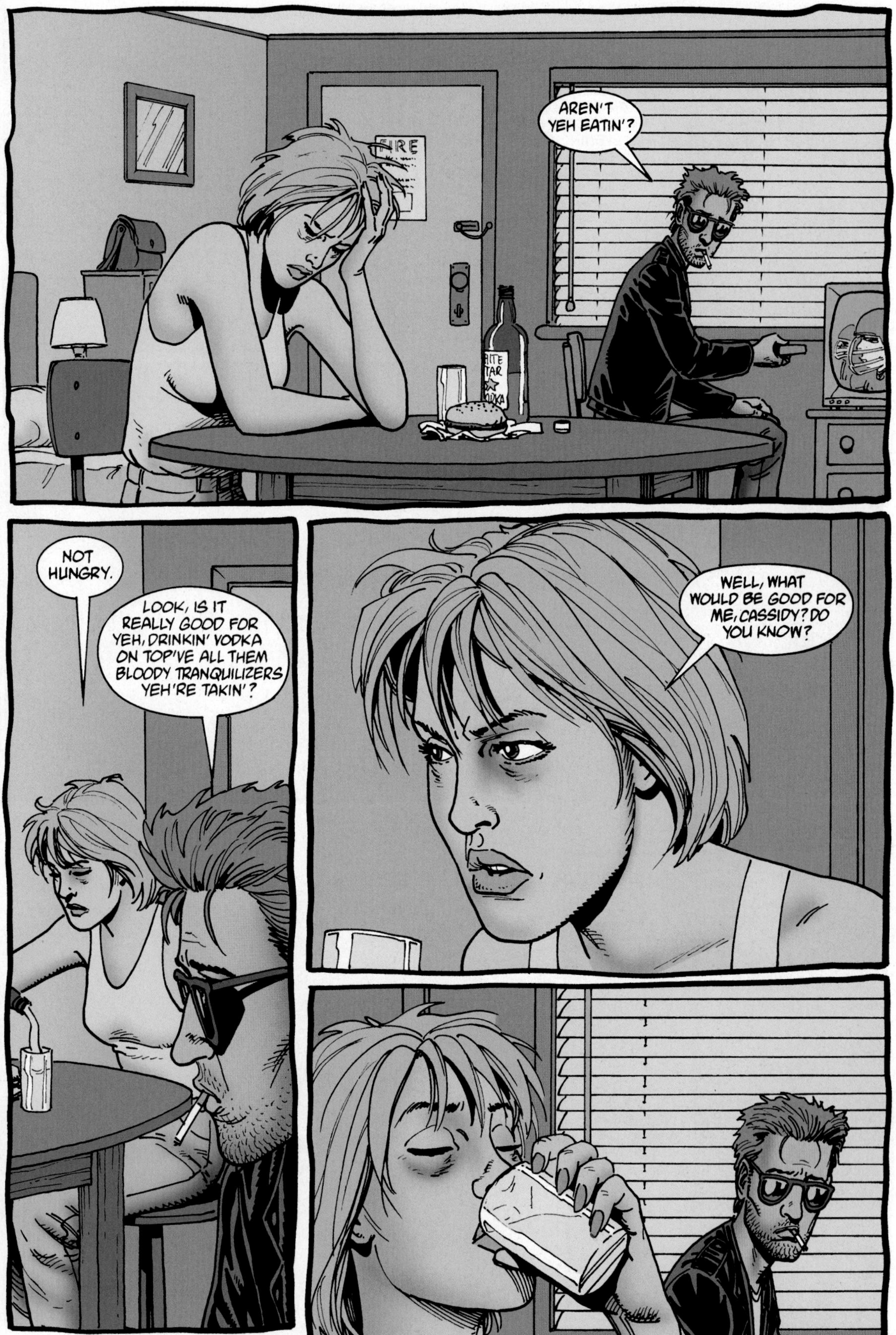
AREN'T YEH EATIN'?
NOT HUNGRY.
LOOK, IS IT REALLY GOOD FOR YEH, DRINKIN' VODKA ON TOP'VE ALL THEM BLOODY TRANQUILIZERS YEH'RE TAKIN'?
WELL, WHAT WOULD BE GOOD FOR ME, CASSIDY? DO YOU KNOW?

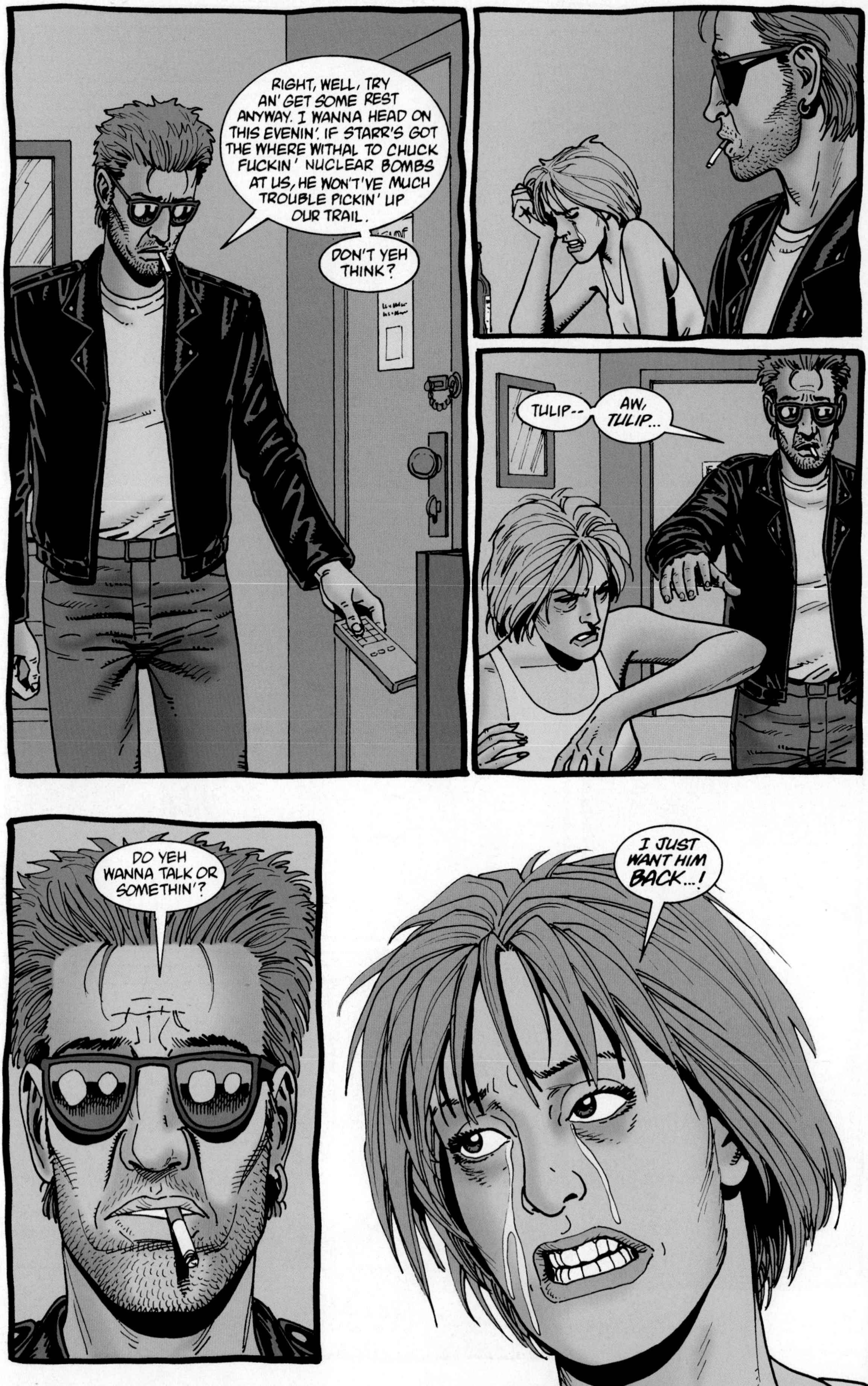
RIGHT, WELL, TRY AN' GET SOME REST ANYWAY. I WANNA HEAD ON THIS EVENIN'. IF STARR'S GOT THE WHERE WITHAL TO CHUCK FUCKIN' NUCLEAR BOMBS AT US, HE WON'T'VE MUCH TROUBLE PICKIN' UP OUR TRAIL.
DON'T YEH THINK?
TULIP--
AW, TULIP...
DO YEH WANNA TALK OR SOMETHIN'?
I JUST WANT HIM BACK...!

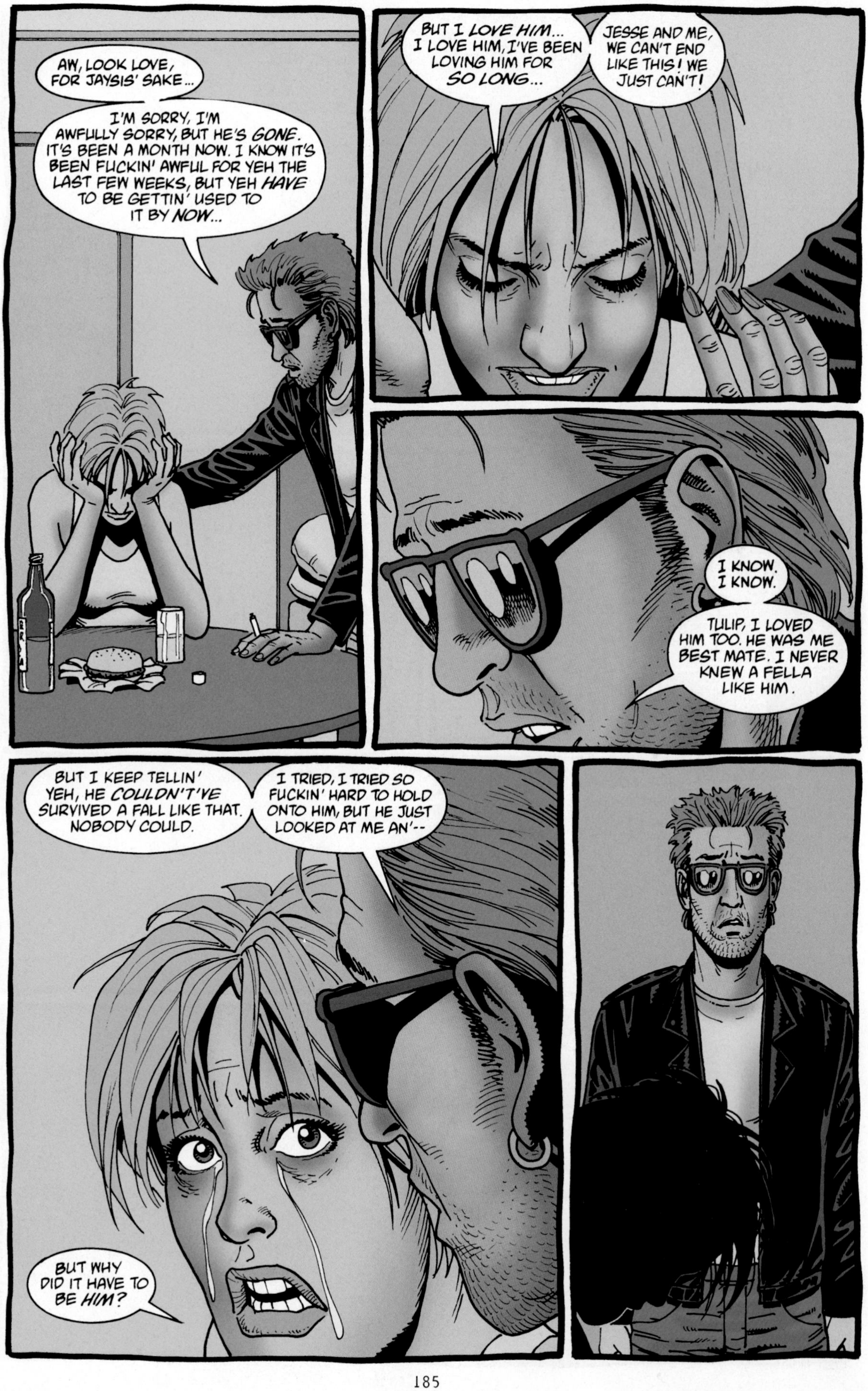
AW, LOOK LOVE, FOR JAYSIS' SAKE...
I'M SORRY, I'M AWFULLY SORRY, BUT HE'S GONE. IT'S BEEN A MONTH NOW. I KNOW IT'S BEEN FUCKIN' AWFUL FOR YEH THE LAST FEW WEEKS, BUT YEH HAVE TO BE GETTIN' USED TO IT BY NOW...
BUT I LOVE HIM... I LOVE HIM, I'VE BEEN LOVING HIM FOR SO LONG...
JESSE AND ME, WE CAN'T END LIKE THIS! WE JUST CAN'T!
I KNOW. I KNOW.
TULIP, I LOVED HIM TOO. HE WAS ME BEST MATE. I NEVER KNEW A FELLA LIKE HIM.
BUT I KEEP TELLIN' YEH, HE COULDN'T'VE SURVIVED A FALL LIKE THAT. NOBODY COULD.
I TRIED, I TRIED SO FUCKIN' HARD TO HOLD ONTO HIM, BUT HE JUST LOOKED AT ME AN'--
BUT WHY DID IT HAVE TO BE HIM?

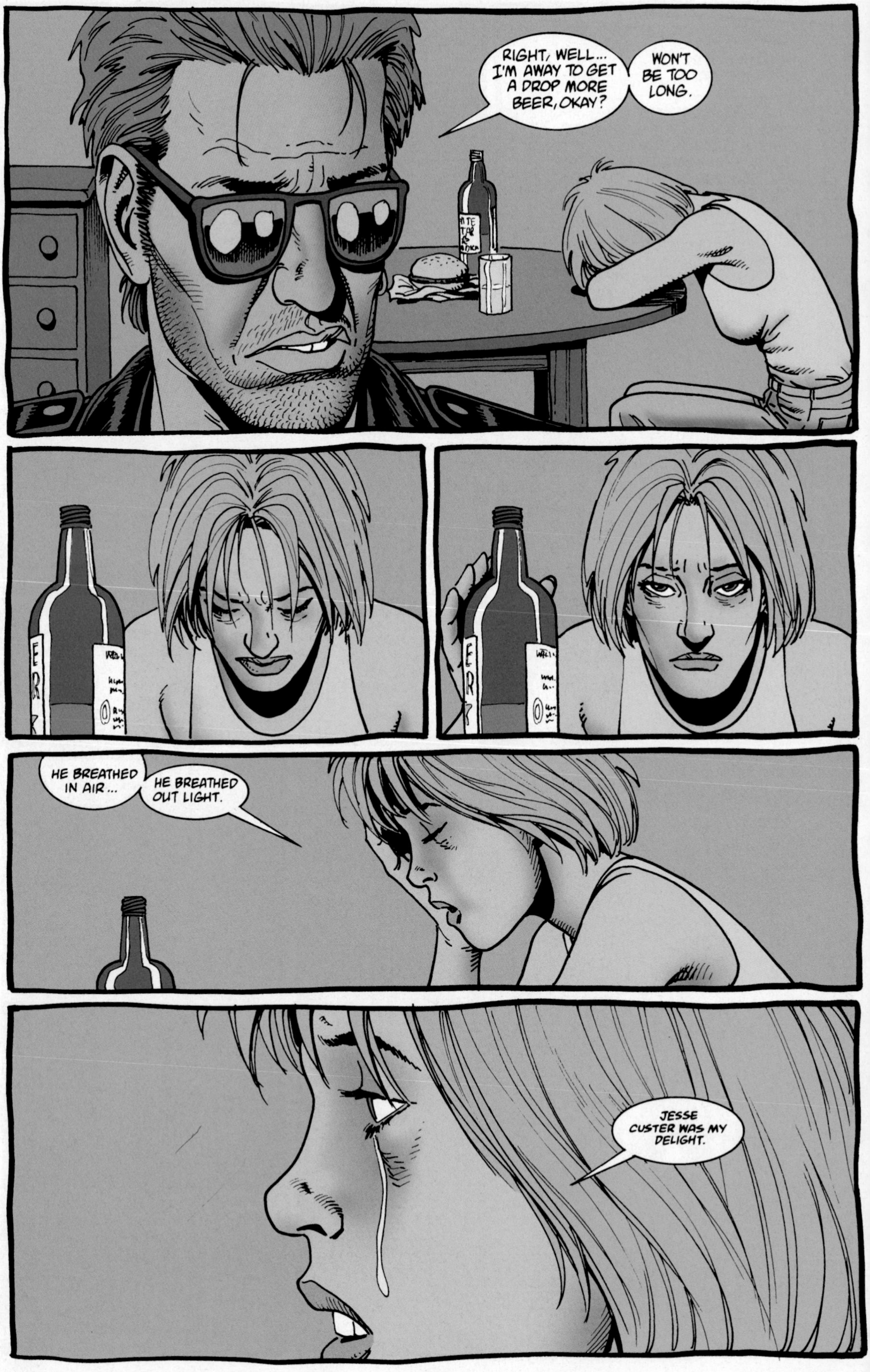
RIGHT, WELL... I'M AWAY TO GET A DROP MORE BEER, OKAY?
WON'T BE TOO LONG.
HE BREATHED IN AIR...
HE BREATHED OUT LIGHT.
JESSE CUSTER WAS MY DELIGHT.

BAD NEWS FOR
ARSEFACE TODAY;
DESPITE HIS SECOND
WEEK AT NUMBER ONE WITH
DEBUT SINGLE YOU OUGHTTA
KNOW, THE DREAMCATCHER
COALITION HAS TURNED
DOWN HIS OFFER TO JOIN
THEIR BENEFIT FOR VICTIMS
OF THE MONUMENT VALLEY
TRAGEDY. A SPOKESPERSON
COMMENTED SIMPLY,
"BE SERIOUS."

SCATTI SUMMERS
WENT FACE TO
ARSEFACE--

SO HOW
DOES THAT
COMMENT
MAKE OO
FEEL?

UH?

DO OO
FINK OO LACK
CWEDIBILITY?

UH JUHZ
WUNUH HULB
PUBBEL--

IF AH MAY SAY
A WORD OR TWO IN
ARSEFACE'S
DEFENSE...

ARSE
POWER

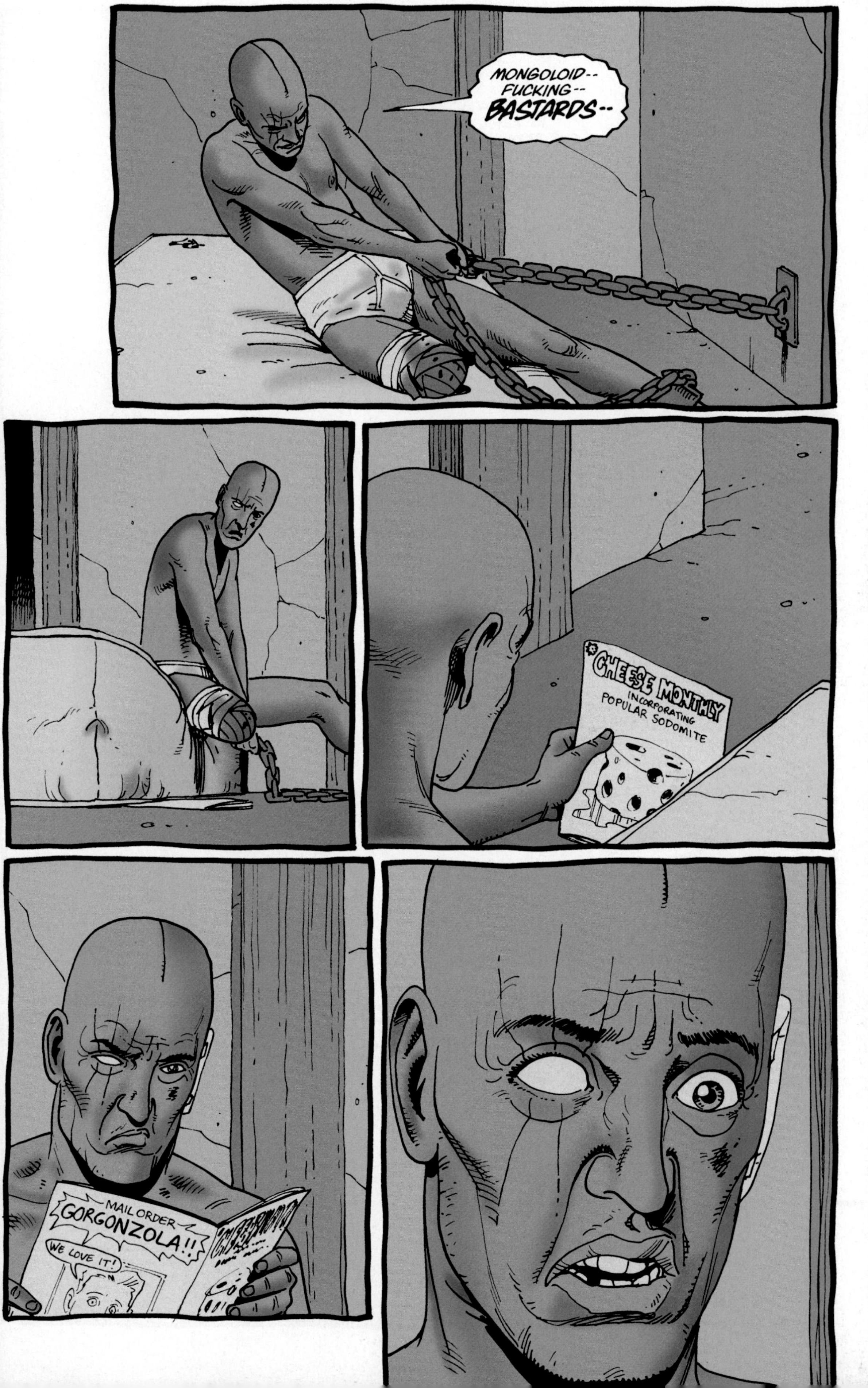
MONGOLOID--
FUCKING--
BASTARDS--
CHEESE MONTHLY
INCORPORATING
POPULAR SODOMITE
MAIL ORDER
GORGONZOLA!!
WE LOVE IT!

190

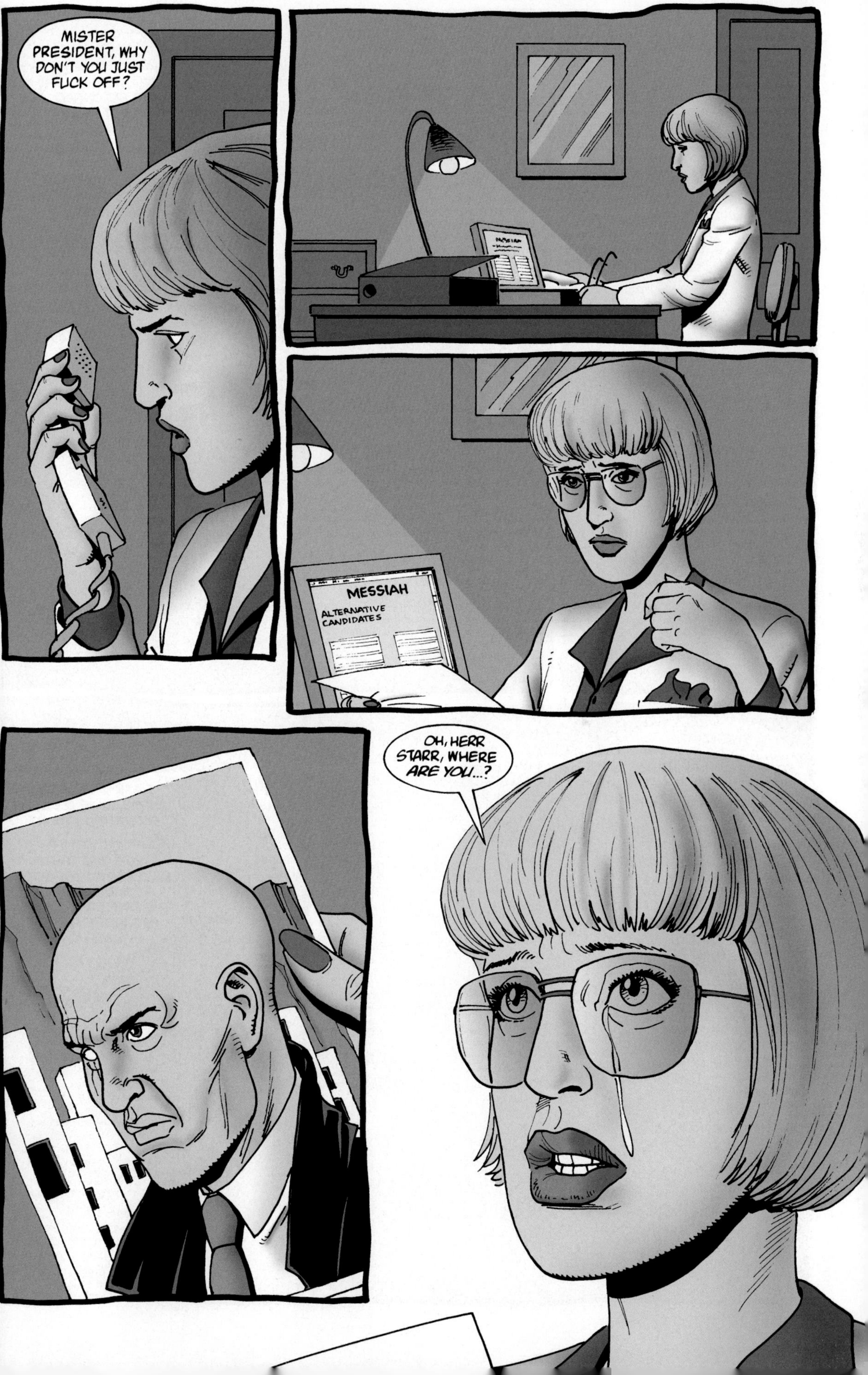
MISTER PRESIDENT, WHY DON'T YOU JUST FUCK OFF?
MESSIAH
MESSIAH
ALTERNATIVE CANDIDATES
OH, HERR STARR, WHERE ARE YOU...?

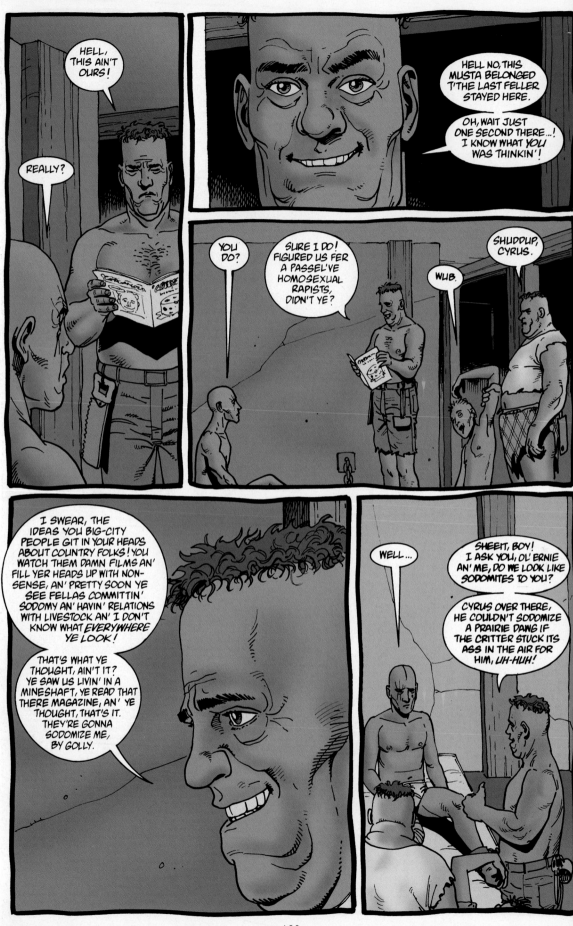

HELL, THIS AIN'T OURS!

REALLY?

HELL NO, THIS MUSTA BELONGED T'THE LAST FELLER STAYED HERE.

OH, WAIT JUST ONE SECOND THERE...! I KNOW WHAT *YOU* WAS THINKIN'!

YOU?

YOU DO?

SURE I DO! FIGURED US FER A PASSEL'VE HOMOSEXUAL RAPISTS, DIDN'T YE?

SHUDDUP, CYRUS.

WUB.

I SWEAR, THE IDEAS YOU BIG-CITY PEOPLE GIT IN YOUR HEADS ABOUT COUNTRY FOLKS! YOU WATCH THEM DAMN FILMS AN' FILL YER HEADS UP WITH NON-SENSE, AN' PRETTY SOON YE SEE FELLAS COMMITTIN' SODOMY AN' HAVIN' RELATIONS WITH LIVESTOCK AN' I DON'T KNOW WHAT *EVERYWHERE* YE LOOK!

THAT'S WHAT YE THOUGHT, AIN'T IT? YE SAW US LIVIN' IN A MINESHAFT, YE READ THAT THERE MAGAZINE, AN' YE THOUGHT, THAT'S IT. THEY'RE GONNA SODOMIZE ME, BY GOLLY.

WELL...

SHEEIT, BOY! I ASK YOU, OL' ERNIE AN' ME, DO WE LOOK LIKE SODOMITES TO YOU?

CYRUS OVER THERE, HE COULDN'T SODOMIZE A PRAIRIE DAWG IF THE CRITTER STUCK ITS ASS IN THE AIR FOR HIM, *UH-HUH!*

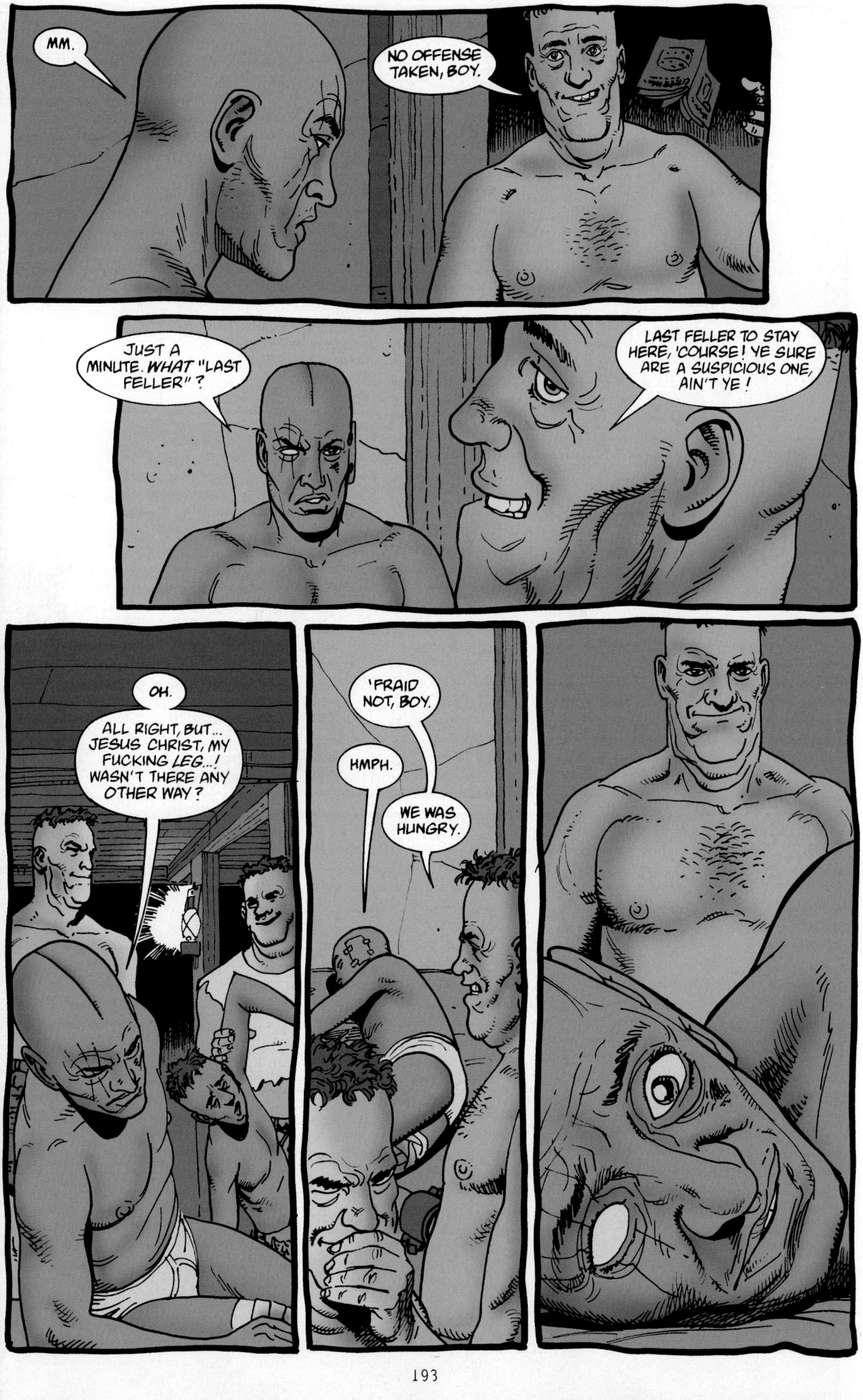
MM.
NO OFFENSE TAKEN, BOY.
JUST A MINUTE. WHAT "LAST FELLER"?
LAST FELLER TO STAY HERE, 'COURSE! YE SURE ARE A SUSPICIOUS ONE, AIN'T YE!
OH.
ALL RIGHT, BUT... JESUS CHRIST, MY FUCKING LEG...! WASN'T THERE ANY OTHER WAY?
'FRAID NOT, BOY.
HMPH.
WE WAS HUNGRY.

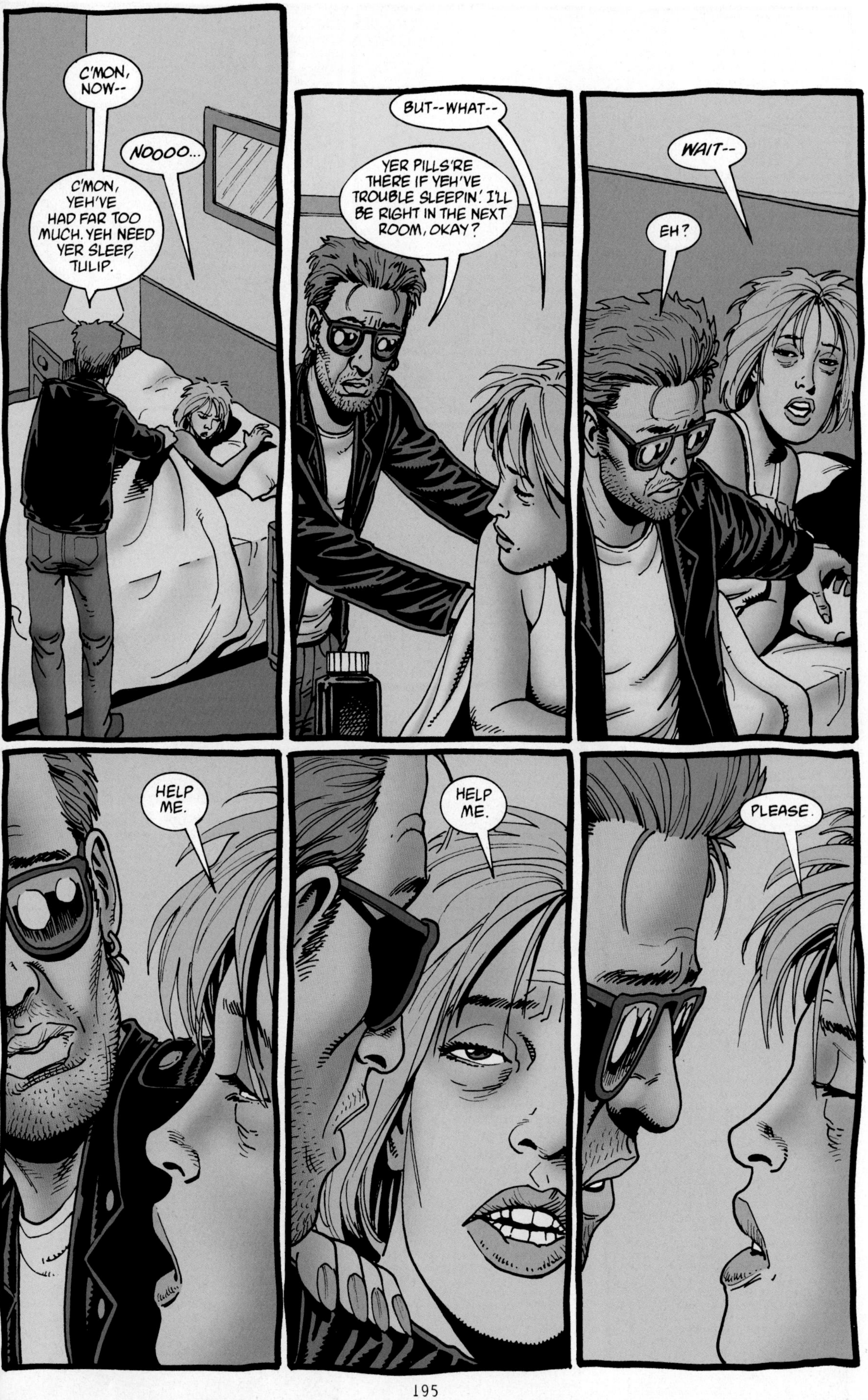
C'MON, NOW--
NOOOO...
C'MON, YEH'VE HAD FAR TOO MUCH. YEH NEED YER SLEEP, TULIP.
BUT--WHAT--
YER PILLS'RE THERE IF YEH'VE TROUBLE SLEEPIN'. I'LL BE RIGHT IN THE NEXT ROOM, OKAY?
WAIT--
EH?
HELP ME.
HELP ME.
PLEASE.

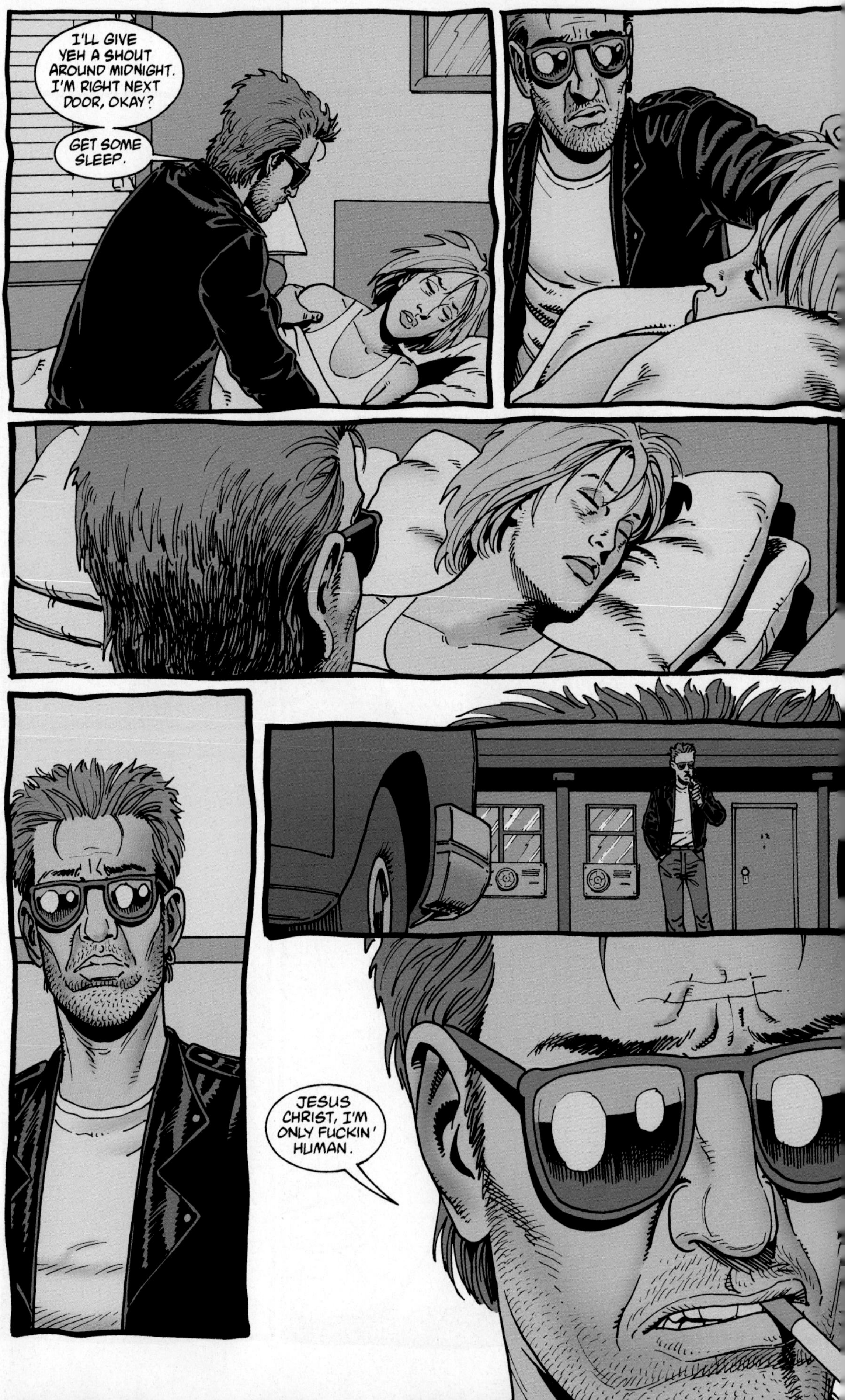
I'LL GIVE YEH A SHOUT AROUND MIDNIGHT. I'M RIGHT NEXT DOOR, OKAY?
GET SOME SLEEP.
JESUS CHRIST, I'M ONLY FUCKIN' HUMAN.

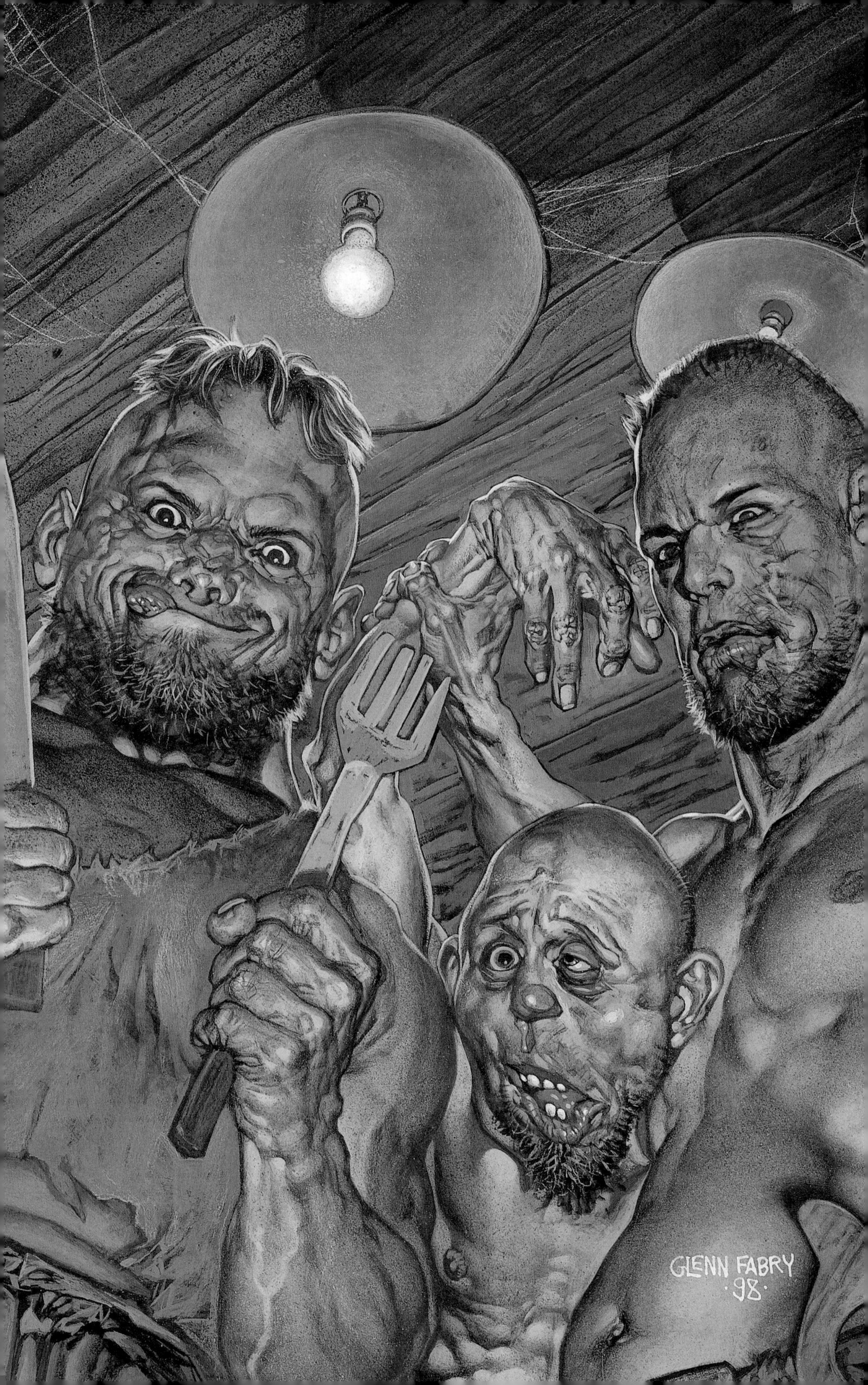
GLENN FABRY
·98·

"For what I am now forced to do,
I will one day wreak vengeance upon God himself."

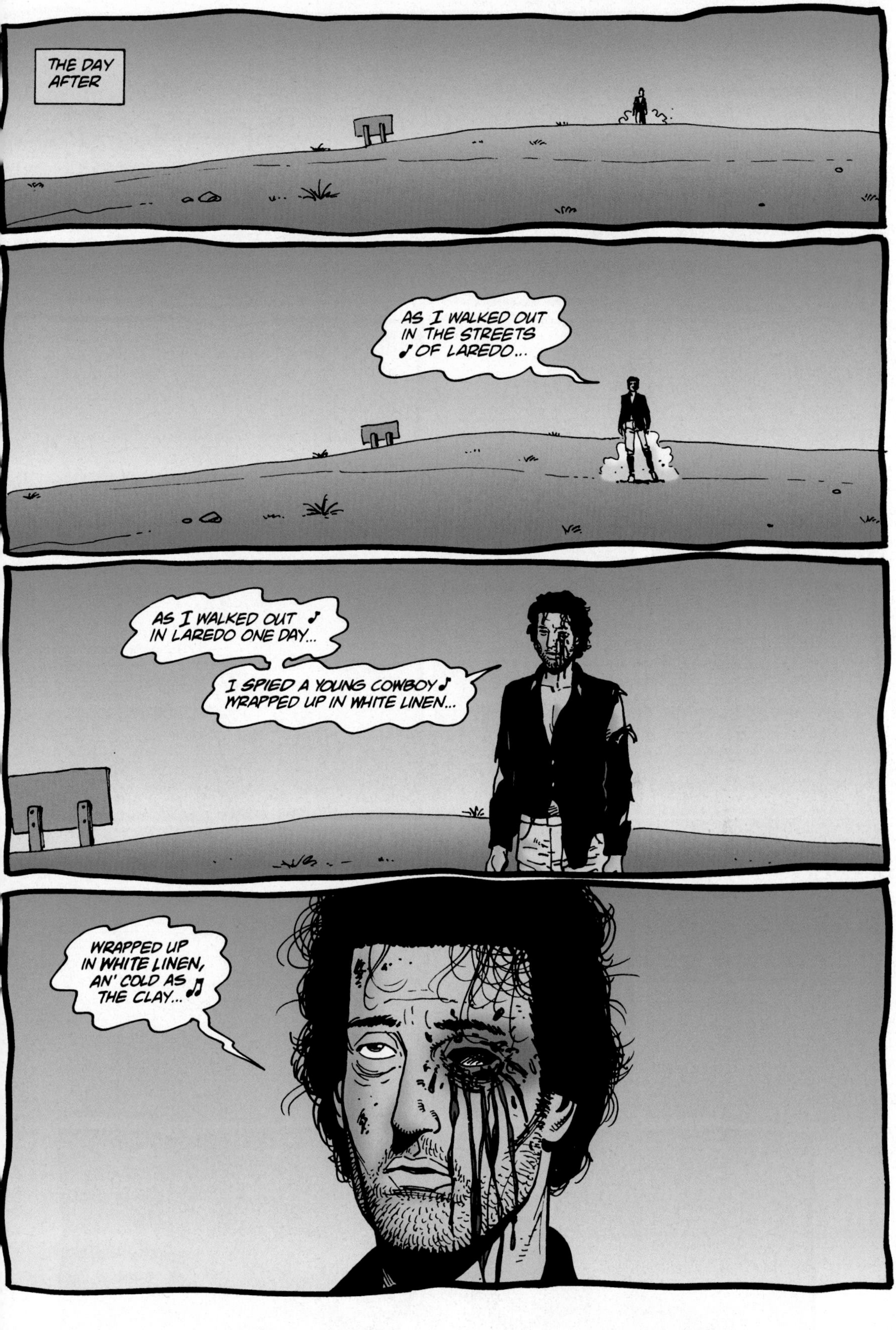
THE DAY AFTER
AS I WALKED OUT IN THE STREETS OF LAREDO...
AS I WALKED OUT IN LAREDO ONE DAY...
I SPIED A YOUNG COWBOY WRAPPED UP IN WHITE LINEN...
WRAPPED UP IN WHITE LINEN, AN' COLD AS THE CLAY...

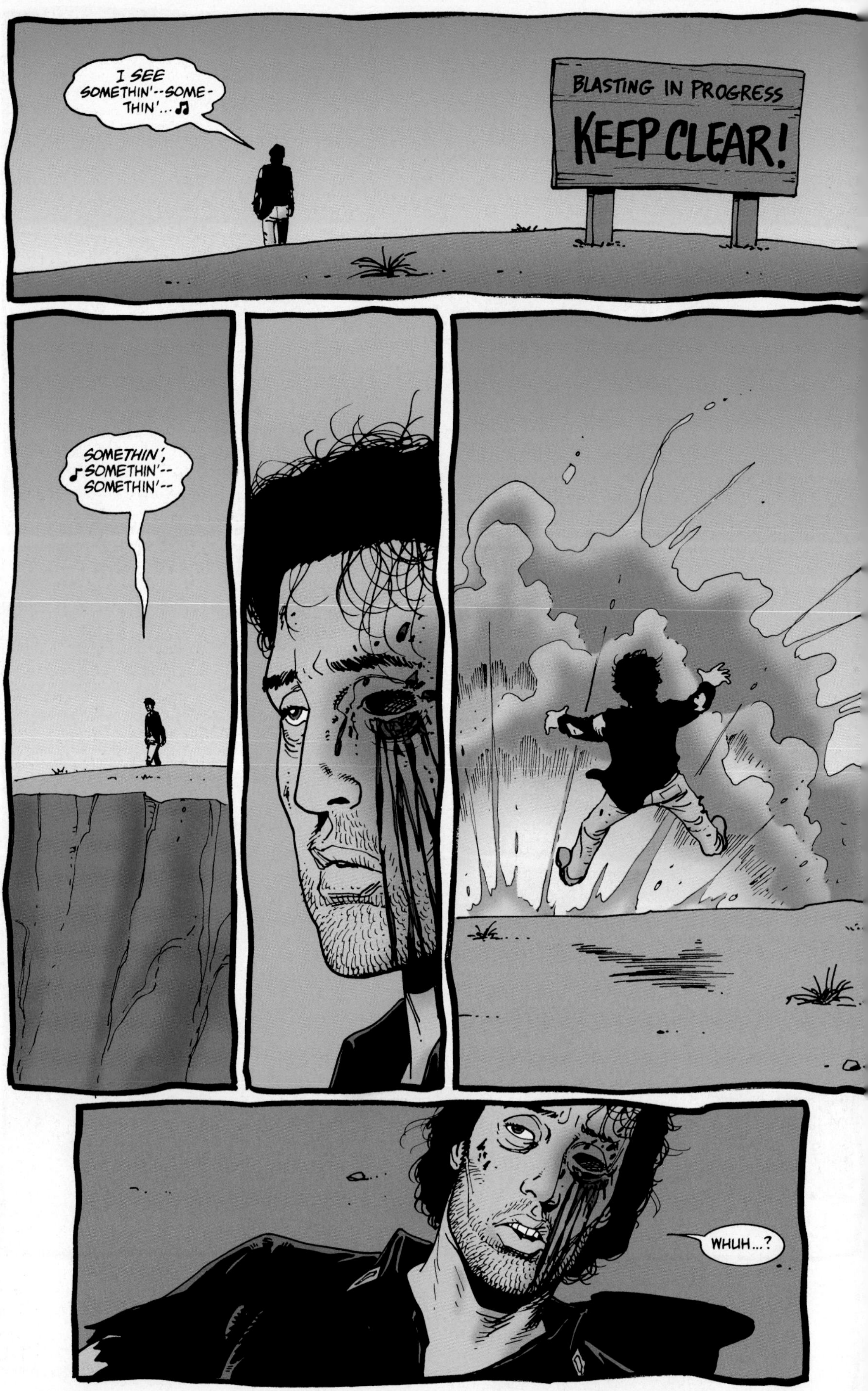
I SEE SOMETHIN'--SOME-THIN'... ♫
BLASTING IN PROGRESS
KEEP CLEAR!
SOMETHIN', ♪ SOMETHIN'-- SOMETHIN'--
WHUH...?

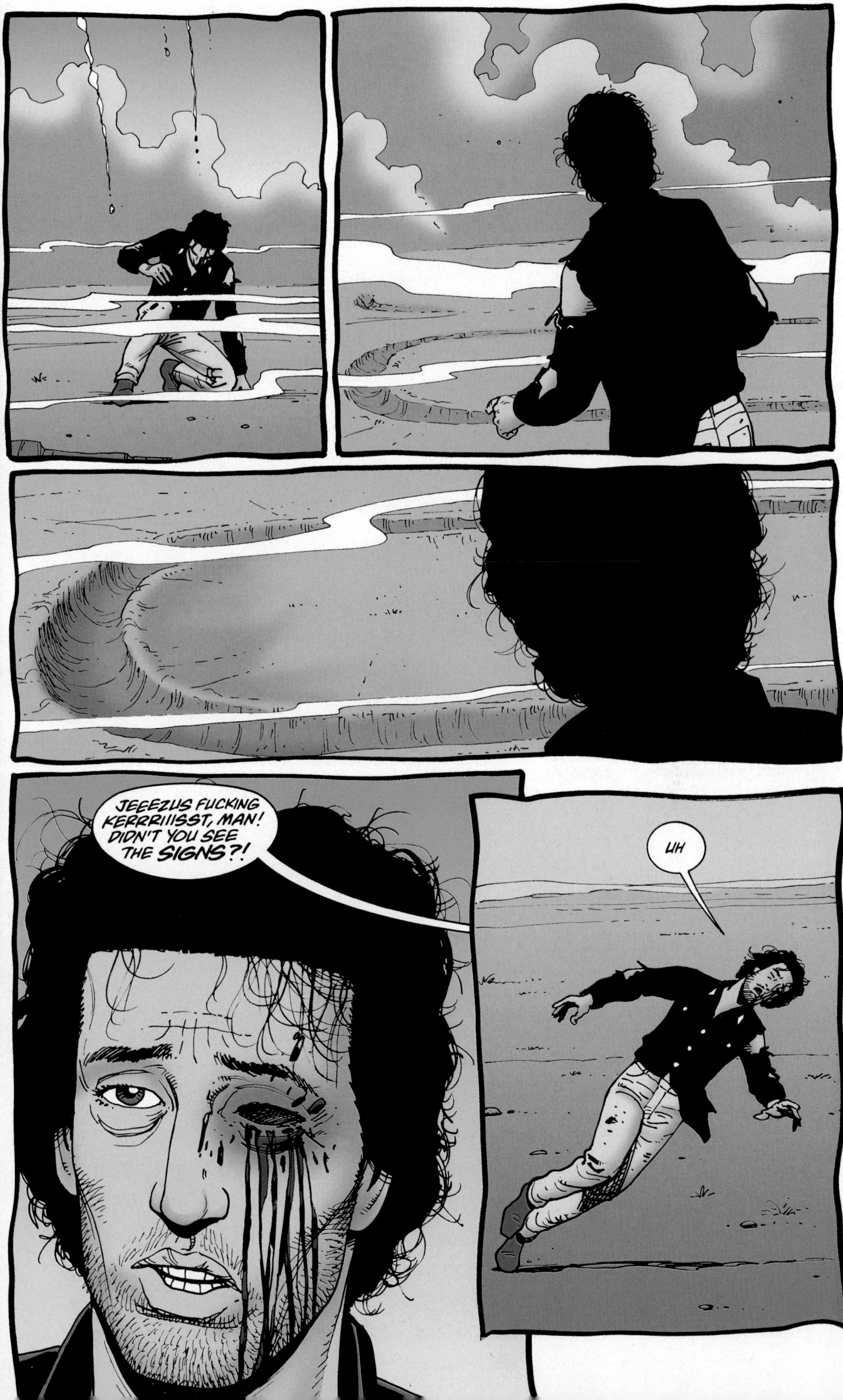
JEEEZUS FUCKING KERRRIIISST, MAN! DIDN'T YOU SEE THE SIGNS?!
UH

FOR ALL MANKIND

GARTH ENNIS-Writer STEVE DILLON-Artist

Pamela Rambo-Colorist, Clem Robins-Letterer, Axel Alonso-Editor

PREACHER created by Garth Ennis and Steve Dillon

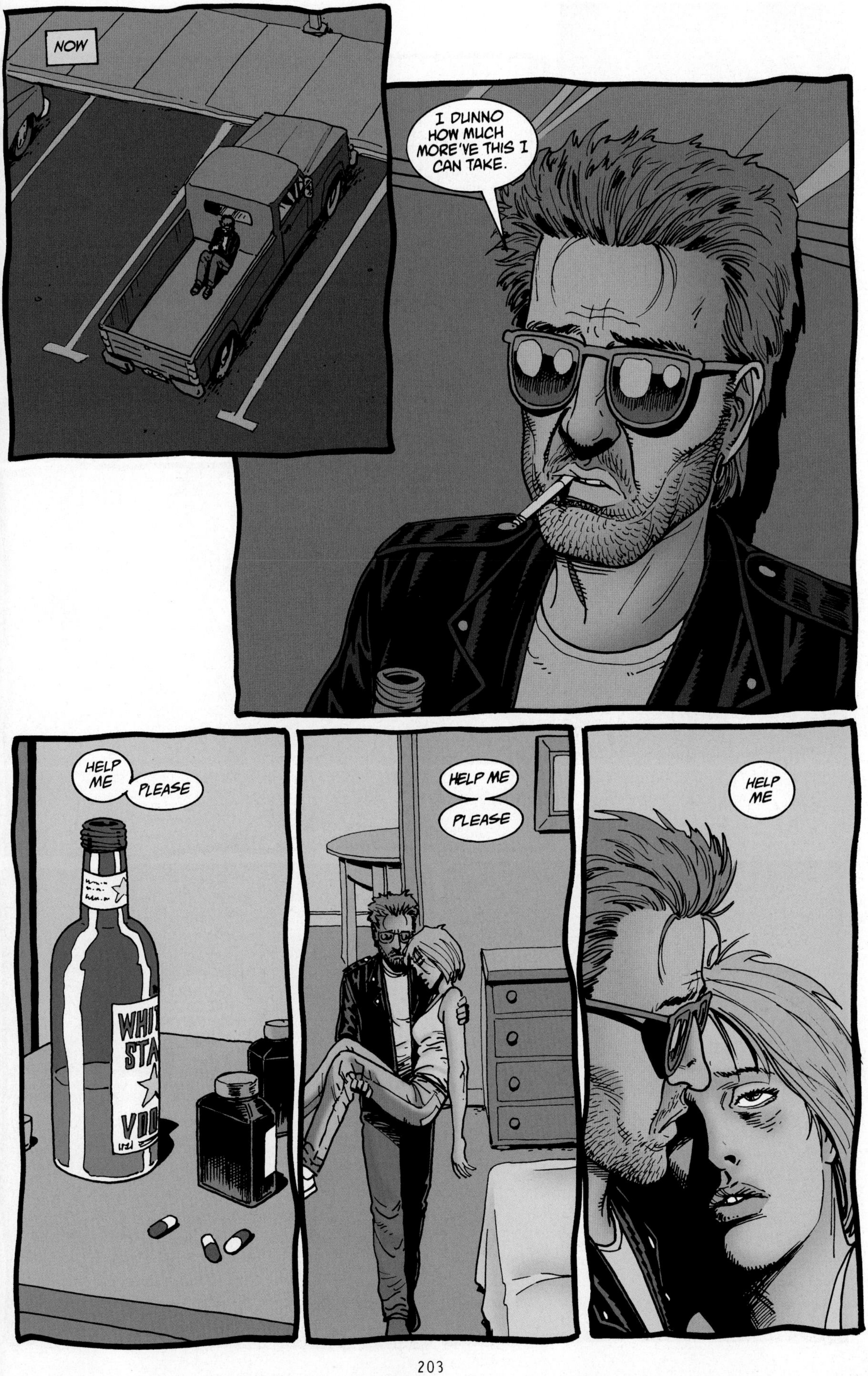
NOW
I DUNNO HOW MUCH MORE'VE THIS I CAN TAKE.
HELP ME
PLEASE
HELP ME
PLEASE
HELP ME

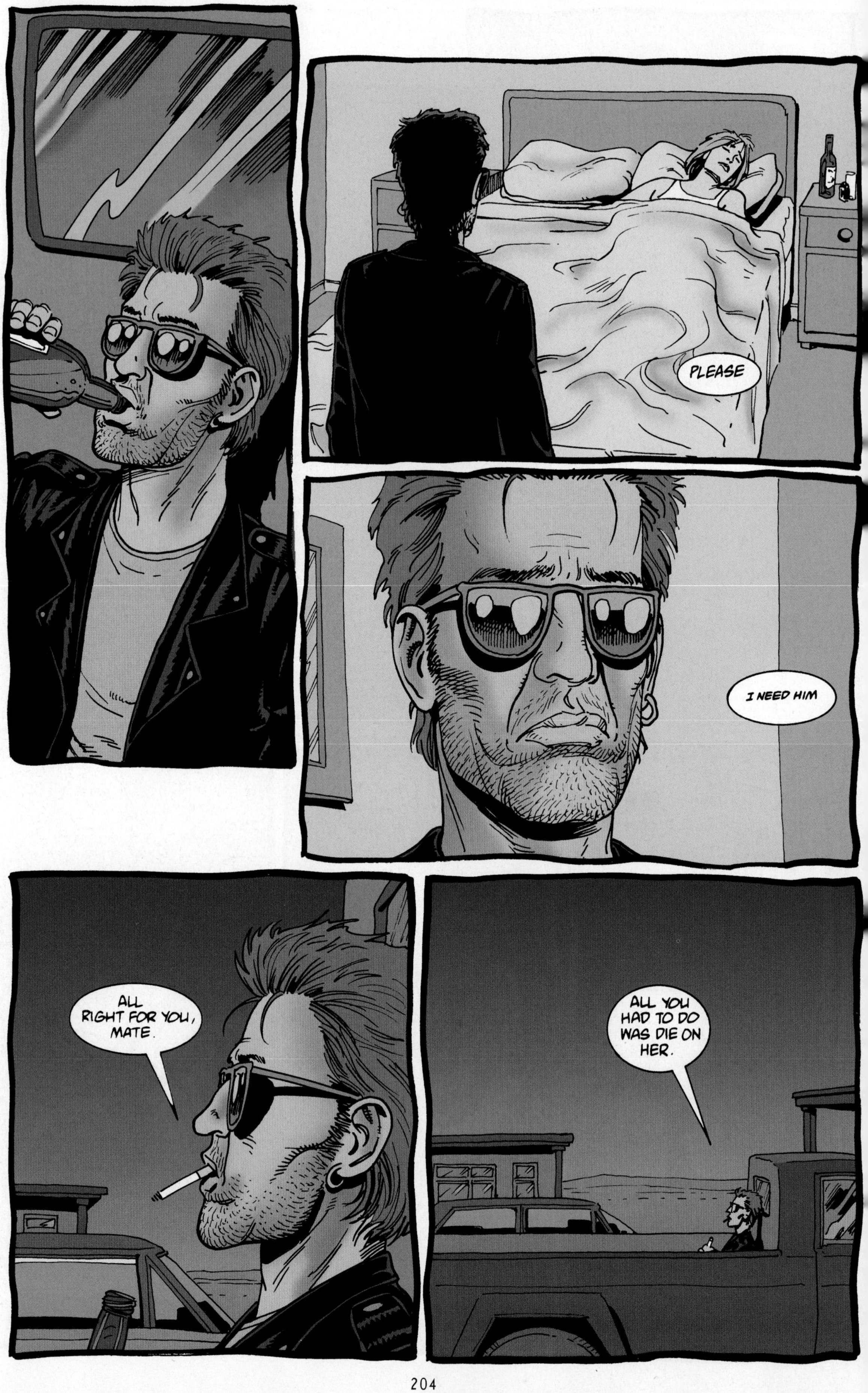
PLEASE
I NEED HIM
ALL RIGHT FOR YOU, MATE.
ALL YOU HAD TO DO WAS DIE ON HER.

205

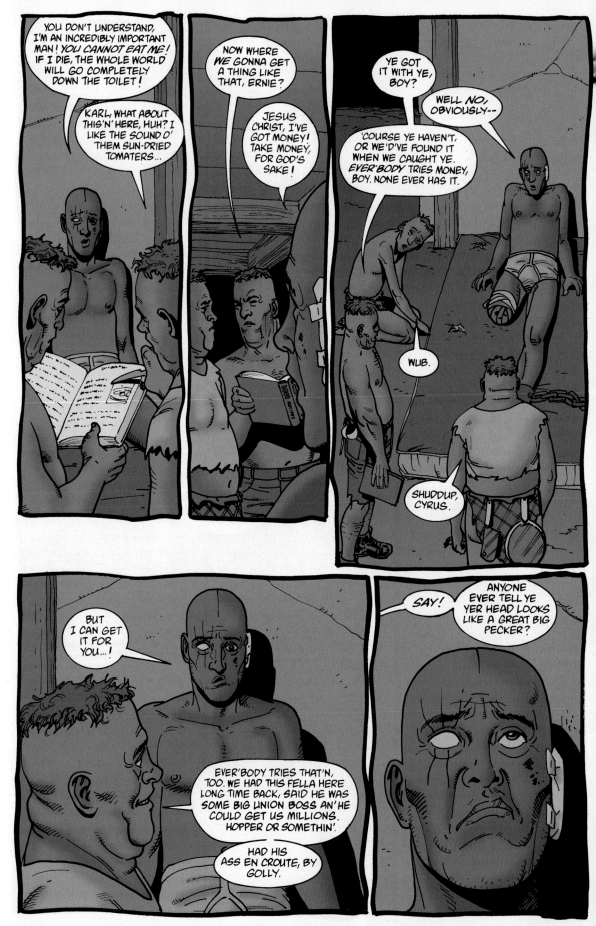

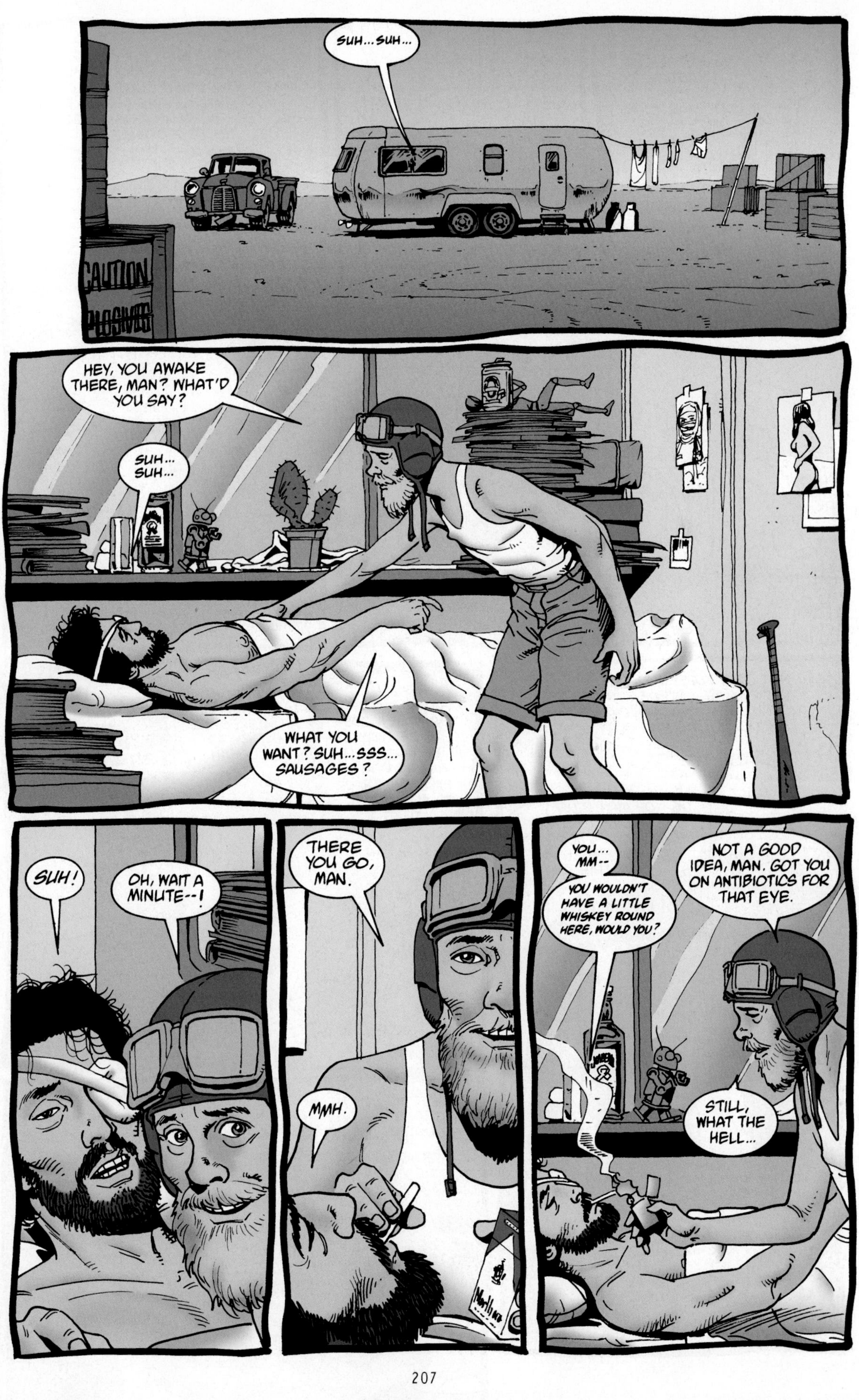
SUH... SUH...
CAUTION
HEY, YOU AWAKE THERE, MAN? WHAT'D YOU SAY?
SUH... SUH...
WHAT YOU WANT? SUH...SSS... SAUSAGES?
SUH!
OH, WAIT A MINUTE--!
THERE YOU GO, MAN.
MMH.
YOU... MM--
YOU WOULDN'T HAVE A LITTLE WHISKEY ROUND HERE, WOULD YOU?
NOT A GOOD IDEA, MAN. GOT YOU ON ANTIBIOTICS FOR THAT EYE.
STILL, WHAT THE HELL...

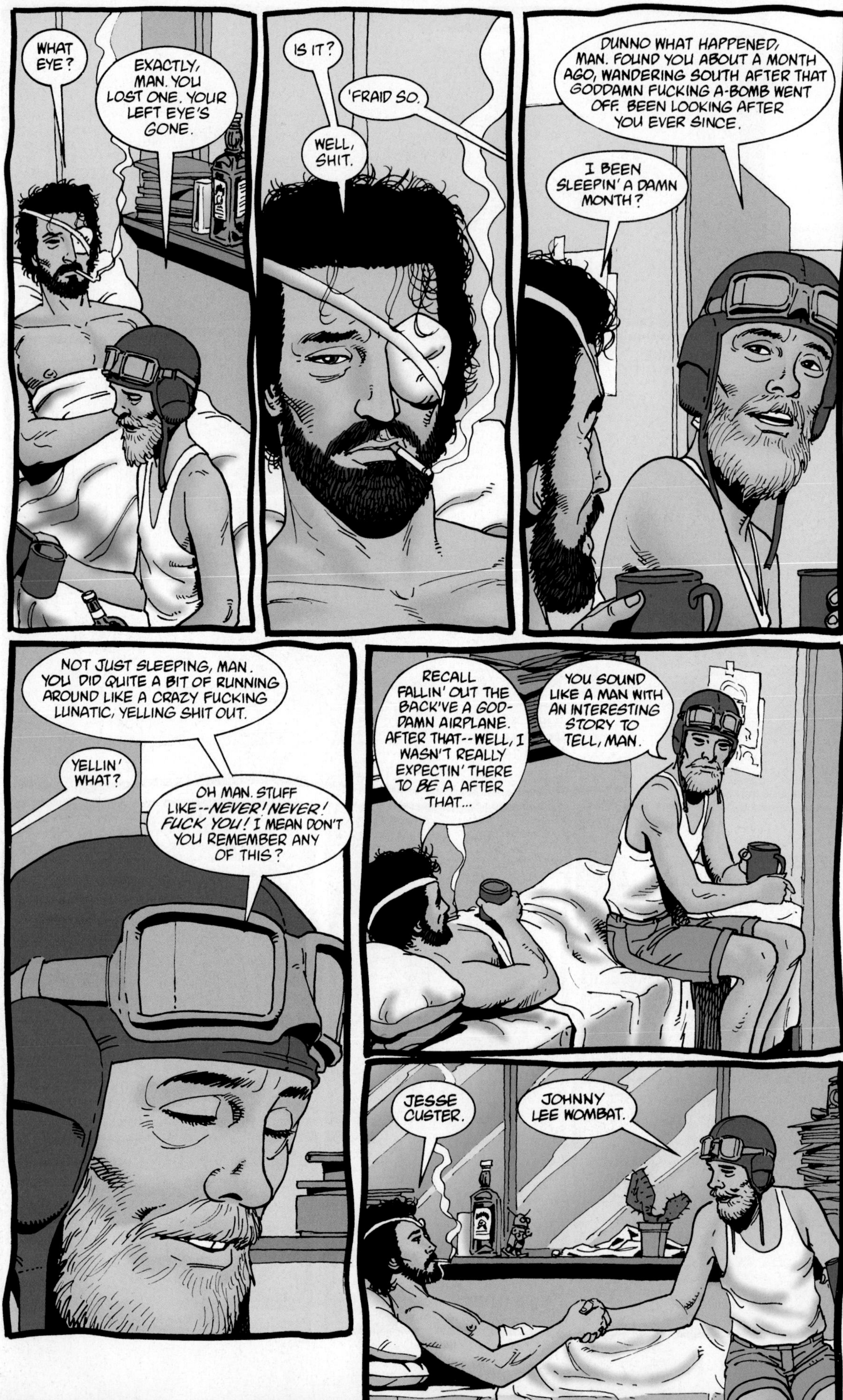

WHAT EYE?
EXACTLY, MAN. YOU LOST ONE. YOUR LEFT EYE'S GONE.
IS IT?
'FRAID SO.
WELL, SHIT.
DUNNO WHAT HAPPENED, MAN. FOUND YOU ABOUT A MONTH AGO, WANDERING SOUTH AFTER THAT GODDAMN FUCKING A-BOMB WENT OFF. BEEN LOOKING AFTER YOU EVER SINCE.
I BEEN SLEEPIN' A DAMN MONTH?
NOT JUST SLEEPING, MAN. YOU DID QUITE A BIT OF RUNNING AROUND LIKE A CRAZY FUCKING LUNATIC, YELLING SHIT OUT.
YELLIN' WHAT?
OH MAN. STUFF LIKE--*NEVER! NEVER! FUCK YOU!* I MEAN DON'T YOU REMEMBER ANY OF THIS?
RECALL FALLIN' OUT THE BACK'VE A GOD-DAMN AIRPLANE. AFTER THAT--WELL, I WASN'T REALLY EXPECTIN' THERE TO *BE* A AFTER THAT...
YOU SOUND LIKE A MAN WITH AN INTERESTING STORY TO TELL, MAN.
JESSE CUSTER.
JOHNNY LEE WOMBAT.

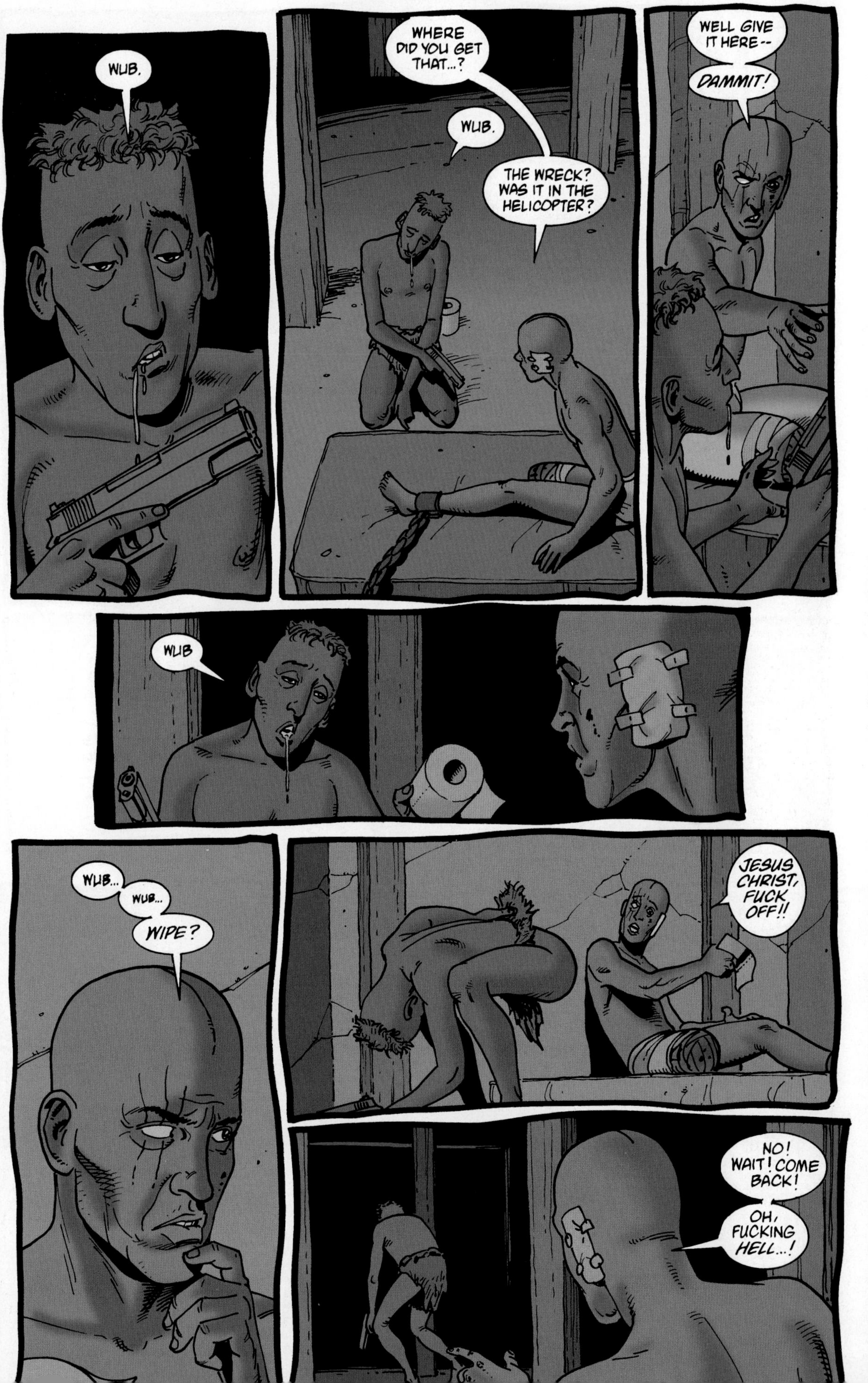
WUB.
WHERE DID YOU GET THAT...?
WUB.
THE WRECK? WAS IT IN THE HELICOPTER?
WELL GIVE IT HERE--
DAMMIT!
WUB
WUB...
WUB...
WIPE?
JESUS CHRIST, FUCK OFF!!
NO! WAIT! COME BACK!
OH, FUCKING HELL...!

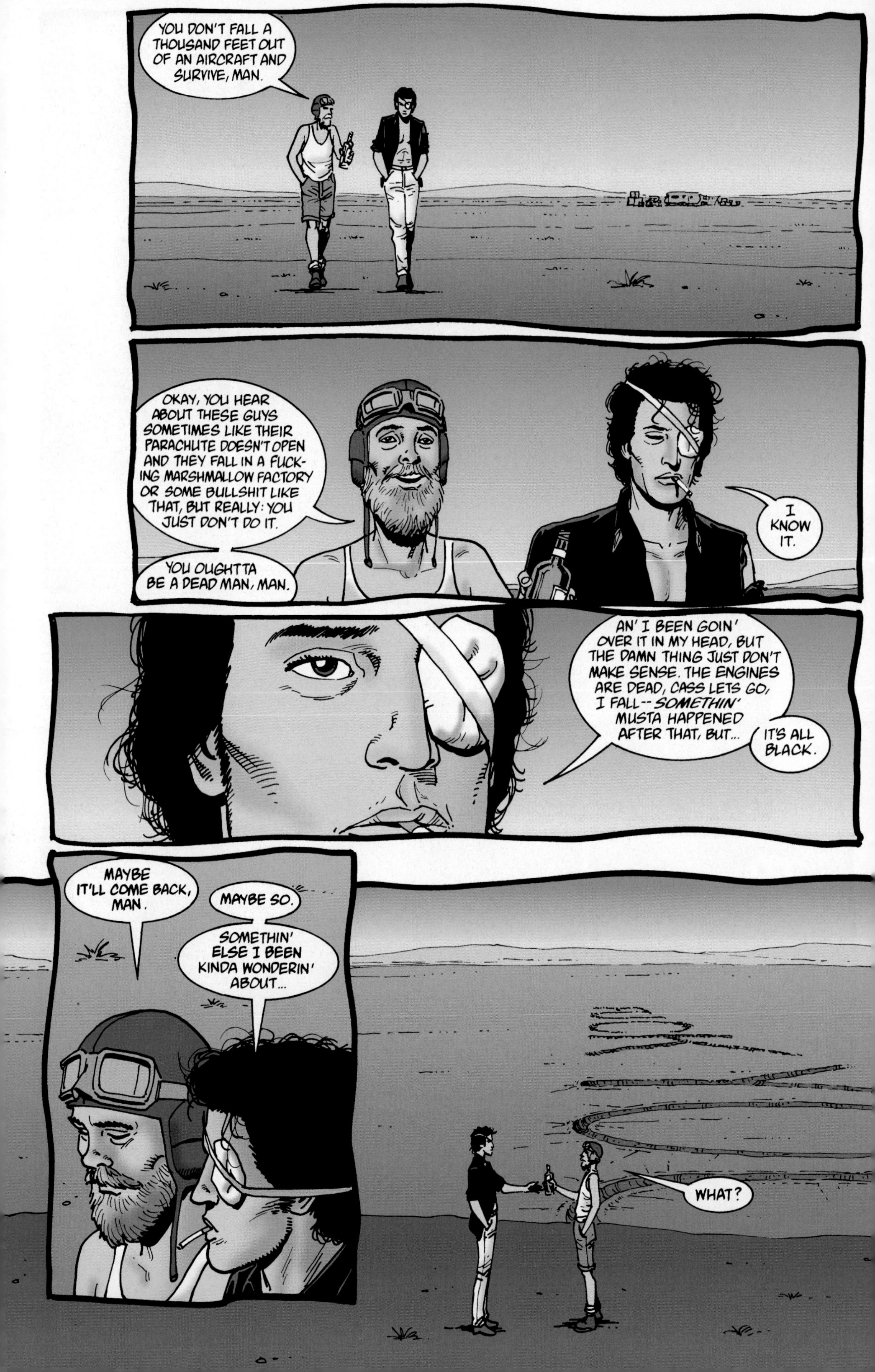
YOU DON'T FALL A THOUSAND FEET OUT OF AN AIRCRAFT AND SURVIVE, MAN.
OKAY, YOU HEAR ABOUT THESE GUYS SOMETIMES LIKE THEIR PARACHUTE DOESN'T OPEN AND THEY FALL IN A FUCKING MARSHMALLOW FACTORY OR SOME BULLSHIT LIKE THAT, BUT REALLY: YOU JUST DON'T DO IT.
YOU OUGHTTA BE A DEAD MAN, MAN.
I KNOW IT.
AN' I BEEN GOIN' OVER IT IN MY HEAD, BUT THE DAMN THING JUST DON'T MAKE SENSE. THE ENGINES ARE DEAD, CASS LETS GO, I FALL-- SOMETHIN' MUSTA HAPPENED AFTER THAT, BUT...
IT'S ALL BLACK.
MAYBE IT'LL COME BACK, MAN.
MAYBE SO.
SOMETHIN' ELSE I BEEN KINDA WONDERIN' ABOUT...
WHAT?

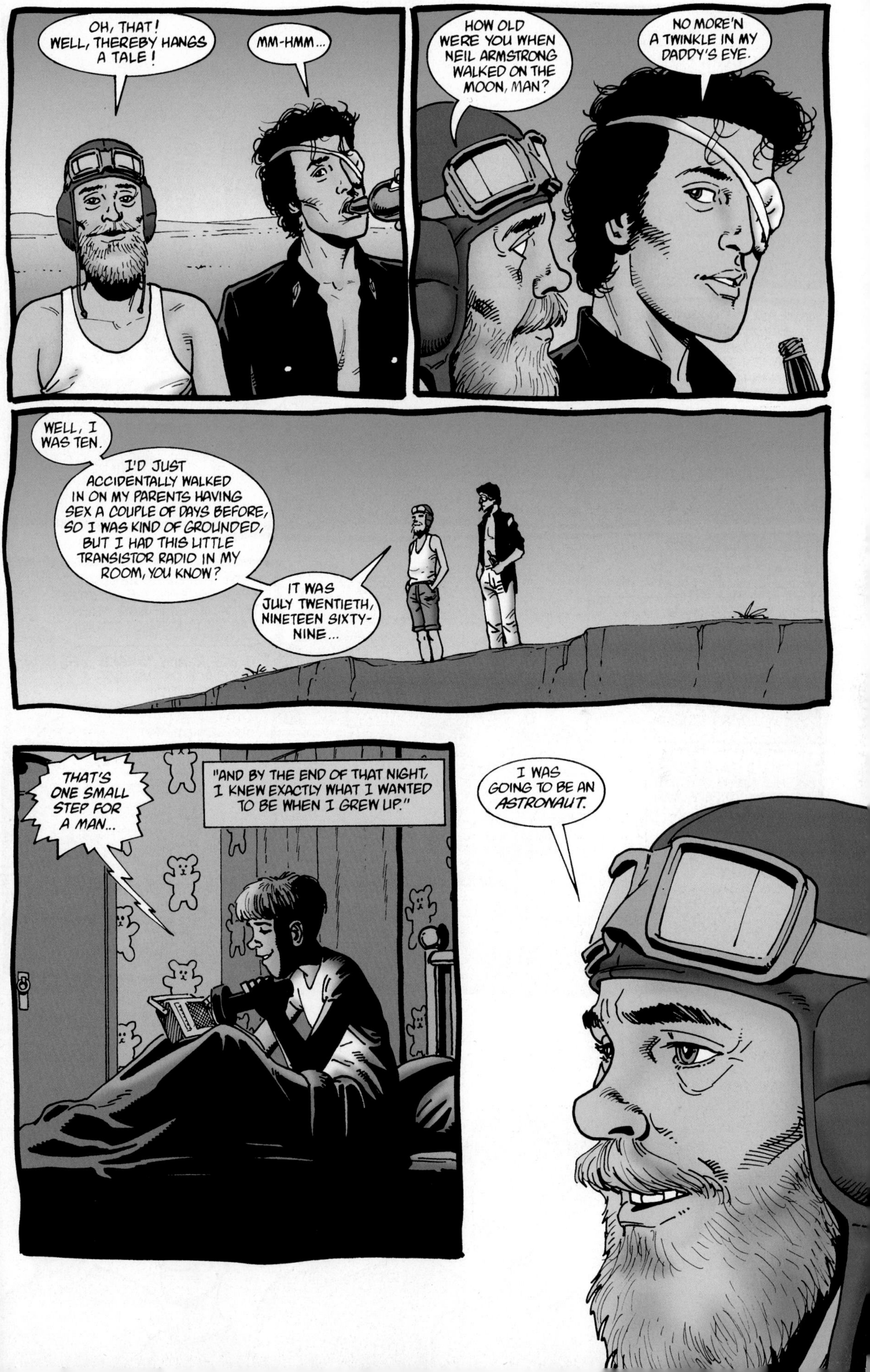
OH, THAT! WELL, THEREBY HANGS A TALE!
MM-HMM...
HOW OLD WERE YOU WHEN NEIL ARMSTRONG WALKED ON THE MOON, MAN?
NO MORE'N A TWINKLE IN MY DADDY'S EYE.
WELL, I WAS TEN.
I'D JUST ACCIDENTALLY WALKED IN ON MY PARENTS HAVING SEX A COUPLE OF DAYS BEFORE, SO I WAS KIND OF GROUNDED, BUT I HAD THIS LITTLE TRANSISTOR RADIO IN MY ROOM, YOU KNOW?
IT WAS JULY TWENTIETH, NINETEEN SIXTY-NINE...
THAT'S ONE SMALL STEP FOR A MAN...
"AND BY THE END OF THAT NIGHT, I KNEW EXACTLY WHAT I WANTED TO BE WHEN I GREW UP."
I WAS GOING TO BE AN *ASTRONAUT*.

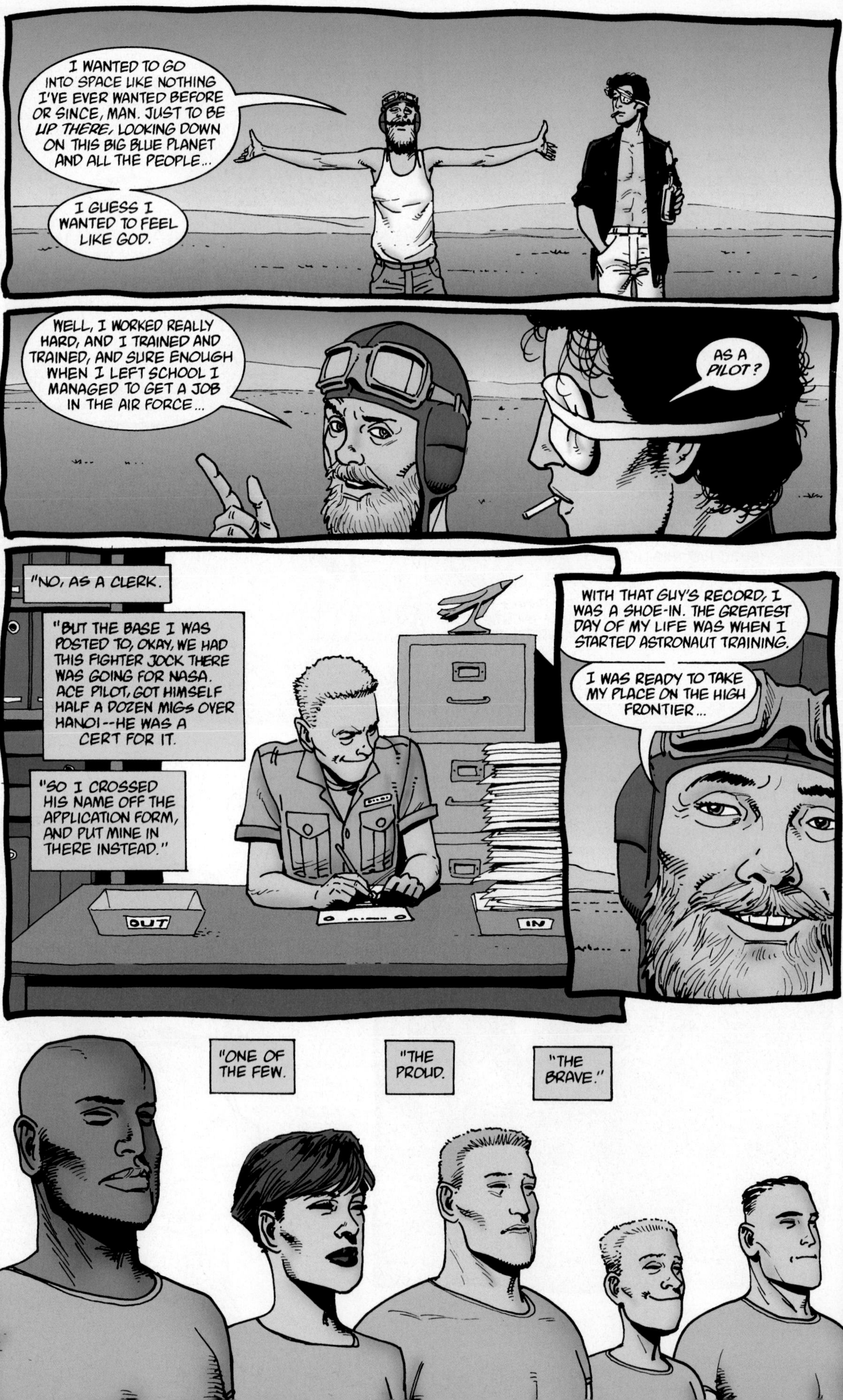
I WANTED TO GO INTO SPACE LIKE NOTHING I'VE EVER WANTED BEFORE OR SINCE, MAN. JUST TO BE *UP THERE*, LOOKING DOWN ON THIS BIG BLUE PLANET AND ALL THE PEOPLE...
I GUESS I WANTED TO FEEL LIKE GOD.
WELL, I WORKED REALLY HARD, AND I TRAINED AND TRAINED, AND SURE ENOUGH WHEN I LEFT SCHOOL I MANAGED TO GET A JOB IN THE AIR FORCE...
AS A *PILOT*?
"NO, AS A CLERK.
"BUT THE BASE I WAS POSTED TO, OKAY, WE HAD THIS FIGHTER JOCK THERE WAS GOING FOR NASA. ACE PILOT, GOT HIMSELF HALF A DOZEN MIGS OVER HANOI--HE WAS A CERT FOR IT.
"SO I CROSSED HIS NAME OFF THE APPLICATION FORM, AND PUT MINE IN THERE INSTEAD."
OUT
IN
WITH THAT GUY'S RECORD, I WAS A SHOE-IN. THE GREATEST DAY OF MY LIFE WAS WHEN I STARTED ASTRONAUT TRAINING.
I WAS READY TO TAKE MY PLACE ON THE HIGH FRONTIER...
"ONE OF THE FEW.
"THE PROUD.
"THE BRAVE."

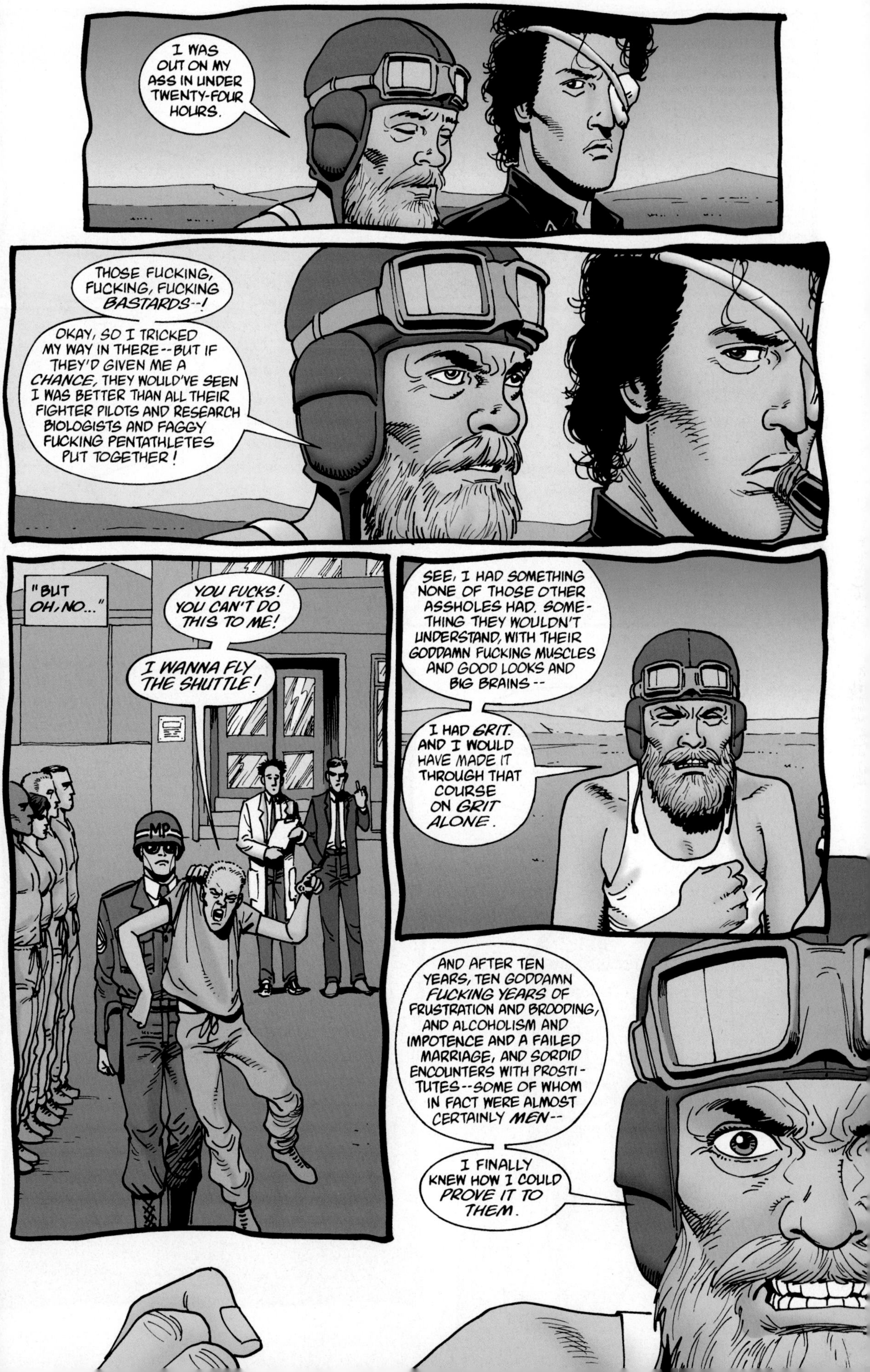
I WAS OUT ON MY ASS IN UNDER TWENTY-FOUR HOURS.
THOSE FUCKING, FUCKING, FUCKING BASTARDS--!
OKAY, SO I TRICKED MY WAY IN THERE--BUT IF THEY'D GIVEN ME A CHANCE, THEY WOULD'VE SEEN I WAS BETTER THAN ALL THEIR FIGHTER PILOTS AND RESEARCH BIOLOGISTS AND FAGGY FUCKING PENTATHLETES PUT TOGETHER!
"BUT OH, NO..."
YOU FUCKS! YOU CAN'T DO THIS TO ME!
I WANNA FLY THE SHUTTLE!
MP
SEE, I HAD SOMETHING NONE OF THOSE OTHER ASSHOLES HAD. SOMETHING THEY WOULDN'T UNDERSTAND, WITH THEIR GODDAMN FUCKING MUSCLES AND GOOD LOOKS AND BIG BRAINS--
I HAD GRIT. AND I WOULD HAVE MADE IT THROUGH THAT COURSE ON GRIT ALONE.
AND AFTER TEN YEARS, TEN GODDAMN FUCKING YEARS OF FRUSTRATION AND BROODING, AND ALCOHOLISM AND IMPOTENCE AND A FAILED MARRIAGE, AND SORDID ENCOUNTERS WITH PROSTITUTES--SOME OF WHOM IN FACT WERE ALMOST CERTAINLY MEN--
I FINALLY KNEW HOW I COULD PROVE IT TO THEM.

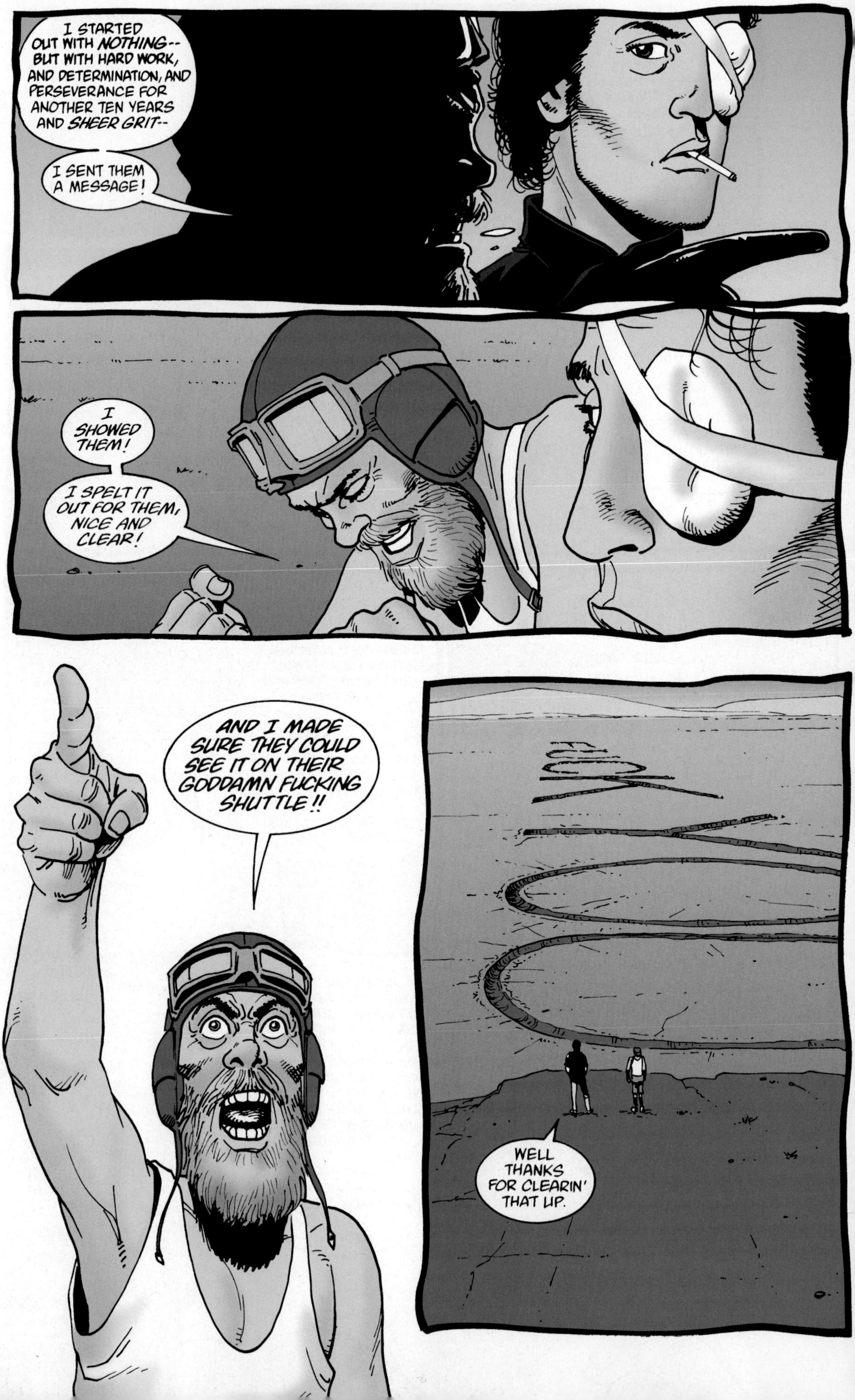
I STARTED OUT WITH NOTHING-- BUT WITH HARD WORK, AND DETERMINATION, AND PERSEVERANCE FOR ANOTHER TEN YEARS AND SHEER GRIT--
I SENT THEM A MESSAGE!
I SHOWED THEM!
I SPELT IT OUT FOR THEM, NICE AND CLEAR!
AND I MADE SURE THEY COULD SEE IT ON THEIR GODDAMN FUCKING SHUTTLE!!
WELL THANKS FOR CLEARIN' THAT UP.

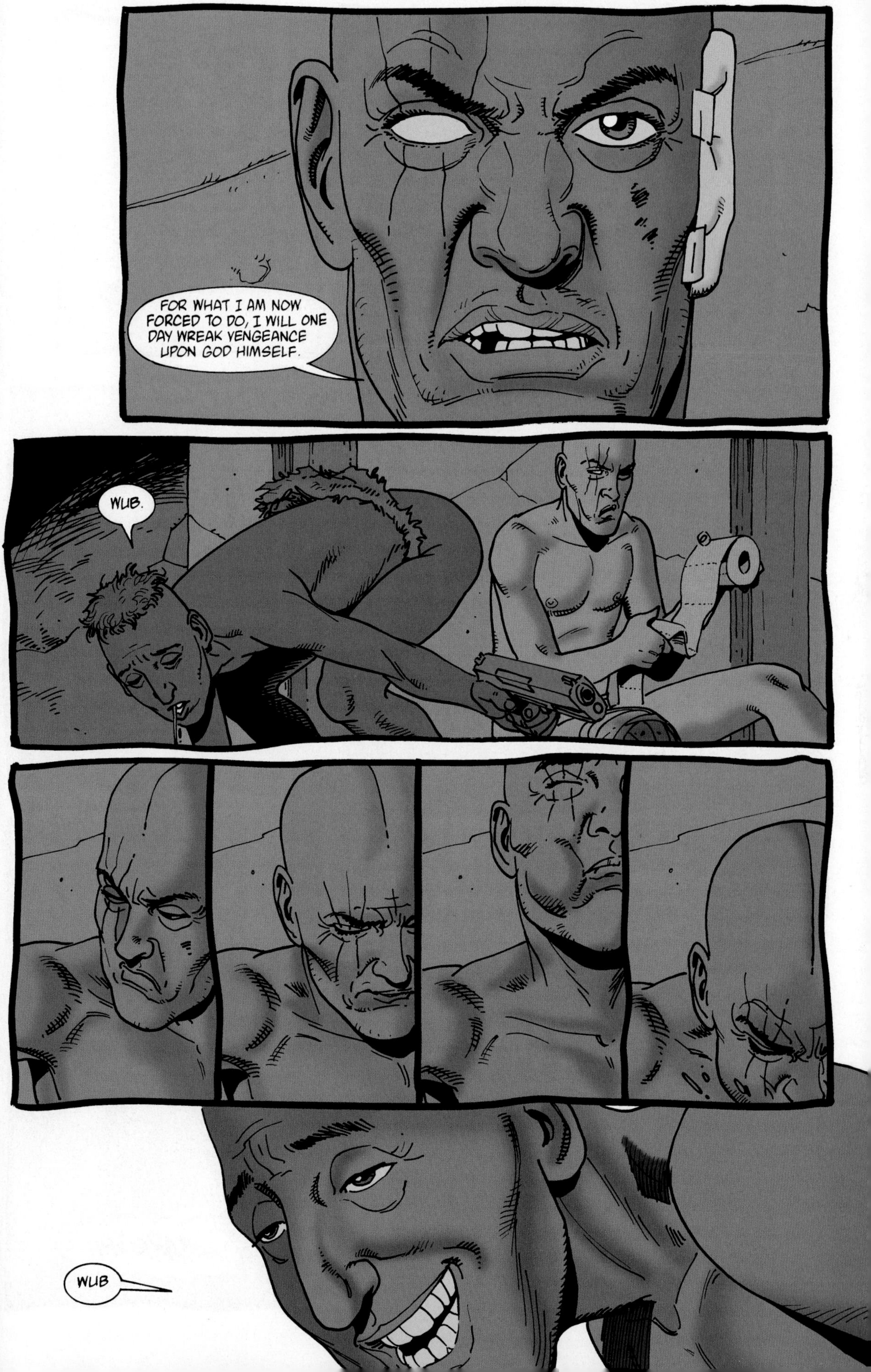
FOR WHAT I AM NOW FORCED TO DO, I WILL ONE DAY WREAK VENGEANCE UPON GOD HIMSELF.
WUB.
WUB

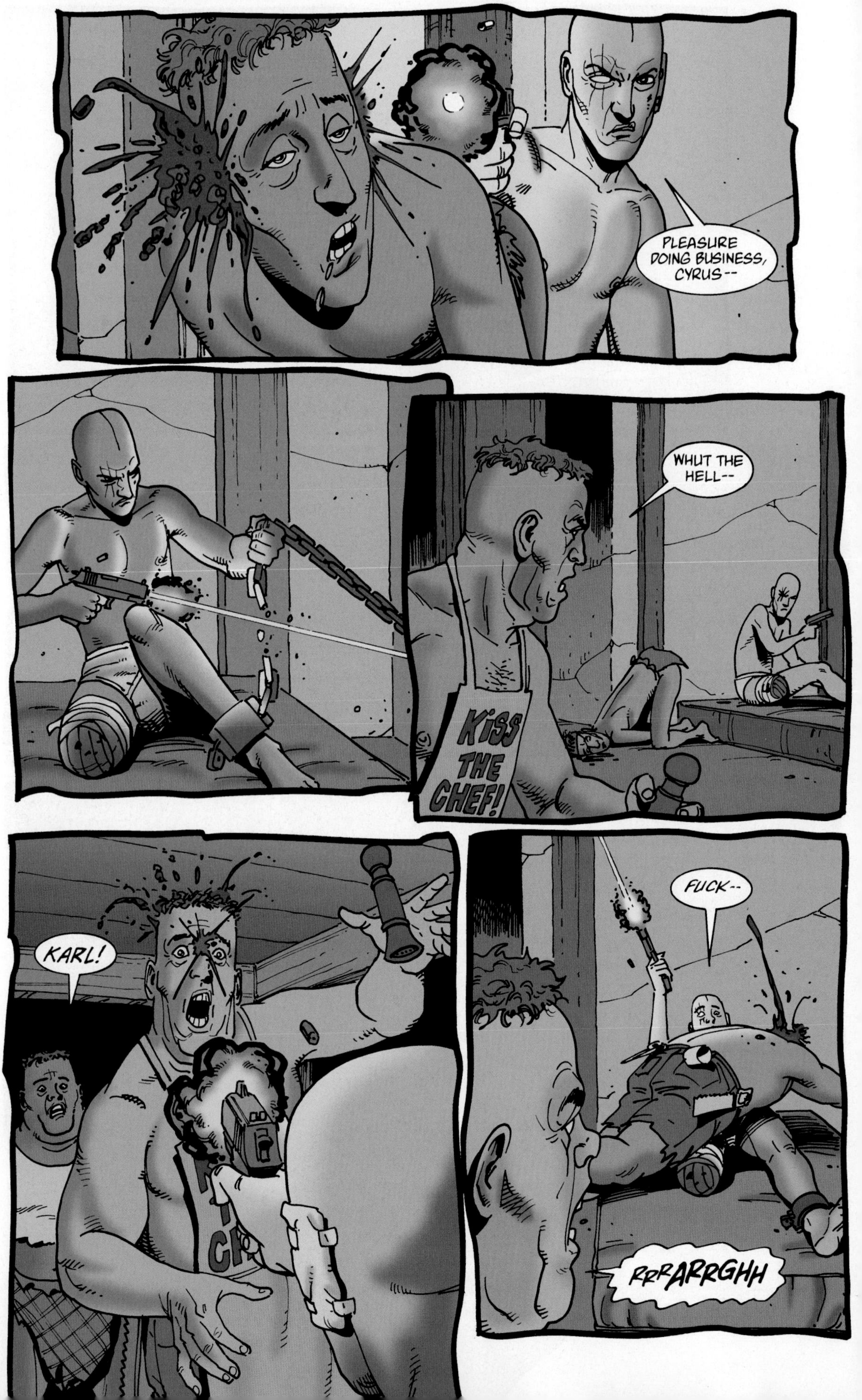
PLEASURE DOING BUSINESS, CYRUS--
WHUT THE HELL--
KISS THE CHEF!
KARL!
FUCK--
RRRARRGHH

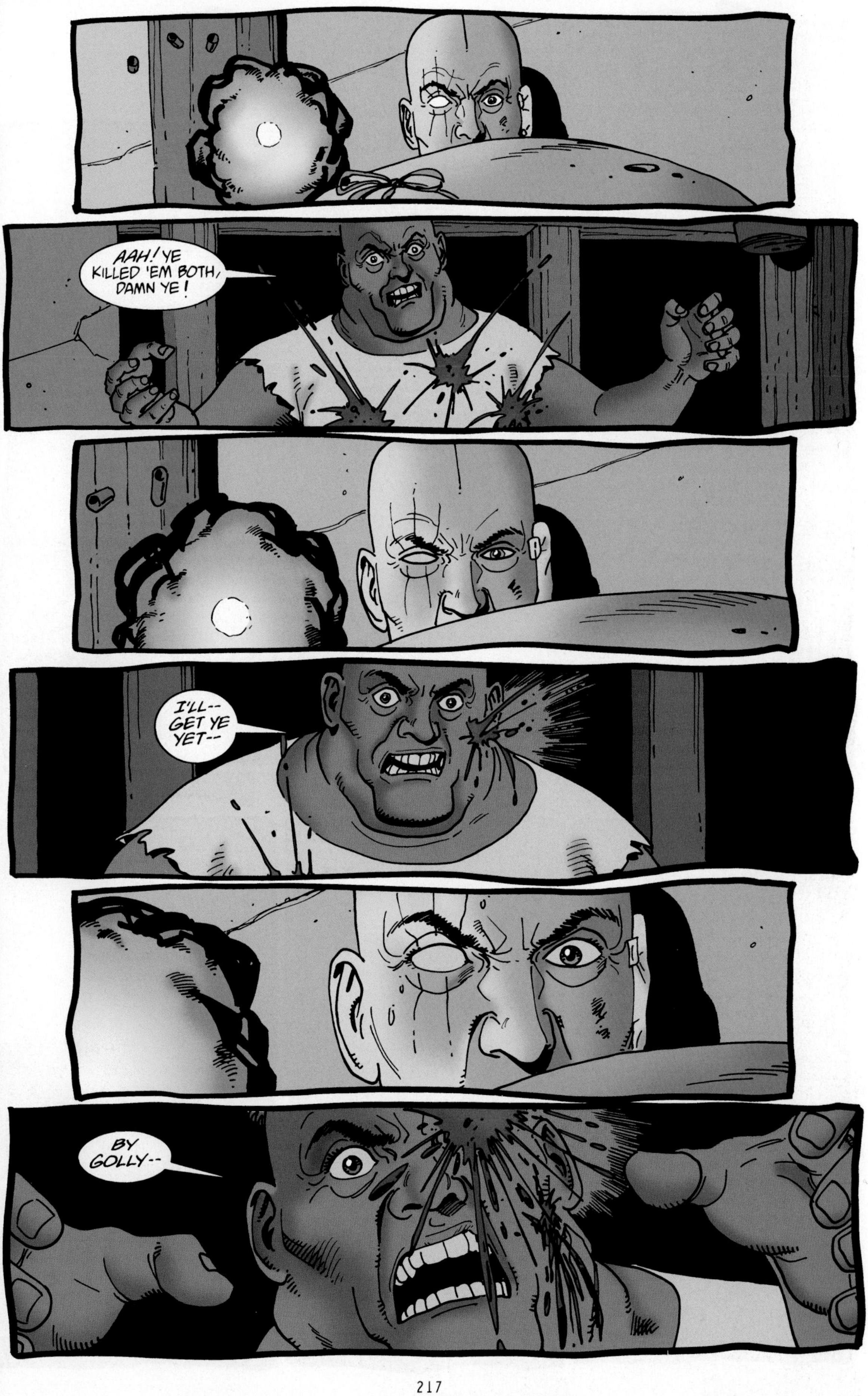
AAH! YE KILLED 'EM BOTH, DAMN YE!
I'LL-- GET YE YET--
BY GOLLY--

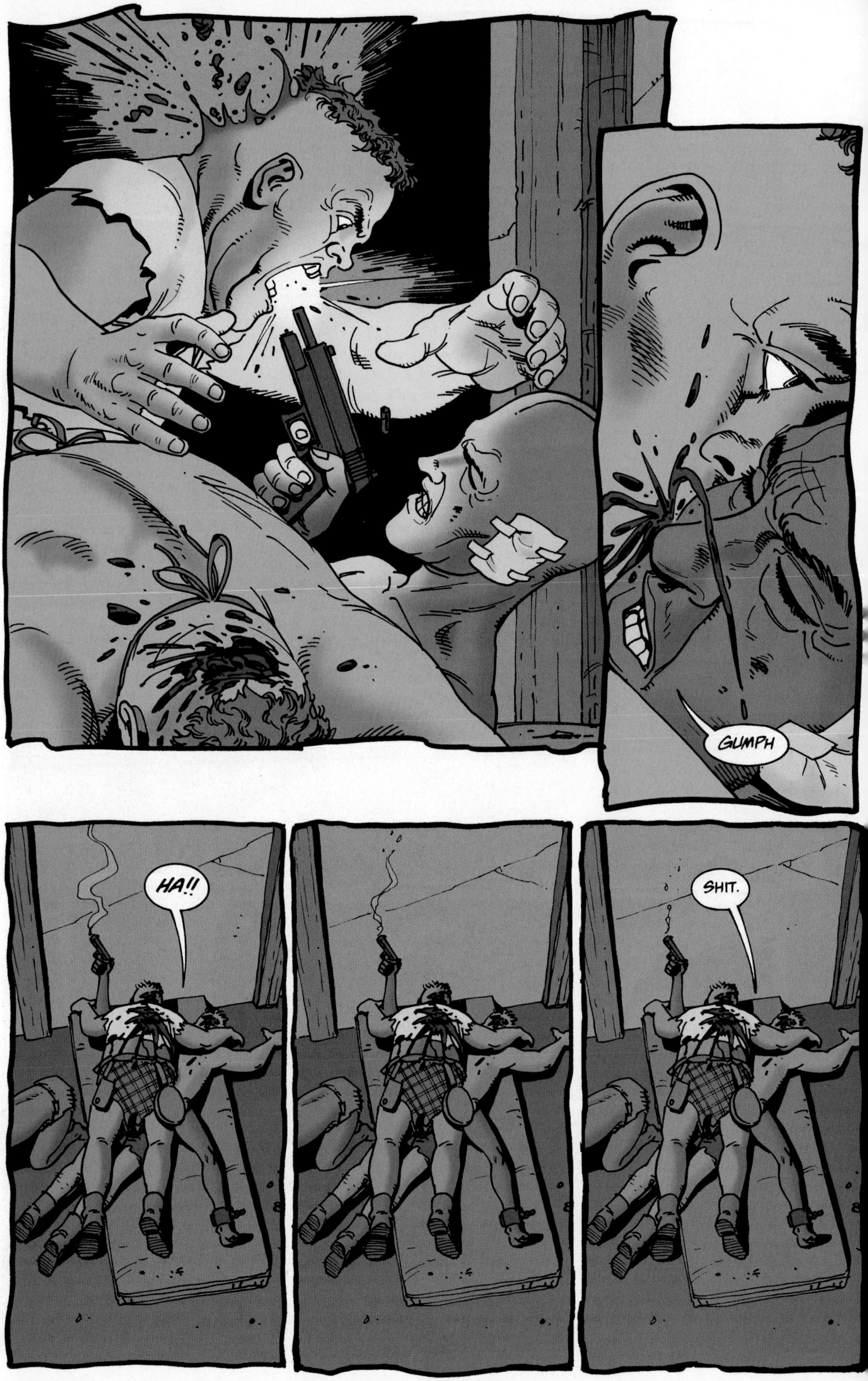
GUMPH
HA!!
SHIT.

219

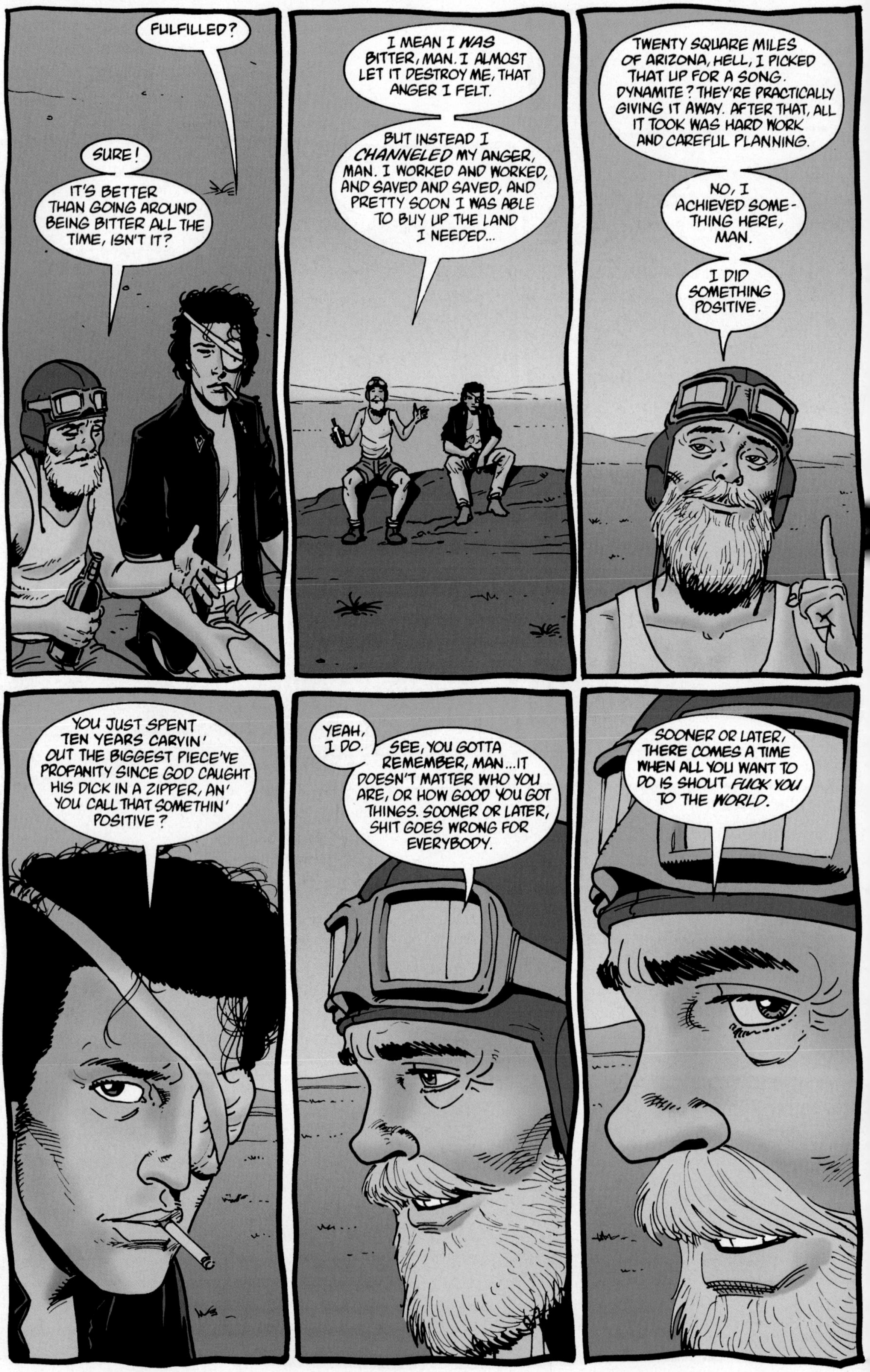
FULFILLED?
SURE!
IT'S BETTER THAN GOING AROUND BEING BITTER ALL THE TIME, ISN'T IT?
I MEAN I WAS BITTER, MAN. I ALMOST LET IT DESTROY ME, THAT ANGER I FELT.
BUT INSTEAD I CHANNELED MY ANGER, MAN. I WORKED AND WORKED, AND SAVED AND SAVED, AND PRETTY SOON I WAS ABLE TO BUY UP THE LAND I NEEDED...
TWENTY SQUARE MILES OF ARIZONA, HELL, I PICKED THAT UP FOR A SONG. DYNAMITE? THEY'RE PRACTICALLY GIVING IT AWAY. AFTER THAT, ALL IT TOOK WAS HARD WORK AND CAREFUL PLANNING.
NO, I ACHIEVED SOMETHING HERE, MAN.
I DID SOMETHING POSITIVE.
YOU JUST SPENT TEN YEARS CARVIN' OUT THE BIGGEST PIECE'VE PROFANITY SINCE GOD CAUGHT HIS DICK IN A ZIPPER, AN' YOU CALL THAT SOMETHIN' POSITIVE?
YEAH, I DO.
SEE, YOU GOTTA REMEMBER, MAN...IT DOESN'T MATTER WHO YOU ARE, OR HOW GOOD YOU GOT THINGS. SOONER OR LATER, SHIT GOES WRONG FOR EVERYBODY.
SOONER OR LATER, THERE COMES A TIME WHEN ALL YOU WANT TO DO IS SHOUT FUCK YOU TO THE WORLD.

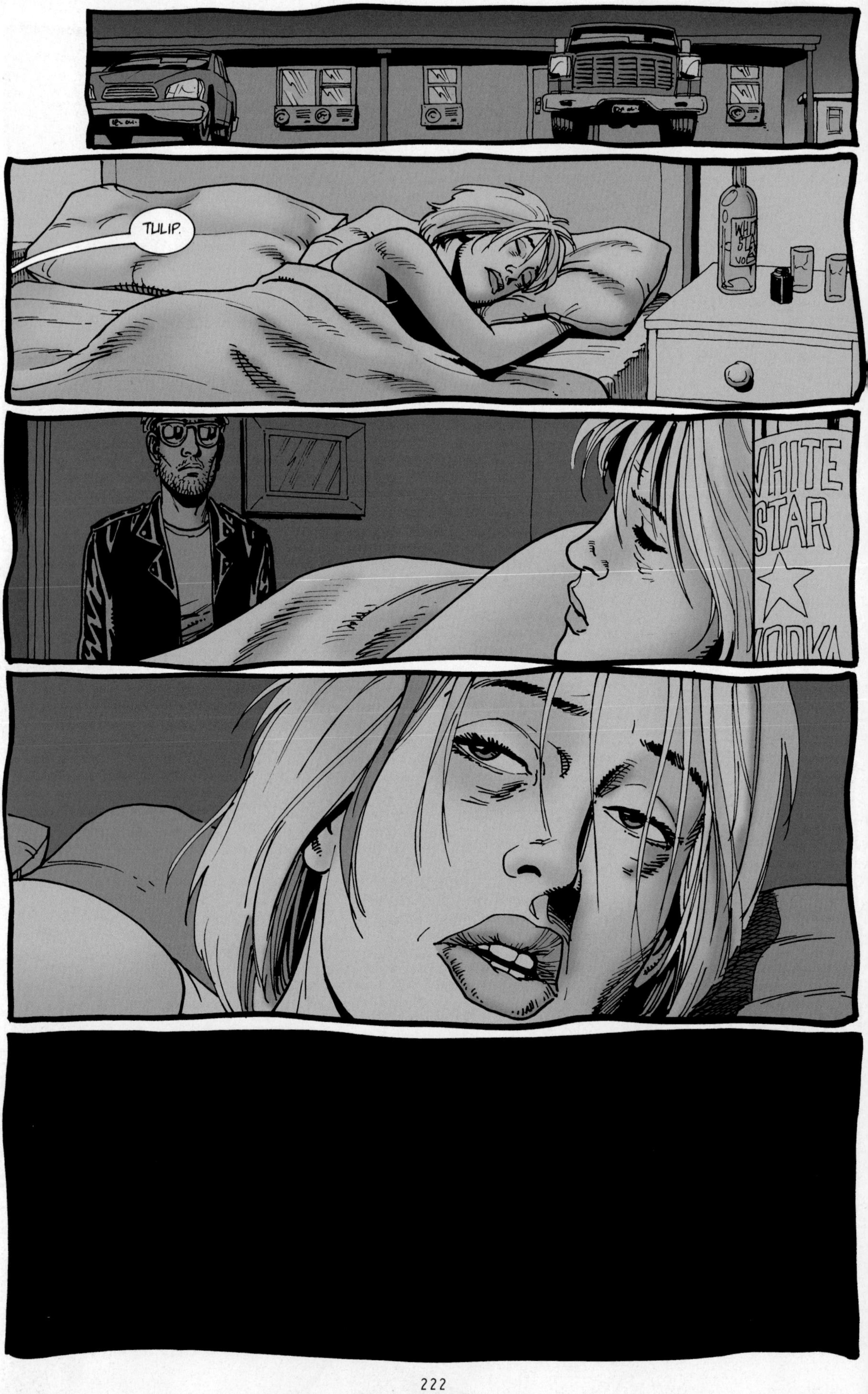
TULIP.
WHITE STAR VODKA

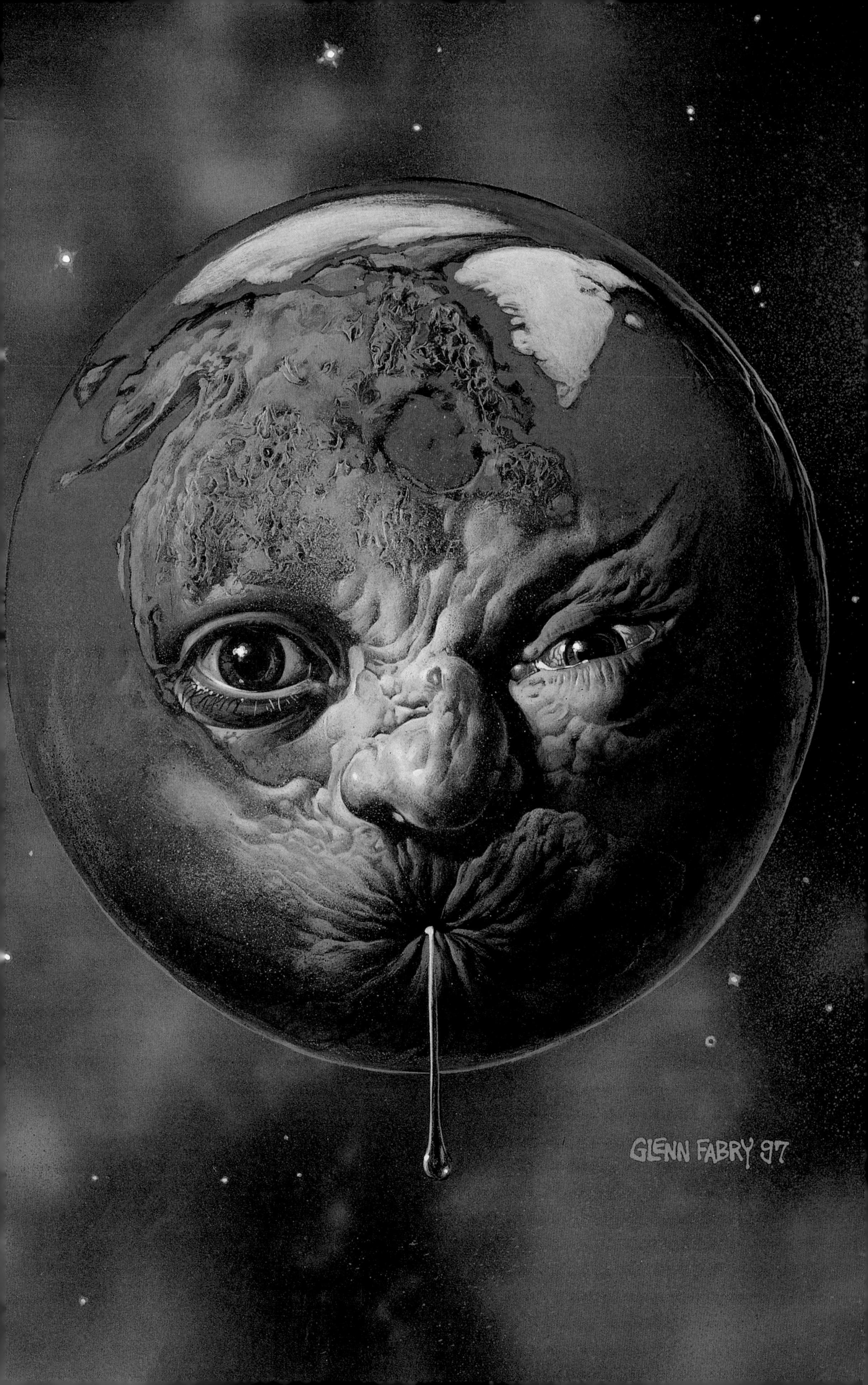
GLENN FABRY 97

"Whuff-whuff-whuff — Fuck! Whuff-whuff-whuff — Fuck! Whuff-whuff-whuff — Fuck!"

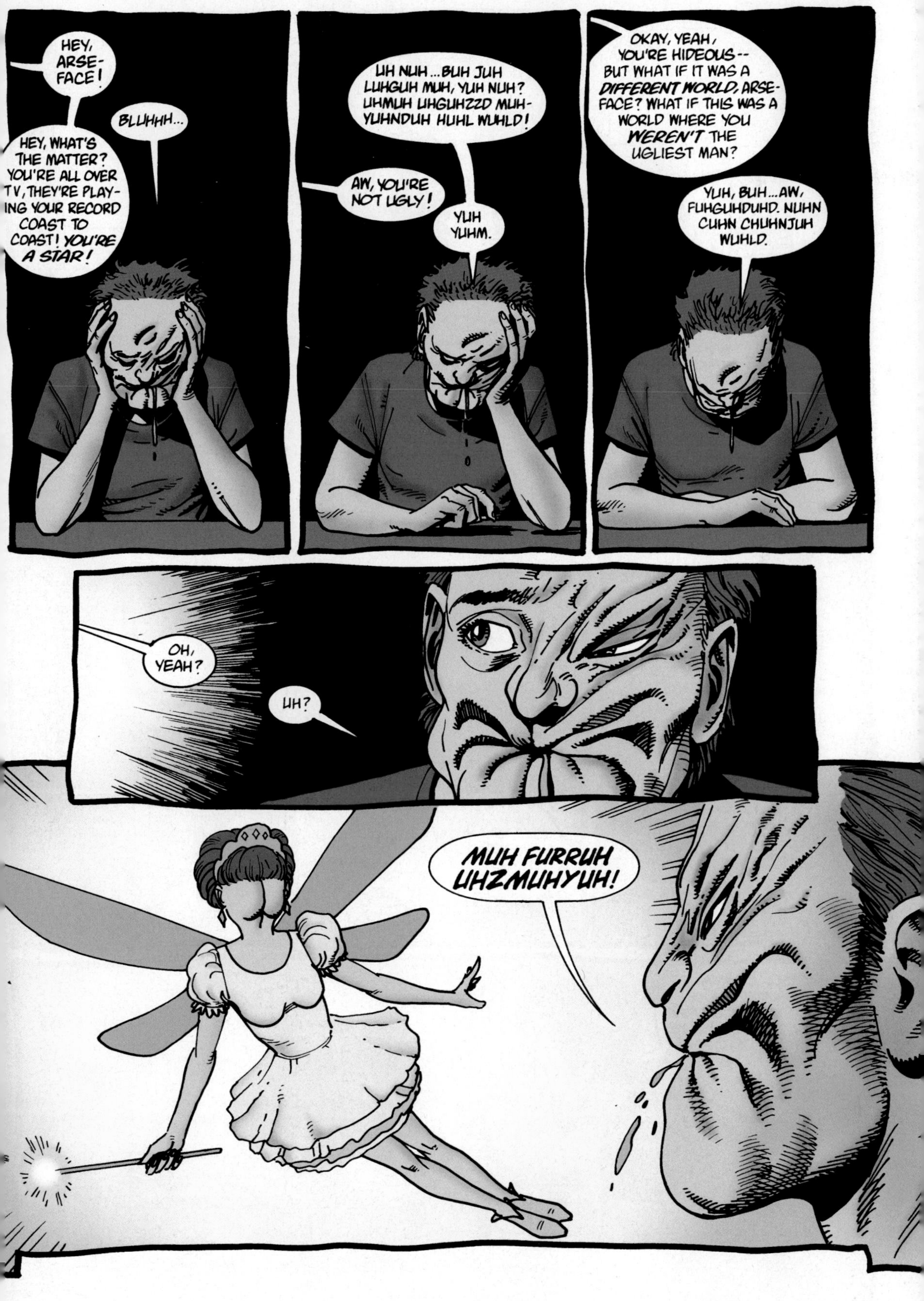
HEY, ARSE-FACE!
BLUHHH...
HEY, WHAT'S THE MATTER? YOU'RE ALL OVER TV, THEY'RE PLAYING YOUR RECORD COAST TO COAST! YOU'RE A STAR!
UH NUH ...BUH JUH LUHGUH MUH, YUH NUH? UHMUH UHGUHZZD MUH-YUHNDUH HUHL WUHLD!
AW, YOU'RE NOT UGLY!
YUH YUHM.
OKAY, YEAH, YOU'RE HIDEOUS-- BUT WHAT IF IT WAS A DIFFERENT WORLD, ARSE-FACE? WHAT IF THIS WAS A WORLD WHERE YOU WEREN'T THE UGLIEST MAN?
YUH, BUH...AW, FUHGUHDUHD. NUHN CUHN CHUHNJUH WUHLD.
OH, YEAH?
UH?
MUH FURRUH UHZMUHYUH!

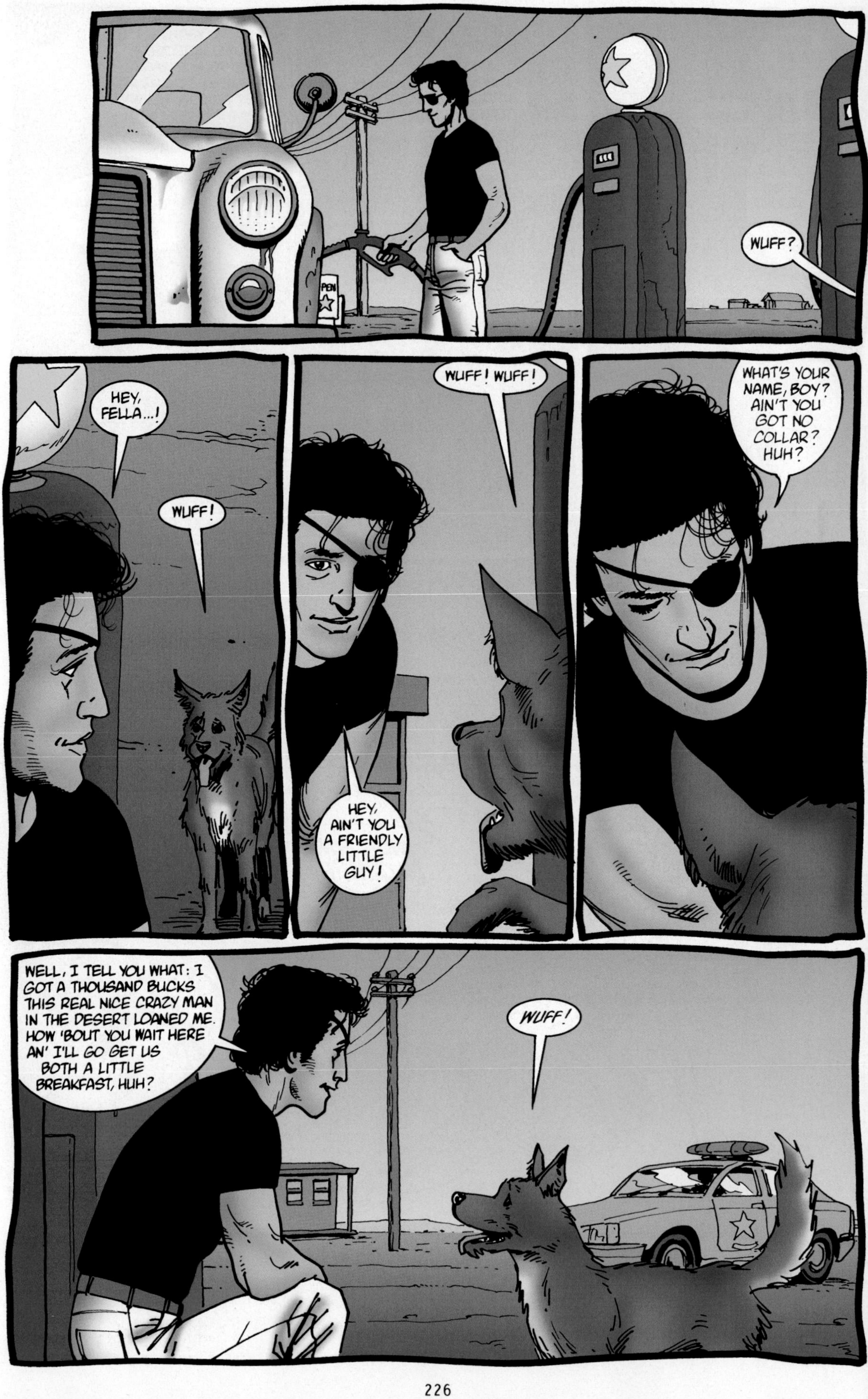
WUFF?
HEY, FELLA...!
WUFF!
WUFF! WUFF!
HEY, AIN'T YOU A FRIENDLY LITTLE GUY!
WHAT'S YOUR NAME, BOY? AIN'T YOU GOT NO COLLAR? HUH?
WELL, I TELL YOU WHAT: I GOT A THOUSAND BUCKS THIS REAL NICE CRAZY MAN IN THE DESERT LOANED ME. HOW 'BOUT YOU WAIT HERE AN' I'LL GO GET US BOTH A LITTLE BREAKFAST, HUH?
WUFF!

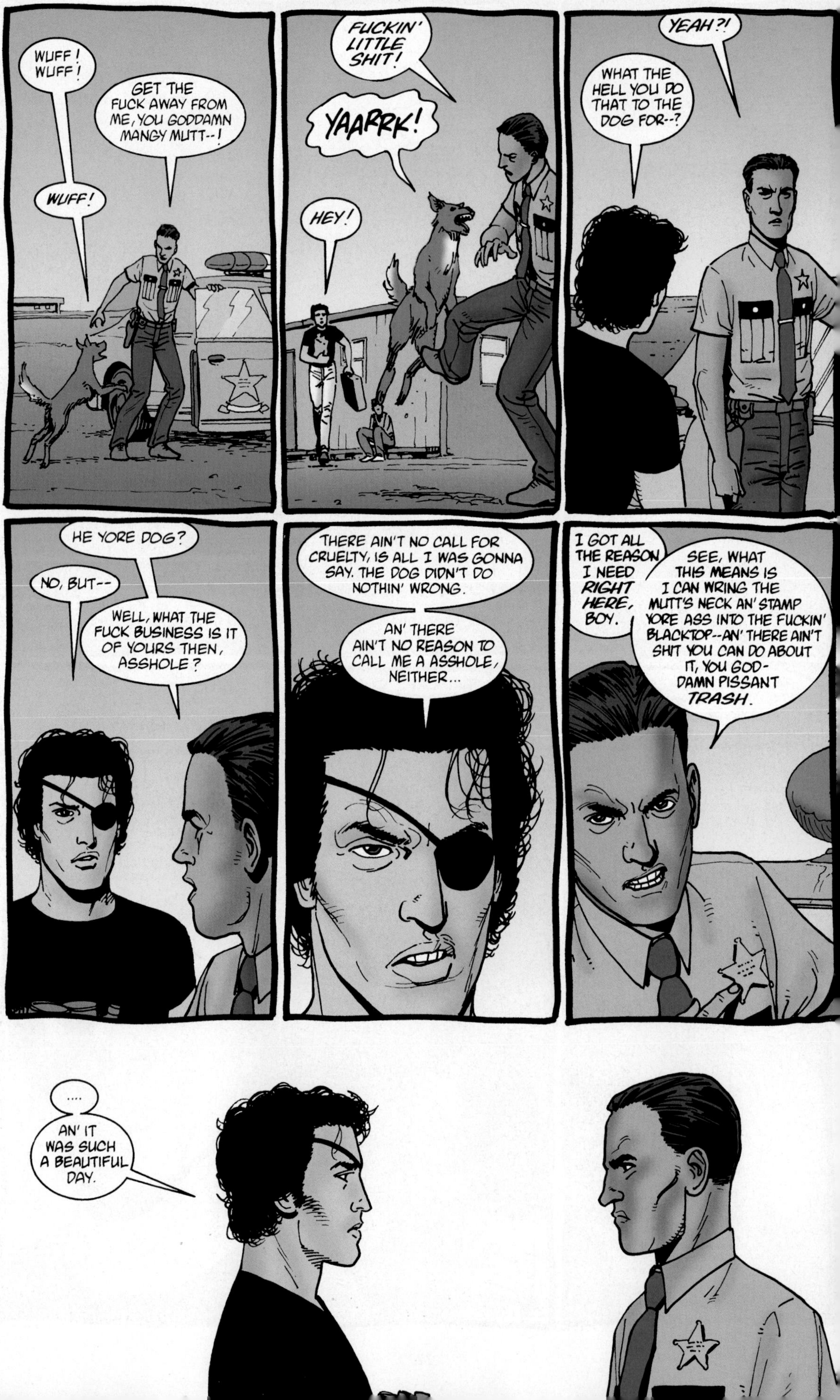

WUFF! WUFF!
GET THE FUCK AWAY FROM ME, YOU GODDAMN MANGY MUTT--!
WUFF!
FUCKIN' LITTLE SHIT!
YAARRK!
HEY!
YEAH?!
WHAT THE HELL YOU DO THAT TO THE DOG FOR--?
HE YORE DOG?
NO, BUT--
WELL, WHAT THE FUCK BUSINESS IS IT OF YOURS THEN, ASSHOLE?
THERE AIN'T NO CALL FOR CRUELTY, IS ALL I WAS GONNA SAY. THE DOG DIDN'T DO NOTHIN' WRONG.
AN' THERE AIN'T NO REASON TO CALL ME A ASSHOLE, NEITHER...
I GOT ALL THE REASON I NEED RIGHT HERE, BOY.
SEE, WHAT THIS MEANS IS I CAN WRING THE MUTT'S NECK AN' STAMP YORE ASS INTO THE FUCKIN' BLACKTOP--AN' THERE AIN'T SHIT YOU CAN DO ABOUT IT, YOU GOD-DAMN PISSANT TRASH.
....
AN' IT WAS SUCH A BEAUTIFUL DAY.

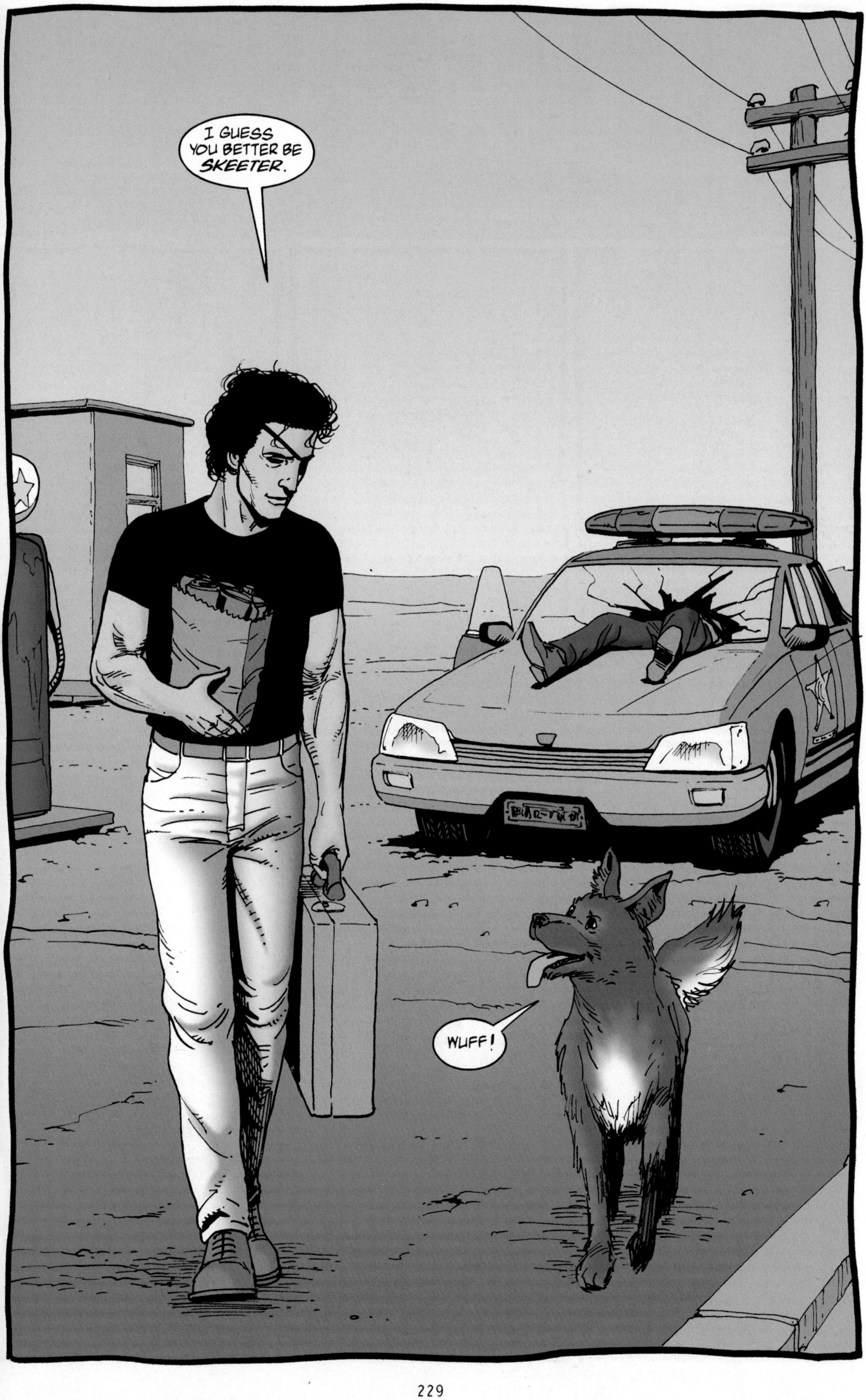
I GUESS YOU BETTER BE SKEETER.
WUFF!

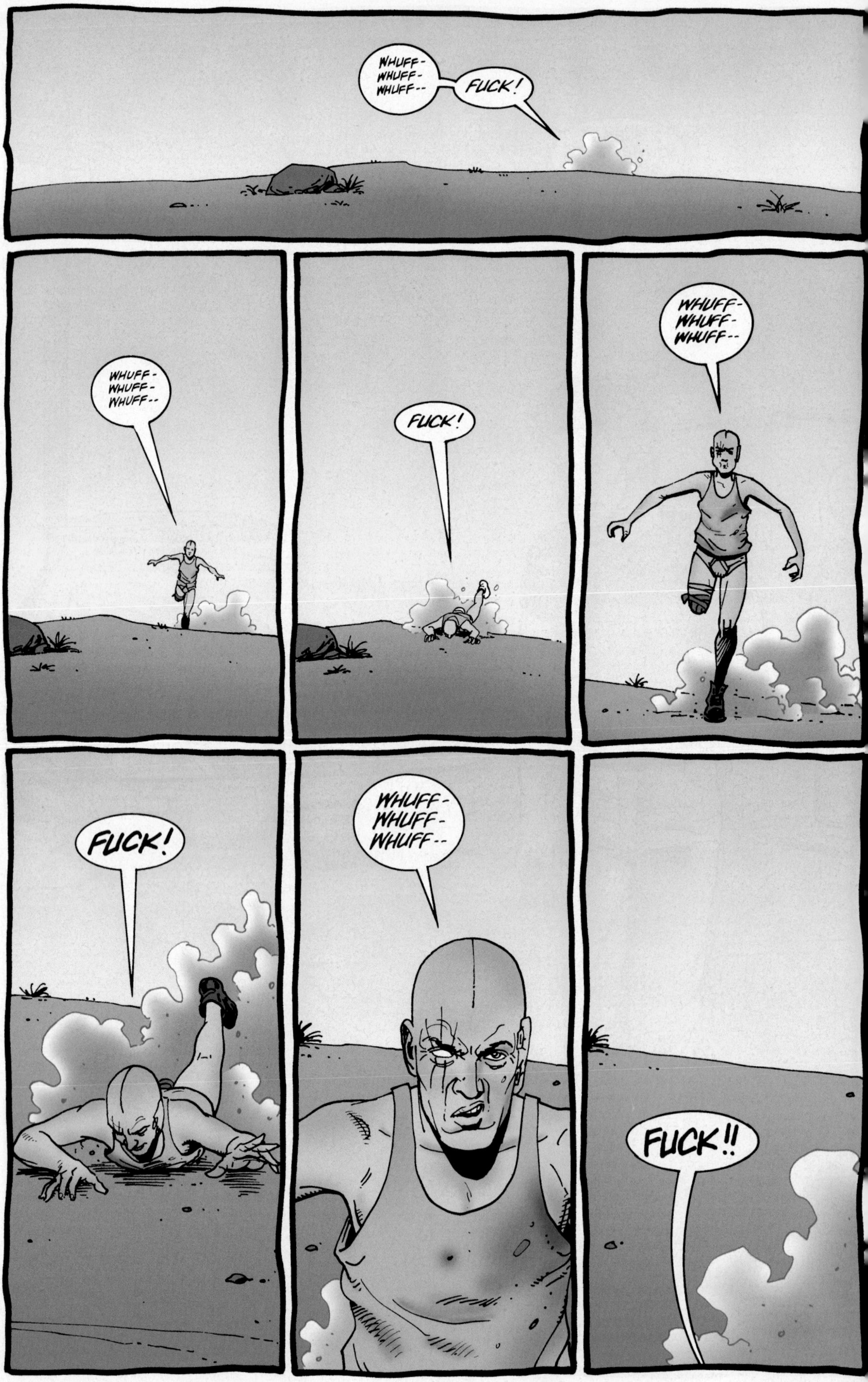
WHUFF-
WHUFF-
WHUFF--
FUCK!
WHUFF-
WHUFF-
WHUFF--
FUCK!
WHUFF-
WHUFF-
WHUFF--
FUCK!
WHUFF-
WHUFF-
WHUFF--
FUCK!!

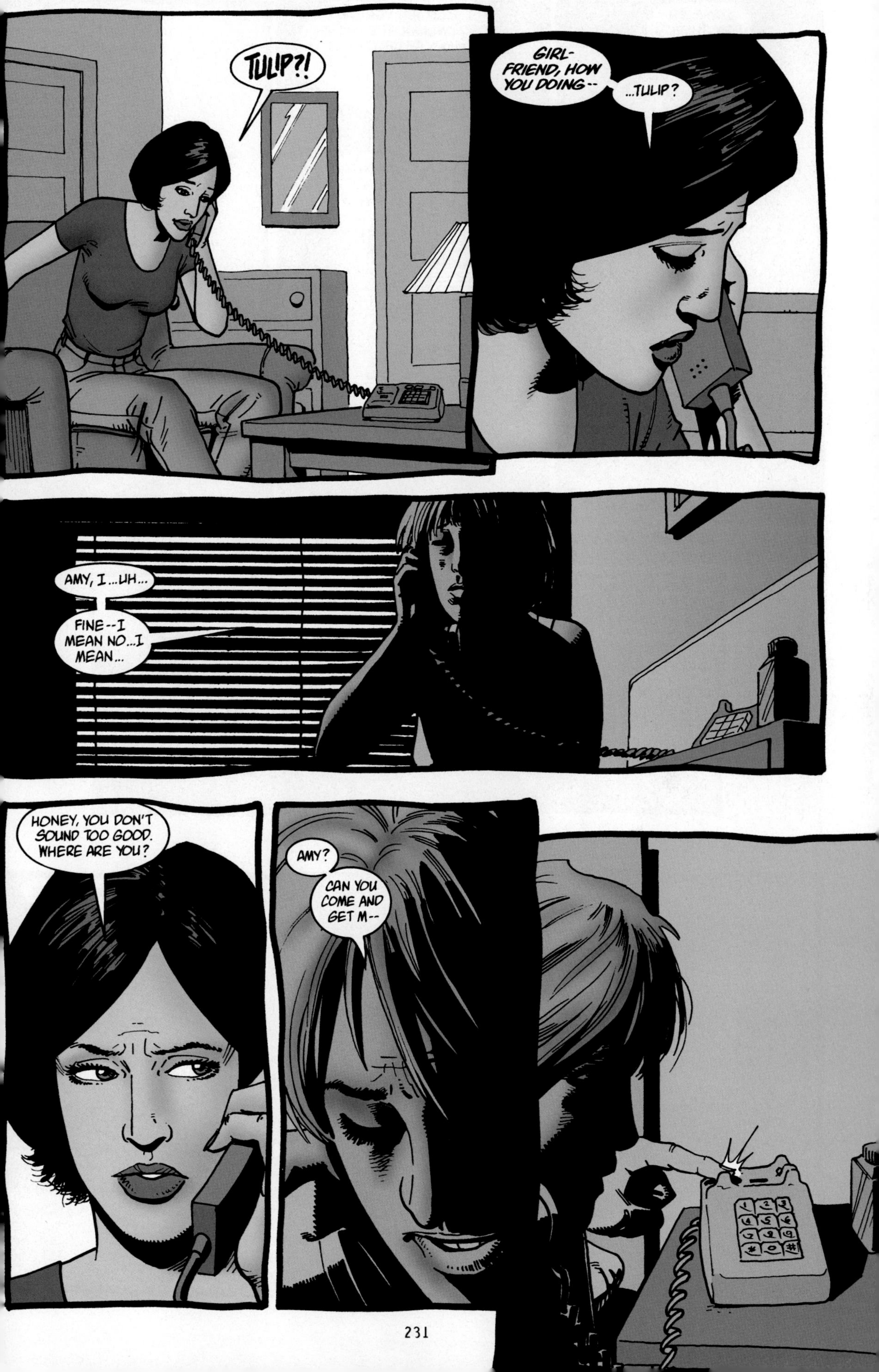
TULIP?!
GIRL-FRIEND, HOW YOU DOING--
...TULIP?
AMY, I...UH...
FINE--I MEAN NO...I MEAN...
HONEY, YOU DON'T SOUND TOO GOOD. WHERE ARE YOU?
AMY?
CAN YOU COME AND GET M--

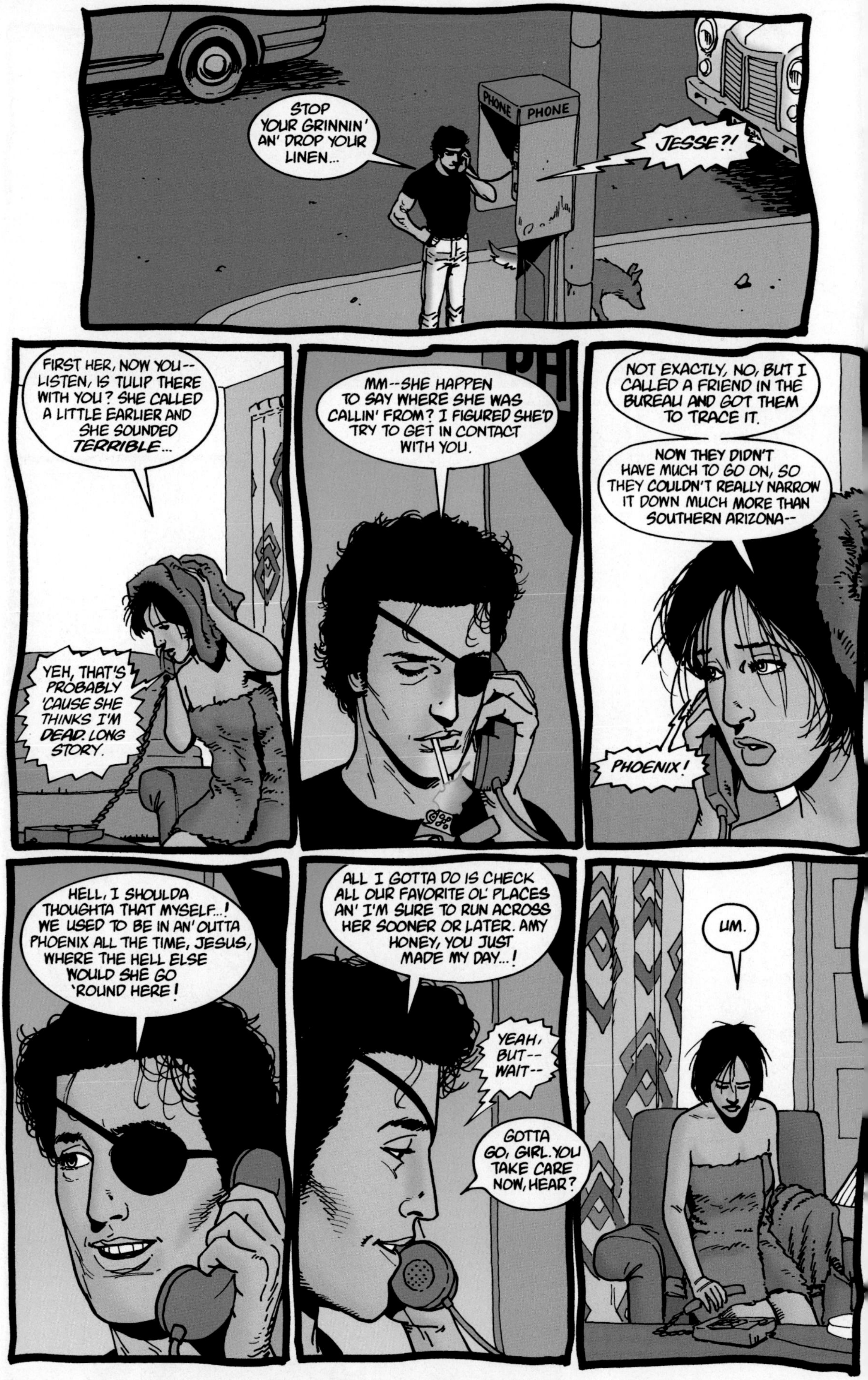
STOP YOUR GRINNIN' AN' DROP YOUR LINEN...
JESSE?!
PHONE
PHONE
FIRST HER, NOW YOU-- LISTEN, IS TULIP THERE WITH YOU? SHE CALLED A LITTLE EARLIER AND SHE SOUNDED TERRIBLE...
YEH, THAT'S PROBABLY 'CAUSE SHE THINKS I'M DEAD. LONG STORY.
MM--SHE HAPPEN TO SAY WHERE SHE WAS CALLIN' FROM? I FIGURED SHE'D TRY TO GET IN CONTACT WITH YOU.
NOT EXACTLY, NO, BUT I CALLED A FRIEND IN THE BUREAU AND GOT THEM TO TRACE IT.
NOW THEY DIDN'T HAVE MUCH TO GO ON, SO THEY COULDN'T REALLY NARROW IT DOWN MUCH MORE THAN SOUTHERN ARIZONA--
PHOENIX!
HELL, I SHOULDA THOUGHTA THAT MYSELF...! WE USED TO BE IN AN' OUTTA PHOENIX ALL THE TIME, JESUS, WHERE THE HELL ELSE WOULD SHE GO 'ROUND HERE!
ALL I GOTTA DO IS CHECK ALL OUR FAVORITE OL' PLACES AN' I'M SURE TO RUN ACROSS HER SOONER OR LATER. AMY HONEY, YOU JUST MADE MY DAY...!
YEAH, BUT-- WAIT--
GOTTA GO, GIRL. YOU TAKE CARE NOW, HEAR?
UM.

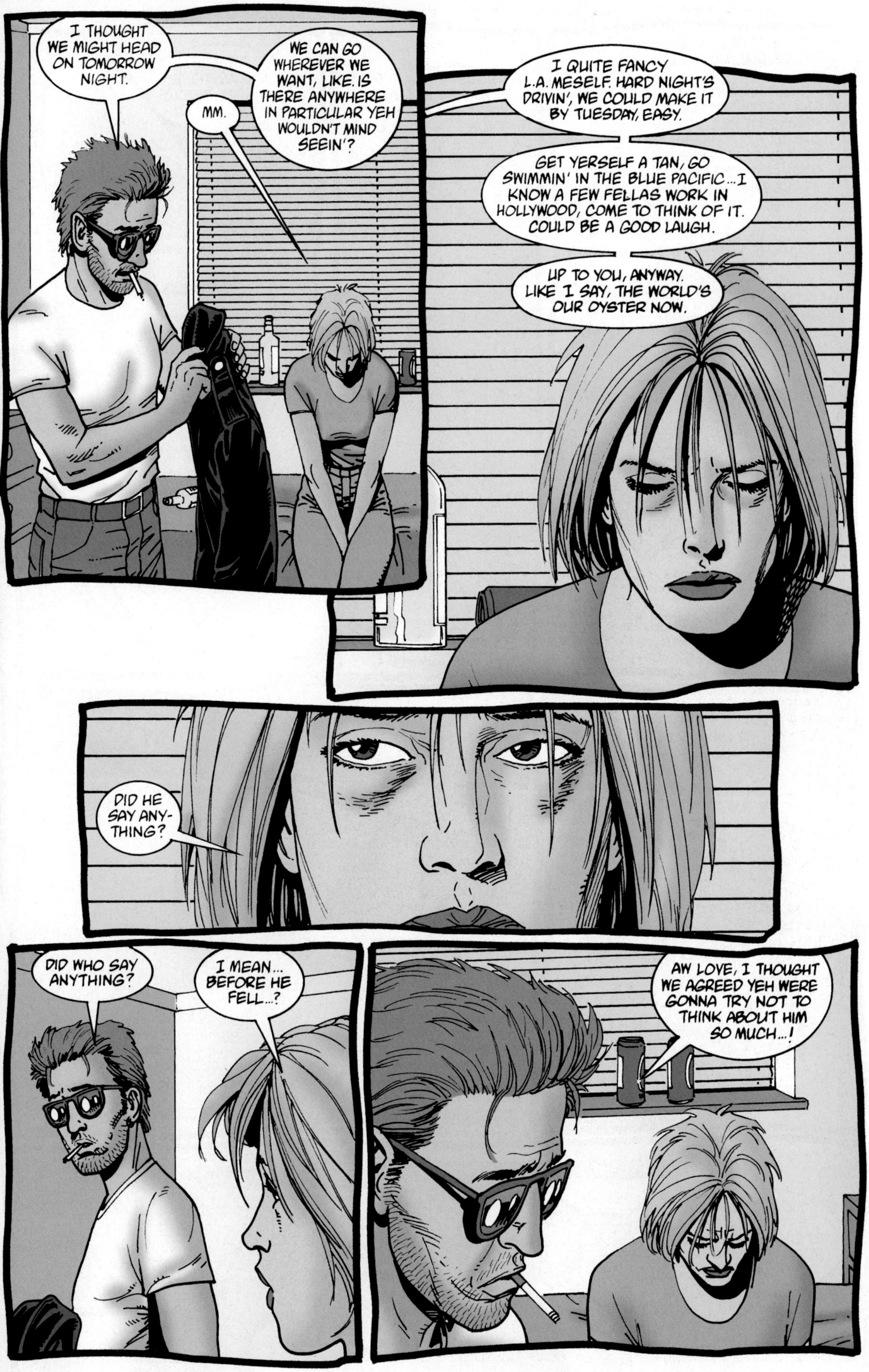
I THOUGHT WE MIGHT HEAD ON TOMORROW NIGHT.
WE CAN GO WHEREVER WE WANT, LIKE. IS THERE ANYWHERE IN PARTICULAR YEH WOULDN'T MIND SEEIN'?
MM.
I QUITE FANCY L.A. MESELF. HARD NIGHT'S DRIVIN', WE COULD MAKE IT BY TUESDAY, EASY.
GET YERSELF A TAN, GO SWIMMIN' IN THE BLUE PACIFIC... I KNOW A FEW FELLAS WORK IN HOLLYWOOD, COME TO THINK OF IT. COULD BE A GOOD LAUGH.
UP TO YOU, ANYWAY. LIKE I SAY, THE WORLD'S OUR OYSTER NOW.
DID HE SAY ANY-THING?
DID WHO SAY ANYTHING?
I MEAN... BEFORE HE FELL...?
AW LOVE, I THOUGHT WE AGREED YEH WERE GONNA TRY NOT TO THINK ABOUT HIM SO MUCH...!

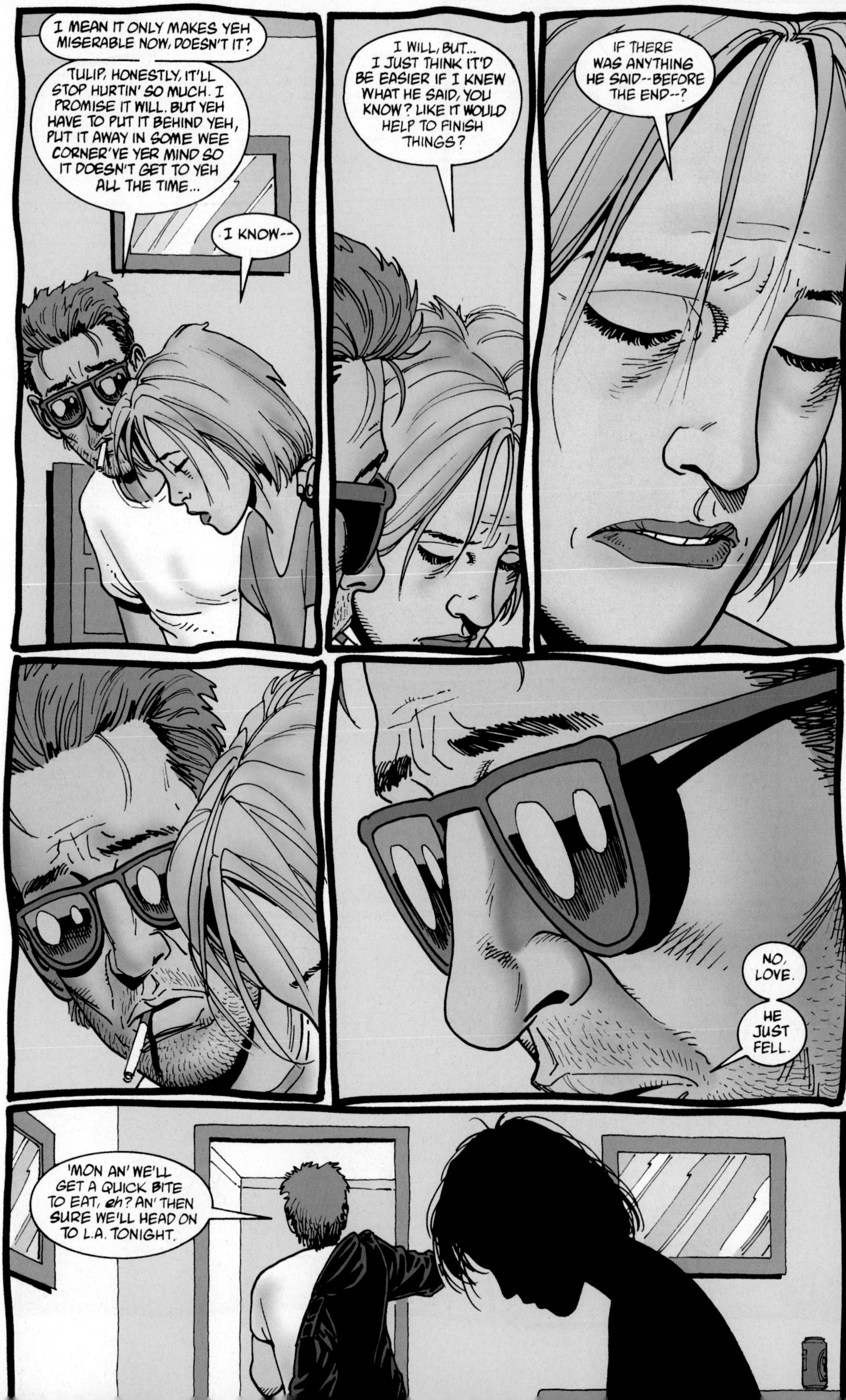
I MEAN IT ONLY MAKES YEH MISERABLE NOW, DOESN'T IT?
TULIP, HONESTLY, IT'LL STOP HURTIN' SO MUCH. I PROMISE IT WILL. BUT YEH HAVE TO PUT IT BEHIND YEH, PUT IT AWAY IN SOME WEE CORNER'VE YER MIND SO IT DOESN'T GET TO YEH ALL THE TIME...
I KNOW--
I WILL, BUT... I JUST THINK IT'D BE EASIER IF I KNEW WHAT HE SAID, YOU KNOW? LIKE IT WOULD HELP TO FINISH THINGS?
IF THERE WAS ANYTHING HE SAID--BEFORE THE END--?
NO, LOVE.
HE JUST FELL.
'MON AN' WE'LL GET A QUICK BITE TO EAT, *eh*? AN' THEN SURE WE'LL HEAD ON TO L.A. TONIGHT.

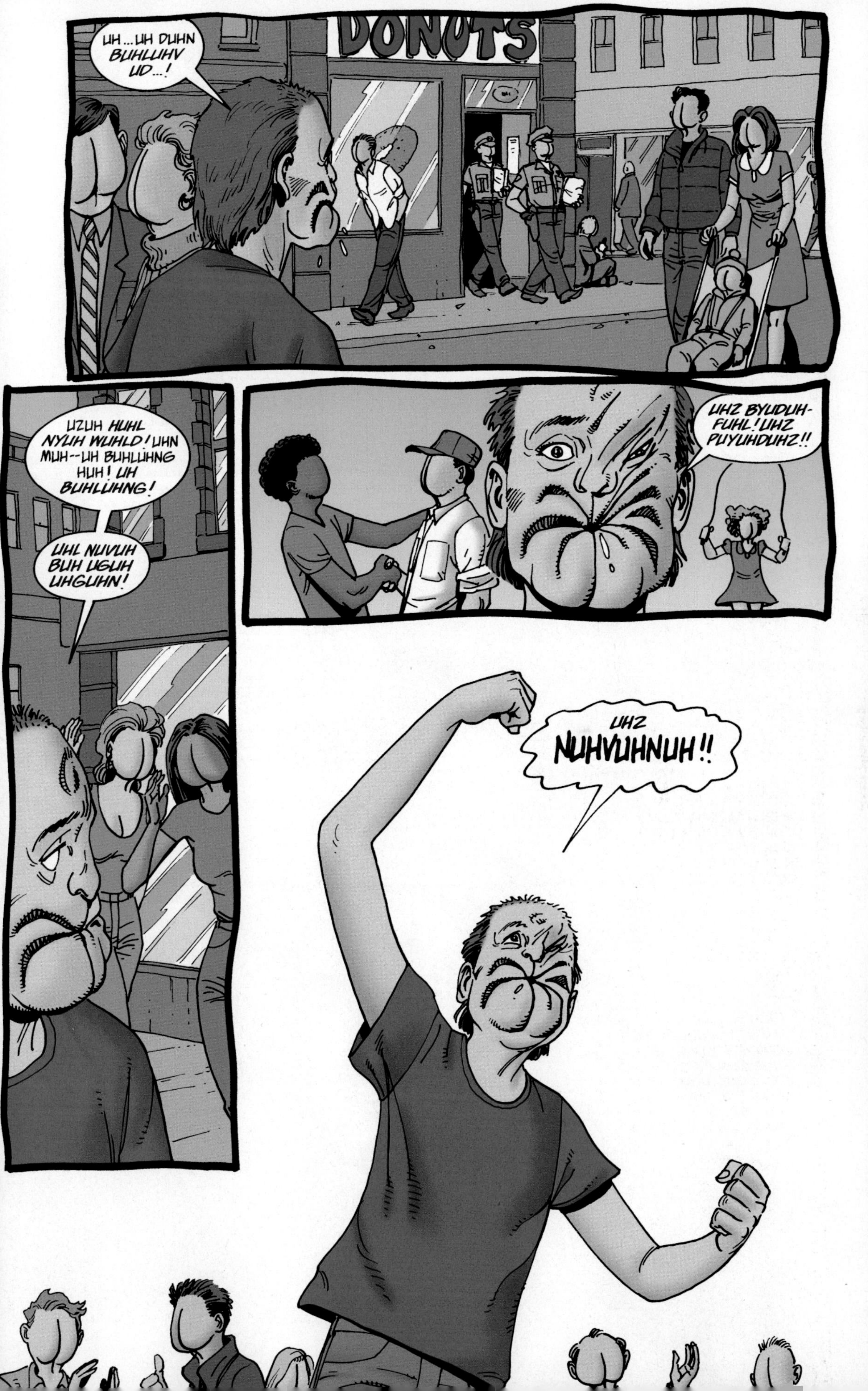
DONUTS
UH...UH DUHN BUHLUHV UD...!
UZUH HUHL NYUH WUHLD! UHN MUH--UH BUHLUHNG HUH! UH BUHLUHNG!
UHL NUVUH BUH UGUH UHGUHN!
UHZ BYUDUH-FUHL! UHZ PUYUHDUHZ!!
UHZ NUHVUHNUH!!

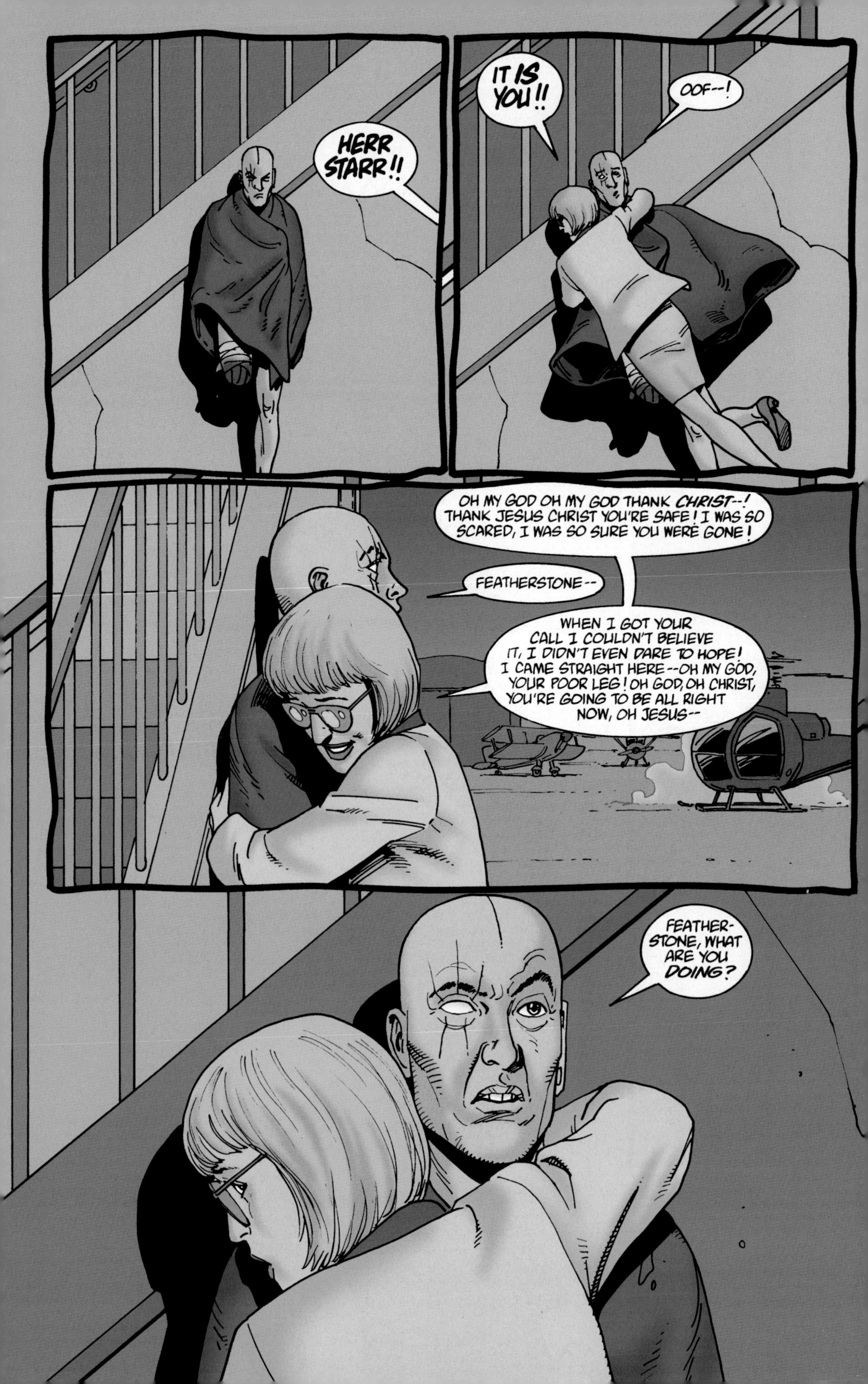
HERR STARR!!
IT IS YOU!!
OOF--!
OH MY GOD OH MY GOD THANK CHRIST--! THANK JESUS CHRIST YOU'RE SAFE! I WAS SO SCARED, I WAS SO SURE YOU WERE GONE!
FEATHERSTONE--
WHEN I GOT YOUR CALL I COULDN'T BELIEVE IT, I DIDN'T EVEN DARE TO HOPE! I CAME STRAIGHT HERE--OH MY GOD, YOUR POOR LEG! OH GOD, OH CHRIST, YOU'RE GOING TO BE ALL RIGHT NOW, OH JESUS--
FEATHER-STONE, WHAT ARE YOU DOING?

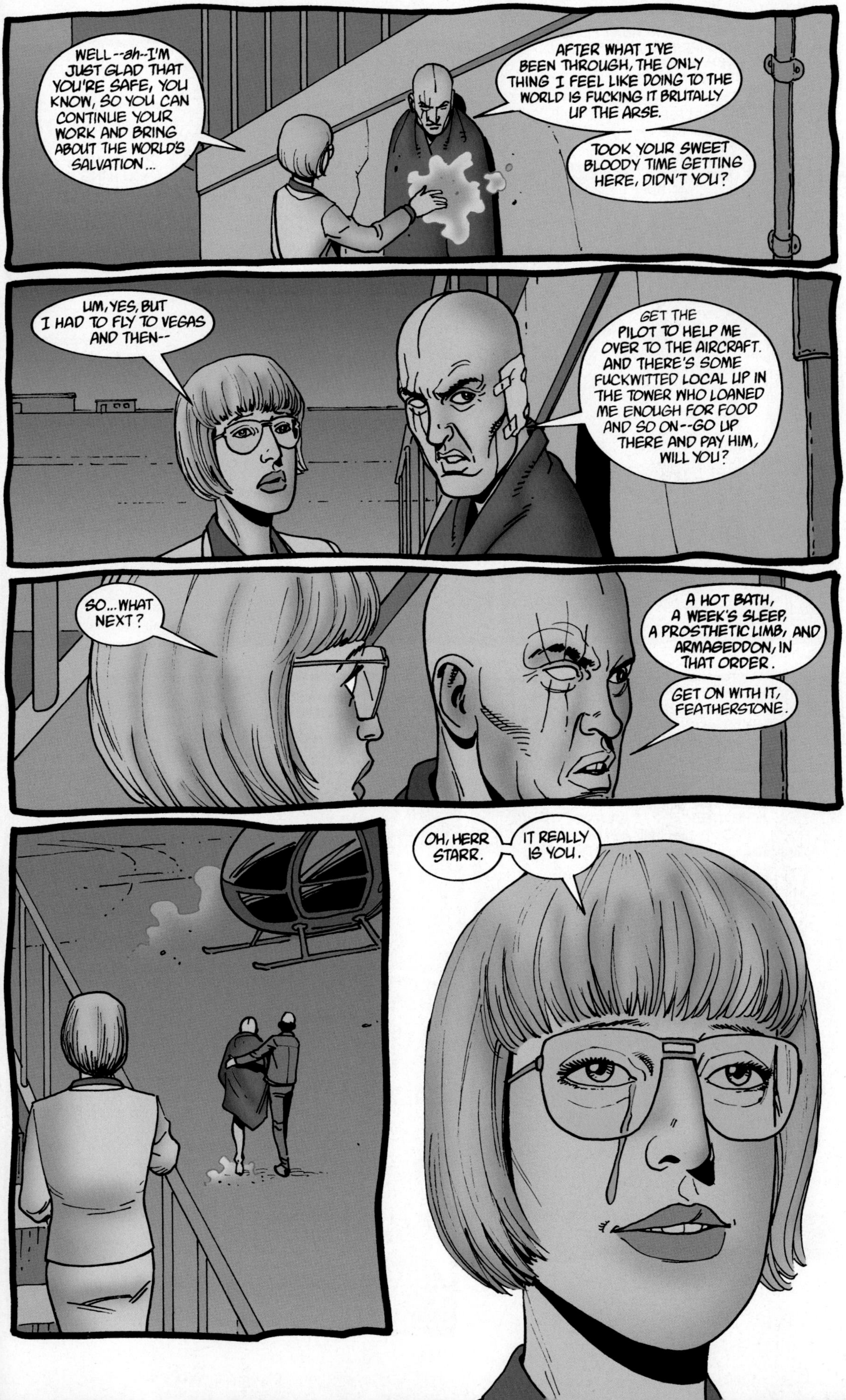
WELL--ah--I'M JUST GLAD THAT YOU'RE SAFE, YOU KNOW, SO YOU CAN CONTINUE YOUR WORK AND BRING ABOUT THE WORLD'S SALVATION...
AFTER WHAT I'VE BEEN THROUGH, THE ONLY THING I FEEL LIKE DOING TO THE WORLD IS FUCKING IT BRUTALLY UP THE ARSE.
TOOK YOUR SWEET BLOODY TIME GETTING HERE, DIDN'T YOU?
UM, YES, BUT I HAD TO FLY TO VEGAS AND THEN--
GET THE PILOT TO HELP ME OVER TO THE AIRCRAFT. AND THERE'S SOME FUCKWITTED LOCAL UP IN THE TOWER WHO LOANED ME ENOUGH FOR FOOD AND SO ON--GO UP THERE AND PAY HIM, WILL YOU?
SO...WHAT NEXT?
A HOT BATH, A WEEK'S SLEEP, A PROSTHETIC LIMB, AND ARMAGEDDON, IN THAT ORDER.
GET ON WITH IT, FEATHERSTONE.
OH, HERR STARR.
IT REALLY IS YOU.

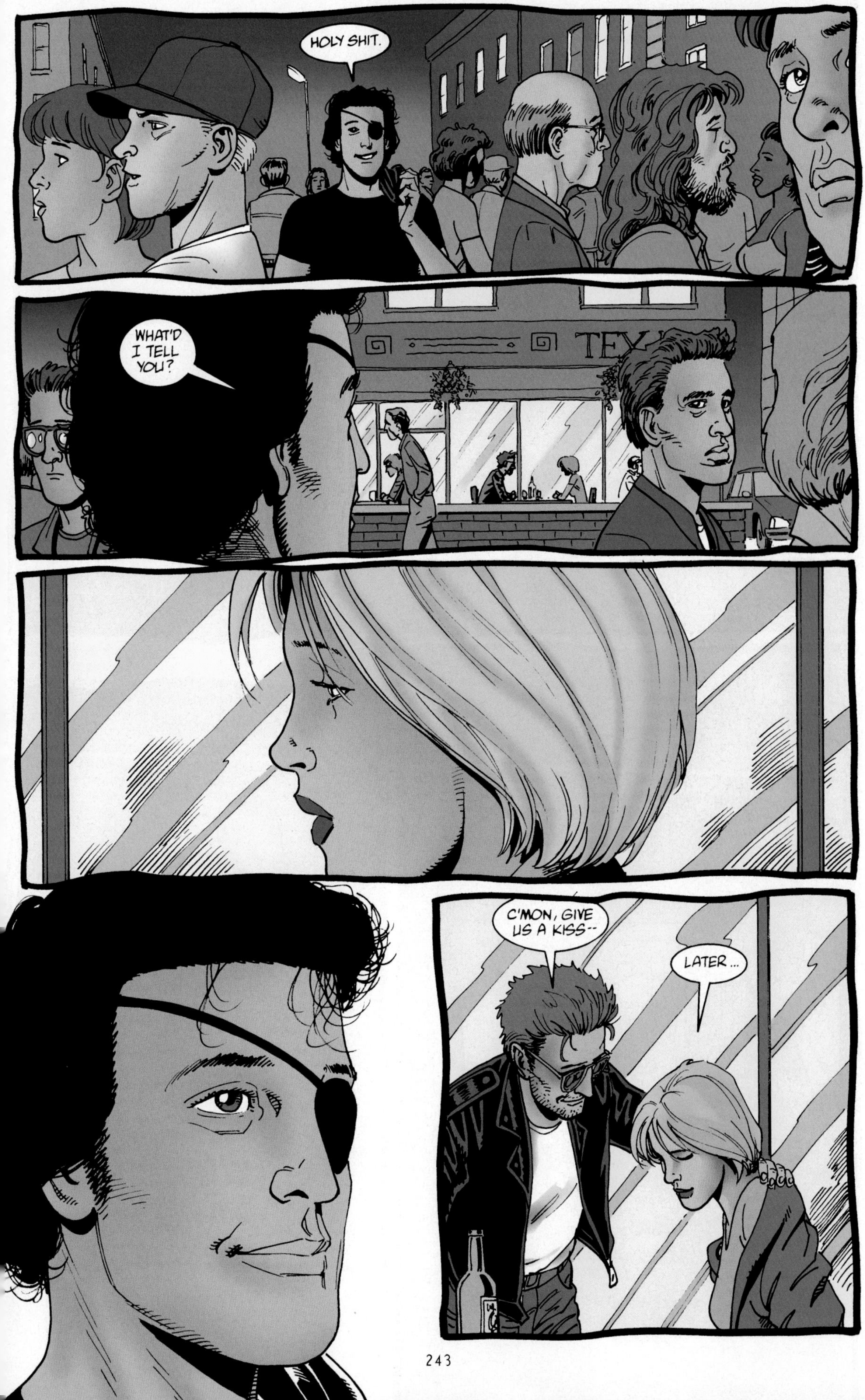
HOLY SHIT.
WHAT'D I TELL YOU?
C'MON, GIVE US A KISS--
LATER...

246

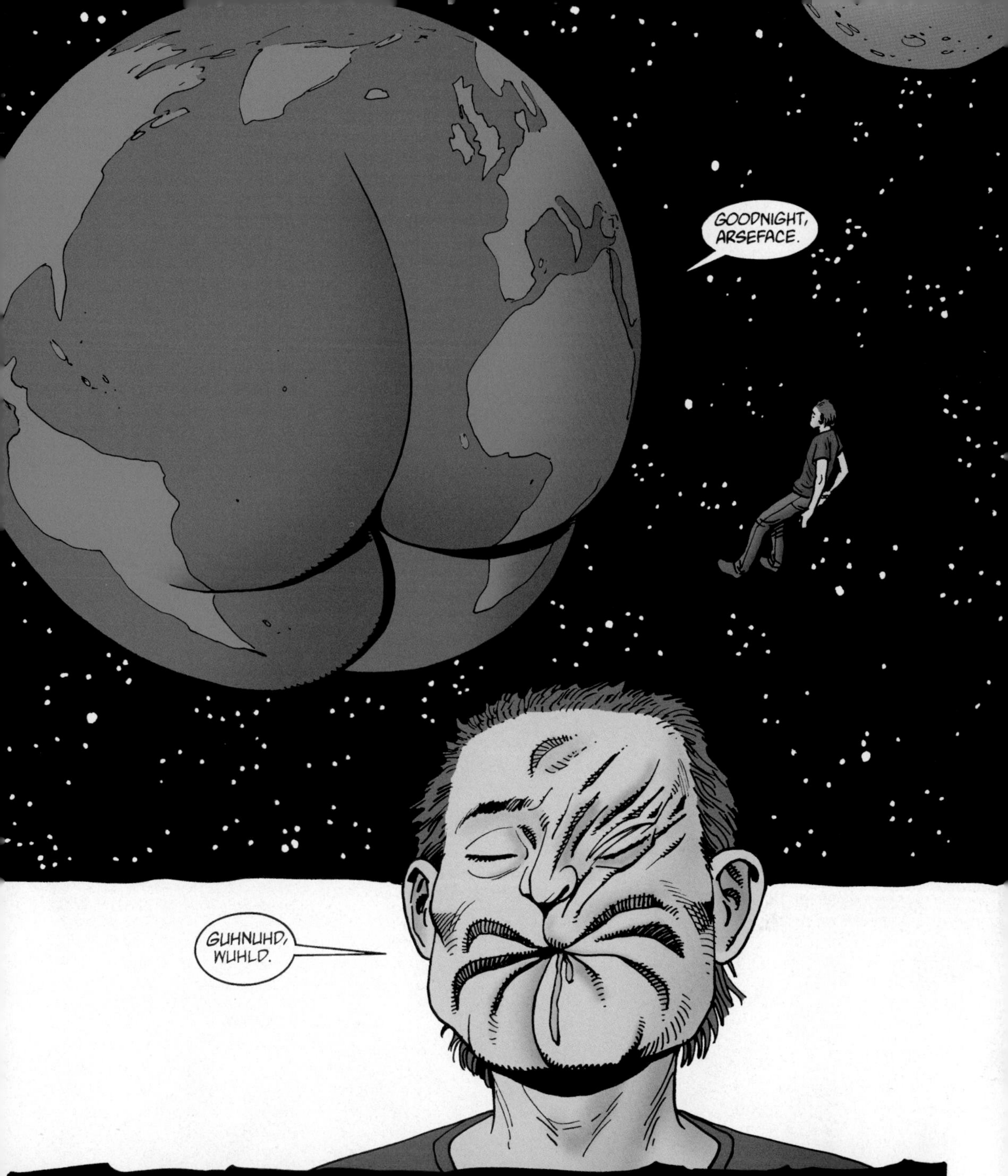
GOODNIGHT, ARSEFACE.
GUHNUHD, WUHLD.

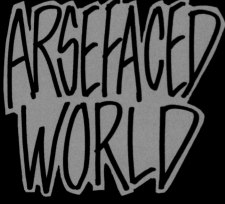

ARSEFACED WORLD

GARTH ENNIS-Writer
STEVE DILLON-Artist

Pamela Rambo-Colorist, Clem Robins-Letterer, Axel Alonso-Editor

PREACHER created by Garth Ennis and Steve Dillon

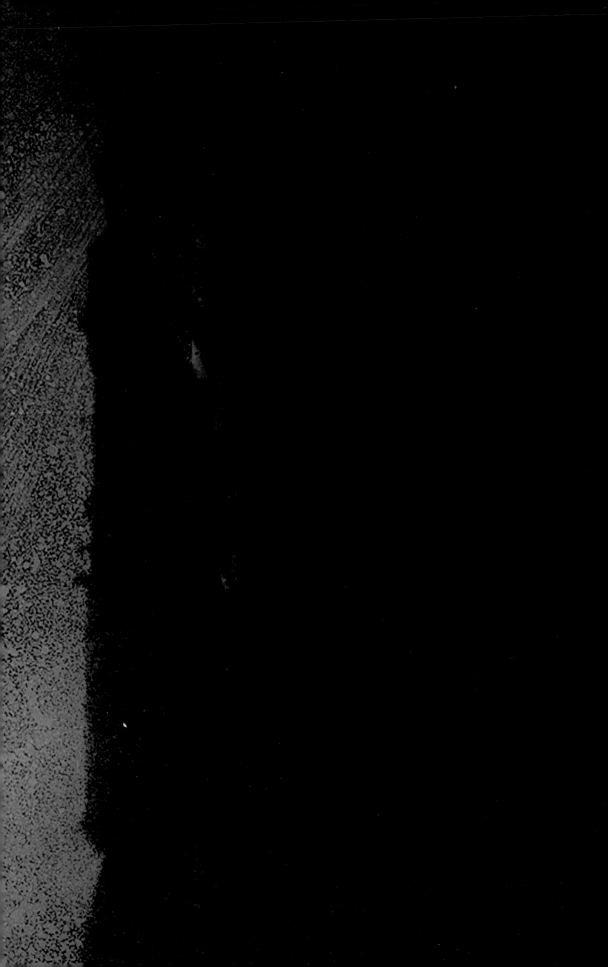

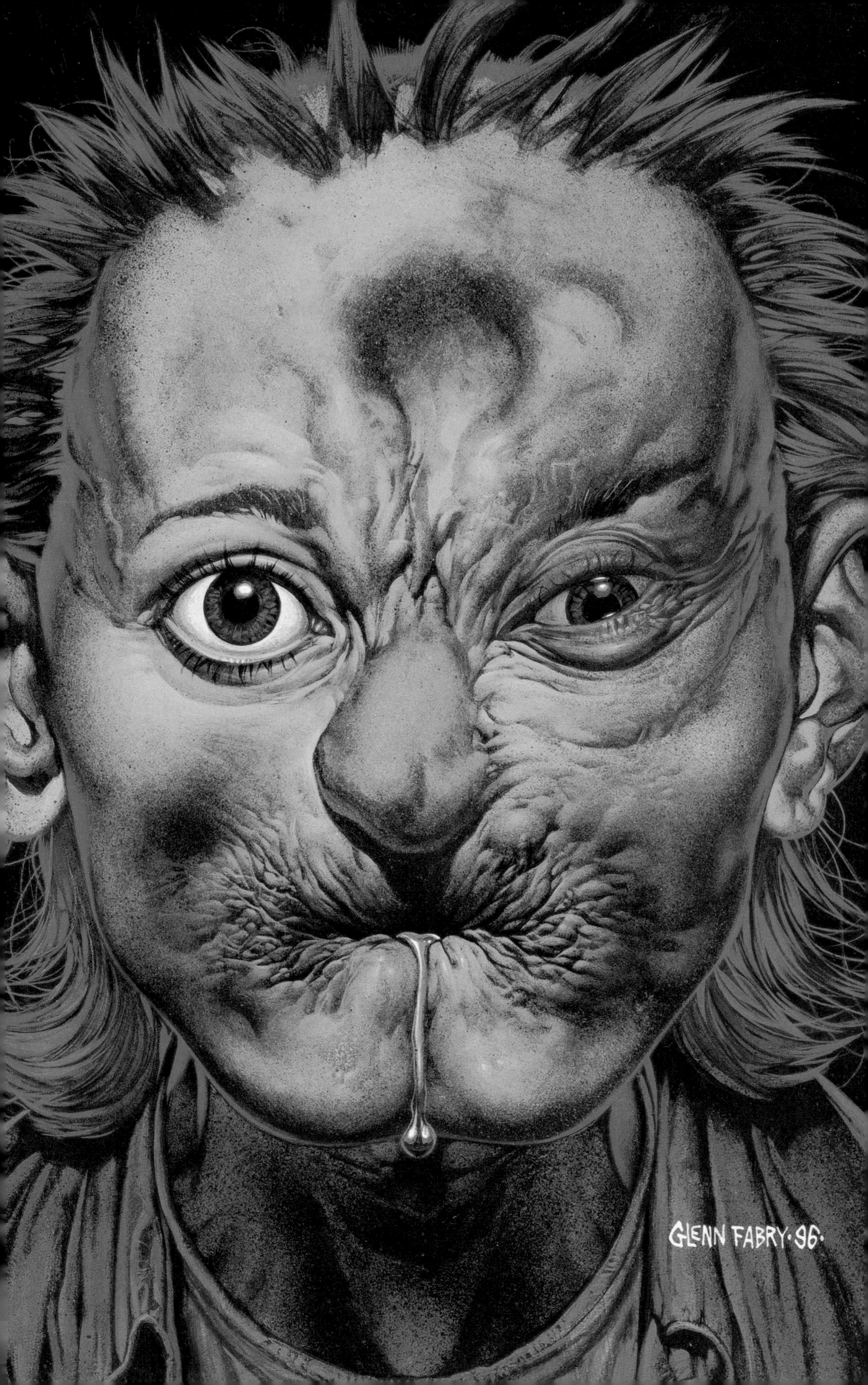
GLENN FABRY·96·

"PS: I lied. Three inches is below average."

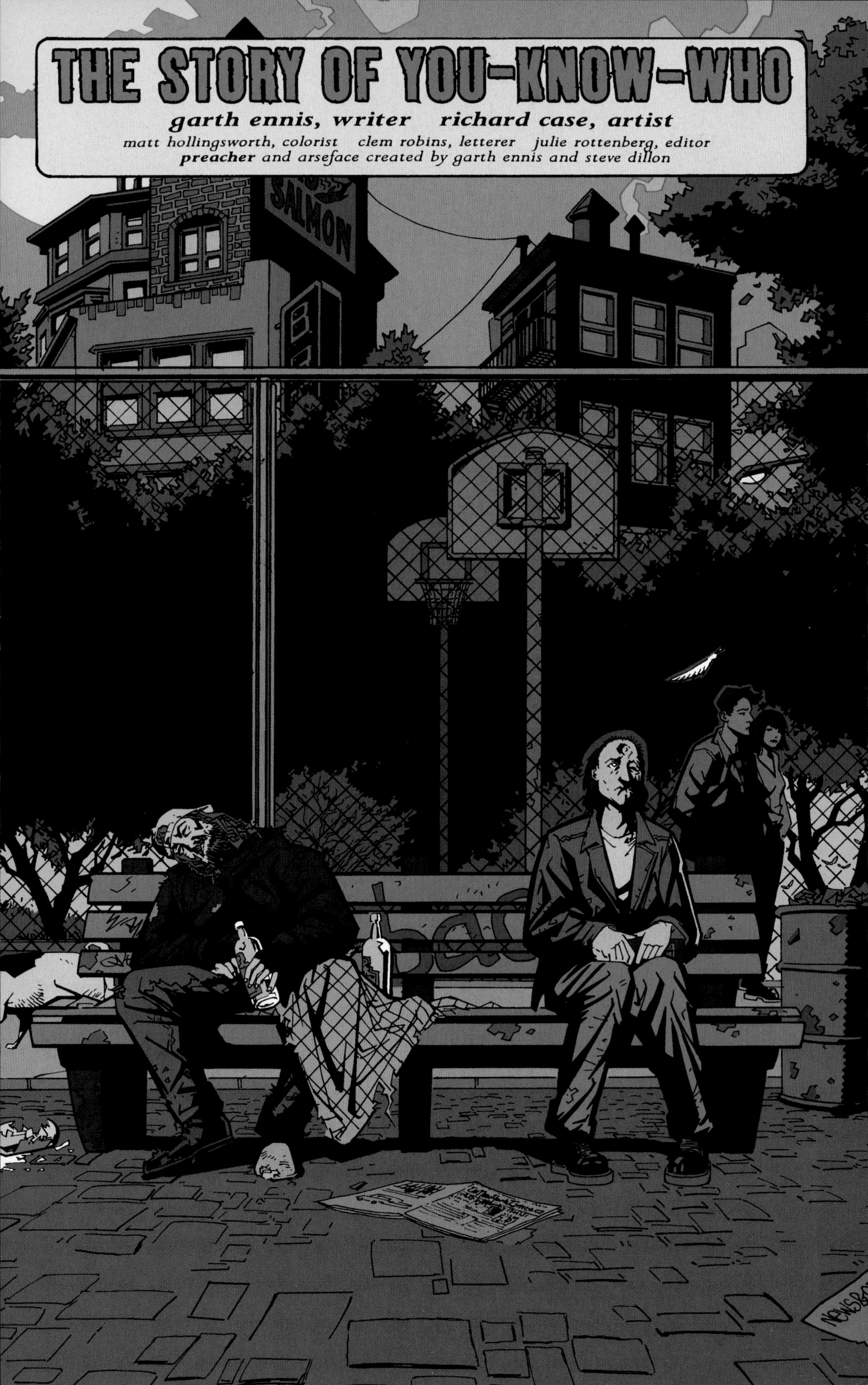
THE STORY OF YOU-KNOW-WHO
garth ennis, writer richard case, artist
matt hollingsworth, colorist clem robins, letterer julie rottenberg, editor
preacher and arseface created by garth ennis and steve dillon
SALMON

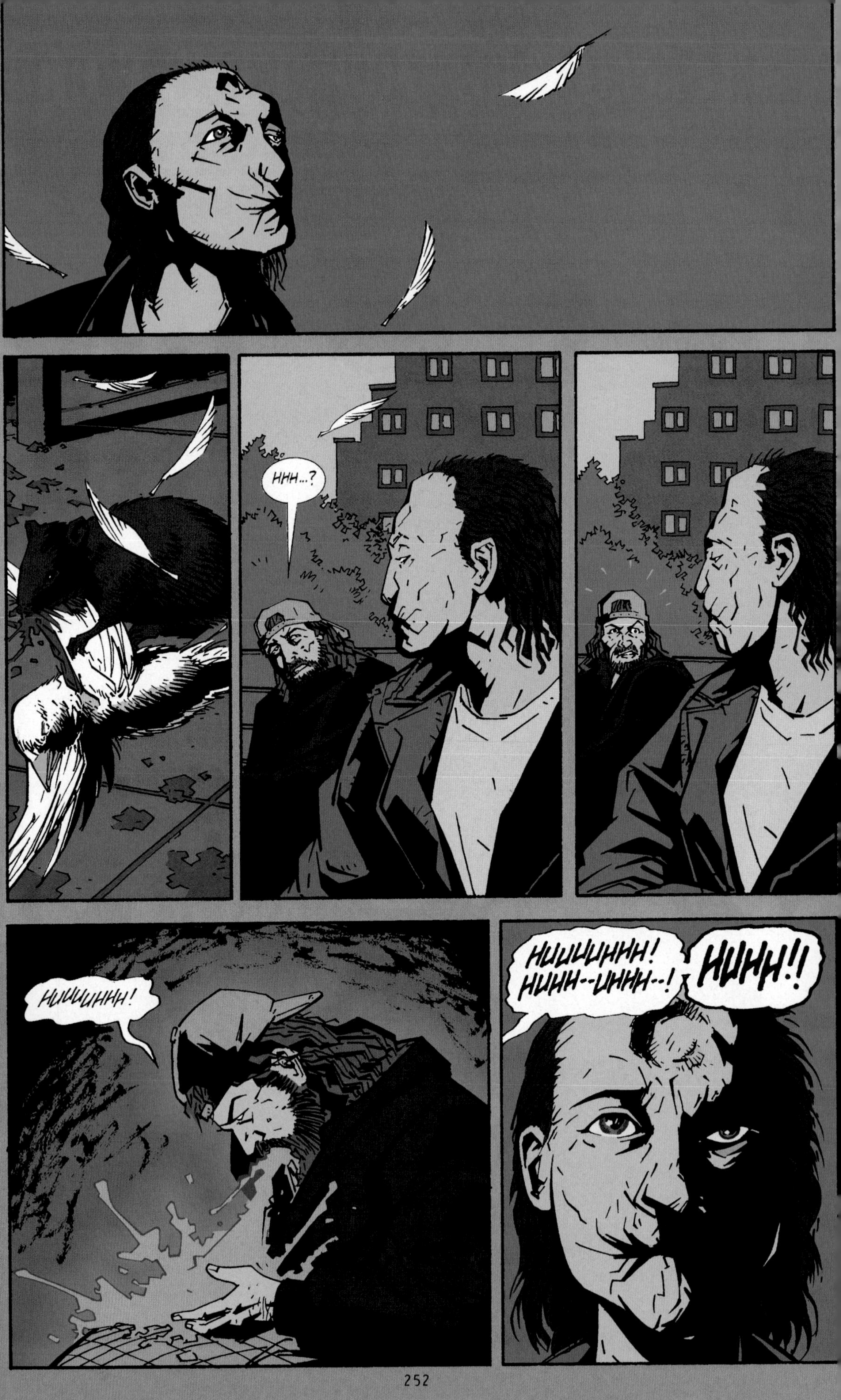
HHH...?
HUUUUHHH!
HUUUUUHHH!
HUHH--UHHH--!
HUHH!!

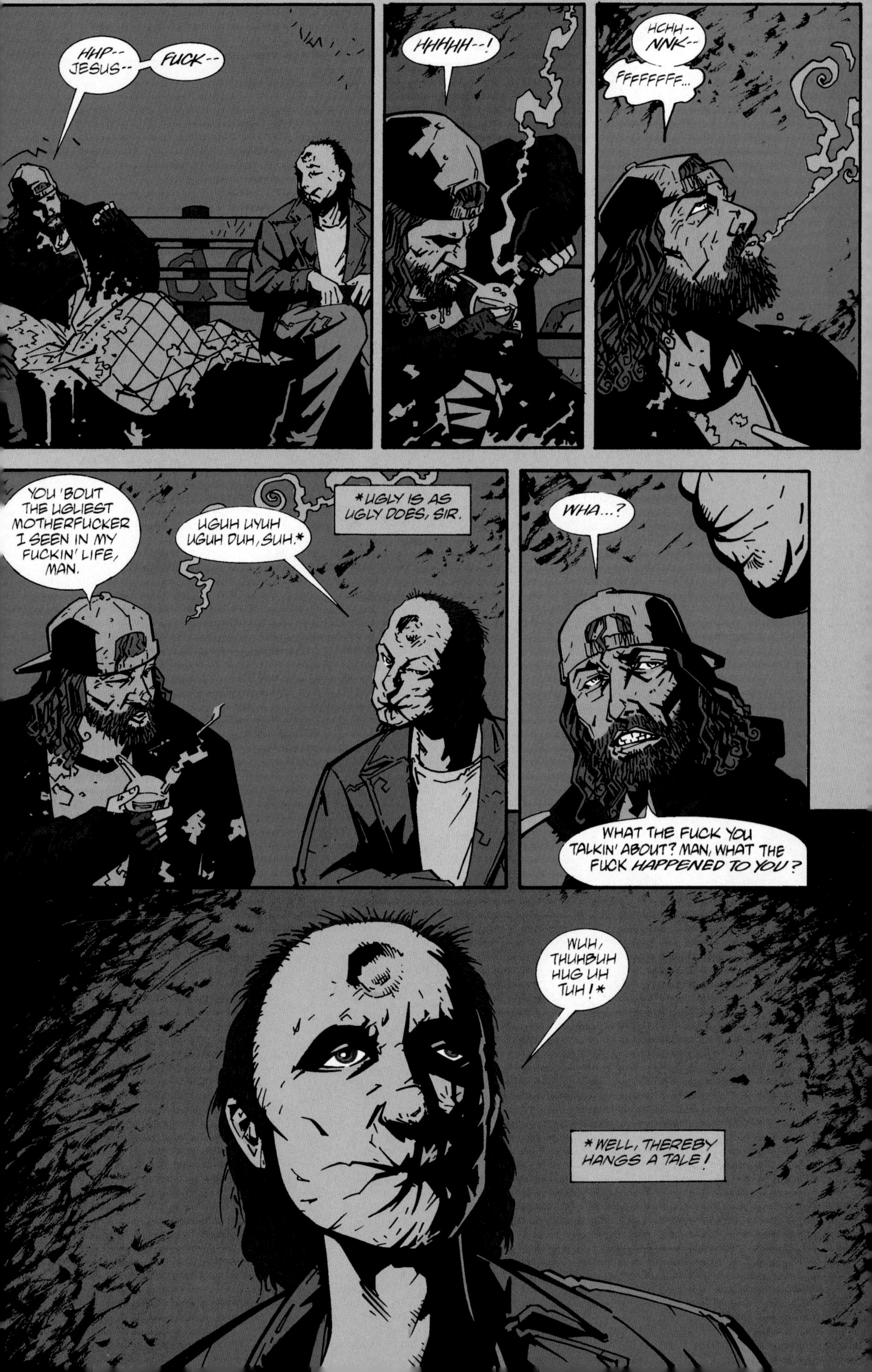
HHP-- JESUS--
FUCK--
HHHHH--!
HCHH-- NNK--
FFFFFFFF...
YOU 'BOUT THE UGLIEST MOTHERFUCKER I SEEN IN MY FUCKIN' LIFE, MAN.
UGUH UYUH UGUH DUH, SUH.*
*UGLY IS AS UGLY DOES, SIR.
WHA...?
WHAT THE FUCK YOU TALKIN' ABOUT? MAN, WHAT THE FUCK HAPPENED TO YOU?
WUH, THUHBUH HUG UH TUH!*
*WELL, THEREBY HANGS A TALE!

1. A Day in the Life

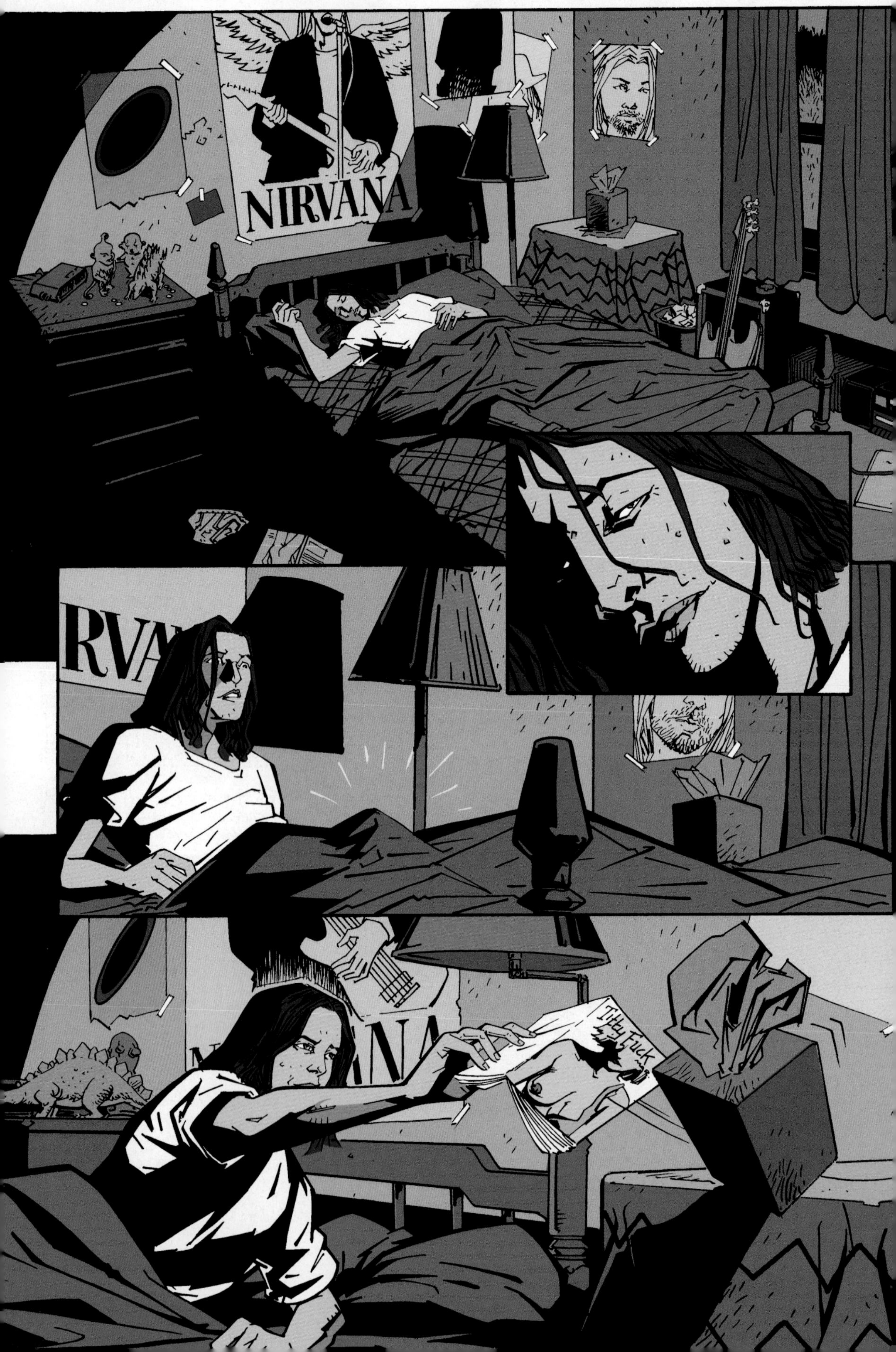
NIRVANA
RVAN
NA
Titty Fuck

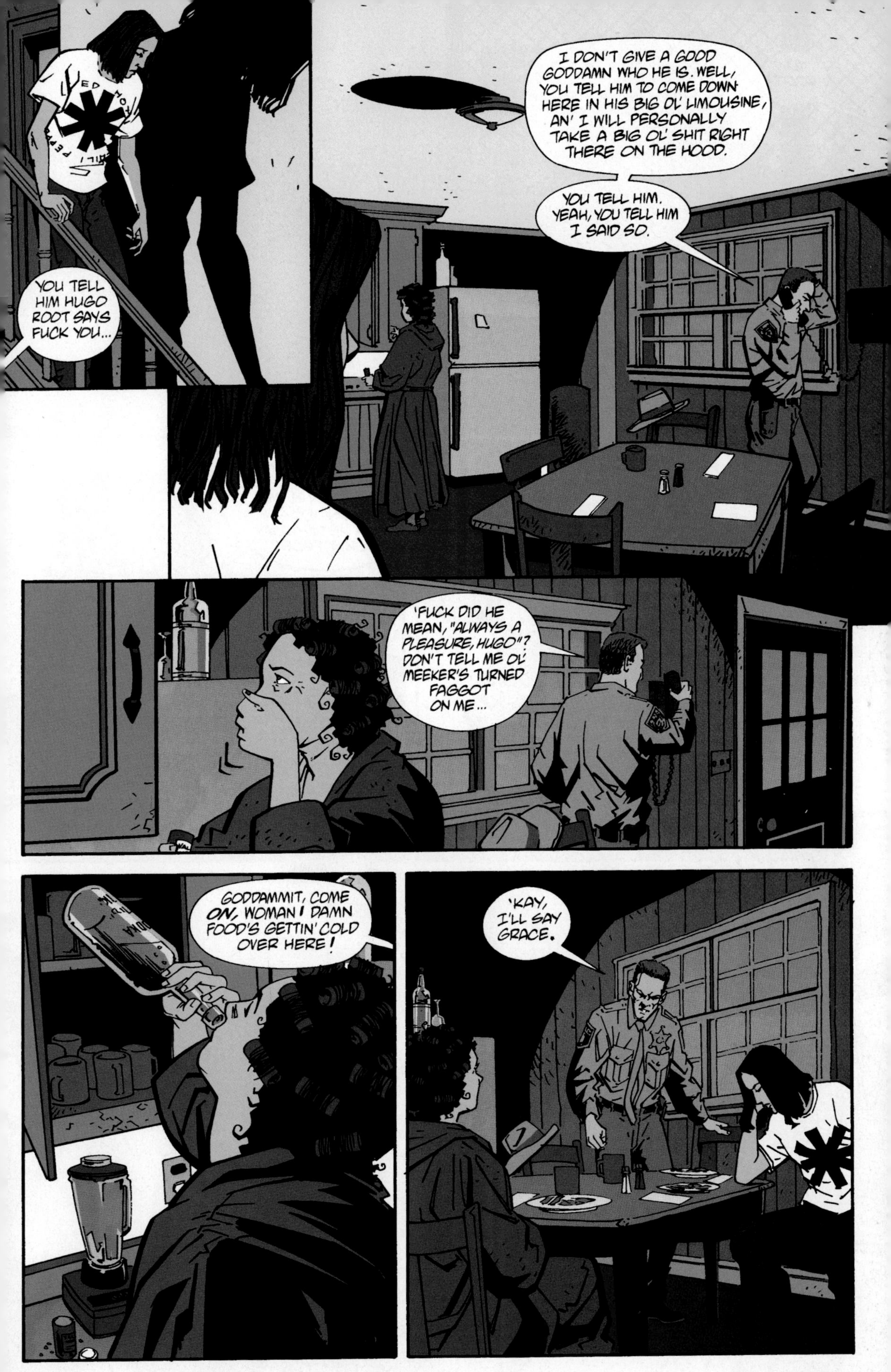

I DON'T GIVE A GOOD GODDAMN WHO HE IS. WELL, YOU TELL HIM TO COME DOWN HERE IN HIS BIG OL' LIMOUSINE, AN' I WILL PERSONALLY TAKE A BIG OL' SHIT RIGHT THERE ON THE HOOD.
YOU TELL HIM. YEAH, YOU TELL HIM I SAID SO.
YOU TELL HIM HUGO ROOT SAYS FUCK YOU...
'FUCK DID HE MEAN, "ALWAYS A PLEASURE, HUGO"? DON'T TELL ME OL' MEEKER'S TURNED FAGGOT ON ME...
GODDAMMIT, COME ON, WOMAN! DAMN FOOD'S GETTIN' COLD OVER HERE!
'KAY, I'LL SAY GRACE.

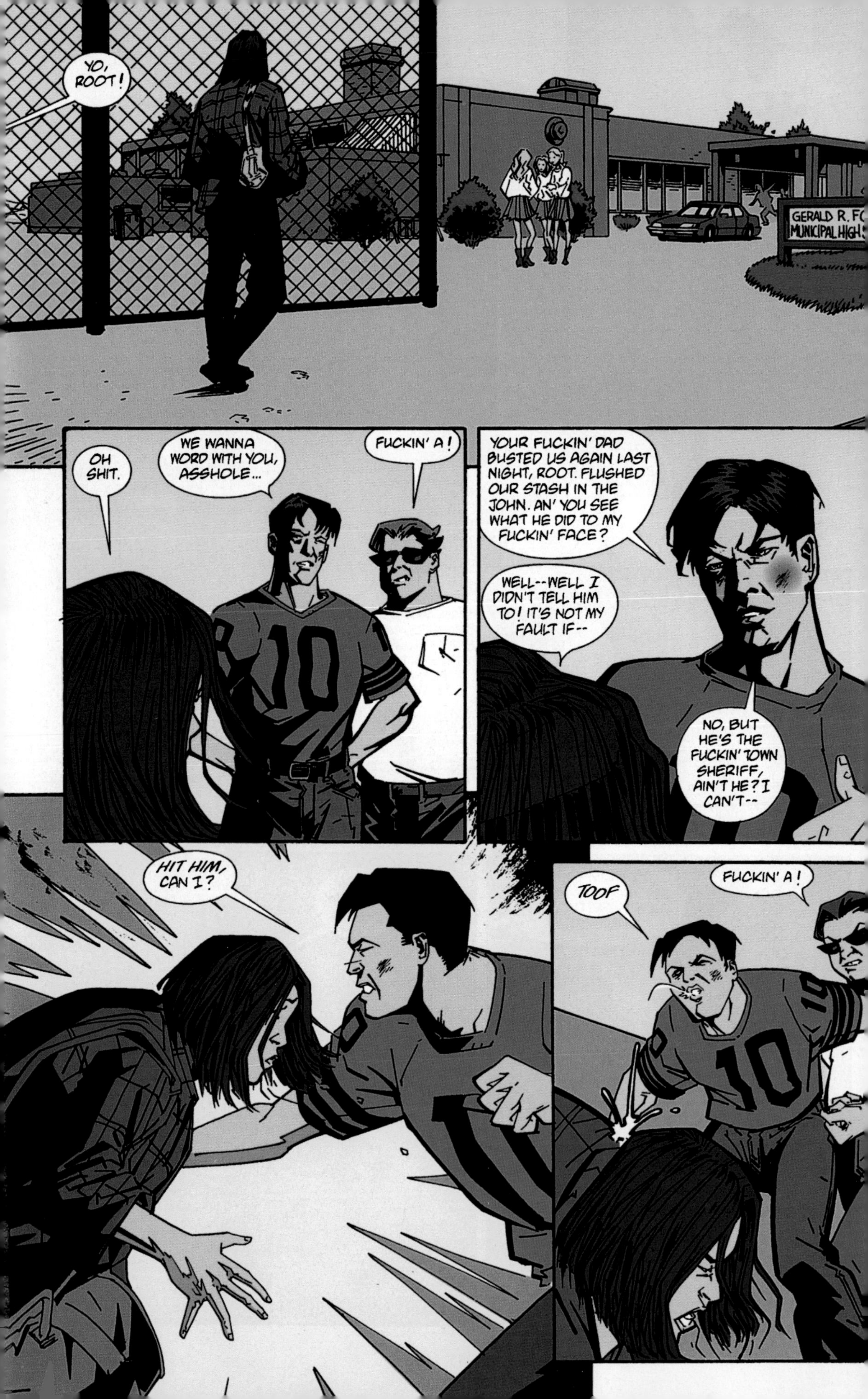
YO, ROOT!
GERALD R. FO
MUNICIPAL HIGH S
OH SHIT.
WE WANNA WORD WITH YOU, ASSHOLE...
FUCKIN' A!
YOUR FUCKIN' DAD BUSTED US AGAIN LAST NIGHT, ROOT. FLUSHED OUR STASH IN THE JOHN. AN' YOU SEE WHAT HE DID TO MY FUCKIN' FACE?
WELL--WELL I DIDN'T TELL HIM TO! IT'S NOT MY FAULT IF--
NO, BUT HE'S THE FUCKIN' TOWN SHERIFF, AIN'T HE? I CAN'T--
HIT HIM, CAN I?
TOOF
FUCKIN' A!

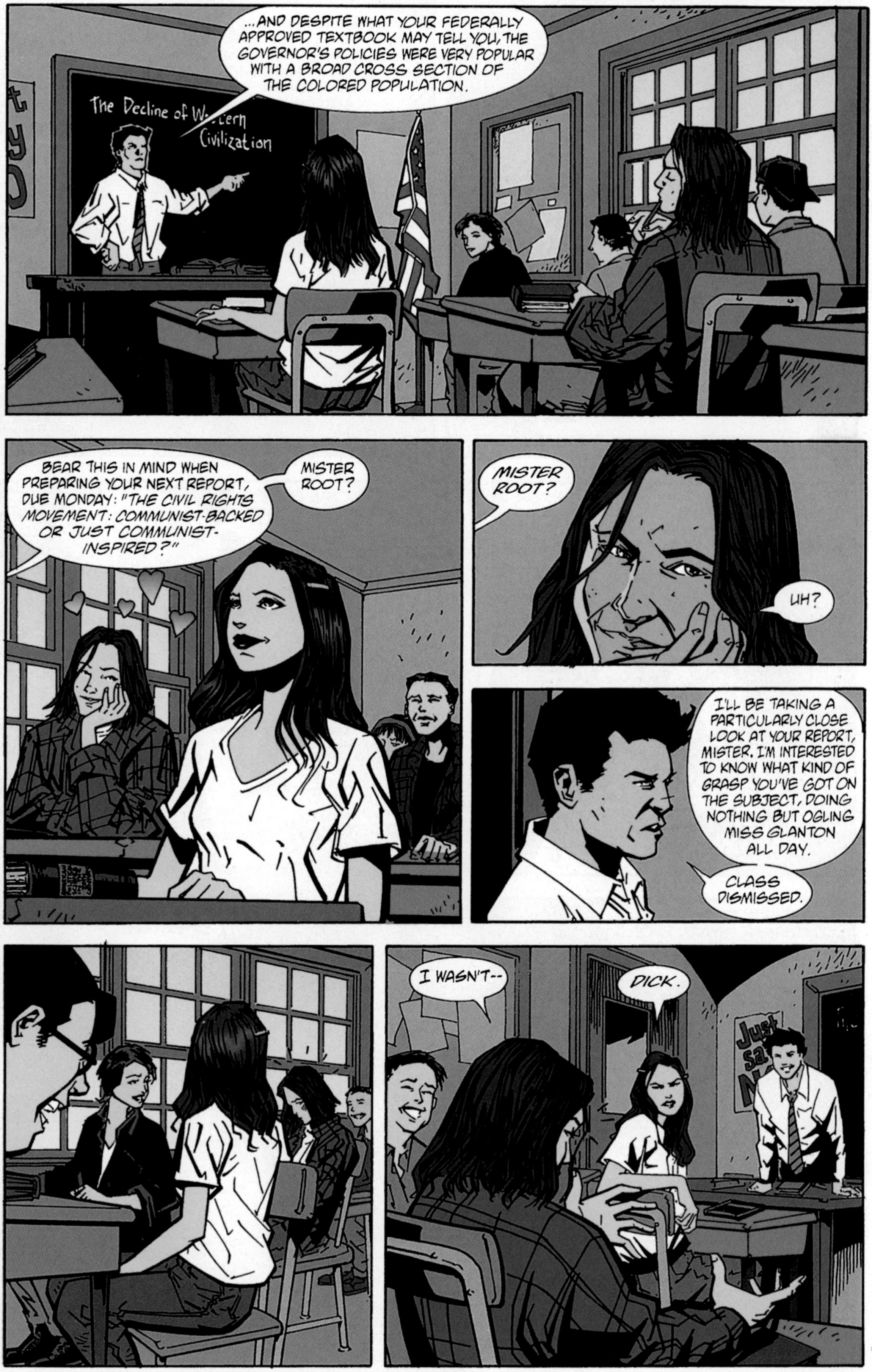
...AND DESPITE WHAT YOUR FEDERALLY APPROVED TEXTBOOK MAY TELL YOU, THE GOVERNOR'S POLICIES WERE VERY POPULAR WITH A BROAD CROSS SECTION OF THE COLORED POPULATION.
The Decline of Western Civilization
BEAR THIS IN MIND WHEN PREPARING YOUR NEXT REPORT, DUE MONDAY: "THE CIVIL RIGHTS MOVEMENT: COMMUNIST-BACKED OR JUST COMMUNIST-INSPIRED?"
MISTER ROOT?
MISTER ROOT?
UH?
I'LL BE TAKING A PARTICULARLY CLOSE LOOK AT YOUR REPORT, MISTER. I'M INTERESTED TO KNOW WHAT KIND OF GRASP YOU'VE GOT ON THE SUBJECT, DOING NOTHING BUT OGLING MISS GLANTON ALL DAY.
CLASS DISMISSED.
I WASN'T--
DICK.

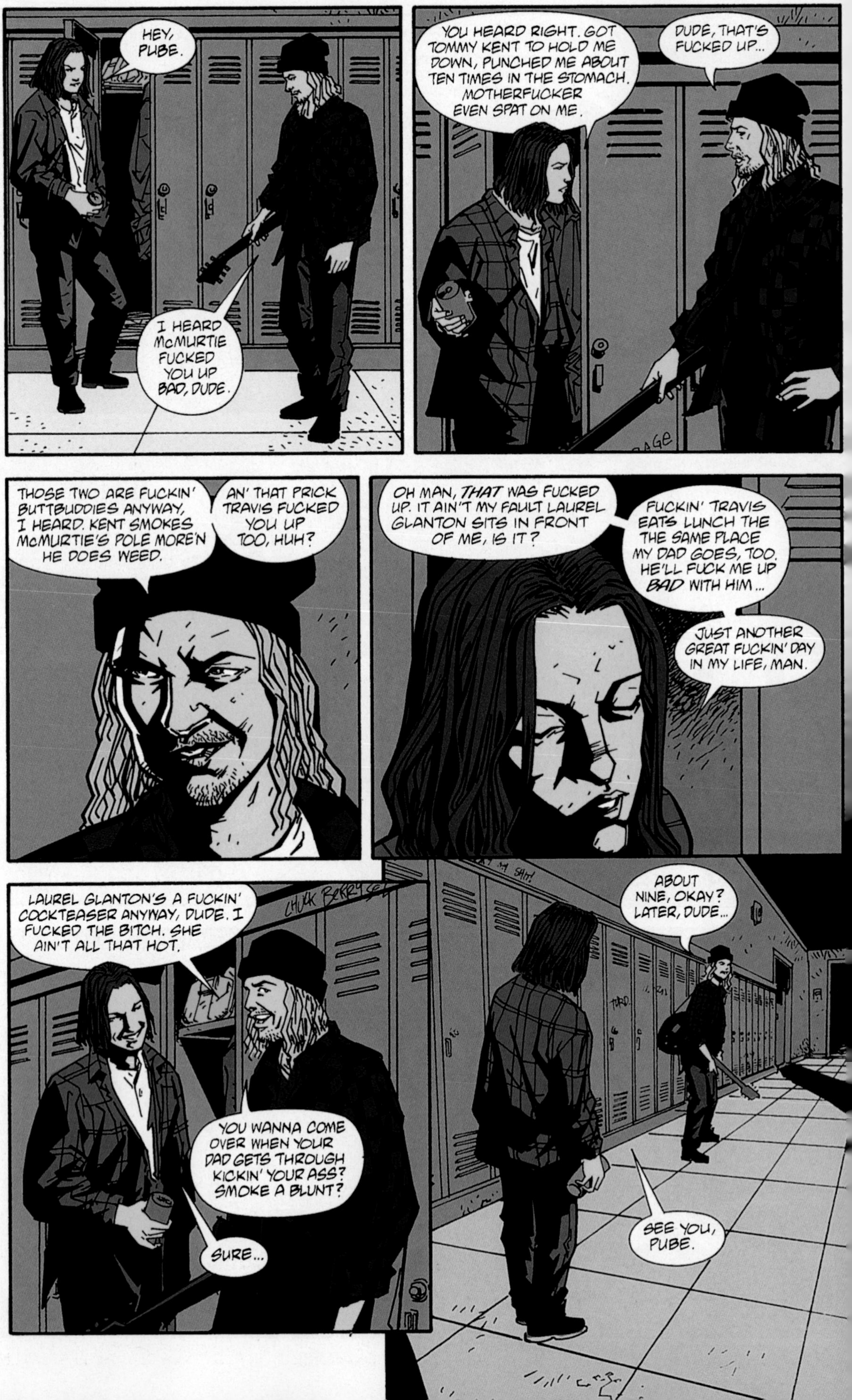
HEY, PUBE.
I HEARD McMURTIE FUCKED YOU UP BAD, DUDE.
YOU HEARD RIGHT. GOT TOMMY KENT TO HOLD ME DOWN, PUNCHED ME ABOUT TEN TIMES IN THE STOMACH. MOTHERFUCKER EVEN SPAT ON ME.
DUDE, THAT'S FUCKED UP...
THOSE TWO ARE FUCKIN' BUTTBUDDIES ANYWAY, I HEARD. KENT SMOKES McMURTIE'S POLE MORE'N HE DOES WEED.
AN' THAT PRICK TRAVIS FUCKED YOU UP TOO, HUH?
OH MAN, THAT WAS FUCKED UP. IT AIN'T MY FAULT LAUREL GLANTON SITS IN FRONT OF ME, IS IT?
FUCKIN' TRAVIS EATS LUNCH THE SAME PLACE MY DAD GOES, TOO. HE'LL FUCK ME UP BAD WITH HIM...
JUST ANOTHER GREAT FUCKIN' DAY IN MY LIFE, MAN.
LAUREL GLANTON'S A FUCKIN' COCKTEASER ANYWAY, DUDE. I FUCKED THE BITCH. SHE AIN'T ALL THAT HOT.
YOU WANNA COME OVER WHEN YOUR DAD GETS THROUGH KICKIN' YOUR ASS? SMOKE A BLUNT?
SURE...
ABOUT NINE, OKAY? LATER, DUDE...
SEE YOU, PUBE.

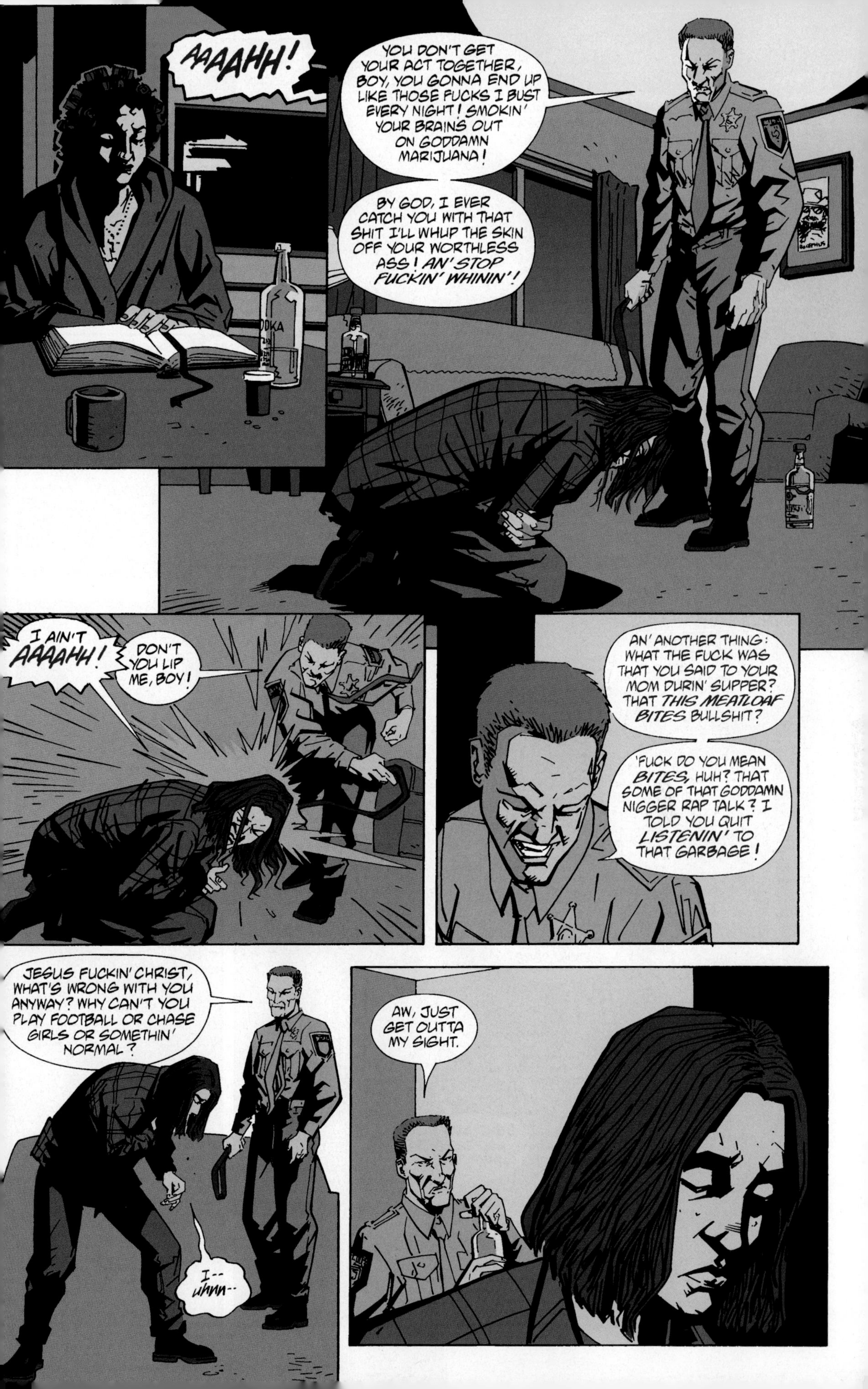
AAAAHH!
YOU DON'T GET YOUR ACT TOGETHER, BOY, YOU GONNA END UP LIKE THOSE FUCKS I BUST EVERY NIGHT! SMOKIN' YOUR BRAINS OUT ON GODDAMN MARIJUANA!
BY GOD, I EVER CATCH YOU WITH THAT SHIT I'LL WHUP THE SKIN OFF YOUR WORTHLESS ASS! AN' STOP FUCKIN' WHININ'!
I AIN'T AAAAHH!
DON'T YOU LIP ME, BOY!
AN' ANOTHER THING: WHAT THE FUCK WAS THAT YOU SAID TO YOUR MOM DURIN' SUPPER? THAT THIS MEATLOAF BITES BULLSHIT?
'FUCK DO YOU MEAN BITES, HUH? THAT SOME OF THAT GODDAMN NIGGER RAP TALK? I TOLD YOU QUIT LISTENIN' TO THAT GARBAGE!
JESUS FUCKIN' CHRIST, WHAT'S WRONG WITH YOU ANYWAY? WHY CAN'T YOU PLAY FOOTBALL OR CHASE GIRLS OR SOMETHIN' NORMAL?
I-- uhnn--
AW, JUST GET OUTTA MY SIGHT.

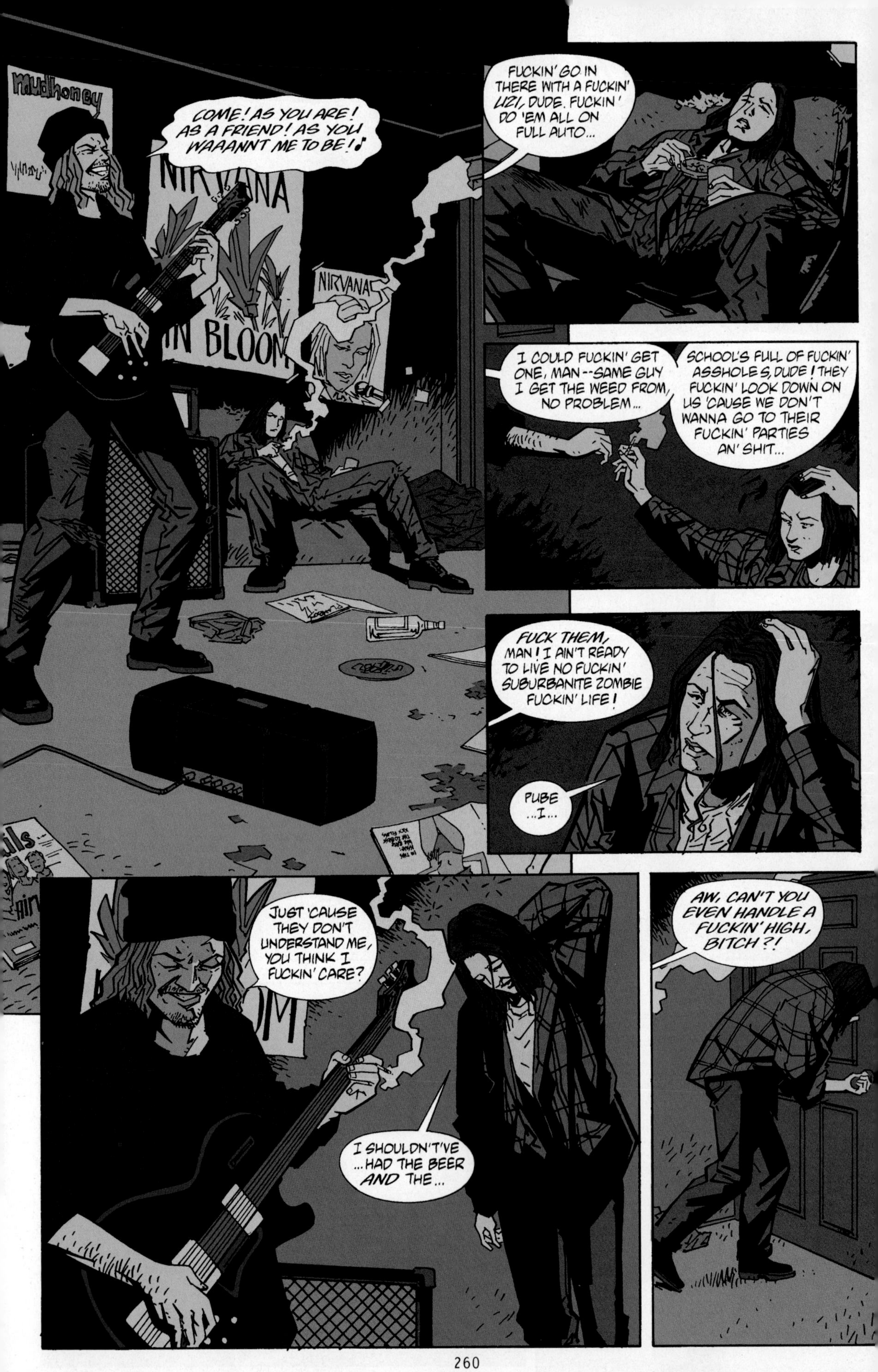

mudhoney
NIRVANA
IN BLOOM
NIRVANA
COME! AS YOU ARE! AS A FRIEND! AS YOU WAAANNT ME TO BE!♪
FUCKIN' GO IN THERE WITH A FUCKIN' UZI, DUDE. FUCKIN' DO 'EM ALL ON FULL AUTO...
I COULD FUCKIN' GET ONE, MAN--SAME GUY I GET THE WEED FROM, NO PROBLEM...
SCHOOL'S FULL OF FUCKIN' ASSHOLES, DUDE! THEY FUCKIN' LOOK DOWN ON US 'CAUSE WE DON'T WANNA GO TO THEIR FUCKIN' PARTIES AN' SHIT...
FUCK THEM, MAN! I AIN'T READY TO LIVE NO FUCKIN' SUBURBANITE ZOMBIE FUCKIN' LIFE!
PUBE ...I...
JUST 'CAUSE THEY DON'T UNDERSTAND ME, YOU THINK I FUCKIN' CARE?
I SHOULDN'T'VE ...HAD THE BEER *AND* THE...
AW, CAN'T YOU EVEN HANDLE A FUCKIN' HIGH, BITCH?!

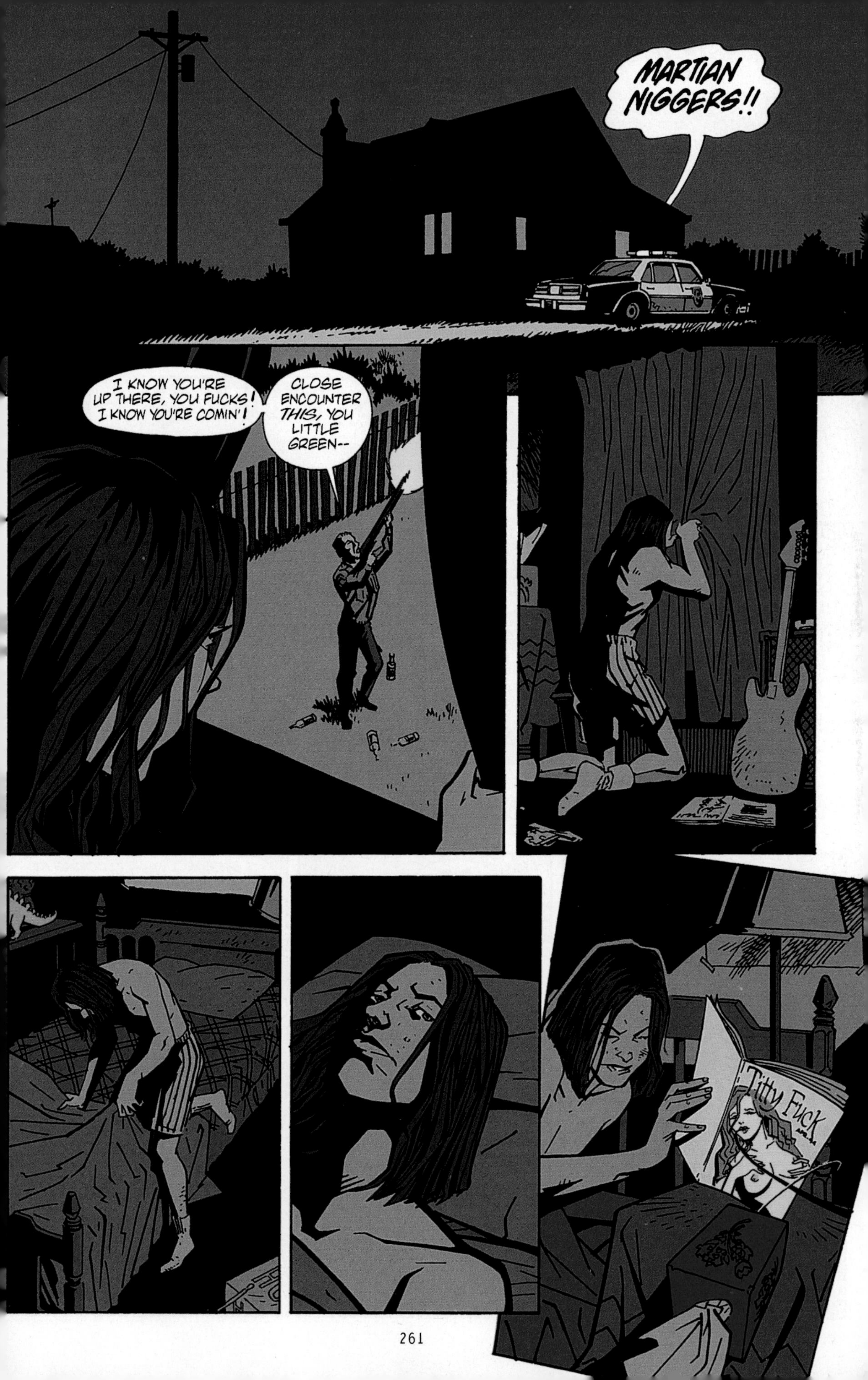
MARTIAN NIGGERS!!
I KNOW YOU'RE UP THERE, YOU FUCKS! I KNOW YOU'RE COMIN'!
CLOSE ENCOUNTER *THIS*, YOU LITTLE GREEN--
Titty Fuck

2. Rebel Rebel

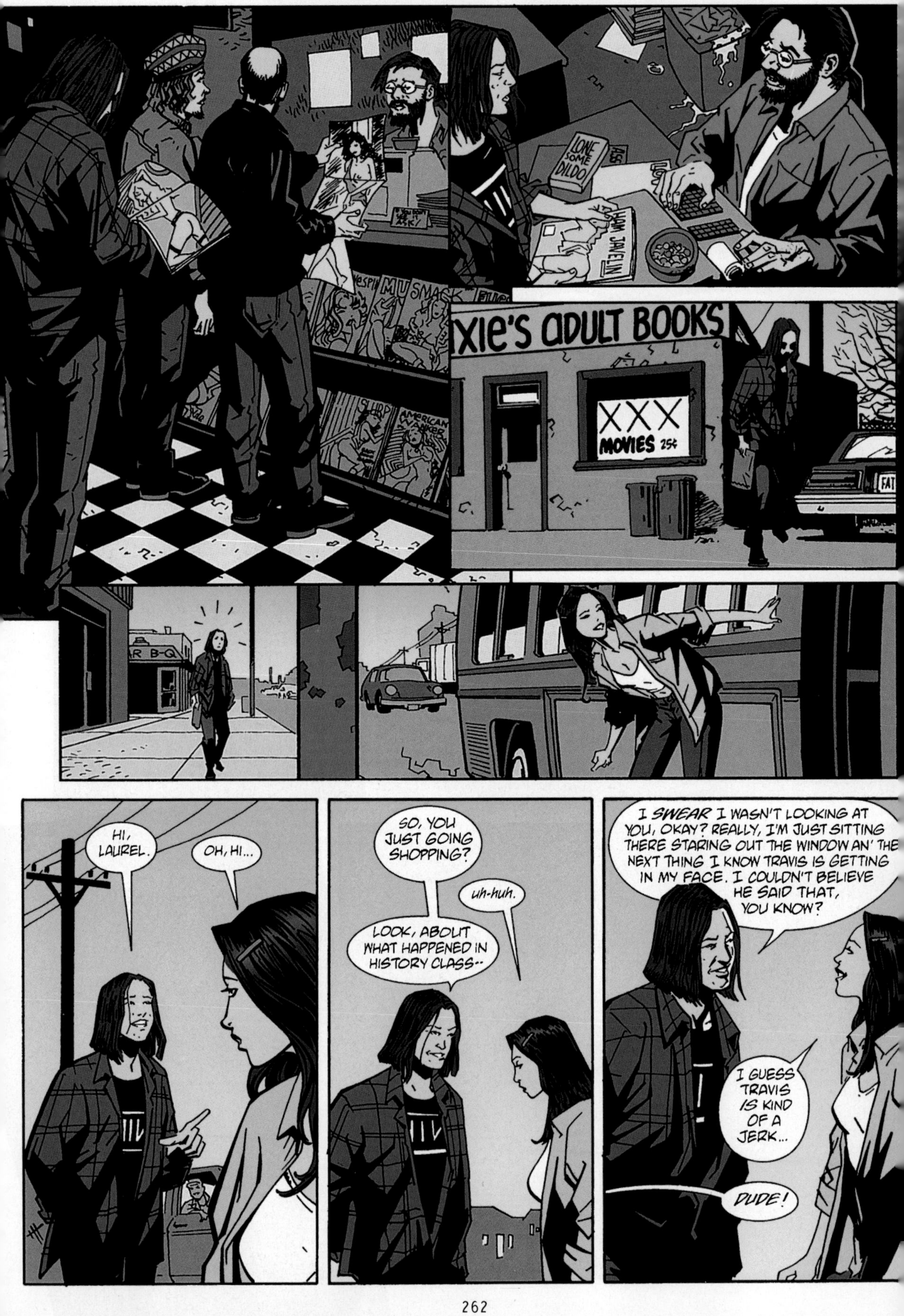

IF YOU DON'T SEE IT ASK!
LONE SOME DILDO
HAM JAVELIN
AMERICAN WANKER
XIE'S ADULT BOOKS
XXX MOVIES 25¢
AR B-Q
HI, LAUREL.
OH, HI...
SO, YOU JUST GOING SHOPPING?
uh-huh.
LOOK, ABOUT WHAT HAPPENED IN HISTORY CLASS--
I SWEAR I WASN'T LOOKING AT YOU, OKAY? REALLY, I'M JUST SITTING THERE STARING OUT THE WINDOW AN' THE NEXT THING I KNOW TRAVIS IS GETTING IN MY FACE. I COULDN'T BELIEVE HE SAID THAT, YOU KNOW?
I GUESS TRAVIS IS KIND OF A JERK...
DUDE!

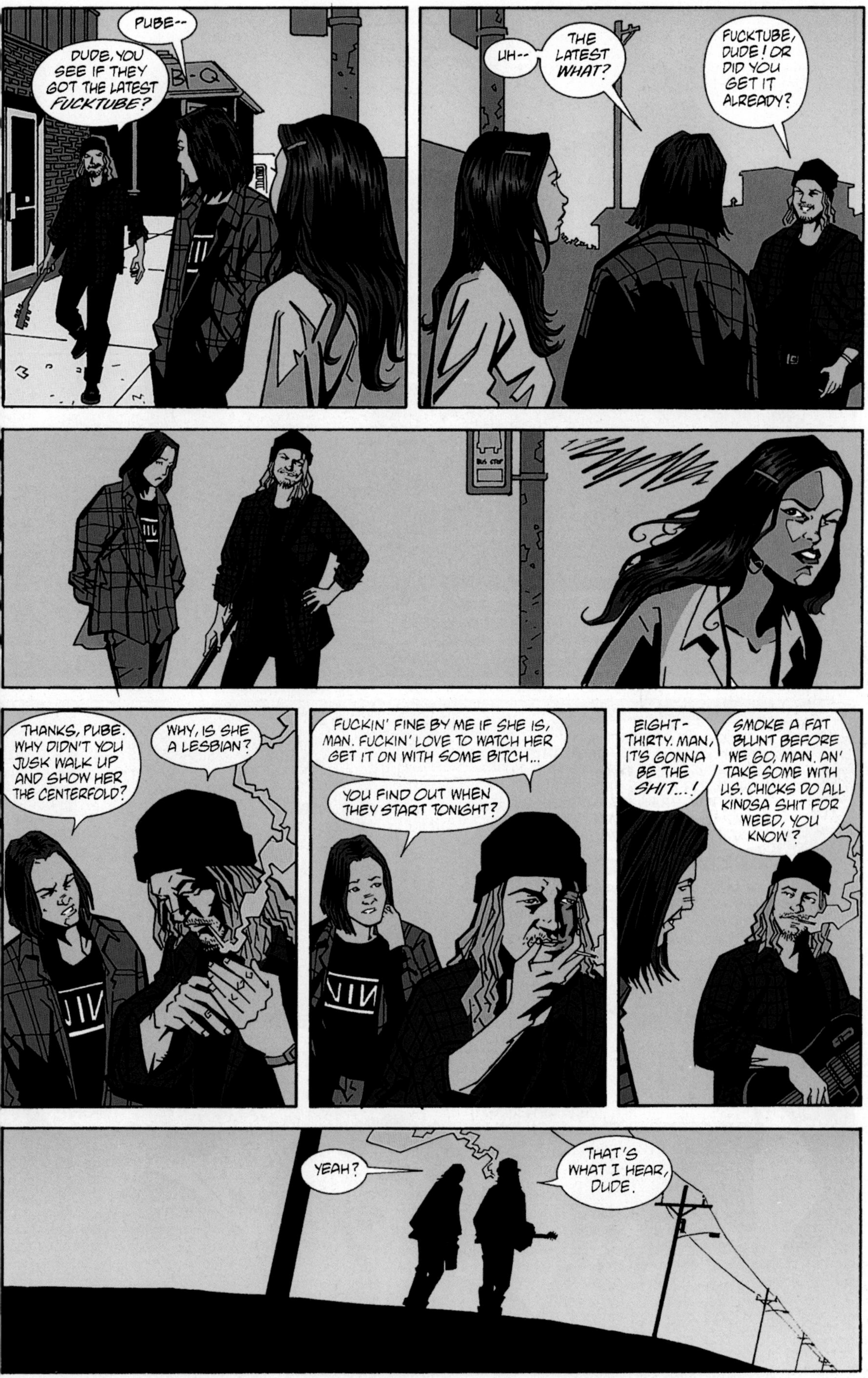
PUBE--
DUDE, YOU SEE IF THEY GOT THE LATEST FUCKTUBE?
UH--
THE LATEST WHAT?
FUCKTUBE, DUDE! OR DID YOU GET IT ALREADY?
BUS STOP
THANKS, PUBE. WHY DIDN'T YOU JUSK WALK UP AND SHOW HER THE CENTERFOLD?
WHY, IS SHE A LESBIAN?
FUCKIN' FINE BY ME IF SHE IS, MAN. FUCKIN' LOVE TO WATCH HER GET IT ON WITH SOME BITCH...
YOU FIND OUT WHEN THEY START TONIGHT?
EIGHT-THIRTY. MAN, IT'S GONNA BE THE SHIT...!
SMOKE A FAT BLUNT BEFORE WE GO, MAN. AN' TAKE SOME WITH US. CHICKS DO ALL KINDSA SHIT FOR WEED, YOU KNOW?
YEAH?
THAT'S WHAT I HEAR, DUDE.

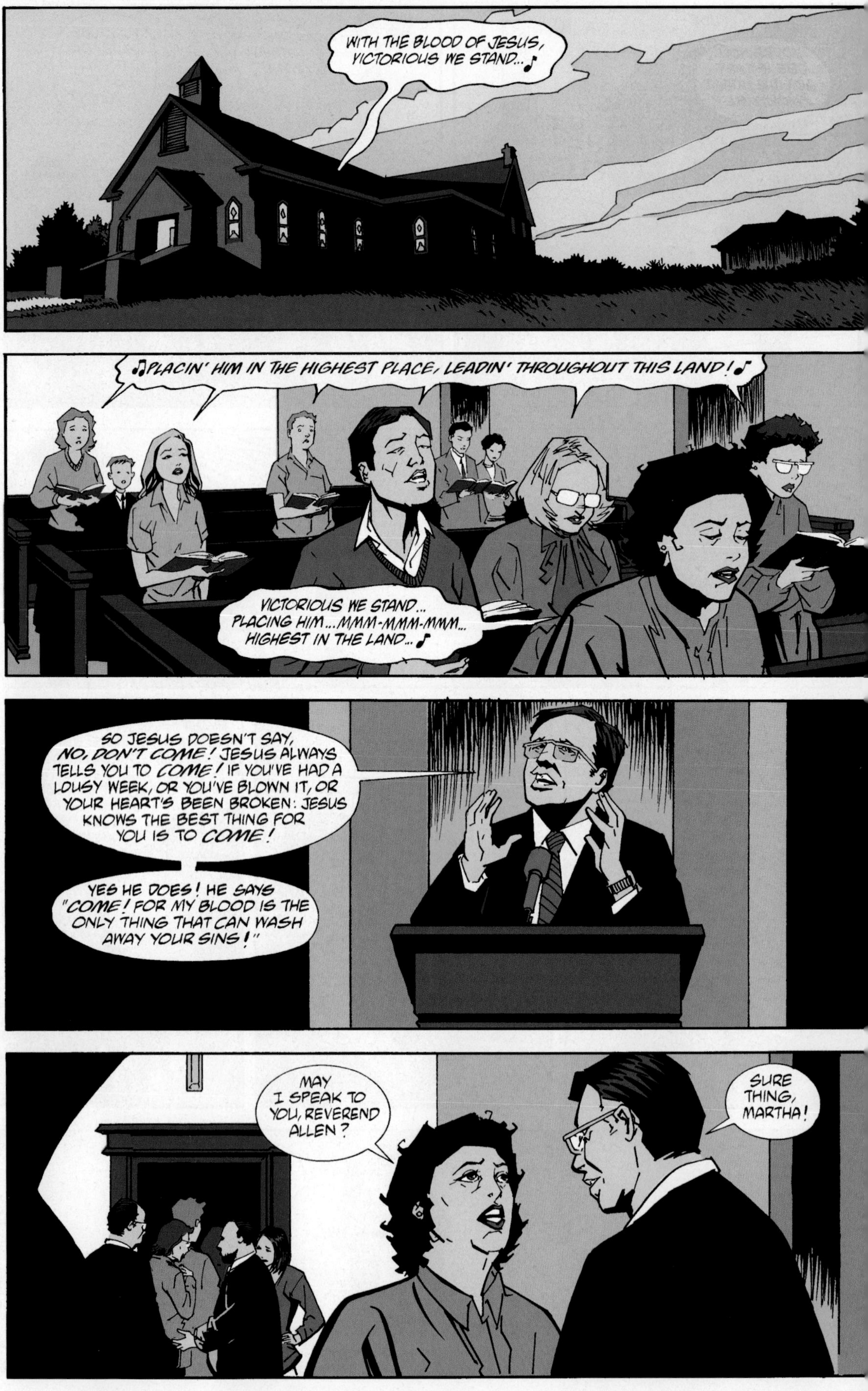
WITH THE BLOOD OF JESUS, VICTORIOUS WE STAND...♪
♫PLACIN' HIM IN THE HIGHEST PLACE, LEADIN' THROUGHOUT THIS LAND!♪
VICTORIOUS WE STAND... PLACING HIM... MMM-MMM-MMM... HIGHEST IN THE LAND...♪
SO JESUS DOESN'T SAY, NO, DON'T COME! JESUS ALWAYS TELLS YOU TO COME! IF YOU'VE HAD A LOUSY WEEK, OR YOU'VE BLOWN IT, OR YOUR HEART'S BEEN BROKEN: JESUS KNOWS THE BEST THING FOR YOU IS TO COME!
YES HE DOES! HE SAYS "COME! FOR MY BLOOD IS THE ONLY THING THAT CAN WASH AWAY YOUR SINS!"
MAY I SPEAK TO YOU, REVEREND ALLEN?
SURE THING, MARTHA!

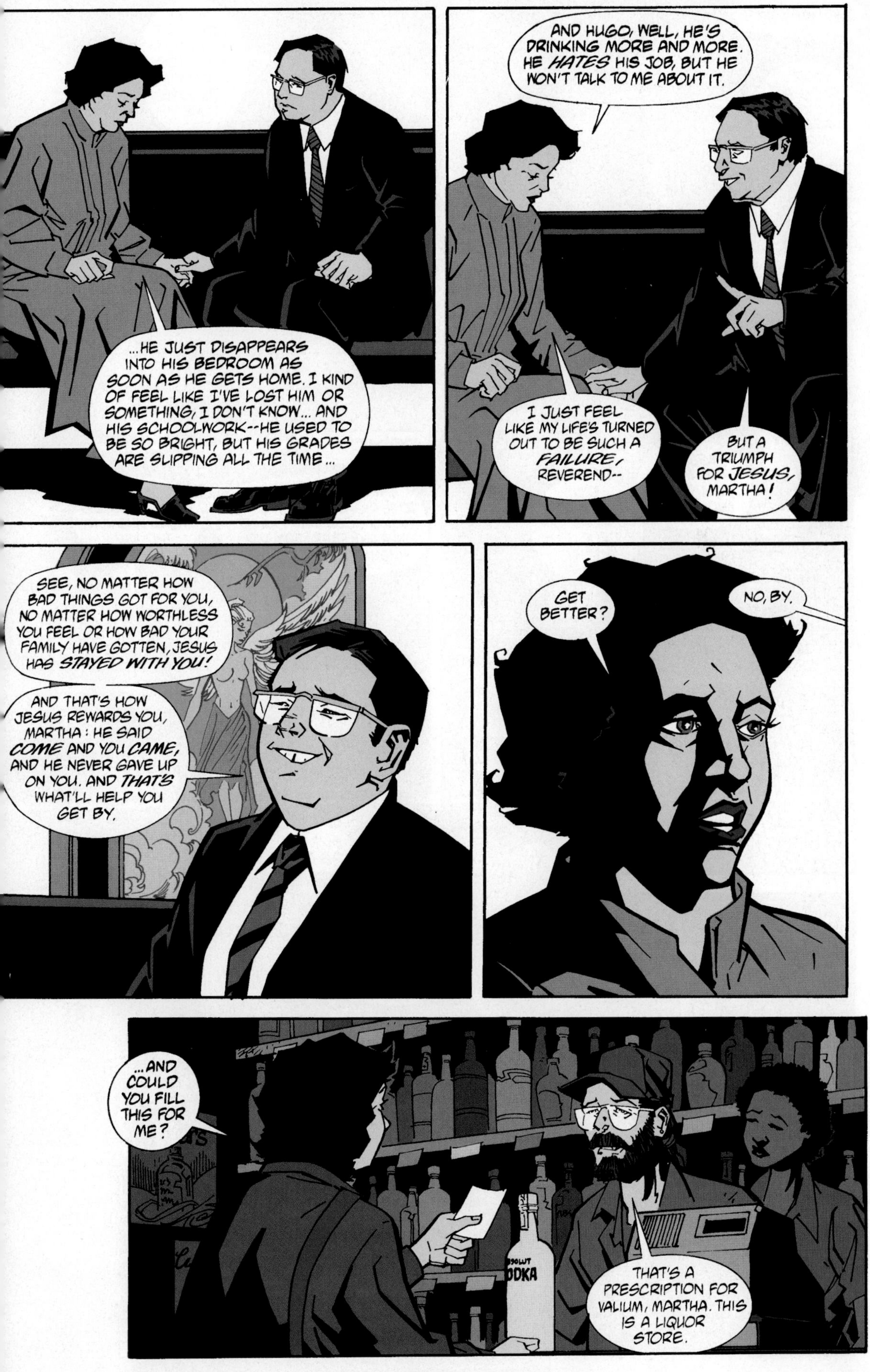
...HE JUST DISAPPEARS INTO HIS BEDROOM AS SOON AS HE GETS HOME. I KIND OF FEEL LIKE I'VE LOST HIM OR SOMETHING, I DON'T KNOW... AND HIS SCHOOLWORK--HE USED TO BE SO BRIGHT, BUT HIS GRADES ARE SLIPPING ALL THE TIME...
AND HUGO, WELL, HE'S DRINKING MORE AND MORE. HE HATES HIS JOB, BUT HE WON'T TALK TO ME ABOUT IT.
I JUST FEEL LIKE MY LIFE'S TURNED OUT TO BE SUCH A FAILURE, REVEREND--
BUT A TRIUMPH FOR JESUS, MARTHA!
SEE, NO MATTER HOW BAD THINGS GOT FOR YOU, NO MATTER HOW WORTHLESS YOU FEEL OR HOW BAD YOUR FAMILY HAVE GOTTEN, JESUS HAS STAYED WITH YOU!
AND THAT'S HOW JESUS REWARDS YOU, MARTHA: HE SAID COME AND YOU CAME, AND HE NEVER GAVE UP ON YOU. AND THAT'S WHAT'LL HELP YOU GET BY.
GET BETTER?
NO, BY.
...AND COULD YOU FILL THIS FOR ME?
THAT'S A PRESCRIPTION FOR VALIUM, MARTHA. THIS IS A LIQUOR STORE.

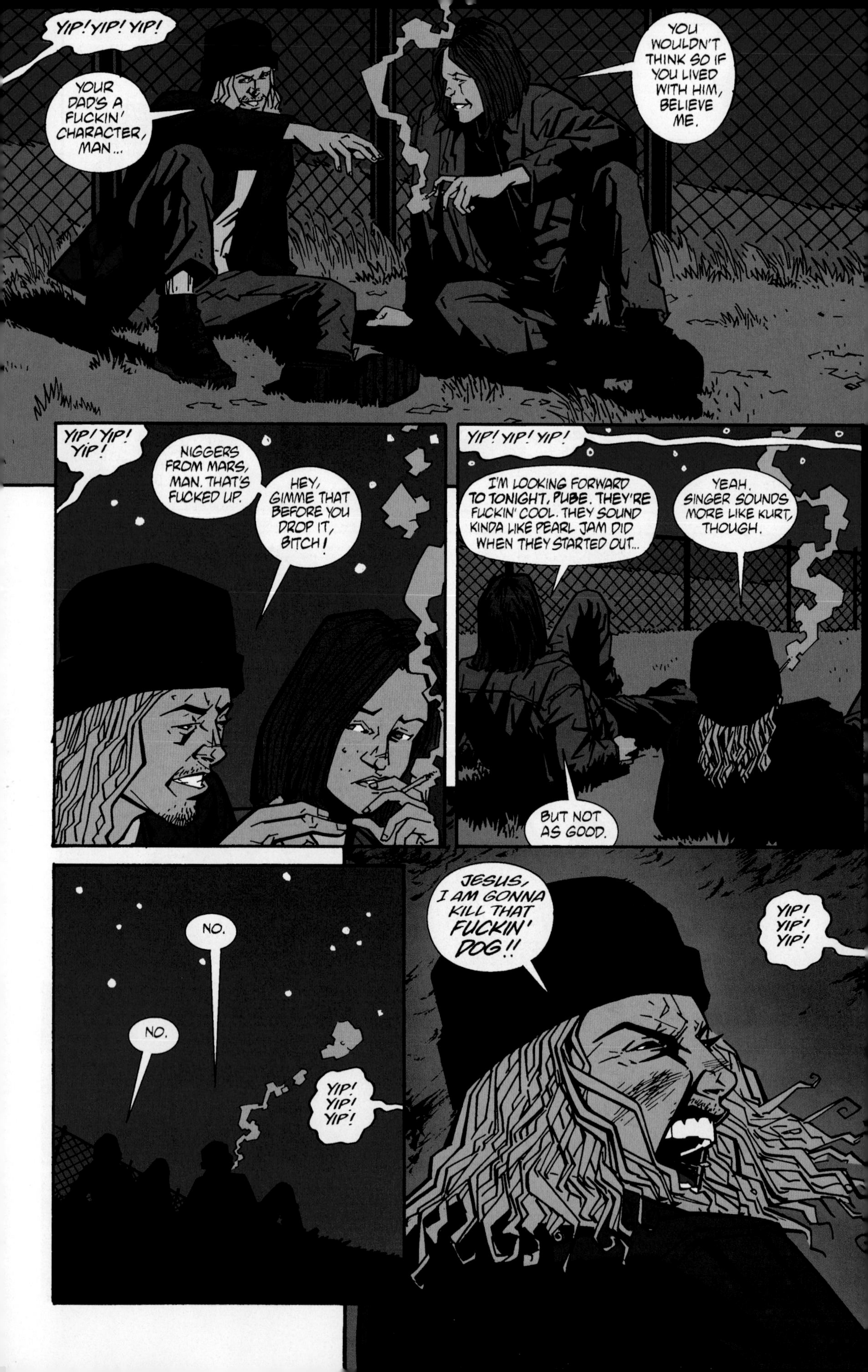
YIP! YIP! YIP!
YOUR DAD'S A FUCKIN' CHARACTER, MAN...
YOU WOULDN'T THINK SO IF YOU LIVED WITH HIM, BELIEVE ME.
YIP! YIP! YIP!
NIGGERS FROM MARS, MAN. THAT'S FUCKED UP.
HEY, GIMME THAT BEFORE YOU DROP IT, BITCH!
YIP! YIP! YIP!
I'M LOOKING FORWARD TO TONIGHT, PUBE. THEY'RE FUCKIN' COOL. THEY SOUND KINDA LIKE PEARL JAM DID WHEN THEY STARTED OUT...
YEAH. SINGER SOUNDS MORE LIKE KURT, THOUGH.
BUT NOT AS GOOD.
NO.
NO.
YIP! YIP! YIP!
JESUS, I AM GONNA KILL THAT FUCKIN' DOG!!
YIP! YIP! YIP!

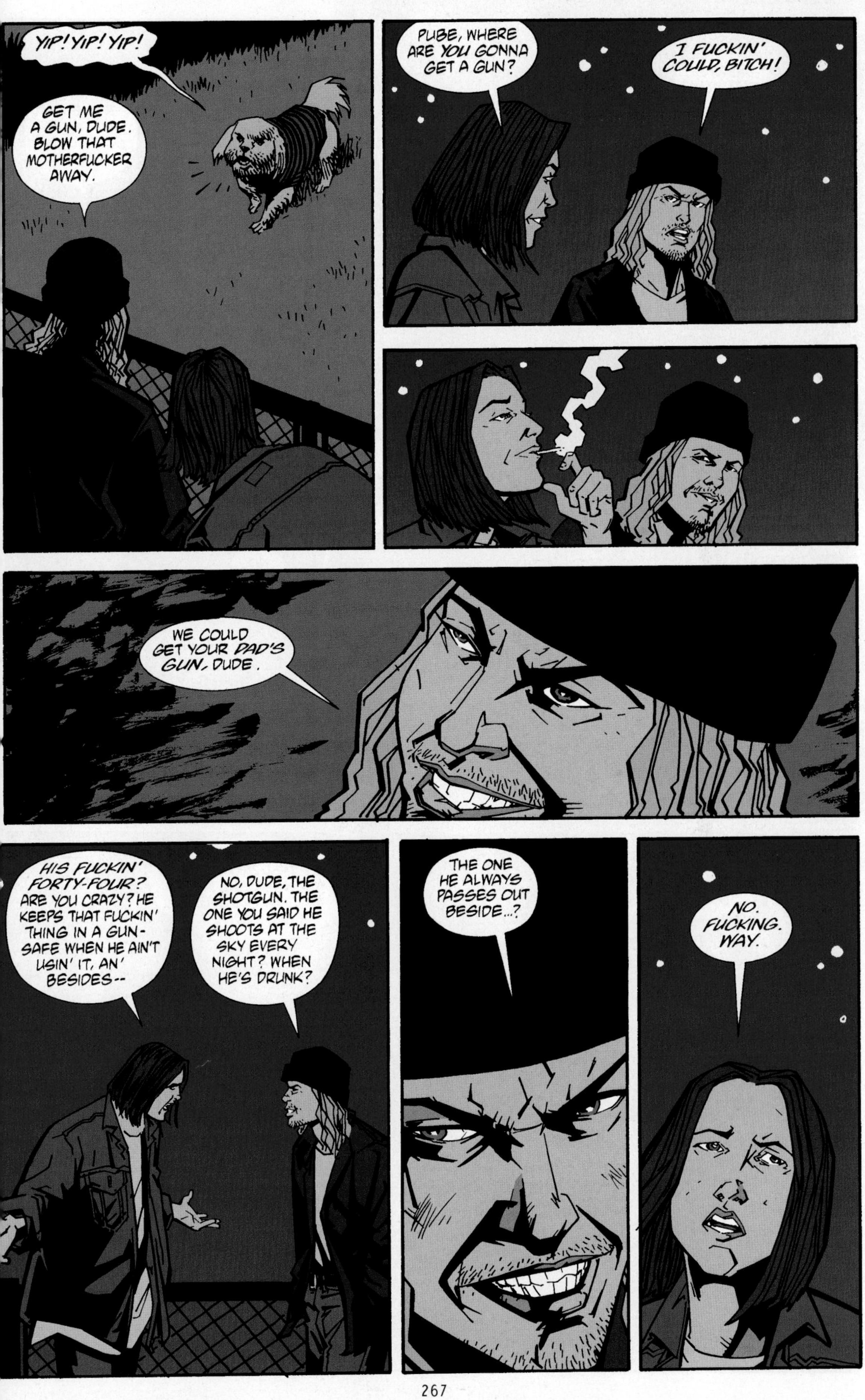
YIP! YIP! YIP!
GET ME A GUN, DUDE. BLOW THAT MOTHERFUCKER AWAY.
PUBE, WHERE ARE YOU GONNA GET A GUN?
I FUCKIN' COULD, BITCH!
WE COULD GET YOUR DAD'S GUN, DUDE.
HIS FUCKIN' FORTY-FOUR? ARE YOU CRAZY? HE KEEPS THAT FUCKIN' THING IN A GUN-SAFE WHEN HE AIN'T USIN' IT, AN' BESIDES--
NO, DUDE, THE SHOTGUN. THE ONE YOU SAID HE SHOOTS AT THE SKY EVERY NIGHT? WHEN HE'S DRUNK?
THE ONE HE ALWAYS PASSES OUT BESIDE...?
NO. FUCKING. WAY.

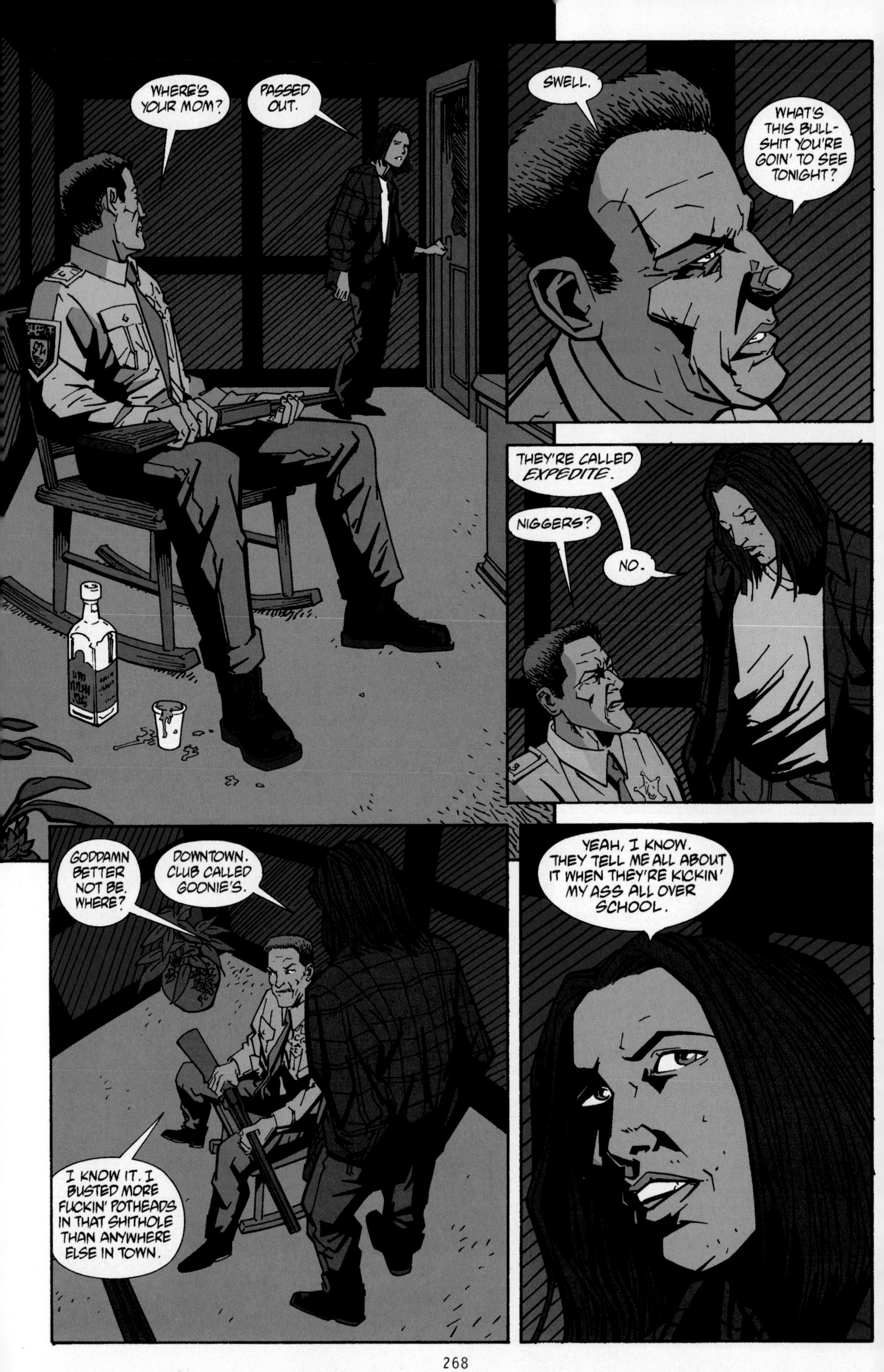
WHERE'S YOUR MOM?
PASSED OUT.
SWELL.
WHAT'S THIS BULL-SHIT YOU'RE GOIN' TO SEE TONIGHT?
THEY'RE CALLED *EXPEDITE*.
NIGGERS?
NO.
GODDAMN BETTER NOT BE. WHERE?
DOWNTOWN. CLUB CALLED GOONIE'S.
I KNOW IT. I BUSTED MORE FUCKIN' POTHEADS IN THAT SHITHOLE THAN ANYWHERE ELSE IN TOWN.
YEAH, I KNOW. THEY TELL ME ALL ABOUT IT WHEN THEY'RE KICKIN' MY ASS ALL OVER SCHOOL.

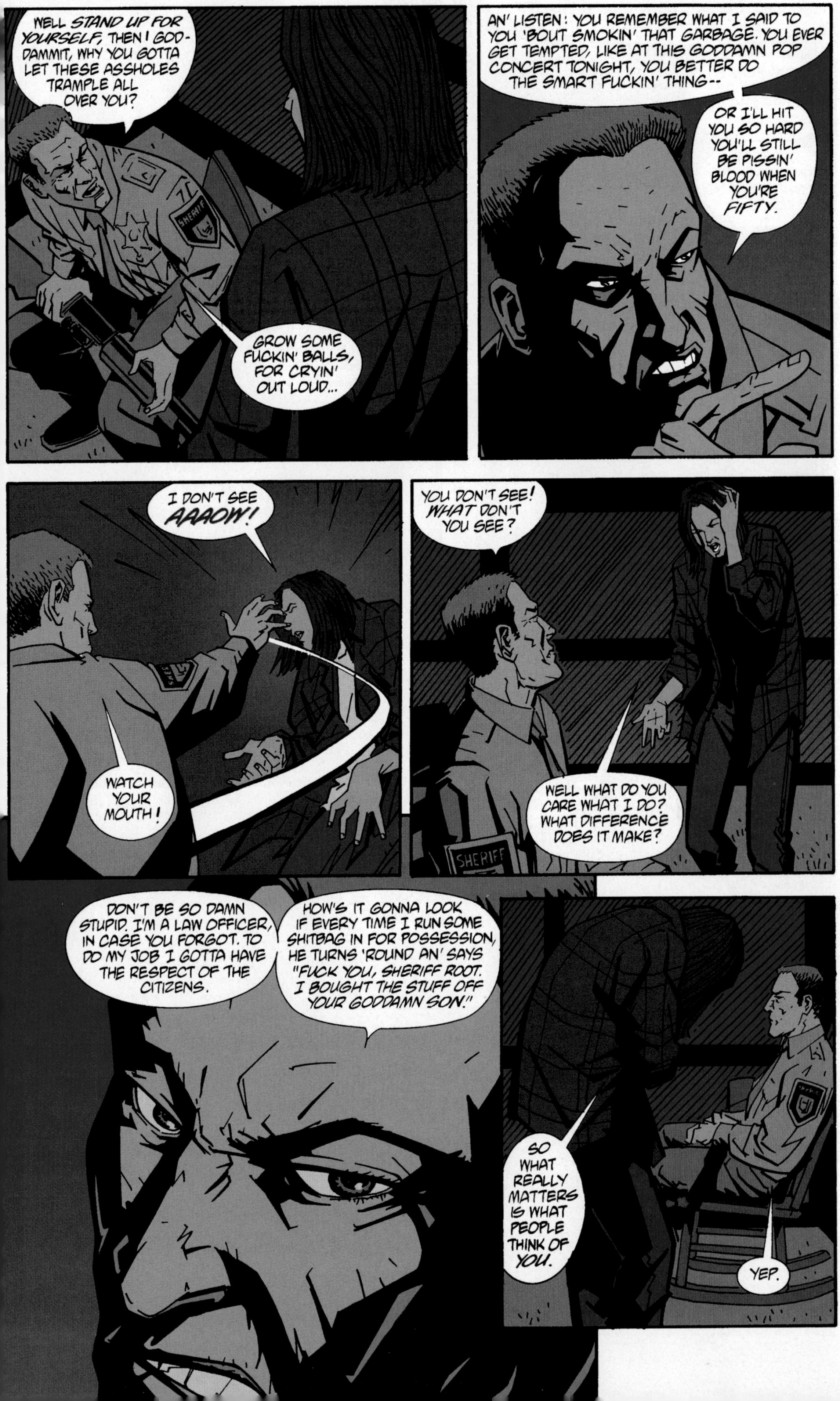
WELL STAND UP FOR YOURSELF, THEN! GOD-DAMMIT, WHY YOU GOTTA LET THESE ASSHOLES TRAMPLE ALL OVER YOU?
GROW SOME FUCKIN' BALLS, FOR CRYIN' OUT LOUD...
AN' LISTEN: YOU REMEMBER WHAT I SAID TO YOU 'BOUT SMOKIN' THAT GARBAGE. YOU EVER GET TEMPTED, LIKE AT THIS GODDAMN POP CONCERT TONIGHT, YOU BETTER DO THE SMART FUCKIN' THING--
OR I'LL HIT YOU SO HARD YOU'LL STILL BE PISSIN' BLOOD WHEN YOU'RE FIFTY.
I DON'T SEE AAAOW!
WATCH YOUR MOUTH!
YOU DON'T SEE! WHAT DON'T YOU SEE?
WELL WHAT DO YOU CARE WHAT I DO? WHAT DIFFERENCE DOES IT MAKE?
SHERIFF
DON'T BE SO DAMN STUPID. I'M A LAW OFFICER, IN CASE YOU FORGOT. TO DO MY JOB I GOTTA HAVE THE RESPECT OF THE CITIZENS.
HOW'S IT GONNA LOOK IF EVERY TIME I RUN SOME SHITBAG IN FOR POSSESSION, HE TURNS 'ROUND AN' SAYS "FUCK YOU, SHERIFF ROOT. I BOUGHT THE STUFF OFF YOUR GODDAMN SON."
SO WHAT REALLY MATTERS IS WHAT PEOPLE THINK OF YOU.
YEP.

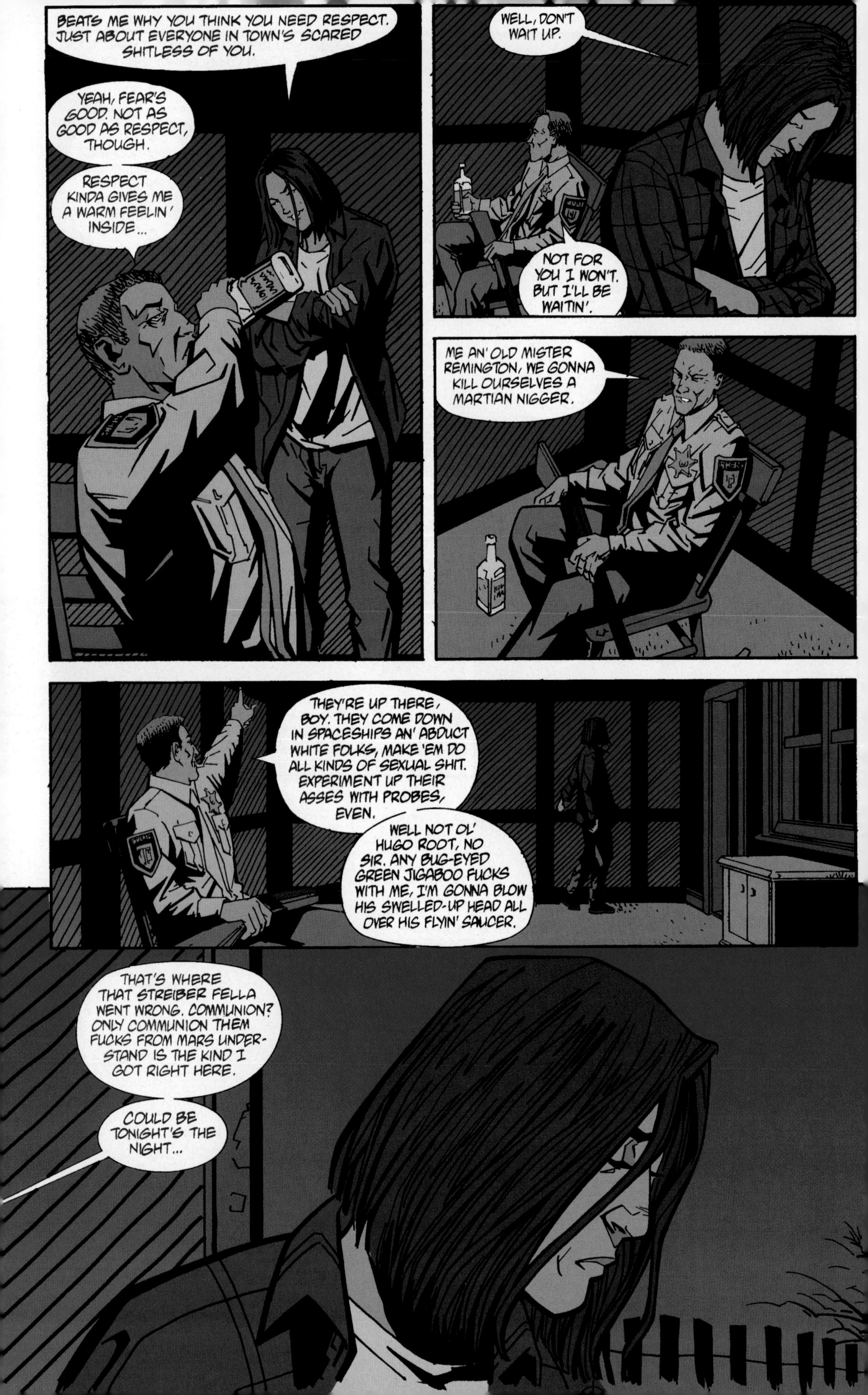
BEATS ME WHY YOU THINK YOU NEED RESPECT. JUST ABOUT EVERYONE IN TOWN'S SCARED SHITLESS OF YOU.
YEAH, FEAR'S GOOD. NOT AS GOOD AS RESPECT, THOUGH.
RESPECT KINDA GIVES ME A WARM FEELIN' INSIDE...
WELL, DON'T WAIT UP.
NOT FOR YOU I WON'T. BUT I'LL BE WAITIN'.
ME AN' OLD MISTER REMINGTON, WE GONNA KILL OURSELVES A MARTIAN NIGGER.
THEY'RE UP THERE, BOY. THEY COME DOWN IN SPACESHIPS AN' ABDUCT WHITE FOLKS, MAKE 'EM DO ALL KINDS OF SEXUAL SHIT. EXPERIMENT UP THEIR ASSES WITH PROBES, EVEN.
WELL NOT OL' HUGO ROOT, NO SIR. ANY BUG-EYED GREEN JIGABOO FUCKS WITH ME, I'M GONNA BLOW HIS SWELLED-UP HEAD ALL OVER HIS FLYIN' SAUCER.
THAT'S WHERE THAT STREIBER FELLA WENT WRONG. COMMUNION? ONLY COMMUNION THEM FUCKS FROM MARS UNDER-STAND IS THE KIND I GOT RIGHT HERE.
COULD BE TONIGHT'S THE NIGHT...

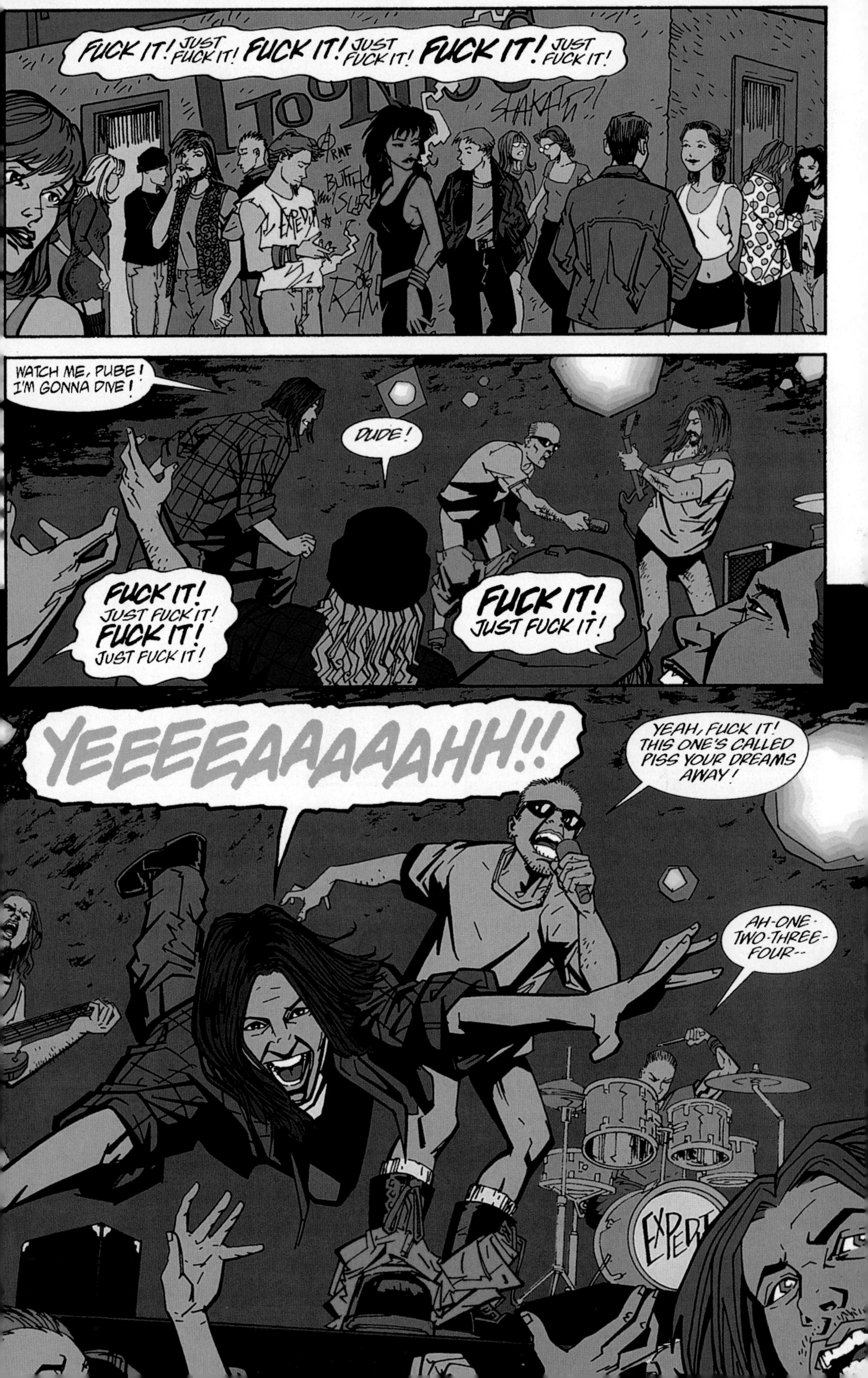
FUCK IT! JUST FUCK IT! FUCK IT! JUST FUCK IT! FUCK IT! JUST FUCK IT!
WATCH ME, PUBE! I'M GONNA DIVE!
DUDE!
FUCK IT! JUST FUCK IT! FUCK IT! JUST FUCK IT!
FUCK IT! JUST FUCK IT!
YEEEEAAAAAAHH!!
YEAH, FUCK IT! THIS ONE'S CALLED PISS YOUR DREAMS AWAY!
AH-ONE-TWO-THREE-FOUR--

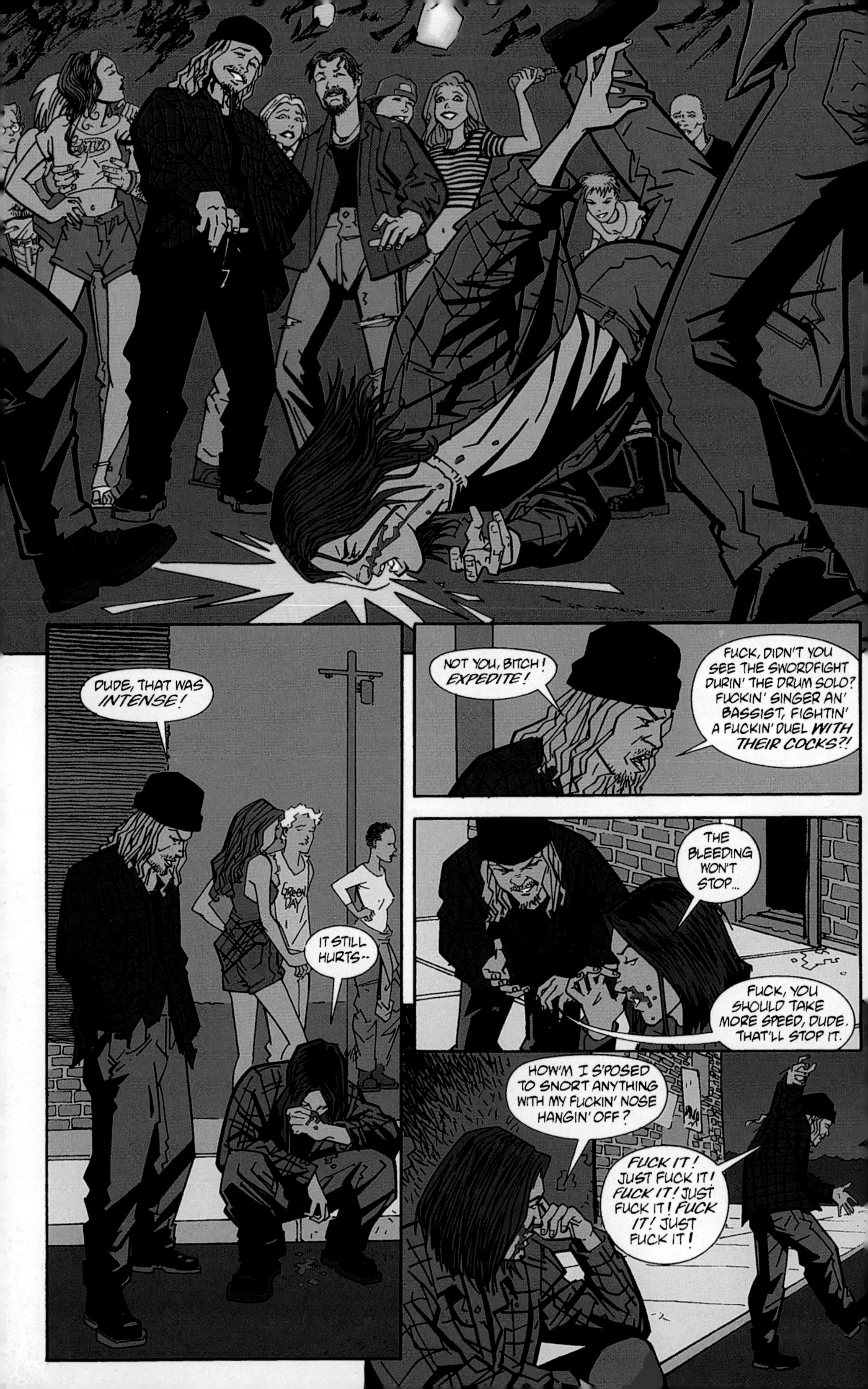
DUDE, THAT WAS *INTENSE!*
IT STILL HURTS--
NOT YOU, BITCH! *EXPEDITE!*
FUCK, DIDN'T YOU SEE THE SWORDFIGHT DURIN' THE DRUM SOLO? FUCKIN' SINGER AN' BASSIST, FIGHTIN' A FUCKIN' DUEL *WITH THEIR COCKS?!*
THE BLEEDING WON'T STOP...
FUCK, YOU SHOULD TAKE MORE SPEED, DUDE. THAT'LL STOP IT.
HOW'M I S'POSED TO SNORT ANYTHING WITH MY FUCKIN' NOSE HANGIN' OFF?
FUCK IT! JUST FUCK IT! *FUCK IT!* JUST FUCK IT! *FUCK IT!* JUST FUCK IT!

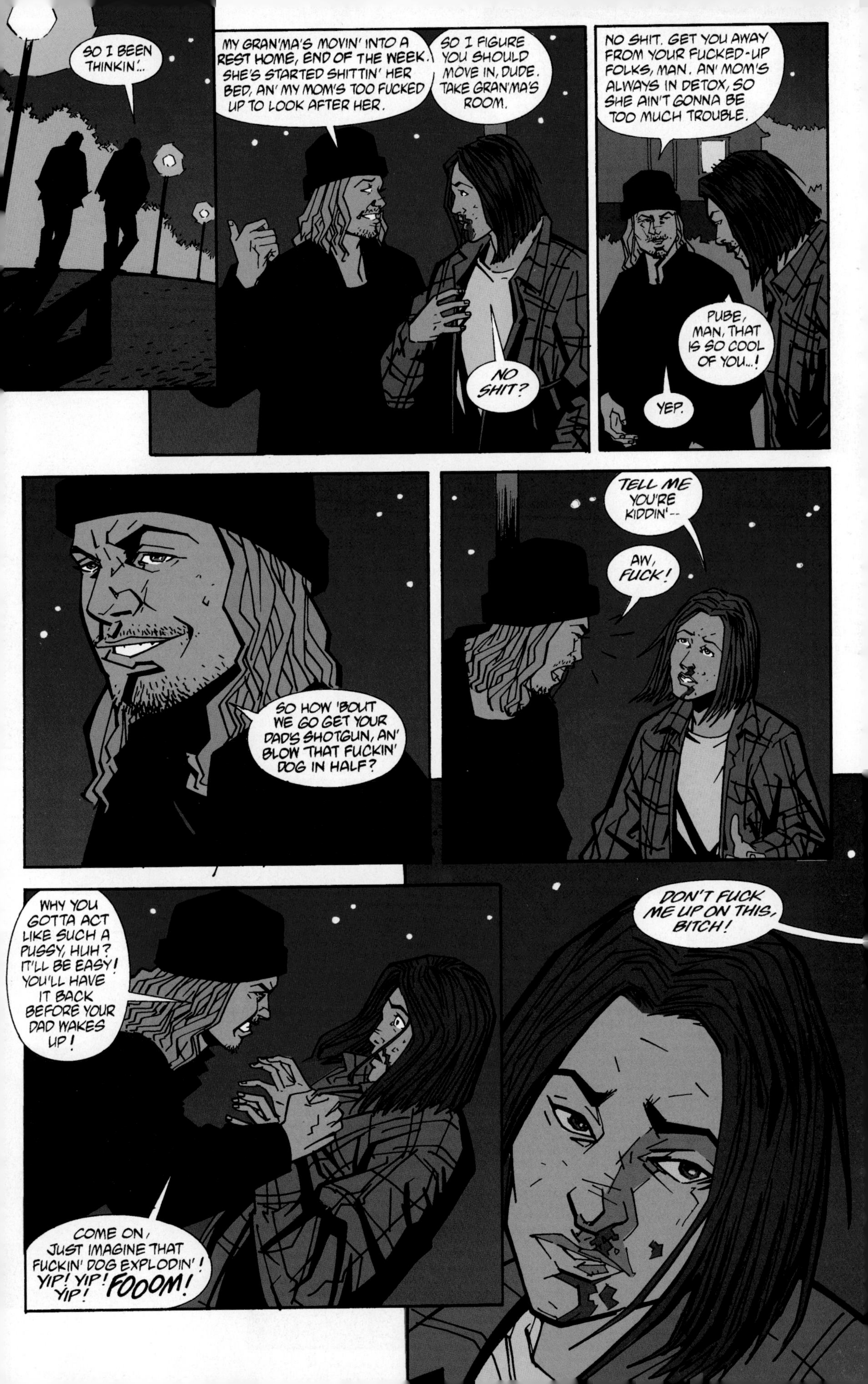
SO I BEEN THINKIN'...
MY GRAN'MA'S MOVIN' INTO A REST HOME, END OF THE WEEK. SHE'S STARTED SHITTIN' HER BED, AN' MY MOM'S TOO FUCKED UP TO LOOK AFTER HER.
SO I FIGURE YOU SHOULD MOVE IN, DUDE. TAKE GRAN'MA'S ROOM.
NO SHIT?
NO SHIT. GET YOU AWAY FROM YOUR FUCKED-UP FOLKS, MAN. AN' MOM'S ALWAYS IN DETOX, SO SHE AIN'T GONNA BE TOO MUCH TROUBLE.
PUBE, MAN, THAT IS SO COOL OF YOU...!
YEP.
SO HOW 'BOUT WE GO GET YOUR DAD'S SHOTGUN, AN' BLOW THAT FUCKIN' DOG IN HALF?
TELL ME YOU'RE KIDDIN'--
AW, FUCK!
WHY YOU GOTTA ACT LIKE SUCH A PUSSY, HUH? IT'LL BE EASY! YOU'LL HAVE IT BACK BEFORE YOUR DAD WAKES UP!
COME ON, JUST IMAGINE THAT FUCKIN' DOG EXPLODIN'! YIP! YIP! YIP! FOOOM!
DON'T FUCK ME UP ON THIS, BITCH!

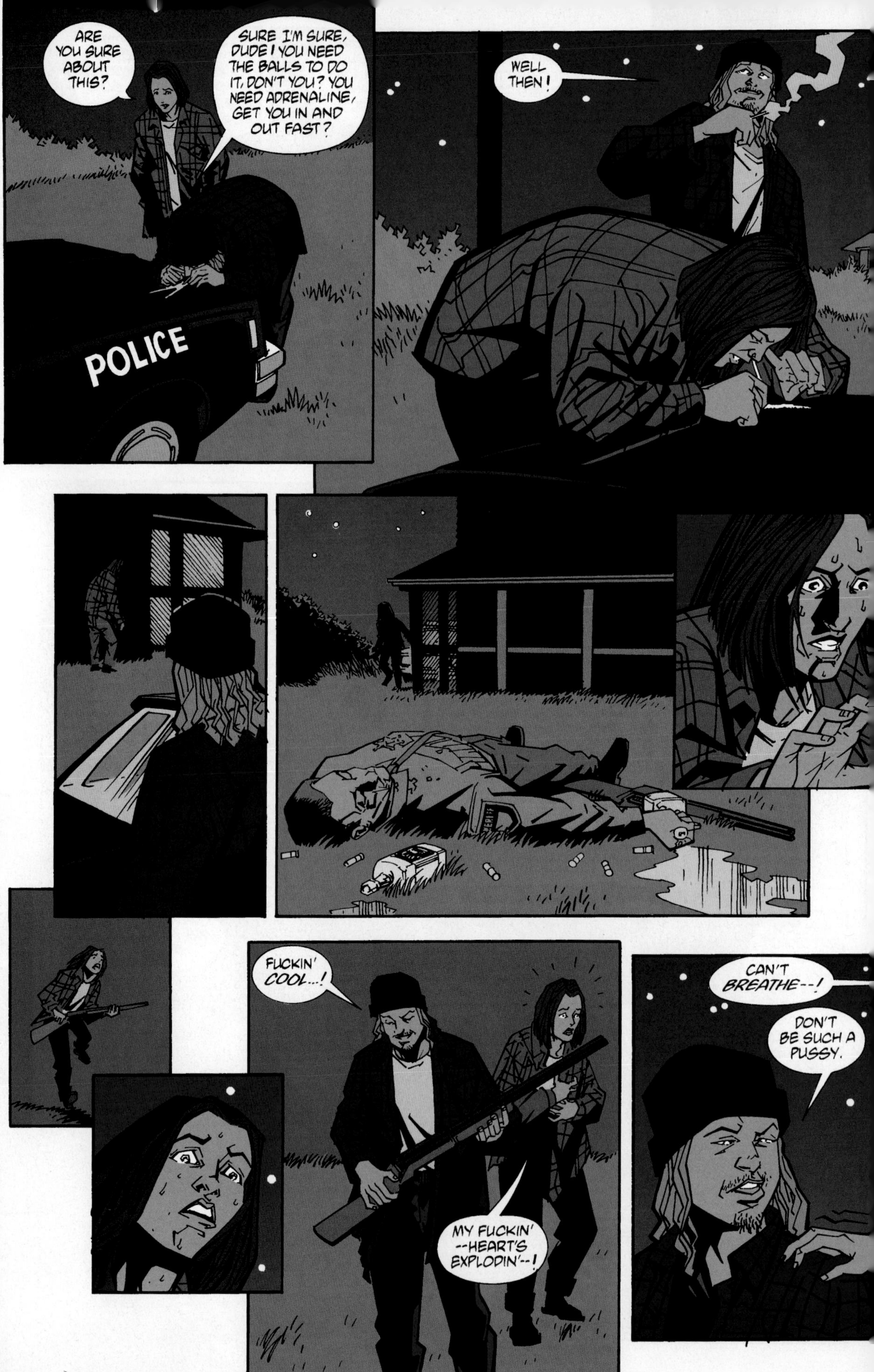
ARE YOU SURE ABOUT THIS?
SURE I'M SURE, DUDE! YOU NEED THE BALLS TO DO IT, DON'T YOU? YOU NEED ADRENALINE, GET YOU IN AND OUT FAST?
POLICE
WELL THEN!
FUCKIN' COOL...!
MY FUCKIN' --HEART'S EXPLODIN'--!
CAN'T BREATHE--!
DON'T BE SUCH A PUSSY.

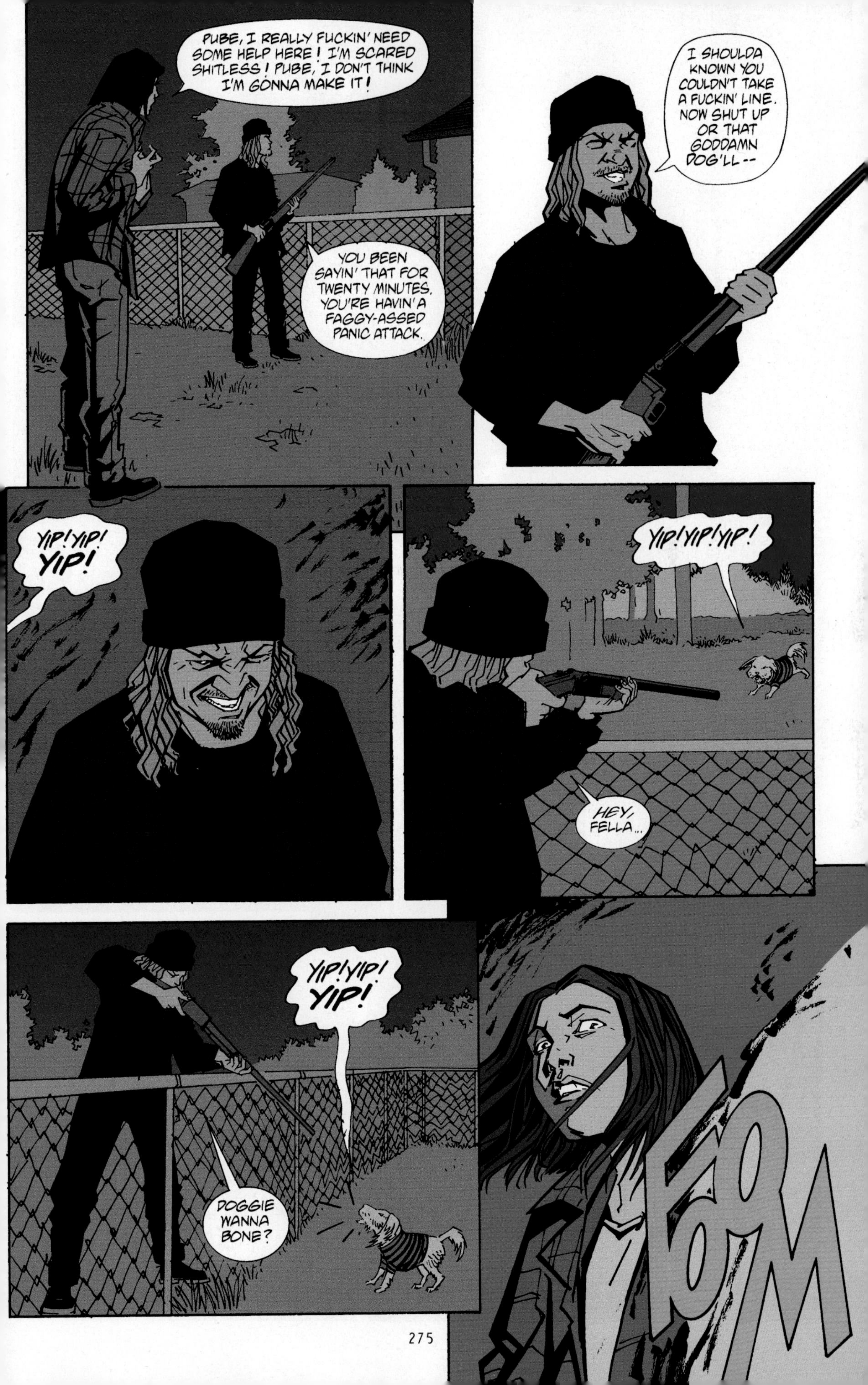
PUBE, I REALLY FUCKIN' NEED SOME HELP HERE! I'M SCARED SHITLESS! PUBE, I DON'T THINK I'M GONNA MAKE IT!
YOU BEEN SAYIN' THAT FOR TWENTY MINUTES. YOU'RE HAVIN' A FAGGY-ASSED PANIC ATTACK.
I SHOULDA KNOWN YOU COULDN'T TAKE A FUCKIN' LINE. NOW SHUT UP OR THAT GODDAMN DOG'LL --
YIP! YIP! YIP!
YIP! YIP! YIP!
HEY, FELLA...
YIP! YIP! YIP!
DOGGIE WANNA BONE?
TOOM

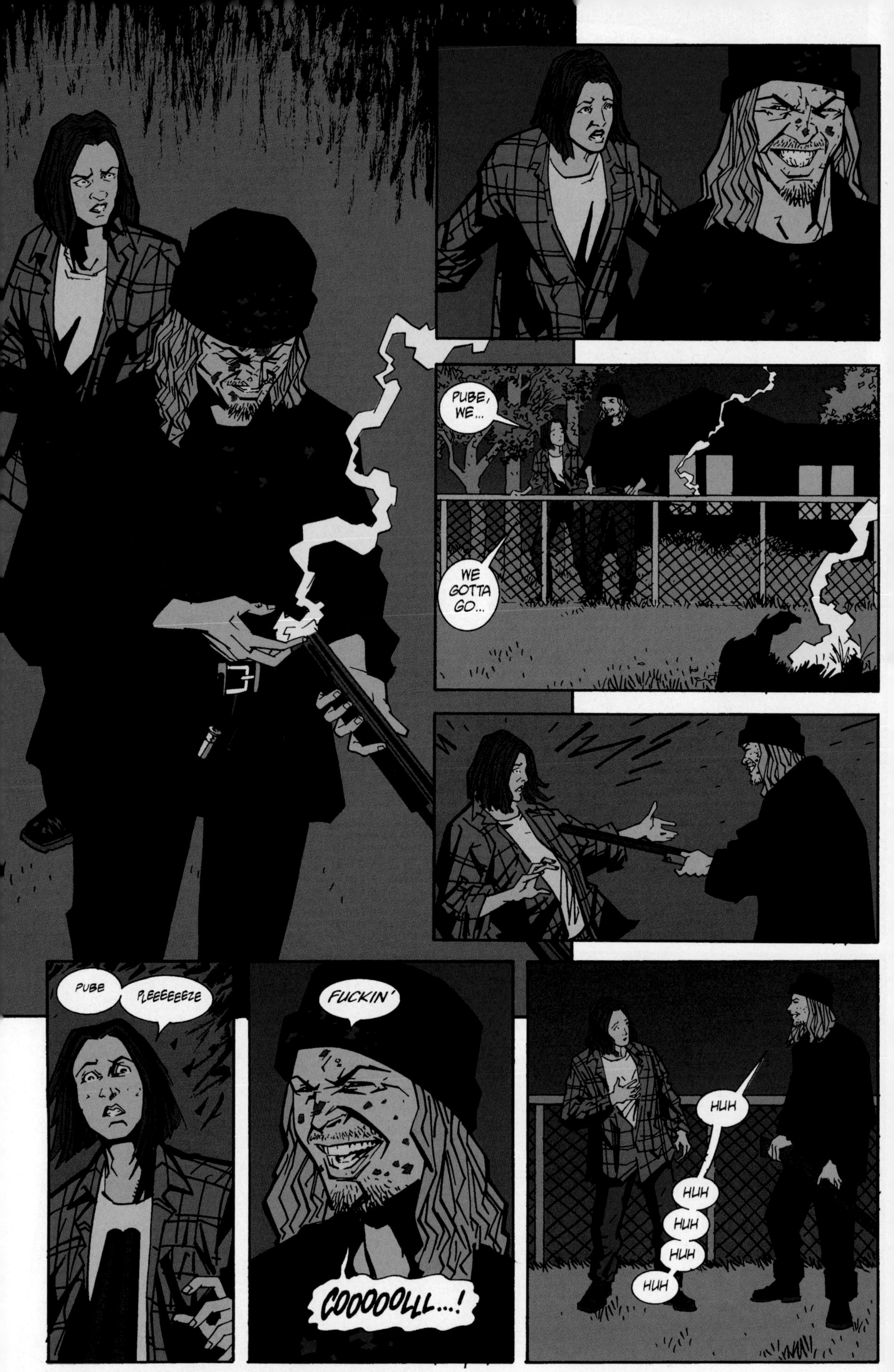
PUBE, WE...
WE GOTTA GO...
PUBE
PLEEEEEEZE
FUCKIN'
COOOOOLLL...!
HUH
HUH
HUH
HUH
HUH

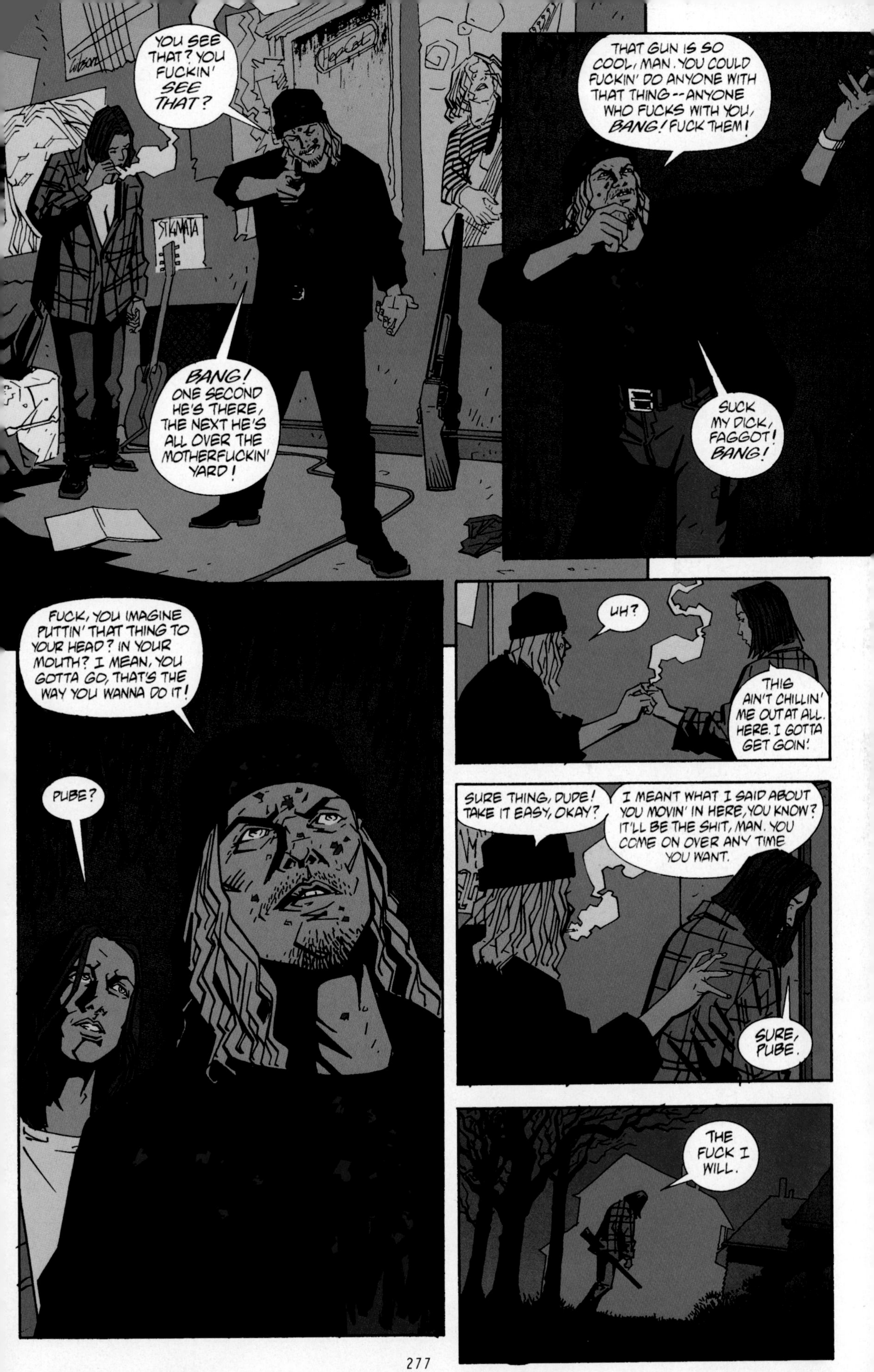

YOU SEE THAT? YOU FUCKIN' SEE THAT?
STIGMATA
BANG! ONE SECOND HE'S THERE, THE NEXT HE'S ALL OVER THE MOTHERFUCKIN' YARD!
THAT GUN IS SO COOL, MAN. YOU COULD FUCKIN' DO ANYONE WITH THAT THING--ANYONE WHO FUCKS WITH YOU, BANG! FUCK THEM!
SUCK MY DICK, FAGGOT! BANG!
FUCK, YOU IMAGINE PUTTIN' THAT THING TO YOUR HEAD? IN YOUR MOUTH? I MEAN, YOU GOTTA GO, THAT'S THE WAY YOU WANNA DO IT!
PUBE?
UH?
THIS AIN'T CHILLIN' ME OUTAT ALL. HERE. I GOTTA GET GOIN'.
SURE THING, DUDE! TAKE IT EASY, OKAY?
I MEANT WHAT I SAID ABOUT YOU MOVIN' IN HERE, YOU KNOW? IT'LL BE THE SHIT, MAN. YOU COME ON OVER ANY TIME YOU WANT.
SURE, PUBE.
THE FUCK I WILL.

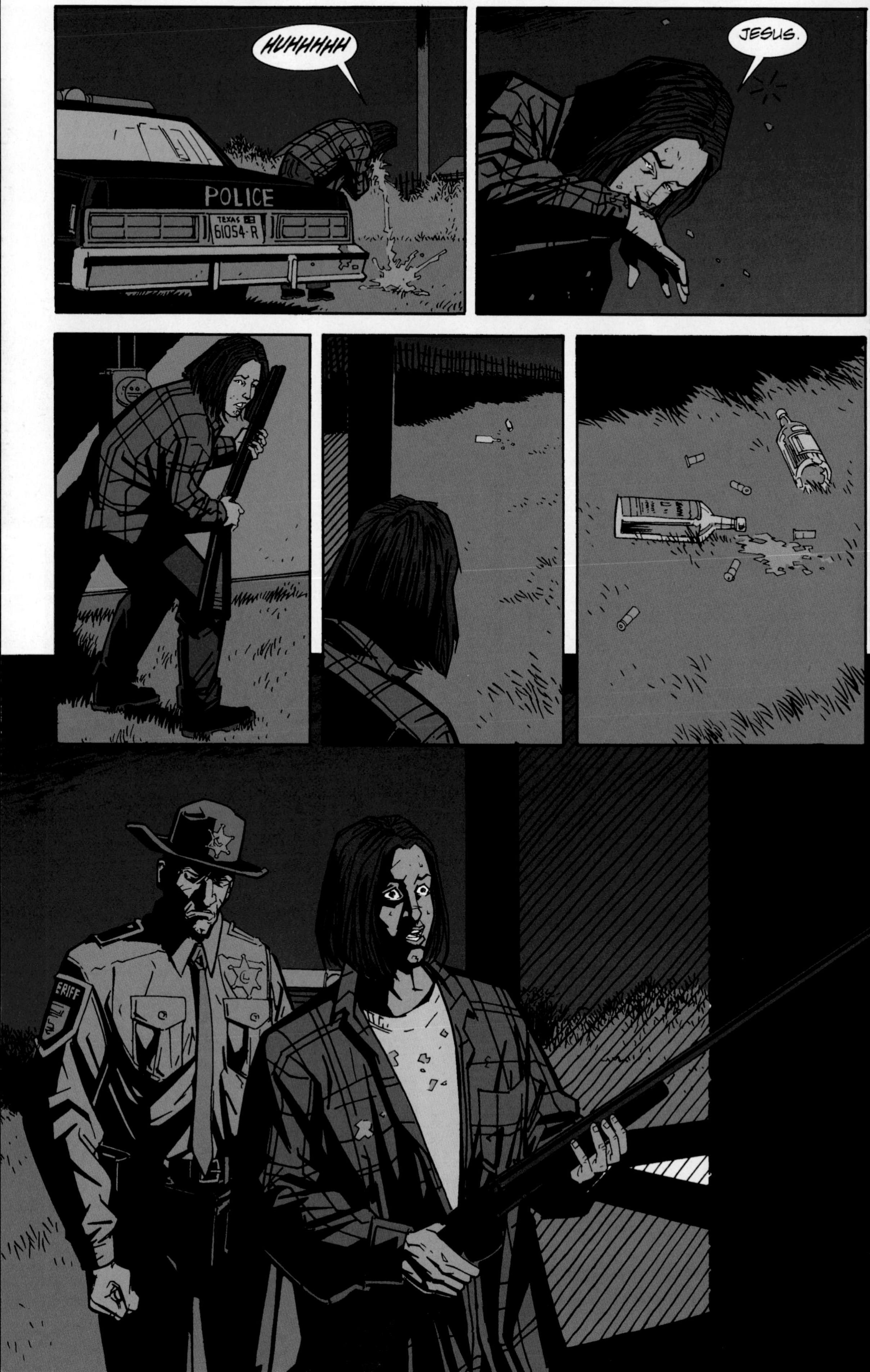
HUHHHHH
POLICE
TEXAS
61054-R
JESUS.
ERIFF

3. New Horizons

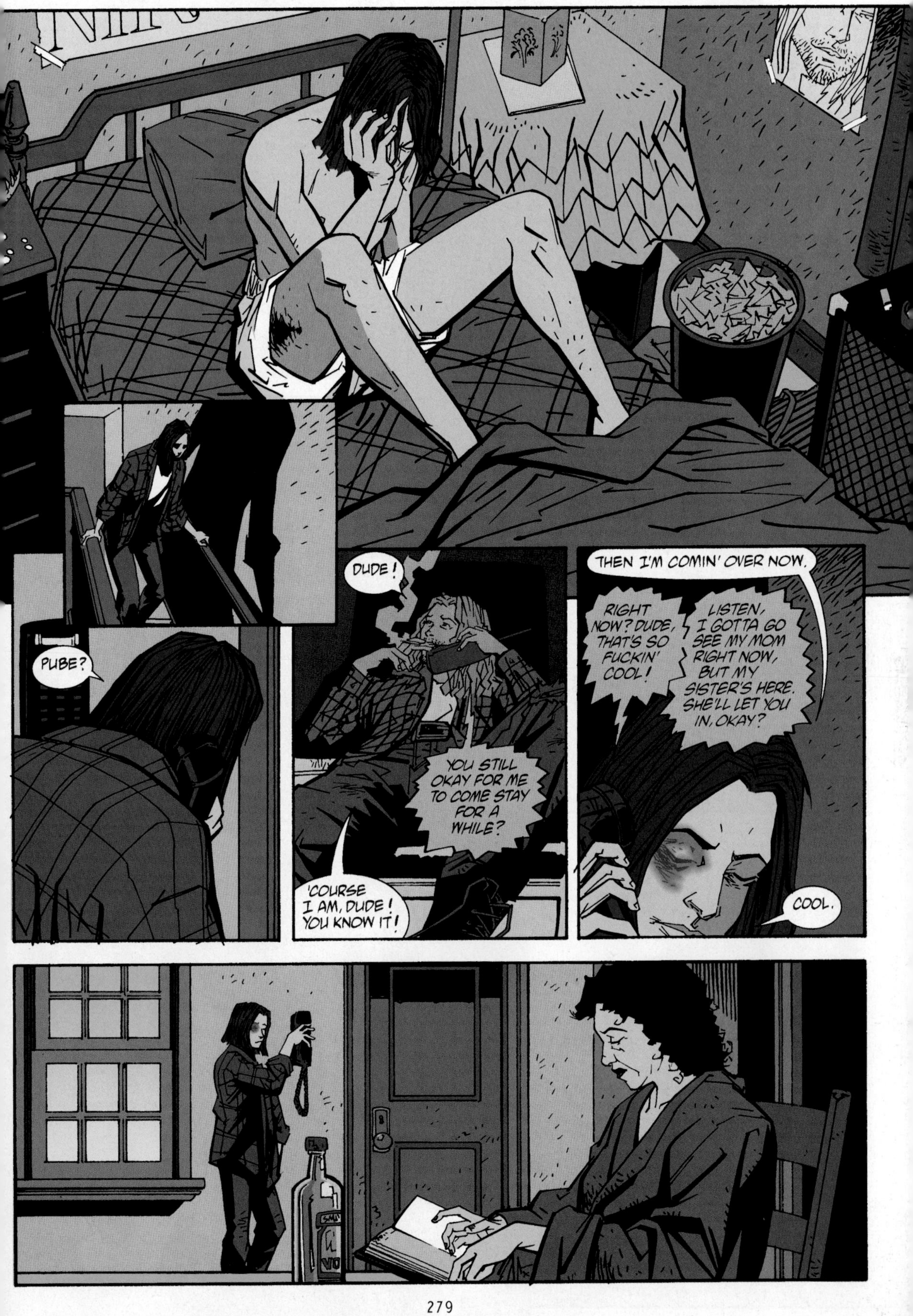

PUBE?
DUDE!
YOU STILL OKAY FOR ME TO COME STAY FOR A WHILE?
'COURSE I AM, DUDE! YOU KNOW IT!
THEN I'M COMIN' OVER NOW.
RIGHT NOW? DUDE, THAT'S SO FUCKIN' COOL!
LISTEN, I GOTTA GO SEE MY MOM RIGHT NOW, BUT MY SISTER'S HERE. SHE'LL LET YOU IN, OKAY?
COOL.

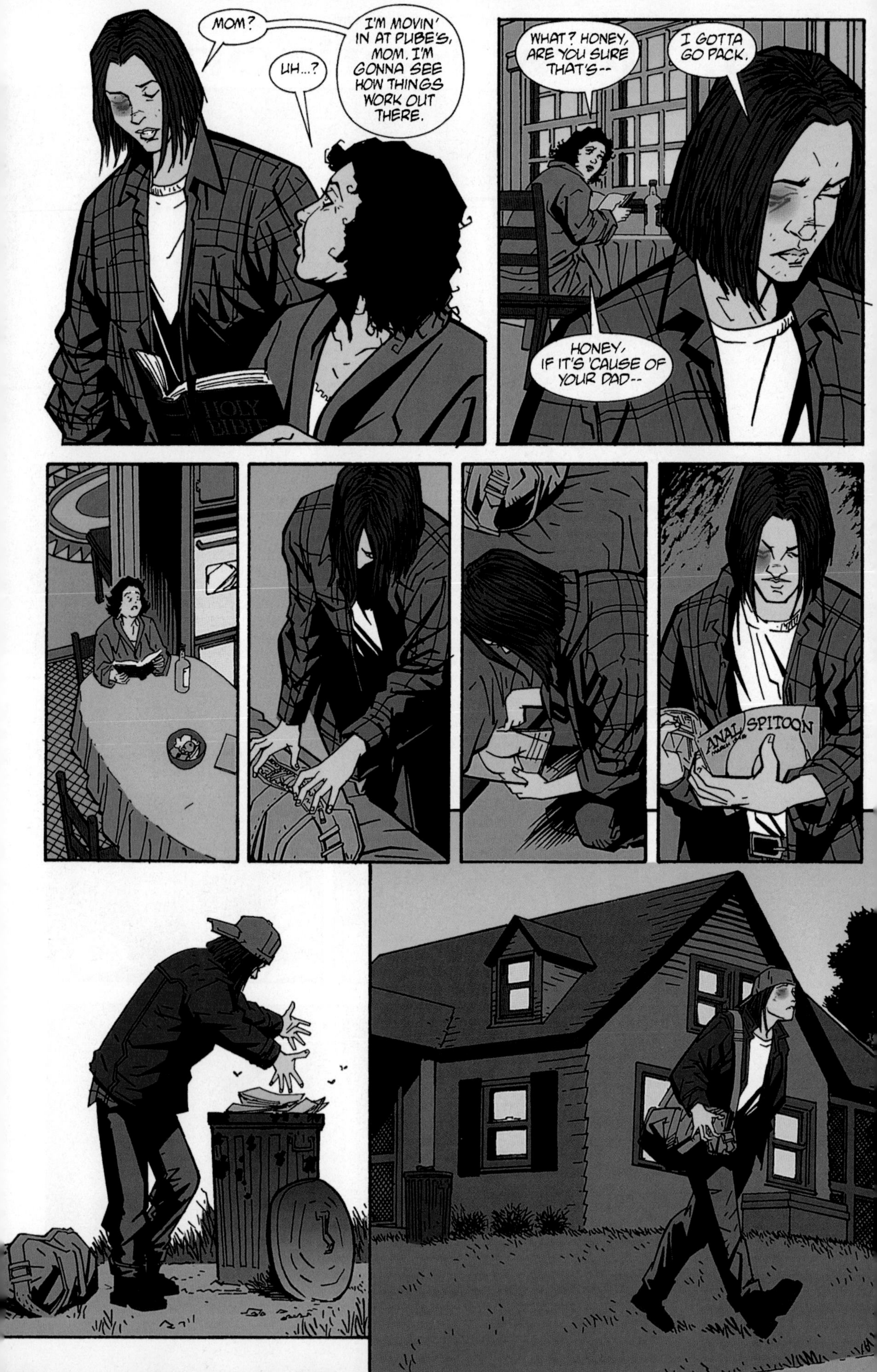
MOM?
UH...?
I'M MOVIN' IN AT PUBE'S, MOM. I'M GONNA SEE HOW THINGS WORK OUT THERE.
WHAT? HONEY, ARE YOU SURE THAT'S--
I GOTTA GO PACK.
HONEY, IF IT'S 'CAUSE OF YOUR DAD--
HOLY BIBLE
ANAL SPITOON

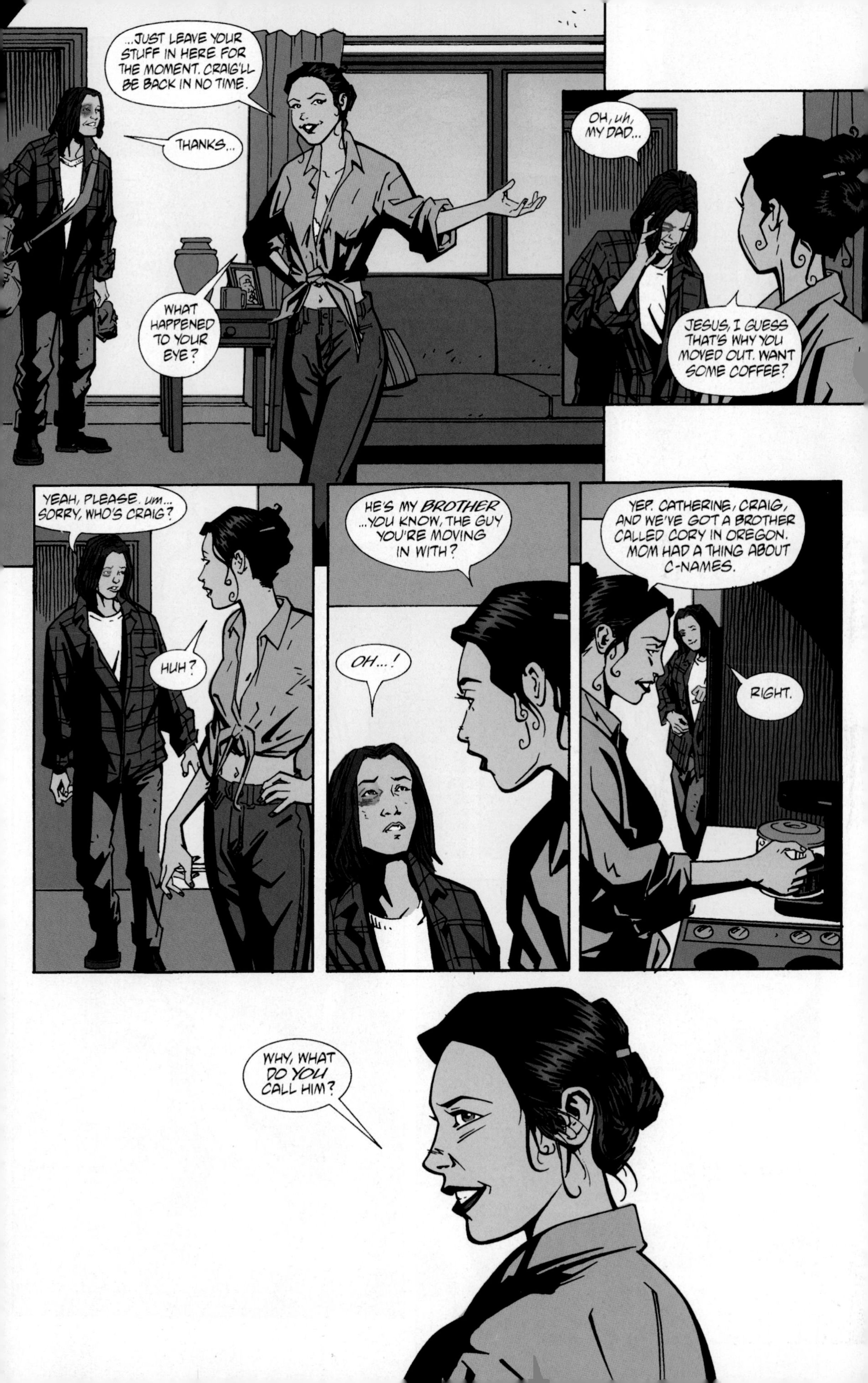
...JUST LEAVE YOUR STUFF IN HERE FOR THE MOMENT. CRAIG'LL BE BACK IN NO TIME.
THANKS...
WHAT HAPPENED TO YOUR EYE?
OH, uh, MY DAD...
JESUS, I GUESS THAT'S WHY YOU MOVED OUT. WANT SOME COFFEE?
YEAH, PLEASE. um... SORRY, WHO'S CRAIG?
HUH?
HE'S MY BROTHER ...YOU KNOW, THE GUY YOU'RE MOVING IN WITH?
OH...!
YEP. CATHERINE, CRAIG, AND WE'VE GOT A BROTHER CALLED CORY IN OREGON. MOM HAD A THING ABOUT C-NAMES.
RIGHT.
WHY, WHAT DO YOU CALL HIM?

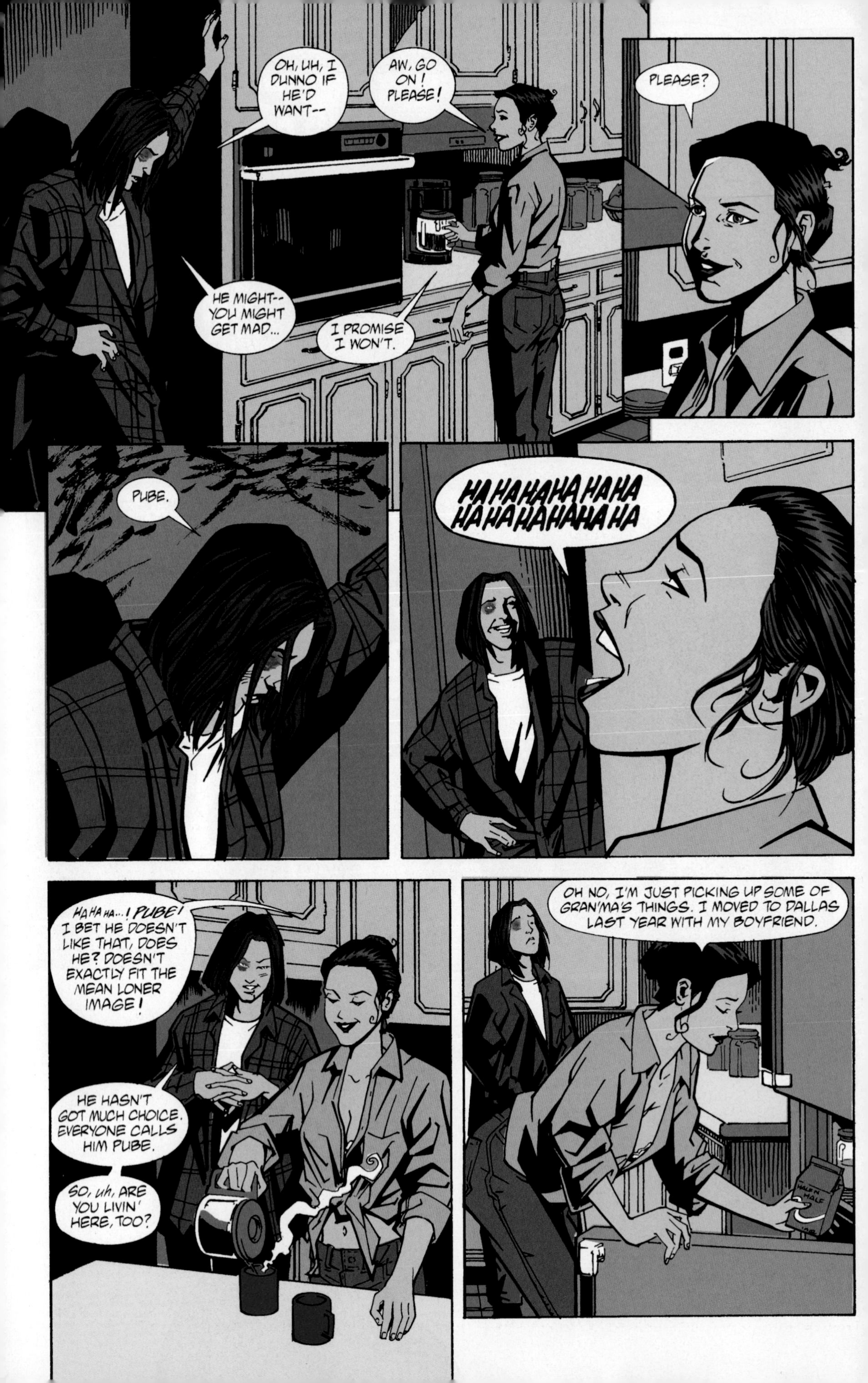
OH, UH, I DUNNO IF HE'D WANT--
AW, GO ON! PLEASE!
HE MIGHT-- YOU MIGHT GET MAD...
I PROMISE I WON'T.
PLEASE?
PUBE.
HA HA HA HA HA HA HA HA HA HA HA HA HA HA HA
HA HA HA...! PUBE! I BET HE DOESN'T LIKE THAT, DOES HE? DOESN'T EXACTLY FIT THE MEAN LONER IMAGE!
HE HASN'T GOT MUCH CHOICE. EVERYONE CALLS HIM PUBE.
SO, UH, ARE YOU LIVIN' HERE, TOO?
OH NO, I'M JUST PICKING UP SOME OF GRAN'MA'S THINGS. I MOVED TO DALLAS LAST YEAR WITH MY BOYFRIEND.

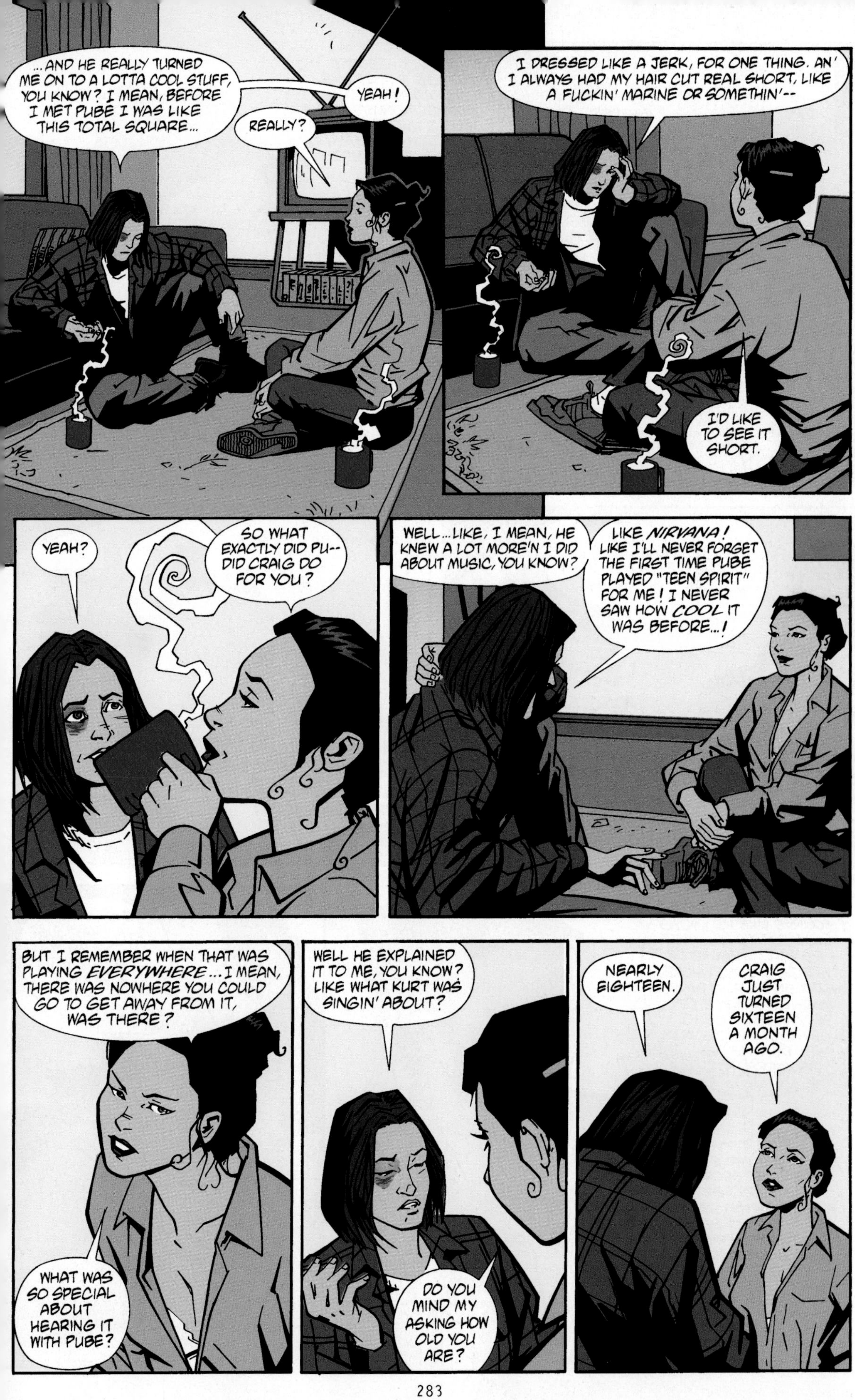
...AND HE REALLY TURNED ME ON TO A LOTTA COOL STUFF, YOU KNOW? I MEAN, BEFORE I MET PUBE I WAS LIKE THIS TOTAL SQUARE...
YEAH!
REALLY?
I DRESSED LIKE A JERK, FOR ONE THING. AN' I ALWAYS HAD MY HAIR CUT REAL SHORT, LIKE A FUCKIN' MARINE OR SOMETHIN'--
I'D LIKE TO SEE IT SHORT.
YEAH?
SO WHAT EXACTLY DID PU-- DID CRAIG DO FOR YOU?
WELL...LIKE, I MEAN, HE KNEW A LOT MORE'N I DID ABOUT MUSIC, YOU KNOW?
LIKE NIRVANA! LIKE I'LL NEVER FORGET THE FIRST TIME PUBE PLAYED "TEEN SPIRIT" FOR ME! I NEVER SAW HOW COOL IT WAS BEFORE...!
BUT I REMEMBER WHEN THAT WAS PLAYING EVERYWHERE... I MEAN, THERE WAS NOWHERE YOU COULD GO TO GET AWAY FROM IT, WAS THERE?
WHAT WAS SO SPECIAL ABOUT HEARING IT WITH PUBE?
WELL HE EXPLAINED IT TO ME, YOU KNOW? LIKE WHAT KURT WAS SINGIN' ABOUT?
DO YOU MIND MY ASKING HOW OLD YOU ARE?
NEARLY EIGHTEEN.
CRAIG JUST TURNED SIXTEEN A MONTH AGO.

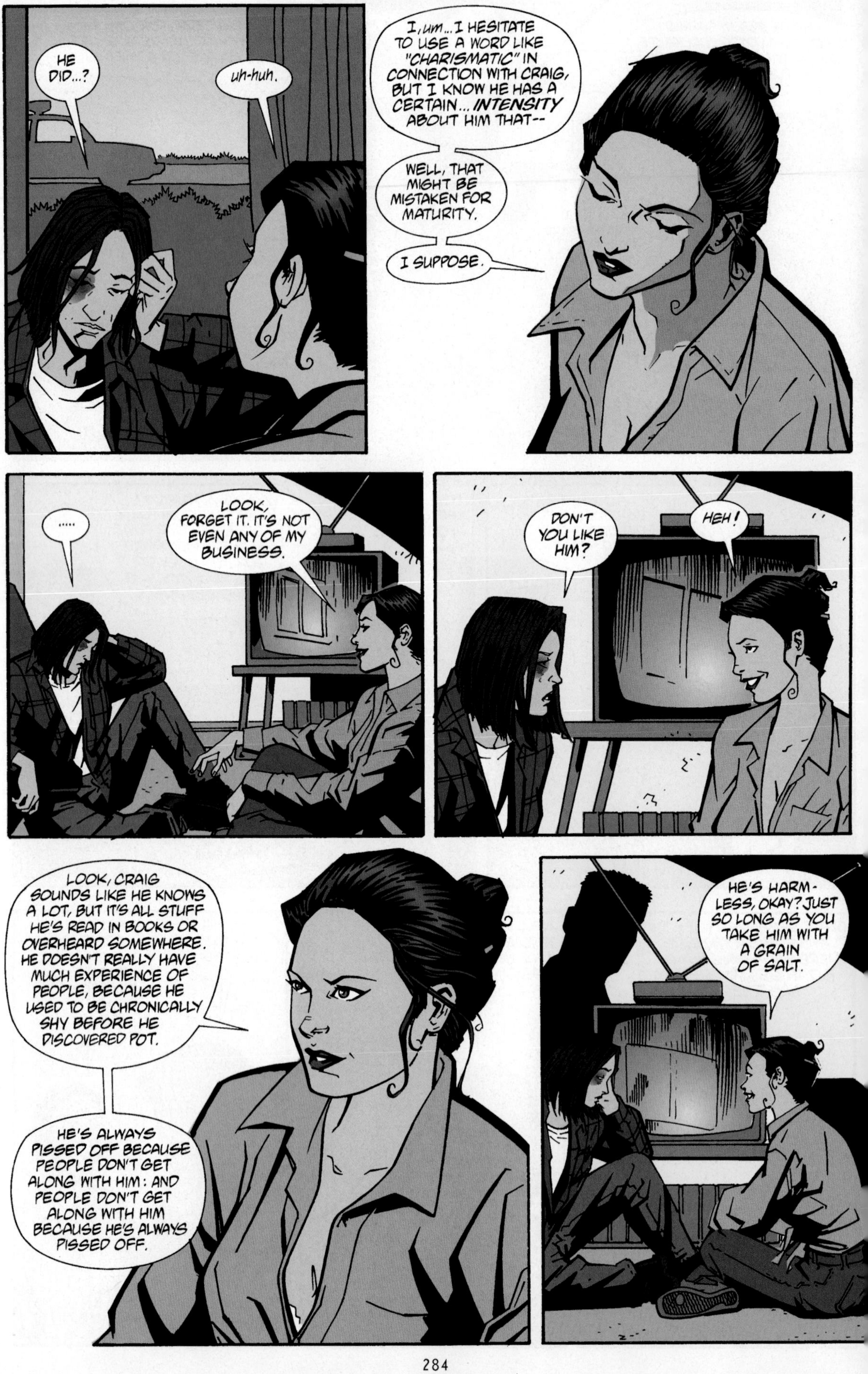
HE DID...?
uh-huh.
I, um... I HESITATE TO USE A WORD LIKE "CHARISMATIC" IN CONNECTION WITH CRAIG, BUT I KNOW HE HAS A CERTAIN... INTENSITY ABOUT HIM THAT--
WELL, THAT MIGHT BE MISTAKEN FOR MATURITY.
I SUPPOSE.
.....
LOOK, FORGET IT. IT'S NOT EVEN ANY OF MY BUSINESS.
DON'T YOU LIKE HIM?
HEH!
LOOK, CRAIG SOUNDS LIKE HE KNOWS A LOT, BUT IT'S ALL STUFF HE'S READ IN BOOKS OR OVERHEARD SOMEWHERE. HE DOESN'T REALLY HAVE MUCH EXPERIENCE OF PEOPLE, BECAUSE HE USED TO BE CHRONICALLY SHY BEFORE HE DISCOVERED POT.
HE'S ALWAYS PISSED OFF BECAUSE PEOPLE DON'T GET ALONG WITH HIM: AND PEOPLE DON'T GET ALONG WITH HIM BECAUSE HE'S ALWAYS PISSED OFF.
HE'S HARMLESS, OKAY? JUST SO LONG AS YOU TAKE HIM WITH A GRAIN OF SALT.

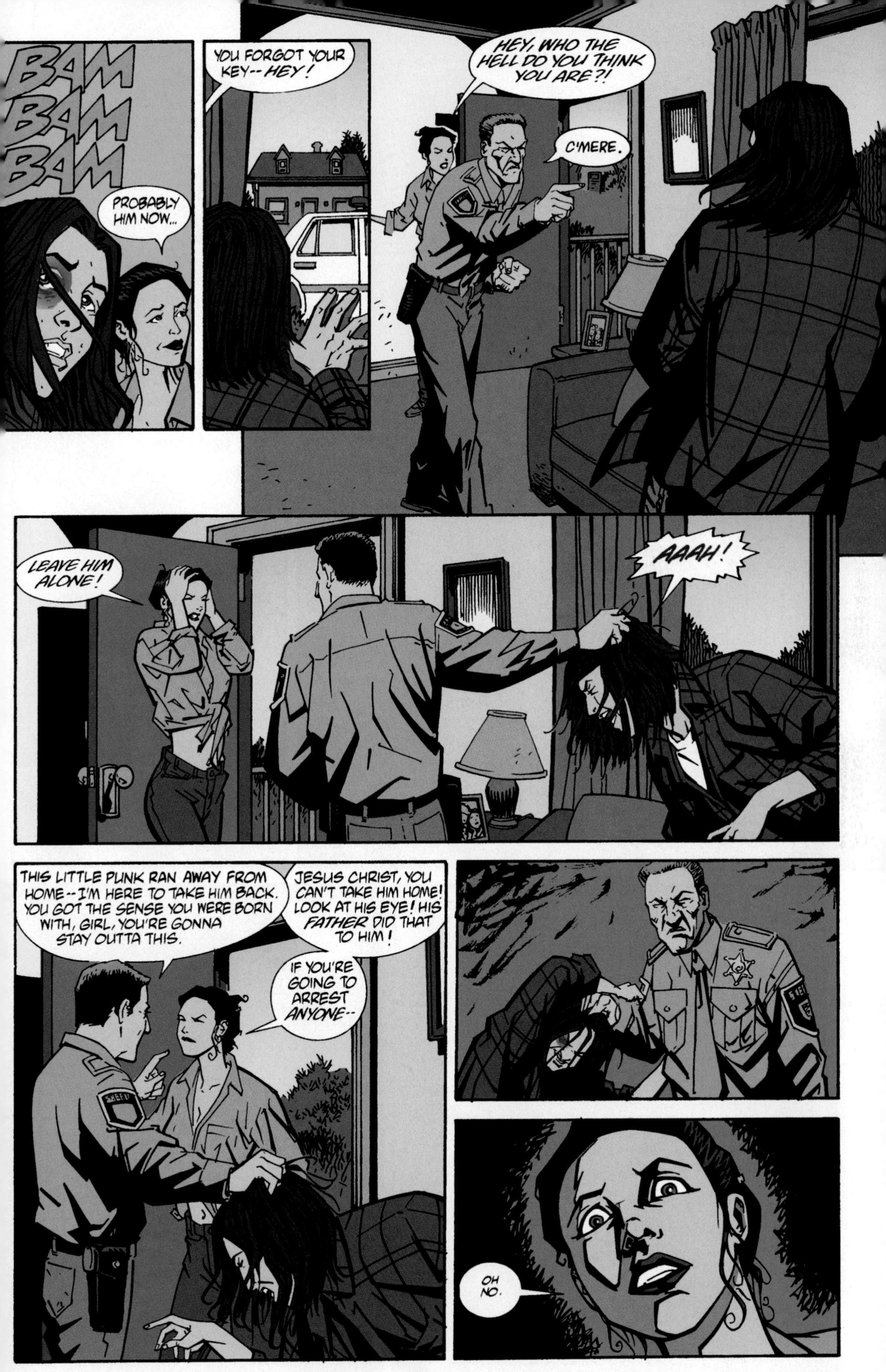
BAM BAM BAM
PROBABLY HIM NOW...
YOU FORGOT YOUR KEY-- HEY!
HEY, WHO THE HELL DO YOU THINK YOU ARE?!
C'MERE.
LEAVE HIM ALONE!
AAAH!
THIS LITTLE PUNK RAN AWAY FROM HOME-- I'M HERE TO TAKE HIM BACK. YOU GOT THE SENSE YOU WERE BORN WITH, GIRL, YOU'RE GONNA STAY OUTTA THIS.
JESUS CHRIST, YOU CAN'T TAKE HIM HOME! LOOK AT HIS EYE! HIS FATHER DID THAT TO HIM!
IF YOU'RE GOING TO ARREST ANYONE--
OH NO.

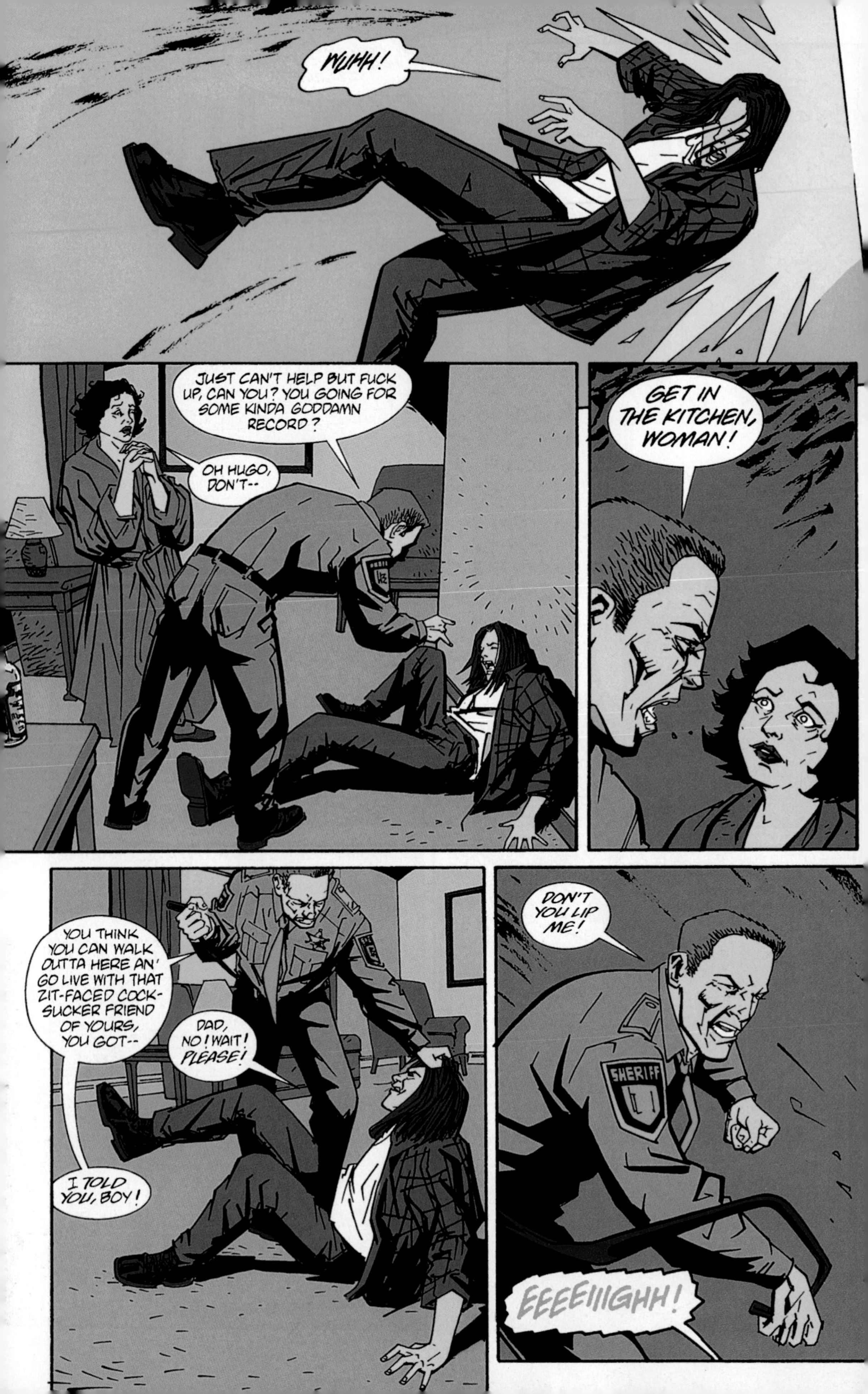
WUHH!
JUST CAN'T HELP BUT FUCK UP, CAN YOU? YOU GOING FOR SOME KINDA GODDAMN RECORD?
OH HUGO, DON'T--
GET IN THE KITCHEN, WOMAN!
YOU THINK YOU CAN WALK OUTTA HERE AN' GO LIVE WITH THAT ZIT-FACED COCK-SUCKER FRIEND OF YOURS, YOU GOT--
I TOLD YOU, BOY!
DAD, NO! WAIT! PLEASE!
DON'T YOU LIP ME!
SHERIFF
EEEEIIIGHH!

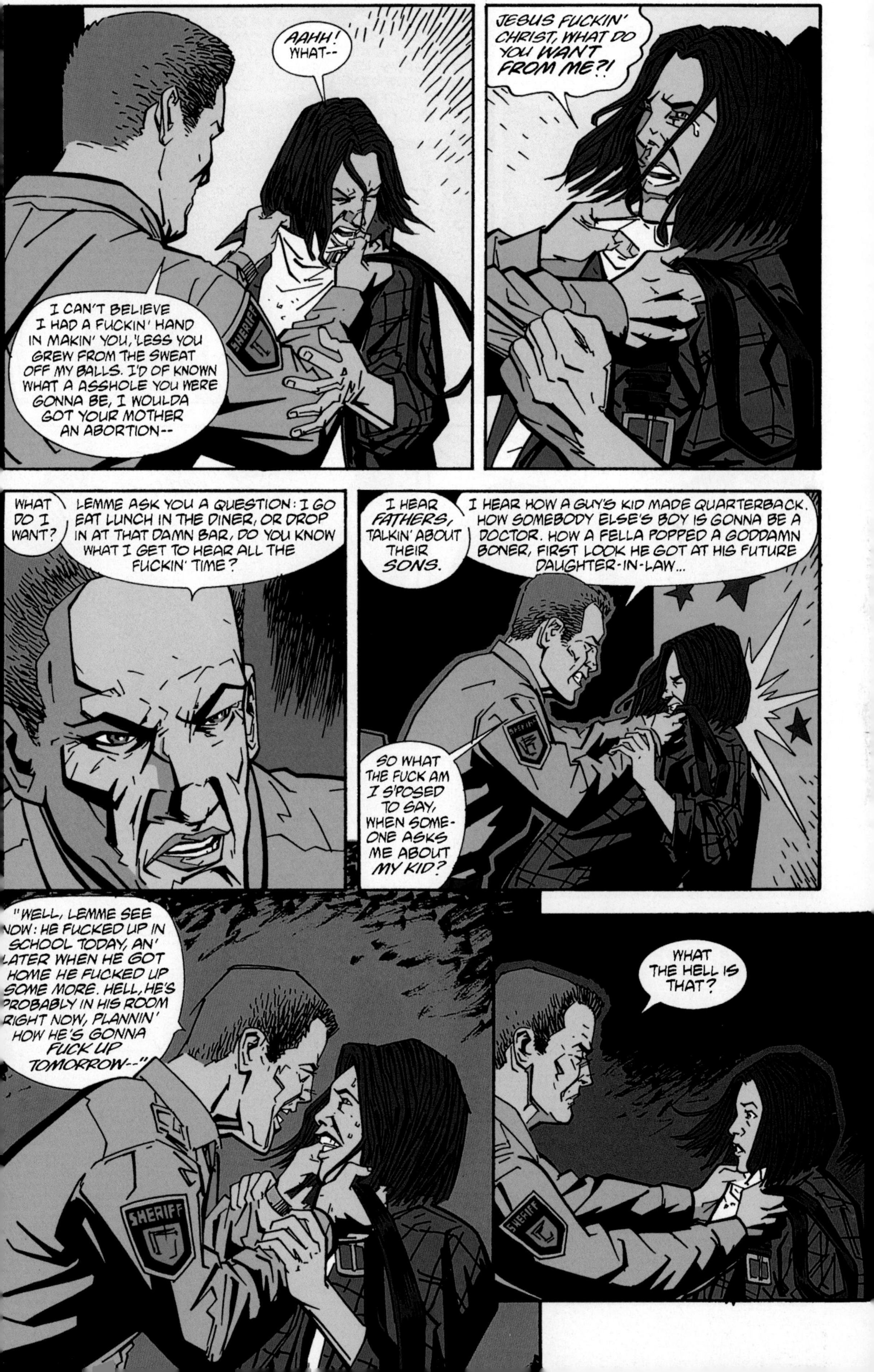
AAHH! WHAT--
I CAN'T BELIEVE I HAD A FUCKIN' HAND IN MAKIN' YOU, 'LESS YOU GREW FROM THE SWEAT OFF MY BALLS. I'D OF KNOWN WHAT A ASSHOLE YOU WERE GONNA BE, I WOULDA GOT YOUR MOTHER AN ABORTION--
JESUS FUCKIN' CHRIST, WHAT DO YOU WANT FROM ME?!
WHAT DO I WANT?
LEMME ASK YOU A QUESTION: I GO EAT LUNCH IN THE DINER, OR DROP IN AT THAT DAMN BAR, DO YOU KNOW WHAT I GET TO HEAR ALL THE FUCKIN' TIME?
I HEAR FATHERS, TALKIN' ABOUT THEIR SONS.
I HEAR HOW A GUY'S KID MADE QUARTERBACK. HOW SOMEBODY ELSE'S BOY IS GONNA BE A DOCTOR. HOW A FELLA POPPED A GODDAMN BONER, FIRST LOOK HE GOT AT HIS FUTURE DAUGHTER-IN-LAW...
SO WHAT THE FUCK AM I S'POSED TO SAY, WHEN SOME-ONE ASKS ME ABOUT MY KID?
"WELL, LEMME SEE NOW: HE FUCKED UP IN SCHOOL TODAY, AN' LATER WHEN HE GOT HOME HE FUCKED UP SOME MORE. HELL, HE'S PROBABLY IN HIS ROOM RIGHT NOW, PLANNIN' HOW HE'S GONNA FUCK UP TOMORROW--"
WHAT THE HELL IS THAT?

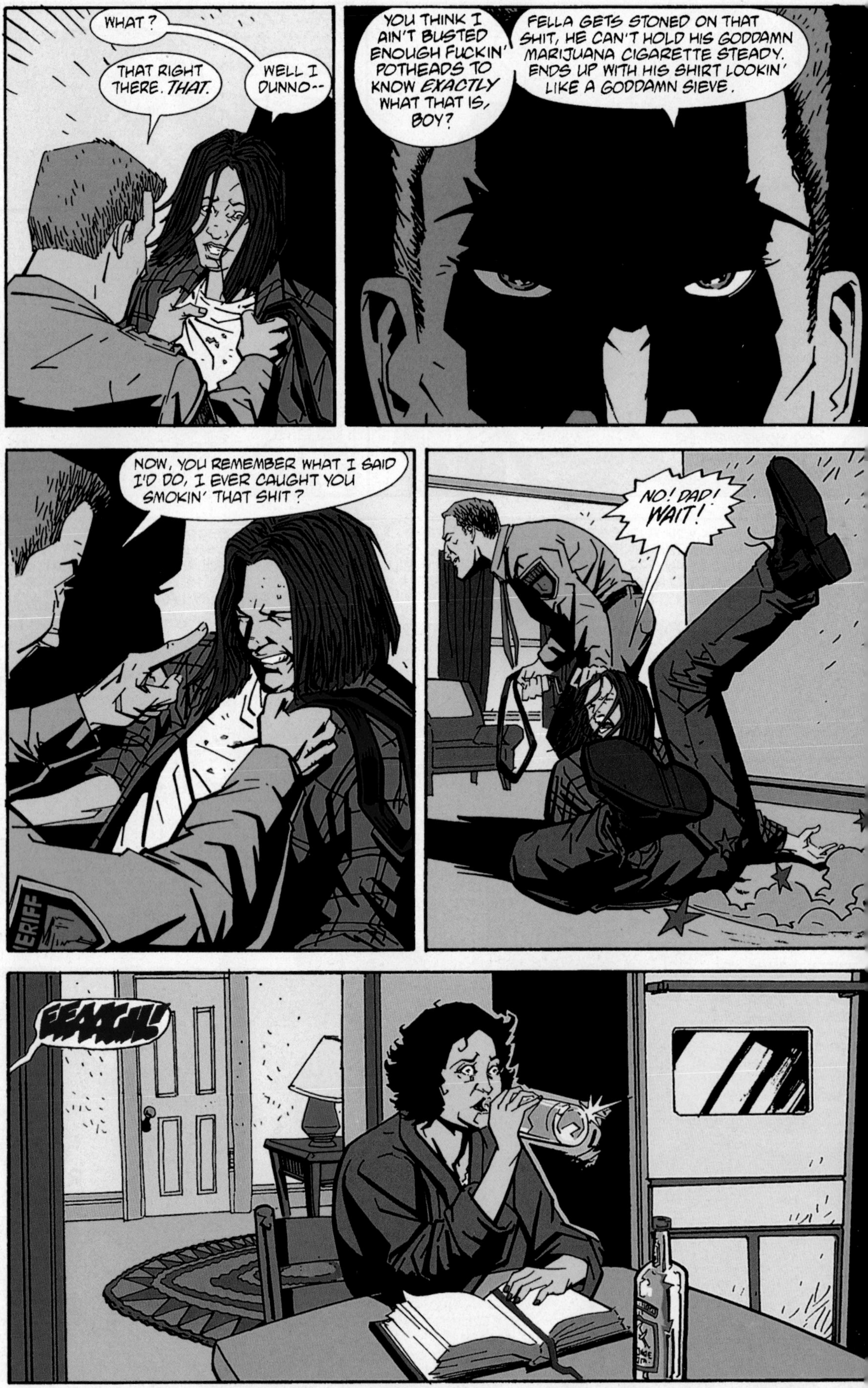
WHAT?
THAT RIGHT THERE. THAT.
WELL I DUNNO--
YOU THINK I AIN'T BUSTED ENOUGH FUCKIN' POTHEADS TO KNOW EXACTLY WHAT THAT IS, BOY?
FELLA GETS STONED ON THAT SHIT, HE CAN'T HOLD HIS GODDAMN MARIJUANA CIGARETTE STEADY. ENDS UP WITH HIS SHIRT LOOKIN' LIKE A GODDAMN SIEVE.
NOW, YOU REMEMBER WHAT I SAID I'D DO, I EVER CAUGHT YOU SMOKIN' THAT SHIT?
NO! DAD! WAIT!
EEAAGH!

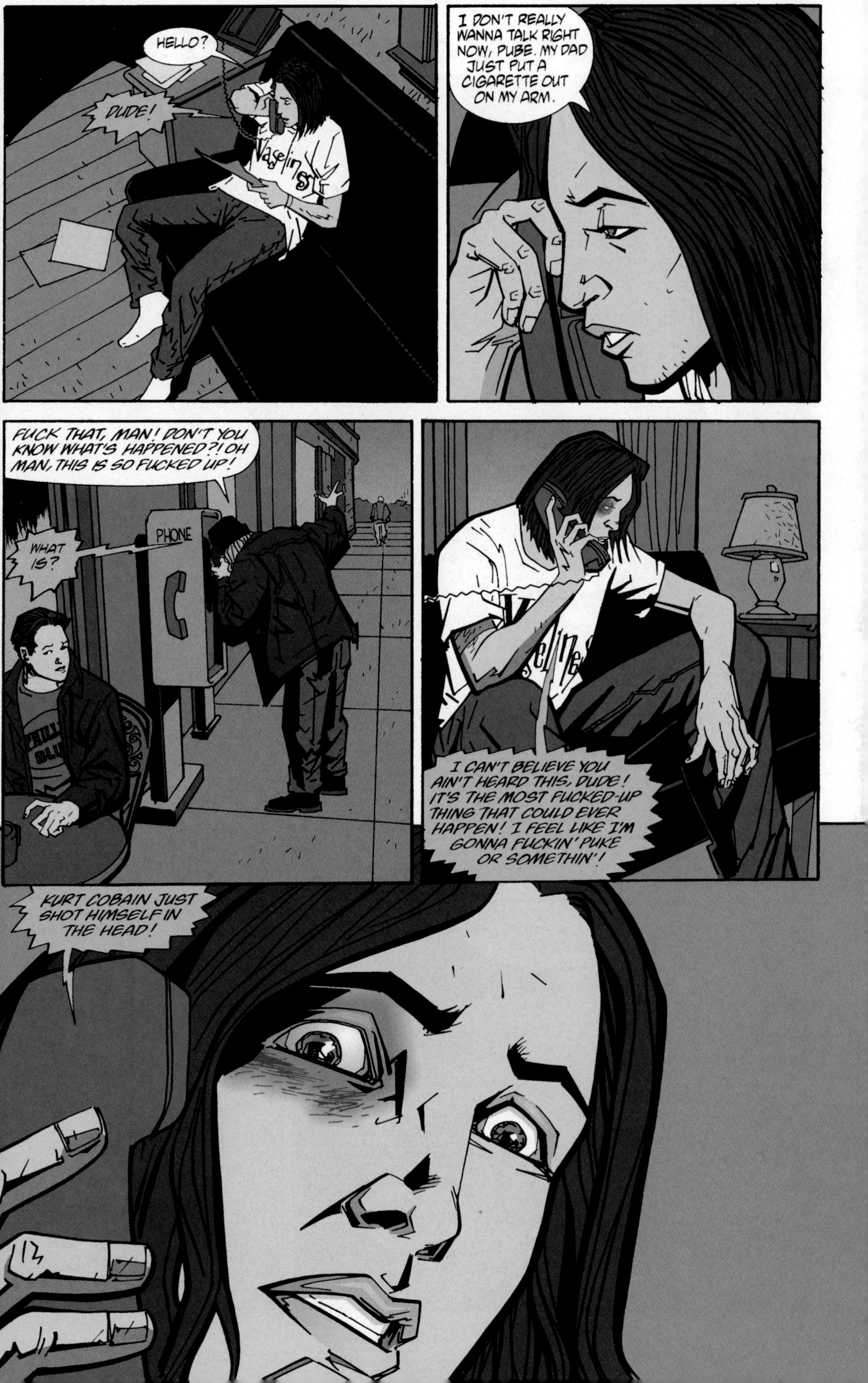
HELLO?
DUDE!
I DON'T REALLY WANNA TALK RIGHT NOW, PUBE. MY DAD JUST PUT A CIGARETTE OUT ON MY ARM.
FUCK THAT, MAN! DON'T YOU KNOW WHAT'S HAPPENED?! OH MAN, THIS IS SO FUCKED UP!
WHAT IS?
PHONE
I CAN'T BELIEVE YOU AIN'T HEARD THIS, DUDE! IT'S THE MOST FUCKED-UP THING THAT COULD EVER HAPPEN! I FEEL LIKE I'M GONNA FUCKIN' PUKE OR SOMETHIN'!
KURT COBAIN JUST SHOT HIMSELF IN THE HEAD!

4. Nevermind

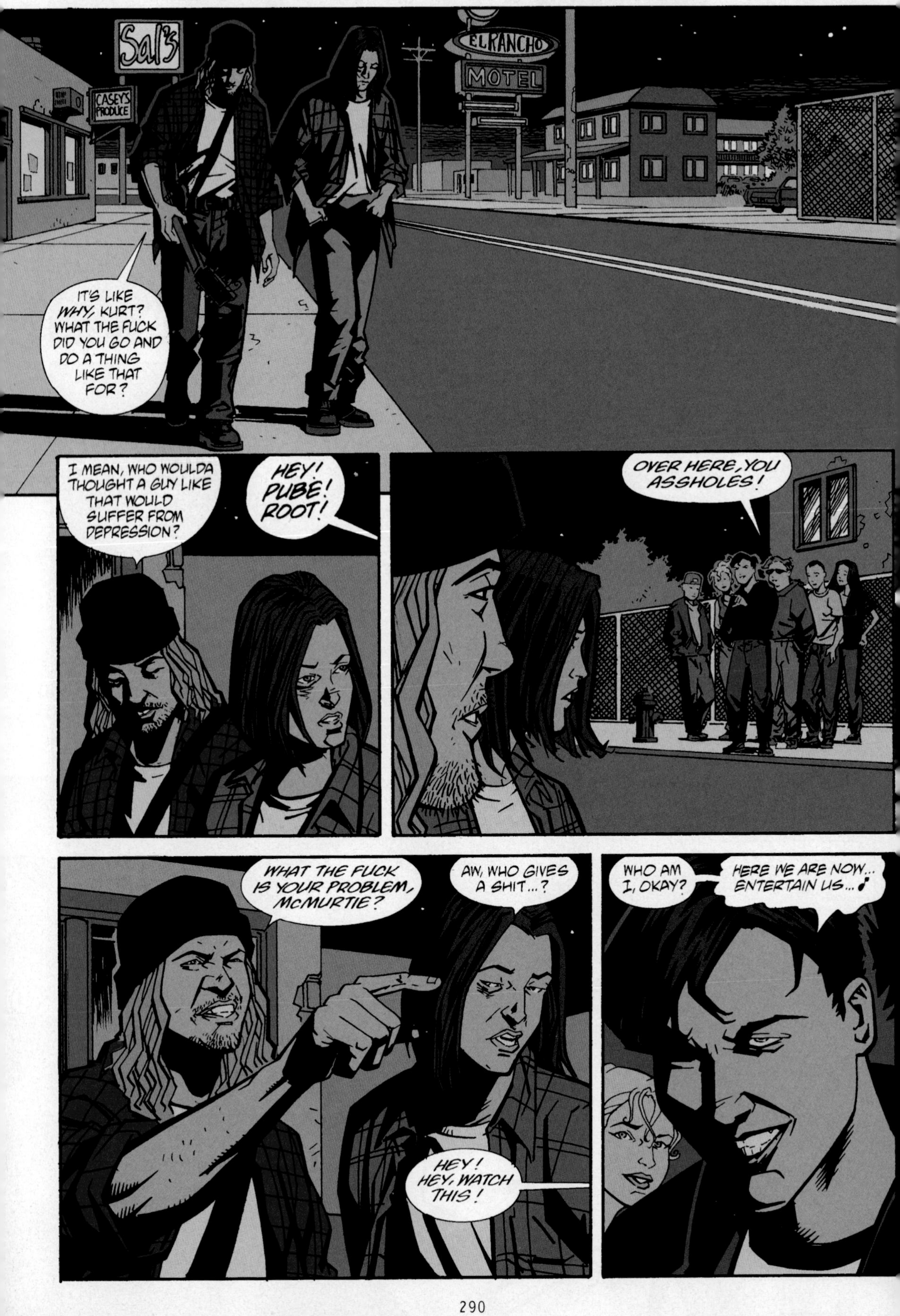

SAL'S
CASEY'S PRODUCE
EL RANCHO
MOTEL
IT'S LIKE WHY, KURT? WHAT THE FUCK DID YOU GO AND DO A THING LIKE THAT FOR?
I MEAN, WHO WOULDA THOUGHT A GUY LIKE THAT WOULD SUFFER FROM DEPRESSION?
HEY! PUBE! ROOT!
OVER HERE, YOU ASSHOLES!
WHAT THE FUCK IS YOUR PROBLEM, McMURTIE?
AW, WHO GIVES A SHIT...?
HEY! HEY, WATCH THIS!
WHO AM I, OKAY?
HERE WE ARE NOW... ENTERTAIN US...

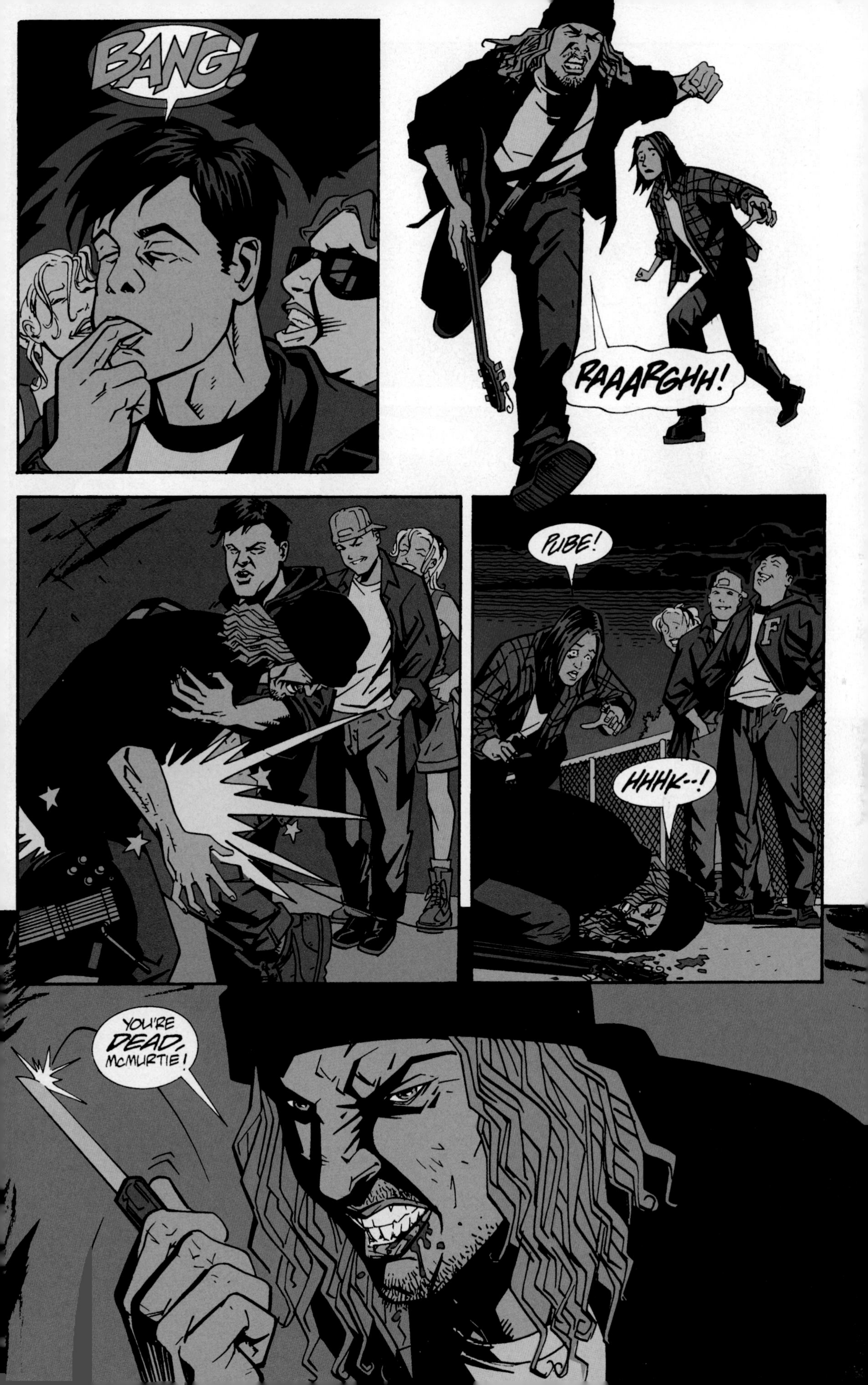
BANG!
RAAARGHH!
PUBE!
HHHK--!
YOU'RE DEAD, McMURTIE!

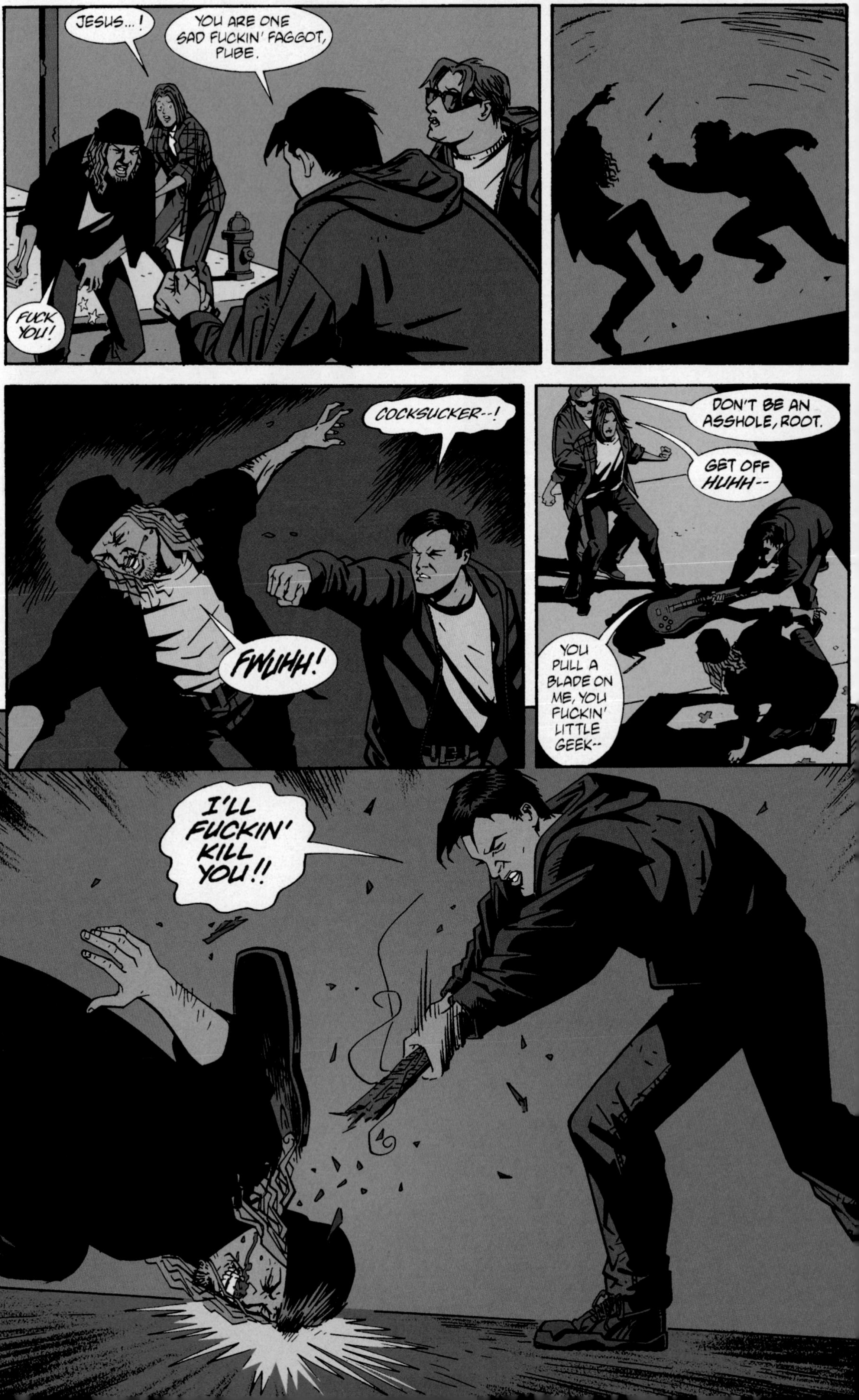
JESUS...!
YOU ARE ONE SAD FUCKIN' FAGGOT, PUBE.
FUCK YOU!
COCKSUCKER--!
FWUHH!
DON'T BE AN ASSHOLE, ROOT.
GET OFF HUHH--
YOU PULL A BLADE ON ME, YOU FUCKIN' LITTLE GEEK--
I'LL FUCKIN' KILL YOU!!

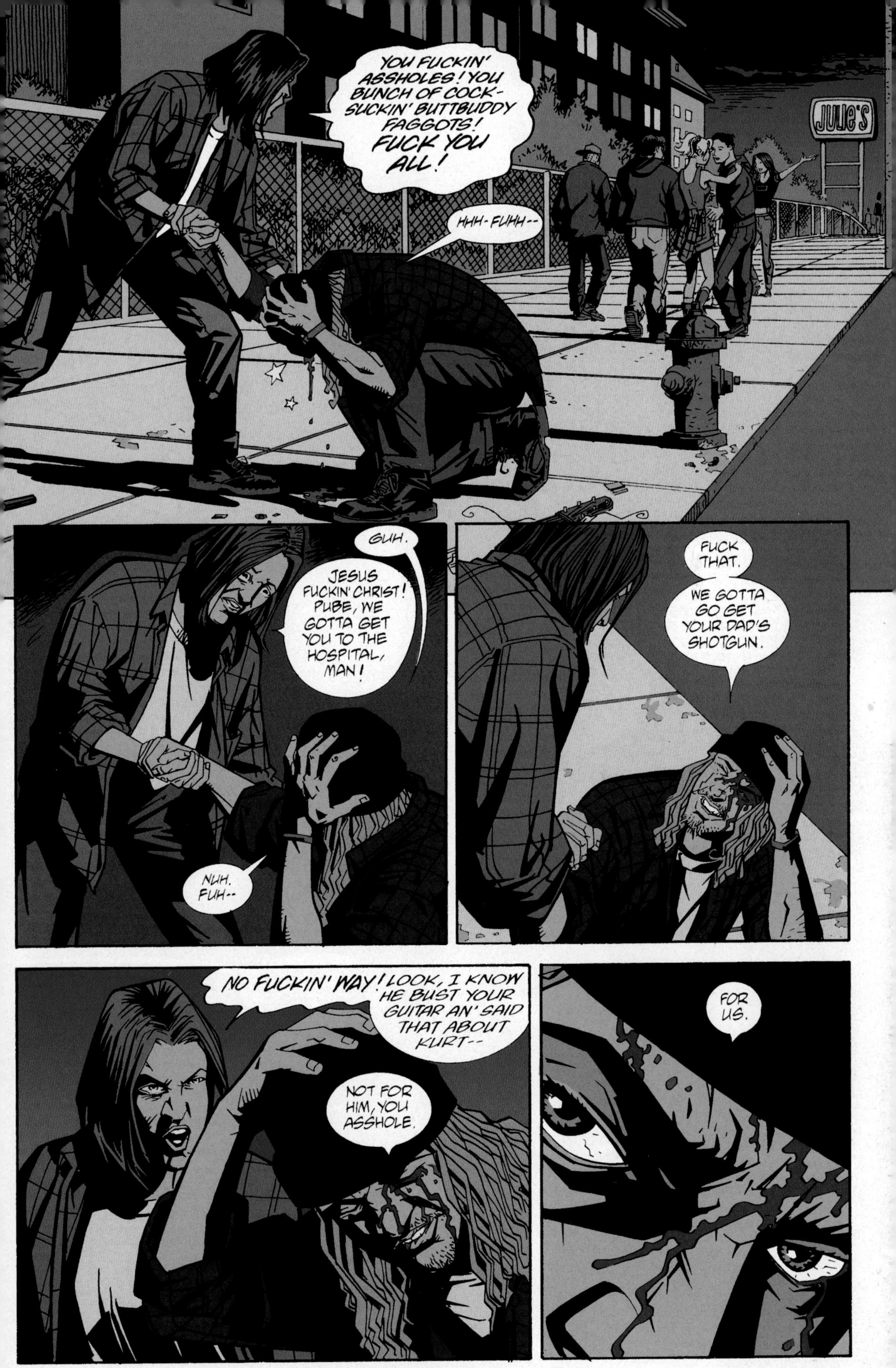
YOU FUCKIN' ASSHOLES! YOU BUNCH OF COCK-SUCKIN' BUTTBUDDY FAGGOTS! FUCK YOU ALL!
JULIE'S
HHH-FUHH--
GUH.
JESUS FUCKIN' CHRIST! PUBE, WE GOTTA GET YOU TO THE HOSPITAL, MAN!
NUH. FUH--
FUCK THAT.
WE GOTTA GO GET YOUR DAD'S SHOTGUN.
NO FUCKIN' WAY! LOOK, I KNOW HE BUST YOUR GUITAR AN' SAID THAT ABOUT KURT--
NOT FOR HIM, YOU ASSHOLE.
FOR US.

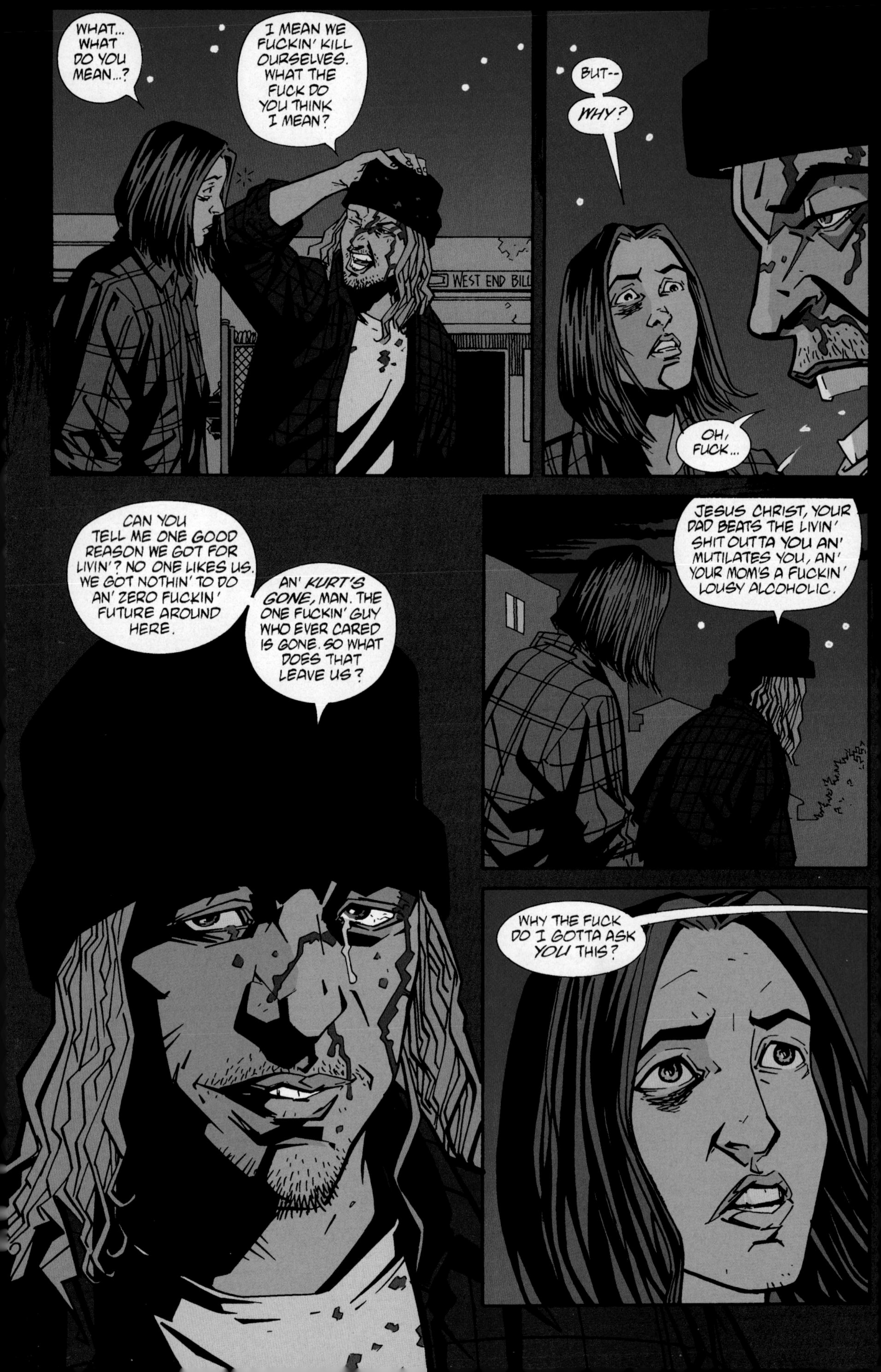
WHAT... WHAT DO YOU MEAN...?
I MEAN WE FUCKIN' KILL OURSELVES. WHAT THE FUCK DO YOU THINK I MEAN?
WEST END BILL
BUT--
WHY?
OH, FUCK...
CAN YOU TELL ME ONE GOOD REASON WE GOT FOR LIVIN'? NO ONE LIKES US. WE GOT NOTHIN' TO DO AN' ZERO FUCKIN' FUTURE AROUND HERE.
AN' KURT'S GONE, MAN. THE ONE FUCKIN' GUY WHO EVER CARED IS GONE. SO WHAT DOES THAT LEAVE US?
JESUS CHRIST, YOUR DAD BEATS THE LIVIN' SHIT OUTTA YOU AN' MUTILATES YOU, AN' YOUR MOM'S A FUCKIN' LOUSY ALCOHOLIC.
WHY THE FUCK DO I GOTTA ASK YOU THIS?

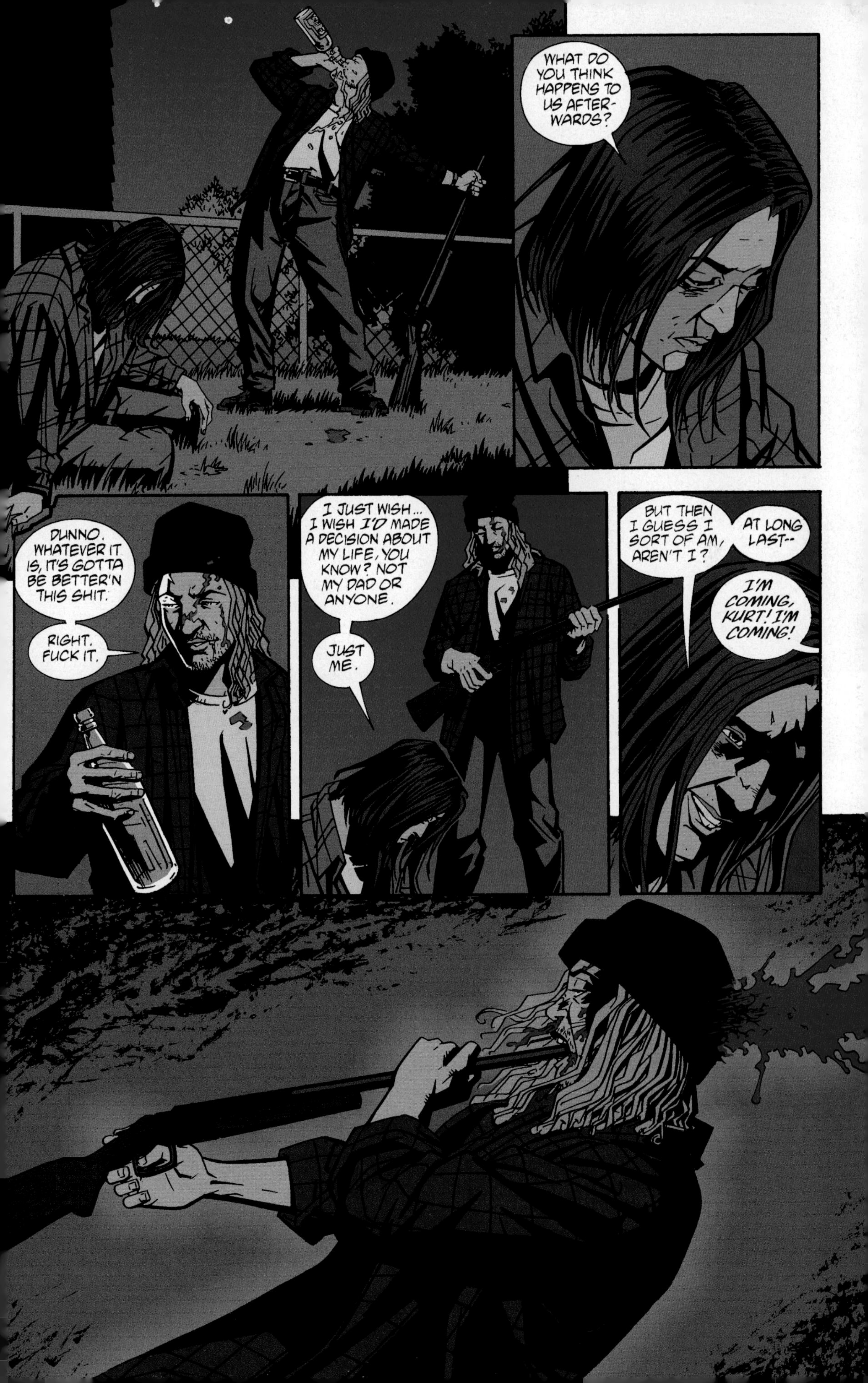
WHAT DO YOU THINK HAPPENS TO US AFTER-WARDS?
DUNNO. WHATEVER IT IS, IT'S GOTTA BE BETTER'N THIS SHIT.
RIGHT. FUCK IT.
I JUST WISH... I WISH I'D MADE A DECISION ABOUT MY LIFE, YOU KNOW? NOT MY DAD OR ANYONE.
JUST ME.
BUT THEN I GUESS I SORT OF AM, AREN'T I?
AT LONG LAST--
I'M COMING, KURT! I'M COMING!

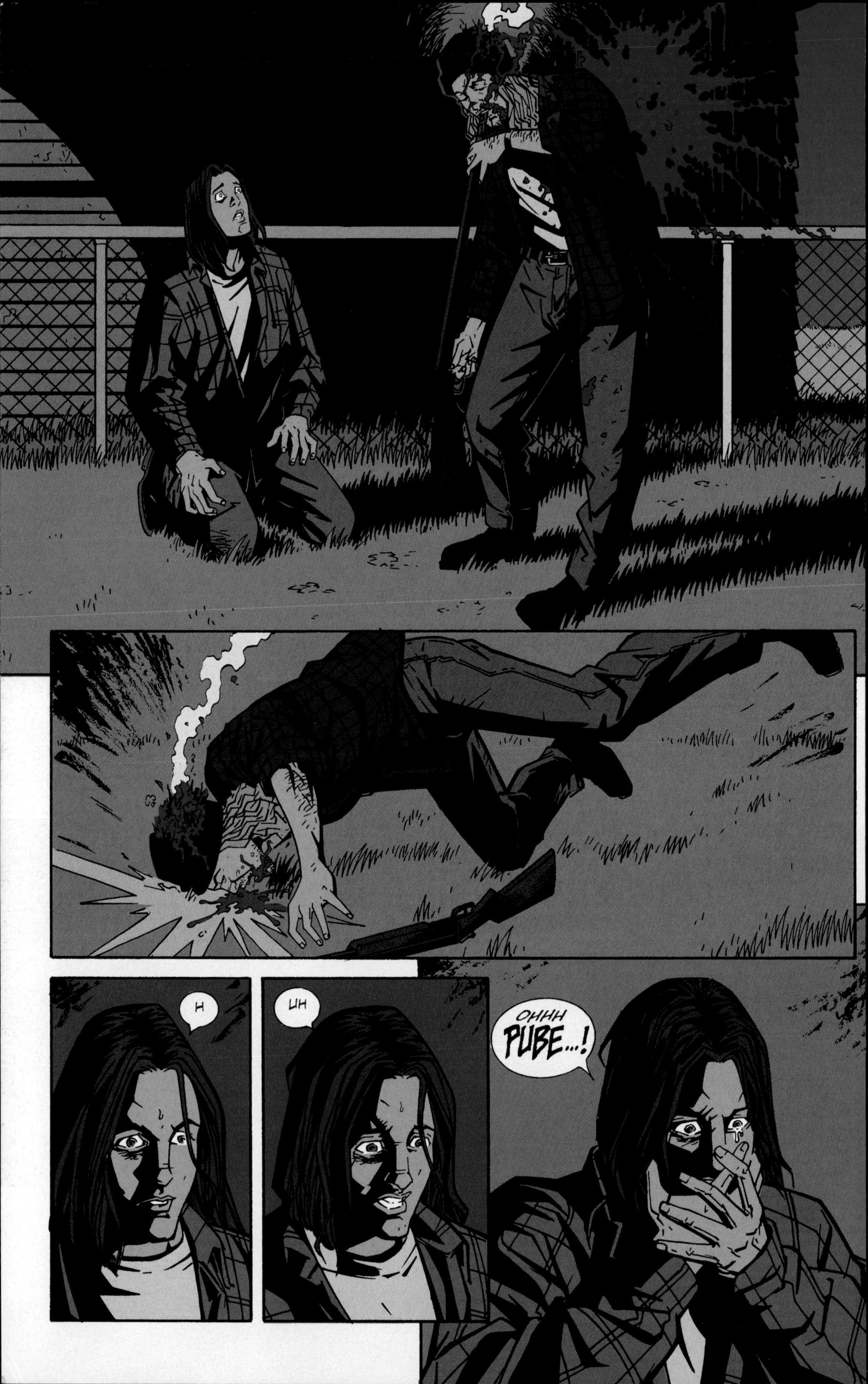
H
UH
OHHH PUBE...!

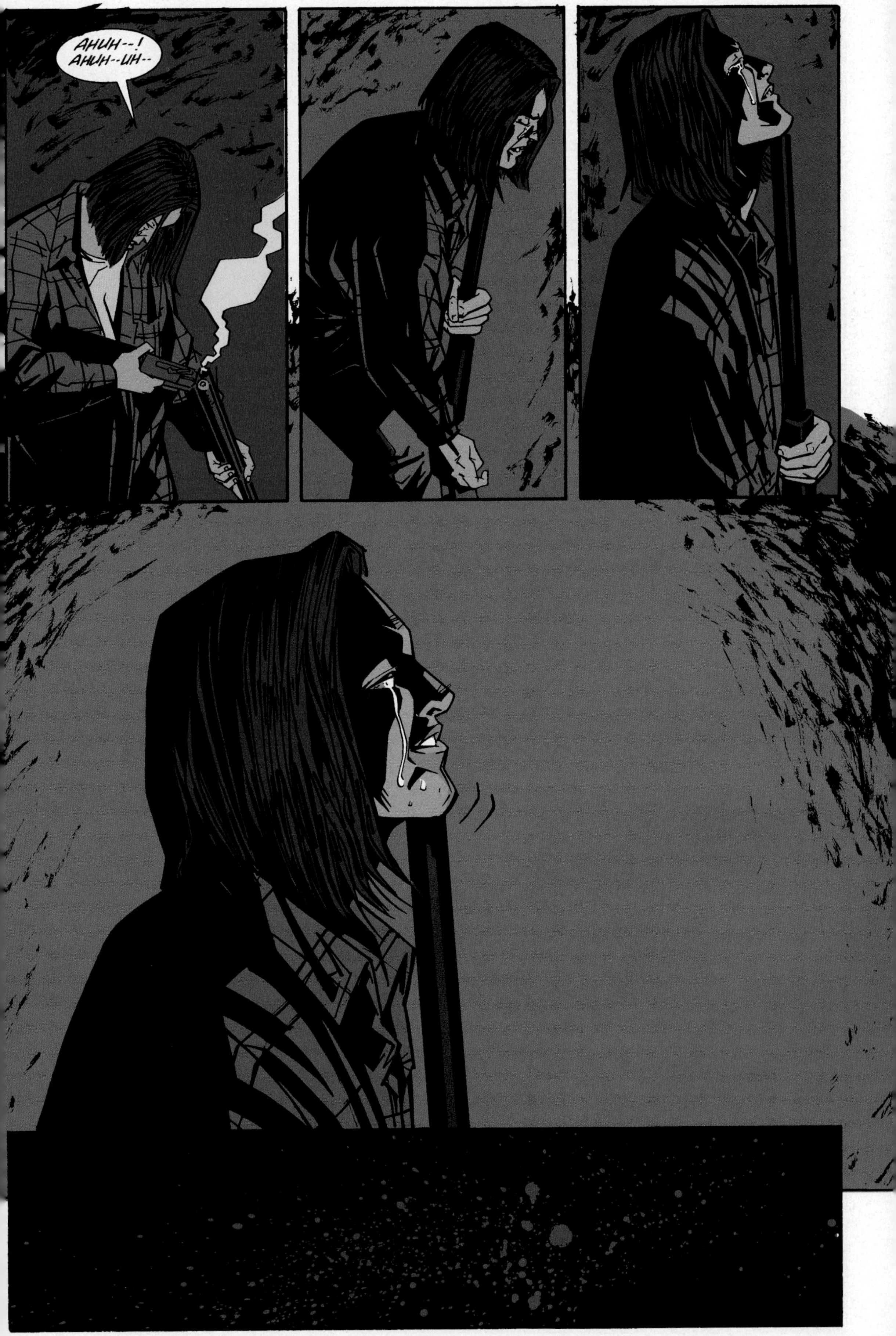
AHUH--! AHUH--UH--

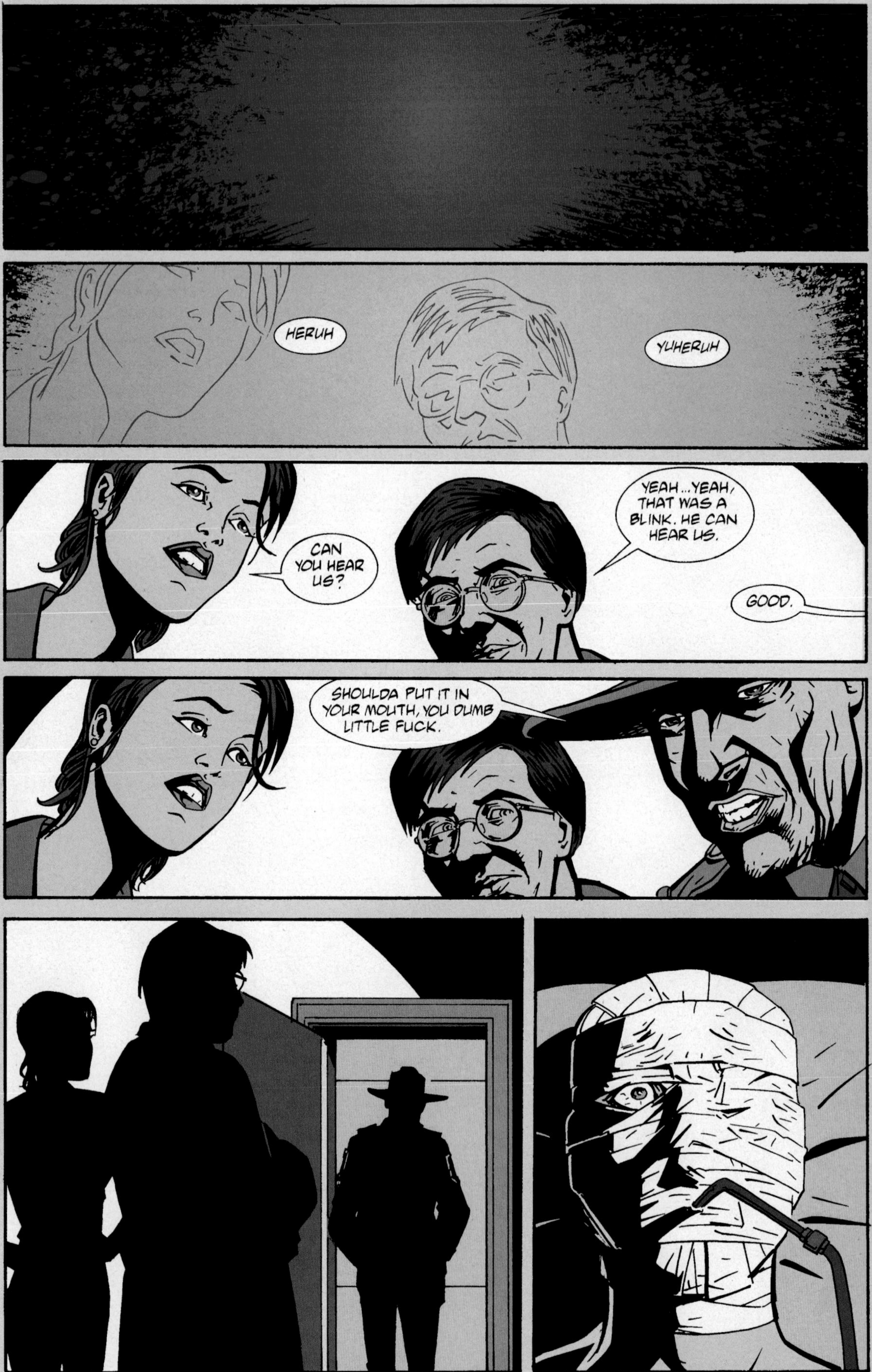
HERUH
YUHERUH
CAN YOU HEAR US?
YEAH...YEAH, THAT WAS A BLINK. HE CAN HEAR US.
GOOD.
SHOULDA PUT IT IN YOUR MOUTH, YOU DUMB LITTLE FUCK.

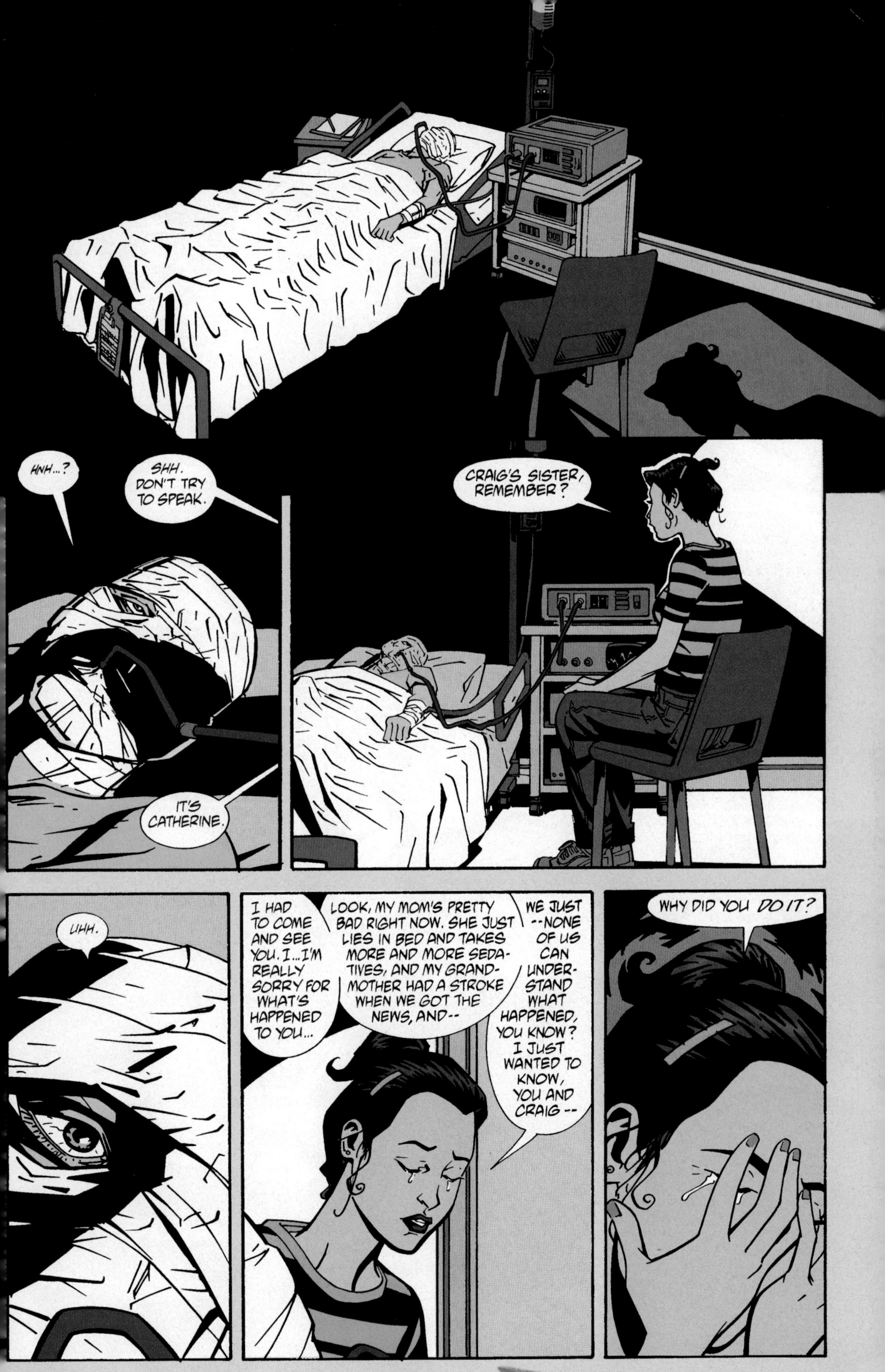
HNH...?
SHH. DON'T TRY TO SPEAK.
CRAIG'S SISTER, REMEMBER?
IT'S CATHERINE.
UHH.
I HAD TO COME AND SEE YOU. I...I'M REALLY SORRY FOR WHAT'S HAPPENED TO YOU...
LOOK, MY MOM'S PRETTY BAD RIGHT NOW. SHE JUST LIES IN BED AND TAKES MORE AND MORE SEDATIVES, AND MY GRANDMOTHER HAD A STROKE WHEN WE GOT THE NEWS, AND--
WE JUST --NONE OF US CAN UNDERSTAND WHAT HAPPENED, YOU KNOW? I JUST WANTED TO KNOW, YOU AND CRAIG --
WHY DID YOU *DO IT?*

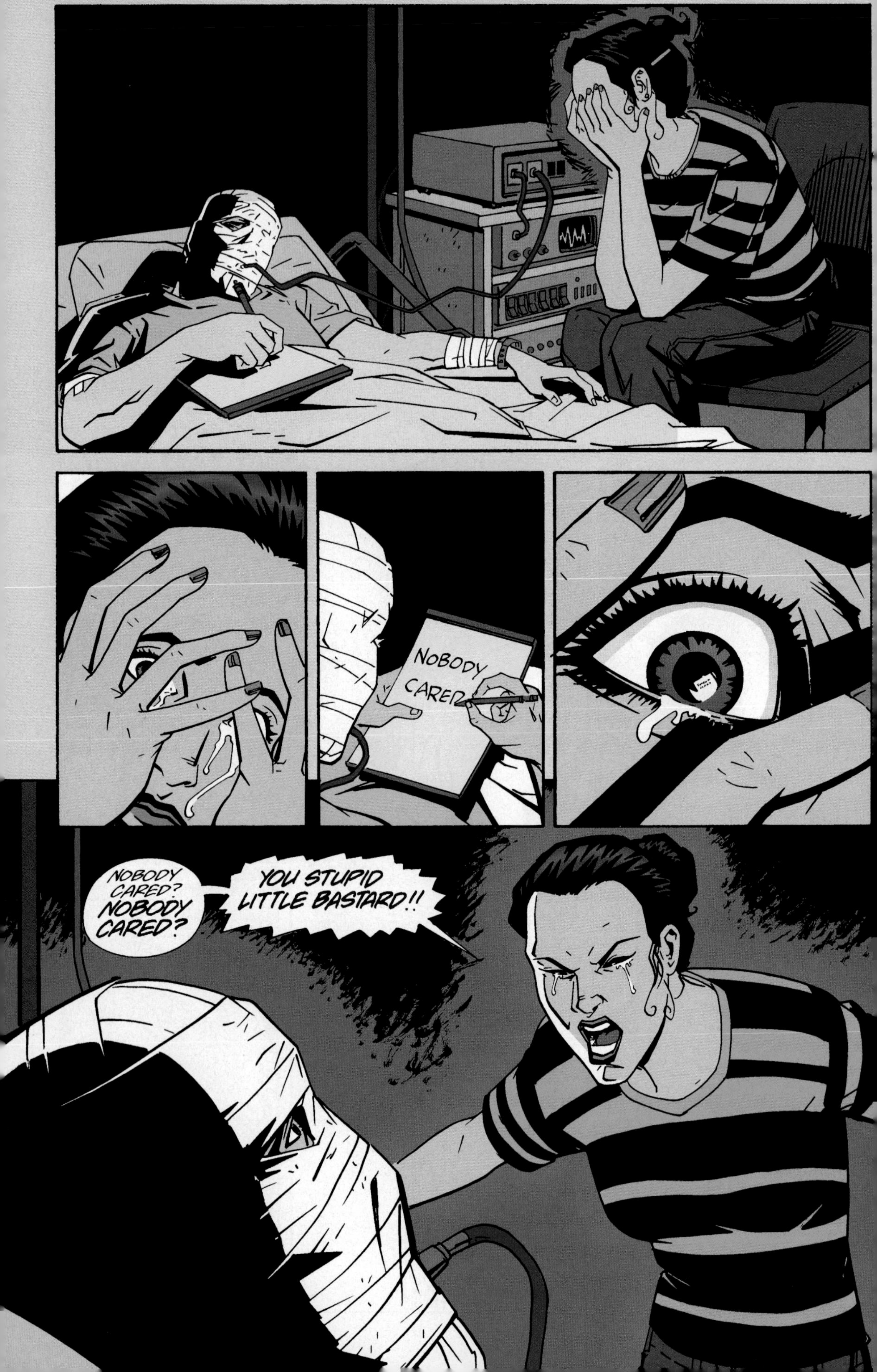
NOBODY CARED
NOBODY CARED? NOBODY CARED?
YOU STUPID LITTLE BASTARD!!

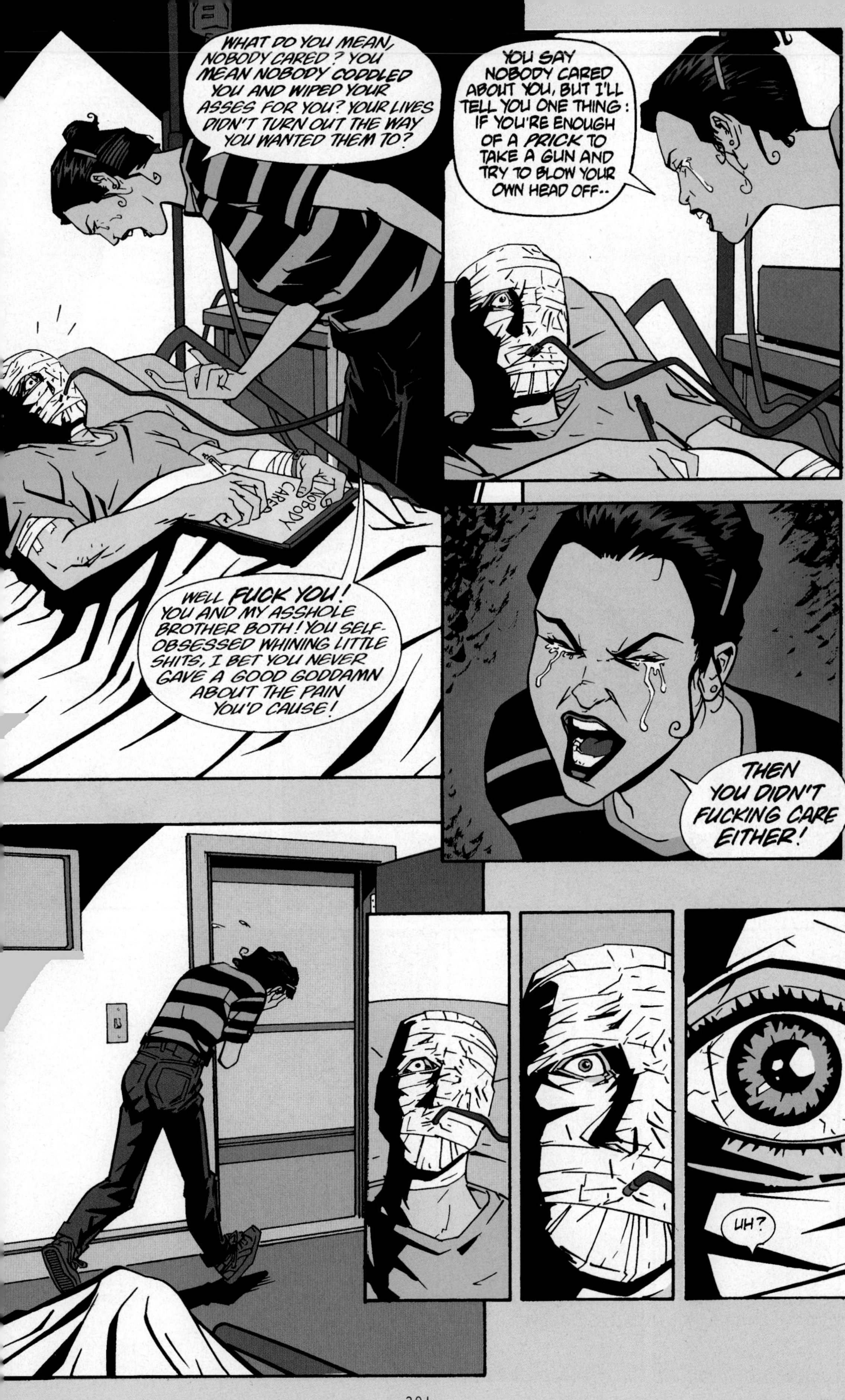
WHAT DO YOU MEAN, NOBODY CARED? YOU MEAN NOBODY CODDLED YOU AND WIPED YOUR ASSES FOR YOU? YOUR LIVES DIDN'T TURN OUT THE WAY YOU WANTED THEM TO?
NOBODY CARED
WELL FUCK YOU! YOU AND MY ASSHOLE BROTHER BOTH! YOU SELF-OBSESSED WHINING LITTLE SHITS, I BET YOU NEVER GAVE A GOOD GODDAMN ABOUT THE PAIN YOU'D CAUSE!
YOU SAY NOBODY CARED ABOUT YOU, BUT I'LL TELL YOU ONE THING: IF YOU'RE ENOUGH OF A PRICK TO TAKE A GUN AND TRY TO BLOW YOUR OWN HEAD OFF..
THEN YOU DIDN'T FUCKING CARE EITHER!
UH?

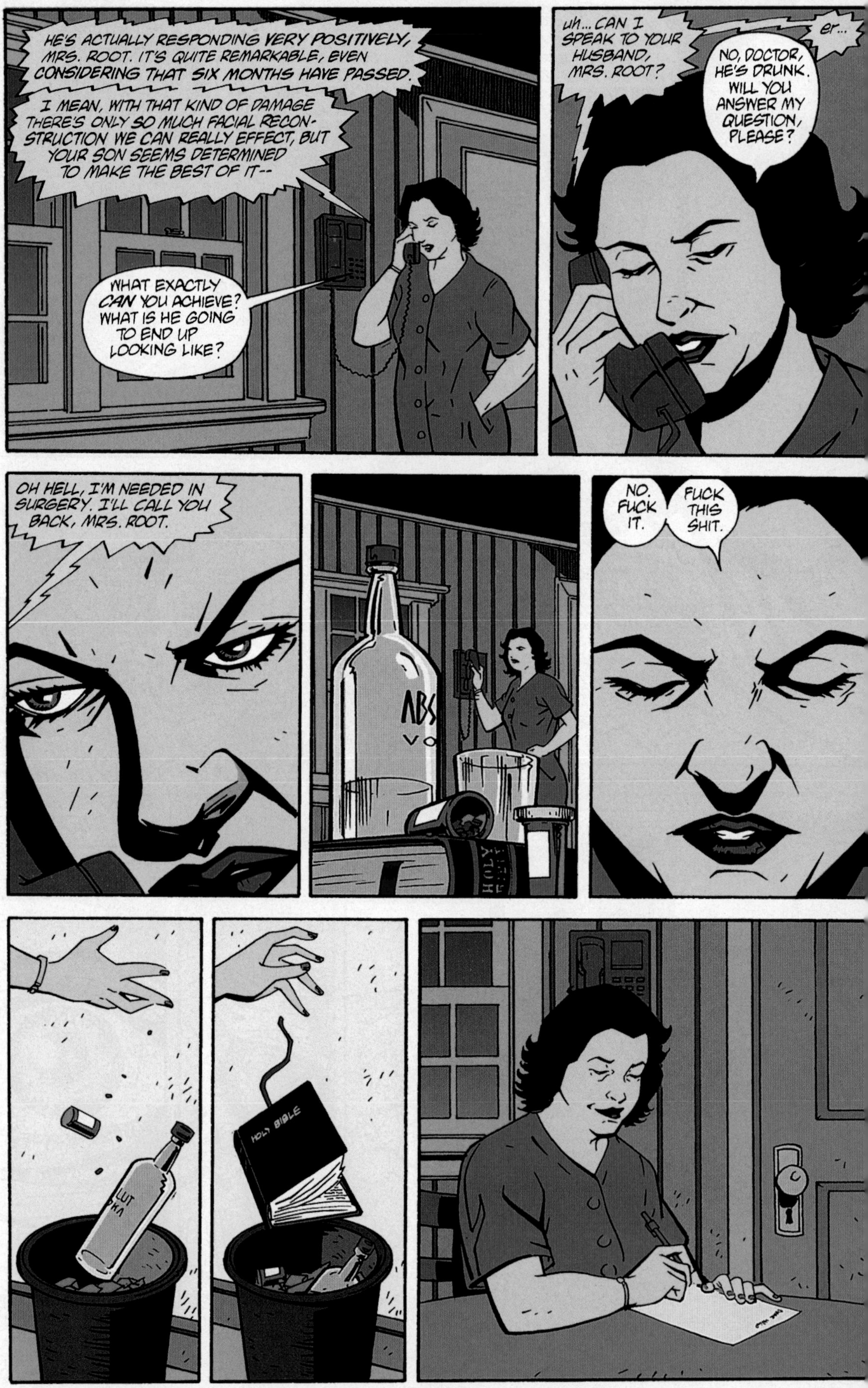
HE'S ACTUALLY RESPONDING VERY POSITIVELY, MRS. ROOT. IT'S QUITE REMARKABLE, EVEN CONSIDERING THAT SIX MONTHS HAVE PASSED.
I MEAN, WITH THAT KIND OF DAMAGE THERE'S ONLY SO MUCH FACIAL RECONSTRUCTION WE CAN REALLY EFFECT, BUT YOUR SON SEEMS DETERMINED TO MAKE THE BEST OF IT--
WHAT EXACTLY CAN YOU ACHIEVE? WHAT IS HE GOING TO END UP LOOKING LIKE?
uh... CAN I SPEAK TO YOUR HUSBAND, MRS. ROOT?
er...
NO, DOCTOR, HE'S DRUNK. WILL YOU ANSWER MY QUESTION, PLEASE?
OH HELL, I'M NEEDED IN SURGERY. I'LL CALL YOU BACK, MRS. ROOT.
NO. FUCK IT.
FUCK THIS SHIT.
HOLY BIBLE

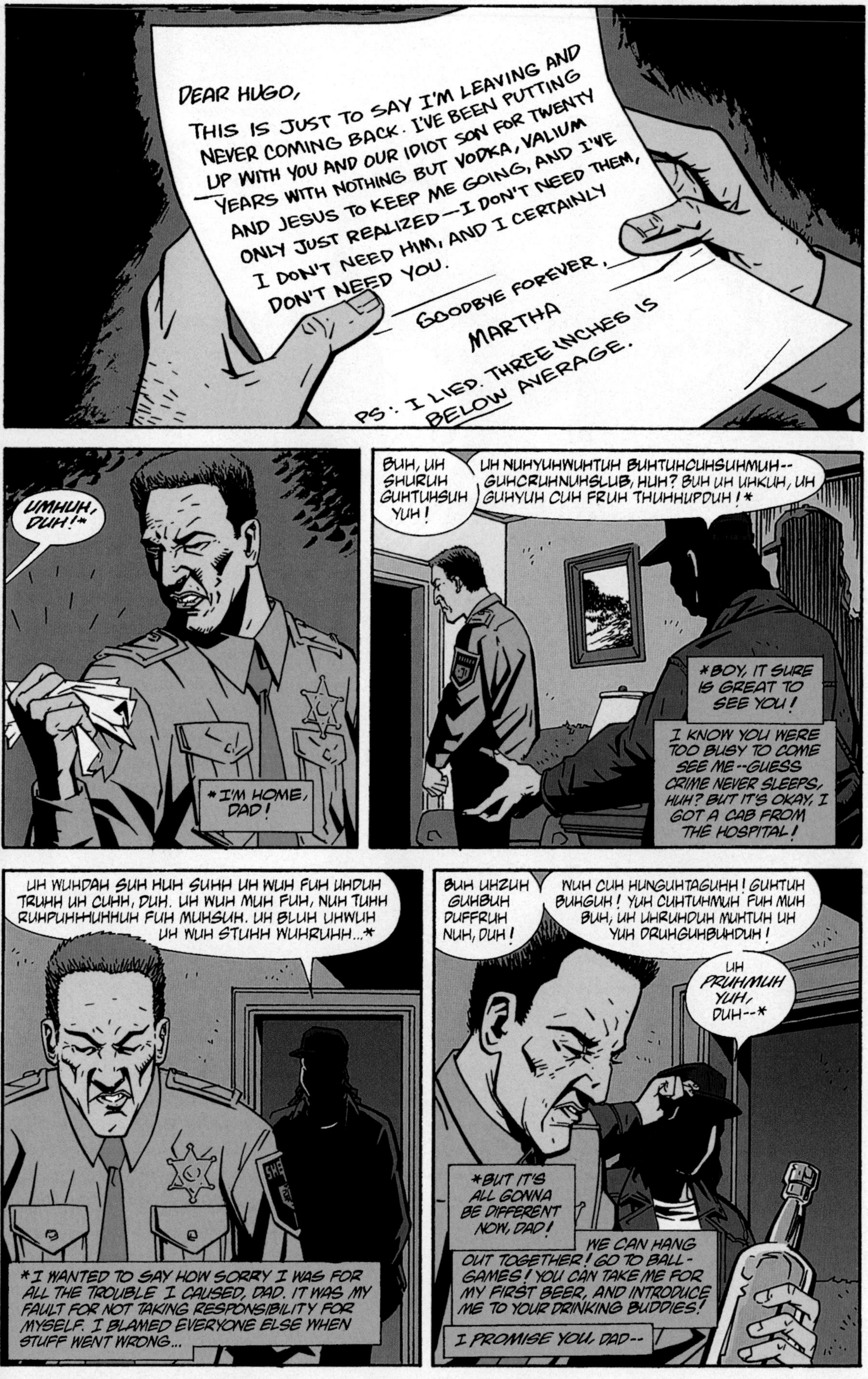
DEAR HUGO,
THIS IS JUST TO SAY I'M LEAVING AND NEVER COMING BACK. I'VE BEEN PUTTING UP WITH YOU AND OUR IDIOT SON FOR TWENTY YEARS WITH NOTHING BUT VODKA, VALIUM AND JESUS TO KEEP ME GOING, AND I'VE ONLY JUST REALIZED -- I DON'T NEED THEM, I DON'T NEED HIM, AND I CERTAINLY DON'T NEED YOU.
GOODBYE FOREVER,
MARTHA
PS: I LIED. THREE INCHES IS BELOW AVERAGE.
UMHUH, DUH!*
*I'M HOME, DAD!
BUH, UH SHURUH GUHTUHSUH YUH!
UH NUHYUHWUHTUH BUHTUHCUHSUHMUH-- GUHCRUHNUHSLUB, HUH? BUH UH UHKUH, UH GUHYUH CUH FRUH THUHHUPDUH!*
*BOY, IT SURE IS GREAT TO SEE YOU!
I KNOW YOU WERE TOO BUSY TO COME SEE ME--GUESS CRIME NEVER SLEEPS, HUH? BUT IT'S OKAY, I GOT A CAB FROM THE HOSPITAL!
UH WUHDAH SUH HUH SUHH UH WUH FUH UHDUH TRUHH UH CUHH, DUH. UH WUH MUH FUH, NUH TUHH RUHPUHHUHHUH FUH MUHSUH. UH BLUH UHWUH UH WUH STUHH WUHRUHH...*
*I WANTED TO SAY HOW SORRY I WAS FOR ALL THE TROUBLE I CAUSED, DAD. IT WAS MY FAULT FOR NOT TAKING RESPONSIBILITY FOR MYSELF. I BLAMED EVERYONE ELSE WHEN STUFF WENT WRONG...
BUH UHZUH GUHBUH DUFFRUH NUH, DUH!
WUH CUH HUNGUHTAGUHH! GUHTUH BUHGUH! YUH CUHTUHMUH FUH MUH BUH, UH UHRUHDUH MUHTUH UH YUH DRUHGUHBUHDUH!
UH PRUHMUH YUH, DUH--*
*BUT IT'S ALL GONNA BE DIFFERENT NOW, DAD!
WE CAN HANG OUT TOGETHER! GO TO BALL-GAMES! YOU CAN TAKE ME FOR MY FIRST BEER, AND INTRODUCE ME TO YOUR DRINKING BUDDIES!
I PROMISE YOU, DAD--

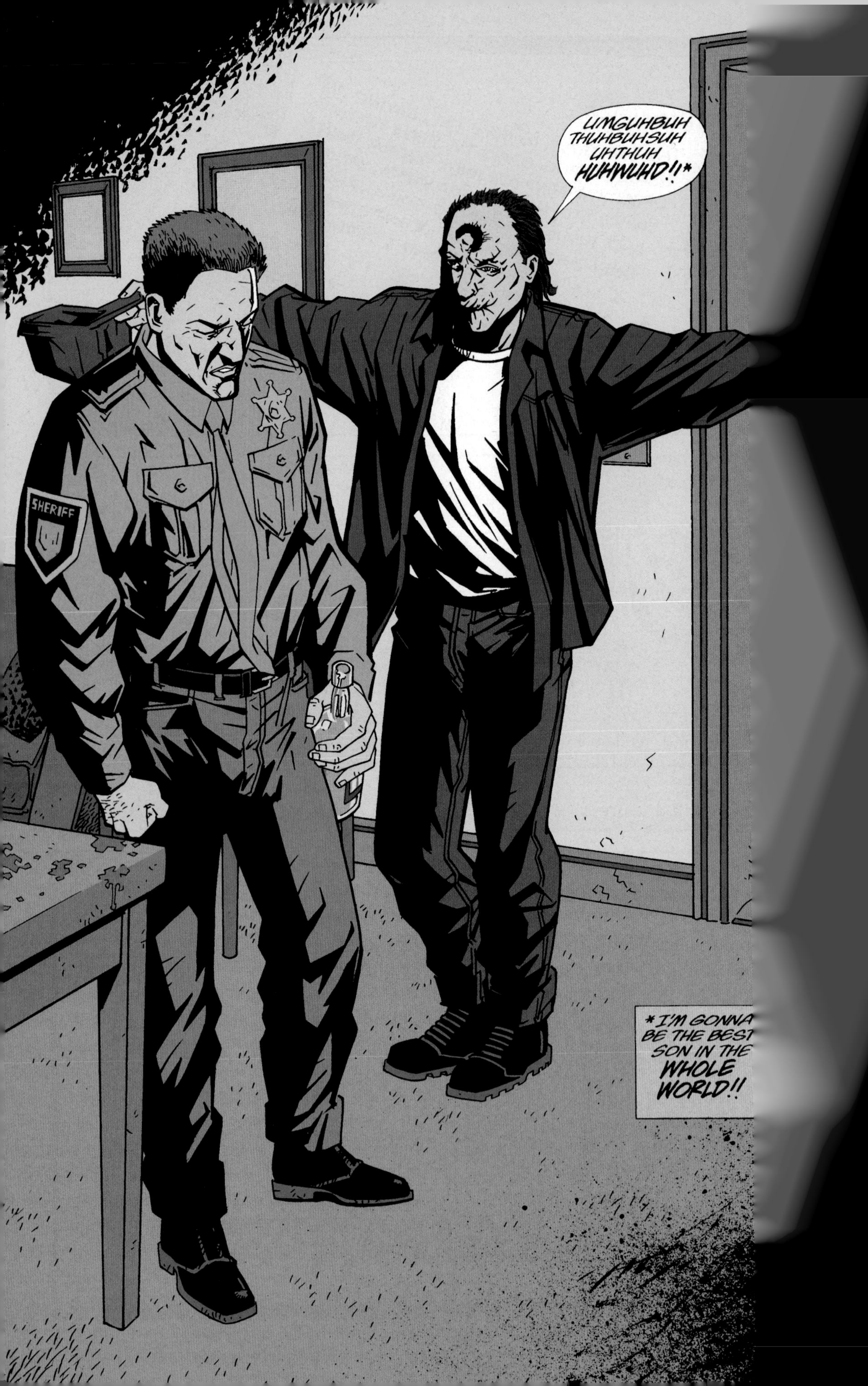
UMGUHBUH THUHBUHSUH UHTHUH HUHWUHD!!*
*I'M GONNA BE THE BEST SON IN THE WHOLE WORLD!!

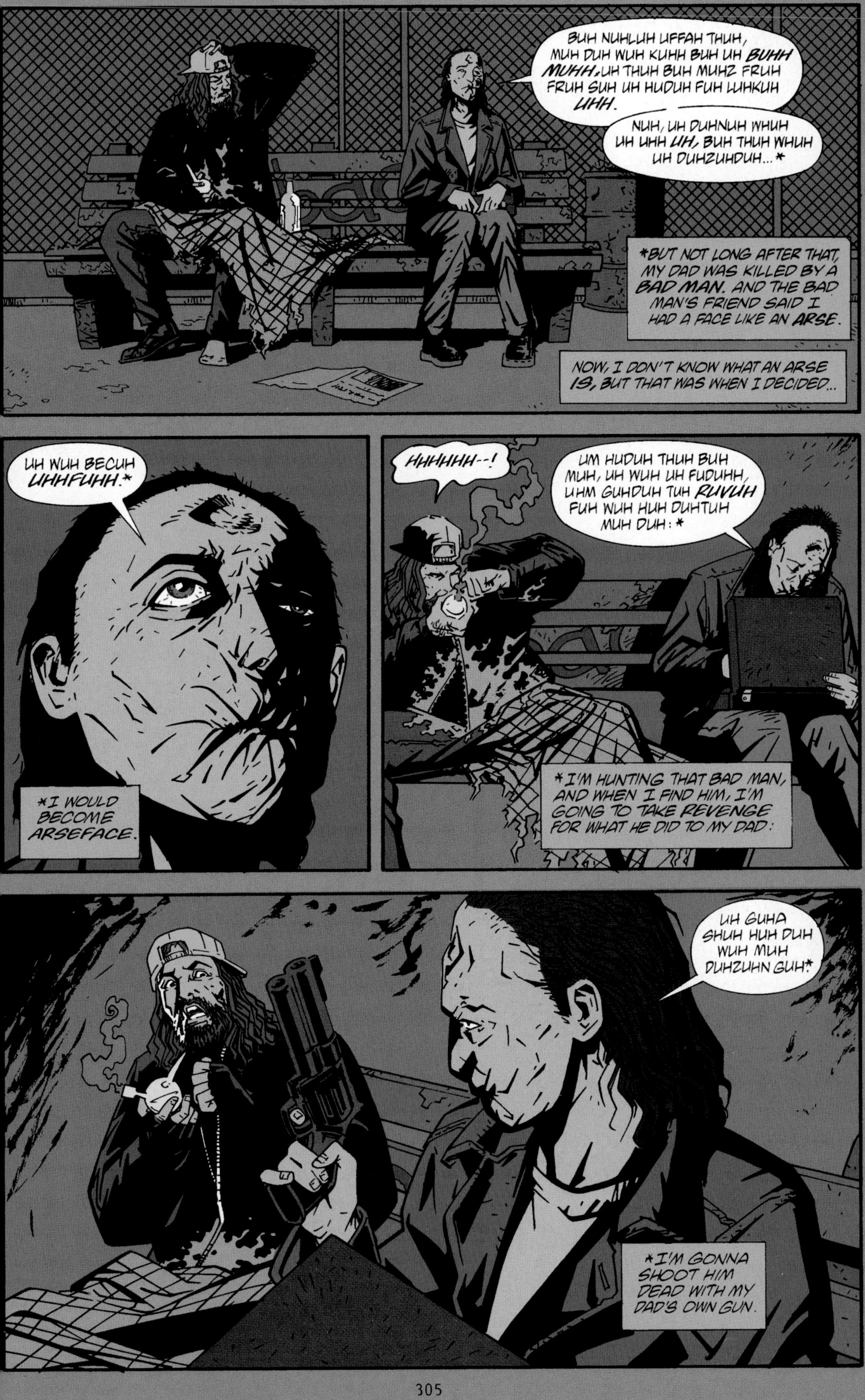

BUH NUHLUH UFFAH THUH, MUH DUH WUH KUHH BUH UH BUHH MUHH. UH THUH BUH MUHZ FRUH FRUH SUH UH HUDUH FUH WHKUH UHH.
NUH, UH DUHNUH WHUH UH UHH UH, BUH THUH WHUH UH DUHZUHDUH...*
*BUT NOT LONG AFTER THAT, MY DAD WAS KILLED BY A BAD MAN. AND THE BAD MAN'S FRIEND SAID I HAD A FACE LIKE AN ARSE.
NOW, I DON'T KNOW WHAT AN ARSE IS, BUT THAT WAS WHEN I DECIDED...
UH WUH BECUH UHHFUHH.*
*I WOULD BECOME ARSEFACE.
HHHHHH--!
UM HUDUH THUH BUH MUH, UH WUH UH FUDUHH, UHM GUHDUH TUH RUVUH FUH WUH HUH DUHTUH MUH DUH:*
*I'M HUNTING THAT BAD MAN, AND WHEN I FIND HIM, I'M GOING TO TAKE REVENGE FOR WHAT HE DID TO MY DAD:
UH GUHA SHUH HUH DUH WUH MUH DUHZUHN GUH.*
*I'M GONNA SHOOT HIM DEAD WITH MY DAD'S OWN GUN.

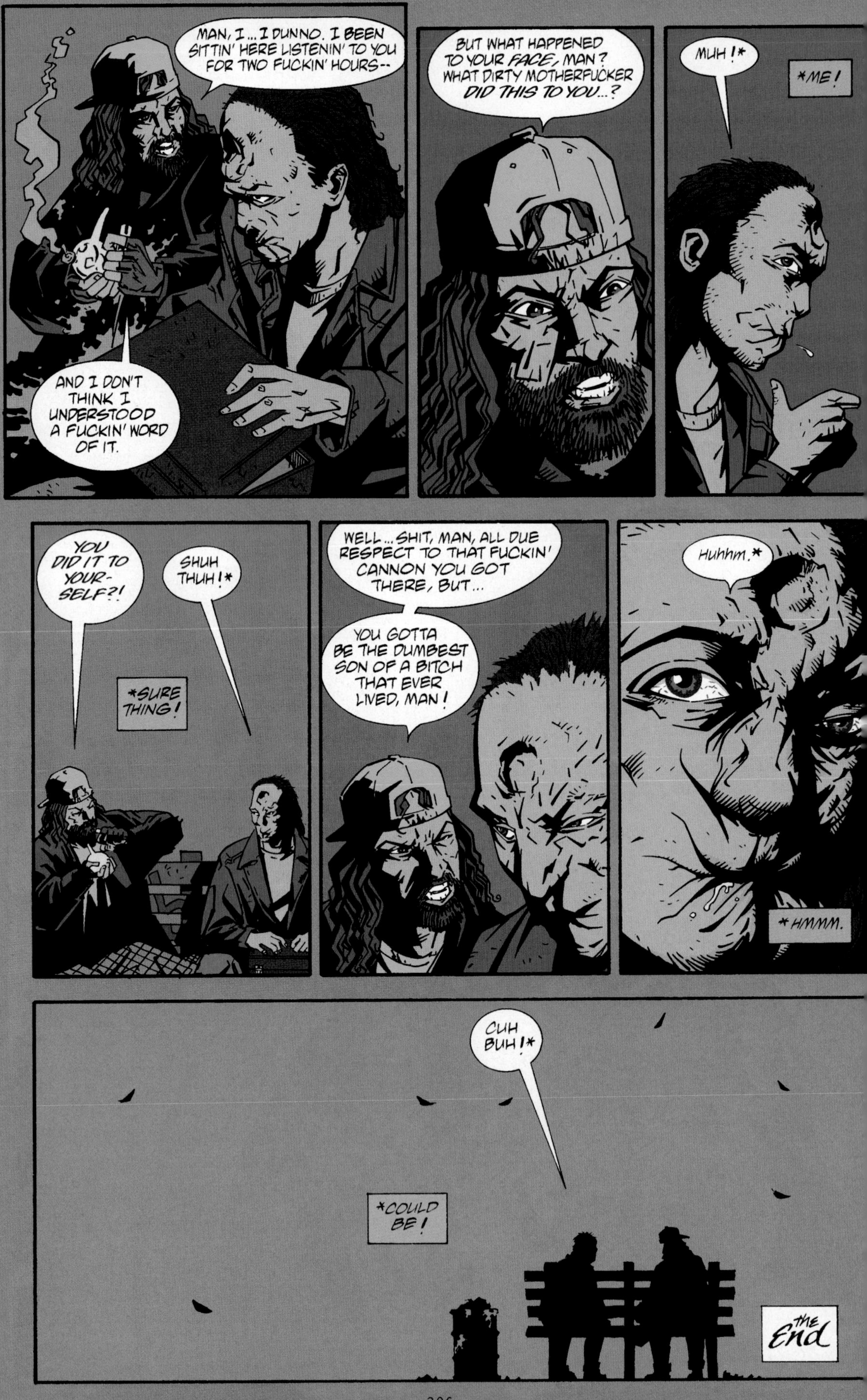
MAN, I... I DUNNO. I BEEN SITTIN' HERE LISTENIN' TO YOU FOR TWO FUCKIN' HOURS--
AND I DON'T THINK I UNDERSTOOD A FUCKIN' WORD OF IT.
BUT WHAT HAPPENED TO YOUR FACE, MAN? WHAT DIRTY MOTHERFUCKER DID THIS TO YOU...?
MUH!*
*ME!
YOU DID IT TO YOUR-SELF?!
SHUH THUH!*
*SURE THING!
WELL... SHIT, MAN, ALL DUE RESPECT TO THAT FUCKIN' CANNON YOU GOT THERE, BUT...
YOU GOTTA BE THE DUMBEST SON OF A BITCH THAT EVER LIVED, MAN!
Huhhm.*
*HMMM.
CUH BUH!*
*COULD BE!
THE End

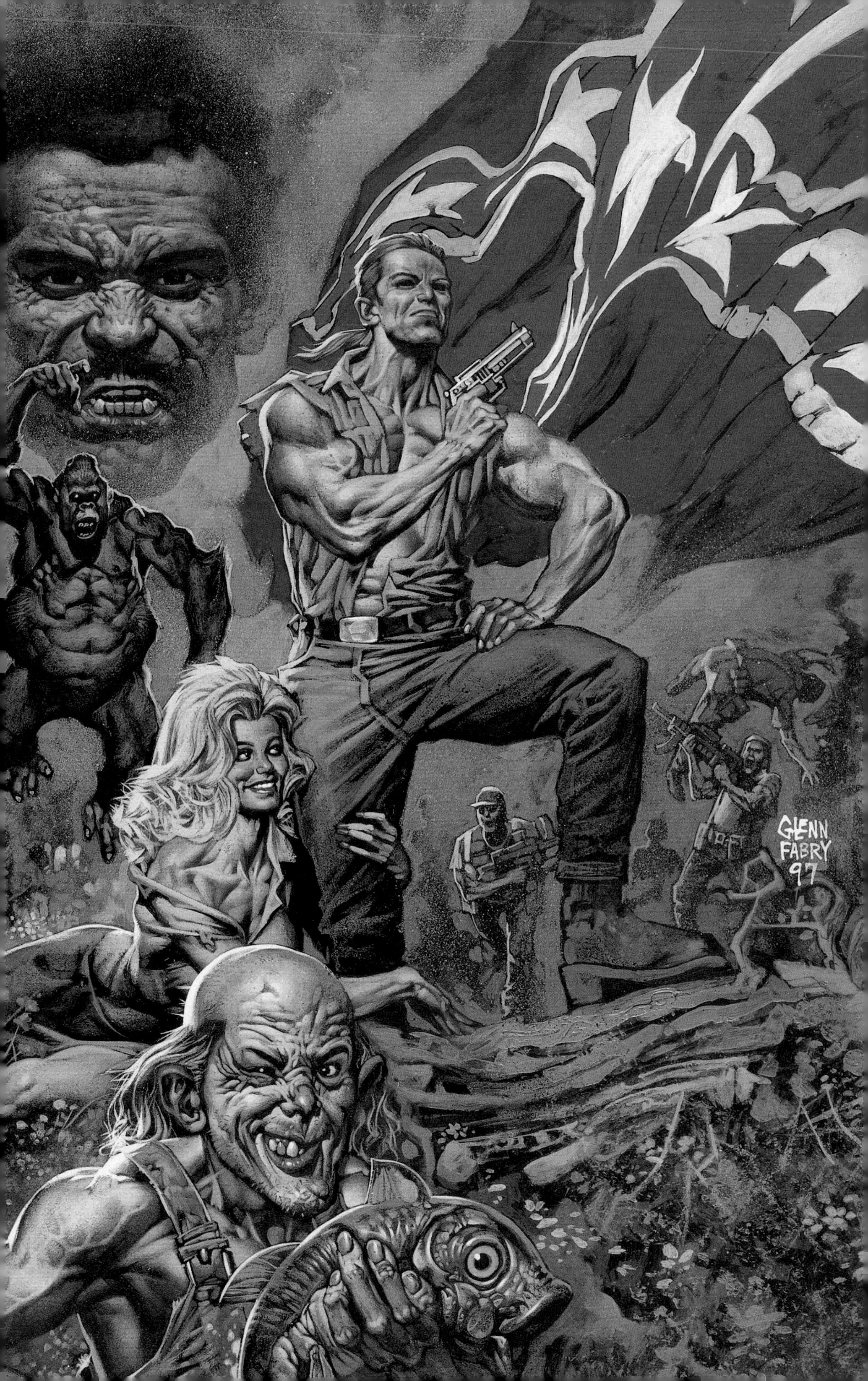
GLENN
FABRY
97

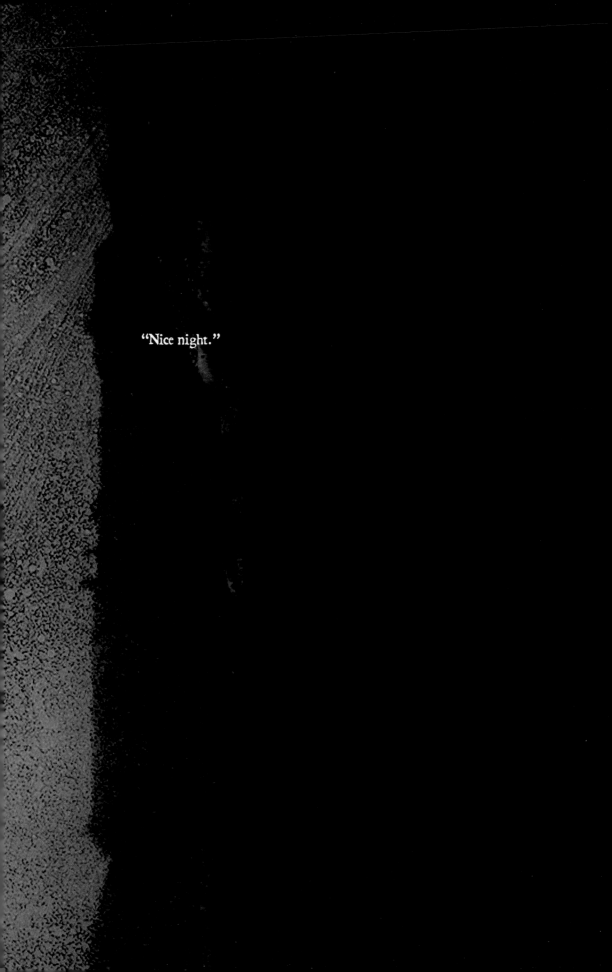

"Nice night."

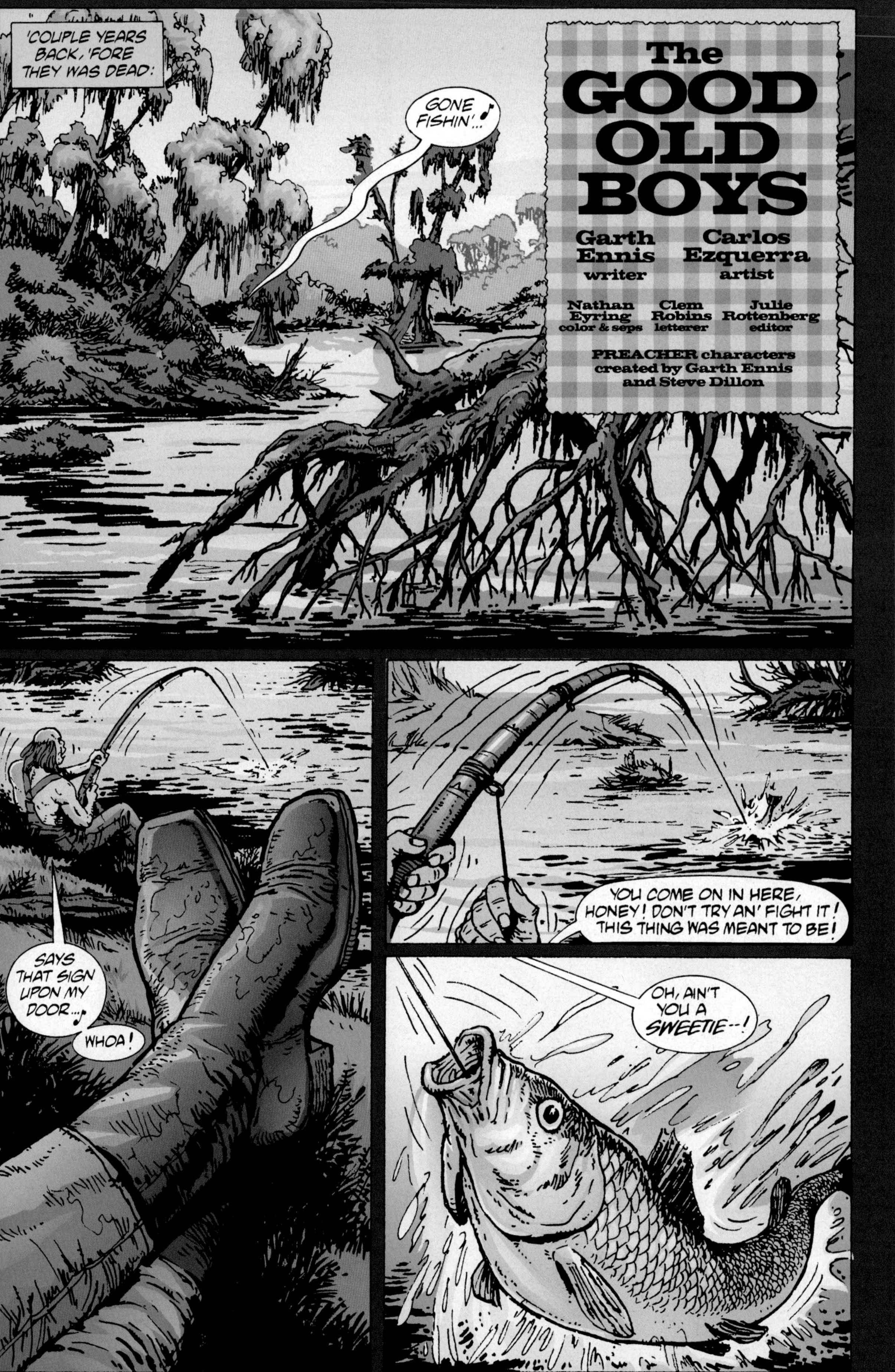

'COUPLE YEARS BACK, 'FORE THEY WAS DEAD:
GONE FISHIN'...
The GOOD OLD BOYS
Garth Ennis writer
Carlos Ezquerra artist
Nathan Eyring color & seps
Clem Robins letterer
Julie Rottenberg editor
PREACHER characters created by Garth Ennis and Steve Dillon
SAYS THAT SIGN UPON MY DOOR...
WHOA!
YOU COME ON IN HERE, HONEY! DON'T TRY AN' FIGHT IT! THIS THING WAS MEANT TO BE!
OH, AIN'T YOU A SWEETIE--!

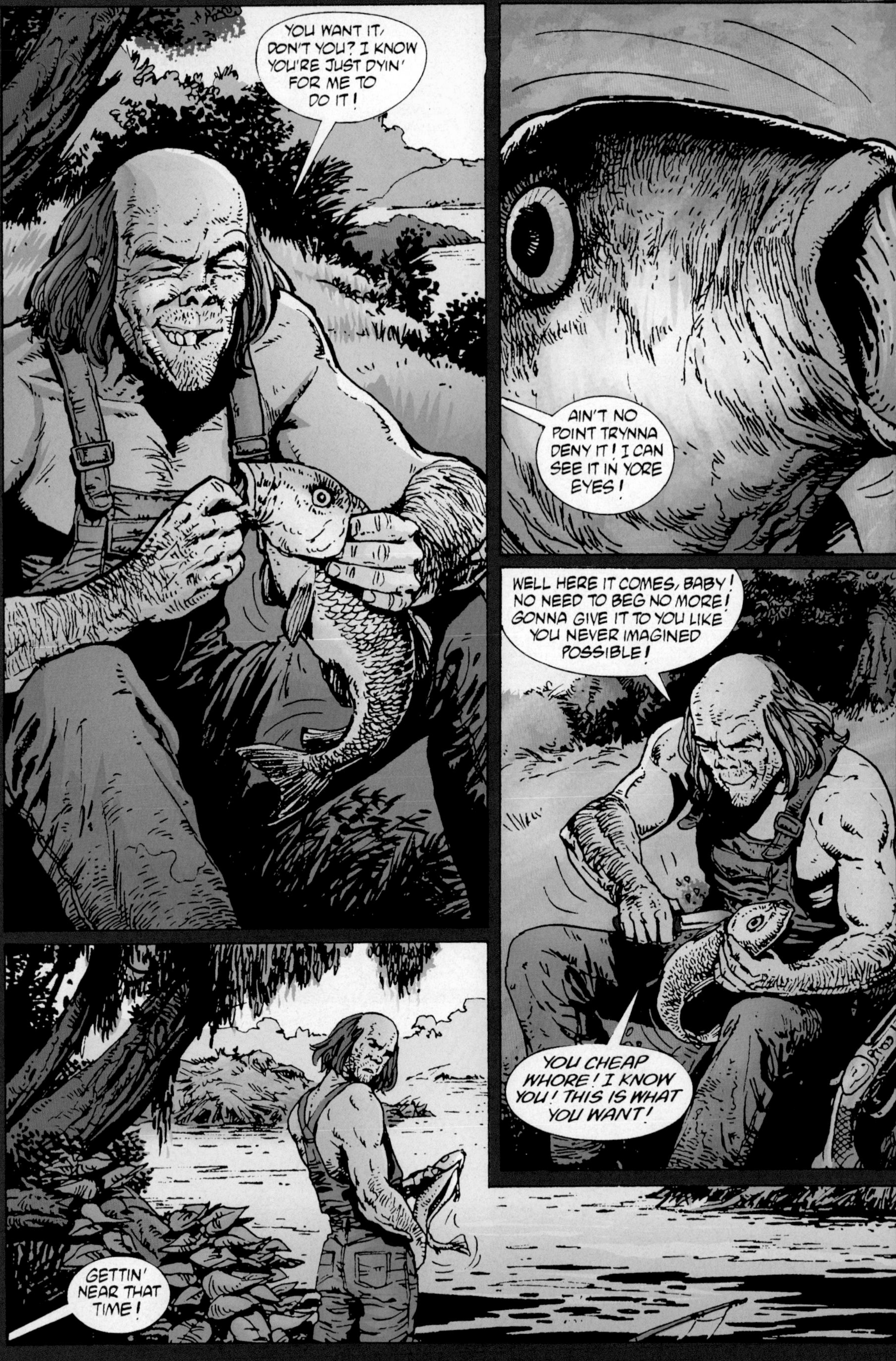

YOU WANT IT, DON'T YOU? I KNOW YOU'RE JUST DYIN' FOR ME TO DO IT!
AIN'T NO POINT TRYNNA DENY IT! I CAN SEE IT IN YORE EYES!
WELL HERE IT COMES, BABY! NO NEED TO BEG NO MORE! GONNA GIVE IT TO YOU LIKE YOU NEVER IMAGINED POSSIBLE!
YOU CHEAP WHORE! I KNOW YOU! THIS IS WHAT YOU WANT!
GETTIN' NEAR THAT TIME!

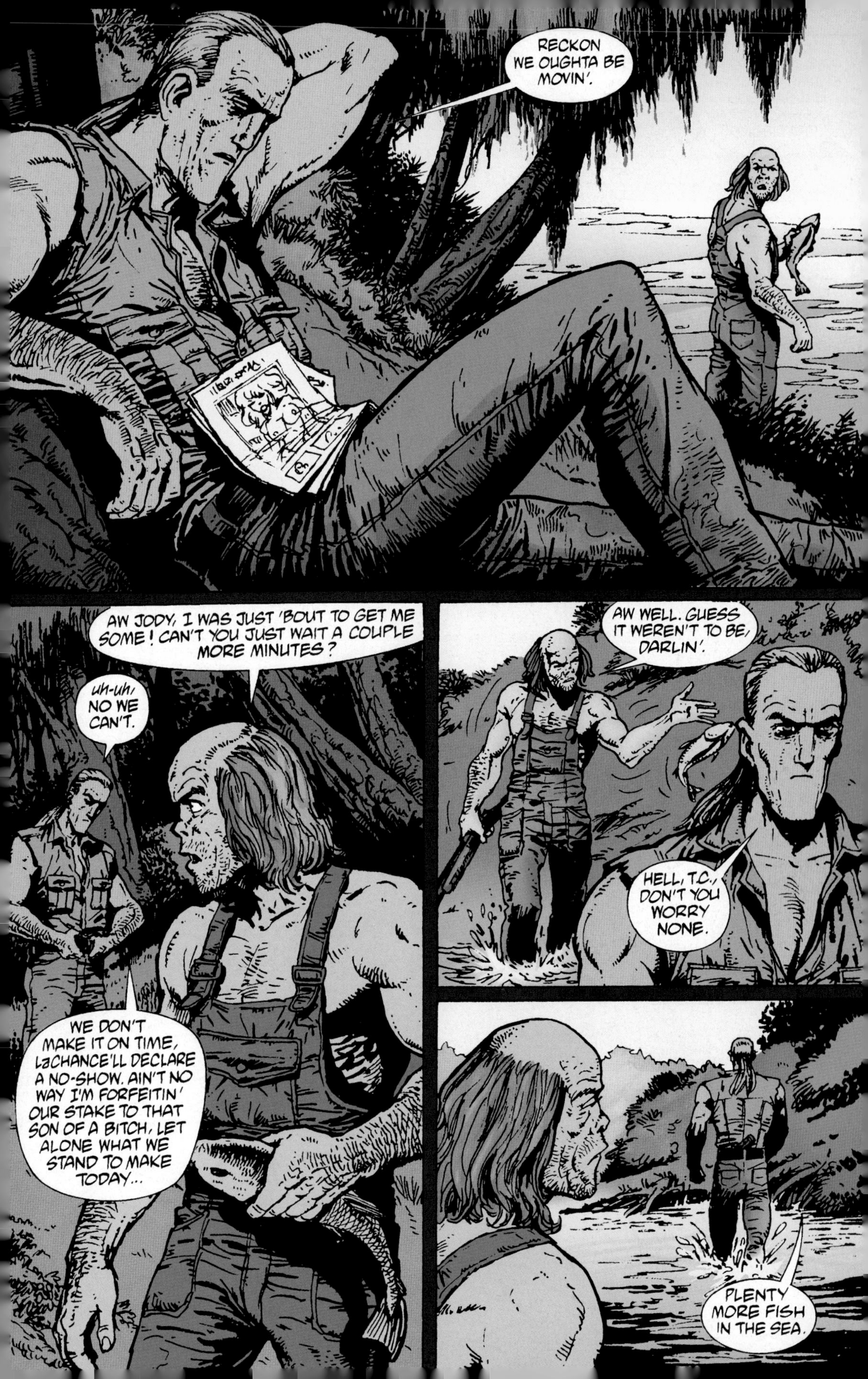
RECKON WE OUGHTA BE MOVIN'.
AW JODY, I WAS JUST 'BOUT TO GET ME SOME! CAN'T YOU JUST WAIT A COUPLE MORE MINUTES?
uh-uh, NO WE CAN'T.
WE DON'T MAKE IT ON TIME, LaCHANCE'LL DECLARE A NO-SHOW. AIN'T NO WAY I'M FORFEITIN' OUR STAKE TO THAT SON OF A BITCH, LET ALONE WHAT WE STAND TO MAKE TODAY...
AW WELL. GUESS IT WEREN'T TO BE, DARLIN'.
HELL, T.C., DON'T YOU WORRY NONE.
PLENTY MORE FISH IN THE SEA.

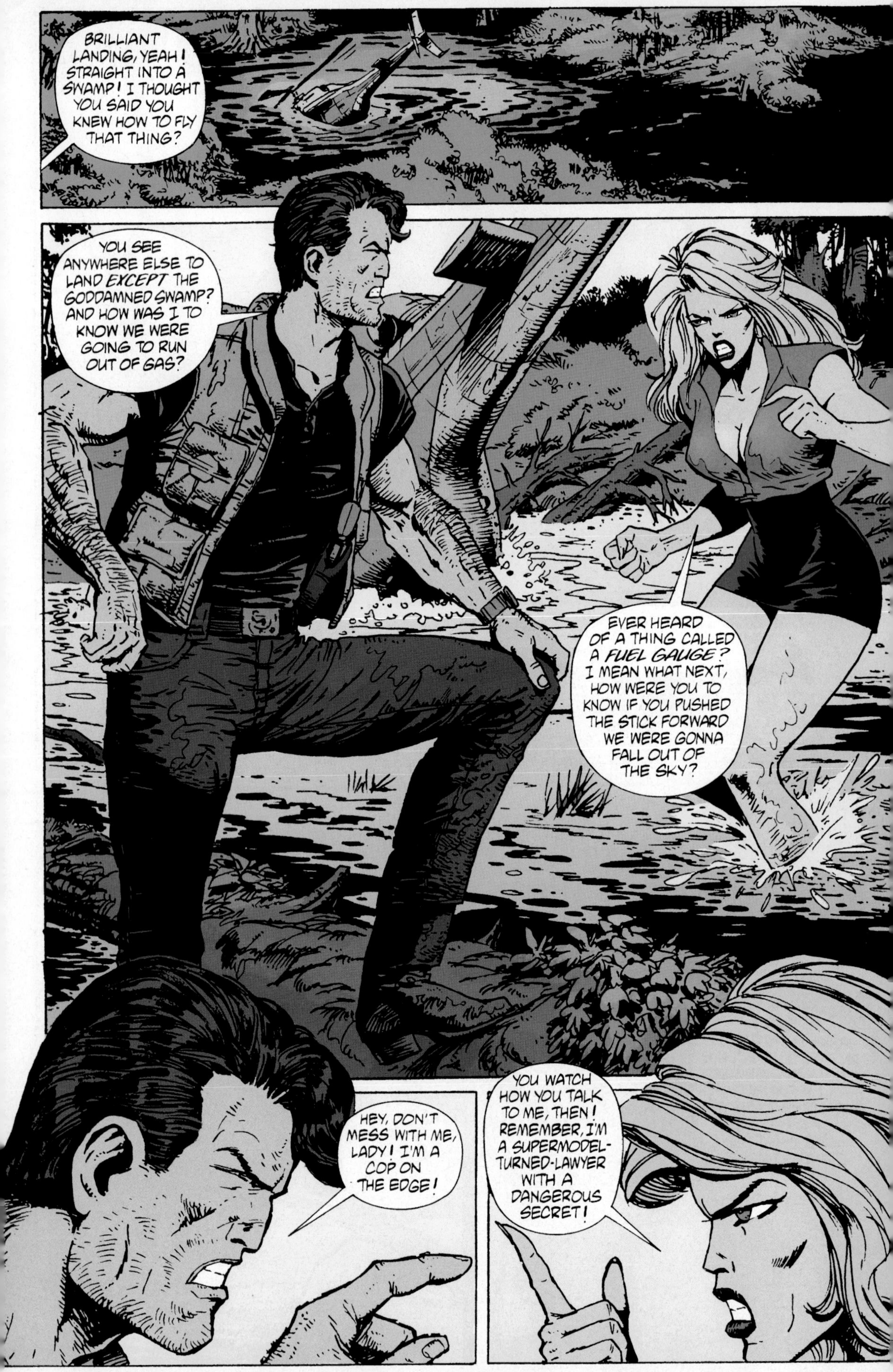
BRILLIANT LANDING, YEAH! STRAIGHT INTO A SWAMP! I THOUGHT YOU SAID YOU KNEW HOW TO FLY THAT THING?
YOU SEE ANYWHERE ELSE TO LAND *EXCEPT* THE GODDAMNED SWAMP? AND HOW WAS I TO KNOW WE WERE GOING TO RUN OUT OF GAS?
EVER HEARD OF A THING CALLED A *FUEL GAUGE*? I MEAN WHAT NEXT, HOW WERE YOU TO KNOW IF YOU PUSHED THE STICK FORWARD WE WERE GONNA FALL OUT OF THE SKY?
HEY, DON'T MESS WITH ME, LADY! I'M A COP ON THE EDGE!
YOU WATCH HOW YOU TALK TO ME, THEN! REMEMBER, I'M A SUPERMODEL-TURNED-LAWYER WITH A DANGEROUS SECRET!

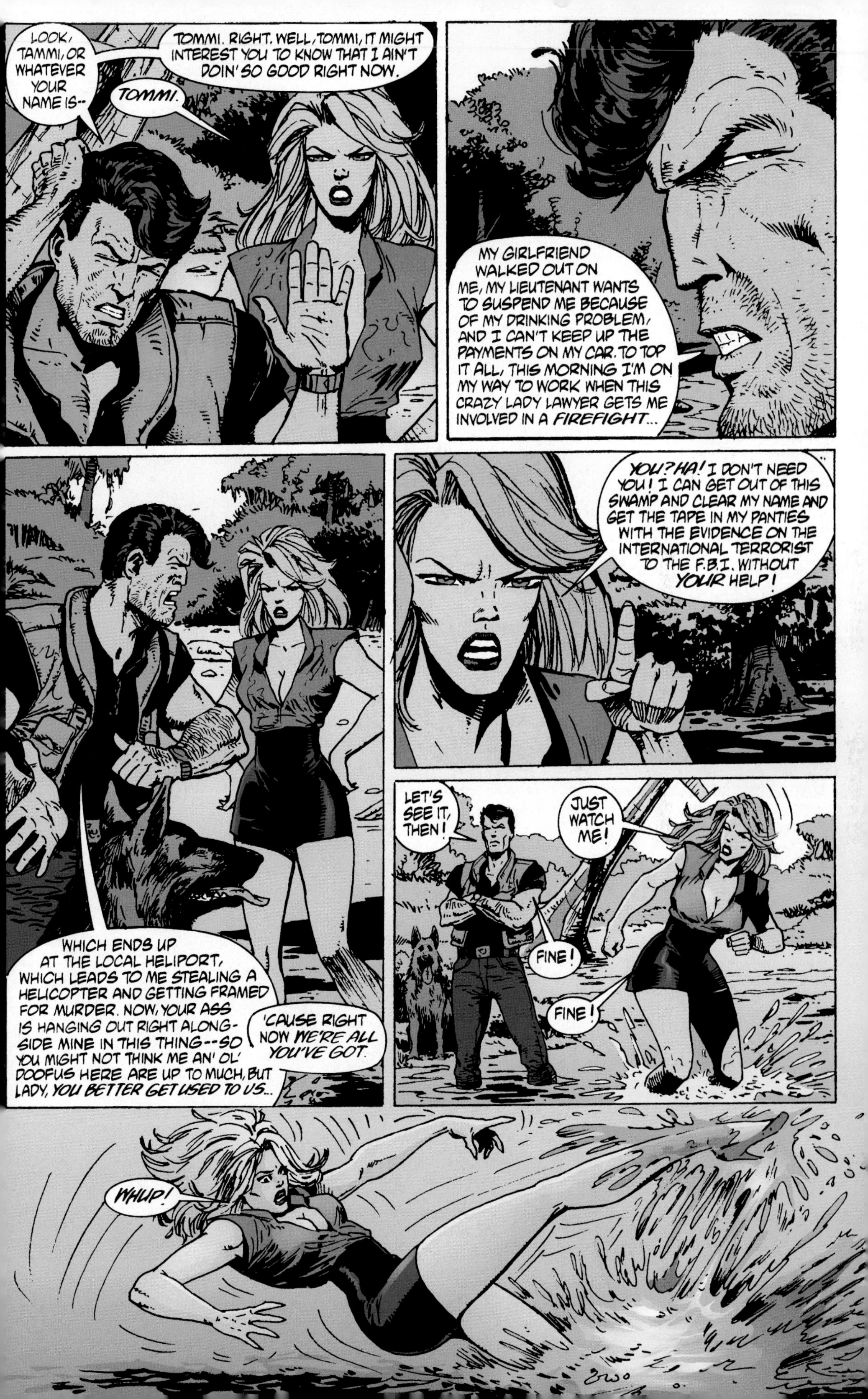
LOOK, TAMMI, OR WHATEVER YOUR NAME IS--
TOMMI.
TOMMI. RIGHT. WELL, TOMMI, IT MIGHT INTEREST YOU TO KNOW THAT I AIN'T DOIN' SO GOOD RIGHT NOW.
MY GIRLFRIEND WALKED OUT ON ME, MY LIEUTENANT WANTS TO SUSPEND ME BECAUSE OF MY DRINKING PROBLEM, AND I CAN'T KEEP UP THE PAYMENTS ON MY CAR. TO TOP IT ALL, THIS MORNING I'M ON MY WAY TO WORK WHEN THIS CRAZY LADY LAWYER GETS ME INVOLVED IN A FIREFIGHT...
WHICH ENDS UP AT THE LOCAL HELIPORT, WHICH LEADS TO ME STEALING A HELICOPTER AND GETTING FRAMED FOR MURDER. NOW, YOUR ASS IS HANGING OUT RIGHT ALONGSIDE MINE IN THIS THING--SO YOU MIGHT NOT THINK ME AN' OL' DOOFUS HERE ARE UP TO MUCH, BUT LADY, YOU BETTER GET USED TO US...
'CAUSE RIGHT NOW WE'RE ALL YOU'VE GOT.
YOU? HA! I DON'T NEED YOU! I CAN GET OUT OF THIS SWAMP AND CLEAR MY NAME AND GET THE TAPE IN MY PANTIES WITH THE EVIDENCE ON THE INTERNATIONAL TERRORIST TO THE F.B.I. WITHOUT YOUR HELP!
LET'S SEE IT, THEN!
JUST WATCH ME!
FINE!
FINE!
WHUP!

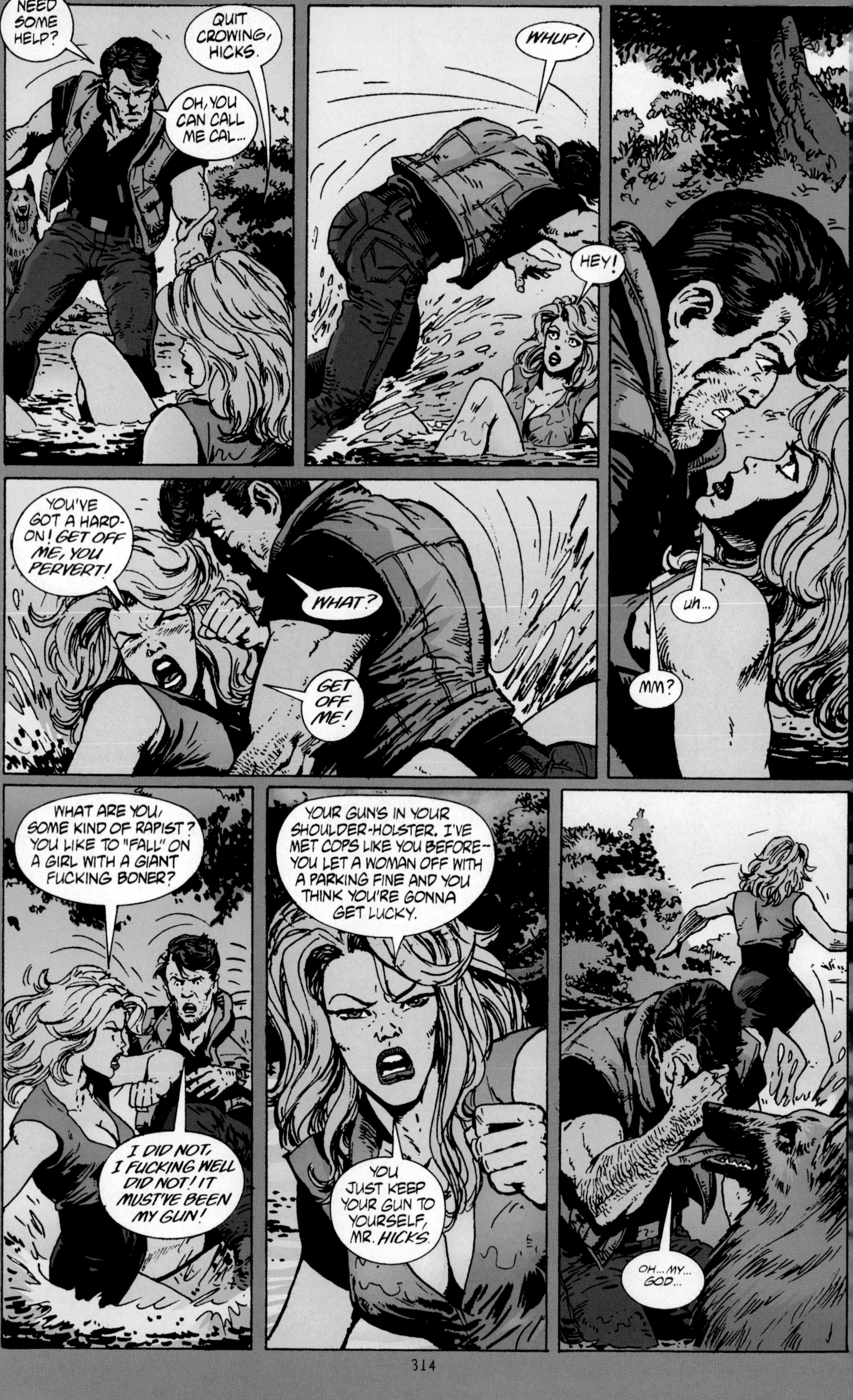
NEED SOME HELP?
QUIT CROWING, HICKS.
OH, YOU CAN CALL ME CAL...
WHUP!
HEY!
uh...
MM?
YOU'VE GOT A HARD-ON! GET OFF ME, YOU PERVERT!
WHAT?
GET OFF ME!
WHAT ARE YOU, SOME KIND OF RAPIST? YOU LIKE TO "FALL" ON A GIRL WITH A GIANT FUCKING BONER?
I DID NOT, I FUCKING WELL DID NOT! IT MUST'VE BEEN MY GUN!
YOUR GUN'S IN YOUR SHOULDER-HOLSTER. I'VE MET COPS LIKE YOU BEFORE-- YOU LET A WOMAN OFF WITH A PARKING FINE AND YOU THINK YOU'RE GONNA GET LUCKY.
YOU JUST KEEP YOUR GUN TO YOURSELF, MR. HICKS.
OH... MY... GOD...

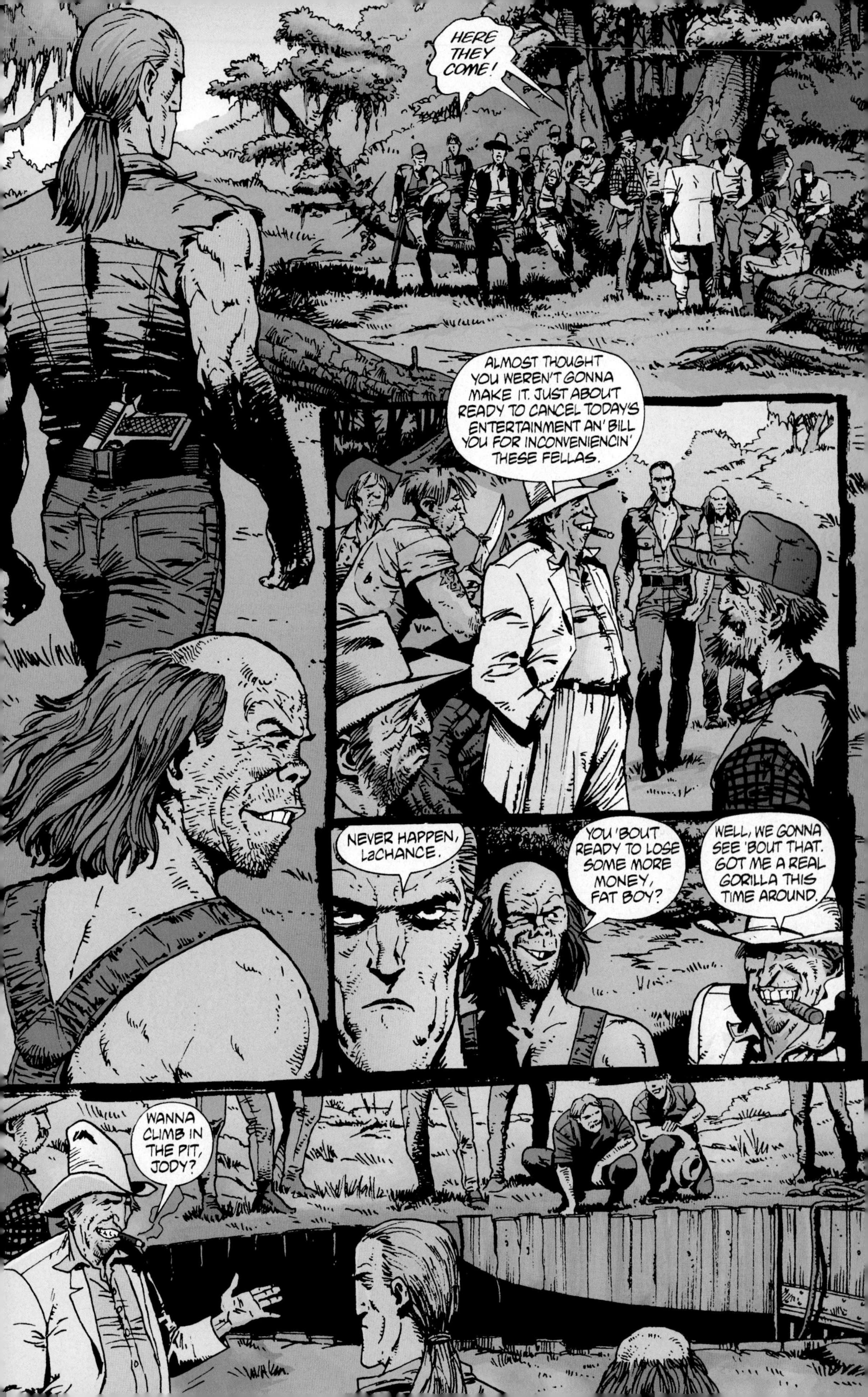
HERE THEY COME!
ALMOST THOUGHT YOU WEREN'T GONNA MAKE IT. JUST ABOUT READY TO CANCEL TODAY'S ENTERTAINMENT AN' BILL YOU FOR INCONVENIENCIN' THESE FELLAS.
NEVER HAPPEN, LaCHANCE.
YOU 'BOUT READY TO LOSE SOME MORE MONEY, FAT BOY?
WELL, WE GONNA SEE 'BOUT THAT. GOT ME A REAL GORILLA THIS TIME AROUND.
WANNA CLIMB IN THE PIT, JODY?

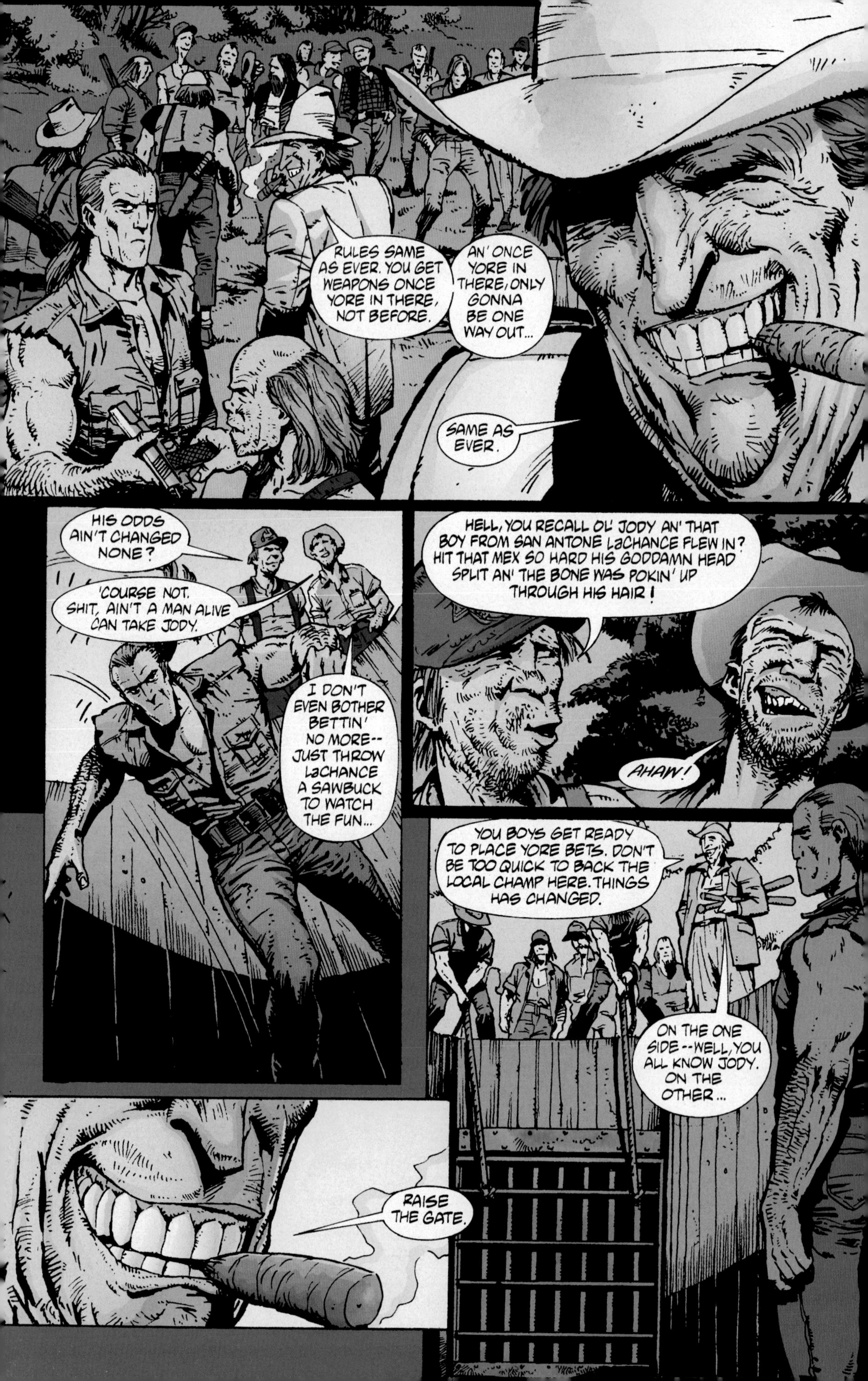
RULES SAME AS EVER. YOU GET WEAPONS ONCE YORE IN THERE, NOT BEFORE.
AN' ONCE YORE IN THERE, ONLY GONNA BE ONE WAY OUT...
SAME AS EVER.
HIS ODDS AIN'T CHANGED NONE?
'COURSE NOT. SHIT, AIN'T A MAN ALIVE CAN TAKE JODY.
I DON'T EVEN BOTHER BETTIN' NO MORE--JUST THROW LaCHANCE A SAWBUCK TO WATCH THE FUN...
HELL, YOU RECALL OL' JODY AN' THAT BOY FROM SAN ANTONE LaCHANCE FLEW IN? HIT THAT MEX SO HARD HIS GODDAMN HEAD SPLIT AN' THE BONE WAS POKIN' UP THROUGH HIS HAIR!
AHAW!
YOU BOYS GET READY TO PLACE YORE BETS. DON'T BE TOO QUICK TO BACK THE LOCAL CHAMP HERE. THINGS HAS CHANGED.
ON THE ONE SIDE--WELL, YOU ALL KNOW JODY. ON THE OTHER...
RAISE THE GATE.

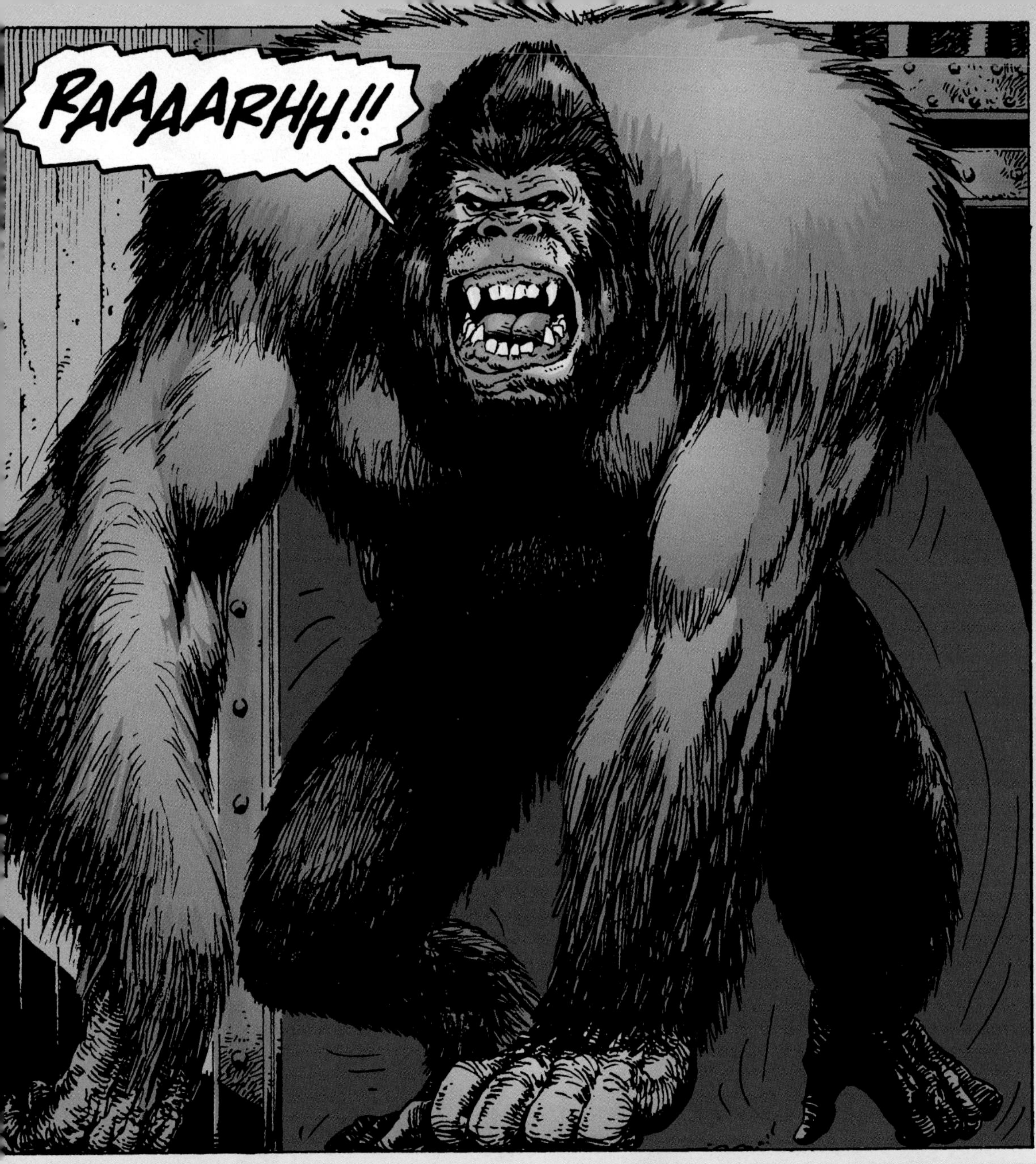
RAAAARHH!!

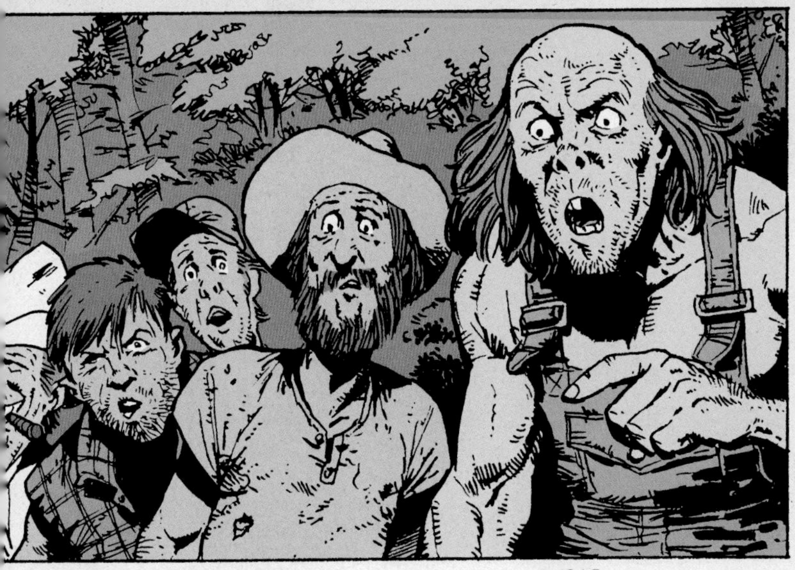

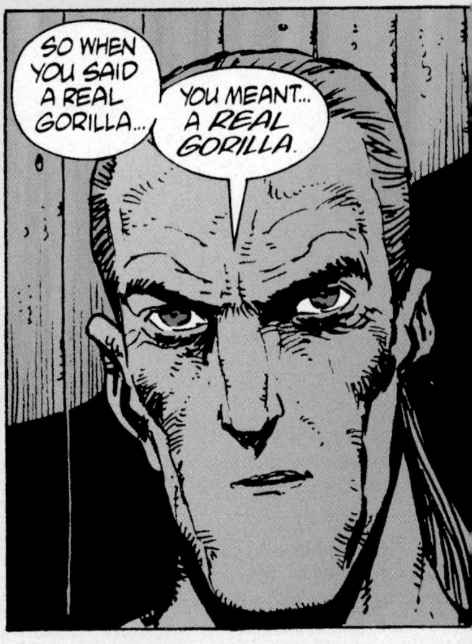
SO WHEN YOU SAID A REAL GORILLA...
YOU MEANT... A REAL GORILLA.

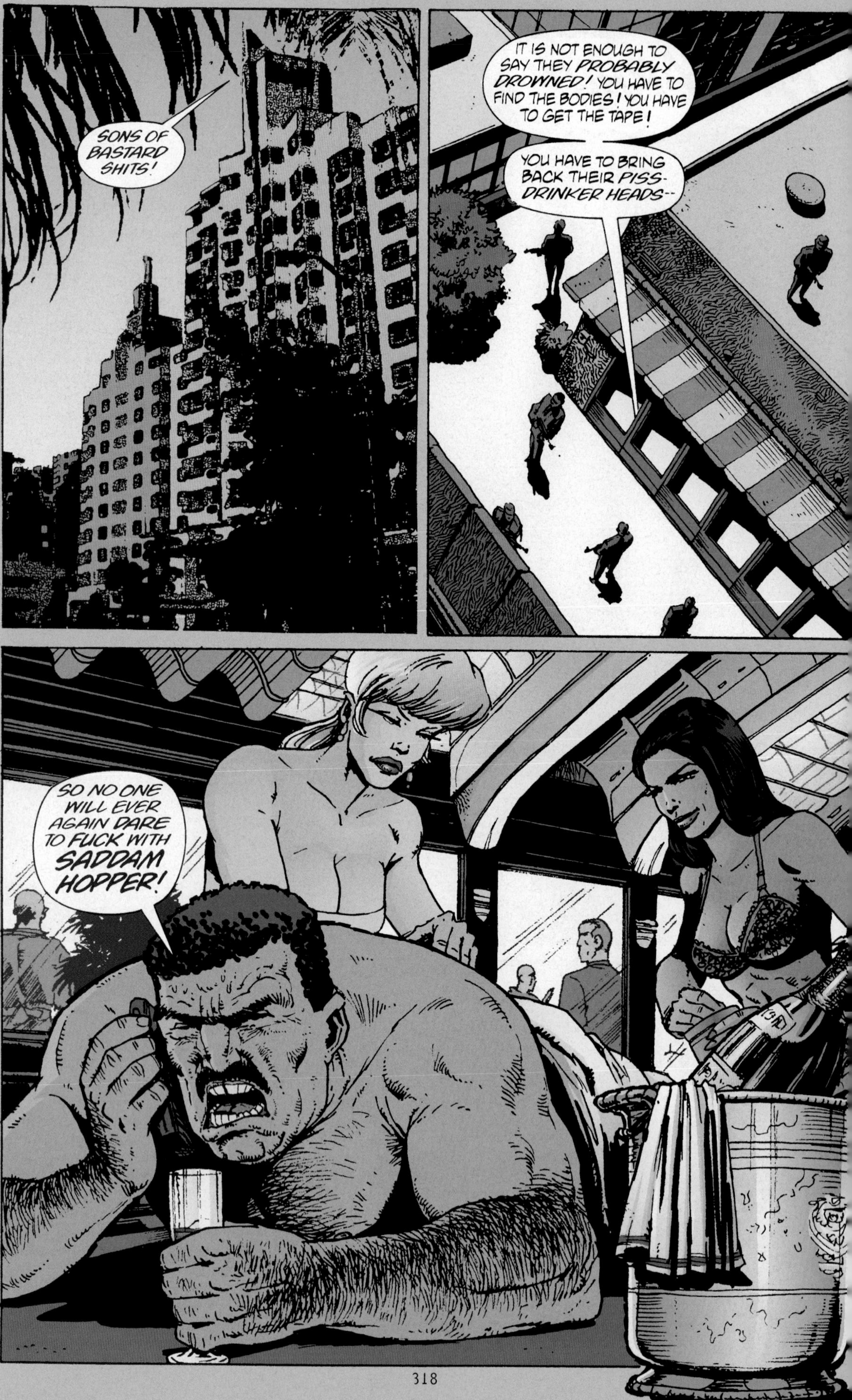
SONS OF BASTARD SHITS!
IT IS NOT ENOUGH TO SAY THEY PROBABLY DROWNED! YOU HAVE TO FIND THE BODIES! YOU HAVE TO GET THE TAPE!
YOU HAVE TO BRING BACK THEIR PISS-DRINKER HEADS--
SO NO ONE WILL EVER AGAIN DARE TO FUCK WITH SADDAM HOPPER!

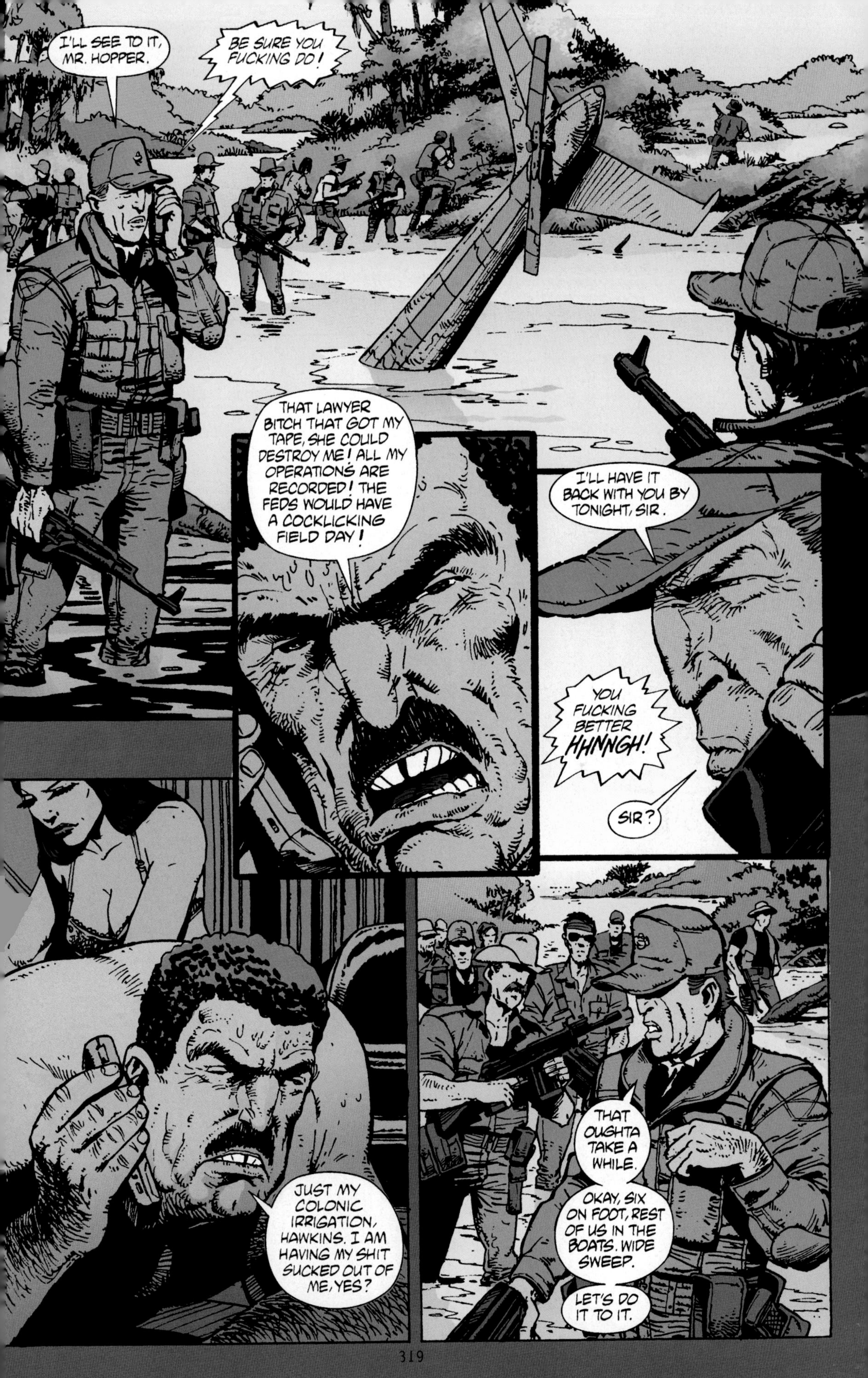
I'LL SEE TO IT, MR. HOPPER.
BE SURE YOU FUCKING DO!
THAT LAWYER BITCH THAT GOT MY TAPE, SHE COULD DESTROY ME! ALL MY OPERATIONS ARE RECORDED! THE FEDS WOULD HAVE A COCKLICKING FIELD DAY!
I'LL HAVE IT BACK WITH YOU BY TONIGHT, SIR.
YOU FUCKING BETTER HHNNGH!
SIR?
JUST MY COLONIC IRRIGATION, HAWKINS. I AM HAVING MY SHIT SUCKED OUT OF ME, YES?
THAT OUGHTA TAKE A WHILE.
OKAY, SIX ON FOOT, REST OF US IN THE BOATS. WIDE SWEEP.
LET'S DO IT TO IT.

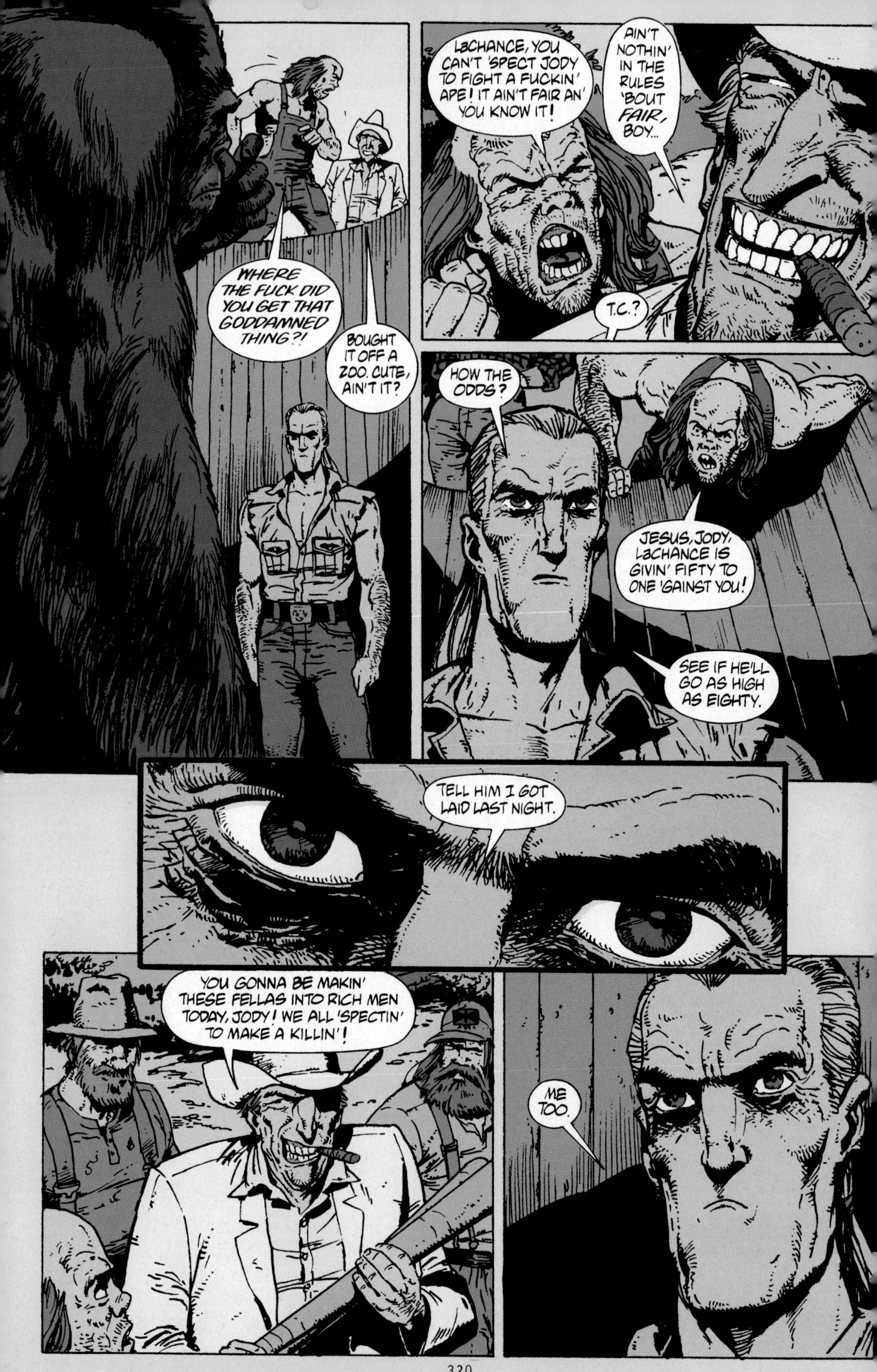
WHERE THE FUCK DID YOU GET THAT GODDAMNED THING?!
BOUGHT IT OFF A ZOO. CUTE, AIN'T IT?
LaCHANCE, YOU CAN'T 'SPECT JODY TO FIGHT A FUCKIN' APE! IT AIN'T FAIR AN' YOU KNOW IT!
AIN'T NOTHIN' IN THE RULES 'BOUT FAIR, BOY...
T.C.?
HOW THE ODDS?
JESUS, JODY, LaCHANCE IS GIVIN' FIFTY TO ONE 'GAINST YOU!
SEE IF HE'LL GO AS HIGH AS EIGHTY.
TELL HIM I GOT LAID LAST NIGHT.
YOU GONNA BE MAKIN' THESE FELLAS INTO RICH MEN TODAY, JODY! WE ALL 'SPECTIN' TO MAKE A KILLIN'!
ME TOO.

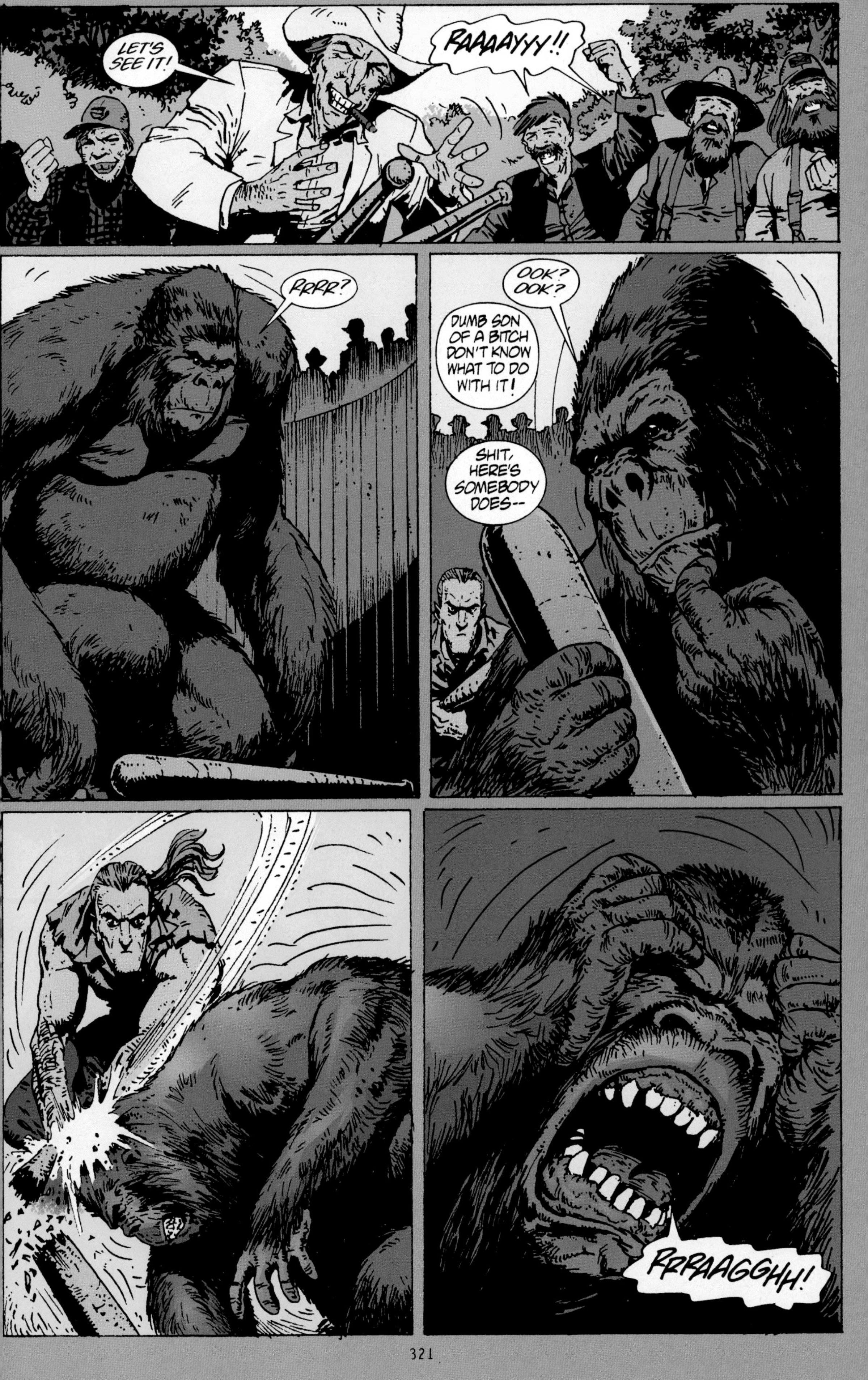
LET'S SEE IT!
RAAAAYYY!!
RRRR?
OOK? OOK?
DUMB SON OF A BITCH DON'T KNOW WHAT TO DO WITH IT!
SHIT, HERE'S SOMEBODY DOES--
RRRAAGGHH!

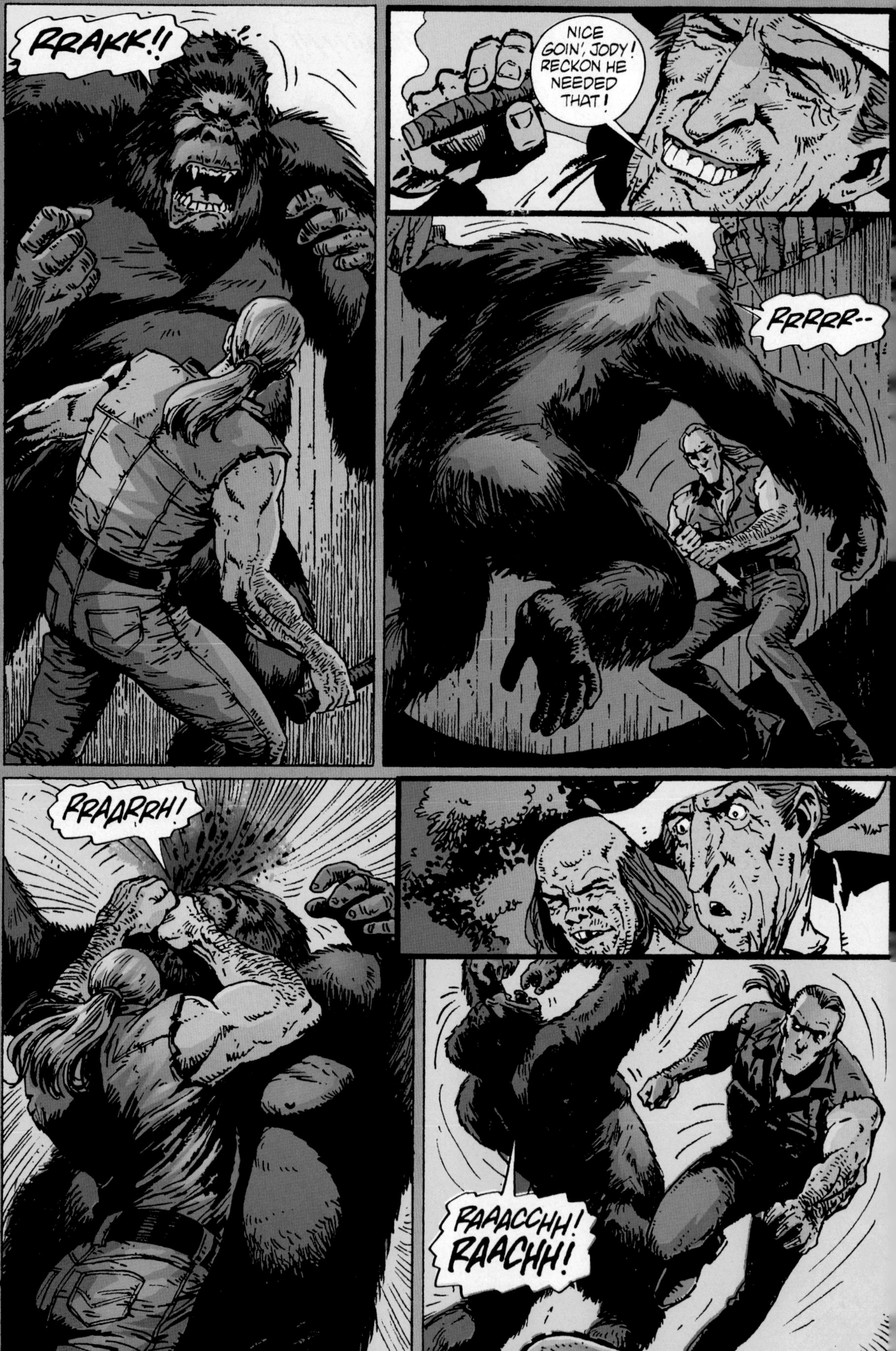
RRAKK!!
NICE GOIN', JODY! RECKON HE NEEDED THAT!
RRRRR--
RRAARRH!
RAAACCHH! RAACHH!

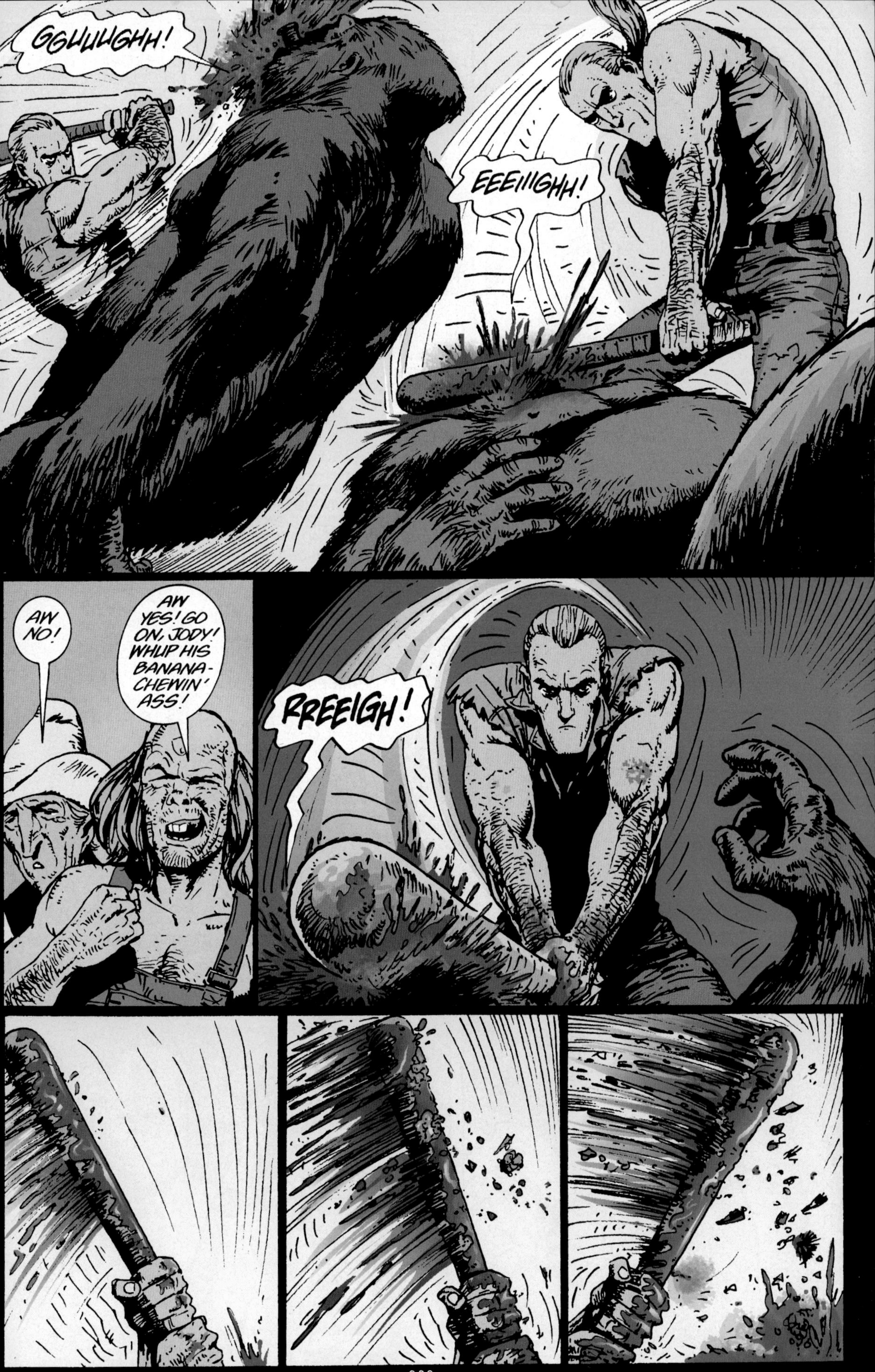
GGUUUGHH!
EEEIIIGHH!
AW NO!
AW YES! GO ON, JODY! WHUP HIS BANANA-CHEWIN' ASS!
RREEIGH!

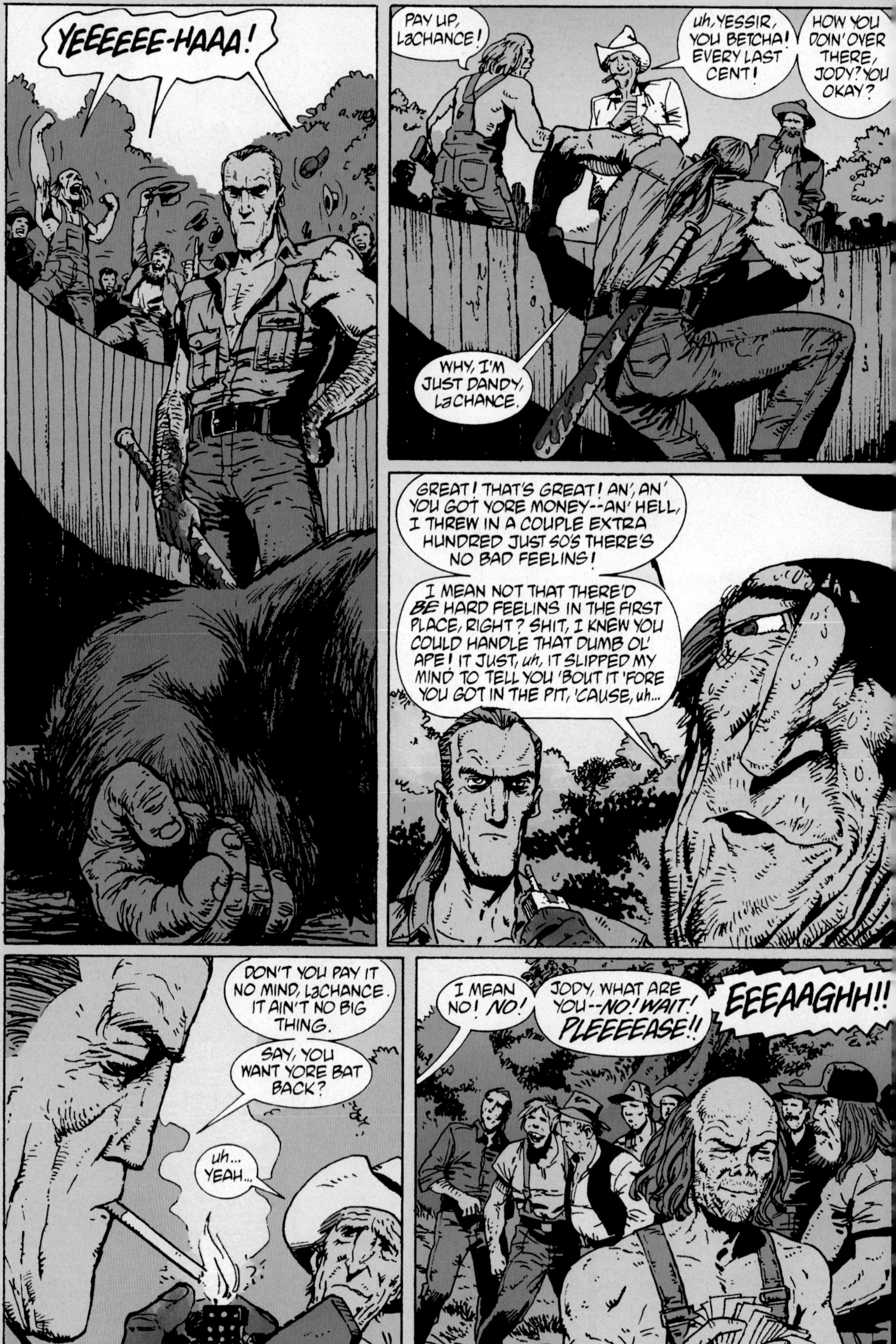
YEEEEEE-HAAA!
PAY UP, LaCHANCE!
uh, YESSIR, YOU BETCHA! EVERY LAST CENT!
HOW YOU DOIN' OVER THERE, JODY? YOU OKAY?
WHY, I'M JUST DANDY, LaCHANCE.
GREAT! THAT'S GREAT! AN', AN' YOU GOT YORE MONEY--AN' HELL, I THREW IN A COUPLE EXTRA HUNDRED JUST SO'S THERE'S NO BAD FEELINS!
I MEAN NOT THAT THERE'D BE HARD FEELINS IN THE FIRST PLACE, RIGHT? SHIT, I KNEW YOU COULD HANDLE THAT DUMB OL' APE! IT JUST, uh, IT SLIPPED MY MIND TO TELL YOU 'BOUT IT 'FORE YOU GOT IN THE PIT, 'CAUSE, uh...
DON'T YOU PAY IT NO MIND, LaCHANCE. IT AIN'T NO BIG THING.
SAY, YOU WANT YORE BAT BACK?
uh... YEAH...
FUCK COMMUNISM
I MEAN NO! NO!
JODY, WHAT ARE YOU--NO! WAIT! PLEEEEASE!!
EEEAAGHH!!

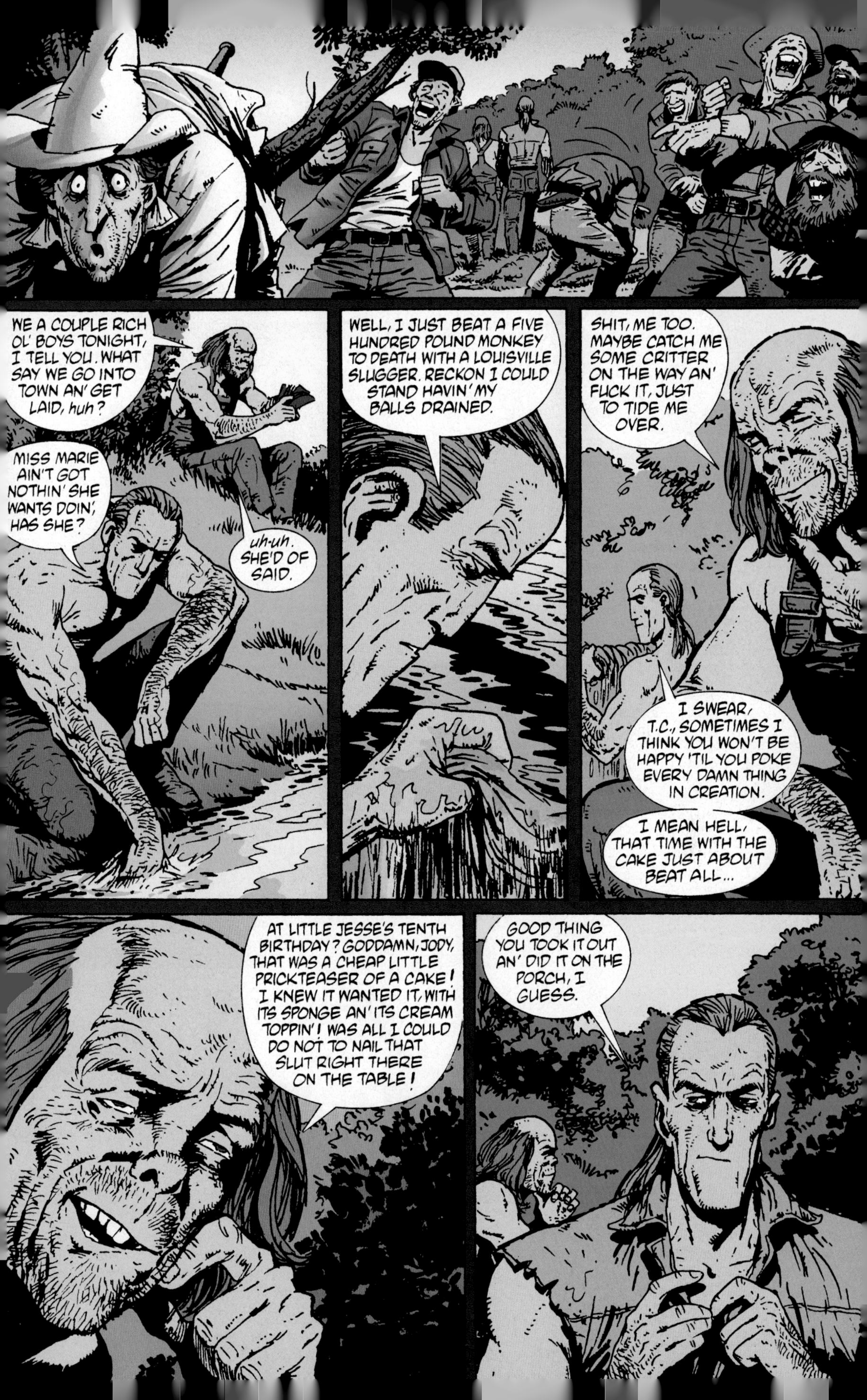
WE A COUPLE RICH OL' BOYS TONIGHT, I TELL YOU. WHAT SAY WE GO INTO TOWN AN' GET LAID, huh?
MISS MARIE AIN'T GOT NOTHIN' SHE WANTS DOIN', HAS SHE?
uh-uh. SHE'D OF SAID.
WELL, I JUST BEAT A FIVE HUNDRED POUND MONKEY TO DEATH WITH A LOUISVILLE SLUGGER. RECKON I COULD STAND HAVIN' MY BALLS DRAINED.
SHIT, ME TOO. MAYBE CATCH ME SOME CRITTER ON THE WAY AN' FUCK IT, JUST TO TIDE ME OVER.
I SWEAR, T.C., SOMETIMES I THINK YOU WON'T BE HAPPY 'TIL YOU POKE EVERY DAMN THING IN CREATION.
I MEAN HELL, THAT TIME WITH THE CAKE JUST ABOUT BEAT ALL...
AT LITTLE JESSE'S TENTH BIRTHDAY? GODDAMN, JODY, THAT WAS A CHEAP LITTLE PRICKTEASER OF A CAKE! I KNEW IT WANTED IT, WITH ITS SPONGE AN' ITS CREAM TOPPIN'! WAS ALL I COULD DO NOT TO NAIL THAT SLUT RIGHT THERE ON THE TABLE!
GOOD THING YOU TOOK IT OUT AN' DID IT ON THE PORCH, I GUESS.

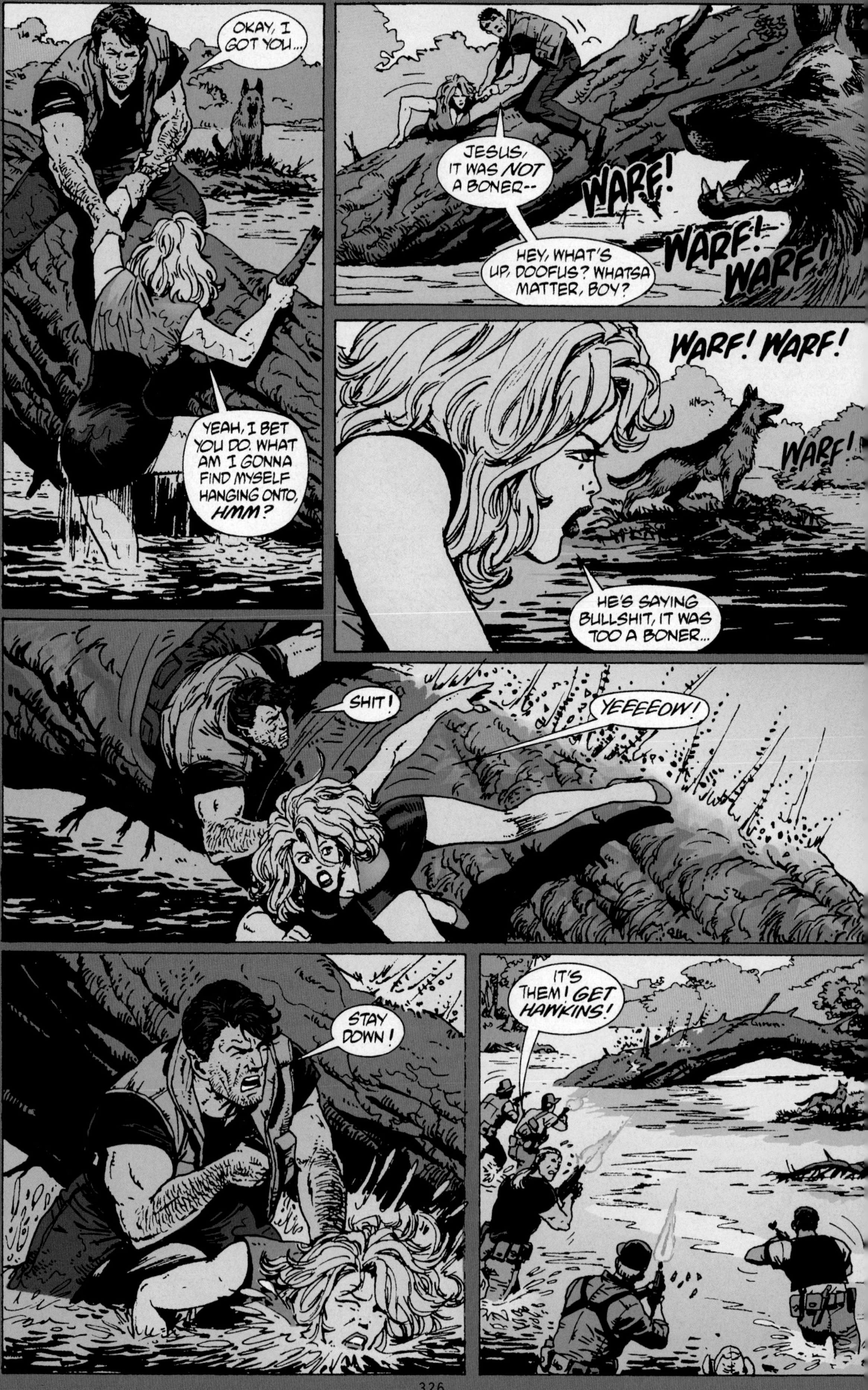
OKAY, I GOT YOU...
YEAH, I BET YOU DO. WHAT AM I GONNA FIND MYSELF HANGING ONTO, HMM?
JESUS, IT WAS NOT A BONER--
HEY, WHAT'S UP, DOOFUS? WHATSA MATTER, BOY?
WARF!
WARF! WARF!
WARF! WARF!
WARF!
HE'S SAYING BULLSHIT, IT WAS TOO A BONER...
SHIT!
YEEEEOW!
STAY DOWN!
IT'S THEM! GET HAWKINS!

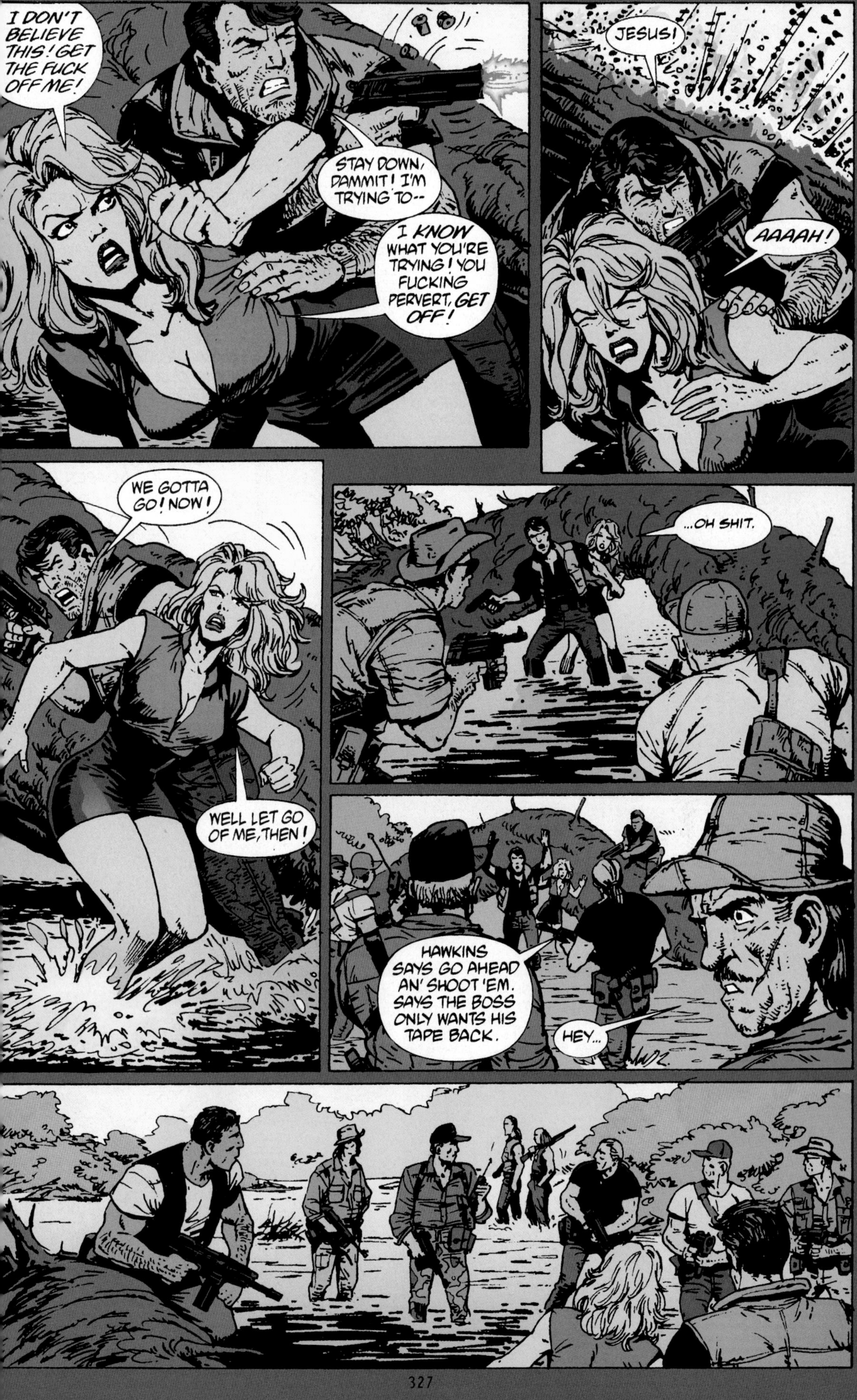

I DON'T BELIEVE THIS! GET THE FUCK OFF ME!
STAY DOWN, DAMMIT! I'M TRYING TO--
I KNOW WHAT YOU'RE TRYING! YOU FUCKING PERVERT, GET OFF!
JESUS!
AAAAH!
WE GOTTA GO! NOW!
WELL LET GO OF ME, THEN!
...OH SHIT.
HAWKINS SAYS GO AHEAD AN' SHOOT 'EM. SAYS THE BOSS ONLY WANTS HIS TAPE BACK.
HEY...

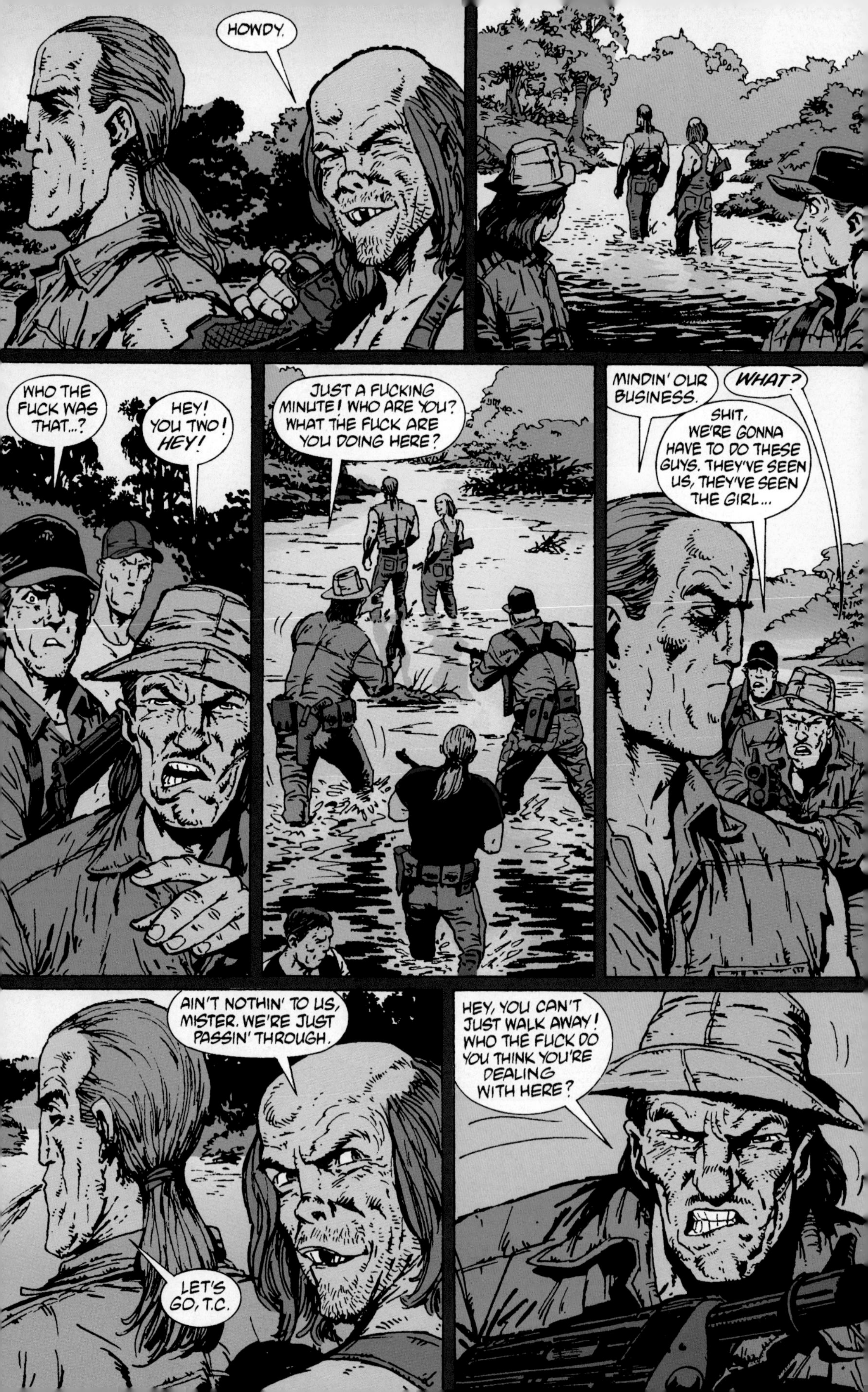
HOWDY.
WHO THE FUCK WAS THAT...?
HEY! YOU TWO! HEY!
JUST A FUCKING MINUTE! WHO ARE YOU? WHAT THE FUCK ARE YOU DOING HERE?
MINDIN' OUR BUSINESS.
WHAT?
SHIT, WE'RE GONNA HAVE TO DO THESE GUYS. THEY'VE SEEN US, THEY'VE SEEN THE GIRL...
AIN'T NOTHIN' TO US, MISTER. WE'RE JUST PASSIN' THROUGH.
LET'S GO, T.C.
HEY, YOU CAN'T JUST WALK AWAY! WHO THE FUCK DO YOU THINK YOU'RE DEALING WITH HERE?

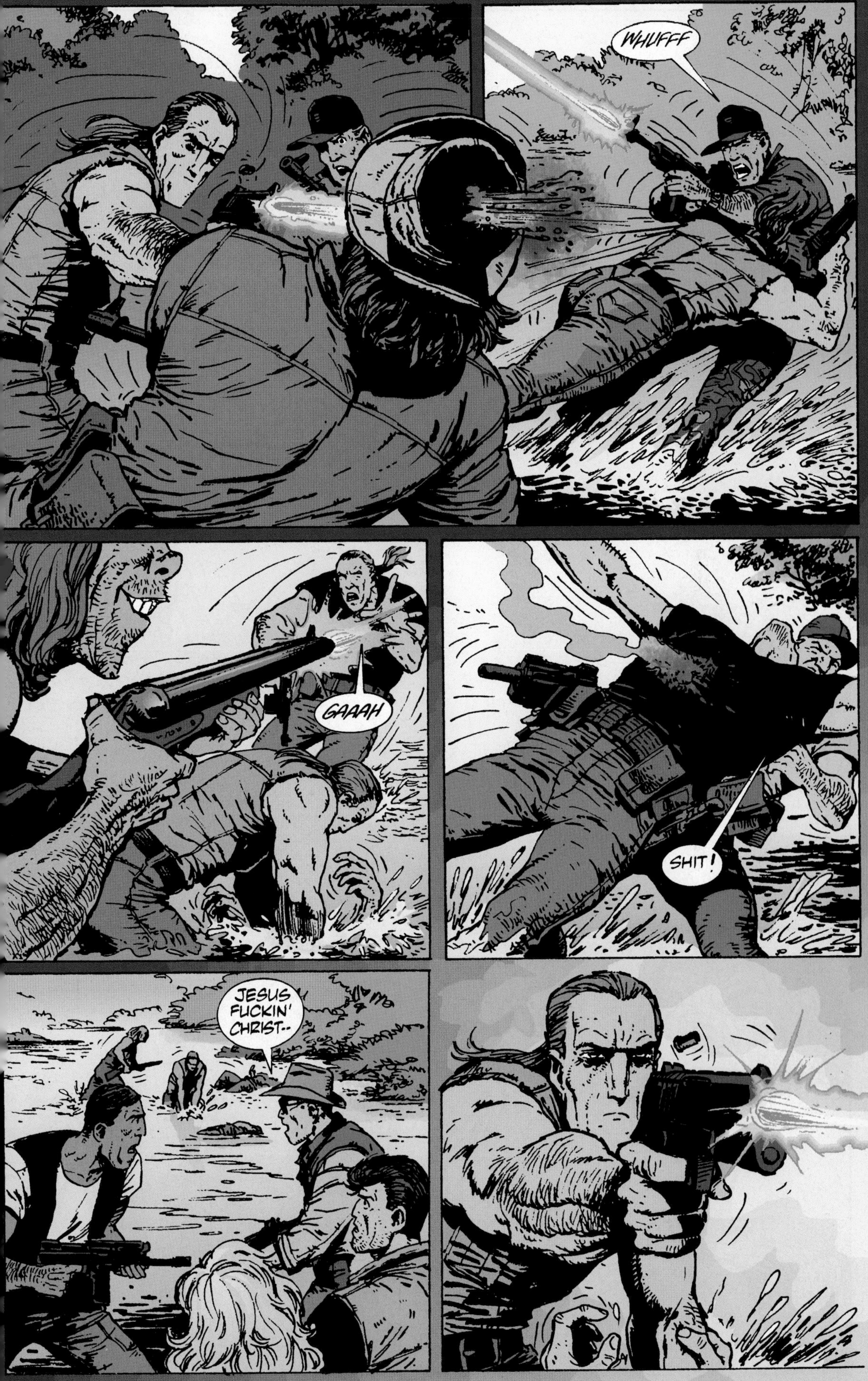
WHUFFF
GAAAH
SHIT!
JESUS FUCKIN' CHRIST--

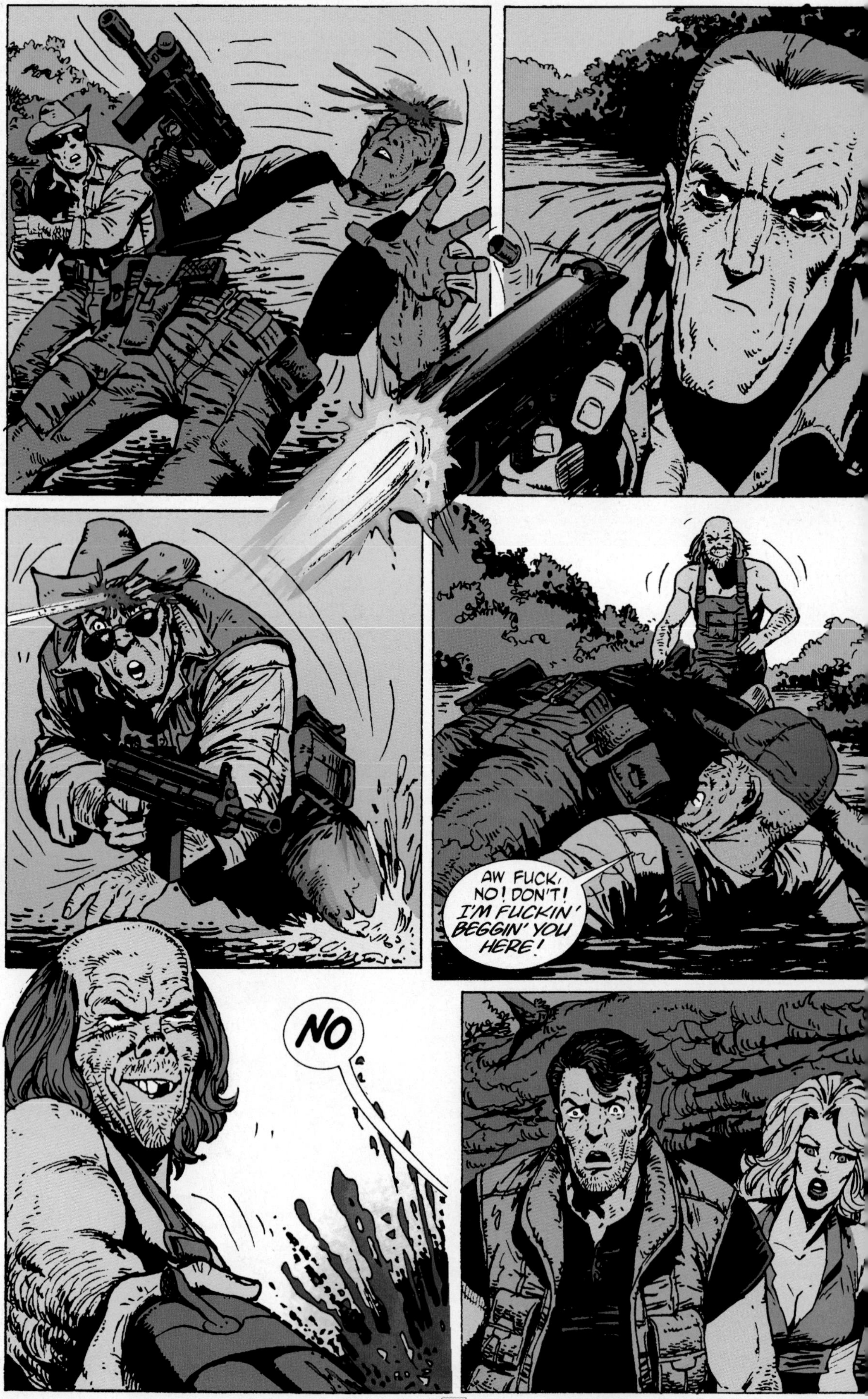
AW FUCK, NO! DON'T! I'M FUCKIN' BEGGIN' YOU HERE!
NO

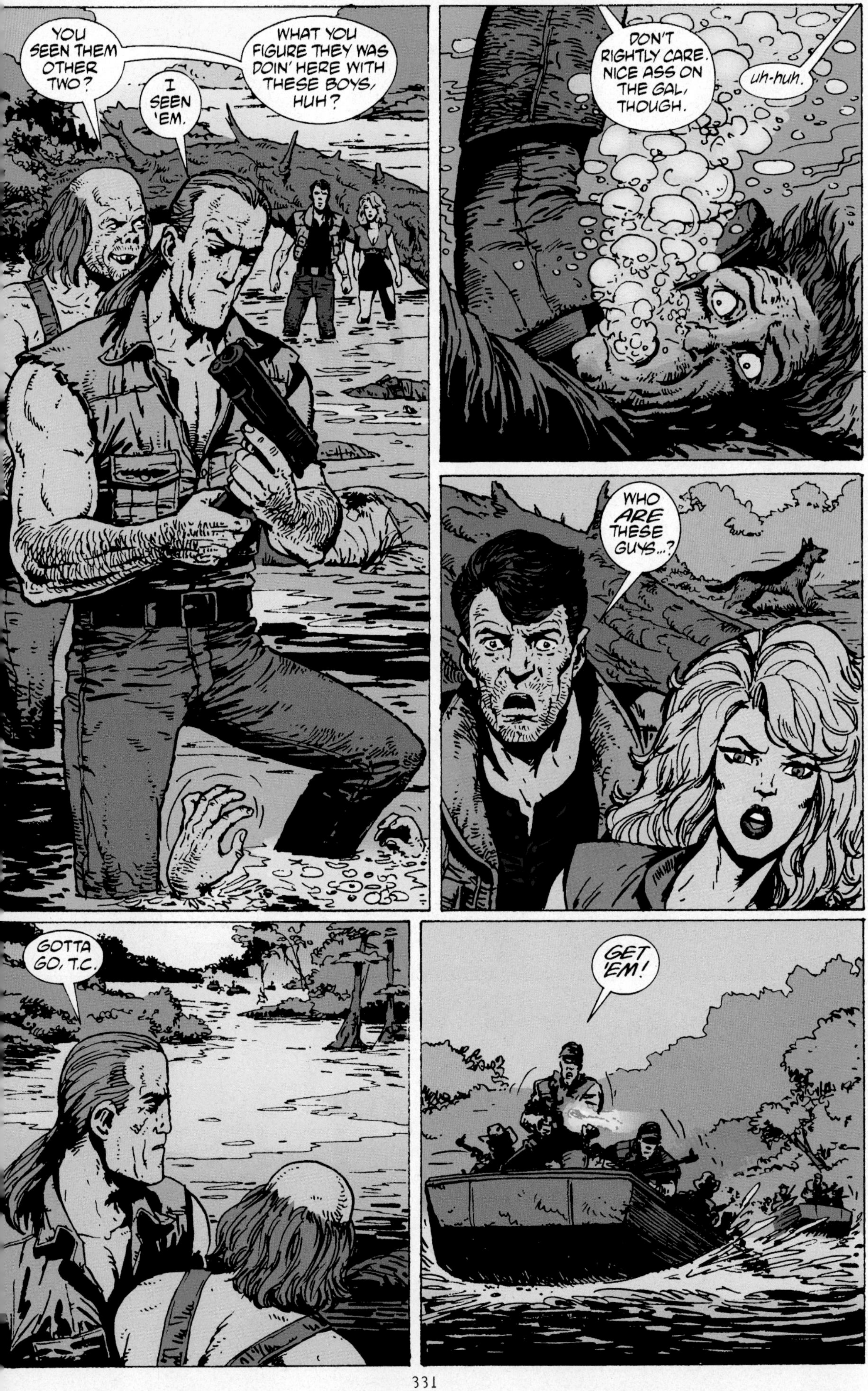
YOU SEEN THEM OTHER TWO?
I SEEN 'EM.
WHAT YOU FIGURE THEY WAS DOIN' HERE WITH THESE BOYS, HUH?
DON'T RIGHTLY CARE. NICE ASS ON THE GAL, THOUGH.
uh-huh.
WHO ARE THESE GUYS...?
GOTTA GO, T.C.
GET 'EM!

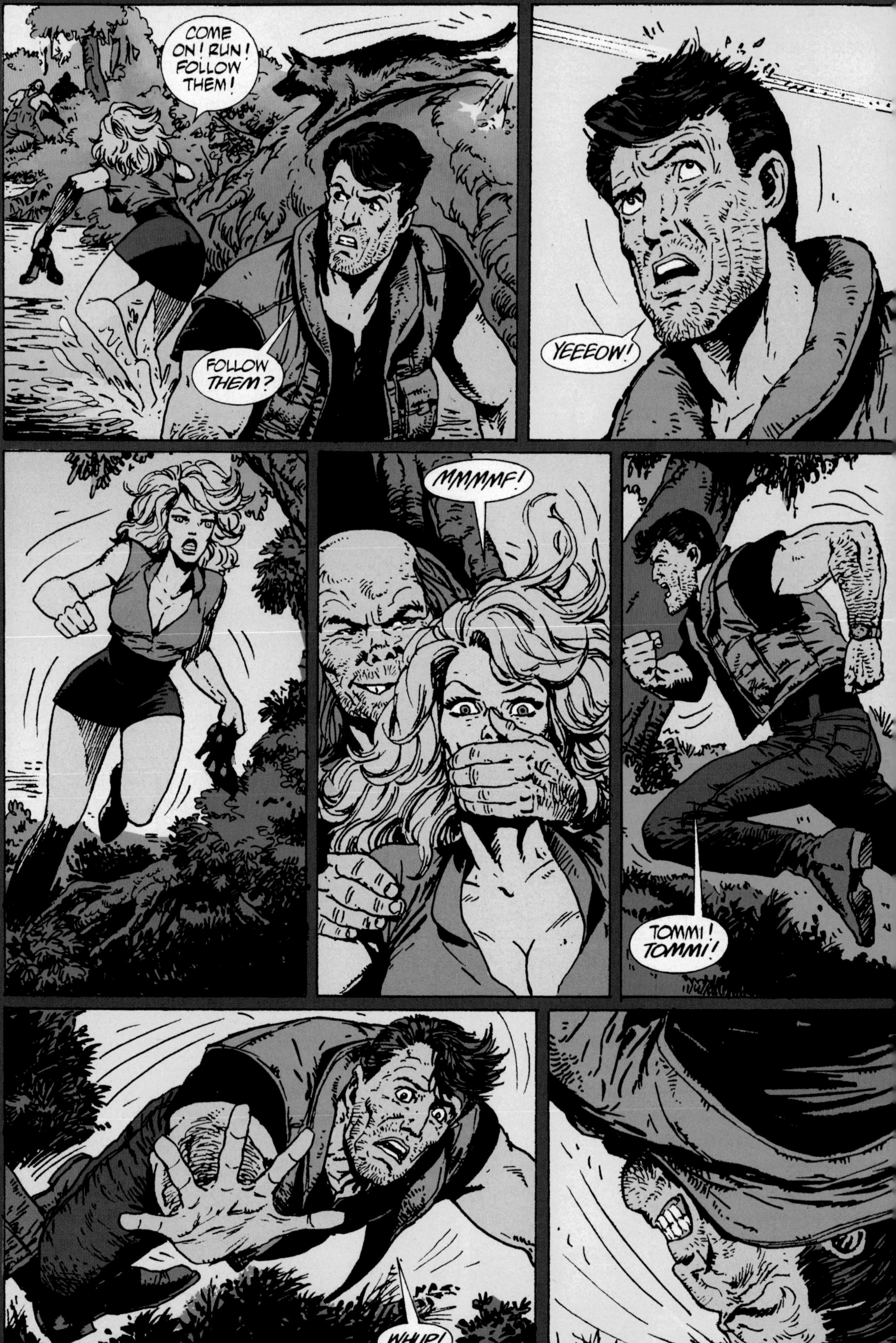

COME ON! RUN! FOLLOW THEM!
FOLLOW THEM?
YEEEOW!
MMMMF!
TOMMI! TOMMI!
WHUP!

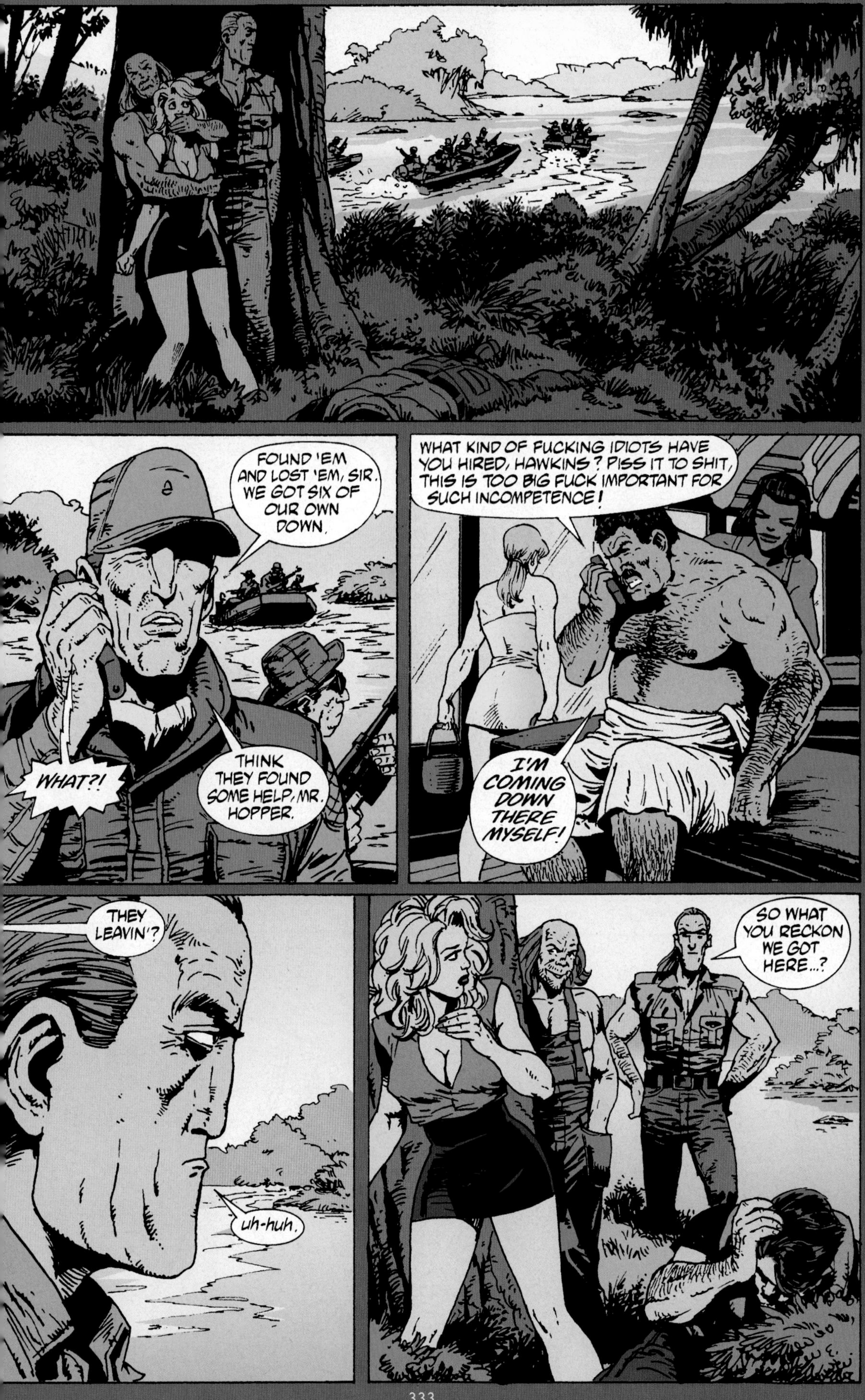
FOUND 'EM AND LOST 'EM, SIR. WE GOT SIX OF OUR OWN DOWN.
WHAT?!
THINK THEY FOUND SOME HELP, MR. HOPPER.
WHAT KIND OF FUCKING IDIOTS HAVE YOU HIRED, HAWKINS? PISS IT TO SHIT, THIS IS TOO BIG FUCK IMPORTANT FOR SUCH INCOMPETENCE!
I'M COMING DOWN THERE MYSELF!
THEY LEAVIN'?
uh-huh.
SO WHAT YOU RECKON WE GOT HERE...?

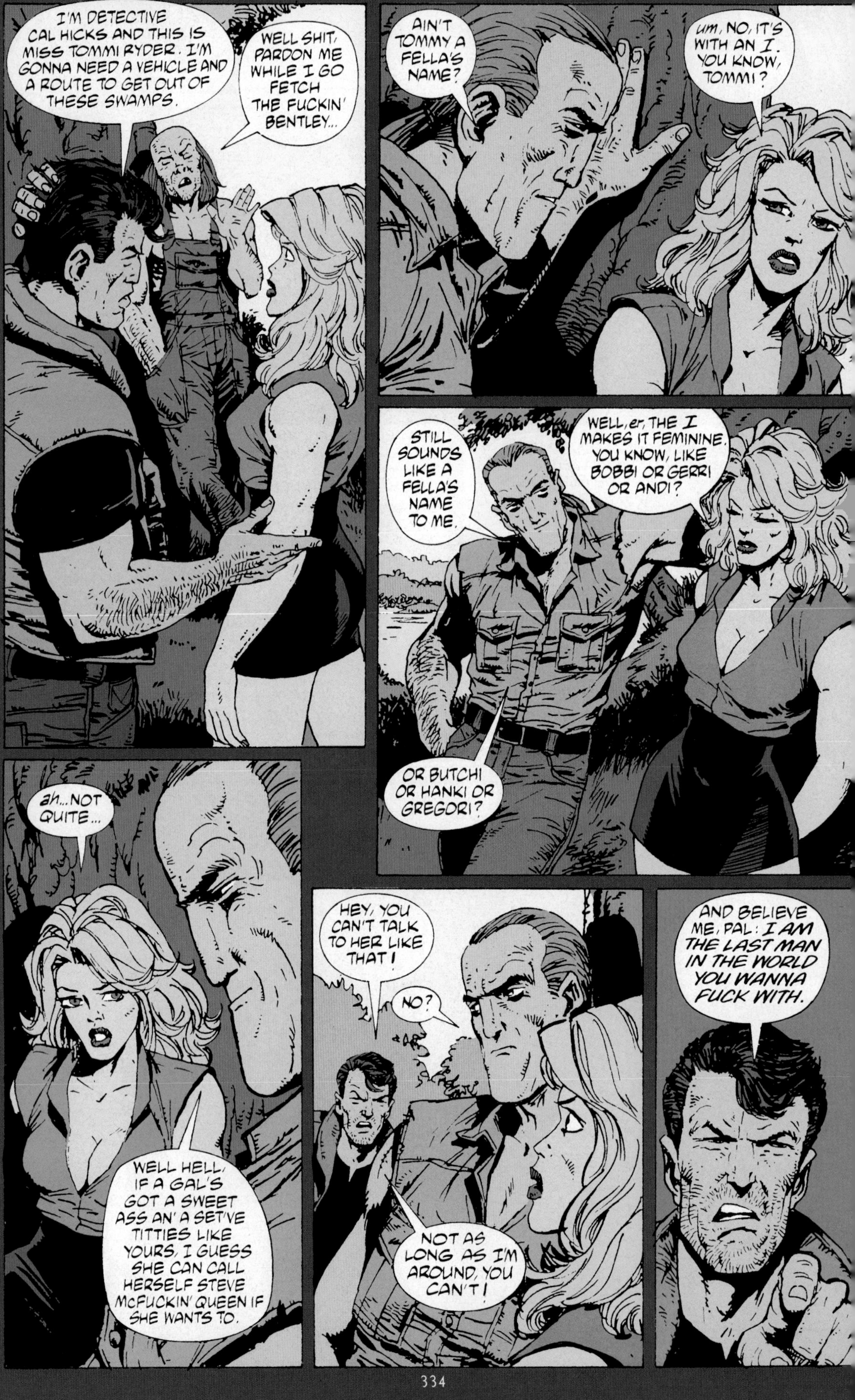
I'M DETECTIVE CAL HICKS AND THIS IS MISS TOMMI RYDER. I'M GONNA NEED A VEHICLE AND A ROUTE TO GET OUT OF THESE SWAMPS.
WELL SHIT, PARDON ME WHILE I GO FETCH THE FUCKIN' BENTLEY...
AIN'T TOMMY A FELLA'S NAME?
um, NO, IT'S WITH AN I. YOU KNOW, TOMMI?
STILL SOUNDS LIKE A FELLA'S NAME TO ME.
WELL, er, THE I MAKES IT FEMININE, YOU KNOW, LIKE BOBBI OR GERRI OR ANDI?
OR BUTCHI OR HANKI OR GREGORI?
ah...NOT QUITE...
WELL HELL, IF A GAL'S GOT A SWEET ASS AN' A SET'VE TITTIES LIKE YOURS, I GUESS SHE CAN CALL HERSELF STEVE McFUCKIN' QUEEN IF SHE WANTS TO.
HEY, YOU CAN'T TALK TO HER LIKE THAT!
NO?
NOT AS LONG AS I'M AROUND, YOU CAN'T!
AND BELIEVE ME, PAL: I AM THE LAST MAN IN THE WORLD YOU WANNA FUCK WITH.

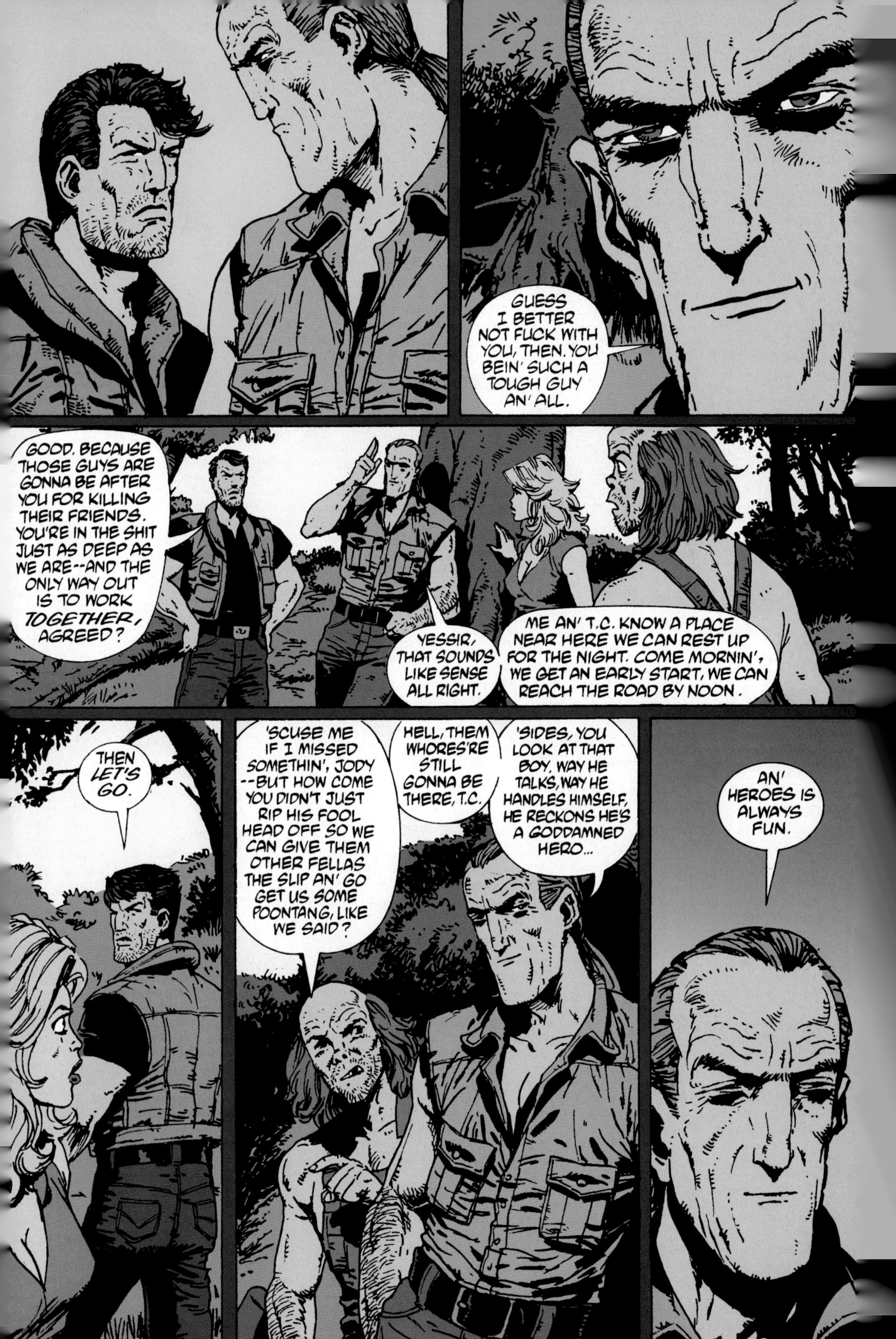
GUESS I BETTER NOT FUCK WITH YOU, THEN. YOU BEIN' SUCH A TOUGH GUY AN' ALL.
GOOD. BECAUSE THOSE GUYS ARE GONNA BE AFTER YOU FOR KILLING THEIR FRIENDS. YOU'RE IN THE SHIT JUST AS DEEP AS WE ARE--AND THE ONLY WAY OUT IS TO WORK *TOGETHER*, AGREED?
YESSIR, THAT SOUNDS LIKE SENSE ALL RIGHT.
ME AN' T.C. KNOW A PLACE NEAR HERE WE CAN REST UP FOR THE NIGHT. COME MORNIN', WE GET AN EARLY START, WE CAN REACH THE ROAD BY NOON.
THEN *LET'S* GO.
'SCUSE ME IF I MISSED SOMETHIN', JODY --BUT HOW COME YOU DIDN'T JUST RIP HIS FOOL HEAD OFF SO WE CAN GIVE THEM OTHER FELLAS THE SLIP AN' GO GET US SOME POONTANG, LIKE WE SAID?
HELL, THEM WHORES'RE STILL GONNA BE THERE, T.C.
'SIDES, YOU LOOK AT THAT BOY. WAY HE TALKS, WAY HE HANDLES HIMSELF, HE RECKONS HE'S A GODDAMNED HERO...
AN' HEROES IS ALWAYS FUN.

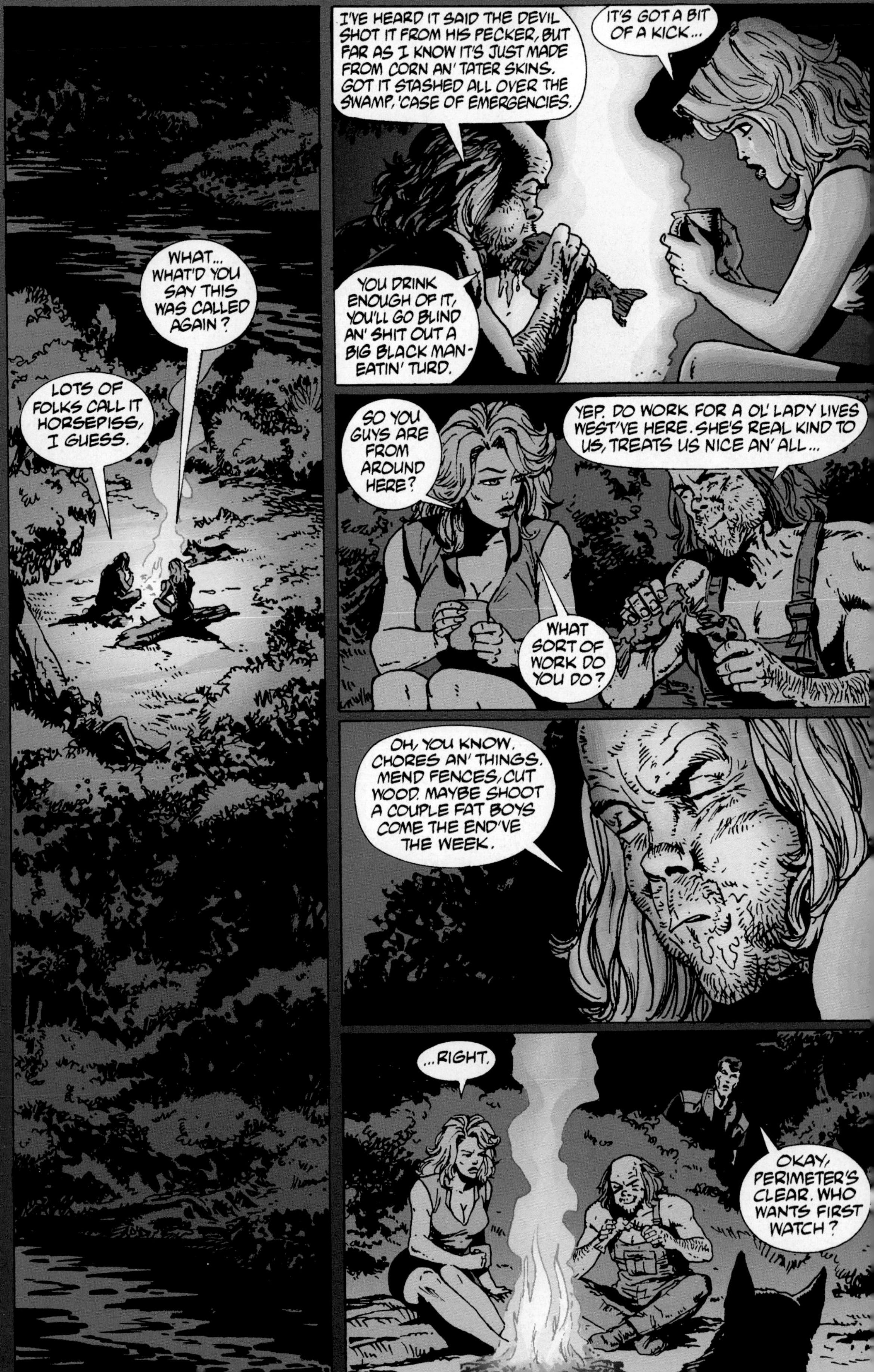
WHAT... WHAT'D YOU SAY THIS WAS CALLED AGAIN?
LOTS OF FOLKS CALL IT HORSEPISS, I GUESS.
I'VE HEARD IT SAID THE DEVIL SHOT IT FROM HIS PECKER, BUT FAR AS I KNOW IT'S JUST MADE FROM CORN AN' TATER SKINS. GOT IT STASHED ALL OVER THE SWAMP, 'CASE OF EMERGENCIES.
IT'S GOT A BIT OF A KICK...
YOU DRINK ENOUGH OF IT, YOU'LL GO BLIND AN' SHIT OUT A BIG BLACK MAN-EATIN' TURD.
SO YOU GUYS ARE FROM AROUND HERE?
YEP. DO WORK FOR A OL' LADY LIVES WEST'VE HERE. SHE'S REAL KIND TO US, TREATS US NICE AN' ALL...
WHAT SORT OF WORK DO YOU DO?
OH, YOU KNOW. CHORES AN' THINGS. MEND FENCES, CUT WOOD. MAYBE SHOOT A COUPLE FAT BOYS COME THE END'VE THE WEEK.
...RIGHT.
OKAY, PERIMETER'S CLEAR. WHO WANTS FIRST WATCH?

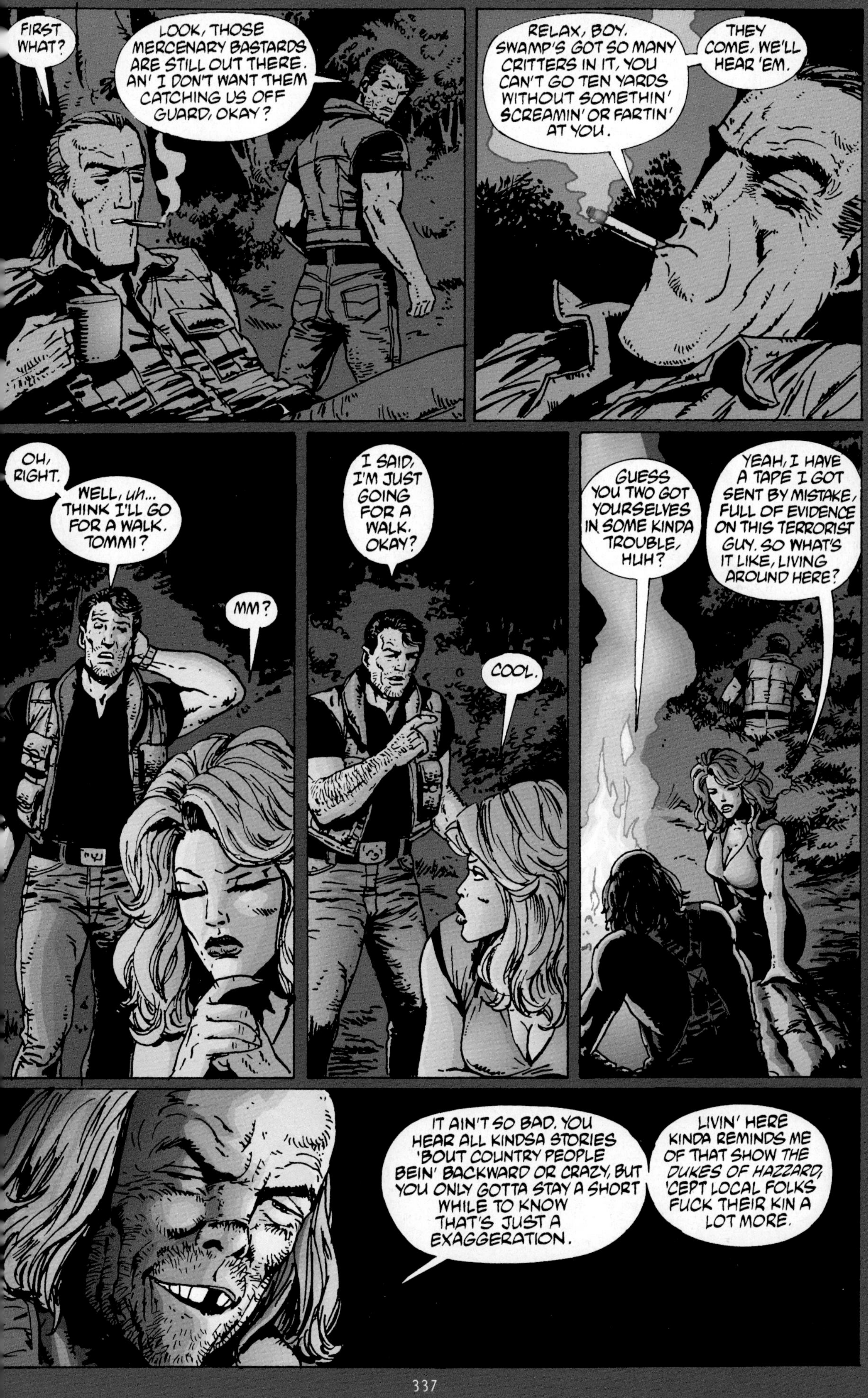
FIRST WHAT?
LOOK, THOSE MERCENARY BASTARDS ARE STILL OUT THERE. AN' I DON'T WANT THEM CATCHING US OFF GUARD, OKAY?
RELAX, BOY. SWAMP'S GOT SO MANY CRITTERS IN IT, YOU CAN'T GO TEN YARDS WITHOUT SOMETHIN' SCREAMIN' OR FARTIN' AT YOU.
THEY COME, WE'LL HEAR 'EM.
OH, RIGHT.
WELL, uh... THINK I'LL GO FOR A WALK. TOMMI?
MM?
I SAID, I'M JUST GOING FOR A WALK. OKAY?
COOL.
GUESS YOU TWO GOT YOURSELVES IN SOME KINDA TROUBLE, HUH?
YEAH, I HAVE A TAPE I GOT SENT BY MISTAKE, FULL OF EVIDENCE ON THIS TERRORIST GUY. SO WHAT'S IT LIKE, LIVING AROUND HERE?
IT AIN'T SO BAD. YOU HEAR ALL KINDSA STORIES 'BOUT COUNTRY PEOPLE BEIN' BACKWARD OR CRAZY, BUT YOU ONLY GOTTA STAY A SHORT WHILE TO KNOW THAT'S JUST A EXAGGERATION.
LIVIN' HERE KINDA REMINDS ME OF THAT SHOW THE *DUKES OF HAZZARD*, 'CEPT LOCAL FOLKS FUCK THEIR KIN A LOT MORE.

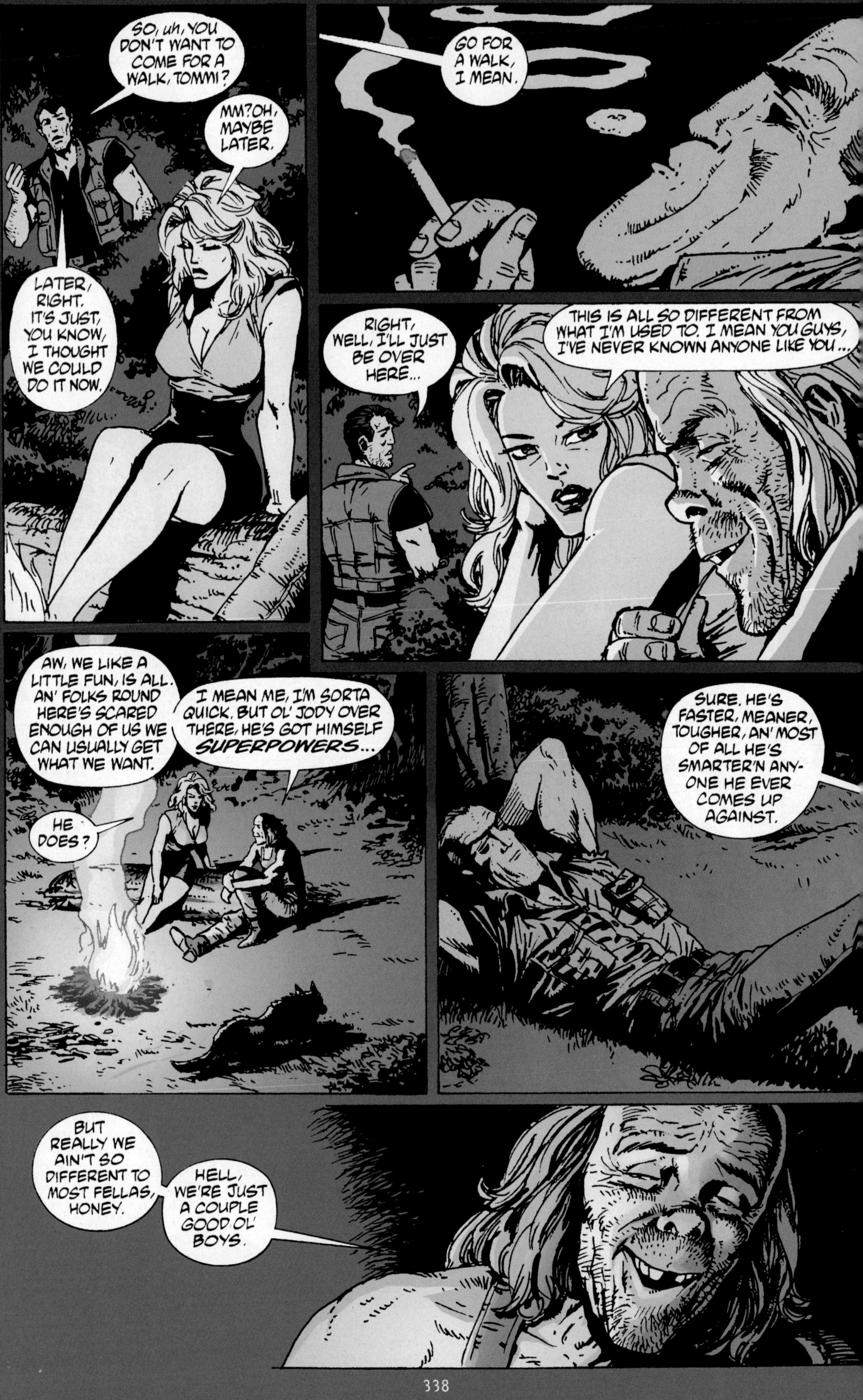
SO, uh, YOU DON'T WANT TO COME FOR A WALK, TOMMI?
MM? OH, MAYBE LATER.
LATER, RIGHT. IT'S JUST, YOU KNOW, I THOUGHT WE COULD DO IT NOW.
GO FOR A WALK, I MEAN.
RIGHT, WELL, I'LL JUST BE OVER HERE...
THIS IS ALL SO DIFFERENT FROM WHAT I'M USED TO. I MEAN YOU GUYS, I'VE NEVER KNOWN ANYONE LIKE YOU...
AW, WE LIKE A LITTLE FUN, IS ALL. AN' FOLKS ROUND HERE'S SCARED ENOUGH OF US WE CAN USUALLY GET WHAT WE WANT.
I MEAN ME, I'M SORTA QUICK. BUT OL' JODY OVER THERE, HE'S GOT HIMSELF SUPERPOWERS...
HE DOES?
SURE. HE'S FASTER, MEANER, TOUGHER, AN' MOST OF ALL HE'S SMARTER'N ANYONE HE EVER COMES UP AGAINST.
BUT REALLY WE AIN'T SO DIFFERENT TO MOST FELLAS, HONEY.
HELL, WE'RE JUST A COUPLE GOOD OL' BOYS.

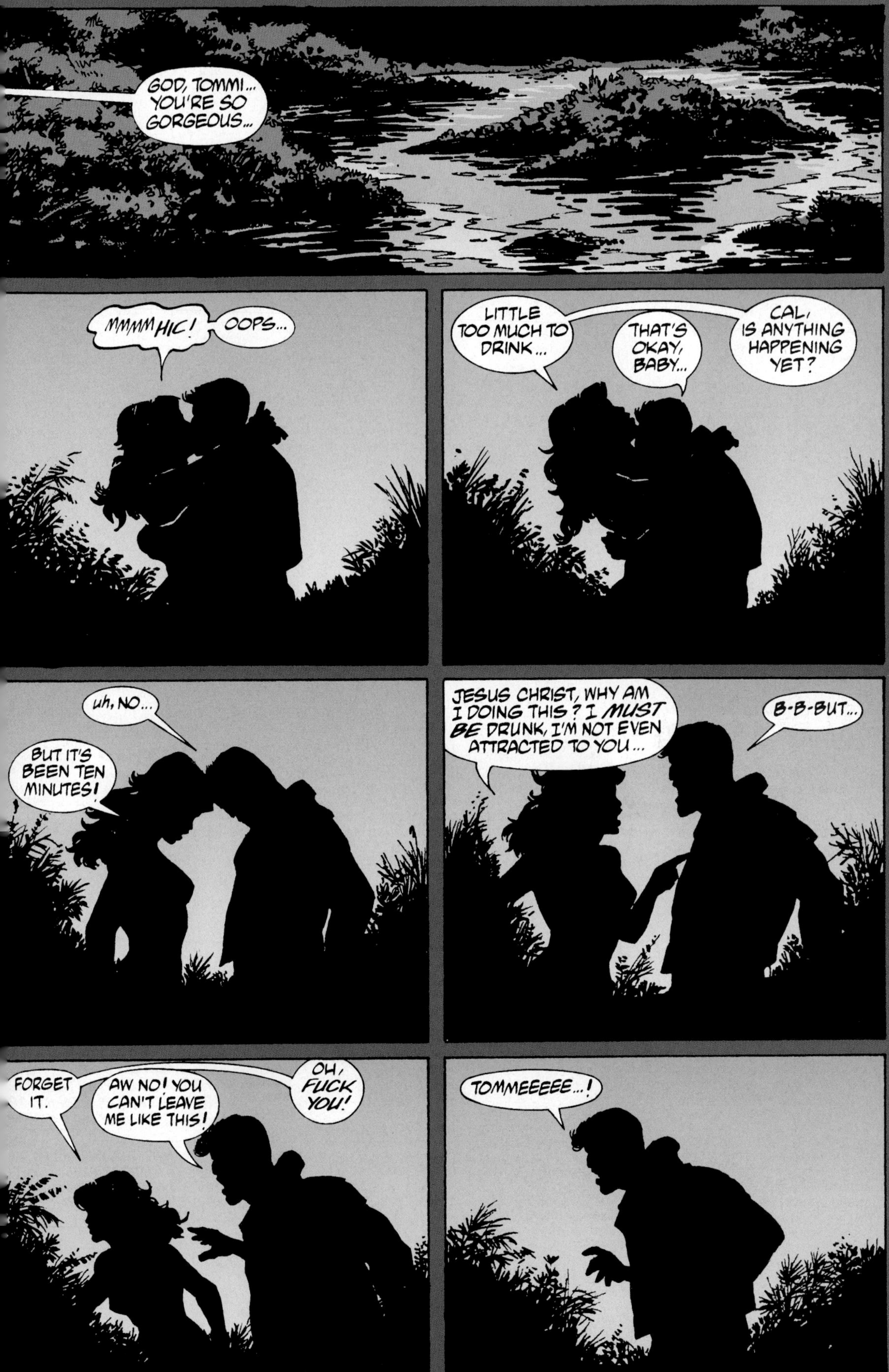
GOD, TOMMI... YOU'RE SO GORGEOUS...
MMMM HIC!
OOPS...
LITTLE TOO MUCH TO DRINK...
THAT'S OKAY, BABY...
CAL, IS ANYTHING HAPPENING YET?
uh, NO...
BUT IT'S BEEN TEN MINUTES!
JESUS CHRIST, WHY AM I DOING THIS? I MUST BE DRUNK, I'M NOT EVEN ATTRACTED TO YOU...
B-B-BUT...
FORGET IT.
AW NO! YOU CAN'T LEAVE ME LIKE THIS!
OH, FUCK YOU!
TOMMEEEEE...!

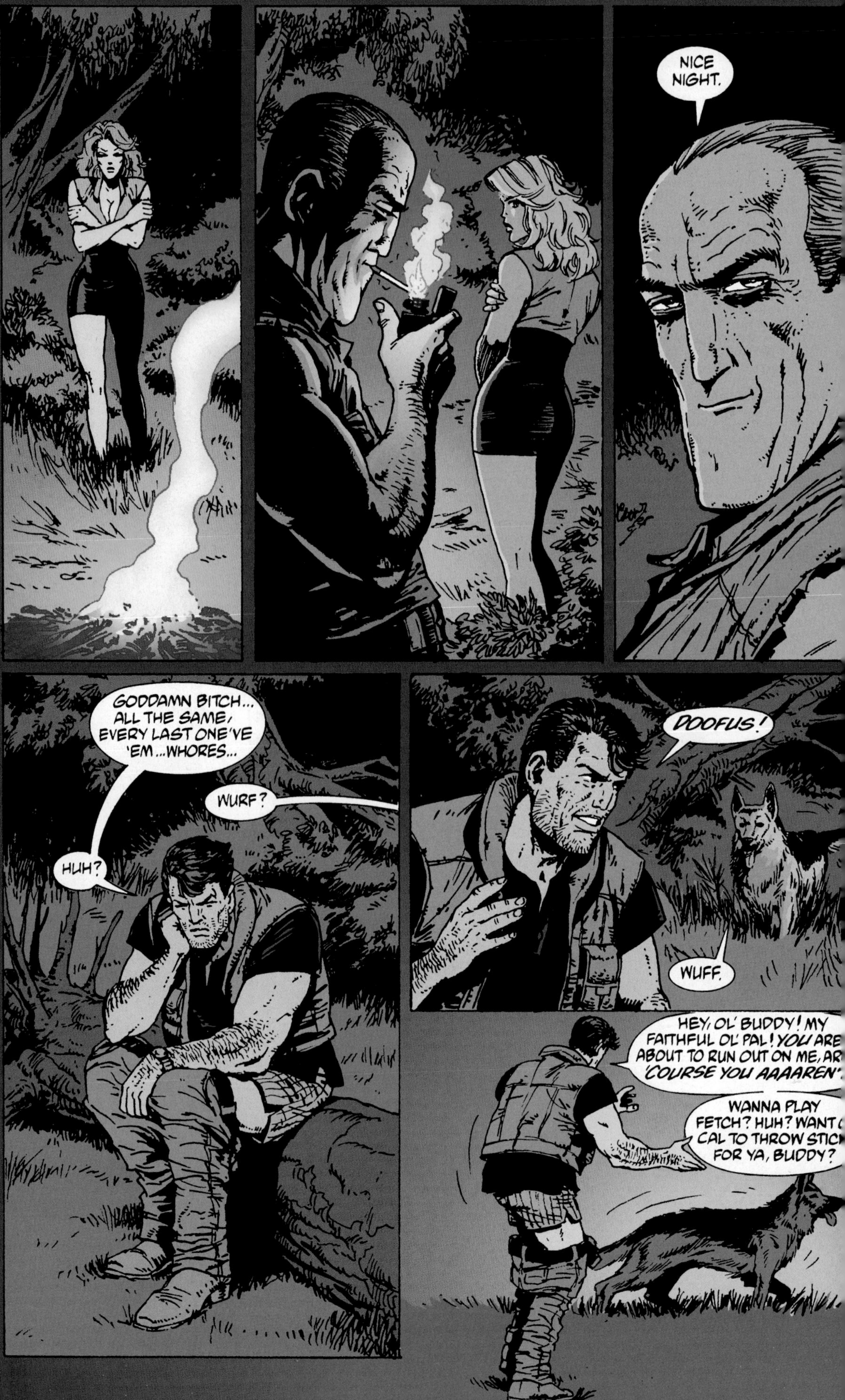
NICE NIGHT.
GODDAMN BITCH... ALL THE SAME, EVERY LAST ONE'VE 'EM...WHORES...
WURF?
HUH?
DOOFUS!
WUFF.
HEY, OL' BUDDY! MY FAITHFUL OL' PAL! YOU ARE ABOUT TO RUN OUT ON ME, AR 'COURSE YOU AAAAREN'
WANNA PLAY FETCH? HUH? WANT CAL TO THROW STIC FOR YA, BUDDY?

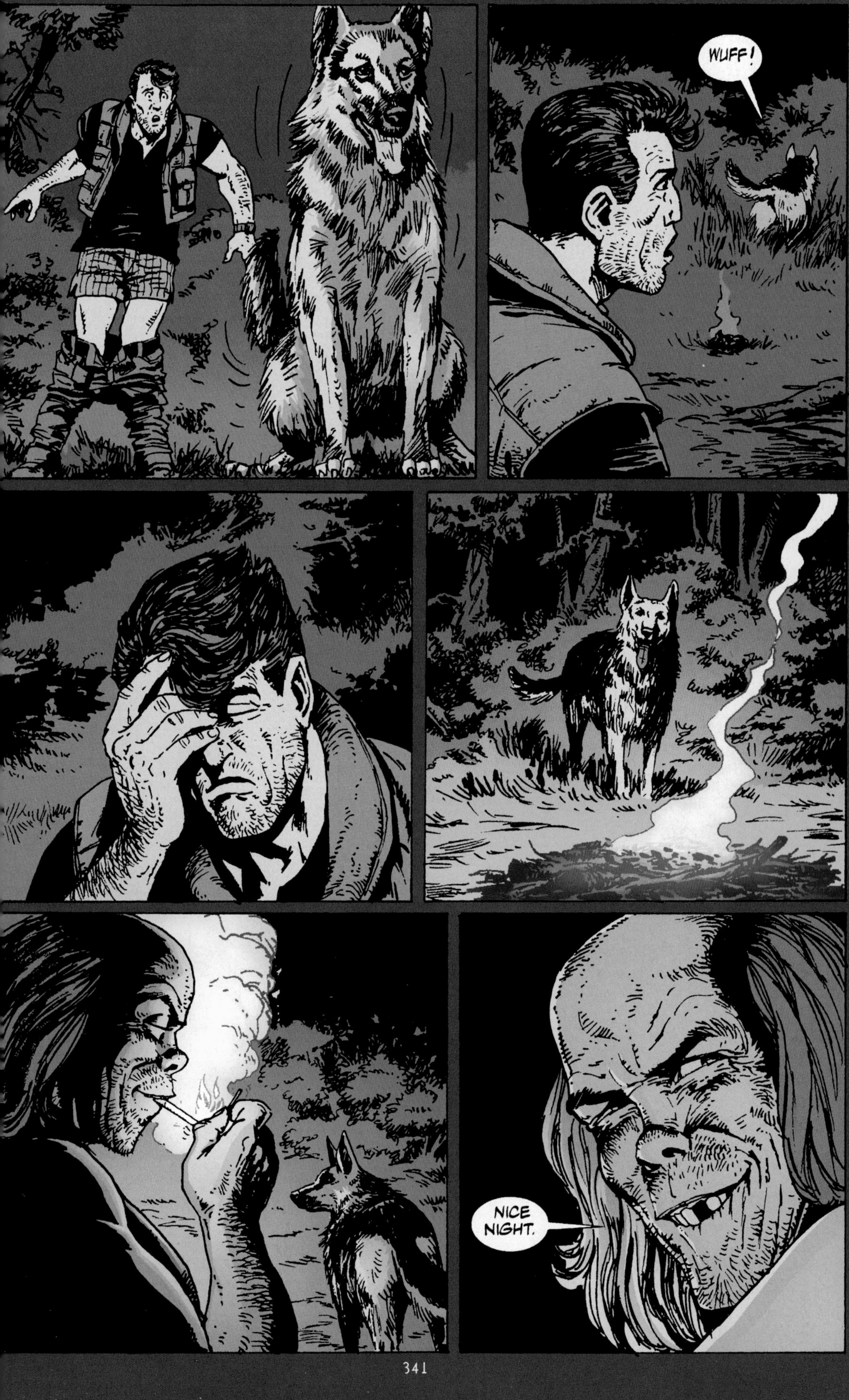
WUFF!
NICE NIGHT.

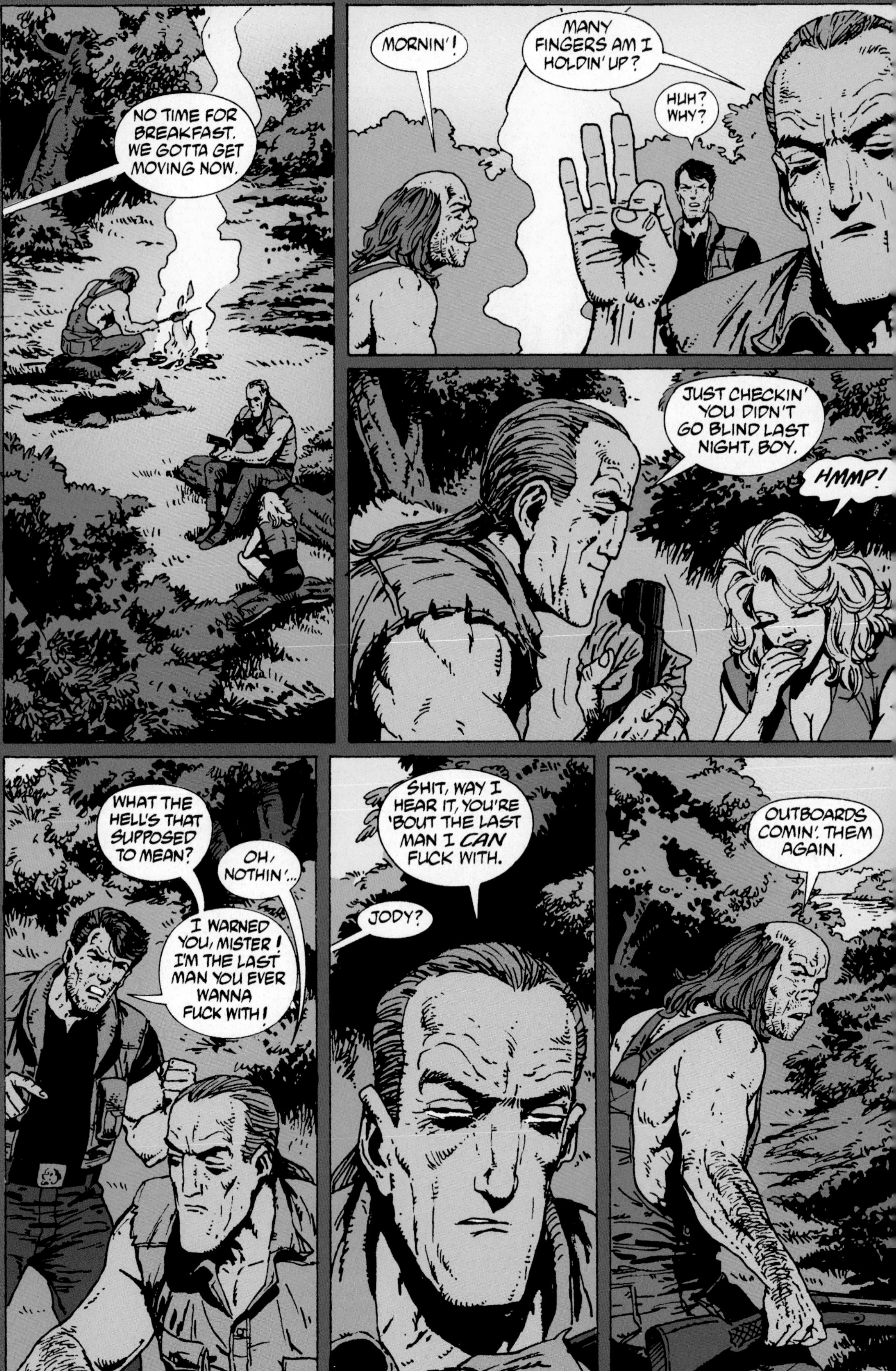
NO TIME FOR BREAKFAST. WE GOTTA GET MOVING NOW.
MORNIN'!
MANY FINGERS AM I HOLDIN' UP?
HUH? WHY?
JUST CHECKIN' YOU DIDN'T GO BLIND LAST NIGHT, BOY.
HMMP!
WHAT THE HELL'S THAT SUPPOSED TO MEAN?
OH, NOTHIN'...
I WARNED YOU, MISTER! I'M THE LAST MAN YOU EVER WANNA FUCK WITH!
SHIT, WAY I HEAR IT, YOU'RE 'BOUT THE LAST MAN I CAN FUCK WITH.
JODY?
OUTBOARDS COMIN'. THEM AGAIN.

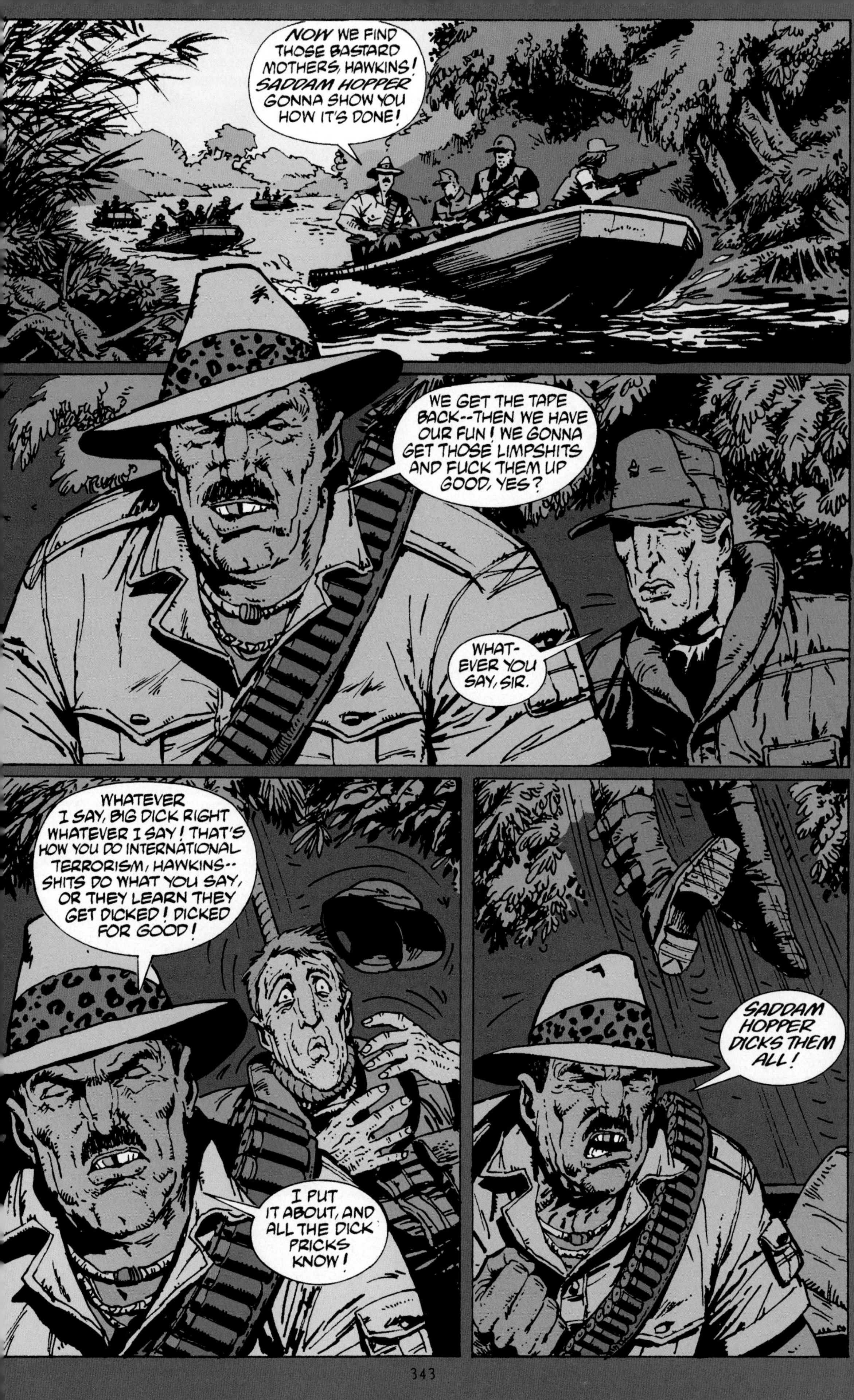
NOW WE FIND THOSE BASTARD MOTHERS, HAWKINS! SADDAM HOPPER GONNA SHOW YOU HOW IT'S DONE!
WE GET THE TAPE BACK--THEN WE HAVE OUR FUN! WE GONNA GET THOSE LIMPSHITS AND FUCK THEM UP GOOD, YES?
WHAT-EVER YOU SAY, SIR.
WHATEVER I SAY, BIG DICK RIGHT WHATEVER I SAY! THAT'S HOW YOU DO INTERNATIONAL TERRORISM, HAWKINS-- SHITS DO WHAT YOU SAY, OR THEY LEARN THEY GET DICKED! DICKED FOR GOOD!
I PUT IT ABOUT, AND ALL THE DICK PRICKS KNOW!
SADDAM HOPPER DICKS THEM ALL!

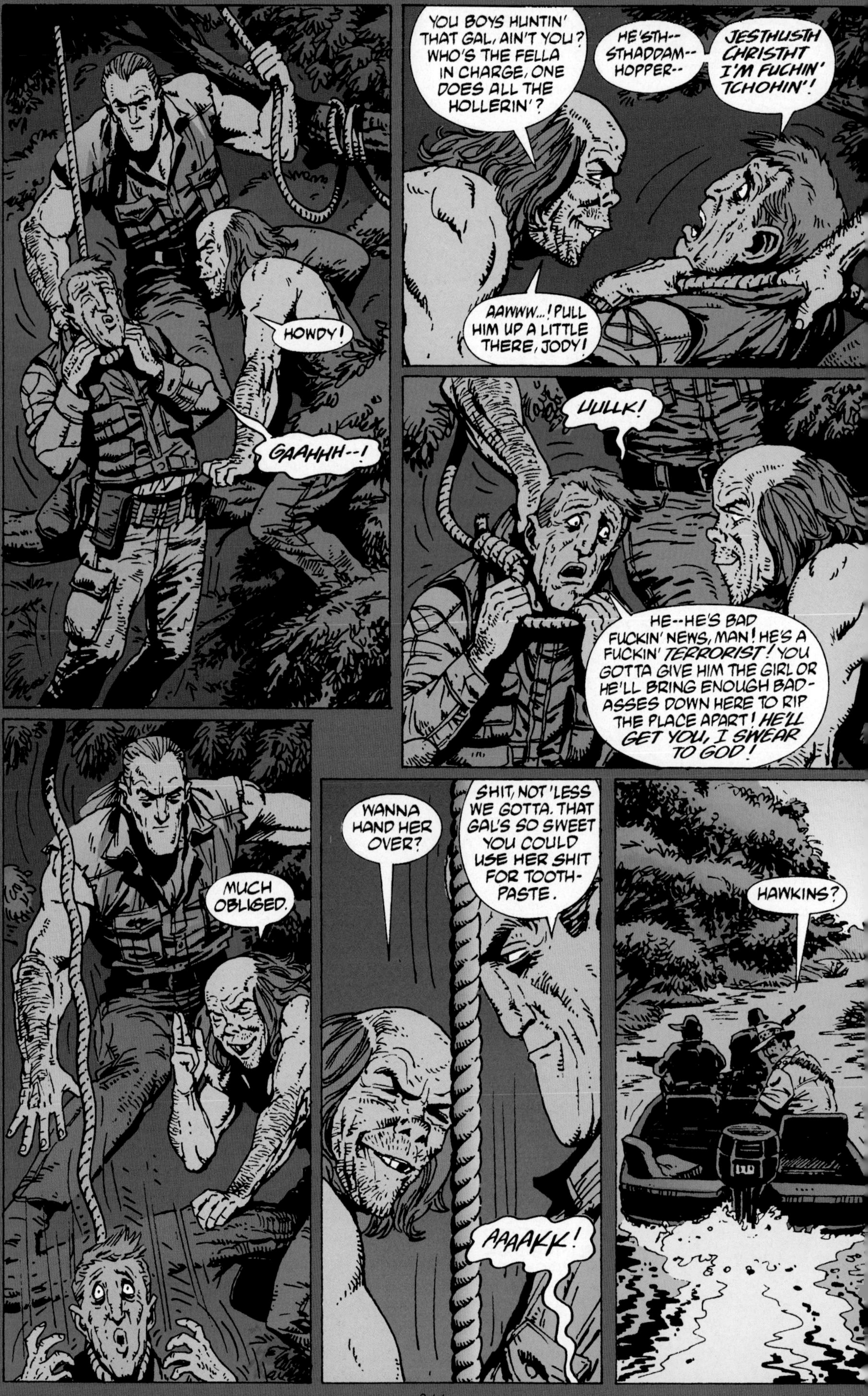
HOWDY!
GAAHHH--!
YOU BOYS HUNTIN' THAT GAL, AIN'T YOU? WHO'S THE FELLA IN CHARGE, ONE DOES ALL THE HOLLERIN'?
HE'STH-- STHADDAM-- HOPPER--
JESTHUSTH CHRISTHT I'M FUCHIN' TCHOHIN'!
AAWWW...! PULL HIM UP A LITTLE THERE, JODY!
UULLK!
HE--HE'S BAD FUCKIN' NEWS, MAN! HE'S A FUCKIN' TERRORIST! YOU GOTTA GIVE HIM THE GIRL OR HE'LL BRING ENOUGH BAD-ASSES DOWN HERE TO RIP THE PLACE APART! HE'LL GET YOU, I SWEAR TO GOD!
MUCH OBLIGED.
WANNA HAND HER OVER?
SHIT, NOT 'LESS WE GOTTA. THAT GAL'S SO SWEET YOU COULD USE HER SHIT FOR TOOTH-PASTE.
AAAAKK!
HAWKINS?

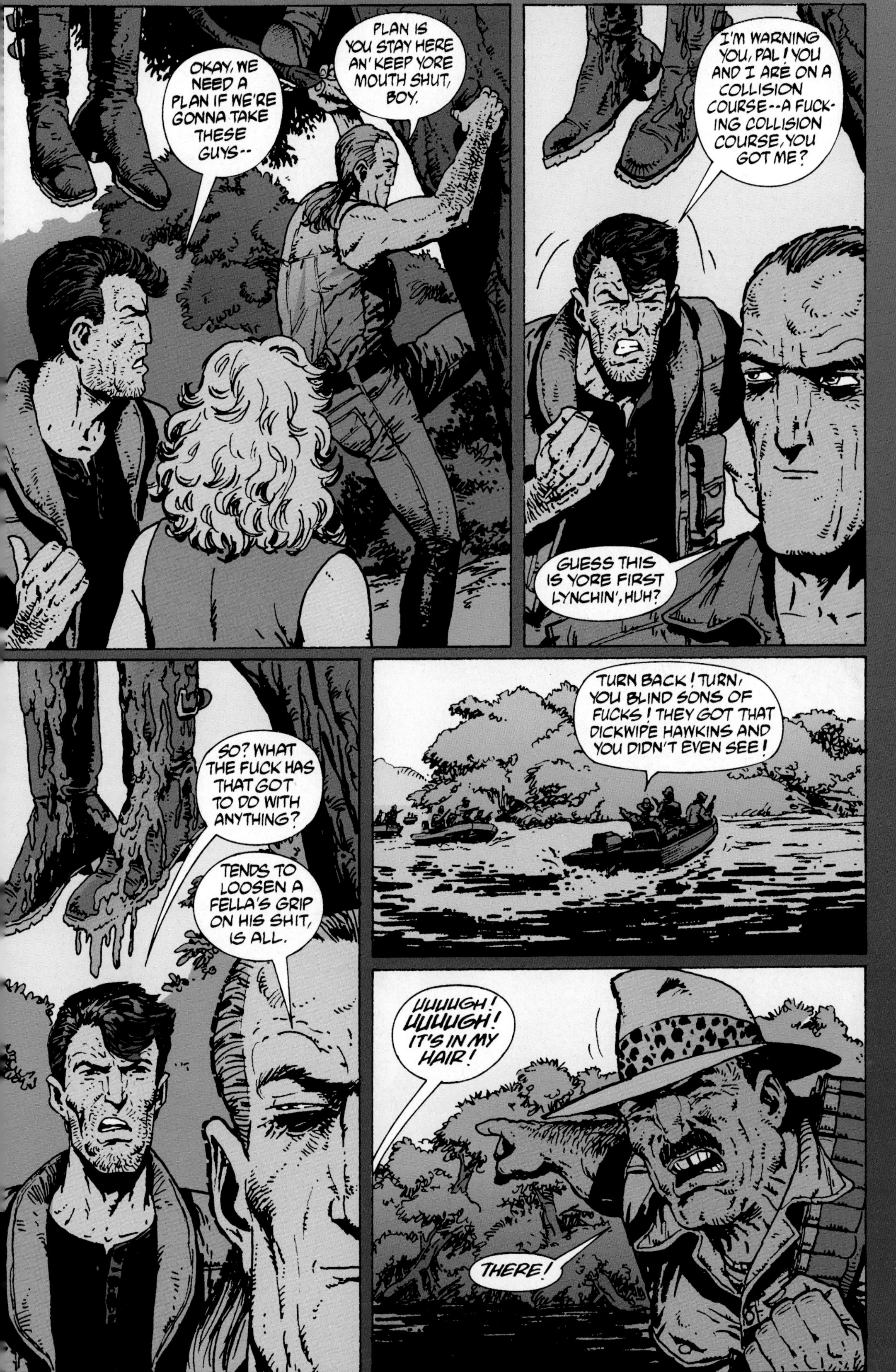
OKAY, WE NEED A PLAN IF WE'RE GONNA TAKE THESE GUYS--
PLAN IS YOU STAY HERE AN' KEEP YORE MOUTH SHUT, BOY.
I'M WARNING YOU, PAL! YOU AND I ARE ON A COLLISION COURSE--A FUCKING COLLISION COURSE, YOU GOT ME?
GUESS THIS IS YORE FIRST LYNCHIN', HUH?
SO? WHAT THE FUCK HAS THAT GOT TO DO WITH ANYTHING?
TENDS TO LOOSEN A FELLA'S GRIP ON HIS SHIT, IS ALL.
TURN BACK! TURN, YOU BLIND SONS OF FUCKS! THEY GOT THAT DICKWIPE HAWKINS AND YOU DIDN'T EVEN SEE!
UUUUGH! UUUUGH! IT'S IN MY HAIR!
THERE!

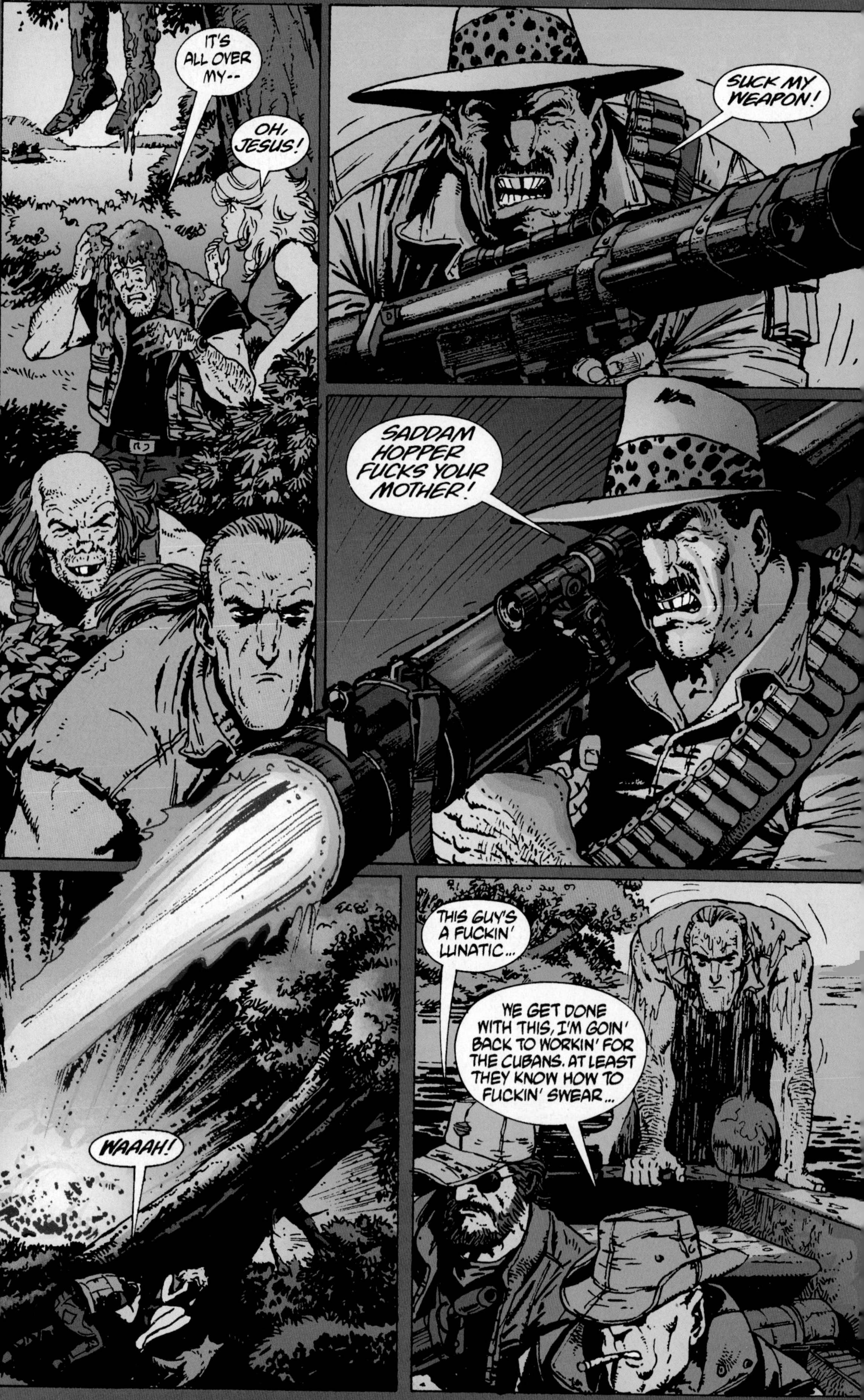
IT'S ALL OVER MY--
OH, JESUS!
SUCK MY WEAPON!
SADDAM HOPPER FUCKS YOUR MOTHER!
WAAAH!
THIS GUY'S A FUCKIN' LUNATIC...
WE GET DONE WITH THIS, I'M GOIN' BACK TO WORKIN' FOR THE CUBANS. AT LEAST THEY KNOW HOW TO FUCKIN' SWEAR...

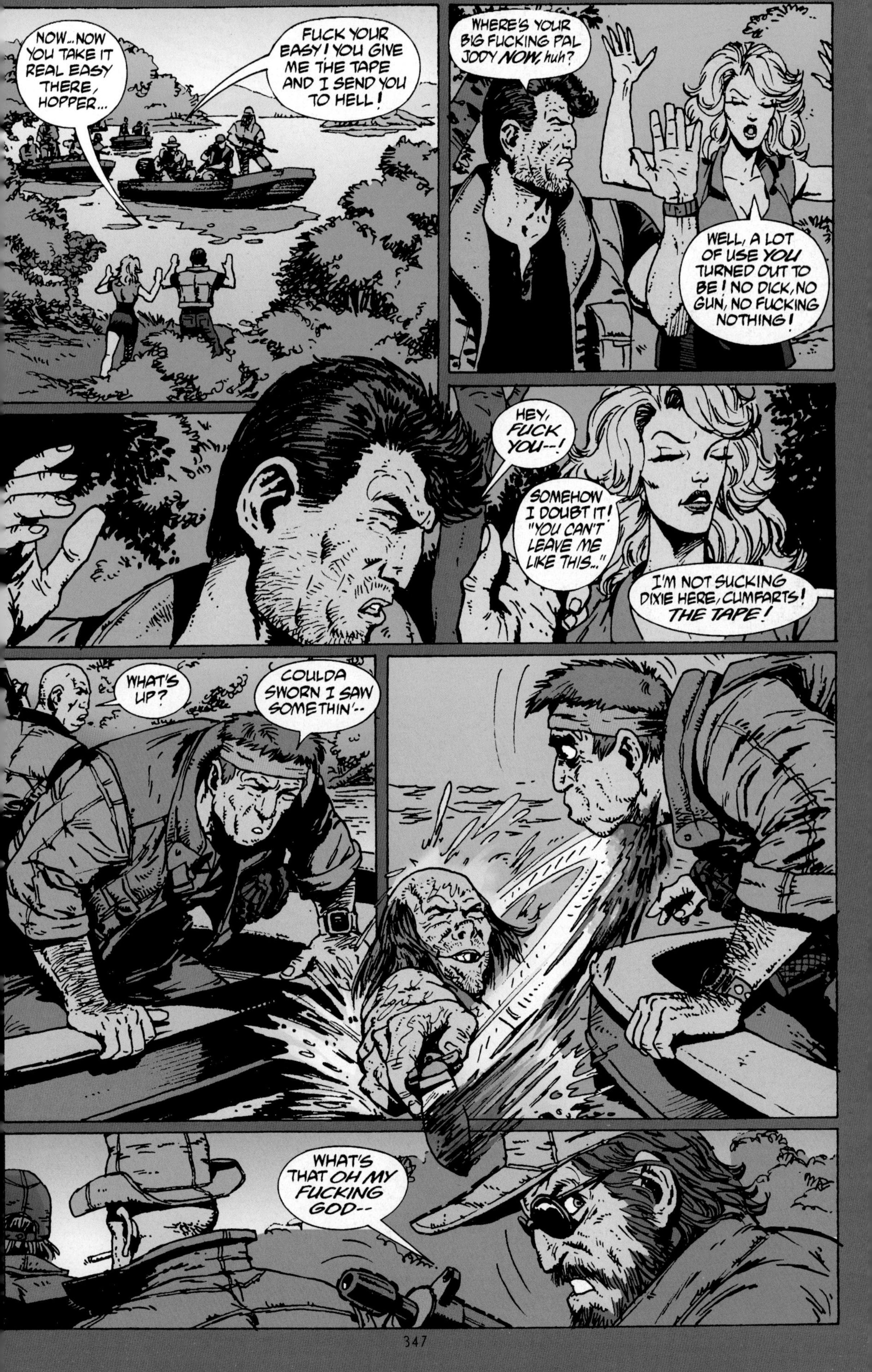
NOW...NOW YOU TAKE IT REAL EASY THERE, HOPPER...
FUCK YOUR EASY! YOU GIVE ME THE TAPE AND I SEND YOU TO HELL!
WHERE'S YOUR BIG FUCKING PAL JODY NOW, huh?
WELL, A LOT OF USE YOU TURNED OUT TO BE! NO DICK, NO GUN, NO FUCKING NOTHING!
HEY, FUCK YOU--!
SOMEHOW I DOUBT IT! "YOU CAN'T LEAVE ME LIKE THIS..."
I'M NOT SUCKING DIXIE HERE, CUMFARTS! THE TAPE!
WHAT'S UP?
COULDA SWORN I SAW SOMETHIN'--
WHAT'S THAT OH MY FUCKING GOD--

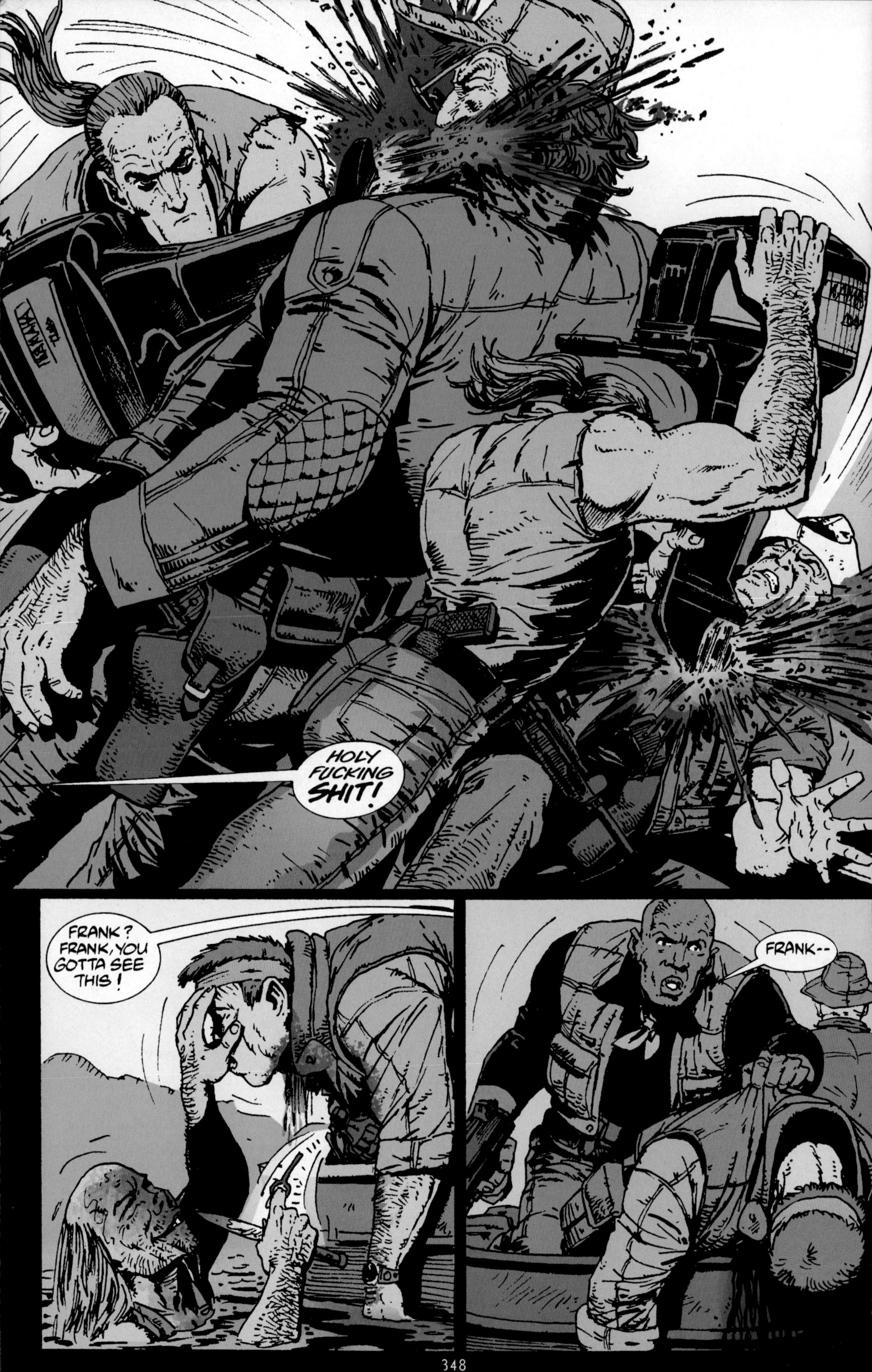
HOLY FUCKING SHIT!
FRANK? FRANK, YOU GOTTA SEE THIS!
FRANK--

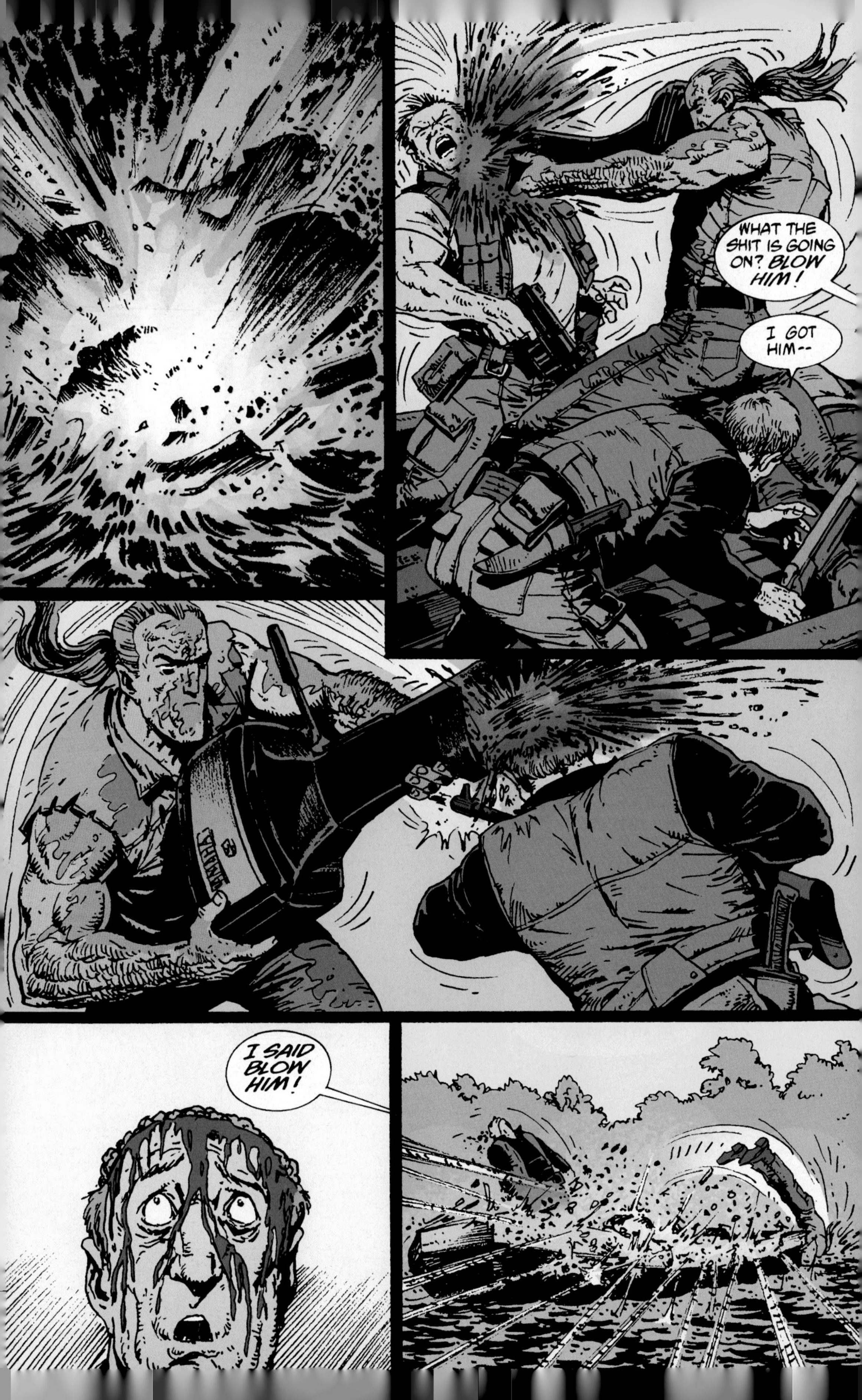
WHAT THE SHIT IS GOING ON? BLOW HIM!
I GOT HIM--
I SAID BLOW HIM!

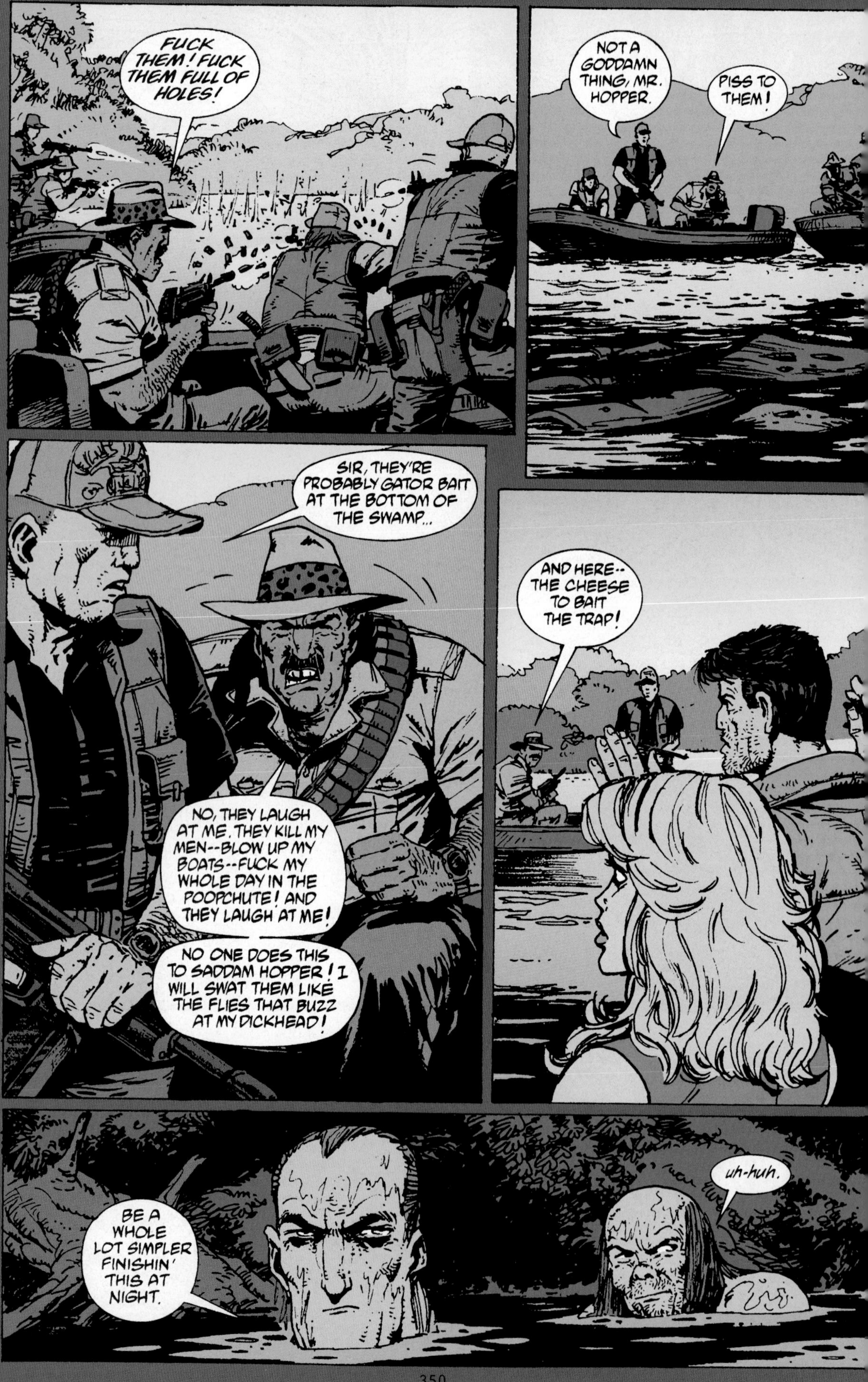
FUCK THEM! FUCK THEM FULL OF HOLES!
NOT A GODDAMN THING, MR. HOPPER.
PISS TO THEM!
SIR, THEY'RE PROBABLY GATOR BAIT AT THE BOTTOM OF THE SWAMP...
NO, THEY LAUGH AT ME. THEY KILL MY MEN--BLOW UP MY BOATS--FUCK MY WHOLE DAY IN THE POOPCHUTE! AND THEY LAUGH AT ME!
NO ONE DOES THIS TO SADDAM HOPPER! I WILL SWAT THEM LIKE THE FLIES THAT BUZZ AT MY DICKHEAD!
AND HERE-- THE CHEESE TO BAIT THE TRAP!
BE A WHOLE LOT SIMPLER FINISHIN' THIS AT NIGHT.
uh-huh.

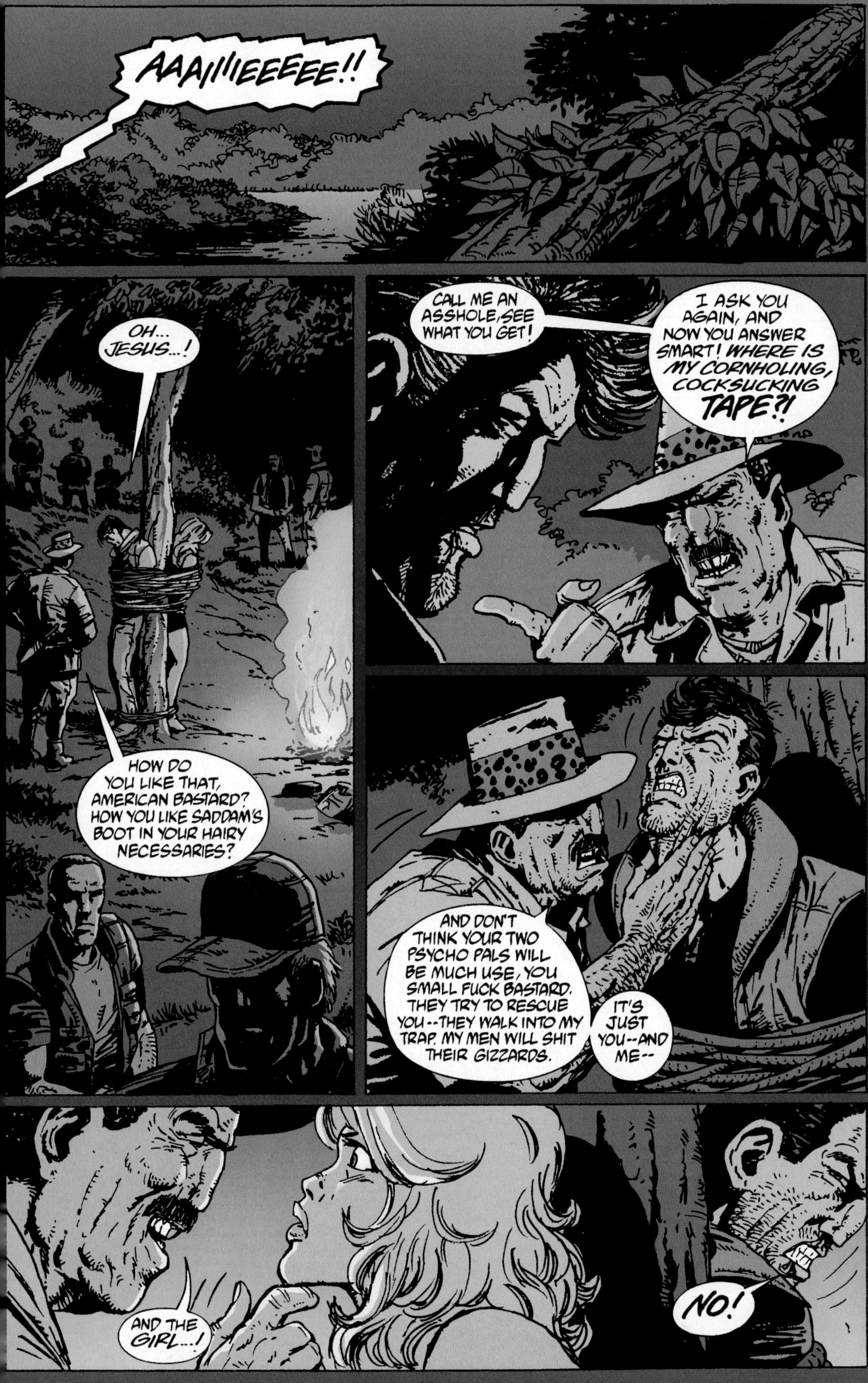
AAAIIIIEEEEEE!!
OH... JESUS...!
HOW DO YOU LIKE THAT, AMERICAN BASTARD? HOW YOU LIKE SADDAM'S BOOT IN YOUR HAIRY NECESSARIES?
CALL ME AN ASSHOLE, SEE WHAT YOU GET!
I ASK YOU AGAIN, AND NOW YOU ANSWER SMART! WHERE IS MY CORNHOLING, COCKSUCKING TAPE?!
AND DON'T THINK YOUR TWO PSYCHO PALS WILL BE MUCH USE, YOU SMALL FUCK BASTARD. THEY TRY TO RESCUE YOU--THEY WALK INTO MY TRAP. MY MEN WILL SHIT THEIR GIZZARDS.
IT'S JUST YOU--AND ME--
AND THE GIRL...!
NO!

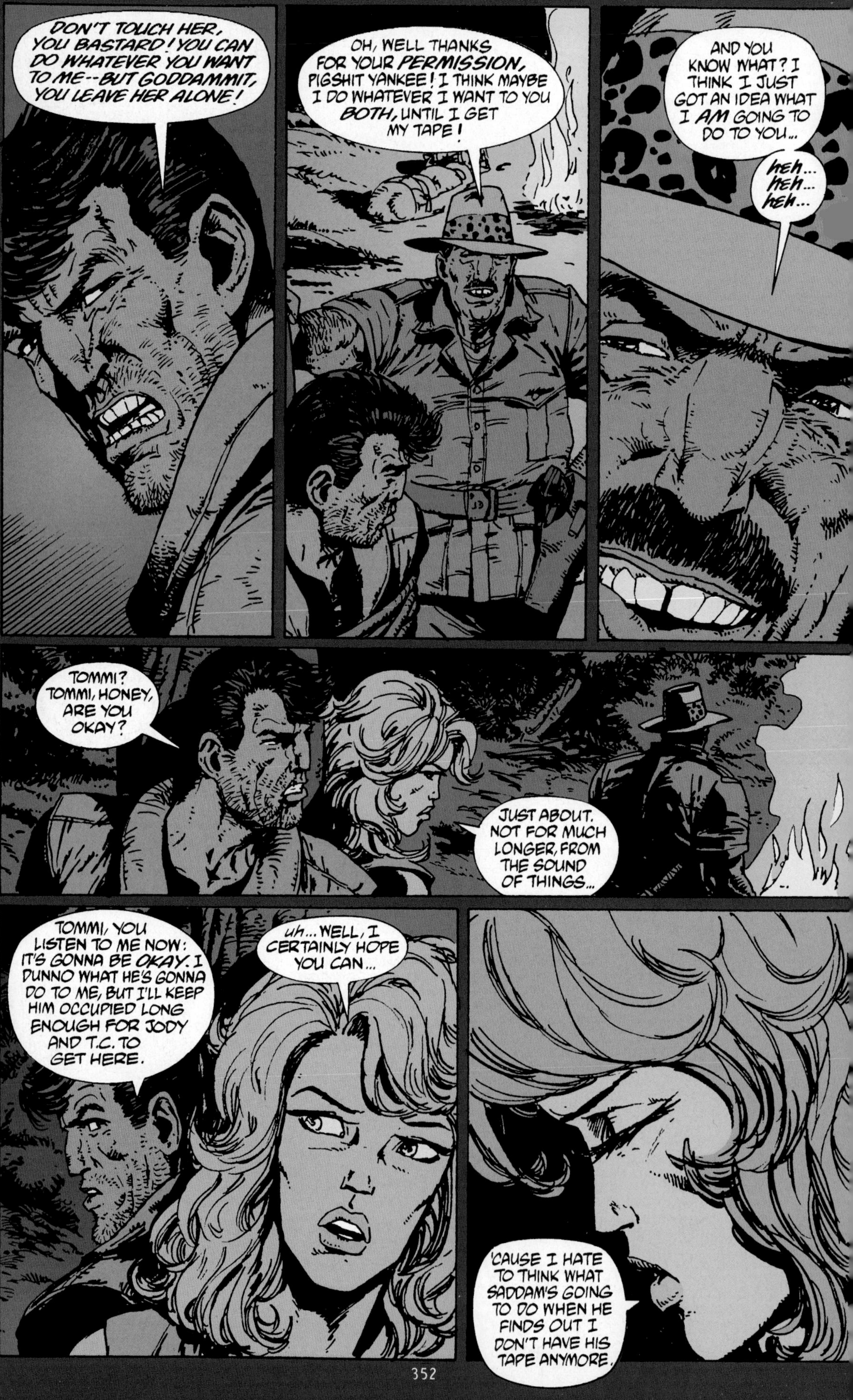
DON'T TOUCH HER, YOU BASTARD! YOU CAN DO WHATEVER YOU WANT TO ME--BUT GODDAMMIT, YOU LEAVE HER ALONE!
OH, WELL THANKS FOR YOUR PERMISSION, PIGSHIT YANKEE! I THINK MAYBE I DO WHATEVER I WANT TO YOU BOTH, UNTIL I GET MY TAPE!
AND YOU KNOW WHAT? I THINK I JUST GOT AN IDEA WHAT I AM GOING TO DO TO YOU...
heh... heh... heh...
TOMMI? TOMMI, HONEY, ARE YOU OKAY?
JUST ABOUT. NOT FOR MUCH LONGER, FROM THE SOUND OF THINGS...
TOMMI, YOU LISTEN TO ME NOW: IT'S GONNA BE OKAY. I DUNNO WHAT HE'S GONNA DO TO ME, BUT I'LL KEEP HIM OCCUPIED LONG ENOUGH FOR JODY AND T.C. TO GET HERE.
uh... WELL, I CERTAINLY HOPE YOU CAN...
'CAUSE I HATE TO THINK WHAT SADDAM'S GOING TO DO WHEN HE FINDS OUT I DON'T HAVE HIS TAPE ANYMORE.

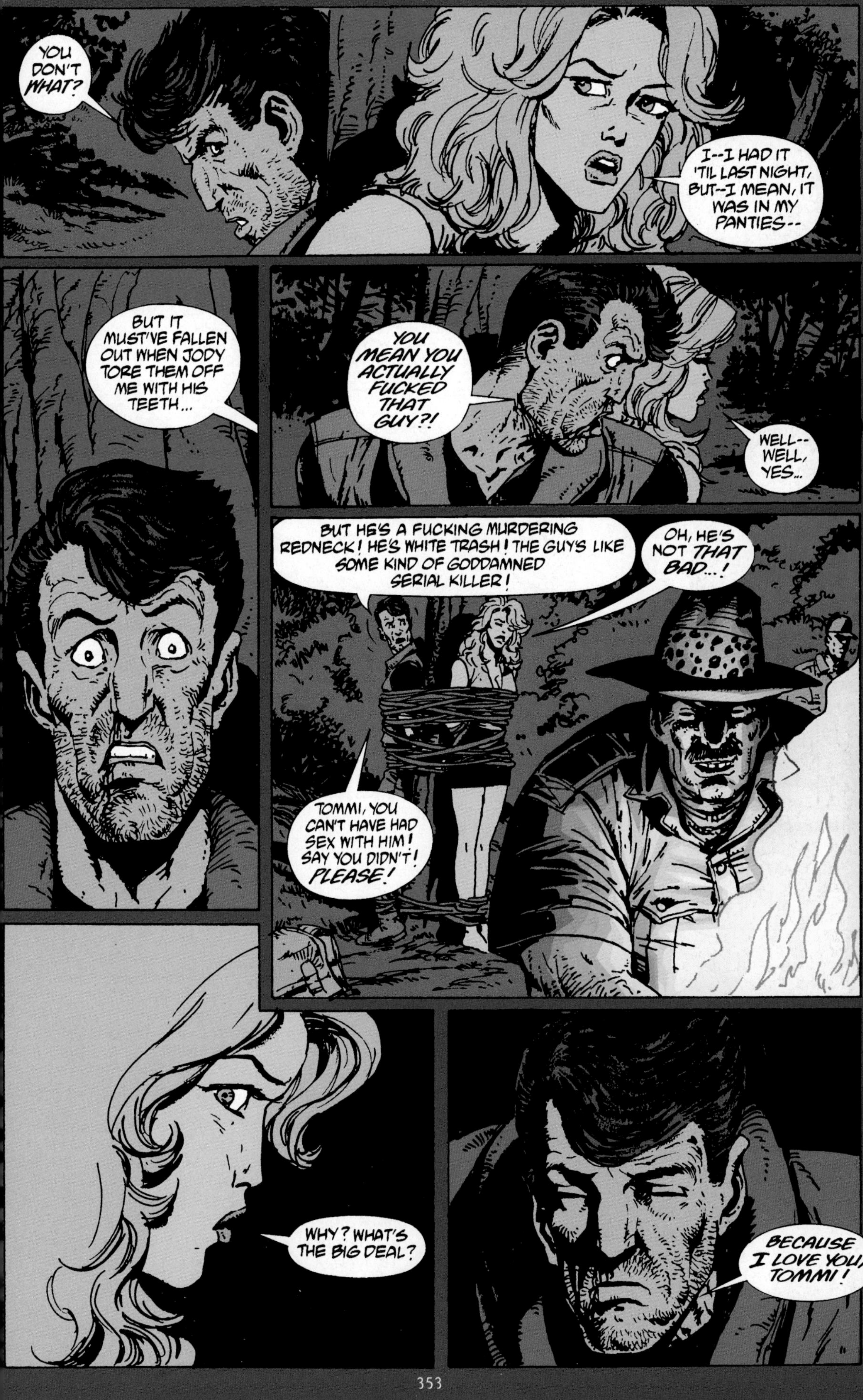

YOU DON'T *WHAT?*
I--I HAD IT 'TIL LAST NIGHT, BUT--I MEAN, IT WAS IN MY PANTIES--
BUT IT MUST'VE FALLEN OUT WHEN JODY TORE THEM OFF ME WITH HIS TEETH...
YOU MEAN YOU ACTUALLY FUCKED THAT GUY?!
WELL-- WELL, YES...
BUT HE'S A FUCKING MURDERING REDNECK! HE'S WHITE TRASH! THE GUY'S LIKE SOME KIND OF GODDAMNED SERIAL KILLER!
OH, HE'S NOT *THAT* BAD...!
TOMMI, YOU CAN'T HAVE HAD SEX WITH HIM! SAY YOU DIDN'T! *PLEASE!*
WHY? WHAT'S THE BIG DEAL?
BECAUSE I LOVE YOU, TOMMI!

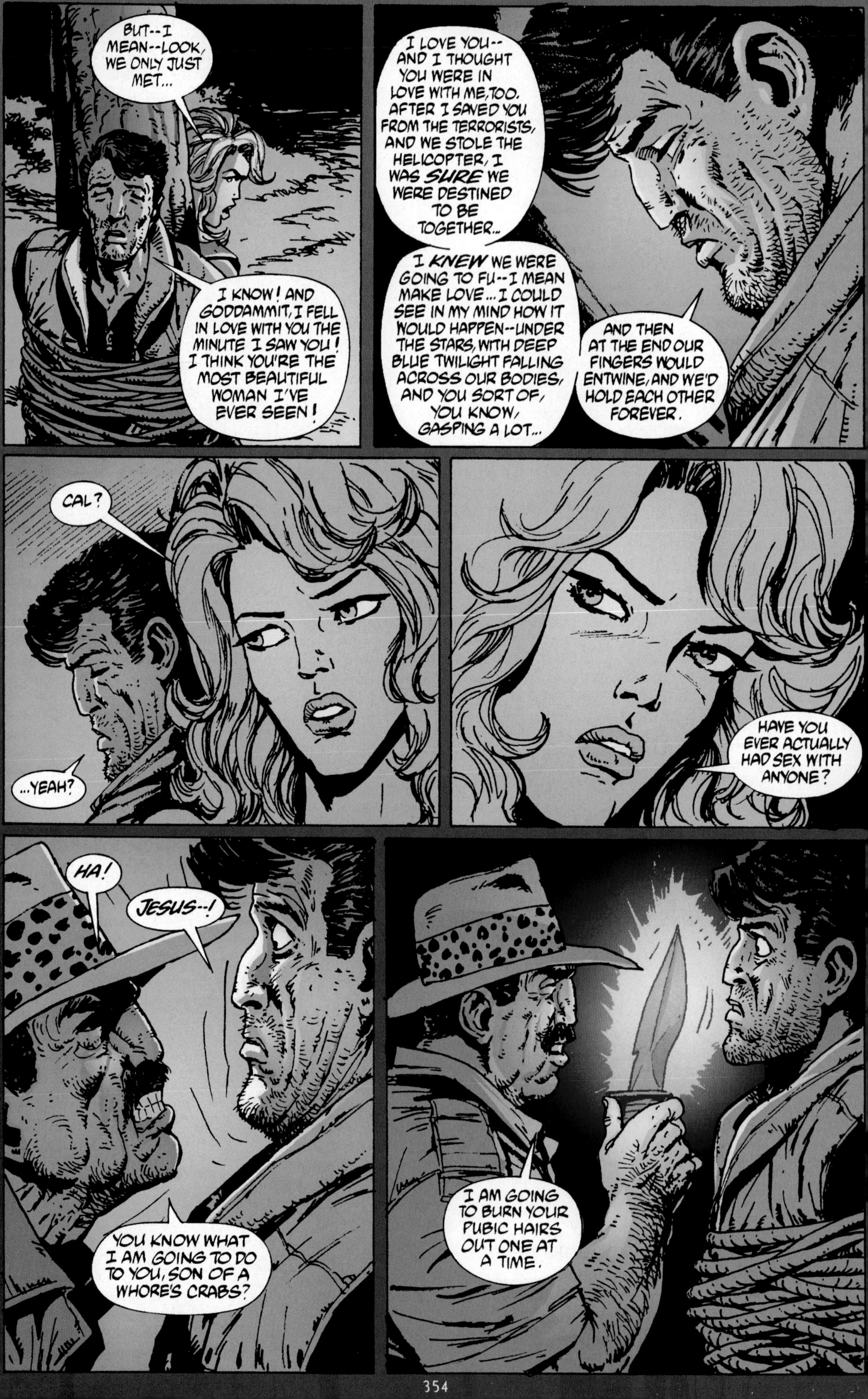

BUT--I MEAN--LOOK, WE ONLY JUST MET...
I KNOW! AND GODDAMMIT, I FELL IN LOVE WITH YOU THE MINUTE I SAW YOU! I THINK YOU'RE THE MOST BEAUTIFUL WOMAN I'VE EVER SEEN!
I LOVE YOU--AND I THOUGHT YOU WERE IN LOVE WITH ME, TOO. AFTER I SAVED YOU FROM THE TERRORISTS, AND WE STOLE THE HELICOPTER, I WAS SURE WE WERE DESTINED TO BE TOGETHER...
I KNEW WE WERE GOING TO FU--I MEAN MAKE LOVE... I COULD SEE IN MY MIND HOW IT WOULD HAPPEN--UNDER THE STARS, WITH DEEP BLUE TWILIGHT FALLING ACROSS OUR BODIES, AND YOU SORT OF, YOU KNOW, GASPING A LOT...
AND THEN AT THE END OUR FINGERS WOULD ENTWINE, AND WE'D HOLD EACH OTHER FOREVER.
CAL?
...YEAH?
HAVE YOU EVER ACTUALLY HAD SEX WITH ANYONE?
HA!
JESUS--!
YOU KNOW WHAT I AM GOING TO DO TO YOU, SON OF A WHORE'S CRABS?
I AM GOING TO BURN YOUR PUBIC HAIRS OUT ONE AT A TIME.

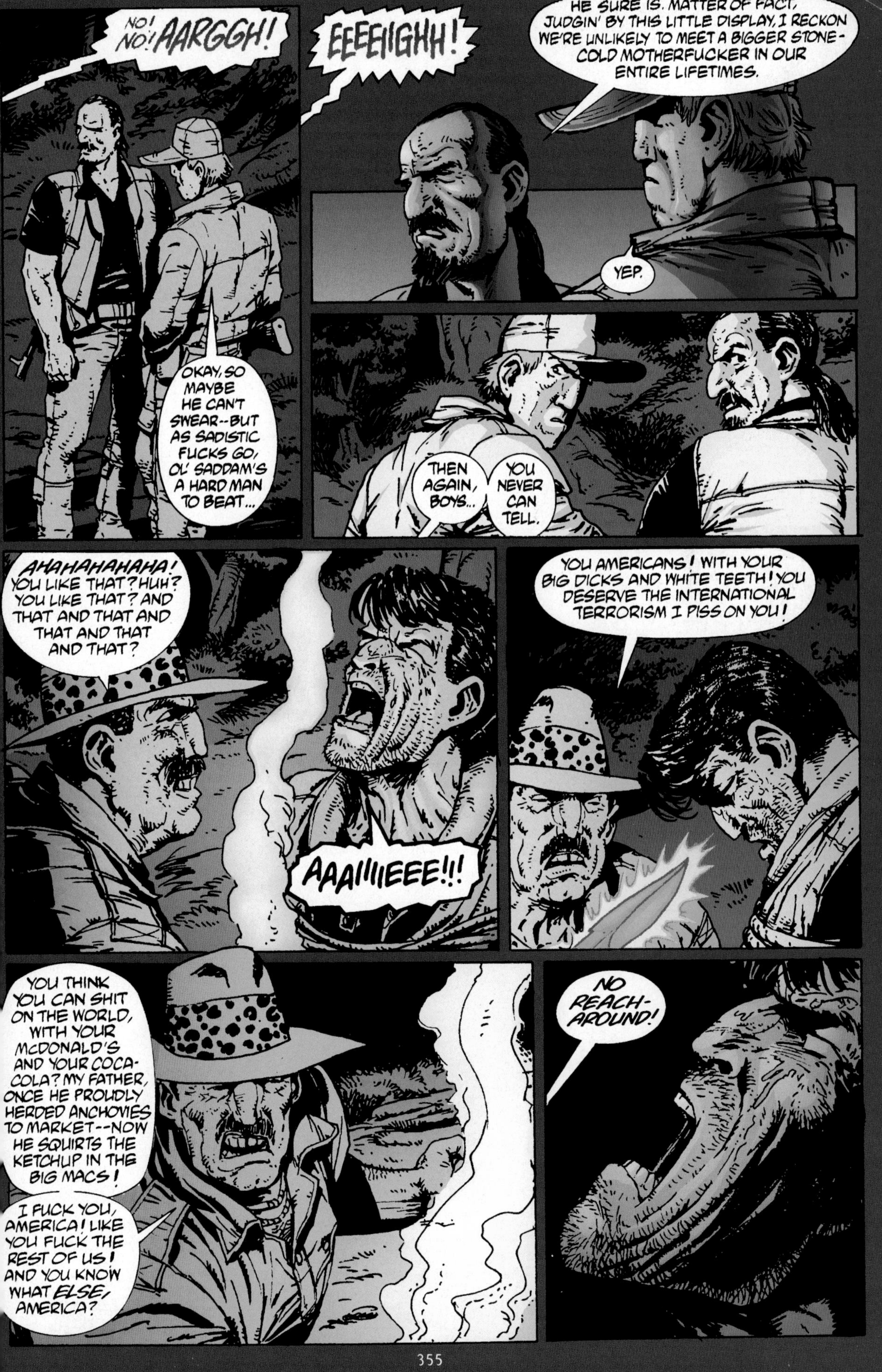
NO! NO! AARGGH!
EEEEIIGHH!
HE SURE IS. MATTER OF FACT, JUDGIN' BY THIS LITTLE DISPLAY, I RECKON WE'RE UNLIKELY TO MEET A BIGGER STONE-COLD MOTHERFUCKER IN OUR ENTIRE LIFETIMES.
YEP.
OKAY, SO MAYBE HE CAN'T SWEAR--BUT AS SADISTIC FUCKS GO, OL' SADDAM'S A HARD MAN TO BEAT...
THEN AGAIN, BOYS...
YOU NEVER CAN TELL.
AHAHAHAHAHA! YOU LIKE THAT? HUH? YOU LIKE THAT? AND THAT AND THAT AND THAT AND THAT AND THAT?
AAAIIIIEEE!!!
YOU AMERICANS! WITH YOUR BIG DICKS AND WHITE TEETH! YOU DESERVE THE INTERNATIONAL TERRORISM I PISS ON YOU!
YOU THINK YOU CAN SHIT ON THE WORLD, WITH YOUR McDONALD'S AND YOUR COCA-COLA? MY FATHER, ONCE HE PROUDLY HERDED ANCHOVIES TO MARKET--NOW HE SQUIRTS THE KETCHUP IN THE BIG MACS!
I FUCK YOU, AMERICA! LIKE YOU FUCK THE REST OF US! AND YOU KNOW WHAT ELSE, AMERICA?
NO REACH-AROUND!

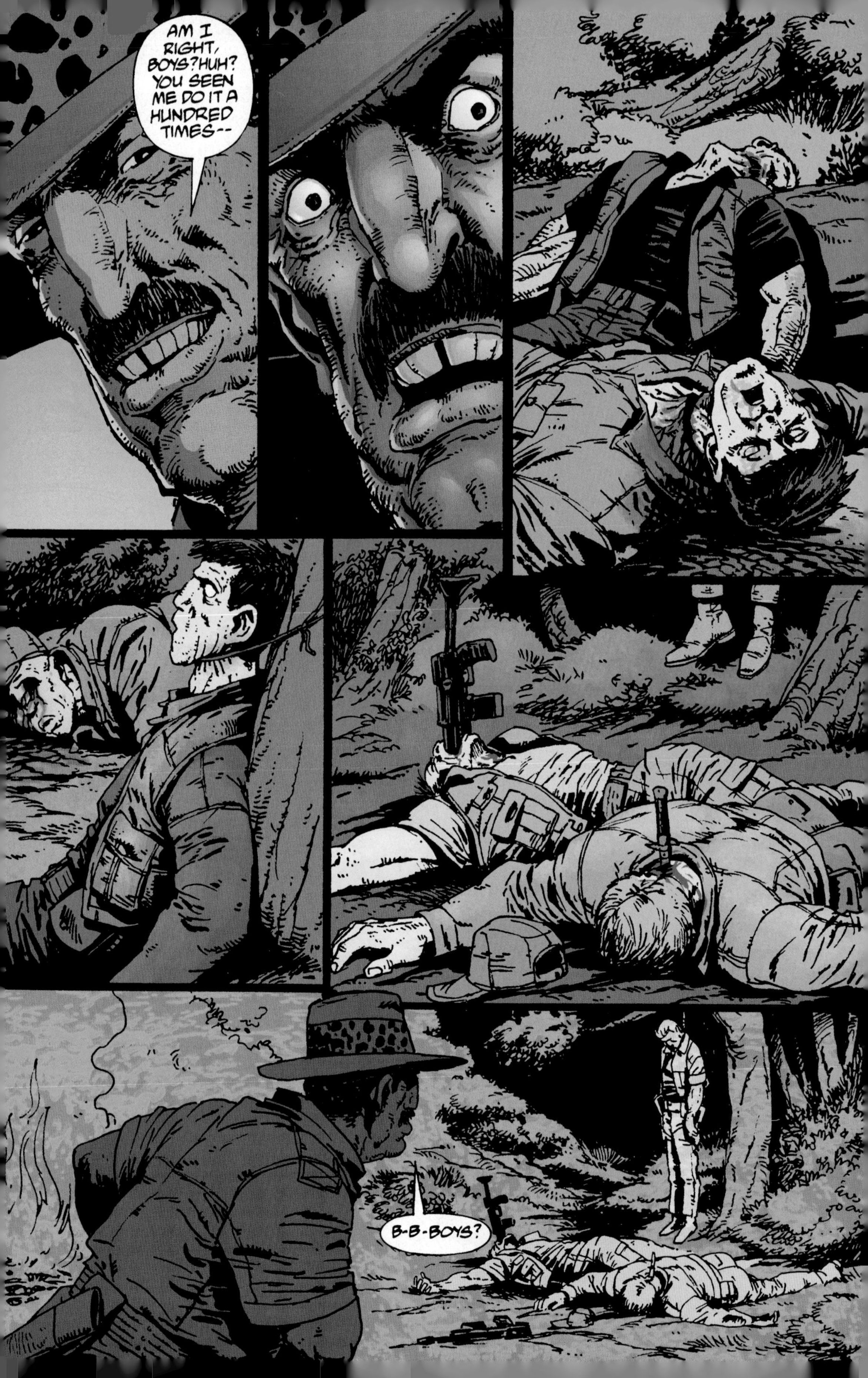
AM I RIGHT, BOYS? HUH? YOU SEEN ME DO IT A HUNDRED TIMES--
B-B-BOYS?

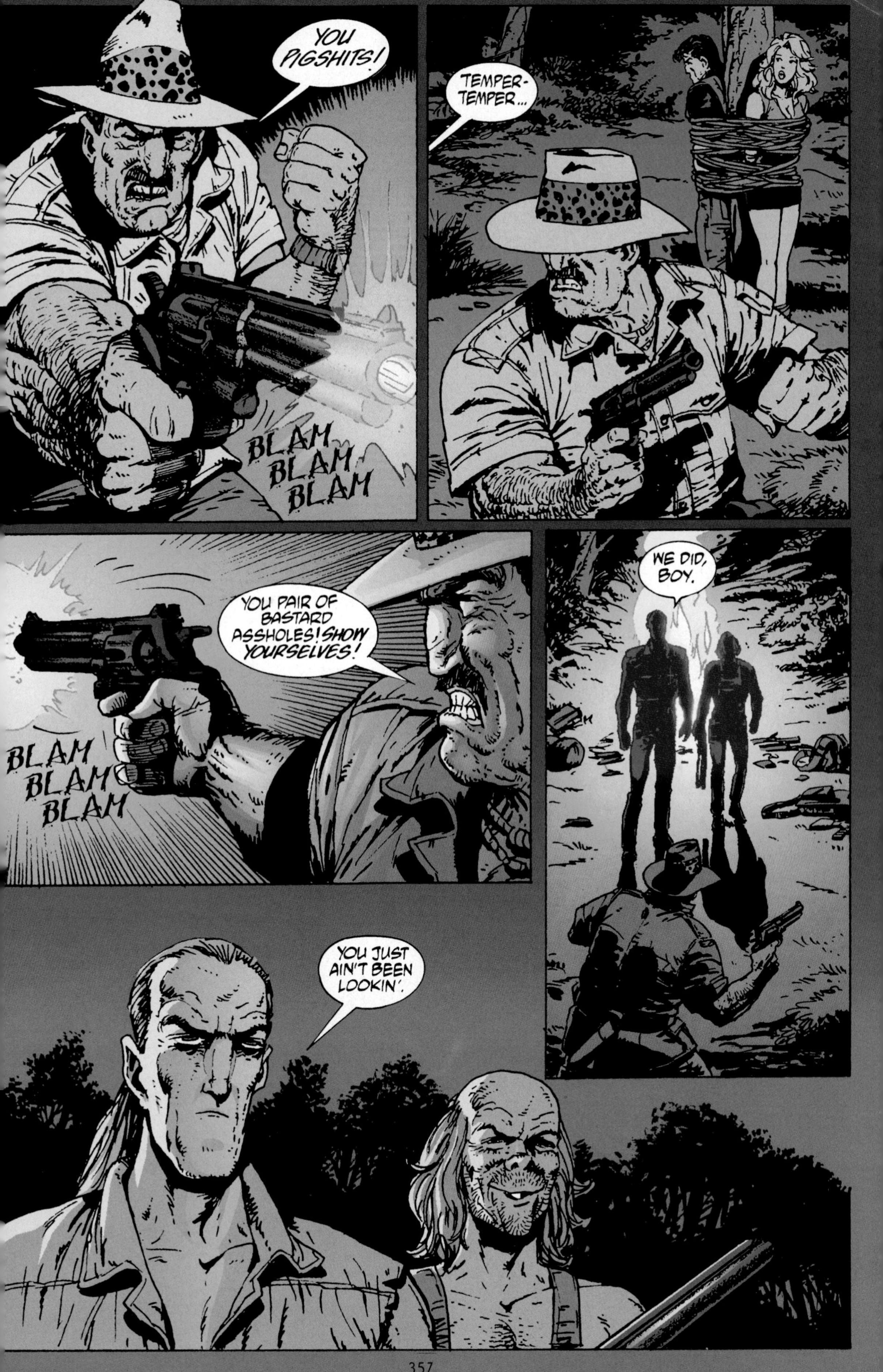
YOU PIGSHITS!
BLAM BLAM BLAM
TEMPER-TEMPER...
YOU PAIR OF BASTARD ASSHOLES! SHOW YOURSELVES!
BLAM BLAM BLAM
WE DID, BOY.
YOU JUST AIN'T BEEN LOOKIN'.

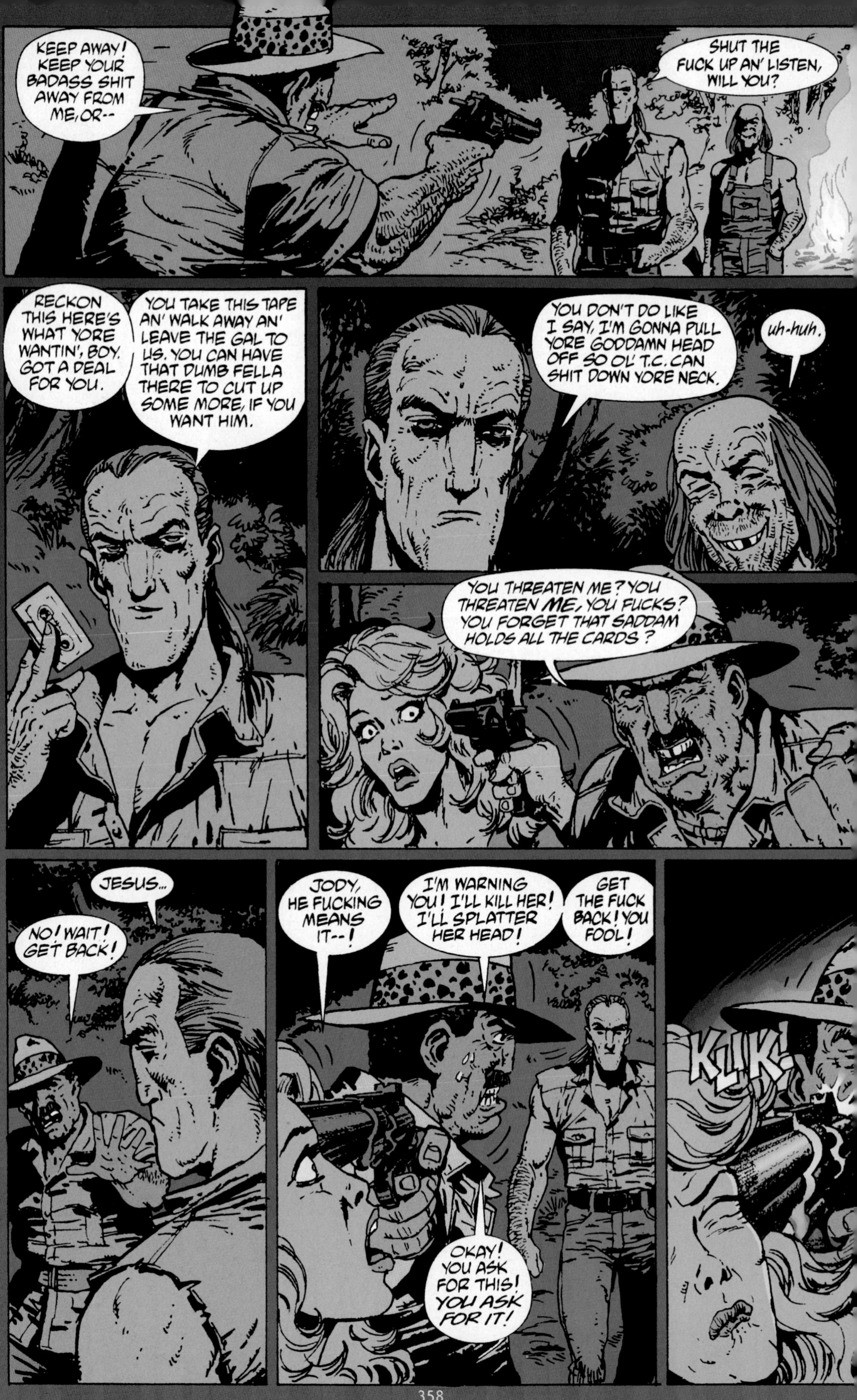
KEEP AWAY! KEEP YOUR BADASS SHIT AWAY FROM ME, OR--
SHUT THE FUCK UP AN' LISTEN, WILL YOU?
RECKON THIS HERE'S WHAT YORE WANTIN', BOY. GOT A DEAL FOR YOU.
YOU TAKE THIS TAPE AN' WALK AWAY AN' LEAVE THE GAL TO US. YOU CAN HAVE THAT DUMB FELLA THERE TO CUT UP SOME MORE, IF YOU WANT HIM.
YOU DON'T DO LIKE I SAY, I'M GONNA PULL YORE GODDAMN HEAD OFF SO OL' T.C. CAN SHIT DOWN YORE NECK.
uh-huh.
YOU THREATEN ME? YOU THREATEN ME, YOU FUCKS? YOU FORGET THAT SADDAM HOLDS ALL THE CARDS?
JESUS...
NO! WAIT! GET BACK!
JODY, HE FUCKING MEANS IT--!
I'M WARNING YOU! I'LL KILL HER! I'LL SPLATTER HER HEAD!
GET THE FUCK BACK! YOU FOOL!
OKAY! YOU ASK FOR THIS! YOU ASK FOR IT!
KLIK!

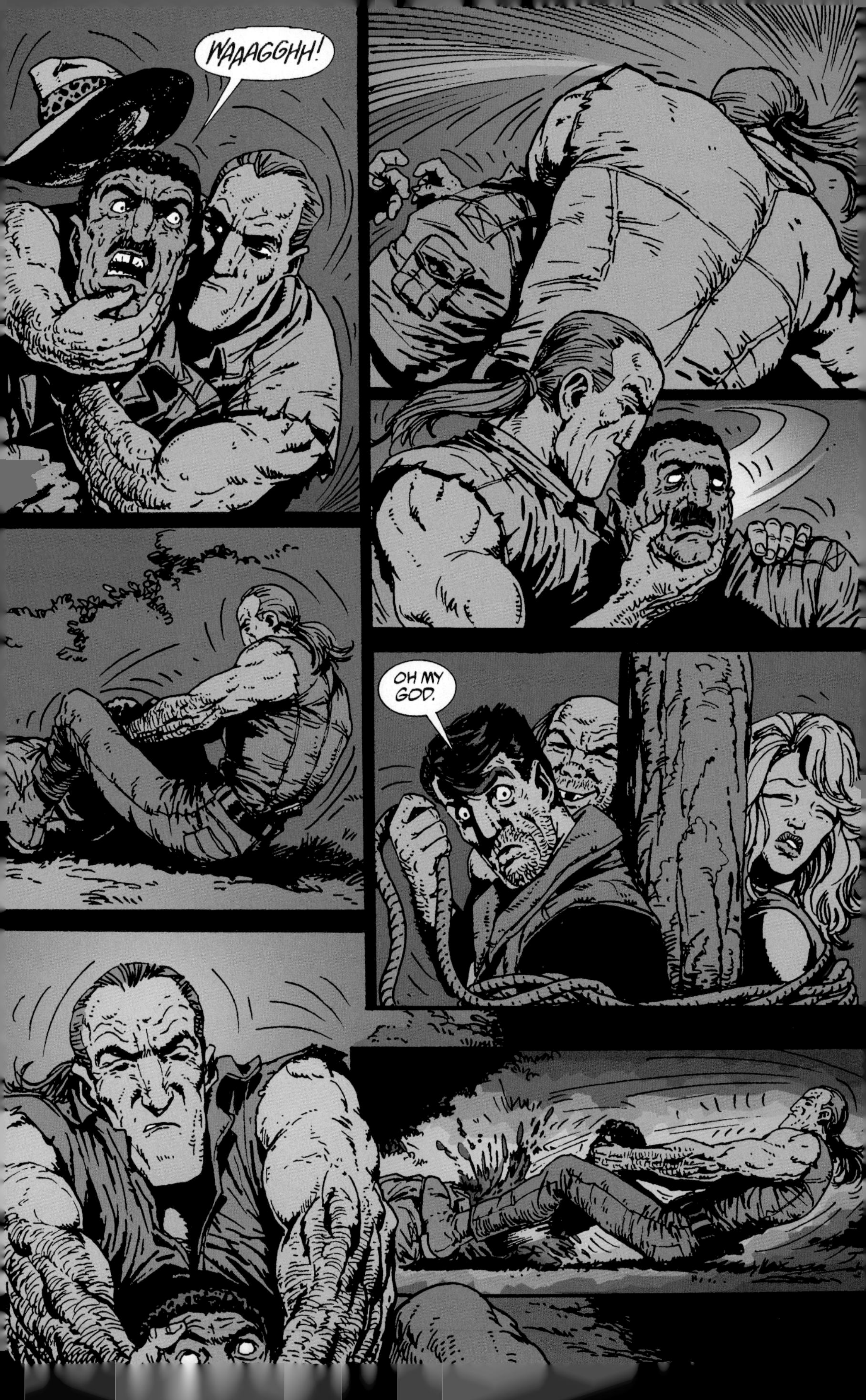
WAAAGGHH!
OH MY GOD.

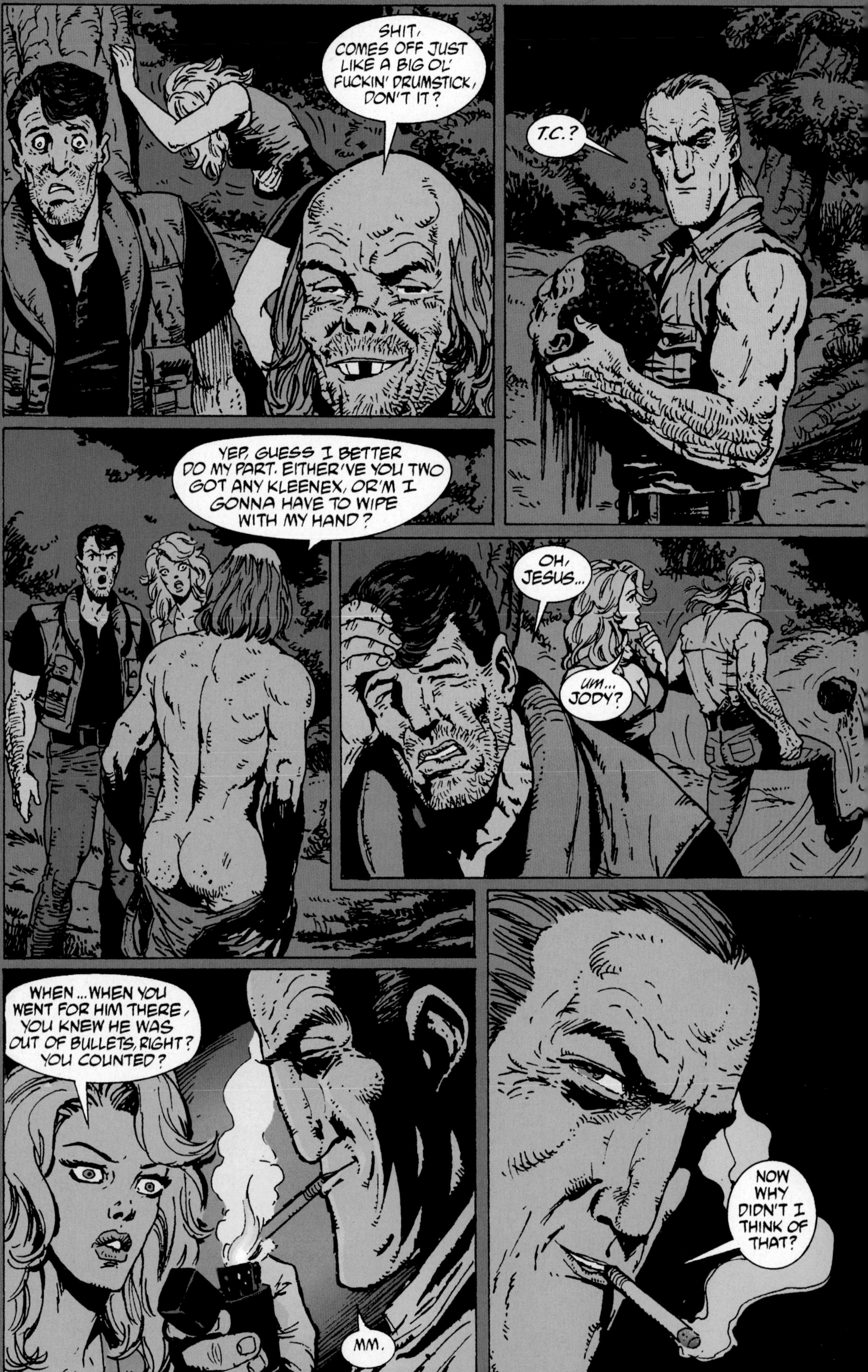
SHIT, COMES OFF JUST LIKE A BIG OL' FUCKIN' DRUMSTICK, DON'T IT?
T.C.?
YEP. GUESS I BETTER DO MY PART. EITHER'VE YOU TWO GOT ANY KLEENEX, OR'M I GONNA HAVE TO WIPE WITH MY HAND?
OH, JESUS...
UM... JODY?
WHEN... WHEN YOU WENT FOR HIM THERE, YOU KNEW HE WAS OUT OF BULLETS, RIGHT? YOU COUNTED?
MM.
NOW WHY DIDN'T I THINK OF THAT?

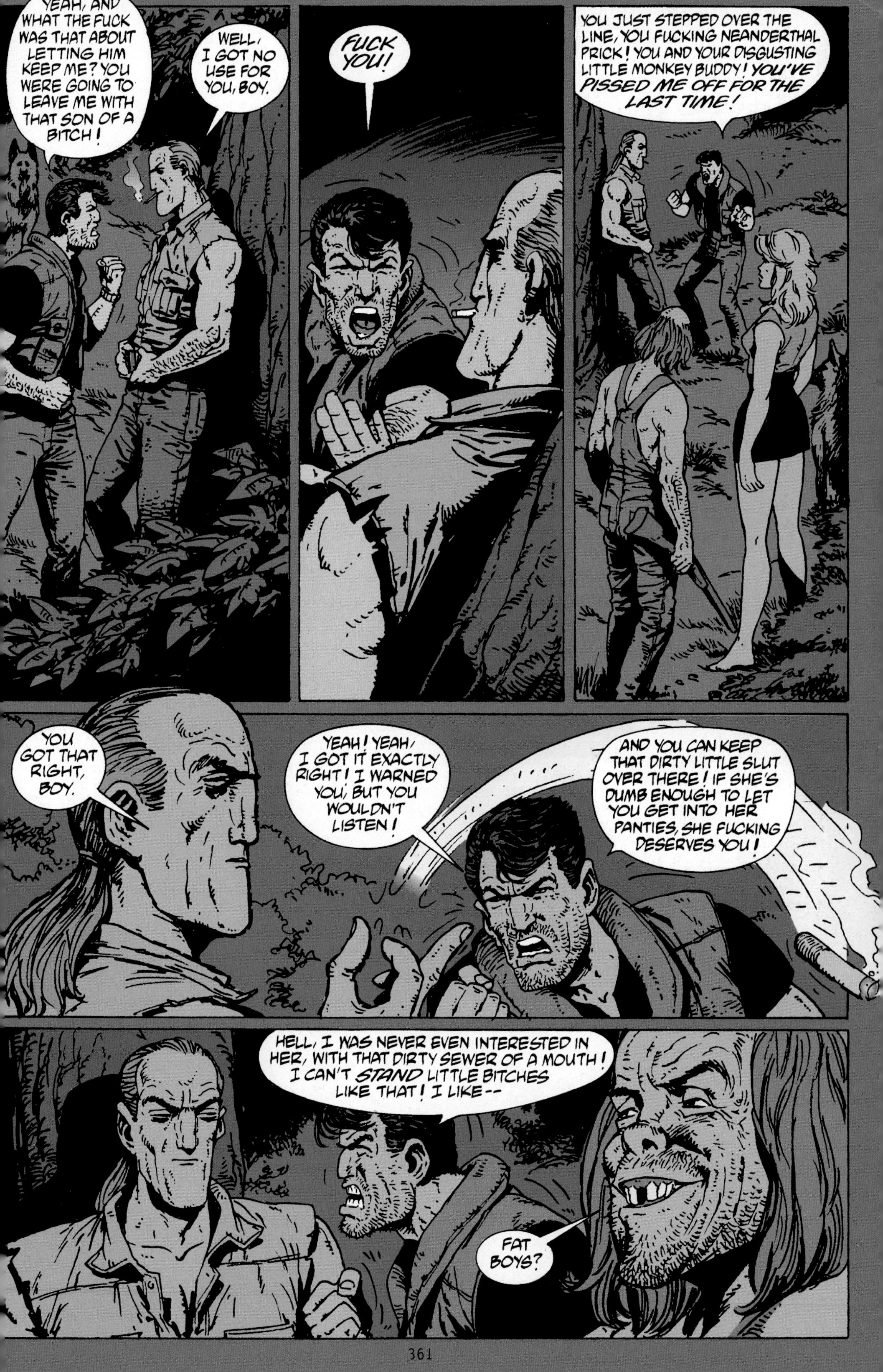
YEAH, AND WHAT THE FUCK WAS THAT ABOUT LETTING HIM KEEP ME? YOU WERE GOING TO LEAVE ME WITH THAT SON OF A BITCH!
WELL, I GOT NO USE FOR YOU, BOY.
FUCK YOU!
YOU JUST STEPPED OVER THE LINE, YOU FUCKING NEANDERTHAL PRICK! YOU AND YOUR DISGUSTING LITTLE MONKEY BUDDY! YOU'VE PISSED ME OFF FOR THE LAST TIME!
YOU GOT THAT RIGHT, BOY.
YEAH! YEAH, I GOT IT EXACTLY RIGHT! I WARNED YOU, BUT YOU WOULDN'T LISTEN!
AND YOU CAN KEEP THAT DIRTY LITTLE SLUT OVER THERE! IF SHE'S DUMB ENOUGH TO LET YOU GET INTO HER PANTIES, SHE FUCKING DESERVES YOU!
HELL, I WAS NEVER EVEN INTERESTED IN HER, WITH THAT DIRTY SEWER OF A MOUTH! I CAN'T STAND LITTLE BITCHES LIKE THAT! I LIKE--
FAT BOYS?

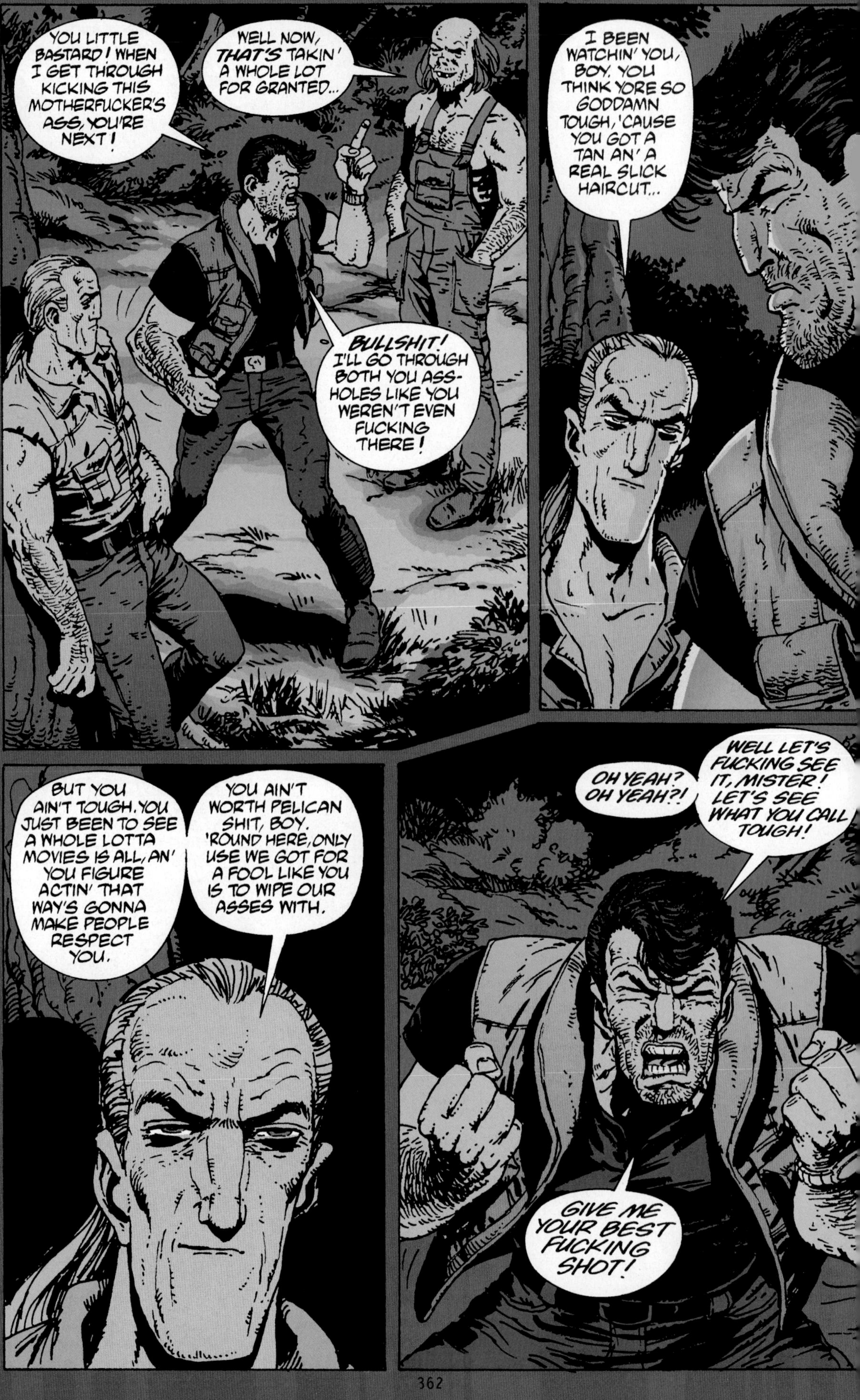
YOU LITTLE BASTARD! WHEN I GET THROUGH KICKING THIS MOTHERFUCKER'S ASS, YOU'RE NEXT!
WELL NOW, THAT'S TAKIN' A WHOLE LOT FOR GRANTED...
BULLSHIT! I'LL GO THROUGH BOTH YOU ASS-HOLES LIKE YOU WEREN'T EVEN FUCKING THERE!
I BEEN WATCHIN' YOU, BOY. YOU THINK YORE SO GODDAMN TOUGH, 'CAUSE YOU GOT A TAN AN' A REAL SLICK HAIRCUT...
BUT YOU AIN'T TOUGH. YOU JUST BEEN TO SEE A WHOLE LOTTA MOVIES IS ALL, AN' YOU FIGURE ACTIN' THAT WAY'S GONNA MAKE PEOPLE RESPECT YOU.
YOU AIN'T WORTH PELICAN SHIT, BOY. 'ROUND HERE, ONLY USE WE GOT FOR A FOOL LIKE YOU IS TO WIPE OUR ASSES WITH.
OH YEAH? OH YEAH?!
WELL LET'S FUCKING SEE IT, MISTER! LET'S SEE WHAT YOU CALL TOUGH!
GIVE ME YOUR BEST FUCKING SHOT!

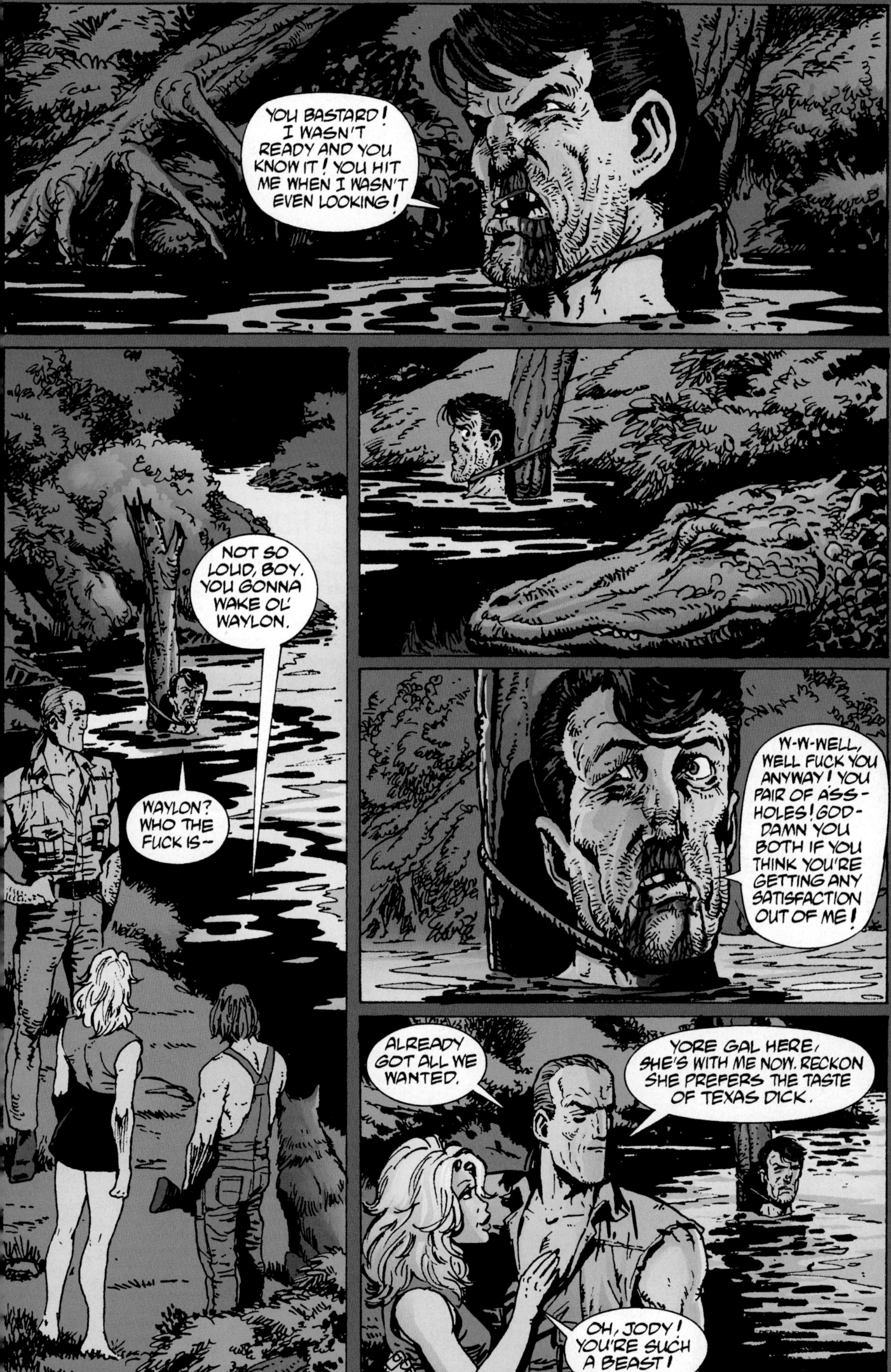
YOU BASTARD! I WASN'T READY AND YOU KNOW IT! YOU HIT ME WHEN I WASN'T EVEN LOOKING!
NOT SO LOUD, BOY. YOU GONNA WAKE OL' WAYLON.
WAYLON? WHO THE FUCK IS--
W-W-WELL, WELL FUCK YOU ANYWAY! YOU PAIR OF ASS-HOLES! GOD-DAMN YOU BOTH IF YOU THINK YOU'RE GETTING ANY SATISFACTION OUT OF ME!
ALREADY GOT ALL WE WANTED.
YORE GAL HERE, SHE'S WITH ME NOW. RECKON SHE PREFERS THE TASTE OF TEXAS DICK.
OH, JODY! YOU'RE SUCH A BEAST!

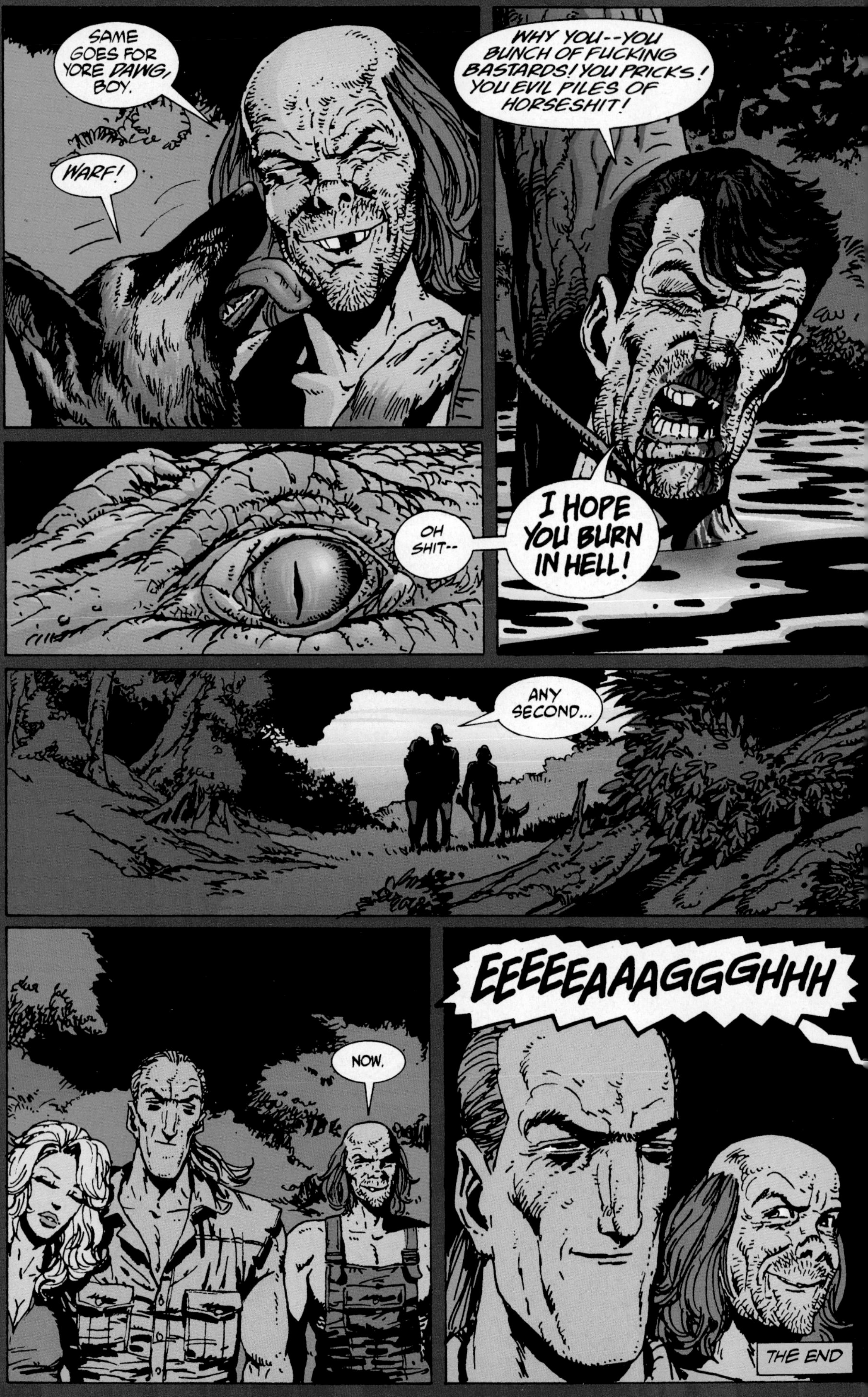
SAME GOES FOR YORE DAWG, BOY.
WARF!
WHY YOU--YOU BUNCH OF FUCKING BASTARDS! YOU PRICKS! YOU EVIL PILES OF HORSESHIT!
OH SHIT--
I HOPE YOU BURN IN HELL!
ANY SECOND...
NOW.
EEEEEAAAGGGHHH
THE END

PINUPS
A PREACHER Gallery by Steve Dillon and Glenn Fabry

Art for the second PREACHER retail poster by Steve Dillon,
released in 1999.
365

Back cover art for the first trade paperback edition of
PREACHER VOL. 4:
ANCIENT HISTORY
by Glenn Fabry
366

Cover art for the first trade paperback edition of
PREACHER VOL. 6:
WAR IN THE SUN
by Glenn Fabry
367

Art by Steve Dillon for the 1995 one-shot
VERTIGO GALLERY: DREAMS AND NIGHTMARES
368

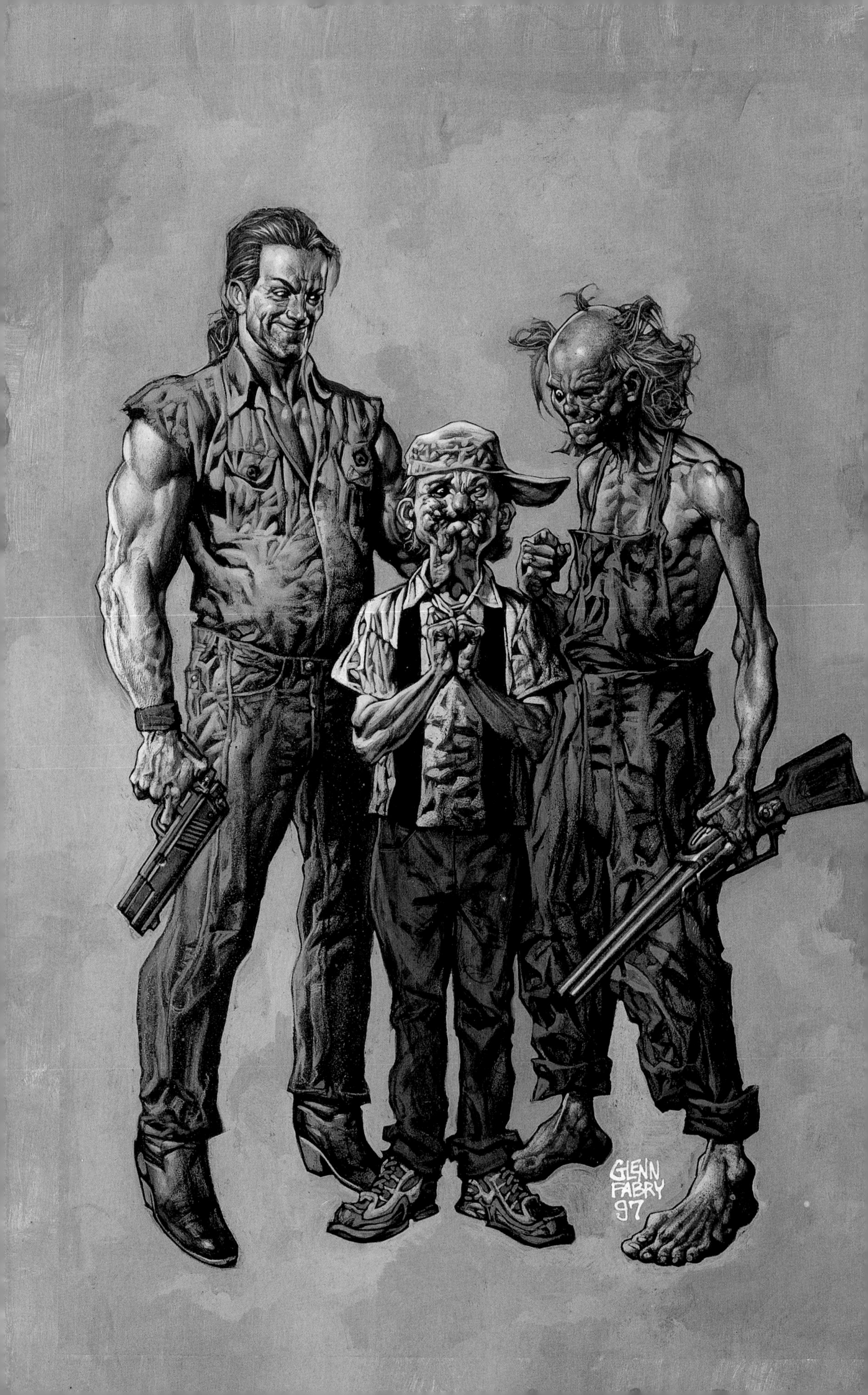
GLENN
FABRY
97

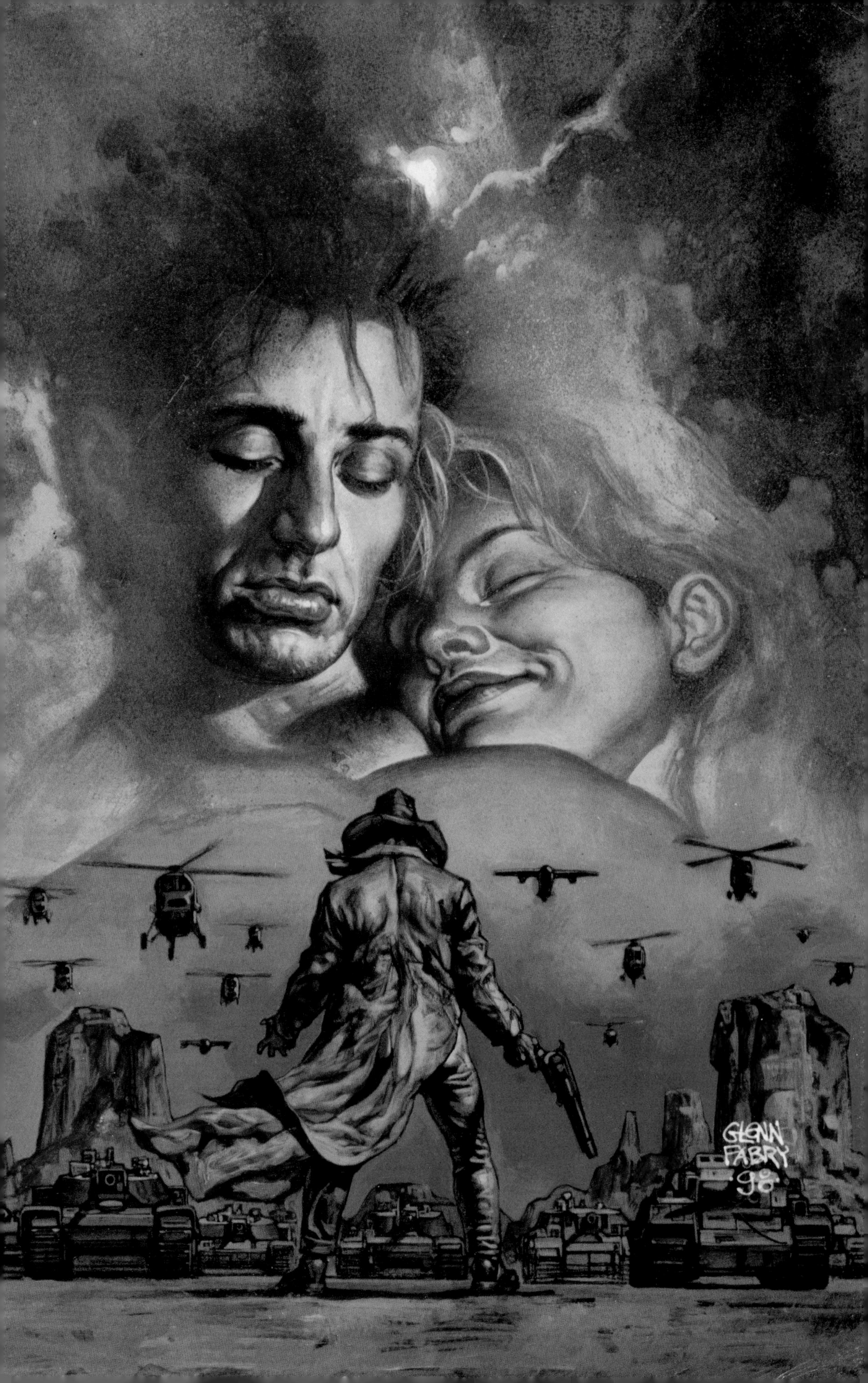
GLENN
FABRY

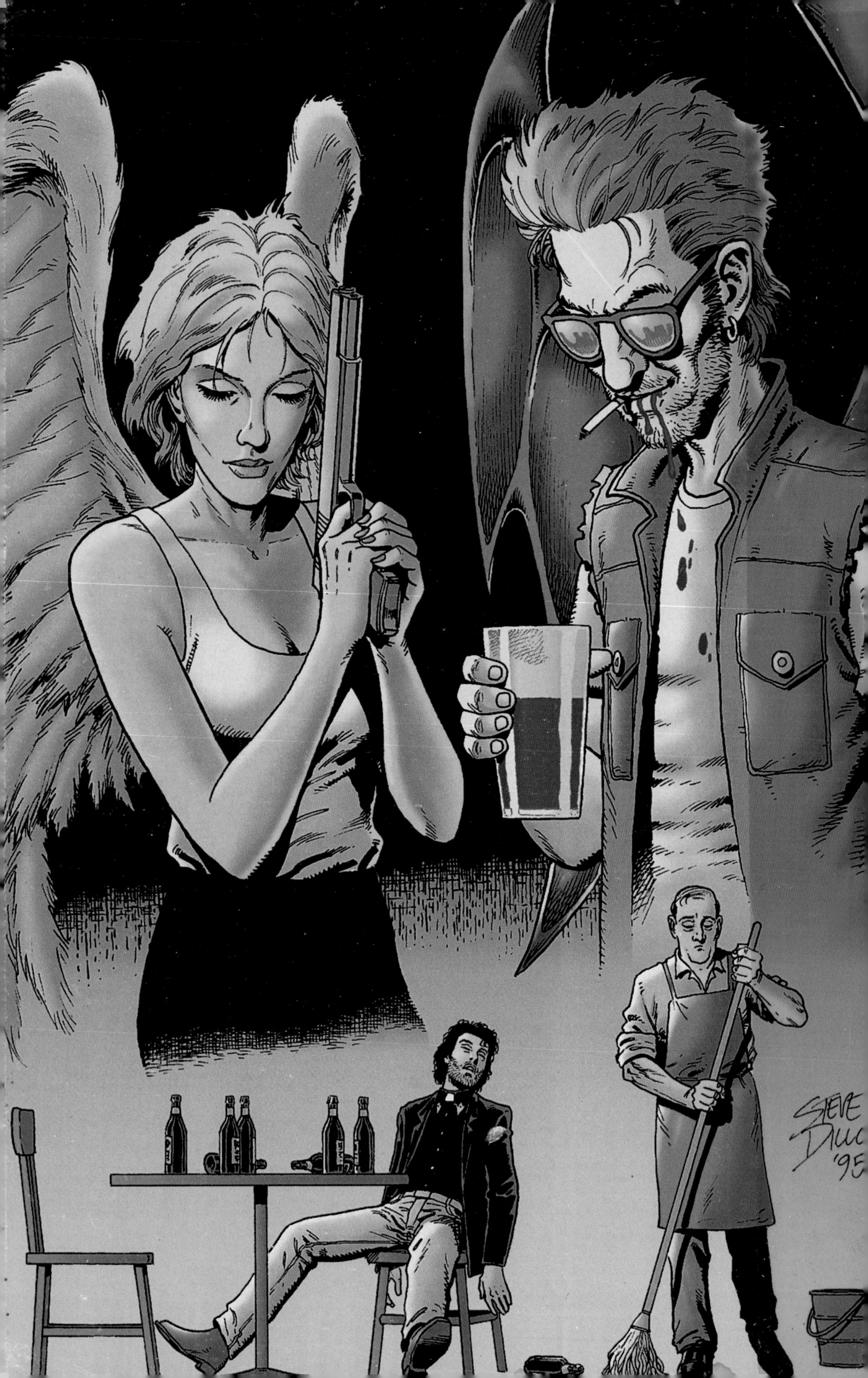
STEVE DILLON '95